Procedures for the Office Professional

Fourth Edition

Fourth Edition

Procedures for the Office Professional

Patsy Fulton-Calkins, Ph.D., CPS
Adjunct Professor
Educational Consultant

Joanna D. Hanks
Dean of Instructional Services
J. Sargeant Reynolds Community College
Richmond, Virginia

Contributing Author

Karin M. Stultz
Northern Michigan University
Marquette, Michigan

VISIT US ON THE INTERNET
www.swep.com
www.thomsonlearning.com

South-Western
EDUCATIONAL PUBLISHING
Thomson Learning™

Australia • Canada • Denmark • Japan • Mexico • New Zealand • Phillipines
Puerto Rico • Singapore • South Africa • Spain • United Kingdom • United States

Project Manager:	Dr. Inell Bolls
Editor:	Carol Spencer
Consulting Editor:	Mary Todd, Todd Publishing Services
Production Coordinator:	Jane Congdon
Art/Design Coordinator:	Darren Wright
Marketing Manager:	Tim Gleim
Photo Editor:	Michelle Kunkler
Publishing Team Leader:	Karen Schmohe
Cover and Internal Design:	Lou Ann Thesing
Cover and Part Opener Illustrations:	Andrew Faulkner, afstudio
Production Services:	Maryland Composition

All Cover Photos © PhotoDisc, Inc.

Copyright © 2000

by SOUTH-WESTERN EDUCATIONAL PUBLISHING

Cincinnati, Ohio

South-Western Educational Publishing is a division of Thomson Learning.
Thomson Learning is a trademark used herein under license.

ISBN: 0-538-72211-8

2 3 4 5 6 7 8 9 0 WT 05 04 03 02 01 00

Printed in the United States of America

For permission to use material from this text or product, contact us by
- web: www.thomsonrights.com
- Phone: 1-800-730-2214
- Fax: 1-800-730-2215

Library of Congress Cataloging-in-Publication Data

Fulton-Calkins, Patsy, 1934-
    Procedures for the office professional/Patsy J. Fulton, Joanna
Davis Hanks.—4th ed.
      p. cm.
    Includes index.
    ISBN 0-538-72211-8 (alk. paper)
    1. Office practice. 2. Secretaries. I. Hanks, Joanna D.
II. Title.
HF5547.5.F842   1999
651—dc21
                                99-30187
                                CIP

The names of all products mentioned herein are used for identification purposes only and may be trademarks or registered trademarks of their respective owners. South-Western Educational Publishing disclaims any affiliation, association, connection with, sponsorship, or endorsement by such owners.

Procedures for the Office Professional

This new edition of **Procedures for the Office Professional** will equip to-day's office professional with skills that will be in demand well into the 21st century. Continued technological advances, a growing global marketplace, and an increasingly diverse labor force are issues that will directly affect all office professionals. Students will learn to conduct a job search, be productive team members, process information via technology, communicate effectively, lead and supervise others, prepare travel arrangements, and assist in the preparation of meetings. Following the comprehensive textbook package list below, you will find more exciting office technology products to consider.

Procedures for the Office Professional
- Textbook w/Template Disk — 0-538-72212-6
- Applications Workbook — 0-538-72213-4
- Instructor's Manual — 0-538-72216-9
- Presentation Software — 0-538-72214-2
- CD-ROM Testing Software — 0-538-72217-7
- Online — 0-538-72215-0

Internet Office Projects
- Text-Workbook — 0-538-72186-3
- Manual w/Bookmark Disk — 0-538-72187-1

Legal Office Projects
- Text-Workbook w/Template Disk — 0-538-72123-5
- Audiocassette for Transcription — 0-538-72122-7
- Instructor's Manual — 0-538-72125-1

Medical Office Projects
- Text-Workbook w/Template Disk — 0-538-72127-8
- Instructor's Manual w/Medisoft Demo CD-ROM — 0-538-72125-1

CNN Video: Interacting in Today's Office — 0-538-72221-5

Proofreading in 10 Hours — 0-538-68924-2

E-Commerce
- Text-Workbook — 0-538-68918-8
- Electronic Instructor CD-ROM — 0-538-68919-6

Book at a Glance

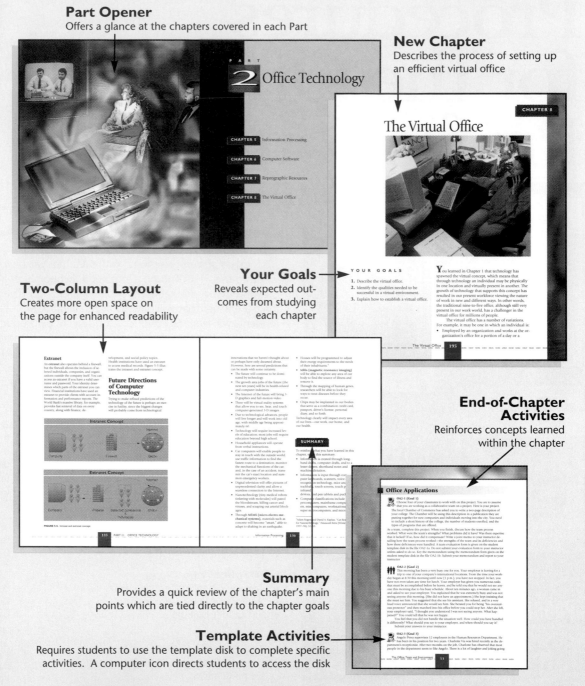

Part Opener
Offers a glance at the chapters covered in each Part

New Chapter
Describes the process of setting up an efficient virtual office

Two-Column Layout
Creates more open space on the page for enhanced readability

Your Goals
Reveals expected outcomes from studying each chapter

End-of-Chapter Activities
Reinforces concepts learned within the chapter

Summary
Provides a quick review of the chapter's main points which are tied directly to the chapter goals

Template Activities
Requires students to use the template disk to complete specific activities. A computer icon directs students to access the disk

Reference Section
Reinforces language arts skills and includes a list of proofreader's marks

What's New?

End-of-Chapter Material

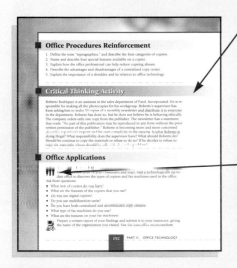

Critical Thinking Activity
Proposes an office case study for analysis. Students present their analysis orally or in writing

Team-Building Icon
Indicates a collaborative activity involving human relations skills

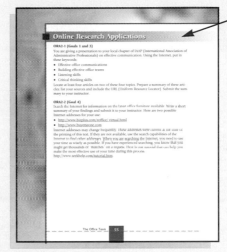

Online Research Applications
Requires students to use the vast resources of the Internet to conduct research

Other Features

Thomson World Class Learning Course
Offers an online course syllabus for distance or distributed learning at www.worldclasslearning.com

CD-ROM Testing Software
Offers the instructor the opportunity to create printed tests and choose questions in rank order

Workbook w/Office Simulation
Depicts realistic office activities with an international focus

Preface

The role of the office professional in the workplace of today is a challenging one. Changes are occurring daily both in the office and the world that will impact your job. Some of these changes are:

- A global marketplace
- Continual advances in technology
- An increasingly diverse labor force

These changes affect not only the overall structure of the organization but also the way in which the organization does business. Consider the changes the Internet has brought to business. Most businesses have a home page on the Internet today. This home page gives information about the products or services, historical background, and organizational structure of the business. A number of businesses sell directly to the consumer from the Internet. Many businesses even post their job openings on the Internet. Additionally, the international operations of many businesses are reflected on the home pages. In fact, many home pages appear in a number of different languages— in the language of the various countries where the organization does business. As a student, you no doubt have used the Internet extensively. Just a few short years ago, this technological innovation was merely a vision in a few individuals' minds. This example is one of many that could be given to demonstrate how businesses are being changed due to technology.

If you are entering the workforce for the first time, you will become aware of the changes that are occurring in the workplace. If you are already employed, you probably have discovered changes. By studying this text and completing the activities, you will be better equipped to handle the changes you encounter. You will learn to:

- Be a productive member of an office team
- Behave ethically
- Process information via technology
- Communicate effectively—both orally and in writing
- Process mail
- Manage records
- Assist in the preparation of meetings
- Prepare travel arrangements
- Do a job search
- Advance on the job
- Lead and supervise others

Text Organization

Procedures for the Office Professional is organized into six parts, with a total of twenty chapters. These parts and chapters are:

PART 1: THE 21ST CENTURY OFFICE
    Chapter 1: A Changing Workplace
    Chapter 2: The Office Team and Environment
    Chapter 3: Productivity in the Office
    Chapter 4: Ethical Behavior

PART 2: OFFICE TECHNOLOGY
    Chapter 5: Information Processing
    Chapter 6: Computer Software
    Chapter 7: Reprographic Resources
    Chapter 8: The Virtual Office

Learning Aids

To assist in the learning process, the following learning aids have been provided throughout this text:

- Goals listed at the beginning of each chapter
- Key terms highlighted in the chapter, with an explanation of the terms, and listed at the end of each chapter
- Numerous illustrations and figures
- Chapter summary tied to chapter goals for each chapter
- Professional pointers
- Office procedures reinforcement, providing items for discussion and/or a written assignment
- Critical thinking addressed through an office case at the end of each chapter and other activities

- Office applications, with each application tied directly to one or more goals of the chapter
- Office applications in each chapter that require work as a team
- Office applications that provide the opportunity to make presentations to the class as individuals or in groups
- Office applications that require the use of a template disk
- Online research applications designed to reinforce the use of the Internet
- End of part activities consisting of vocabulary review and language skills
- Reference Section at the back of the text that serves as a resource on abbreviations, capitalization, numbers, often misused words and phrases, plurals and possessive, proofreaders' marks, punctuation, spelling, and word division

Supplementary Items

To assist in student learning, these supplementary items are provided:

- An *Applications Workbook* that contains:
  - additional information needed to complete certain office applications
  - supplemental exercises
  - vocabulary review
  - language skills practice
- Student template disk containing information for certain office applications, letterhead, and forms
- CD-ROM testing software for each part of the text
- Presentation Software (PowerPoint®

Slides) that emphasize key concepts from each chapter

New Features in this Edition

- An integrated learning system that includes:
  - Learning activities tied directly to goals
  - Emphasis on critical thinking and team building skills throughout the text
  - Activities that support critical thinking and team building skills, with the critical thinking activities identified by a blue color bar and the team building activities identified by icons
  - Emphasis on technical skills, with online research activities and template disk activities
  - Disk activities identified by an icon
  - End-of-part tests that include an optional case for students to solve as a team
  - Web-based Online Course Syllabus containing course information and Power-Point slides.
- New chapter—Chapter 8: The Virtual Office
- Online research applications identified with a blue color bar
- Office simulation with an international focus in the *Applications Workbook*
- Expanded instructor's manual

Student Message

This book has been written in a format designed to help you learn, with these aids to assist you in the learning process:

- Goals at the beginning of each chapter
- Key terms highlighted and defined within the chapter and listed at the end of the chapter for a quick review
- Illustrations and figures that provide reinforcement to the concepts presented
- A summary at the end of each chapter
- Professional pointers related to the information presented in the chapter
- Questions for you to answer that will help you learn the concepts
- Case studies designed to improve your critical thinking skills
- Office applications tied to the goals to reinforce your learning
- Online research applications to reinforce your use of technology
- Vocabulary Review and Language Skills practice at the end of each part

We, the authors, hope that you not only learn in this course but that you also enjoy the experience. We wish you every success in this course and as you enter the world of work or continue in your chosen career path.

The Authors

Dr. Patsy J. Fulton-Calkins' experience in the field is extensive. Her past experience in the office includes working as a secretary for large corporations; she holds the CPS certification. Her teaching experiences include work at the university, community college, and high school levels. She has taught multicultural and management courses at the collegiate level; community college courses in business communications, office procedures, keyboarding, shorthand, and CPS review; and high school level courses such as business law, general business, and vocational office education.

In addition to her teaching experience, she has worked as an administrator in the following positions:

- Chancellor of Oakland Community College, the chief executive office, Oakland County, Michigan
- President of Brookhaven College, Dallas, Texas
- Vice President of Instruction, El Centro College and Cedar Valley College, Dallas, Texas
- Division Chairperson of Business and Social Science, Cedar Valley College, Dallas, Texas

Her present position involves consulting with universities and community colleges across the nation and adjunct teaching at the collegiate level.

Her educational credentials include a BBA, an MBEd and a PhD. Honors include Outstanding Alumnus, University of North Texas; Transformational Leader in Community Colleges; Outstanding Women in Management; Paul Harris Fellow of Rotary International; Piper Professor; Business Teacher of the Year; Who's Who in American Universities and Colleges; and numerous other honors. She has held many leadership roles in the community.

Joanna D. Hanks is Dean of Instructional Services at J. Sargeant Reynolds Community College in Richmond, Virginia. She has been a secretary, a high school business teacher, and a professor of Office Administration at the community college level for 20 years where she has taught office procedures, punctuation and proofreading skills, effective writing, supervision, and quality management. Prior to her current position, she was Dean of Economic Development and Extended Studies. She also held administrative appointments as Director of the Center for Office Development and Director of Economic Development and Public Relations. She is very active in civic affairs. Her educational background includes a BS, MS, and an EdS. She is among Who's Who in the Southwest, Outstanding Young Women in America, a Chancellor's Leadership Fellow, and a Paul Harris Fellow of Rotary International.

The Reviewers

Thanks to the following reviewers for their thorough review of the chapters and their insightful comments during the writing of this textbook. Their contributions have made it a book that will give the students an opportunity to learn, grow, and become better office professionals.

Dr. Mitsy Ballentine
Greenville Technical College
Greenville, SC 29606

Mrs. Rose Corgan
University of Cincinnati,
Raymond Walters College
Cincinnati, OH 45236

Dr. Raenelle Hanes
Pikes Peak Community College
Colorado Springs, CO 80921

Mrs. Gloria E. Smith
Southern Ohio College
Cincinnati, OH 45215

Contents

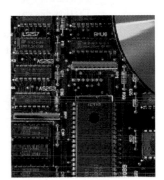

Chapter 17:
Travel Arrangements 454

Chapter 18:
Financial Documents 482

Part 6 • The Office Professional's Career

Chapter 19:
Employment and Advancement 514

Chapter 20:
Leadership and Management 555

Reference Section 583

Index 601

Acknowledgments

The following companies are gratefully acknowledged for the use of their photographs on the part and chapter opener pages:

© CORBIS
Pages 2, 29, 56, 84, 112, 142, 195, 222, 242, 394, 482, 555

Courtesy of GTE Spacenet Corp.
Page 110

Courtesy of International Business Machines Corporation
Page 220

© Digital Vision
Page 358

© EyeWire
Page 420

© PhotoDisc, Inc.
Pages 168, 269, 294, 328, 418, 454, 512, 514

1 The 21st Century Office

CHAPTER I

A Changing Workplace

The workplace of the twenty-first century promises to change at a rapid pace due to major technological advances and increasing globalization. Your role as an office professional in this world can be both challenging and exciting. It will demand that you continue to learn. In fact, the term **lifelong learning** will have great relevance for you. In order for workers to remain competitive and productive, it has been estimated that they will have to accumulate learning equivalent to 30 credit hours of instruction every seven years.[1]

[1]Michael G. Dolence and Donald M. Norris, *Transforming Higher Education: A Vision for Learning in the 21st Century* (Ann Arbor: Society for College and University Planning, 1995), 25.

YOUR GOALS

1. Describe the forces that are changing the office environment.

2. Identify career opportunities in the office field.

3. Define the skills and knowledge needed to succeed in the office.

4. Develop a career plan with short- and long-range goals.

5. Engage in effective decision making.

Whether you are preparing to enter the office after finishing your studies or you are presently employed in the office field either full- or part-time, the increased cultural diversity of the environment will be apparent to you. The population of the United States is more diverse today than it has ever been; and that diversity is expected to increase due to several factors, some of which are:

- Increases in the Asian and Hispanic populations as a percent of the total population of the United States
- Continued immigration to the United States from other countries
- Increased longevity of our people

The number of white non-Hispanics in our nation as a percent of our total population has been declining slightly for many years. The trend is expected to accelerate in the twenty-first century. By 2020, according to Census Bureau projections, white non-Hispanics will comprise slightly more than 64 percent of our total population, with African-Americans comprising 12.9 percent, Asians comprising 6.5 percent, and Hispanics comprising 16 percent.[2]

The increased diversity in the population means an increase in the diversity in the workforce. In addition, our workforce is made more diverse by a growing number of women and older people in the workforce. This increased diversity can have a very positive impact on all of us. It allows us to learn and grow as we understand people who come from different backgrounds and experiences than our own. This greater diversity in the workplace, along with the constant expansion of United States corporate operations to countries abroad, suggests that we must increase our communication, team building, and human relation skills.

Your career may take very different directions than in the past. For example, you may not work in the typical office at all but in a **virtual environment** where work can be performed anywhere and at any time using technology, including working from home. This concept will be discussed in greater detail later in this chapter. Also, rather than building a lifelong career with one company, you may work for a number of companies. In fact, you may develop specialized skills that allow you to work for a number of companies simultaneously. For example, you may become a communication specialist contracted by several companies to assist office professionals in improving their written and verbal communications. The changes in the workplace are opening up a variety of options for the office professional.

As an office professional employed in this technological and international workplace, your goals must be proficiency in your field; commitment to lifelong learning; and development of strong communication, critical thinking, and human relations skills. This chapter will help you understand more about the directions of the office and the skills that you must acquire to be successful as an office professional.

The Information Age Office

We live in the **Information Age**—a time where there has been a great explosion of knowledge. One of the results of this is an increase in the amount of information

[2]Richard W. Judy and Carol D'Amico, *Workforce 2020: Work and Workers in the 21st Century* (Indianapolis: Hudson Institute, 1997), 107–108.

The microchip will allow us to have continuous communications anywhere on earth and at any time. *Courtesy of ©*
Digital Vision.

available to us. Technology is an integral part of this Information Age, which exists because of the growth of technology. Technology has spawned the **digital era**— a world fueled by numbers. In this world, we wallow in numbers—account numbers, credit card numbers, **PINs** (personal identification numbers), Social Security numbers, checking account numbers, and telephone numbers, to name a few. The invention that unleashed the digital era is the **microchip**—a device the size of a fingernail that empowers our technological equipment. These microchips will continue to become more powerful and impact the way our world operates to an ever greater degree. In the not-so-distant future, the microchip will allow us to have continuous communications anywhere on earth and at any time.

Think for a moment about the vast changes in the office that have occurred because of the technological explosion that is continuing to be fueled by the microchip. In addition to the telephone, we communicate with people within and outside our offices via:

- **Email** (electronic mail)
- **Fax** machines (facsimile)
- Cellular phones
- Voice mail

Although we continue to have conferences with groups of people in face-to-face settings, we also have conferences via:

- **Video conferencing** (transmitting audio and video communication between individuals at distant locations)
- **Audio conferencing** (using telephones and speakerphones to transmit communications)
- **Computer conferencing** (linking of participants via a computer)
- **Virtual conferencing** (linking of participants through the **Internet** and **chat rooms** to transmit information and discuss issues) A chat room is a special area established on the Internet that allows a group of people to converse on issues.

Throughout this text, you will learn more about these and other technological innovations that have changed the way the office professional works.

As you begin employment in the office, you will discover that computer technology influences:

- The procedures used to produce work
- The techniques used to communicate both within and outside the office
- The amount and type of information available for making decisions

The changes in our work environment today are just as dramatic and dynamic as the changes caused by technology. As you begin your office work, or if you are working in an office at the present time, here are some of the changes taking place in the work environment that you need to understand.

- The people who make up the labor force are more diverse than ever before; projections are that the increased diversity will continue into the foreseeable future.

- Increased education will be necessary in order to achieve a salary that will provide a comfortable living.
- The types of businesses and their structure are changing. You need to understand what the growth areas of the job market are for the future. For example, the service and professional specialty occupations are expected to grow faster than other areas of the job market.
- Businesses are operating with fewer employees and a flatter organizational structure; this flatter structure will be explained in more detail later in this chapter.
- There is an increased focus on quality. This focus demands that the office worker understands that high standards of performance are essential.
- There is more flexibility in the workweek than ever before. A number of organizations have implemented modified workweeks, with the expectation that organizations offering the modified workweek to their employees will increase in the future.
- As business continues to downsize, more individuals will be contracted specialists, who move from company to company to perform specific contracted assignments.

To understand in more detail what these changes in the office environment will mean, carefully read the next sections.

Increasingly Diverse Labor Force

According to the 1998–99 *Occupational Outlook Handbook*, by the year 2006[3]:

[3]U.S. Department of Labor, *Occupational Outlook Handbook* (Washington, D.C.: Bureau of Labor Statistics, 1998–99), 1–2.

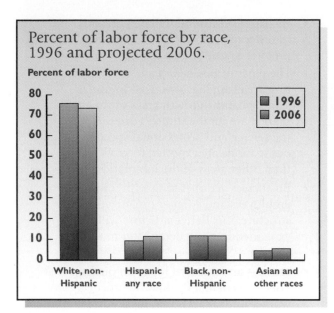

Percent of labor force by race,
1996 and projected 2006.

Percent of labor force

■ 1996
■ 2006

White, non-Hispanic   Hispanic any race   Black, non-Hispanic   Asian and other races

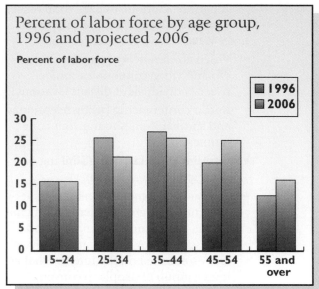

Percent of labor force by age group,
1996 and projected 2006

Percent of labor force

■ 1996
■ 2006

15–24   25–34   35–44   45–54   55 and over

FIGURE 1-1 Percent of labor force by race, 1996 and projected 2006. Source: U.S. Department of Labor, *Occupational Outlook Handbook* (Washington, DC: Bureau of Labor Statistics, 1998–99), 1–2.

FIGURE 1-2 Percent of labor force by age group, 1996 and projected 2006. Source: U.S. Department of Labor, *Occupational Outlook Handbook* (Washington, DC: Bureau of Labor Statistics, 1998–99), 2.

- The number of Hispanics and Asians in the workforce will increase.
- Between 1996 and 2006, women's share of the labor force is projected to increase from 46 to 47 percent, continuing a pattern that began in 1976.
- Workers over age 45 will account for a larger share of the labor force as the baby-boom generation ages.
- Two age groups with large numbers of baby boomers will grow by more than 30 percent—people 45 to 54 and 55 to 64.

Figures 1-1 and 1-2 depict these changes graphically.

The average age of retirement will no longer be 65. People are already living longer than ever before; and with the advances in the medical field on understanding and controlling the aging process, it is believed that we may live well beyond 100 years in the foreseeable future. With longer life spans and the shortages expected in the Social Security fund, working beyond 65 will become the norm rather than the exception.

Our country will become home to many more immigrants. Thus, in addition to the growth of Hispanics, Asians, and African-Americans in the workforce, we can expect an increasingly diverse group of workers from numerous countries outside the United States whose native language is not English.

Increased Education

In the future we will not be able to classify workers under the blue-collar/white-collar division that has been used to separate professional from labor jobs. The labor area jobs such as assembly work will continue to dwindle. According to Robert

Reich, former Labor Secretary, there will be a new class of workers in the middle that are referred to as technicians.[4] Almost all technician jobs will involve computers. These jobs will require more training than high school but less than a college degree. Community colleges and business schools will train many of these workers.

Changing Businesses

The service industry will increase faster than other industries, with growth projected to be nearly 30 percent. Service and retail trade industries will account for 14.8 million out of a total projected growth of 17.5 million wage and salary jobs. Business (including the computer field), health-care services, and education services will account for 70 percent of the growth within the service industry.[5] The projected increases in business, health, education services, and computer services are as follows:

- Health-care services will increase 30 percent and account for 3.1 million new jobs by 2006, the largest numerical increase of any industry. Factors contributing to continued growth in this industry include the aging population and the increased use of innovative medical technology for intensive diagnosis and treatment.
- Educational services are projected to increase by 1.8 million jobs.
- Computer services will add over 1.3 million jobs from 1996 to 2006.

Other trends in business will be:

- More multinational corporations

- Greater emphasis on quality
- A flattened and more efficient organizational structure
- More flexible workweeks
- Larger number of employees working in virtual office situations
- Contracted specialists

Multinational Corporations. An increasing number of businesses in the United States are no longer confined to state or national boundaries. The term **multinational** means that a business operates both within and outside the United States. As businesses look for the most efficient ways to deliver a product or service, they are looking increasingly at the resources available in other countries. These resources include people and natural resources. The technologies available in our world make it more profitable to consider the world as the marketplace. This international orientation demands that we know more about the people of other nations and their cultures.

Due to the technology available, "multinational" has a new and broader context today. International **telecommunities** are being formed. These communities are built on shared international interests via technology. They include such areas as patient-doctor networks, banking (virtual banks), merchandising, homecare at a distance, and education, to name a few. Telecommunities are **metanational** in scope since they bring together many different nations. It is expected that telecommunities will continue to increase and will impact not only our economy but our international relations as well.[6]

[4]"Workers of the World, Get Online," *Newsweek Extra 2000* (Winter 1997–1998), 34.
[5]U.S. Department of Labor, *Occupational Outlook Handbook* (Washington, D.C.: Bureau of Labor Statistics, 1998–99), 2.

[6]George Bugliarcello, "Telecommunities: The Next Civilization," *The Futurist* (September-October 1997), 23–26.

Quality Focus. It is imperative in our competitive society that businesses focus on quality. Competitors are surpassing organizations that fail to provide quality products and services at reasonable costs. An American statistician, the late Dr. W. Edwards Deming, began the quality movement. Deming first introduced his concepts to businesses in the United States but failed to receive their support. In the 1950s, he took his concepts to Japan, where industrialists received him and his ideas enthusiastically. Significant productivity results began to emerge in the Japanese industries. Japan today is a major industrial force, producing quality products that are distributed worldwide. In recent years, Americans have become aware of the need to focus on the quality of goods and services produced. Organizations are now applying Deming's quality principles across a spectrum of production and service industries. Figure 1-3 gives Deming's 14 principles for management. This approach to organizational improvement is now referred to as **TQM (total quality management)** or **CQM (continuous quality management).** This quality movement is affecting the way work is structured and performed.

How does TQM affect the office professional? How does it change your work?

- The office professional is more involved in decisions that affect the direction of the businesses.
- The office professional may have a major role as a member of a team that is responsible for producing a service or product.
- The office professional is more involved in meeting the needs of the customer.
- The office professional has the opportunity to be creative in helping to solve the problems of the organization.

The total quality cycle first involves identifying what the customer requires. Next, a plan of action is developed to achieve these requirements. Finally, the customer receives the product or service. The cycle is continually repeated so that feedback from the customer is being considered at all times. You will learn more about the management concepts associated with TQM in Chapter 20.

Flattened Organizational Structure. The Information Age, with its emphasis on quality, is producing changes in organizational structure. For years we have talked about the organization as a hierarchy. A **hierarchy** is organized according to rank or authority. Figure 1-4 shows a traditional hierarchical organization. Such a structure assumes that knowledge and information flow from the top down—from the president or CEO (chief executive officer) of the company to the workers. In the Information Age, this organizational structure is less effective than in the past. The president or CEO cannot have all the knowledge or information necessary to produce the product or service; our world is too complex. The employees within the organization have specialized skills and knowledge that may be far different from those of the CEO. Out of this situation, an organizational structure has evolved in which employees work in teams to complete a particular project or deliver a particular service.

The flattened organizational structure has fewer levels than the traditional structure. In the past, the optimum number of individuals reporting to any person was six to eight. Organizations now have as many as 25 to 30 people reporting to one individual. Because of the knowledge and skill that each individual worker possesses and the worker's involvement in the

DEMING'S 14 PRINCIPLES FOR AMERICAN MANAGEMENT

1. Create constancy of purpose toward improvement of product and service, with the aim to become competitive and to stay in business and to provide jobs.

2. Adopt a new philosophy. We are in a new economic age. Western management must awaken to the challenge, must learn their responsibilities and take on leadership for change.

3. Cease dependence on inspection to achieve quality. Eliminate a need for inspection on a mass basis by building quality into the product in the first place.

4. End the practice of awarding business on the basis of price tag. Instead minimize the total cost. Move toward a single supplier for any one item, on a long term relationship of loyalty and trust.

5. Improve constantly and forever the system of production and service, to improve quality and productivity, and thus constantly decrease costs.

6. Institute training on the job.

7. Institute leadership. The aim of leadership should be to help people and machines and gadgets to do a better job. Leadership of management is in need of overhaul, as well as leadership of production workers.

8. Drive out fear so that everyone may work effectively for the company.

9. Break down barriers between departments. People in research, design, sales, and production must work as a team, to foresee problems of production and use that may be encountered with the product or service.

10. Eliminate slogans, exhortations, and targets for the work force, asking for zero defects and new levels of productivity.

11. Eliminate work standards on the factory floor. Substitute leadership. Eliminate management by objective. Eliminate management by numbers, numerical goals, substitute leadership.

12. Remove barriers that rob the hourly worker of his pride of workmanship. The responsibility of the supervisor must be changed from sheer numbers to quality. Remove barriers that rob people in management and engineering of their right to pride of workmanship. This means, among other things, abolishment of the annual or merit rating and of management by objective, management by numbers.

13. Institute a vigorous program of education and self-improvement.

14. Put everyone in the company to work to accomplish the transformation. The transformation is everyone's job.

FIGURE 1-3 Deming's 14 Principles for American Management.

planning and decision-making process of the organization, there is much less need for close supervision than in the past.

Within a workgroup of 25 to 30 people, there may be as many as five teams of people (each with five or six members) working on individual projects at a particular time. The individual members of each team are supportive of and helpful to each other in getting the task performed. Ideally, such an arrangement allows an organization to spend fewer dollars on management with no loss in efficiency.

This flattened organizational structure with the team concept is shown in Figure 1-5. Notice that there are fewer levels of management than in Figure 1-4. An office professional in this flattened

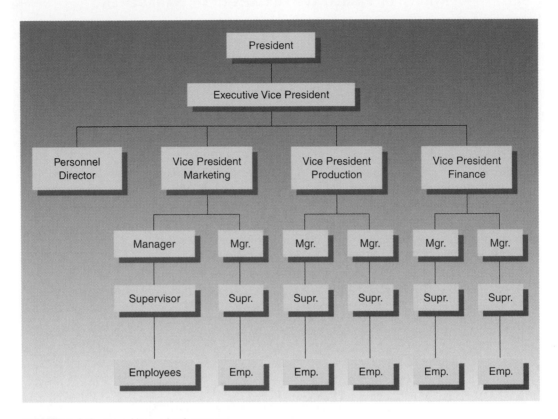

FIGURE 1-4 Traditional hierarchical structure.

structure has increased communication within the workgroup, as well as more knowledge of the customer's needs. The result is more knowledge of the product or service produced.

Flexible Workweek. Although a number of offices still adhere to the traditional five-day workweek and 8 or 9 a.m. to 5 p.m. office hours, the tradition is changing. The change is due largely to the increasing numbers of women in the workforce. Companies have begun to establish more flexible hours to accommodate changing family structures and needs. Several alternatives to the traditional workweek are gaining in popularity. These alternatives include the compressed workweek, flextime, and job sharing.

With a **compressed workweek,** employees work the usual number of hours (35 to 40), but the hours are compressed into fewer than five days. For example, a 40-hour week may consist of 4 days of 10 hours each, and a 36-hour week may be 3 days of 12 hours each.

Flextime is another departure from the eight-to-five workday. With flextime, working hours are staggered. Each employee must work the full quota of time but at periods convenient for the individual and the company. Under this plan, all employees do not report to or leave work at the same time. For example, with a 40-hour week, one employee may come to work at 7:30 a.m. and work until 4:00 p.m. (with 30 minutes for lunch). **Core hours** (hours when everyone is in the office) may be from 9:30 a.m. until 2:30 p.m. Flextime helps reduce traffic congestion at the traditional peak hours and allows employees needed flexibility in their schedules.

Still another departure from the traditional work schedule is **job sharing.** Under this arrangement, two part-time employees perform a job that otherwise one full-time employee would hold. For example, job sharing might be two people working five half days or one person working two full days and another person working three full days. Such a plan can be suitable for families with small children where one or both spouses want to

work on a part-time basis. Also, it can be suitable for workers who want to ease into retirement by reducing the length of their workday or workweek. Both the employees and the organization can profit from job sharing. For example, the company can save on benefit costs since full-time benefits do not have to be paid to part-time employees.

The Virtual Office. Technology has spawned the virtual concept, meaning that through technology an individual may be physically in one location and **virtually** in another location. To help you understand the concept, consider two academic situations. You may communicate **asynchronously** (not at the same time—telecommunication signals are traveling at different times) with other students through chat rooms set up on the Internet. Or you may take an interactive TV course

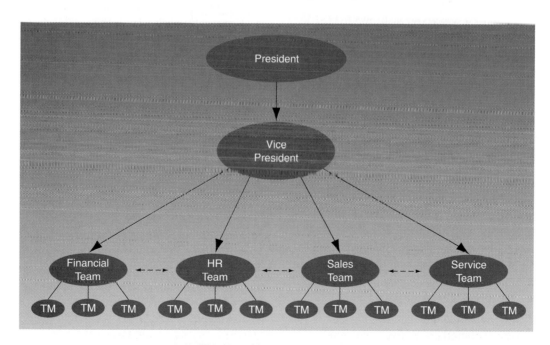

FIGURE 1-5 Flattened organizational structure.

where you communicate **synchronously** (at the same time—with telecommunication signals going back and forth simultaneously) with the instructor who is communicating from another city. In both incidences, you are not physically in the same location with those persons with whom you are communicating. Through technology, you communicate virtually with one or a number of people.

Millions of people now work in virtual situations, and the number working virtually is projected to increase in the future. These virtual situations can vary significantly. The most common example consists of the individual worker who is equipped with a laptop, notebook, or handheld computer for traveling; a cellular phone; pager; fax machine; email; and voice mail system, with the workplace varying. For example, the employee may work at the company office for a portion of a day or a week and at home for the remainder of the time. Or the employee may work exclusively from the home. The hours worked may be just as varied as the work environment. An employee with small children may work hours when they are sleeping or attending school or opposite hours from the spouse so that one parent is available for the children. The individual may be employed by a company or be self-employed.

Telecommuting is another term very similar in concept to the virtual office. However, in telecommuting, the individual is always employed by an organization. In the virtual office, the individual may be:

- Employed by an organization
- Self-employed
- A contracted specialist

Telecommuting involves individuals working at home, at a customer's office, or at some location other than the major office of the business and employed by the business. Communicating with the main office occurs via computers or other technological equipment, such as fax machines and cellular telephones.

According to a 1997 survey, 11 million Americans are telecommuting at least one day a month. On the average, telecommuters work 19 hours a week from home, spending the other time in the office. Government officials have projected that by the year 2002, the federal government will have 15 percent of its employees working from home (approximately 250,000 workers).[7] Businesses that are introducing telecommuting programs are making it work by offering training for both the supervisor and the telecommuting employee.

The advantages of working in a virtual situation include:

- Greater flexibility with the work schedule
- Less or no lost time in driving to and from work
- Ability to provide primary child care while continuing a career
- Increased individual productivity by reducing commute time
- Improved employee morale due to ability to establish the work schedule
- Ability to be your own boss

Some disadvantages are:

- Limited face-to-face communication with other employees and/or the employer
- Isolation from others—lack of feeling of being part of a larger family of workers

---

[7]"Telecommuting Grows in Popularity," *Managing Office Technology* (October 1997), 8.

- Interruptions in work by family and friends if working from home
- Need to set up portion of home for office—space may be an issue

Contracted Specialists. A research project by the Human Resource Institute found that just 61 percent of the large companies surveyed expected to have more than three-quarters of its workforce as full-time, regular employees a decade from now. This percentage is a considerable decrease from the present figure of 84 percent of the workforce being full-time, regular employees.[8] More individuals will be freelance specialists who move from organization to organization to perform contracted jobs. These individuals may be working mainly from their home offices—their virtual office—visiting the contractor's office only occasionally. Or they may be **portfolio** employees who take their skills to special temporary agencies that have contracts with the companies, with the temporary agencies taking care of payroll and benefits.

---

[8]"Workers of the World, Get Online," *Newsweek Extra 2000* (Winter 1997–98), 33–34.

Career Opportunities

There are many types of career opportunities available in the office. To make wise career choices, you need to understand what these opportunities are, the skills needed for the various specialty areas, and some of the professional growth opportunities available.

More and more employees are working in virtual situations. *Courtesy of © PhotoDisc, Inc.*

Types of Positions Available

Career opportunities for office professionals exist in almost every type of business or industry you can name. Since the service industries are growing so extensively and will be major sources of job opportunities for you, presented here are office positions in several service sectors.

According to information from the *Occupational Outlook Handbook,*[9] occupations in the computer field are projected to be the fastest-growing between 1996 and 2006, with the second-fastest-growing field being health occupations. Other service areas where job opportunities are projected to be good include:

- Legal
- Education
- Travel and tourism

Still another area of promise for challenging jobs is the international market. With the continued growth of multinational companies, opportunities for employment for the office professional become global in scope.

Technical.   The technical office professional may work in these fields: computer technology, engineering, aerospace, nuclear energy, or chemistry. As was noted earlier, the computer field is projected to be the major growth field through 2006. The job possibilities here are many and varied. They include positions in the computer department of a large company, computer software company, and peripheral equipment-manufacturing firms. Working for a retail distributor of computing equipment is another possibility.

---

[9]U.S. Department of Labor, *Occupational Outlook Handbook* (Washington, D.C.: Bureau of Labor Statistics, 1998–99), 4.

Health Occupations.   The health occupations industry is not only experiencing considerable growth, but is changing dramatically due to technology and increased costs of health services. In addition to the traditional job possibilities of working in the office of a medical doctor and in the hospital, groups of doctors are now organized into health-care providing agencies called **HMOs** (health maintenance organizations). Job opportunities exist with these groups of health providers.

Positions are also available in health-related organizations such as insurance companies and medical departments of large corporations that provide health-care services. Administrative support responsibilities vary from organization to organization. Duties may include:

- Performing receptionist duties in greeting patients
- Maintaining medical reports and histories
- Completing insurance forms
- Handling the business operations
- Maintaining payment records of patients

Most medical secretaries need to be familiar with insurance rules, billing practices, and hospital or laboratory procedures.

The American Association of Medical Assistants (AAMA) provides certification (CMA—Certified Medical Assistant) for medical support personnel. The examination tests medical, administrative, and clinical knowledge. Another professional growth opportunity available to medical support personnel is sponsored by the American Association for Medical Transcription (AAMT), with the certification being the Certified Medical Transcriptionist (CMT).

Legal.   Growth in the legal service industries is expected to offer employment

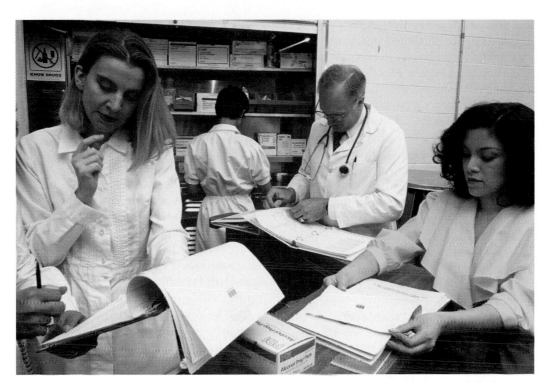

Positions in health occupations are projected to increase through 2006. *Courtesy of © PhotoDisc, Inc.*

growth for legal support personnel. The legal field is very specialized, with specialties including criminal, matrimonial, probate, negligence, environmental, patent, corporate, malpractice, public interest, and computer law.

Job responsibilities in the legal office include preparing legal documents such as complaints, motions, subpoenas, affidavits, and briefs. Typical duties include:

- Processing of documents using the computer
- Performing administrative support functions, such as recordkeeping and telephone contacts
- Assisting with legal research, such as verifying quotes and citations in legal briefs

- Filing court papers
- Taking notes on proceedings

An avenue of continual growth and learning for you in the legal field is obtaining certification. Certification information is available from these organizations:

- National Association of Legal Secretaries
  2448 East 81st Street, Suite 3400
  Tulsa, OK 74137-4238
  Homepage: http://www.nals.org
- Legal Secretaries International, Inc.
  8902 Sunnywood Drive
  Houston, TX 77088-3729
  Homepage:
  http://www.compassnet.com/legalsec/

In addition to office assistant positions, the legal field offers paralegal/legal assistant possibilities for the office professional. Many community colleges offer paralegal programs with the course of study being two years. These positions are readily available, and the salaries are generally higher than office assistant positions. The work involves heavy research, taking depositions, and other duties.

Education. There are a wide variety of office professional positions available in the education field, both in public and private institutions. These institutions include elementary, high school, and higher education. Although salaries of office professionals in the education field have not traditionally been as high as in other fields, there are some advantages that offset this drawback. For example, there are usually more holidays. Many schools provide winter and spring breaks and have no session between Christmas and New Year's. Some positions run nine or ten months, particularly those in elementary schools.

Office professional positions in the legal profession are projected to grow. © 1998–1999 Tony Stone Images. All Rights Reserved.

These positions usually involve a great deal of interaction with both the internal and external public. Office professionals work closely with teachers, administrators, board members, community representatives, parents, and students. Duties consist of:

- Preparing correspondence
- Setting up meetings and conferences
- Keeping records
- Ordering supplies

Support personnel in the education field may belong to the National Association of Educational Office Personnel (NAEOP). This association sponsors a Professional Standards Program (PSP) to encourage professional growth among its members.

Travel and Tourism. The travel and tourism industry is growing dramatically due to increased globalism, an economy that allows individuals more discretionary money for travel, and a larger retired population that are living longer and have time and money for travel. In fact, travel and tourism is one of the world's largest service industries. The job opportunities are varied and can provide opportunities for travel, both within the United States and abroad. For example, you might work in a computer center on a cruise ship. Fluency in a second language can be helpful in this field, as well as good communication, human relations, and computer skills. The entire industry is computerized, with instant communication across the world made possible through technological means.

Salaries. Although salaries vary significantly depending on the type of job and the size and location of the company, here are some general statements that can be made concerning the fields listed here. Positions in the technical (computer) and legal fields pay the highest salaries, followed by the health occupations field. Travel/tourism and education are the lowest-paying fields of the five, although they do offer some advantages in benefits and flexibility; for example, travel opportunities in the tourism field and flexibility in work times in the education field.

One method of finding specific salary information is to search the Web. For example, one location that you might try is http://www.nbew.com. From this location, you can search for a job by title and area of the country where you would like to work. Salary ranges are given on most job listings. This location is only one example; there are numerous locations on the Web where you can search for jobs. To do so, merely put in the key words "job search," and you will discover several sites.

Twenty-First Century Skills

There are certain skills needed in all office professional positions. These skills include the following:

- Communication (listening, speaking, and writing)
- Human relations
- Time and organizational management
- Critical thinking
- Decision making
- Creative thinking
- Technology
- Lifelong learning

Communication Skills. Office professionals spend a major part of their time communicating with others. Communications may be written letters and memorandums, faxes, voice mail, email, telephone calls, or face-to-face conversations. Regardless of the form it takes, you must

be extremely proficient in the communications area. You must express yourself accurately and concisely in written correspondence, and you must state your needs clearly and tactfully in verbal communications.

Another important communication skill is listening. Although most of us think we spend an inordinate amount of time listening, research studies show that we only listen with 25 to 50 percent efficiency. In other words, 50 to 75 percent of what we hear is never processed. Moreover, even when we do process what we hear, we may not grasp the full implications of the meaning. The office professional needs to understand the importance of listening and practice good listening techniques. Several such techniques are given on page 34, Chapter 2. Refer to these now and begin to practice them.

Human Relations Skills. As an office professional, you will interact with many people. Within the company, you will work with coworkers, your supervisor, and executives. Contacts outside the company will include customers and other visitors to your office. All these people will be different; they will have different backgrounds and experiences. They will be of different cultures, races, and ethnicities. If you are to be effective, you will need to accept, understand, and work well with these individuals. Human relations skills are like most of our other skills; we must constantly be developing and improving them if we are to grow in our abilities. Chapter 2 will help you improve your human relations skills.

Time and Organizational Management Skills. Another important skill is the ability to organize your time and work. As an efficient office professional, you will need to organize your time, paper, electronic files, and calendar so that work flows more smoothly and tasks are finished on time. Chapter 3 will help you develop your time and organizational management skills.

Critical Thinking Skills. Critical thinking can be defined as a unique kind of purposeful thinking in which the thinker systematically chooses conscious and deliberate inquiry. Critical comes from the Greek word **"krinein,"** which means to separate, to choose. To think critically about an issue means to try to see it from all sides before coming to a conclusion. As an office professional working in a highly technical and rapidly changing workplace, it is imperative that you daily think critically about the issues facing you. Not only can doing so save you time and make your life easier as an individual working in this office, these skills can also make you a valuable employee for your company—one who is recognized and promoted. As you are learning and practicing critical thinking skills, a systematic process of asking appropriate questions will help you. Several of these questions are listed in Figure 1-6. Take a few moments to read them and then begin to practice and improve your critical thinking skills.

Decision-Making Skills. In your role as an office professional, you will make decisions daily. If you are to be effective in that process, you must understand and implement the steps in decision making. These steps are given in the next section of this chapter. Study them and then practice these skills throughout this course so that you may use them effectively in the office.

Creative Thinking Skills. Creativity is defined in the dictionary as "having the ability or the power to cause to exist." Creativity is a process. It is a way of think-

---

CREATIVE THINKING QUESTIONS

- What is the purpose of my thinking?
- What problem or question am I trying to answer?
- What facts do I need to address this problem or these questions?
- How do I interpret the facts or information I receive?
- What conclusions can I make from the information received?
- Are my conclusions defensible?
- Have I dealt with the complexity of the situation?
- Have I avoided thinking in simple stereotypes?
- What will be the consequences if I put my conclusions into practice?

FIGURE 1-6 Critical thinking questions.

ing and of doing. It is a way of making new connections or new links. It is solving a problem in a new and different way. A creative person understands that multiple options exist in most situations and is free to choose from a wide variety of options. He or she is not bound by one set of rules or one method of getting a job done.

Consider this situation. You have decided to take advantage of your company's offer to work virtually for three days a week. You are expected to be extremely productive as you work from your home; you will have no support from your colleagues. You have two young children who are in the first and second grades. You will be responsible for being the primary caregiver when they return from school each afternoon. In this situation, how do you think creatively about accomplishing your job at the highest level of productivity? How do you set up your office at home to provide for maximum efficiency? How do you provide for your children's needs and still get your job done? Notice the creative thinking tips that appear in Figure 1-7. Take a few moments to read them. Throughout this course, use these tips as you make decisions. This process will help you use them on the job.

Technology Skills. If you are to succeed in the office, you must be technologically competent and current in your knowledge and skills of the technology as it applies to your job. You must be:

- Extremely proficient on a computer, both a personal computer and a laptop or notebook, and on current software packages, including word processing, integrated software, spreadsheets, graphics, communications (online services, email, voice mail, and so forth), presentation software, and personal in-

formation management software
- Proficient in the telecommunications area
- Competent in using fax machines, copiers, scanners, and calculators

This technological competence involves continual learning due to the rapid changes in technology. It requires thinking critically about new equipment and software that needs to be purchased and how the integration of the two takes place in the office.

Lifelong-Learning Skills. If you are to continue to learn and grow in your professional development, you must participate in courses and activities that provide these opportunities for you. You learned earlier about certifications that are available in the medical, legal, and education fields. A widely respected certification that applies to all office fields is the CPS (Certified Professional Secretary). The letters CPS after an office professional's name are indicative of the achievement of the highest professional standard within the field. International Association of Administrative Professionals (IAAP) gives the exam. Figure 1-8 has more details about this certification.

Software certifications can also make you more marketable in the business world. For example, a number of business schools and community colleges offer short courses leading to certification in software such as Word, Excel, and Access.

Your Career Path

Now that you understand some of the opportunities available in the office field and some of the skills that are necessary, consider your career path. What are your goals? Where do you want to be in five

---

CREATIVE THINKING TIPS

- Have faith in your own creativity.
- Attack barriers to creativity. Self-judgment and judging others are both barriers to creativity.
- Pay attention to everything around you.
- Ask questions constantly.
- Tackle tasks that are not easy and that require effort.

  Break tasks into small pieces.

  Do one thing at a time.

  Make a game of tasks.

  Know when to stop.

- Stop worrying.
- Block irrelevant thoughts.
- Pay attention to your intuition.
- Concentrate intently on the activity at hand.

FIGURE 1-7 Creative thinking tips.

years? in ten years? What steps do you need to take to get there? If you are to get to your destination, it is important that you set goals and make effective decisions about reaching these goals. Over time you should continue to evaluate your attainment or lack of attainment in reaching your goals.

Set Appropriate Goals

Personal goal setting involves setting both long- and short-range goals. In order to set goals, you need to take a good look at yourself. Determine what makes you tick. Take an inventory of your needs, wants, interests, and abilities. Let's say that in developing your master plan you decide that you want your life to consist of career success, good health, financial security, and happiness. You must set some long-range goals that will help you in realizing those desires. These goals, for example, may include becoming an office manager, having a family, and staying well. But to become an office manager, have a family, and be well takes hard work and the accomplishment of many short-range goals.

THE CERTIFIED PROFESSIONAL SECRETARY

WHAT: Certification is granted to individuals who pass a written examination and have certain verified minimum secretarial experience. The certificate and CPS designation signify a standard of achievement, the accomplishment of a professional goal, and pride in one's promotion.

HOW: To take the examination an application must be submitted to the IAAP Institute for certification. Certain minimum requirements must be satisfied before taking the examination; fee is payable in advance.

The examination is given twice a year at over 250 locations in the United States, Puerto Rico, Jamaica, Malaysia, the Virgin Islands, and Canada. It is administered on one day in the months of May and November.

The CPS examination is made up of three parts:

      I.   Finance and Business Law

      II.   Office Systems and Administration

      III. Management

Recertification is mandatory every five years, with requirements for recertification given at the time of certification. Upon recertification, an applicant is awarded a dated certificate that is valid for five years.

An educational review program at a local community college or university is advised prior to taking the examination.

WHY: CPS holders may receive special consideration for promotions and salary increases. Many holders of the certificate have used it as a stepping stone into supervisory and/or management positions. Many colleges grant college credits to individuals with CPS certificates. The CPS designation leads to opportunities for leadership positions within professional organizations oriented toward office and secretarial work.

FIGURE 1-8 CPS—What, how, and why.

How do you set short-range goals? You begin by considering the following:

- Your strengths and weaknesses
- Your motivation
- Your energy level
- Your ultimate desire to succeed in what you've planned for yourself

Consider the long-range goal of becoming an office manager. To do so will require experience, commitment, hard work, and time. Thus, a logical short-range goal may include getting a job that will allow you to use the skills and knowledge you've gained, in addition to providing you with work experience for future opportunities. Salary in your first job may not be your highest priority since you are seeking experience. Money may become a higher priority as you work toward your long-range goal.

In setting long- and short-range goals, you may begin by asking yourself these questions:

- What are my strong points?
- What are my weak points?
- What are my achievements?
- What is my motivation?
- What do I enjoy doing?
- Where do I want to be in five years? ten years?

Keep in mind that your goals will change over time and that you will not always reach all of your long- or short-range goals. However, if you go through life never setting goals, you will never accomplish much.

Make Effective Decisions

In your role as an office professional, you will make decisions daily. It is important that you make good decisions. These decisions may range from deciding the type of format to use in preparing a report, to deciding how to handle a difficult customer, to determining the type of records management system to establish. You learned earlier in this chapter that the office is constantly changing as advances in technology occur. You also learned that with the flattened organizational structure, the office professional needs to understand the directions of the organization and be able to make sound decisions. These directions lead to increased complexity of the office assistant role, with more difficult decisions facing the support worker. To help you make these decisions more effectively, an understanding of the decision-making process is beneficial.

A **decision** is the outcome or product of a problem, concern, or issue that must be addressed and solved. The process by which a decision is reached includes five steps, which are depicted in Figure 1-9 and presented in the following section. You should systematically follow these steps in making a decision.

Define the Problem or the Purpose. This step may sound simple, but it is usually the most difficult of the steps. In attempting to define the purpose or problem, it is helpful to ask yourself a series of questions:

- What purpose am I trying to achieve or what problem am I trying to solve?
- Why is this decision necessary?
- What will be the outcome of this decision?

Assume that you are completing your education and are ready to look for a position as an office professional. You know that you want to enter the medical field. You have two job offers—one in a small medical office in the suburbs and one in a large city hospital. The people in the

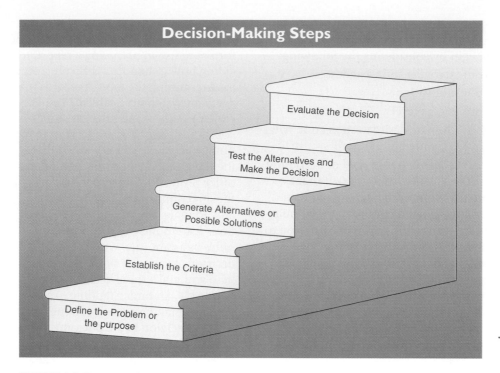

Decision-Making Steps

- Evaluate the Decision
- Test the Alternatives and Make the Decision
- Generate Alternatives or Possible Solutions
- Establish the Criteria
- Define the Problem or the purpose

FIGURE 1-9 Decision-making steps.

hospital seem very nice, but the pace seems to be hectic. The medical office has a very informal, yet professional, atmosphere therefore; you will be able to dress casually. Your answers to the three questions might be:

- I am trying to solve the problem of finding a suitable position in the medical field. I want a job that provides good promotional opportunities and challenging work. Since I have a small child who will be staying with a babysitter, I don't want to drive long distances to work. I want to be able to spend as much time as possible with my child. I would rather work in a small office—a more family-type environment. Also, I would like to be able to dress casually.

- The decision is necessary because: (a) I am finishing my education; (b) I need money to help support my family; and (c) I want employment in meaningful work.

- The outcome of the decision will be that I am employed in a position that provides me challenges and opportunities, with an appropriate starting salary and benefits (vacation, sick leave, contributions to saving plans).

When you finish answering the questions, it is a good idea to frame the problem in a statement form. Your statement might be:

My purpose is to find an office professional position in the medical field within reasonable proximity of my home. This position should be one that provides challenges and opportunities in addition to satisfying my financial needs. I prefer to work in a small office, with a casual atmosphere.

Establish the Criteria. The next step in the decision-making process is to determine the criteria you need to make a sound decision. In setting your criteria, here are three questions you may ask:

- What do I want to achieve?
- What do I want to preserve?
- What do I want to avoid?

Your answers to these questions in the situation given might be:

- I want employment in a medical office professional position where promotions are possible.
- I want to use the skills that I have.
- I want to avoid traveling more than 30 minutes to and from work each day.
- I want to work in a small office, with a casual environment.

By asking and answering these questions, you can determine several criteria that are important to you as you look for a position.

Generate Alternatives or Possible Solutions. The next step in the decision-making process is to begin generating alternatives or possible solutions. For example, you might list the job duties of each position, promotional opportunities available, and the starting salaries available. Next, drive to each location at the times when you would be going to and from work. Determine how long the drive will take.

Test the Alternatives and Make the Decision. The effective decision-maker tests each alternative using this system:

- Eliminate alternatives that are unrealistic or incompatible with your needs or the situation.
- Give more thought to the alternatives that seem appropriate in the situation.

- Select the alternative that appears the most realistic, creative, or appealing.

For example, you might discover that one of the positions has only one promotional opportunity with a very limited salary increase. You would then consider carefully the other position. Does it provide the challenges and opportunities you want? Is it within 30 minutes driving distance? Is the atmosphere a friendly, casual one? If the answers to all questions are *yes*, you make the decision to accept the position. If the answers to one or more questions are *no*, you probably will decide to decline both positions and continue your job search.

Evaluate the Decision. The last step in the decision-making process is evaluating the decision. Evaluation serves two purposes:

- It helps you decide if you have made the right decision for the immediate situation.
- It helps you improve your decision-making skills for the future.

In evaluating your decision, here are some questions you can ask yourself:

- What was right about this decision? What was wrong?
- How did the decision-making process work? What improvements are necessary? What was learned from the decision? What changes need to be made for the future?

Setting appropriate goals and making effective decisions allow you to move in the direction you wish in your career. This approach also helps you deal realistically with your strengths and weaknesses and to minimize the latter as you reach your career goals.

SUMMARY

To reinforce what you have learned in this chapter, study this summary.

- The Information Age has brought vast change to the office. One example of this change can be seen in the way we communicate—through email, fax, cellular phones, video conferencing, and virtual conferencing. Just a few short years ago, these methods of communication were not available.

- Changes in the office environment include an increasingly diverse labor force, growth of the service industries, more multinational corporations, greater emphasis on quality, a flattened and more efficient organizational structure, more flexible workweeks, virtual employment opportunities, and contracted specialists.

- Career opportunities for the office professional can be expected in the growing service industries, such as the computer, health occupations, legal, education, and travel and tourism fields.

- Twenty-first century skills are needed in the areas of communication, human relations, time and organizational management, critical thinking, decision-making, creative thinking, technology skills, and lifelong learning.

- In planning your career, you should set appropriate goals and make effective decisions.

- Decision-making steps include defining the problem, establishing the criteria, generating alternatives, testing the alternatives and making the decision, and evaluating the decision.

Key Terms

- Lifelong learning
- Virtual environment
- Information Age
- Digital era
- PINs
- Microchip
- Email
- Fax
- Video conferencing
- Audio conferencing
- Computer conferencing
- Virtual conferencing

- Internet
- Chat rooms
- Multinational
- Telecommunities
- Metanational
- TQM (total quality management)
- CQM (continuous quality management)
- Hierarchy
- Compressed workweek

- Flextime
- Core hours
- Job sharing
- asynchronously
- synchronously
- Telecommuting
- portfolio
- HMOs
- Critical thinking
- Krinein
- Creativity
- Decision

Professional Pointers

Planning your career will require that you look into your future using a wide-area camera lens. Try to see the world of possibilities that are available to you. Don't make the mistake of considering just your current circumstances or abilities. You should:

- Practice creative dreaming of where you wish to be in your professional life 10 or even 20 years from the current date.
- Know your own beliefs and personal goals; pay attention to what you value.
- Focus on your achievements and your strengths.
- Learn from your failures.
- Create a vision for your future.

Office Procedures Reinforcement

1. Define and explain the following terms:
   a. Virtual environment
   b. Information Age
   c. Digital era
2. Describe four characteristics of the labor force of 2006.

3. List four ways in which the office environment is changing.
4. Explain the difference between a hierarchy and a flattened organizational structure.
5. List six skills required of the office professional; explain their importance.

Critical Thinking Activity

Carlotta Zapata graduated from high school two years ago. While in school she maintained a solid B grade point average. She was president of the Student Government during her senior year. After graduation Carlotta decided to work for a few years before going to college. She thought she needed a break from school, and she also needed the money.

Carlotta started working as a receptionist in the Student Services Department of Long Island Community College. During her two years at Long Island, she has received two promotions and is now working as a clerk in the Admissions Office. She enjoys talking with students and has been given excellent evaluations by her supervisors. However, Carlotta has discovered that she cannot receive another promotion without a two-year associate degree. One of the benefits of Long Island is that employees are allowed to take courses without a tuition charge. Carlotta wants to get a degree in Office Information Systems. She would then like to work as a legal assistant in a large firm, with a long-term goal of becoming an office manager in a law firm. Carlotta presently lives in a small city in Michigan; her career plans involve moving to Chicago. Carlotta is single and does not have a serious relationship at the present time.

1. List the experiences and achievements that Carlotta has had that affect her career plan.
2. What steps might Carlotta take to enhance her chances of achieving her short- and long-term goals?
3. What skills should Carlotta develop to ensure success in the legal field? How should she go about developing these skills?

Office Applications

OA1-1 (Goals 1 and 3)
Interview three office professionals who are currently working in the field. If you have access to email, you may choose to do these interviews that way since almost all office professionals have email addresses. Ask them the following questions:

- How long have you worked as an office professional?
- What changes in the office environment have you seen since you began working?

- How have you handled these changes?
- What skills do you need to be effective on your job?
- How do you keep current in your field?
- What are the advantages/disadvantages of your current position?
- What advice would you give to a student to help prepare for the same type of career that you have?

Write a summary of your findings, giving the names of the office professionals you interviewed and their company affiliation. Present the report to the class. Submit your summary to your instructor. Write thank you letters to the interviewees.

OA1-2 (Goal 1)
Using the information provided on page 1 of the Applications Workbook, prepare a chart showing graphically the percent of the labor force by race from 1996 and projected through 2006.

OA1-3 (Goal 2)
Using the classified ad section of the Sunday paper, research for three weeks the job openings that are listed. Compile a list of these openings by the type of business. For example, list all office professional jobs that you found in the medical field, the legal field, and the computer field. Note the entry salaries (If given) and the qualifications required for each job. Present these findings orally to the class; submit your compiled list (noting the name and dates of the newspaper) to your instructor.

OA1-4 (Goal 3)
To help you understand what your strengths and weaknesses are, rate yourself using the self-evaluation chart provided on page 3 of your Applications Workbook. Discuss your evaluation with a trusted friend, coworker, or family member to see if the person agrees with your ratings. Keep your self-evaluation; you will rate yourself again at the end of the course to determine if you have increased your strengths and lessened your weaknesses.

OA1-5 (Goals 4 and 5)
Outline your career plan beginning with your current status, and describe how you made the decision to enroll in your current course or program. Note where you plan to be in your career in three years and how you expect to accomplish this goal. Conclude your outline with your career expectations in ten years and ways that you can make your goals a reality. Print a copy of your outline and submit it to your instructor. Save your career plan, and make updates to it as you progress through this course.

Online Research Applications

ORA1-6 (Goal 1)

Select two or three of your classmates to work with on this project. Using the Internet, research the use of the virtual environment in offices today. Write a synopsis of your findings and present them orally to the class. Submit your synopsis to your instructor, citing the resources you used from the Internet.

ORA1-7 (Goal 2)

Using the Internet, check the office positions that are listed. One address that you may use is <u>http://www.careermosaic.com/cm/</u>. Print the listing of the office positions from the Internet and submit it to your instructor. Internet addresses change frequently; this address is current at the time of the printing of this text. If it is not available as you prepare to do this job, use the search capabilities of the Internet to find another address.

CHAPTER 2

The Office Team and Environment

YOUR GOALS

1. Demonstrate how to work effectively with internal and external teams.

2. Demonstrate how to be effective with office visitors.

3. Describe and engage in productive communication.

4. Describe the role of ergonomics, safety, and health in the office.

Two major factors that influence your productivity and happiness on the job are your relationships with the people with whom you work and the physical environment in which you work. As an office professional, you will work not only with people within the company, but with external people such as clients or customers. None of your responsibilities will be more challenging than learning to work effectively with these people. Good communication and human relations skills are built each day by consciously striving to improve your understanding of yourself and people with whom you come in contact. These are skills you constantly improve and refine throughout your life.

You learned in Chapter 1 that our world is becoming more and more diverse, and this diversity means that each individual has to constantly seek to understand others who are different in race, ethnicity, gender, age, background, and experience. It is not an easy task, but one well worth your effort. Remember you will likely spend a large part of each day working with others, whether face-to-face or through various telecommunication contacts. If you are to be a productive and happy contributor in your work environment, it is essential that you continue to learn how to communicate with others.

Additionally, the physical environment in which you work is important to your health, happiness, and productivity. None of us can be maximally productive and happy if we feel ill or unsafe in our environment. In this chapter, you will discover ways in which you can be healthy and safe in your work environment.

The Internal Team

What does the word **team** mean? In the office, a team is a group of individuals who work together to achieve defined goals. To be effective the team must understand and accept each other, work productively together, and consistently achieve the goals established. These three elements are examined separately in the following sections.

Understanding and Accepting Others

People who are going to work together must understand and accept the differences that each individual brings to the team. These range from differences in age, gender, and ethnicity to physical and mental differences.

Individual perceptions also vary. Each person sees the world from a perspective determined by his or her values. **Values** are principles and qualities that you consider important. Your values are learned from significant people in your life and from your experiences. Consider the following situation in which different backgrounds cause individuals to view work differently.

Hugo grew up in Canada. He is from a large family; he has five brothers and two sisters. As he was growing up, he was taught that the family unit was always to be valued. Every week the family came together to discuss the chores for the next week. If there were serious disagreements during the week, a family council was held to settle the differences. Hugo has always approached his work life in the same way. He believes that all individuals within the company should work together for the good of the company.

Sarah grew up in a small family; she has one sister. Both of her parents worked outside the home while she was growing up. Everyone was taught to be totally independent. The family unit was not discussed. They rarely even ate together; each person had his or her own schedule. The primary values Sarah was taught were respect for the individual and the ability to operate independently.

Recently, Sarah served as chair of a team on which Hugo was a member. Sarah was an efficient chair, assigning each individual team member a task and expecting it to be done. However, even though they were supposed to be working as a team, Sarah never encouraged teamwork. Team members came to a meeting, received the assignment from Sarah, and reported on their assignment at the next meeting. After three team meetings, Hugo voiced his concern that they were not working together. Sarah didn't seem to understand what he was saying. She suggested that the two of them discuss his concerns after the meeting. Hugo became upset and told Sarah she was not listening to him. Sarah then responded angrily that he was not doing his assignments.

Value clashes such as this one are caused by differences in background and experience. Such incidents can cause misunderstandings among the office team that make it difficult for individuals to work together. As you work with others in the office, you must recognize and understand these differences. You do not need to adopt someone else's values or behaviors, but you do need to be nonjudgmental of that person for behaving in ways that are consistent with his or her background, experiences, and values. When clashes occur, you need to be willing to attempt to find the solution to the problem rather than lashing out at the individual for his or her behavior.

Working Together

Members of the workplace team form a working unit. The design of almost all offices forces individuals into physical proximity. You usually will work on some tasks with those people who are physically close to you. You also are generally part of a larger department, such as Human Resources. Each individual within the department works independently and interdependently to accomplish a variety of tasks. For example, you may be updating a report on the number of employees hired within the last six months; you work with the Assistant Director of Human Resources to obtain the correct figures. However, working together has much broader implications than proximity and similar job tasks. To work together effectively, the group must have a common goal or purpose. This concept is considered next.

Achieving Goals

What are the goals of the workplace team? Two groups of goals to consider are individual goals and organizational goals. You join a company with certain goals of your own. They are probably both short- and

Differences in the backgrounds and experiences of individuals result in different values that can cause misunderstandings. *Courtesy of © PhotoDisc, Inc.*

long-term. One of your short-term goals may be to learn your job as quickly as possible or to be highly productive in your job. One of your long-term goals may be to be promoted to a high-level position in the company.

In addition to individual goals, the organization has goals. A major long-term goal of all businesses is to serve their customers or clients well so that they may make an adequate profit and remain in business. A short-term goal of a company may be to increase sales by $1 million over the next six months. In order to do so, the company must engage in numerous activities such as producing its products quickly and at a low cost, acquiring its share of the market, and keeping labor costs low.

For an individual to work effectively as a member of the office team, the individual's goals and the organization's goals should be compatible. However, this is not always the case. Consider the following example:

> Assume that one of your goals is to develop social relationships with your coworkers. To achieve this goal you make it a habit to go to lunch each day with people who satisfy your social needs. After you have worked several months, the Advertising Department (where you work) begins a major advertising campaign to market a new product. The campaign is behind schedule; your department head asks you to shorten your lunch hour by thirty minutes and work overtime for two hours every evening for a week.

At this point, your goals and your employer's goals are conflicting. By shortening your lunch break, you will not be able to engage in your usual social activities. You can reconcile your goals and the organization's goals only by postponing your social needs for a week and by adjusting your schedule to meet the demands of your job. Reconciling conflicting goals may require adjustments on both your part and that of the organization. This adjustment may be a small price to pay for becoming a productive and essential team member who will be given first consideration when promotional opportunities arise.

Composition of the Workplace Team

In addition to understanding the definition of the workplace team, you must also understand the composition of the team. There are three basic types of internal teams that you will work with formally or informally. These teams are the **project team,** the **office professional and supervisor team**, and the **office professional and coworker team.**

The Project Team

We have become a global economy, competing and collaborating in a world marketplace. This world marketplace has spawned a need for businesses to increase productivity and **worker empowerment** if they are to succeed. The project team is one response to meeting these needs for increased productivity and worker empowerment.

Empowerment implies that the worker has access to the information needed to do his or her job and the authority and responsibility to do it without checking constantly with a supervisor. The empowered worker is trusted to do the job well and make decisions consistent with achieving the goals established. This concept is much different than the hierarchical concept defined in Chapter 1 where a strict organizational structure is followed and very few decisions are made at the lower level of the organization.

Just as worker empowerment is a relatively new term, so is the project team a fairly recent phenomenon in American business. It is defined as a group of employees, approximately 6 to 18, fully responsible for turning out a well-defined segment of work. The segment may be a final product, such as a human resources manual, or it may be a service, such as providing training for customers on a new product. If the project team is to be successful, there are certain essential criteria. Some of these criteria include:

- Clarity of purpose
- Training
- Commitment

Clarity of Purpose. The purpose of the project team must be established clearly before the team begins its work. Here are some questions that need to be asked and satisfactorily answered.

- What is the team to accomplish?
- When is the team to complete its work?
- What standards will be used in determining a successful project completion?
- Who will be evaluating the project?
- What additional resources does the team need outside the organization?
- What is the budget of the team?

As the project team operates, its membership collectively must:

- Have a clear sense of the team identity.
- Be certain that team efforts are consistent with corporate-wide objectives.
- Ensure accountability of the team and each member in it.

- Make certain that the team conforms to fiscal, legal, and other critical guidelines.

Training. Training is essential for a team. In fact, project teams can fail if members do not receive the training they need at the start-up of the team. This training needs to include technical, administrative, and interpersonal skills. Also, many times it is necessary to provide ongoing training for team members, particularly if they are involved in highly technical work.

Technical Skills. Each member of the team must have the necessary technical skills to perform the jobs assigned during the duration of the project. Also, generally there is some **cross-training** (training on different jobs within the team) necessary for the entire team. The most accomplished team member in each skill should conduct this training.

Administrative Skills. Administrative skill training includes the processing of paperwork, interpreting financial data, analyzing budgets, and other similar types of administrative work. As the team assumes wider responsibilities, the list of administrative skills can grow. There will usually be at least one team member who is proficient in these skills. It becomes his or her responsibility to cross-train others in the team.

Interpersonal Skills. The importance of interpersonal skills cannot be stressed too strongly. In fact, studies for many years have shown that individuals lose their jobs more because of the inability to get along with others than for lack of technical ability to do the work. Team members must be able to do the following:

- Listen to each other
- Give performance feedback
- Speak clearly in a team meeting

- Solve group problems
- Learn new skills
- Counsel each other
- Conduct team meetings
- Resolve conflict
- Work collaboratively

To help you in developing listening skills, resolving conflicts, and working collaboratively in teams, read the tips given in Figures 2-1, 2-2, and 2-3. These interpersonal skills are only some of the essentials. As the team works together,

LISTENING TECHNIQUES

- Listen for facts.
- Listen for feelings.
- Withhold evaluation.
- Direct your attention to the speaker.
- Maintain eye contact with the speaker.
- Watch for nonverbal communication.
- Remove distractions.
- Ask questions when you are not sure of what was said.
- Paraphrase what the speaker has said.
- Ask open questions.
- Don't anticipate the speaker.
- Organize what you hear.
- Try to understand the words the speaker uses.
- Don't get angry.
- Don't criticize.
- Take notes if appropriate.
- Set aside your own preconceptions about the topic being discussed.
- Use the listening time productively. People speak at about 150 words per minute; we think at about 500 words per minute. Use the time to think about what the speaker is saying.

FIGURE 2-1. Listening techniques.

CONFLICT RESOLUTION TECHNIQUES

- Attempt to understand the basis of the conflict.
- Listen carefully to all individuals involved in the conflict.
- State your views truthfully but diplomatically.
- Be supportive of the attempt to resolve the conflict.
- Don't be critical.
- Don't get emotional.
- Separate the person(s) from the problem.
- Discuss individual perceptions.
- Initiate a process that examines both sides of the issue.
- Identify points of agreement and work from these points first.
- Hold sessions on neutral turf.

FIGURE 2-2. Conflict resolution techniques.

TIPS FOR WORKING COLLABORATIVELY

- Define the purpose of the collaborative project.
- Choose a chairperson or group leader.
- Determine each group member's skills and expertise.
- Assign tasks to each group member.
- Establish guidelines for completing the task.
- Determine a timeline for completion.
- Determine how the product produced by the group will be evaluated.
- Determine how the group members will be evaluated.
- Praise in public and criticize in private.

FIGURE 2-3. Tips for working collaboratively.

numerous other interpersonal skills will be needed.

Sometimes individuals fail to pay much attention to these skills, believing that human interactions will take care of themselves. However, these interpersonal skills are often the most difficult to learn. Employees bring with them habits, experiences, and values that impact interpersonal skills. If such skills are a problem within the team, attention must be given immediately to improving the situation so that the work of the team can be accomplished.

Commitment. Each individual in the team must be committed to:

- Accomplishment of the task of the team
- Individuals within the team

If each person truly is committed to the accomplishment of the task, he or she will willingly share information about the job to be done. The team members will take risks and express their opinion. Individual members and the team will share accountability for the results.

In demonstrating commitment to each other, the team members will trust each other. They will listen when another team member expresses his or her ideas and opinions. By working together in an open and trusting environment, the contribution of each member can be maximized.

The Office Professional and the Supervisor

A second type of team in the workplace is the office professional and the supervisor team. As an employee, you need to be clear about what you owe your immediate supervisor and what your supervisor owes you. Your relationship with your supervi-

It is extremely important that the office professional and the executive work together as a team. *Courtesy of © PhotoDisc, Inc.*

sor is of primary importance. Unless it is satisfactory, you will not perform at top capacity.

The Office Professional's Obligations to the Employer. Every employer wants to be accepted and respected. Employers also want employees who are loyal, dependable, and understanding.

Acceptance. Your employer is a person with the same basic needs that you have. Try to accept your employer and avoid letting personality differences interfere with your relationship. Do not categorize your employer because of gender, age, race, or any other single characteristic.

Respect. You owe your employer respect simply because of the responsible position the person holds in the company. You need to show respect for your employer's decision-making role although you may not always understand or agree with the decisions made.

Loyalty. **Loyalty** between the office professional and employer is a must. Loyalty means that you handle office matters confidentially. A person who cannot keep business or personal secrets should not expect to advance to a responsible position. If your employer cannot give you confidential work with the assurance that information will not be divulged, you will never have his or her full confidence.

Loyalty also means that you do not circumvent the chain of command. For example, if you have a concern about something that is happening in the workplace, you need to discuss your concerns with your employer. A basic rule here is: **Never surprise your employer.** Always go first to your immediate supervisor with an issue or concern.

Dependability. **Dependability** in the office means that you observe the company rules regarding office hours, coffee breaks, sick leave, vacations, and the like. You are expected to work during the hours set by the company and to observe the designated break times. You are also expected not to abuse the sick leave or vacation policies.

Honesty. **Honesty** means that you do not take office supplies home with you for your personal use. You do not use the telephone excessively for personal calls. You do not play games on your computer or "surf the Internet" for personal uses such as making your own travel arrangements or doing your shopping. You do not use email to send a friend personal notes.

Personality Traits. Personality traits tend to carry over into how people do their jobs. Understanding your supervisor's personality will help make the work go more smoothly. For example, if your employer is a **procrastinator** and you like to get things done immediately, you may have to adjust your style or at least accept that work will not always be finished in your timeframe. On the other hand, if it is your tendency to procrastinate, you must try very hard to overcome this tendency and adjust to the expectations of your boss.

The Supervisor's Obligations to the Office Professional. The office professional/supervisor relationship is not one-sided. There are certain things that your supervisor owes you.

Respect. Your employer should be aware of your needs and show respect for you and your abilities. You were hired because you had the qualifications to handle the job. Your employer must give you the chance to prove that you can.

Feedback. Your employer should let you know how your performance is being evaluated. If you have done something well, you should be told. If you have not performed satisfactorily, your employer should honestly tell you about it. You, in turn, must be able to take constructive criticism. If your employer honestly and sincerely tells you about your progress or lack of it, you will benefit in the long run.

Loyalty. Just as your employer deserves your loyalty, you deserve your employer's loyalty. Your employer should present you in a positive light to all individuals. For example, loyalty means that your employer does not criticize you either professionally or personally to other people. If there is a criticism of your work, the employer needs to talk with you—not to other people.

The Office Professional and Coworkers

A third important team consists of you and your coworkers. What type of relationship should you have with other employees? Have you ever been in a work situation where one employee who had nothing to do refused to help another employee who was overloaded with work? Have you ever been in a situation in which coffee breaks and lunch hours were spent gossiping about other employees? Have you ever worked in an environment where small cliques existed? Ridiculous? Yes, but if you have worked at all, you have probably encountered at least some of these situations. These problems can never be avoided entirely, but they can be reduced considerably if you apply human relations principles.

Acceptance. You will come in contact with many different people in an office. Their backgrounds and interests may be quite different from yours. You may not understand many of these people at first. Because you do not understand them, you may dislike or disapprove of them. As a successful office professional, you need to accept other employees without judging them. You should recognize and respect people who are different from you. If you sincerely listen to others, you will learn more about them and avoid conflicts that result from a lack of understanding.

Cooperation. You should have a cooperative attitude in working with other employees in the office. Since few jobs are performed in isolation, cooperation is necessary in order to attain company goals. You should assist other employees willingly in meeting job deadlines when the situation demands. If one employee has a rush job that cannot be finished without help, you should offer that help, provided you have no top-priority work to complete. Through cooperation, office professionals establish informal working

arrangements for such responsibilities as answering the telephones and covering the reception desk during lunch.

Tact. Tact is skill and grace in dealing with others. Tact demands sensitivity to the needs of others. You should consider the impact of what you say and attempt to avoid statements that will offend people. The tactful office professional emphasizes others' positive traits rather than their negative traits. If you are tactful, you think before you speak. For example, if one of your fellow employees has just returned to the office after a serious illness, let the person know that you are happy that he or she is back; but avoid asking prying or possibly upsetting questions about the illness.

Fairness. The fair person does not take advantage of others. You may get an idea from someone else; but if you are fair, you will not take credit for it. Instead, you will give credit to the individual who gave you the idea. You also assume your share of responsibility without attempting to get coworkers to do jobs that are yours.

The External Team

Although the external team cannot be considered as closely a constructed network as the internal team, it nevertheless has some elements of a team. It is composed of one or more individuals within a company who work with individuals outside the company to achieve specified company goals.

An example of external teams can be seen in the **outsourcing** that is taking place frequently in business now. Outsourcing refers to utilizing an outside company or consultant to complete a portion of a project or a total project. One example of outsourcing is a company that engages an outside consultant to assist in a five-year strategic planning effort. Other examples of outsourcing include a computer department that outsources its programming projects and a college that outsources its food service.

Working with the external team requires the same human relations skills as working with internal teams. Good communication skills and an understanding of the relationship between the outsourcing companies and your company are crucial. As an office professional, you may handle the details of these relationships—telephoning, faxing, processing contracts and payments, monitoring schedules, and the like.

Good Public Relations

In working with the external team, good **public relations** is essential. Public relations is defined as the technique of inducing the public to have understanding for and goodwill toward a person, firm, or institution. Favorable public relations is crucial to any organization. In fact, organizations are so concerned about maintaining a favorable public image that many companies have internal public relations departments or employ professional public relations firms to handle this aspect of their business.

The office professional must use good public relations when dealing with the external team as well as with visitors, clients, customers, or prospective customers of the company. Office professionals can increase the likelihood of a prospective customer becoming a customer and an established customer becoming a repeat customer through effective public relations.

Office Visitors

In many large organizations, a receptionist initially greets all office visitors. The receptionist generally keeps a register in which the name of the visitor, company affiliation, nature of the visit, person the visitor wishes to see, and date of the visit are recorded. This information usually is maintained on the computer. After obtaining this information from the visitor, the receptionist notifies the office professional that the caller has arrived. If this is a first-time visit, the office professional's job may include going to the reception area and escorting the visitor to the executive's office.

If you are employed as an office professional in a small company, you also may serve as the receptionist. You may have the responsibility of greeting all visitors to the company and seeing that they are directed to the proper persons. Regardless of whether you work in a large or small company, here are some techniques for receiving office visitors.

- When the visitor enters your office, greet the person graciously with a simple "Good morning" or "Good afternoon."

- Learn the visitor's name quickly and call him or her by name. One good way to help you learn names quickly is to ask the visitor for a business card. Attach this card to an index card with notations about the caller. If you have numerous visitors, you may prefer to transfer the card information and the notations to the computer. Make notations that will help you remember the person. You might describe the person's appearance briefly—tall, dark brown hair, slight build, ruddy complexion, and so forth. Remember, however, that your comments may be seen by others, so never enter any negative information (i.e., fat, bald, and so forth).

- Determine the purpose of the visit when it is unscheduled. Avoid blunt questions such as, "What do you want?" More appropriately, you might say, "Could you please tell me what company you represent and the purpose of your visit?"

- Make appropriate introductions. If the visitor has not met your employer, you should introduce the two. See the Reference Section, page 598 for introduction rules.

- Be pleasant to a difficult visitor. Be wary of an office visitor who tries to avoid your inquiries with evasive answers such as, "It's a personal matter." You may respond, "I'm sorry, but my employer sees visitors only by appointment. She needs to know the purpose of a call before I'm permitted to schedule an appointment." If the visitor still refuses to reveal the purpose of the visit, you may offer a sheet of paper and suggest that a note be written that you can then deliver to your employer.

- Handle interruptions well. If you need to interrupt your employer with a message when visitors are present, do so as quietly as possible. You may call your employer on the office phone or knock on the door and hand a note to your employer

- Let angry or upset visitors talk. Listen; try to understand the visitor's viewpoint. Once the anger has dissipated (and it might if you let the person talk while you really listen), help the person with the concern.

- Do not disclose specific information about the company or your employer to unidentified visitors. An appropriate response is, "Company policy does not permit me to disclose that information, but perhaps you would like to speak with Mrs. Browne about it."

Organizational Communication

All organizations have formal and informal communication channels, and you should understand how they function. Also, you should be aware of communication techniques that can help you continue to build your skills in this area.

Formal Communication

Formal communication channels in an organization may be upward, downward, or horizontal. **Downward communication** consists of messages that flow from management to the employees of the company. **Upward communications** are messages that travel from the employees to management. **Horizontal communication** involves messages that flow from coworker to coworker or from manager to manager.

Informal Communication

In addition to formal communication in an organization, there are also informal channels, often called the grapevine. The origin of the term **grapevine** goes back to the time of the Civil War. Messages were transmitted by telegraph wires that were strung like a grapevine from tree to tree. These messages were often garbled. Today

Always greet a visitor to the office in a gracious manner. *Courtesy of © PhotoDisc, Inc.*

them is to keep the lines of formal communication open. Management needs to give employees the information required to do their jobs and to be kept informed about the direction of the company.

The grapevine can be a positive form of organizational communication. For example, change is never easy for individuals within an organization. If upper management knows that considerable changes are going to be made, the grapevine sometimes can be used effectively to help employees adjust over a period of time. For example, if there will be a reorganization, certain elements of it can be fed into the grapevine, with the details of the organization being given to the employees through the formal communication channels at a later point. However, when using the grapevine in this way, management must be extremely careful to be certain that the information fed into the grapevine will be a more positive way of communicating temporarily and that people within the organization will not be unduly upset by the grapevine format.

Informal communication can also take place at company-sponsored social events. For example, your company may have an annual picnic, holiday dinner, or award ceremony for outstanding employees. These events provide an opportunity for camaraderie in a relaxed setting. However, you should remember that these events are company ones, and you should always behave professionally. Profane language or suggestive behavior is never appropriate.

Communication Techniques

Communication within an organization can be improved if all individuals use

the grapevine has come to mean messages that may or may not be true and that originate from an unknown source.

The grapevine is a natural and normal outgrowth of people working together. The worst feature of the grapevine is the untrue communication or rumor that is often started. Such untruths or rumors can hurt an organization and its employees. Since rumors can never be squelched entirely, the best way to reduce

good techniques. Several of these techniques are discussed in this section.

Understand the Organizational Structure.   When you join a company, ask for an organization chart if one is not made available to you. This chart will show you the structure of the company, the relationship between departments, and the level of administrative authority. Remember that, as you learned in Chapter 1, there is a trend today to flatten the organization and to use teams in the accomplishment of projects. Thus, certain portions of the organization chart may change from time to time, depending on the projects of the company. These changes are usually reflected in dotted lines showing new relationships based on the project.

Understand the Organizational Climate.   The top and middle managers of an organization can have a considerable influence on the amount and type of communication in an organization. The managers of one organization, for example, may encourage individuals to express themselves and to participate in the decisions of the company. This leadership style is called **participative**, and the climate in such an organization is usually open and communicative.

Although most organizations today are moving toward more teamwork and greater participation, some organizations still use an **autocratic** style of management. Even if a participative style is used as a general management style, individual managers within the company may be autocratic. Such managers discourage participation except in a very limited sense. They tend to tell people what needs to be done rather than asking for input. You will learn more about leadership in Chapter 20.

Write and Speak Clearly.   As an office professional you will frequently engage in both spoken and written communications. Be certain that your communications are as clear as possible. Keep your words simple; refrain from using difficult words to impress others. If you use difficult words, you usually do not impress people—you merely confuse them. Express your thoughts, opinions, and ideas concisely. Tell others exactly what you mean. If you think you do not understand the speaker, repeat what you think the person said in your own words. Ask the speaker to confirm the accuracy or inaccuracy of your statements. If you think the listener has not understood you, tactfully ask the person to repeat what you have said. For example, you might say, "I know I am not always clear in my communication. Perhaps it would be helpful if we checked my communication skills by your repeating what you heard me say."

Be Word Conscious.   Words can mean different things to different people. You need to consider how the communicator interprets and uses words. The intended meaning of a supervisor may be misinterpreted by an employee unless both persons are using the same point of reference. It is always a good idea to check your communication with the receiver of the communication. Review the communication techniques shown in Figure 2-4, and begin to practice them now.

Consider Multicultural Differences. As you learned in Chapter 1, our world is becoming more and more diverse. Projections are that the diversity within our country will continue to grow. Effectiveness in working with people demands that we be open to **multicultural differences** and willing to continue to learn about people from other races, ethnicities, and other countries. People from other countries, because they have

COMMUNICATION TECHNIQUES

• Understand the organizational structure.

• Understand the organizational climate.

• Write and speak clearly.

• Be word conscious.

• Consider multicultural differences.

FIGURE 2-4. Communication techniques.

different backgrounds and experiences, often view the world very differently from the way we do. Words can mean different things to them. Consider the differences listed here.

• People from Asia believe it is disrespectful to be addressed by their first name. Older persons expect to be addressed by their titles.

• In Middle Eastern styles of doing business, negotiation continues even after a formal agreement has been reached.

• In Korea, wives retain their maiden names, and the family name comes before the given name.

• Asians often feel uncomfortable and embarrassed when receiving praise. They may even consider praise as a form of subtle criticism.

• In Mexico, when a woman marries, she keeps her maiden name and adds her husband's name.

• In the Middle East, the first response to a question or statement may not be the real answer. It may be intended merely as an opening formality.

• Some Asian cultures consider it rude to say no and will go to extremes to avoid doing so.[1]

[1]Norine Dresser, *Multicultural Manners* (New York: John Wiley & Sons, Inc., 1996), 151–156.

As you work in a multicultural office, be sensitive to different cultures and alert to the differences in the meaning of words and the way they are used.

Physical Environment

A pleasant work environment contributes to the growth of the office team. How? Everyone prefers to work in an attractive, safe, and healthy physical environment. If our environment is unattractive, unsafe, and unhealthy, our productivity is affected. We are sick more, absent more, and our morale is lower. For the employer, an unsafe and unhealthy environment results not only in lost productivity but increased costs in the form of greater medical expenses and disability payments. The impact of the physical environment is enormous and greatly affects the office team.

To understand more about the importance of the office environment, consider some of the health issues that we are facing today. Technological factors are not only influencing the way we perform our work, but they are also affecting our health. **Cumulative trauma disorders (CTDs)** caused by repetitive strain injury are increasing. CTDs typically involve pain or discomfort in hands, wrists, arms, shoulders, or neck. In the past this type of illness was linked to industrial occupations such as meatpacking and poultry processing. Today, however, CTDs are prevalent in the office. Improper techniques at the computer such as poor posture and sitting for a long period of time without appropriate breaks may cause CTDs. Other health problems that may occur include vision and hearing problems, fatigue, depression, and stress-related disorders.

The most effective way to deal with these health problems in the office is to keep them from happening. In this next section, you will learn ways to prevent these illnesses.

Ergonomics

Ergonomics, from the Greek words **ergos** (work) and **nomos** (natural laws), means the bringing together of the physiological factors that make an effective work environment and the psychological factors that explain how workers react to their environment. Ergonomics simply stated is the fit between people, the tools they use, and the physical setting where they work. The physiological factors in the office include the utilization of space and color, the arrangement of furniture and equipment, and the regulation of lighting and noise. Ergonomics is treated succinctly here; an in-depth approach would take several chapters. As an office worker, you should understand how ergonomics affects you and the office team.

Color.   Color influences the way visitors regard a company as well as the productivity and morale of its employees. Attractive, cheerful, and efficient-looking offices tend to inspire confidence and trust. In contrast, drab or poorly painted offices can arouse doubt or mistrust. Tones of gray tend to put workers to sleep. Warm colors such as yellow, red, and orange create cheerful surroundings. Cool colors such as green and blue produce a calm and tranquil atmosphere. Studies have shown that productivity increases and absenteeism is reduced as a result of improved color in the office. Notice the office photos on this page and page 44. The photo above shows an office in which cheerful colors have been used. Drab colors have been used in the photo on the next page.

Warm colors in an office such as yellow, red, and orange create cheerful surroundings. *Courtesy of © PhotoDisc, Inc.*

Lighting.   In order to process information in an office, an adequate lighting system must be maintained. Improper lighting can cause headaches, eye fatigue, neck and shoulder muscle strain, and irritability. If improper lighting conditions continue over a period of time, productivity and morale are lowered, which in turn can cost a business considerable dollars. For example, a 1 percent productivity loss with a $1 million per year workforce will cost a company $10,000 annually.[2]

The office worker of the past spent a large percentage of time looking down at materials. Today, with computer screens, the office worker spends most of his or her time looking straight ahead. Glare

---

[2]John Phillip Bachner, "Eliminate Those Glaring Errors," *Managing Office Technology* (April 1998), 16.

Drab colors used in an office can arouse doubt or mistrust. *Courtesy of © PhotoDisc, Inc.*

reflected from a computer screen could be a major problem. Glare can be caused by overhead lighting, light bouncing off objects such as picture frames and mirrors, and even glare bouncing off a glossy magazine. There are a number of techniques that can be used to reduce glare including:

- Relocating items on the wall or framing artwork with nonglare glass

- Reorienting workstations

- Using screen filters

- Replacing overhead lighting with flexible systems so that lights can be easily repositioned and brightened or dimmed as appropriate[3]

- Using screens and draperies that diffuse light and deflect glare

---

[3]Bachner 18.

Acoustics.   Sound in the office can be good or bad. For example, background music and subdued conversations are necessary in the office and do not disrupt the workday. Street sounds and clattering machines can irritate and disturb employees. In the short run, offensive noise diminishes the worker's efficiency and decreases productivity. In the long run, noise can have serious effects on the employee's health. Noise interferes with communication, makes concentration difficult, and causes irritation and fatigue. High levels of noise impair hearing, cause sleep loss, and can induce emotional damage. In contrast, the control of noise levels can increase efficiency, decrease errors, and reduce turnover.

In order to control noise, various measures are used, including:

- Installing partitions with acoustical panels between workstations
- Installing carpeting, draperies, and acoustical ceilings
- Placing noisy equipment in separate rooms
- Providing conference rooms for small and large group meetings

Floor Plans.   The technological revolution demands that floor plans be as flexible as possible. To provide maximum flexibility, office planners are using furnishings that can be moved easily. Large, open rooms are sectioned off by movable partitions. These partitions can be rearranged easily as needs change. The photo below shows a workstation that can be quickly changed, depending on the needs of the individual and the company. Flexible furnishings offer the office professional some control over the work environment. The professional has the capability to organize the workspace, within limits, to create a comfortable and pleasant environment.

Furniture and Equipment.   Much of the office furniture of today is modular. Desktops, shelves, and cabinets attach to partitions, and these units can be adjusted for height, efficiency, and attractiveness. Pneumatically operated ergonomic chairs that are fully adjustable for seat height and tilt, back height and tilt, and arms

Flexible office furniture design allows for quick changes in arrangement to be made easily. *Courtesy of © PhotoDisc, Inc.*

that are continuously height adjustable should be purchased. It is also important that the chair's seat and back move independently of each other so that the most appropriate adjustments can be made.

The seat upholstery on the chairs should be very firm. Each person should be fitted for a chair independently of the work surface. The person's specific seat height is determined by sitting with both feet flat on the floor and the knees slightly higher than the hips to reduce curvature in the lower back. The front edge of the chair seat should be tilted slightly down to avoid pressure behind the knees. The person should sit well back in the seat to support the lower back. Notice Figure 2-5, which gives a workstation checklist.

Computers and other technological equipment used constantly in the office today have introduced new ergonomic factors that must be considered. As an office professional, you will be spending a major portion of your workweek on the computer. Your productivity and well-being depend on your using proper techniques and taking positive steps to insure your good health. You will learn more about computer ergonomic considerations in Chapter 6, where a section is devoted to this topic.

Safety and Health Issues

In 1970, the Occupational Safety and Health Act was passed to ensure American workers a safe and healthy workplace. **OSHA** (Occupational Safety and Health Administration), established by the act, was directed to encourage states to develop and operate their own job safety and health programs. OSHA requires that employers furnish a place of employment free from recognized hazards that are likely to cause death or serious injury.

> **WORKSTATION CHECKLIST**
>
> - Is there sufficient space to perform tasks?
> - Is there sufficient space for equipment?
> - Can all items that are used frequently be easily reached?
> - Is there flexibility to rearrange the workstation if needed?
> - Is the lighting sufficient?
> - Is the height of the work surface appropriate?
> - Is the height of the chair appropriate?
> - Can the chair be adjusted easily?
> - Can the work surface height be adjusted easily?
> - Is the computer screen free of glare?
> - Is the work surface depth adequate to allow the computer screen to be placed at an appropriate distance?
> - Are document holders provided?
> - Is the furniture light in color?
> - Is the equipment suitable for the work to be done?
> - Can the computer screen be tilted?
> - Is adequate storage space provided?

FIGURE 2-5. Workstation checklist.

Employers are required to keep records of work-related deaths, illnesses, and accidents. They are also required to maintain records of employee exposure to materials and when the toxic effects exceed the set standards. Trained safety inspectors, employed by the government, make unannounced visits to companies to see that safety standards are maintained. If problems are found, the company is required to correct the problems.

Carpal Tunnel Syndrome. You learned earlier that CTDs are considered the occupational illness of the decade. Included in the CTD category is **carpal tunnel**

syndrome. This syndrome is a condition that occurs due to the compression of a large nerve, the median nerve, as it passes through a tunnel composed of bone and ligaments in the wrist. Symptoms include a gradual onset of numbness and a tingling or burning in the thumb and fingers.

Eyestrain. Symptoms of eyestrain include visual discomfort, irritation, problems in focusing, blurring, double vision, and headaches. Eyestrain problems can be caused by uncorrected vision and/or long periods at the computer without breaks.

Fatigue. Fatigue while sitting at a **VDT (video display terminal)** has something to do with the type of work that is being done in addition to the time that is spent at the VDT. Some studies have found that scientists, engineers, and programmers experience less fatigue while working at a VDT than do data entry operators. Reasons as to why this situation occurs vary. The data entry work may be more monotonous and the operator may not be as involved with the subject matter as the engineer or programmer. Programmers also are probably more tolerant of system delays and error messages than data entry operators since they have more knowledge of what is happening with the computer. Software packages that are not user-friendly can cause frustration that leads to

The office worker should maintain a viewing distance of 24 to 28 inches from the computer screen in order to avoid eyestrain and fatigue. *Courtesy of © PhotoDisc, Inc.*

fatigue, as can office furniture that is poorly designed and uncomfortable.

Tips. Here are some tips to assist in lessening the possibility of carpal tunnel syndrome, eyestrain, and fatigue.

- Be certain that the light on the screen is good—not too dark, not too light.
- Take a short rest period (10 to 15 minutes) every two to three hours.
- Stand up every half hour.
- Be certain your chair is adjusted properly for you.
- Organize your workstation.
- Use good posture.
- Look away from the screen for a short period of time every 30 minutes.
- If eye problems persist, get an eye examination.
- Focus on distant objects occasionally as an exercise to relieve eye muscles.
- Maintain a viewing distance of 24 to 28 inches from the eye to the computer screen.
- Eliminate any glare on the computer screen.
- Use proper hand and wrist position when keyboarding.

Smoking. Another health issue that is causing much concern in offices now is smoking. Studies have shown that breathing secondhand smoke is unhealthy and point out the linkages to emphysema and lung disease from secondhand smoke. Nonsmokers complain of eye, nose, and throat irritations resulting from secondhand smoke. They are making it known that they believe smoking should be banned from the workplace, and many offices are taking a strong stand in this regard by adopting no-smoking policies. For

businesses that still allow smoking (for example, those in the service industries such as hotels and restaurants), it is usually restricted to a specific location.

Substance Abuse. Substance abuse is a problem of monumental proportions. This term refers to the use of alcohol or drugs to the extent that it is debilitating for the individual using the substance. The result of substance abuse in the office is higher absenteeism and illness. Drug-and-alcohol-affected employees are absent an average of two to three times more than the normal employee. Staff turnover is greater. Chemically dependent people often lead disorganized lives and frequently quit rather than face detection. Drug-and-alcohol-affected employees perform at about two-thirds of their actual work potential; thus, productivity is lowered. Shoddy work and material waste are evident with such individuals. Mental and physical agility and concentration deteriorate with substance abuse. Chronic drug abuse creates wide mood swings, anxiety, depression, and anger. Employees who abuse drugs are more likely to steal equipment and materials in order to get money for their substance habit. They are also over three times more likely to cause accidents. Even small quantities of drugs in the system can cause deterioration of alertness, clear mindedness, and reaction speed.

Substance Abuse Laws. In 1988, the federal government imposed sweeping anti-drug rules on private employers in an effort to curb employee substance abuse. The Drug-Free Workplace Act of 1988 requires most federal government contractors, as well as recipients of federal grants, to take steps to ensure a drug-free workplace.

Security

The office should also be secure. Security efforts should be cooperative ones between managers and employees. Security issues involve personnel, equipment and information, and emergency procedures.

Personnel

It is common for employees to work outside the regular office hours of the company. Employees may arrive early and stay late to finish a rush job. Companies have a variety of procedures to protect their employees. Security guards may be stationed at doors to monitor who enters and exits. Special badges or passes may be issued to visitors. Some companies have television screens and cameras in particular locations within the company. Personnel monitor these screens for suspicious individuals or behaviors.

Regardless of your company policies or procedures, to ensure safety and security, you should establish some practices of your own. Here are some recommended ones.

- If you work late, notify the security staff. It is also wise to notify someone at your home that you are working late. Call the person just before you leave to say that you are on your way home.
- If you drive to work, walk to your car with someone else if possible. Someone from the security staff may be willing to accompany you if you work in a high crime area. Have your car keys ready to unlock your car; then lock it immediately after getting in.
- Situate yourself near others who are working late if possible.

- Work next to a telephone and have emergency numbers handy.
- Keep all doors to your office locked while working.
- If you hear strange noises, call for help. Do not investigate on your own.

Equipment and Information

With the increase in electronic equipment used in the office, theft is a grave concern. Small office equipment such as personal computers and calculators can be taken easily. In order to help prevent theft, it is suggested that companies affix serial-numbered tags with the company name to pieces of equipment. Information pilferage is also a major concern. Computer codes or access devices should be used for confidential information. Shredders should be used to destroy confidential printouts.

Caution should be taken also that information will not be lost due to equipment malfunction. Anti-static floor mats, sprays, and dustcovers should be used to control static electricity that can cause electronic equipment memory loss and produce inaccurate data.

Emergency Procedures

Emergencies such as fires demand that businesses have evacuation procedures. These procedures should be printed and distributed to all personnel, and there should be periodic reminders of them. For illnesses or accidents, emergency procedures should include a list of employees who can administer first aid and phone numbers for ambulances, hospitals, and physicians. Oxygen kits and first aid kits should be located so that they are readily available to employees.

SUMMARY

Study this summary to reinforce what you have learned in this chapter.

- The workplace team is composed of a group of individuals working together to achieve defined goals.

- The workplace team is composed of the internal team and the external team.

- The internal workplace team includes three different types of teams: the project team, the office professional and supervisor team, and the office professional and coworker team.

- If the project team is to be successful, there must be a clear purpose and commitment to the task and team.

- In the office professional and supervisor team, both individuals have obligations to each other. For the office professional, these obligations include acceptance, respect, loyalty, dependability, and acceptance of personality traits. For the supervisor, these obligations include respect, feedback, and loyalty.

- The office professional and coworker should accept each other, cooperate, and use tact and fairness in dealing with each other.

- The external team is composed of one individual or several individuals within a company who work with individuals outside the company to achieve specified company goals.

- Public relations is defined as the technique of assisting the public in understanding and having goodwill toward a person, firm, or institution. Favorable public relations is crucial to all businesses.

- Receptionist responsibilities include receiving the visitor, understanding the supervisor's expectations, determining the purpose of the visit, learning names, making introductions, handling interruptions, and handling the difficult visitor.

- Communication within the office is both formal and informal.

- Communication within the office can be improved by: (1) understanding organizational structure and climate, (2) writing and speaking clearly, (3) being word conscious, and (4) understanding multicultural differences.

- A pleasant work environment contributes to the growth of the office team.

- Important elements to consider in the physical environment are color, lighting, acoustics, floor plan, and furniture and equipment.

- Health issues such as carpal tunnel syndrome, eyestrain, and fatigue are becoming common in the technological office.

- Smoking and substance abuse are hazardous to your health and can cause absenteeism and illness.

- The office should be a safe and secure environment.

Key Terms

- Team
- Values
- Project team
- Office professional and supervisor team
- Office professional and coworker team
- Worker empowerment
- Cross-training
- Loyalty
- Dependability
- Honesty
- Procrastinator
- Tact
- Fair
- Outsourcing
- Public relations
- Formal communication
- Downward communication
- Upward communication
- Horizontal communication
- Grapevine
- Participative
- Autocratic
- Multicultural differences
- Cumulative trauma disorders (CTDs)
- Ergonomics
- Ergos
- Nomos
- OSHA
- Carpal tunnel syndrome
- VDT (video display terminal)
- Substance abuse

Professional Pointers

Business is a team sport, and it takes a team to make a superstar! No one individual in an organization can be successful without the support of their fellow employees, but a group of individuals is not necessarily a team. A team is a group of people who agree on a goal and agree that the best way to achieve it is by working together.

These pointers will help you learn the skills necessary to be an effective team member.

- Every member of a team must be involved.
- The best way to get everyone involved is through communication.
- No one person has all the answers; all team members' opinions are valuable.
- There is no "I" in the word TEAM.
- Teamwork is not about seeking credit for one's individual contributions but about the team succeeding.

Office Procedures Reinforcement

1. Define team; list and explain the standard types of internal teams that exist in an office.
2. Describe your obligations as an office professional to your supervisor.
3. Explain the difference between three kinds of communication: downward, upward, and horizontal.
4. Define ergonomics; give three ways that ergonomics impacts the office professional.
5. Identify and explain three types of health issues that may affect the office professional.

Critical Thinking Activity

Hatcher & Edwards is a 15-year old company providing pharmaceutical supplies both in the United States and Canada. The company is progressive; it has been very successful over the last five years. In this time period, its stock has increased dramatically, an average of 25 percent each year. The company attributes part of its success to its emphasis on solving problems through a team-based approach. Employees serve on project teams that address methods to improve various work processes.

Ben Capner has been asked to serve on an eight-member team to examine the company's employee evaluation procedures. Ben is very pleased about serving on this team; he feels he has several good suggestions that will improve the evaluation procedures. However, the team leader is Jennifer Anvil, supervisor in the Records Management Department. Ben has little respect for Jennifer; he feels she is a poor supervisor. He has heard stories from several people who report to her about how unfair she is with employees. Although Ben has not had direct experience with her as a supervisor, two trusted employees have told him of several incidences where she behaved unfairly. Ben feels that Jennifer is an unacceptable team leader.

What should Ben do?

1. Request to be taken off the team? Why or why not?
2. Talk with others on the team about his concerns? Why or why not?
3. Talk with Jennifer's supervisor? Why or why not?
4. Say nothing and concentrate on being an effective team member? Why or why not?

In answering these questions, use these critical thinking principles.

Critical thinking assumes:

- Open-mindedness, intellectual curiosity
- Willingness to entertain new ideas
- Willingness to acquire new information
- Willingness to evaluate assumptions and inferences

Office Applications

OA2-1 (Goal 1)

Choose four of your classmates to work with on this project. You are to assume that you are working as a collaborative team on a project. Here is your project.

The local Chamber of Commerce has asked you to write a two-page description of your college. The Chamber will be using this description in a publication they are putting together for new companies and individuals moving into the city. You need to include a short history of the college, the number of students enrolled, and the types of programs that are offered.

As a team, complete this project. When you finish, discuss how the team process worked. What were the team's strengths? What problems did it have? Was there expertise that it lacked? If so, how did it compensate? Write a joint memo to your instructor detailing how the team process worked—the strengths of the team and its deficiencies and how these deficiences were handled. A team evaluation form is given on the student template disk in the file OA02-1a.doc. Do not submit your evaluation form to your instructor unless asked to do so. Key the memorandum using the memorandum form given on the student template disk in the file OA02-1b.doc. Submit your memorandum and report to your instructor.

OA2-2 (Goal 2)

This morning has been a very busy one for you. Your employer is leaving for a trip to one of your company's international locations. From the time your work-day began at 8:30 this morning until now (1 p.m.), you have not stopped. In fact, you have not even taken any time for lunch. Your employer has given you numerous tasks that must be accomplished before he leaves, and he told you that he would not see any-one this morning due to his busy schedule. About ten minutes ago, a woman came in and asked to see your employer. You explained that he was extremely busy and was not seeing anyone this morning. (She did not have an appointment.) She kept insisting that she must see him. You suggested that she see his assistant. She refused, and in a very loud voice announced that she would see him. She berated you for being "his overzeal-ous protector" and then marched into his office before you could stop her. After she left, your employer said, "I thought you understood I was not seeing anyone. What hap-pened?" You could tell that he was not happy.

You feel that you did not handle the situation well. How could you have handled it differently? What should you say to your employer, and when should you say it?

Submit your answers to your instructor.

OA2-3 (Goal 3)

Angelo Perez supervises 12 employees in the Human Resources Department. He has been in his position for two years. Charlotte Via was hired recently as the de-partment's receptionist. After two months on the job, Charlotte has observed that most people in the department seem to like Angelo. There is a lot of laughter and joking going on. However, the department does not seem to be a highly productive one. Here are some of the things that Charlotte has observed.

- Angelo shows favoritism to Juanita, with whom he has a lot in common. Juanita is frequently late for work. When she does come in, she and Angelo tend to have a 20- to 30-minute conversation before she begins work. The conversation is often conducted at Juanita's workstation. Charlotte can overhear the conversation, and it is always a personal one about what Juanita did the evening before, a new movie she has seen, or what she is planning to do over the weekend. Charlotte has been told that Angelo never docks Juanita's pay for being late.

- Angelo seems to want all employees in the office to like each other. Every Friday, he encourages everyone to meet after work for "happy hour." Charlotte is a single parent who must pick up her child from day care by 6 p.m. Besides, she really does not like to socialize in such a way with her coworkers.

Assume that you are Angelo's supervisor. Charlotte has complained to you about Angelo's behavior. You do know that he socializes with his employees after hours, but you do not know that the other statements that Charlotte has told you are true. You know very little about Charlotte. However, Angelo has told you that her performance during the two months that she has been with the company has been "superior." Answer the following questions as to how you, as Angelo's supervisor, should handle the situation.

- What should you say to Charlotte?
- Should you talk with Angelo? If so, what should you say to him?
- Are there communication problems in Angelo's department? If so, what are they?
- What suggestions would you make to Angelo to improve communications within his unit?

OA2-4 (Goal 3)
On pages 10–12 of your Applications Workbook is the draft of an article for People First International's company newsletter. Cecilia Ivon, the company's Chief Executive Officer, coauthored the article with Hugh Minor, vice president of communications. Key the article in an appropriate format; prepare the chart, using graphics. Submit the keyed article to your instructor.

OA2-5 (Goal 4)
Select one of the following topics to research:

- Ergonomics
- Safety and/or health issues within the office

Using three current periodicals, prepare a summary of the articles; list your references. Present your findings orally to the class. Prepare a cover memorandum for your instructor, using the memorandum form on the student template disk in the file OA2-5. Explain in the memorandum why you chose the particular topic that you did and how you might use the information you received in your present job or in a future job. Turn in both the memorandum and the report to your instructor.

Online Research Applications

ORA2-1 (Goals 1 and 3)

You are giving a presentation to your local chapter of IAAP (International Association of Administrative Professionals) on effective communication. Using the Internet, put in these keywords:

- Effective office communications
- Building effective office teams
- Listening skills
- Critical thinking skills

Locate at least four articles on two of these four topics. Prepare a summary of these articles; list your sources and include the URL (Uniform Resource Locator). Submit the summary to your instructor.

ORA2-2 (Goal 4)

Search the Internet for information on the latest office furniture available. Write a short summary of your findings and submit it to your instructor. Here are two possible Internet addresses for your use:

- http://www.bizplus.com/zoffice/ virtual.html
- http://www.buyerszone.com

Internet addresses may change frequently. These addresses were current at the time of the printing of this text. If they are not available, use the search capabilities of the Internet to find other addresses. When you are searching the Internet, you need to use your time as wisely as possible. If you have experienced searching, you know that you might get thousands of "matches" on a request. Here is one tutorial that can help you make the most effective use of your time during this process.
http://www.seekhelp.com/tutorial.htm.

CHAPTER 3

Productivity in the Office

You learned in Chapter 1 that rapid change will continue in the workplace of the twenty-first century due to technological advances and our global economy. In this workplace, the office professional is expected to:

- Produce a large amount of work quickly, accurately, and efficiently
- Keep current on new technology and equipment
- Maintain a cheerful, helpful attitude while working with diverse people and situations

Stress is inevitable in this world of change and high expectations. The way in which you handle stress affects not only your productivity but also your emotional and physical health.

This chapter will help you learn how to manage your stress and become the productive, healthy

YOUR GOALS

1. Determine why managing stress and time is important in the workplace.

2. Apply appropriate coping techniques to minimize negative stress.

3. Establish time and stress management action plans.

employee that you are capable of being. Techniques for coping with stress are presented. Since one of the major techniques for helping you cope with multiple pressures is the ability to manage your time well, time management techniques and systems are discussed in detail. As you continue this course, you will want to review this chapter frequently to determine if you are applying the skills and techniques you have learned, on your job, at home, and in school. Used appropriately and consistently, the techniques presented in this chapter can significantly improve the quality of your life.

The Office Professional and Stress

Stressful situations do occur in an office. These stressful situations may be challenging or debilitating for you. For example, no matter how competent and capable you are, there will be workdays in which nothing seems to go right. It may seem as if everything you touch falls apart in your hands; you make one error after another. Such days can produce negative stress that causes even more errors. All of us have had difficult days, and all of us will continue to experience them. However, through understanding and applying effective stress management techniques, we can lessen our own negative stress in tough situations. Part of lessening your stress is understanding the difference between good stress and bad stress and what bad stress can do to our bodies if it continues over a prolonged period of time.

Stress Defined

Stress is the response of the body to a demand made upon it. Wants, needs, and desires are derived from stress of some kind. You cannot avoid stress. However, stress does not always have a negative effect. For example, if you didn't feel a need for friends, you wouldn't join social groups. If you didn't feel a need to make good grades in your courses, you wouldn't study. If you didn't feel a need to achieve, you wouldn't take a challenging job. All of these situations are examples of stress that can make a positive impact on your life. Through needs, wants, or desires that you have, you feel pressure to satisfy those needs and respond in a positive way to obtain satisfaction.

Now consider negative stress, often referred to as **distress** due to the negative impact it has on our lives. For example, if someone you love is sick, you feel distress. If you are unable to keep up with new technology in your office, you feel distress. If you receive a negative performance review on your job, you feel distress. Even the stresses of driving to work in heavy traffic or getting you and your family ready for work each morning can cause negative stress. If we are unable to cope with our stresses, we can become physically, mentally, and/or emotionally ill. It is important to achieve an appropriate balance between the distress in our life and the ability to cope with this distress. Figure 3-1 graphically illustrates appropriate and inappropriate balances. This section will help you understand more about stress and how to maintain the appropriate balance.

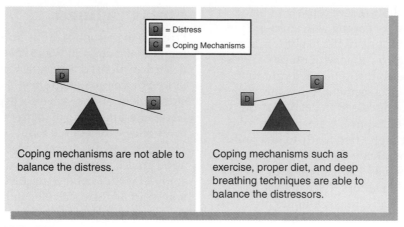

FIGURE 3-1. Maintain an Appropriate Balance.

Types of Negative Stress

There are two types of negative stress:

- Acute stress
- Chronic stress

Acute Stress.   Acute stress occurs when a person has to respond instantaneously to a crisis situation. For example, if your car goes into a skid on an icy road, you must react quickly. As you experience acute stress, two chemicals are produced in your body—adrenaline and noradrenaline. These chemicals have stimulated people to perform incredible acts in a crisis, from lifting extremely heavy objects off injured people (objects they would not be able to lift in an ordinary situation) to fighting off ferocious animals. Immediately after the crisis, however, these heroic persons may become weak, their hands shake, and their knees quiver. They may even collapse.

Chronic Stress.   Chronic stress occurs when a distressful situation is prolonged with no rest or recuperation for the body. Chronic stress triggers the production of different biochemicals in our bodies.

While our bodies can break down adrenaline and noradrenaline, the chemicals produced by chronic stress cannot be broken down, and they remain in our system where they are capable of damaging our bodies. Chemicals produced by chronic stress can cause.

- High blood pressure
- Kidney damage
- Cardiovascular disease
- Migraine headaches
- Ulcers
- Elevated cholesterol
- Weakening of the immune system
- Cancer[1]

Chronic stress can also cause emotional problems, such as:

- Depression
- Withdrawal
- Deep-seated anger
- Loss of self-esteem
- Self-rejection

---

[1]Christine K. Nowroozi, "How Stress May Make You Sick," *Nation's Business* (December 1994), 82.

Cost of Stress

The price of stress is high for both the organization and the individual. For the organization, the price can be absenteeism and loss of productivity; for the individual, the price can be illness and temporary loss of work.

To the Organization. According to surveys done by the American Stress Institute, job stress costs U.S. businesses between $200 billion and $300 billion each year due to:

- Absenteeism
- Reduced productivity
- Employee turnover
- Accidents
- Worker compensation and medical, legal, and insurance fees[2]

On an average workday, one million employees are absent because of stress-related problems, according to the National Safety Council. Between 75 and 90 percent of all visits to primary-care physicians are for stress-related problems. Job stress is related to 40 percent of employee turnover. Between 60 and 80 percent of on the job accidents are stress related[3] Notice that Figure 3-2 illustrates these statistics graphically.

In an attempt to reduce employee stress, many organizations offer stress-reduction programs in the workplace. These programs are based on exercise, diet, and stress-reduction techniques such as meditation. Some organizations even offer programs designed to increase fun in the workplace.

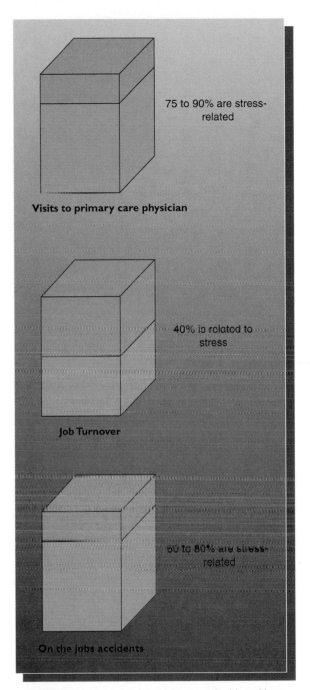

Visits to primary care physician

75 to 90% are stress-related

Job Turnover

40% is related to stress

On the jobs accidents

60 to 80% are stress-related

FIGURE 3-2. Stress-related problems cause health problems, employee turnover, and job accidents.

---

[2] Aaron Fischer, "Is Your Career Killing You?" *Data Communications* (February 1998), 52.

[3] "Is Stress Destroying Your Team?" *Dartnell's Teamwork* (August 1998), 3.

COMMON SYMPTOMS OF STRESS

- Heart palpitations
- Muscle tension
- Excessive perspiration
- Upset stomach
- Headache
- Cold, clammy hands
- Rash
- Fatigue
- Shifting sleep patterns
- Overeating or loss of appetite
- Boredom
- Irritation

FIGURE 3-3. Common Symptoms of Stress. Source: Shirley Siluk Gregory, "Are You a Team of 'Worrywarts'?" *Dartnell's Teamwork* (August 1998), 4.

To the Individual. The vast majority of workers in America say they experience stress on the job. According to statistics gathered by the American Institute of Stress:

- Eighty-nine percent of adults say they experience high levels of stress, with one in four saying they feel this stress on a daily basis.

- Seventy-eight percent of Americans say their jobs are stressful.[4]

Notice Figure 3-3, which lists some of the common symptoms of stress. The next sections of this chapter address factors that contribute to stress, along with coping techniques to decrease the negative stress.

---

[4]"Is Stress Destroying Your Team?" *Dartnell's Teamwork* (August 1998), 3.

Contributing Factors

Some of the factors that contribute to stress on the job are

- Role ambiguity
- Job insecurity
- Working conditions and relationships
- Work overload
- Personal problems
- Dual-career families and single parents
- Economic pressures

Role Ambiguity. Role ambiguity exists when an individual has inadequate information about his or her work role—when there is lack of clarity about work objectives and expectations. As an office professional, you may experience some role ambiguity. You may not understand exactly what is expected of you. When this situation occurs, it is up to you to find out what your job is. Many companies write **job descriptions** detailing the duties to be performed on the job. If one exists for your position, read it. If there is no job description, ask your employer what he or she expects of you.

Job Insecurity. Another factor that contributes to stress on the job is job insecurity. Many organizations today are **downsizing** (reducing the number of employees). Perhaps your company has had recent profit losses and is in the process of laying off employees. You may wonder, "Will I be the next to go?" If you have these thoughts, you probably are not able to give your best efforts to your job. You are in a distressful situation that can cause reduced productivity.

Working Conditions and Relationships. A number of studies have shown that there is a relationship between working conditions and an employee's physical and mental health. Health is impaired by

- A dehumanizing environment—one in which people are treated as objects rather than as individuals
- A poor working relationship with the supervisor
- An unsatisfactory working relationship with colleagues
- Lack of trust among people who must work together
- Lack of support from coworkers
- Work overload

Dual-Career Families, Single Parents, and Extended Families. In the majority of two-parent families, both parents work. This means that the day-to-day pressures of the job must be balanced against time with children and juggling the demands of housework, grocery shopping, meal preparation, yardwork, and so forth.

In our society, divorce is commonplace, which means that there are numerous single parents who must also juggle the job, home, and children. The pressures on these single parents can become tremendous.

Still another factor that can cause negative stress is the need to take care of aging parents. People are living longer today than ever before, and due to the advances in medical science, longevity is expected to increase. This phenomenon often means that there are both children and aging parents, many times with health problems, who need care. These aging parents often live in the same household, which can result in constant demands being made on the caregiver.

Economic Pressures. Even in dual-career families, it is sometimes difficult to balance the personal budget. Individuals must work longer hours (and sometimes two jobs) to bring in adequate money to meet the needs of the family. The economic pressures on single parents can be even greater, and extended families may have increased health-care costs due to aging family members.

Stress Coping Techniques

Since negative stress is so prevalent, each of us must learn how to cope with stress. It is extremely important that we give time and attention to techniques that can make our life less stressful. Here are some suggestions.

Do a Stress Audit. Make a list of the circumstances that contribute to your negative stress. Ask yourself which of the circumstances you can do something about. Concentrate your time on these items. Prepare a plan of action detailing what you plan to do to decrease your stress. Attempt to minimize the circumstances over which you have no control. For example, if you are in a job where you are very unhappy and there is nothing you can do to make the situation better, look for another job.

Maintain a Proper Diet. What you eat or do not eat affects your overall health. Excessive intake of fat, sugar, salts, and caffeine contributes to poor health and to certain diseases such as hypertension and heart disease. The average cup of regular coffee contains 100 to 150 milligrams of caffeine. Nervousness, insomnia, headaches, sweaty palms, and perhaps ulcers have been related to as little as 250 milligrams of caffeine.

The average American consumes more than 126 pounds of sugar a year. Excessive sugar consumption can lead to an increase in triglyceride levels in the blood, which can lead to cardiovascular disease. Too much salt can lead to an increase in blood pressure and to the development of hypertension. The wisest course of action for an individual is to lower the intake of fat, sugar, salt, and caffeine in the diet.

In addition, it is important to maintain a diet that is rich in fruits and vegetables. Eating fiber-rich vegetables, fruits, cereals, and legumes helps you maintain a high level of fiber in your diet. A number of these foods are listed in Figure 3-4.

Set Up an Exercise Program.
Cardiovascular specialists have found that regular exercise can

- Lower your blood pressure
- Decrease fats in the blood
- Reduce joint stiffness
- Lessen your appetite
- Decrease fatigue

Exercise helps reduce stress. *Courtesy of © PhotoDisc, Inc.*

HIGH FIBER FOODS

Vegetables	*Cereals*
Artichokes	Oat Bran
Sweet potatoes	Oatmeal
Turnips	Raisin Bran
Acorn squash	All Bran
Brussels sprouts	
Broccoli	
Carrots	*Legumes*
	Lima beans
Fruits	Butter beans
Strawberries	Black beans
Figs	Navy beans
Oranges	Lentils
Pears	
Blackberries	
Mangos	
Plums	

FIGURE 3-4. High Fiber Foods.

There are many exercises that are good for your body—swimming, bicycling, jogging, and walking, to name a few. Participate in an exercise that you enjoy. Determine a regular time of day that you will exercise and then do it. When you begin exercising, go slowly. Train your body—don't strain it. If you have any medical problems, be sure to consult your doctor about the type of exercise that is best for you.

Get the Proper Amount of Sleep.   In India, there is a saying that sleep "nurses all living beings."[5] The proper amount of

[5]Edward Claflin, ed., *Age Protectors* (Pennsylvania: Rodale Press, Inc., 1998), 141.

sleep is essential to mental and physical health. Although the amount of sleep needed varies by individual, studies have shown that people who sleep seven to eight hours a night tend to live longer than people whose sleep is longer or shorter.[6] Yet, a number of us have problems getting the proper amount of sleep due to our busy schedules and stressful lives. And many times even when we go to bed at the proper hour, getting to sleep is difficult. We often have trouble turning off our minds. We rethink what went wrong in our day or begin to plan for the next day. Practicing the following techniques will help you get to sleep.

- Set aside the hour before bed for quiet activities such as reading.
- Take a hot bath.
- Turn off the TV in the bedroom and/or turn down the TV in an adjoining room.
- Practice deep breathing exercises.
- Create a relaxing scene in your head— waves rolling up on a beach or a mountain stream.
- Be certain that your mattress and pillow are right for you—the proper firmness or softness.
- Pay attention to the amount of coffee, tea, cola, and chocolate you are consuming these drinks can lead to sleep deprivation.

Use Visualization.   Visualization is using your imagination to help you relax. Through visualization, you block out unwanted thoughts. In order to achieve the maximum benefits from visualization, you must get into a comfortable position, relax any muscles that feel tense, and then

[6]Edward Claflin, ed., *Age Protectors* (Pennsylvania: Rodale Press, Inc., 1998), 143.

DEEP BREATHING TECHNIQUES

- Sit in a comfortable position with your back straight and your eyes lightly closed.
- Focus your attention on your breathing, and follow the contours of the cycle through inhalation and exhalation, noting, if you can, the points at which one phase changes into the other.
- Do the breathing exercise for five minutes once a day.

FIGURE 3-5. Deep Breathing Techniques. Source: Andrew Weil, *8 Weeks to Optimum Health* (New York: Alfred A. Knopf, Inc., 1997), 60.

begin to visualize a pleasant scene. For example, you might imagine a sky of white fluffy clouds, ocean waves licking a golden beach, the sun glistening on a snow-covered mountain, or a beautiful sunset over your favorite lake. Focus on the scene you select for several minutes to block out the tensions of the day. As you visualize, it is also a good idea to practice deep breathing techniques. Figure 3-5 lists some deep breathing techniques.

Clarify Values.   Whether or not you think about it daily, you live by a set of values. Generally, these values developed at an early age. You acquired your values through the teaching of significant others in your life (your parents, other relatives, and close friends) and through observing their behaviors. **Values** are principles that guide your life, such as honesty, fairness, love, security, and belief in a higher being. If you have not given much thought to your values recently, try answering these questions:

- What are the highest priorities in my life?
- Of these priorities, which are the most important?

Your thoughtful answers to these questions will identify your values. In our hectic day-to-day lives, we often lose track of what is most important to us. We may find that our present reality has little to do with our core values. However, psychologists tell us that when we bring together what we do or how we live on a daily basis with what we really value, we experience an inner peace and happiness that impacts every area of our lives.

If you are working in a company where the values that are lived out by management and employees are inconsistent with your own, you are probably very unhappy. Take time now to assess your values. List what you value in life—what you are committed to regardless of the many pressures that you face. Now ask yourself if you live these values in your daily life. If not, why not? Consistently paying attention to your values and being committed to living them daily will significantly reduce the negative stressors that you face.

Reduce Organizational Dependency. Do not depend totally on the organization. Educate and train yourself to be employable by a number of companies. Engage in continuing education to keep you up-to-date on technology and other skills needed in the workplace. This education may be formal, at a college or university; informal, such as reading professional books and periodicals; attending workshops and seminars; and/or participating in company staff development programs.

Understand Role Relationships. Be sensitive to the needs of your employer and your coworkers. Know what they expect of you. Know how you fit into the organizational structure. Be familiar with the organization chart; know who reports to whom. Accept people; be tolerant; strive to communicate openly and honestly.

Time Management

You learned earlier that time management can help you reduce your stress and be more productive on your job. This section will help you understand:

- Time management as a concept
- Some of your time wasters
- Time inventory analysis
- Time management techniques
- Time management systems

Time—A Resource

In order to control time more effectively, we must understand something about time. We never seem to have enough time, yet we have all the time there is. **Time** is a resource that cannot be bought, sold, rented, borrowed, saved, or manufactured. It cannot be changed, converted, or controlled. It can only be spent. Each of us receives an equal amount of time every day. We spend it, even if we accomplish nothing. **Managing time** is really a misnomer. In actuality, managing time means *managing yourself* in relation to your time.

Time Wasters

Every day we waste time in a variety of ways. If, as individuals, we understand our own time wasters, we can become more effective in managing ourselves in relation to our time. Listed here are several common time wasters.

Socializing. If you presently have a job, do you go to work and get busy accomplishing the tasks of the day? Or do you report to work promptly and then spend

Socializing at inappropriate times on the job can be a time waster. *Courtesy of © PhotoDisc, Inc.*

the first 30 minutes of your workday talking to your coworkers about what happened the night before? Certainly it is important to have some time to talk about items other than business in the workplace, but socializing can be done on morning and afternoon breaks or at noon. In most organizations, too much time is wasted in excessive socializing at times when employees should be accomplishing the work of the organization.

Disorganization. "I had that letter just a few minutes ago, and now I can't find it. It couldn't have disappeared into thin air." Have you ever made such a statement and then proceeded to rummage through the clutter on your desk for 30 minutes in an

attempt to find the paper you never should have misplaced? A disorganized and cluttered desk can be a major time waster for the office professional. You should know what goes into your desk, what stays on top of your desk, and what should be placed in the file cabinet. Do not clutter your desk with papers that should be in file drawers. Efficiently organize incoming and outgoing materials.

Part of organization is also organizing your day appropriately. For example, if you try to process a report, plan a meeting, do a month's filing—all at the most hectic part of the day—when the telephone is ringing constantly and callers are coming and going, the result will be time wasted, nothing accomplished, frayed nerves, and total frustration. When you have a detailed task to accomplish, plan to do it during a time when interruptions are minimal.

Ineffective Communication. As an office professional, you will communicate both orally and in writing with people both within and outside the office—your employer, coworkers, and customers or clients. It is important that the lines of communication between you and others are open and easily understood. Communication in the office of today is extremely complex in part due to the various modes of communication that are available—for example, email, fax, telephone,

Time can be lost in looking for papers on a disorganized desk.
Courtesy of © PhotoDisc, Inc.

COMMUNICATION ISSUES

- Employees say their work is interrupted by 34 percent of the communications they receive.

- 45 percent of surveyed employees say they experience difficulty because of the number of messages they receive.

- 43 percent complain about receiving multiple communications with the same message.

- 54 percent say they have difficulty with the work that has to be done in response to messages received.

- 46 percent say they have trouble because they don't receive messages in their preferred format.

- Employees use an average of 8.7 different types of communication tools.

FIGURE 3-6. Communication Issues. Source: Pitney Bowes Inc. "Workplace Communications in the 21st Century" (1998), conducted by the Institute of the Future.

voice mail, Internet, and **hard copy** (paper) such as letters, reports, and company newsletters, in addition to face-to-face communication. Another factor adding to the communication complexity is the number of people with whom the average employee communicates each day. A study by Pitney Bowes of employees at 1,000 companies in the U.S., Canada, and the United Kingdom shows that:

- Employees communicate with an average of 24 people per day.

- Communications arrive primarily electronically (72 percent) rather than by paper (28 percent).

- Employees are interrupted an average of six times an hour during the average workday.[7]

Additional statistics from this study are given in Figure 3-6.

---

[7]"Soothing Yourself: 7 Simple Ways to Ease Your Mind," *Dartnell's Teamwork* (August 1998), 2.

Lack of communication or misunderstood communication can cause confusion and loss of productivity. For example, think of the time that you waste if you key and format a report incorrectly because you misunderstood instructions from your employer. Or think of the profits that the company may lose if you make a customer unhappy and lose an account due to poor communication.

Procrastination. Procrastination means trying to avoid a task by putting it aside with the intention of doing it later. It can be the number-one time waster. Procrastination takes many forms, but people who habitually procrastinate actually invite interruptions. They will prolong telephone conversations, talk with coworkers, take a long coffee break, or seek all kinds of excuses to avoid doing what must be done.

Time Inventory

Now that you have examined some of the major time wasters, consider how you spend your time. Unless you know how you spend your time, you cannot expect to become more efficient in managing it.

Time Log Preparation. One way to determine how you spend your time is to chart how long you spend each day in various activities. Some companies actually pay employees based on how much they produce; a time log may be used to chart your production. Figure 3-7 shows a time log that was prepared and maintained on the computer by an office professional. Maintaining a time log on the computer for a period of one to two weeks is an efficient and effective way to discover exactly how you are spending your time. You may also record your time manually; Figure 3-8 shows a manual time log. Whichever method you use, the important consideration is to accurately record the time you

---

Work with the Schedule

Calendar for: *Katrina Fulton*

Date: *10/19/96* *Monday*

Type any changes to the schedule below.

BEGIN	END	DESCRIPTION
8:00AM	9:00AM	Staff Meeting
9:30AM	10:30AM	Meeting: Agenda Review - TJ/DJ/LM
10:30AM	11:30AM	Meeting: J. Valentino
NOON	1:30PM	CONF: F. Gersten (Troy City manager) @ Patricks
1:30PM	2:00PM	CONF: Office time
2:00PM	2:30PM	Meeting: Enrollment Services, (D.M. McCall, etc.)
2:45PM	3:15PM	Meeting: J. Mann, Carolyn Wang
3:30PM	5:00PM	Meeting: United Way

FIGURE 3-7. Computer Time Log.

TIME LOG		

Monday, Oct. 25

	Total Time per Day	Total Time per Week
Keyboarding 9:00–10:05, 11:00–11:30, 1:00–2:15, 4:00–4:25	3hrs. 10min.	17.5hrs
Filing 10:15–10:25, 11:30–11:40, 12:00–12:10, 2:15–2:25	40min.	3.0hrs.
Composing 8:10–8:25, 3:05–3:30	40min.	4.5hrs
Meeting arrangement 8:25–9:05	40min.	4.0hrs.
Incoming mail 10:25–10:40, 3:30–3:45	30min.	2.5hrs.
Outgoing mail 11:40–12:00, 3:45–3:55	30min.	2.5hrs.
Incoming calls	30min.	1.00hrs
Outgoing calls 9:16–9:18, 10:40–10:44, 2:37–2:40	15min.	.5hrs.
Financial records		.5hrs.
Office host duties		.5hrs.
Copying 3:30–3:55	25min.	1.25hrs.
Working with others		1.25hrs.
Miscellaneous		1.0hrs.

FIGURE 3-8. Manual Time Log.

spend in each activity for a period of one to two weeks. Take the time to notice when you start and stop each activity; the time you spend in the process will be well worth the information you are able to glean as you analyze your time log.

Log Analysis. Your second step is to analyze your time log in an attempt to discover ways in which you can improve the management of your time. Ask yourself these questions.

- What was the most productive period of the day? Why?
- What was the least productive period of the day? Why?
- Who or what accounted for the interruptions?

- Can the interruptions be minimized or eliminated?
- What activities needed more time?
- On what activities could I spend less time and still get the desired results?
- Do I have all my supplies and materials ready before beginning an activity?

Action Plan. After you analyze your log, you must do something about how you spend your time. Make an action plan for yourself. Determine the positive steps you will take to increase your time management efficiency. In deciding how you will manage your time more efficiently, you may want to use some of the time management techniques given in the next section.

Time Management Techniques

If you consistently use the techniques presented here as you perform your daily tasks, you will discover that it is much easier to get your work done quickly and accurately while feeling in control of your time.

Set Priorities

Many times it will be impossible for you to do everything that you are asked to do in one day. You must be able to determine the most important items—which tasks should be done first, which can wait until tomorrow or next week. If you are new to a job, you probably will need some help from your employer to determine what items are the most important. But once you learn more about the job and your employer, you should be able to establish priorities on your own. Part of your responsibility as an office professional is to be able to set priorities.

Prepare Daily To-Do Lists

Each afternoon before you leave for the day, it is a good idea to prepare a to-do list for the next day. List all of the tasks, activities, and projects that you need to accomplish the next day. Then review your list. Mark the items in this manner.

- Most important matters—A
- Less important items—B
- Remaining items—C

Those projects that have a deadline of the following day will be in Category A. In addition, you may have a very large project that is due next week; however, in order to get it done on time, you must break it into parts. For example, one part might be given a Category A priority and completed tomorrow. The following day another part might be given a Category A priority and completed the next day. By breaking it into parts and assigning priorities to those parts, the project becomes manageable. What once seemed overwhelming has been accomplished in an orderly and timely fashion.

You must be able to determine the most important items—which tasks should be done first, which can wait until tomorrow or next week. CATHY © Cathy Guisewite. Reprinted with permission of UNIVERSAL PRESS SYNDICATE. All rights reserved.

Category B consists of those items that would be nice to complete the next day, but no serious consequences will result if they are not completed. Category C consists of things that are either fairly unimportant or that may be delegated. If you are going to delegate the items, be clear with the individual who will be doing the task exactly what is expected. If the project is a complex one, you might want to give the individual written instructions; or ask the individual to take your verbal instructions and write them down for your review before beginning the project.

If you are having trouble setting priorities, you might want to try the procedure given in Figure 3-9.

Use your numbered list, with priorities, to:

- Arrange papers on your desk in priority order, with the A's in one pile, B's in another, and C's in another
- Mark telephone message slips with A, B, or C

The next day as you complete the items on your to-do list, mark them off (if you keep a manual list) or delete them on your

---

DEVELOPING PRIORITIES

This tool can be useful if you are having difficulty setting priorities. It might be helpful for both you and your supervisor to go through the exercise. It is not intended to be used daily. However, if you are new to the process of setting priorities or are having difficulty, it helps you break down the process into small increments.

Step 1

Make a list of ten things for which you must set priorities; order is not important at this point; however, do give each item a number, with the numbers being one through ten.

Step 2

Compare number one with number two and circle the number that you believe is most important.

Step 3

Compare number two with number three and circle the number you believe is most important. Note: You probably will be circling a number several times; as you circle a second time, make your circle bigger, since it will be important later to count the number of times you circled each item.

Step 4

Compare number three with number four; circle the number that is the most important of this pair. Compare two with four; circle the number that is most important. Compare number one with number four; circle the number that is most important.

Steps 5-10

Continue to go through the items on your list comparing each item with every other item and circling the most important of each set of two.

Last Step

Count the number of ones, number of twos, number of threes, and so forth. Your priority list will begin with the number you have circled the most. The last item on your list (least important item) will be the number on the list that you circled the least number of times.

FIGURE 3-9. Developing Priorities.

computer. This step gives you a sense of accomplishment in addition to calling your attention to what still needs to be done. As you prepare your to-do list for the next day, use the present to-do list. If there are items that you have not been able to accomplish, transfer these items to the to-do list for the next day.

Use Slack Time

If you have slack time, you should use it productively. Accomplish those tasks that you have been unable to do during your peak workload periods. These tasks may be cleaning out your desk, rearranging the files, organizing supplies, or reading articles related to your business or the technology you use on your job.

Handle Paperwork as Few Times as Possible

Many time management experts claim that handling paper over and over—putting it in piles on your desk, reshuffling, rehandling, rereading—is the biggest paperwork time waster. The basic rule is: handle paper once. Read it, route it, file it, or answer it—but get it off your desk as quickly as possible without handling it over and over.

Simplify Repetitive Work

If you find yourself keyboarding a form numerous times, simplify the process. Prepare a form on the computer and store it on a disk so that you may call it up when needed. If you find yourself looking up the same address or telephone number several times, make a list of frequently used addresses and telephone numbers. Whatever the repetitive task, simplify it.

Such an approach takes time to organize initially, but in the long run, the time savings are significant.

Perform Work Correctly the First Time

At times, the office professional may have to redo work that could have been done right the first time. How do you prevent the need to redo work? Get appropriate instructions or procedures before beginning the work. If you do not have the information readily available to you, ask someone who does. Ask your employer or a coworker for assistance if necessary. Read the file on similar correspondence. It is much better to take some initial time before doing the project to understand how to do it. If you do not have the time to do it right the first time, when will you have the time to redo it? Not only do you become frustrated in the process of redoing, but also it costs both you and your employer valuable time.

There are times when you must redo work because your supervisor has changed his or her mind about what should be done. If such is the case, do not let yourself become upset or frustrated. Just remember that there are times when jobs must be redone. Never place blame or make excuses when a mistake has been made or work must be redone for any reason. Keep your attitude right and redo the job.

Develop a Procedures Book

There are usually specific tasks that you will perform each week or each month. It is a good idea to develop a procedures book outlining the steps and information

If you have to redo work, keep your attitude right. *Courtesy of ©
PhotoDisc, Inc.*

relate to other projects. Put these materials in a file folder, label the folder with the name of the project, and place the folder in your drawer. It is not easy to work with stacks of paper around you. You need a flat, uncluttered surface on which to work. Limit the items on your desk.

Your Supplies.   Label the trays on your desk so that it is clear which is for incoming material and which is for outgoing material. If space permits, you may wish to have a file tray or alphabetic file sorter for materials to be filed. The center drawer of your desk should hold frequently used supplies, such as pencils, erasers, and paper clips. The top side drawer is generally equipped with sloping partitions for paper.

Your Work Area.   The way you arrange your work area will have much to do with your efficiency in getting work done. The

needed in performing these tasks. For example, when you are making travel arrangements for your employer, the types of accommodations that he or she wants may be standard. List the travel procedures in your book. This list might include the travel agency name and phone number; preferences of your employer for airlines, hotels, rental cars; and so forth. Preparing a procedures book saves you time and serves as a ready "how to" reference.

Organize Your Workstation and Your Reading

Organizing your workstation is not an easy task, but it must be done if you are to make the most efficient use of your time.

Your Desk.   When you are working on a project, clear your desk of materials that

Organize your supplies.

modular workstations that are used extensively today in offices allow for great flexibility. Panels may be rearranged and equipment moved to provide for the most efficient work arrangement possible.

Your Reading.   As an office professional, numerous items to be read will pass your desk. In reading the correspondence and other materials, organize the material in order of importance. Prepare folders, noting the dates when the materials must be read.

Practice speed reading when reading the materials. Read for the main thought or idea. If you are reading a periodical or company literature, scan the table of contents first. Then practice selective reading techniques. Read carefully only the sections that will enhance your knowledge of your job and your company.

Use Good Communication Techniques

A few communication tips are given here. By studying Chapters 9, 10, and 11, you will learn much more about the entire communication process.

- Transmit ideas in simple, clear terms.
- Define terms if necessary.
- Listen carefully.
- Repeat what you think you have heard and ask for clarification if necessary.
- Be sensitive to the communicator's body language as well as to the words being spoken.
- Keep your mind open to new ideas.
- Do not pass judgment on what the speaker is saying.

Figure 3-10 gives some tips on managing your email.

TIPS ON MANAGING YOUR EMAIL

- Keep email messages on one screen.
- When preparing a list, use a bulleted or numbered list.
- If you must send a long message, attach the file as an enclosure.
- Don't send copies of messages unless absolutely needed.
- Don't type your message in capital letters. Capitals are considered shouting in the email world, and people do not appreciate shouting.
- If you are sending email to more than one person, put the names in alphabetical order.
- Send only work-related messages at work—no jokes or invitations to nonwork-related events.
- If your message is very important, controversial, or confidential, use the telephone or set up a face-to-face meeting.

FIGURE 3-10. Tips on Managing E-Mail. Source: Jeffrey J. Mayer, *Time Management for Dummies* (Chicago. IDG Books Worldwide, Inc., 1995), 164–165.

Time Management Systems

In addition to the techniques that have been presented in the previous section, you will want to establish a system that will allow you to utilize your time more effectively. The system may be manual or electronic.

Manual Systems

There are a number of manual time management systems that are easy to set up and efficient to use. These systems include calendars and tickler files.

Calendars.   You need a calendar for your desk that has a separate page for each day with the hours of the day given. A calendar of this type is shown in Figure 3-11. Such a calendar allows you to schedule appointments for your supervisor and yourself, telling at a glance when time is available.

There are also calendars that display a full week or a full month at a glance. These calendars are usually the size of a notebook with space for brief entries. If it is important for you to be able to see a full week or a month at once, you will want to have one of these calendars. Usually daily calendars are maintained even if it is necessary to maintain weekly and monthly calendars, too.

Most businesses use some type of master calendar that includes the important dates for the year. These dates may include board meeting dates, planning and budgeting dates, personnel evaluation dates, special events, and holidays. As an office professional, you may have the responsibility of calling your employer's attention to those dates on the master calendar that impact your department or area.

Tickler Files. Another type of daily reminder is the tickler file. A **tickler file** is a chronological record of items to be completed. Such a file is shown in Figure 3-12. A guide for the current month is placed in the front of the file followed by a separate guide for each day of the month. At the back of the file are guides for each month of the year.

To use this file, notes are written on index cards and filed behind the appropriate dates. For example, assume you need to send a memorandum concerning a meeting on October 15. The memorandum needs to reach the participants 10 days prior to the meeting. You would place an index card with the notation "Send memorandum for October 15 sales meeting to all sales representatives" behind the guide card labeled "5."

Electronic Systems

Electronic time management systems that allow you to organize your work quickly and efficiently are known as **PIM (personal information manager)** systems. **PIM** software generally integrates several components of time and task management including:

- Calendaring and scheduling meetings
- Emailing and faxing
- Tracking notes and tasks
- Accessing data
- Storing contact information

A brief description of some of these features is given here. To develop a working knowledge of PIM systems, you will need to spend several hours understanding and using the system available to you.

Calendaring and Scheduling Meetings. The calendaring function allows you to create calendars and schedule meetings for one person or a whole company. Calendars can be viewed for the day, the week, or one or two months. Notice the calendar screen shown in Figure 3-13. When scheduling meetings, you put in the name of the attendees, the subject and location of the meeting, and the start and end times. PIM software is "smart" in that you can type in phrases such as "next Monday" or "two weeks from today" and the program will put in the appropriate date. If the meeting is to be a recurring one, you can tell the program to add this appointment on any automatic schedule you set up. The program lets you know if an attendee is not available for the meeting and if rooms are not available. You can also track the attendees' responses to the meeting invitation.

Emailing and Faxing. PIM software allows you to send and receive email and

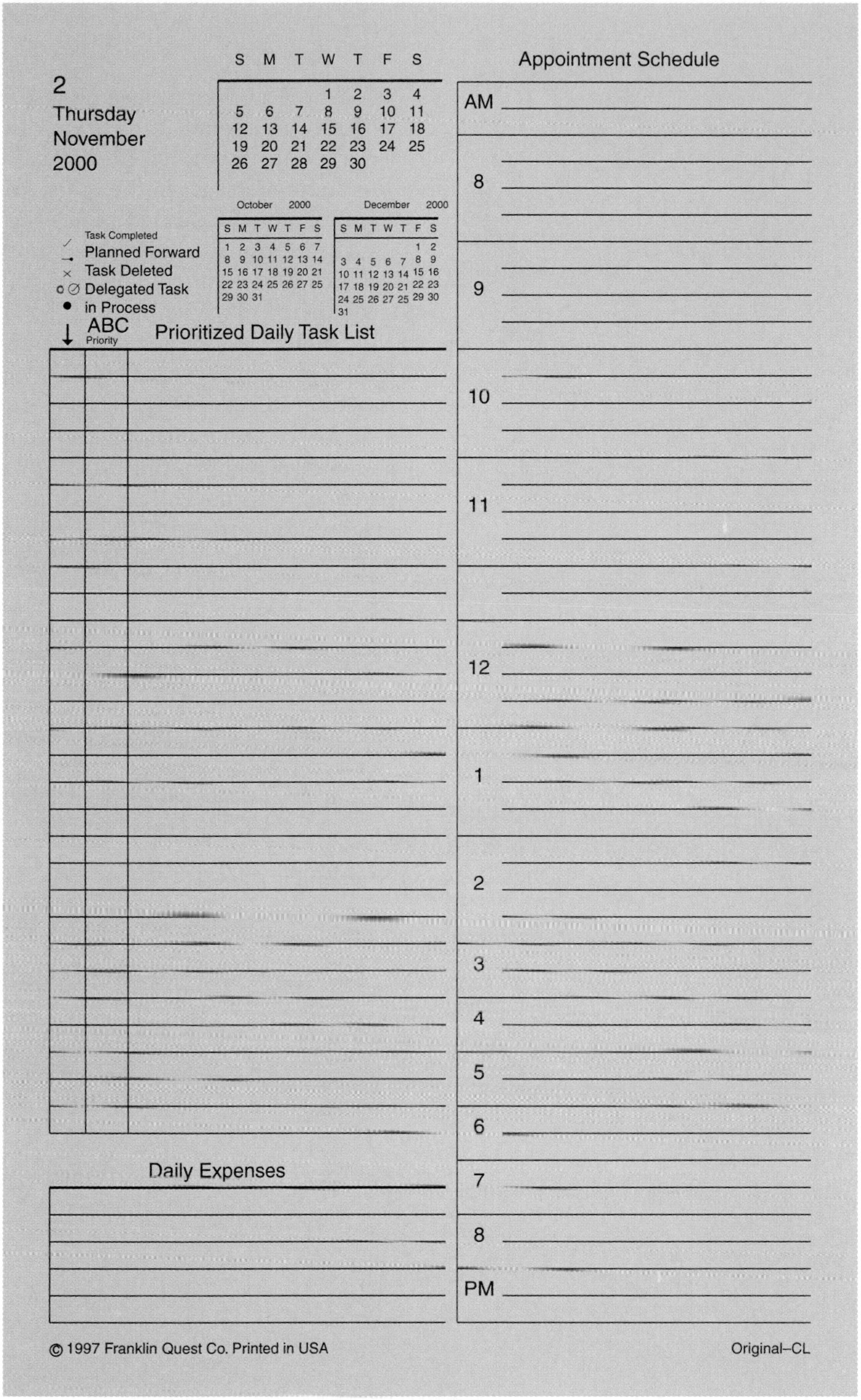
2
Thursday
November
2000

S	M	T	W	T	F	S
			1	2	3	4
5	6	7	8	9	10	11
12	13	14	15	16	17	18
19	20	21	22	23	24	25
26	27	28	29	30		

October 2000

S	M	T	W	T	F	S
1	2	3	4	5	6	7
8	9	10	11	12	13	14
15	16	17	18	19	20	21
22	23	24	25	26	27	28
29	30	31				

December 2000

S	M	T	W	T	F	S
					1	2
3	4	5	6	7	8	9
10	11	12	13	14	15	16
17	18	19	20	21	22	23
24	25	26	27	28	29	30
31						

✓ Task Completed
→ Planned Forward
× Task Deleted
○ ⊘ Delegated Task
● in Process

↓ ABC Priority — Prioritized Daily Task List

Daily Expenses

Appointment Schedule

AM
8
9
10
11
12
1
2
3
4
5
6
7
8
PM

Original–CL

FIGURE 3-11. Daily Calendar.

FIGURE 3-12. Tickler File.

faxes. You can add colors, graphics, and tables to your email. The system can automatically check your electronic mailbox and dump messages in the inbox folder. The program also has **templates** (pre-designed forms) that allow you to choose a format for outgoing mail. You can attach a completed file to your email. You can write messages and send them out in the future; you can also save messages for rereading at a later point. Screens are available on some PIM software that allow you to display upcoming appointments, pending tasks, and the unread email messages waiting for you. This information is organized in one "at a glance" location.

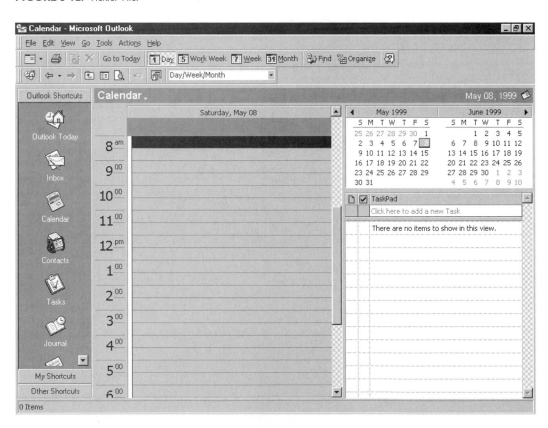

FIGURE 3-13. PIM Calendar Screen.

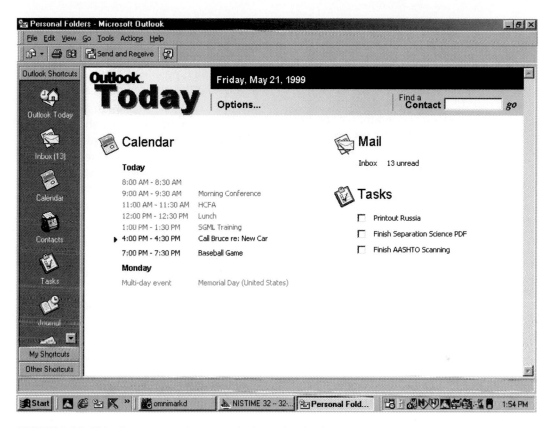

FIGURE 3-14. PIM software screen showing a calendar, mail, and tasks.

Figure 3-14 shows a screen that gives this information.

With PIM software, you can send and receive faxes from your computer without touching a piece of paper and without waiting your turn at the fax machine in your office. A fax **wizard** (help mechanism) is available to help you compose and send faxes. Fax applications also can work with other applications. For example, you can compose a document on your word processing package, mailmerge it with a contacts list, and then fax it to each contact.

Tracking Notes and Tasks. Using this function of PIM software, you can put on your daily, weekly, and/or monthly to-do lists. You can assign categories and priorities to these tasks. The task modules work with the calendar modules to allow you to enter due dates or recurring appointments. The task modules automatically shuttle events into the calendar and are smart enough to use a reminder window to tell you when the task is due. The notes portion of PIM software is the electronic equivalent of writing a note on a sticky pad. It allows you to jot down a reminder or a phone number.

Accessing Data. You can access the **World Wide Web** through PIM software. For example, if you use one location on the Internet often, you can get there quickly through using PIM software. The software can store the **uniform resource locator (URL)** as a **hyperlink,** which will automatically open a file for viewing. You can go directly to the Web site with one click on the software program; you do not have to surf the Web for the information. It is also possible to locate specific files on your own system by using PIM software.

Storing Contact Information.   Like a simple card file, PIM software allows you to store names, addresses, phone numbers, email addresses, fax numbers, and pager numbers of your coworkers and customers. You can also store notes concerning specific contacts.

Whether the time management systems you use are manual or electronic (and most office professionals will use a combination of both systems), these systems are invaluable in helping you improve your productivity and reduce the stress in your life. Start now to practice the skills you have learned in this chapter. By doing so, you will be ready to use these skills effectively in the workplace.

SUMMARY

To reinforce what you have learned in this chapter, study this summary.

- Stress is the response of the body to a demand made upon it. Stress can be positive as well as negative. Negative stress is sometimes called distress.

- Negative stress can be categorized into two types—acute and chronic. Acute stress occurs when a person has to respond instantaneously to a crisis situation. Chronic stress occurs when a dis-

tressful situation is prolonged with no rest or recuperation for the body.

- Chronic stress can cause physical and emotional problems, such as cardio-vascular disease and depression.

- The cost of stress to the organization is great due to employee absenteeism; reduced productivity; employee turnover; accidents; and worker compensation and medical, legal, and insurance fees.

- Factors that contribute to negative stress include:
  a. Role ambiguity
  b. Job insecurity
  c. Working conditions and relationships
  d. Dual-career families and single parents
  e. Economic pressures

- Suggestions for coping with stress include:
  a. Doing a stress audit
  b. Maintaining a proper diet
  c. Setting up an exercise program
  d. Using visualization
  e. Clarifying values
  f. Reducing organizational dependency
  g. Understanding role relationships

- Time is a resource that cannot be bought, sold, rented, borrowed, saved, or manufactured. It is spent by each of us. Managing time means managing ourselves so that we utilize the time that we have to the optimum.

- Time wasters include socializing, disorganization, ineffective communication, and procrastination.

- You may learn more about how you spend time by keeping a time log for a period of time and then analyzing your entries on the log.

- Time management techniques include:
  1. Setting priorities
  2. Preparing daily to-do lists
  3. Using slack time
  4. Handling paperwork as few times as possible
  5. Simplifying repetitive work
  6. Performing work correctly the first time
  7. Developing a procedures book
  8. Organizing your workstation and your reading
- Both manual and electronic systems are available to help you manage your time. Electronic systems provide calendaring, scheduling, emailing, faxing, tracking notes and tasks, accessing data, and storing contact information functions.

Key Terms

- Stress
- Distress
- Acute stress
- Chronic stress
- Role ambiguity
- Job description
- Downsizing
- Visualization
- Values
- Time
- Managing time
- Hard copy
- Procrastination
- Tickler file
- PIM (personal information manager)
- Templates
- Wizard
- World Wide Web
- Uniform resource locator (URL)
- Hyperlink

Professional Pointers

Try these time and stress management suggestions to help you work more productively.

- Concentrate more on what you do with your time and why you do it, rather than how much you are doing. Self-management is the best offensive strategy in controlling stress.
- Identify the time of the day when you are generally at your "peak." Plan to tackle your most difficult jobs during your peak period.
- Do not over-schedule yourself. Allow an hour or two of uncommitted time each day.
- Take shorter and more frequent breaks, especially if your job requires you to sit at a computer for long periods.
- Try writing about stressful situations. Keep a journal in which you write regularly; writing in private can be like talking to a trusted friend.
- Balance your professional life with a fulfilling personal life. Make time to pursue personal interests and to relax apart from your career.

Office Procedures Reinforcement

1. Explain why the workplace can be stressful and the difference between negative stress (including acute and chronic stress) and positive stress.
2. List and explain five strategies that will help you cope with stress.
3. Define time and explain four time wasters.
4. List and explain five time management techniques.
5. Describe how PIM software can help you manage your time.

Critical Thinking Activity

Beverly Teo began her career as an office professional after obtaining a degree in business, with office systems as a major. She served as an administrative assistant for a car dealership for three years. In this position, Beverly was required to greet customers, process sales records for the 30 salespeople, and handle the clerical work required by the service technicians. The job was stressful, but Beverly was happy, felt in control of her work, and was productive on the job.

Due to her outstanding performance in the job, Beverly was offered the position of assistant to the president of the dealership. Beverly knew that the job would be challenging and that there would be much to learn. The job requires supervising two office professionals, who have clerical responsibilities, as well as preparing numerous sales reports on spreadsheet software and keeping track of the myriad activities that her employer, Mr. Evans, handles. Beverly was not current on spreadsheet software, so before beginning the position, she took a short course and received certification on Excel software. She has never supervised any employees and feels that she has lots to learn. During the six months that Beverly has been the assistant to Mr. Evans, she has worked very hard and logs at least five hours each week in overtime. She now finds that she is tired, depressed, and generally unhappy. Some days she feels like telling Mr. Evans that she is leaving immediately. Compounding the stressful workload is her boss. Mr. Evans is a nice man, but he is very demanding, a workaholic, and a perfectionist. It seems to Beverly that he has no life outside the company.

1. Describe the factors that contribute to the stress Beverly is feeling.
2. What steps can she take to help her cope with the stress?
3. If you were Beverly, how would you attempt to get control of the job?

Office Applications

OA 3-1 (Goal 1)

If you are working at the present time, interview your supervisor concerning stress and time management. Ask your supervisor these questions:

1. Is stress a problem in the workplace? If so, how do the employees in the company exhibit stress?
2. What is the cost of stress to the company?
3. Does the company offer any workshops or seminars for employees in handling stress and managing time appropriately?
4. Do you have suggestions for helping employees deal with stress and manage time?

Write a short report of this interview and present your report orally to the class. Turn in your written report to your instructor, giving the name and company of the person interviewed.

If you are not working at the present time, read two recent articles (within the last two years)—one about the cost of stress to companies and one about time management techniques. Write a short summary of these articles, noting your sources. Present the report orally to the class, and submit the written report to your instructor.

OA 3-2 (Goals 2 and 3)

In your Applications Workbook, p. 15, there is a Stress Audit. Respond to the items given and then score your Stress Audit by using the points listed on p. 18 of your workbook. After you have completed and scored your Stress Audit, prepare an action plan listing the steps you will take in an attempt to reduce your stress level. An Action Plan form is given on the student template disk in file OA03-2.doc. Do not turn in either item to your instructor. Make a commitment to completing these steps during this course. Keep your Stress Audit. At the end of the course, you will retake the Stress Audit to determine if you have been able to reduce your stress.

OA3-3 (Goal 2)

On the student template disk in file OA03-3a.doc is a list of items that need to be accomplished. Prioritize the items by assigning an "A" to the items requiring immediate attention, "B" to those items that should be dealt with this week, and "C" to those items that you should begin work on but that have no deadline.

On the student template disk in file OA03-3b.doc is an email message from your supervisor. After viewing the message, reclassify the priorities on your "to-do" list.

Write a short paragraph justifying your reassignment of the priorities. Turn in a copy of your priorities and the justification to your instructor.

OA3-4 (Goal 3)

Refer to the Daily Time Logs provided on pages 19–21 of your Applications Workbook. For the next five days, log the time you spend in various activities on the form. Record each day's activities on a different form. If you are employed, log the time you spend in activities at work. If you are not employed, log the way you use your personal time.

Analyze the way you spent your time during the five days by answering the questions on the Time Management Analysis on page 23 of your Applications Workbook. Using the Action Plan form on the student template disk in file OA03-4.doc, prepare an action plan listing techniques you will use to better manage your time. Submit your action plan to your instructor.

Online Research Applications

ORA3-5 (Goal 1)

Using the Internet, research the following:

- Stress coping techniques
- Time management techniques

Summarize two recent articles (within the past two years) from your search. Submit your summary to your instructor, listing the sources you used.

ORA3-6 (Goal 2)

Using the Internet, research the cost of stress to business. The American Stress Institute is one organization that conducts surveys on this topic. Check to see if you can find any articles from this Institute. If none are available, surf the Net for other references. Present your research in an oral report to the class.

CHAPTER 4

Ethical Behavior

Ethical behavior in business is defined as doing
what is right, not merely what is profitable. Since
"right" and "wrong" have very different connotations
depending on people's values, the culture of the business, and even the country in which the business is
located, ethical behavior is interpreted in vastly different ways. However, what is not in dispute today is the
importance of ethical behavior in business. It has become a necessity. Charles Wilson, owner of SeaRail
International Inc. of Houston, Texas, has this to say
about ethics:

> Ethics is what's spearheading our growth. It creates
> an element of trust, familiarity and predictability
> in the business. We're in an industry where a lot of
> people cut corners. It's easy to misrepresent prod-
> ucts and be less than upfront with customers about

YOUR GOALS

1. Explain the importance of ethical
   behavior in the workplace.

2. Identify the characteristics of an
   ethical organization.

3. Identify the characteristics of an
   ethical office professional.

4. Determine how to achieve ethical
   change.

the condition of goods. I just don't think that's good for business. You don't get a good reputation doing things that way. And eventually, customers won't want to do business with you.[1]

The social responsibility ethic of the late 1980s and 1990s is partly responsible for the concern with ethical behavior in business today. **Social responsibility** is defined as the trustworthiness of business to assume accountability for the impact it has on people, the community in which it exists, and the larger world in which it operates. In other words, a business is not merely responsible for producing a product or service that sells to the public and makes a profit for the company; it is also responsible for providing a product that is safe and does not harm the environment. For example, business is responsible for not polluting our environment through disposing of chemicals in unsafe ways or putting an unsafe toy on the market.

Three additional reasons for the importance of business ethics today are:

- With our **transnational ecology** (worldwide), what happens in one country affects the ecology of another country. For example, raging forest fires in Mexico in 1998 not only caused major air pollution problems in Mexico but also affected the quality of air in Texas and portions of Oklahoma. As a result, the elderly and those individuals with respiratory and heart disease were urged to avoid any physical exertion. Parents were also advised to watch their children for health problems if they played outside for any extended period of time.

- Consumers demand ethical behavior from business. According to one poll, 70 percent of consumers would not buy—at any price—from a company that was not socially responsible.[2]

- Employees expect ethical behavior from the company where they work. In a Walker Information survey, 86 percent of the respondents who had favorable opinions of their companies' ethics were strongly committed to their organizations. Of the respondents, 42 percent stated that a company's ethical integrity would directly influence their choice of employers.[3]

In this chapter, ethics is considered a **pragmatic** topic—one to be understood conceptually and also practiced in the day-to-day operation of a business and in the lives of employees within the business. You are provided a framework that allows you to understand the importance of ethics and the characteristics of ethical organizations. The chapter also provides practical suggestions for you as an office professional in behaving ethically.

Business Ethics

Ethics is the systematic study of moral conduct, duty, and judgment—what is right and what is wrong, what is good and what is bad. Practically, **business ethics** is the study of just and unjust behavior in business. Business ethics requires that judgment be exercised about a proposed act and the anticipated consequences of the act. It means that individuals within an organization, collectively and singularly, are socially responsible for their conduct and are focused on what is right.

[1]Gayle Sato Stodder, "Goodwill Hunting," *Entrepreneur* (July 1998), 118–126.

[2]Stodder, 118–126.
[3]Stodder, 118–123.

A Historical Evolution of Business Ethics

To help you understand how much of our ethical thought and behavior has evolved, you need to look briefly at history. The major roots of our ethical principles today stem from religion and philosophy. For example, the major religions of the world are in basic agreement on the fundamental principles of ethical doctrine. Buddhism, Christianity, Judaism, Confucianism, and Hinduism all teach the importance of acting responsibly toward all peoples and contributing to the general welfare of our world. In fact, the work ethic that is still practiced by many in the United States came from what was called the **Protestant ethic.** It began as a religious teaching in the fourteenth century and was carried to the American colonies. The Protestant ethic encouraged hard work, thrift, and dedication to the task. This philosophy still holds true for millions of Americans.

The great philosophers in history have also added to the body of knowledge concerning ethics and have impacted the way we think about it. Here are a few examples of their influence:

- Socrates taught that virtue and ethical behavior were associated with wisdom.
- Plato taught that justice can be discovered through intellectual effort.
- Jeremy Bentham and John Mills taught that morality resides in its consequences and one must maximize the greatest benefit for the greatest number of people.
- Immanuel Kant taught that one must behave in a way that one's actions can become a universal law.
- Saint Thomas Aquinas taught that ethical behavior in business was necessary to achieve salvation.

In addition to the religious and philosophical roots of ethical behavior, our cultures and our systems of government teach us ethical behavior—for example, the Golden Rule: Do unto others as you would have them do unto you, came from many ancient cultures. Our Declaration of Independence states that there are certain "inalienable rights" such as "life, liberty, and the pursuit of happiness."

The study of ethics began in the classroom in the 1970s. In the 1980s it was integrated into the business curriculum, where it has progressed from religious and philosophical theory into the pragmatic study of ethical behavior and decision making within the business organization.

The Why

Why be ethical? This question is a deep and difficult one in ethical philosophy, but it is more than an academic question. At some point, all of us—individuals and businesses—must answer it. There are numerous ways to do so. You might answer it from a religious or philosophical view as noted in the previous section. You might also answer it from your own value perspective or from a personal satisfaction view. However, for purposes of this text, the question will be answered from a pragmatic view.

As we begin the twenty-first century, medical science has expanded so far that questions of ethics are of major consideration. With the cloning of Dolly the sheep in 1997, the possibility of cloning humans is now imminent. How do we as a society address this very real ethical issue? Obviously, there are numerous other areas of society where ethical questions arise daily. Great wisdom is required now and

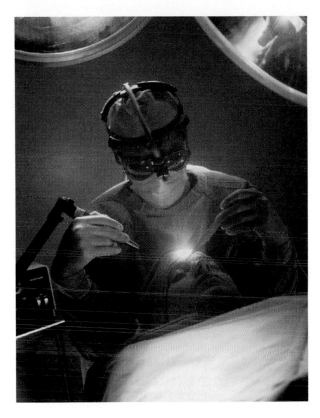

The advances in medical science are raising some ethical questions.
Courtesy of © PhotoDisc, Inc.

recognize the importance of behaving ethically and how ethical or unethical behavior can impact our nation. You can understand the corporate culture in which you work and the philosophies of the leaders within the organization. You can understand how to achieve ethical change from within. You can behave ethically when dealing with your supervisor, your peers, and the customers, vendors, and clients of your company. You can constantly examine your own ethical standards and determine if you are consistently behaving in ethical ways. As Margaret Mead, a preeminent anthropologist of the twentieth century, stated:

> "Never doubt that a small group of thoughtful, committed citizens can change the world; indeed, it's the only thing that ever has."

The Ethical Organization

What are the characteristics of an ethical organization? There are a number of them; a few of the most important are mentioned here.

Environmentally Responsible

The organization that is environmentally responsible is constantly aware of the dangers that are possible in the business and takes all possible precautions to see that the environment is not polluted. The organization pays attention to OSHA (Occupational Safety and Health Association) regulations regarding the careful disposal of waste products. The organization makes it a top priority when building new buildings to cut down as

in the future to overcome the ethical dilemmas that we face. An understanding of our own principles of **morality** (a set of ideas of right and wrong) is vitally important. We must all do whatever we can to strengthen our ethical understandings and **moral integrity** (consistently adhering to a set of ideas of right and wrong), both within the workplace and outside it.

The How

How can you as an office professional make a difference on this globally important ethical issue? First of all, you can

The ethical organization is environmentally responsible. *Courtesy of © CORBIS.*

few trees as possible and to protect wetland areas and other areas that are important to the ecology.

Internationally Aware

The ethical organization is aware that ethical behavior has different meanings in different countries. For example, bribes are often an accepted business practice in some countries. Human rights are given very different interpretations in different countries. In some countries, there is no consideration of gender equity. Harassment and discrimination are not considered ethically wrong. Such awareness on the part of an American business operating in another country does not mean that it adopts the ethical standards of that country. It does mean that the American business must be knowledgeable of the practices that occur and carefully formulate their own practices and behaviors.

An ethical organization is aware of differences in cultures and business customs in other countries. The ethical organization understands the importance of learning the culture and business customs of the country and respects the differences

that exist. For example, when dealing with the People's Republic of China, it is important to understand that:

- Status and title are important. (Titles such as "Vice President" or "Bureau Chief" are often used before the surname.)
- Business deliberations are cautious. (The Chinese may spend several months on a matter that would take a week in the United States.)
- Formality is important. (Individuals are not addressed by their first names; the leader of a delegation speaks before any member of the delegation speaks.)
- Punctuality is a given. (It is not acceptable to be ten minutes late; to be late is to show disrespect.)

Culturally Committed to Behaving Ethically

Organizational culture is defined as the ideas, customs, values, and skills of a particular organization. All organizations have a culture, which may be committed to behaving ethically or give little thought to the matter. In an ethical organization, employees are well aware of the ethical stance of the organization and realize that they are held accountable for upholding the ethics espoused by it. The preparation and dissemination of a values statement is one communication vehicle that companies use to inform their employees and customers of their ethics. Consider the following information from Johnson & Johnson concerning their Credo (values statement):

For more than 50 years, Our Credo has helped us in fulfilling our responsibilities to customers, employees, communities and stockholders. Our worldwide family of companies shares this value system in 36 languages spreading across Africa, Asia/Pacific, Eastern Europe, Europe, Latin America, Middle East and North America.[4]

Johnson & Johnson has published the Credo and information about it on the Web; see Figure 4-1. It appears not only in English but also in the language of those countries where Johnson & Johnson is located. For example, in Europe, Johnson & Johnson has locations in Belgium, Denmark, Finland, France, Germany, Greece, Hungary, Ireland, Italy, Netherlands, Norway, Poland, Portugal, Spain, Sweden, and the United Kingdom. By clicking on the appropriate country, the citizens of that country may read the Johnson & Johnson Credo in their native language.

Johnson & Johnson lives the values expressed in its Credo in its daily operations. One example of the organization living its values is apparent in the company's reaction to the Tylenol crisis in 1982 and 1986. Someone, not an employee, tampered with Tylenol bottles, lacing them with cyanide. Several deaths occurred as a result. Johnson & Johnson immediately removed all Tylenol capsules from the United States market—even though the deaths were confined to one area of the United States—at an estimated cost of over $100 million. They also mounted a massive communication effort to alert the public and deal with the problem. The company responded swiftly, responsibly, and effectively. They not only contained the crisis, but they came out of it with a better image than they had before the crisis. The Johnson & Johnson Credo continues to be lived today; it is also evaluated periodically by employees to judge how well the company performs its Credo responsibilities.

Another example of a company that lives by a set of principles is the ice cream company Ben and Jerry's. Each year, the company plants enough trees to replace those cut down to make its ice cream sticks.

Once you know your company's values, it is your responsibility to behave in ways that support them. If you find yourself in a company where you cannot support the values, it is time for you to find another job.

Honest

An ethical organization is honest in dealing with employees and other organizations and individuals. For example, it makes its personnel policies clear to all employees. Employees understand salary and promotion policies. In a sales organization, for example, product specifications and pricing structures are clearly stated and communicated to external organizations and individuals. An ethical organization holds employees accountable for honesty. Honest employees do not falsify expense reports, time reports, or personnel records.

Committed to Diversity

The ethical organization is concerned that equal treatment be afforded to all individuals, regardless of race, ethnicity, age, gender, sexual orientation, or physical challenge. For example, women often face obstacles in the workplace that occur not because of their performance but because of their gender and how others perceive them. Gays and lesbians often face discrimination based not on who they are or

[4]Taken from the World Wide Web, http://www.jnj.com.

JOHNSON & JOHNSON
OUR CREDO

We believe our first responsibility is to the doctors, nurses and patients,
to mothers and fathers and all others who use our products and services.
In meeting their needs everything we do must be of high quality.
We must constantly strive to reduce our costs
in order to maintain reasonable prices.
Customers' orders must be serviced promptly and accurately.
Our suppliers and distributors must have an opportunity
to make a fair profit.

We are responsible to our employees,
the men and women who work with us throughout the world.
Everyone must be considered as an individual.
We must respect their dignity and recognize their merit.
They must have a sense of security in their jobs.
Compensation must be fair and adequate,
and working conditions clean, orderly and safe.
We must be mindful of ways to help our employees fulfill
their family responsibilities.
Employees must feel free to make suggestions and complaints.
There must be equal opportunity for employment, development
and advancement for those qualified.
We must provide competent management,
and their actions must be just and ethical.

We are responsible to the communities in which we live and work
and to the world community as well.
We must be good citizens—support good works and charities
and bear our fair share of taxes.
We must encourage civic improvements and better health and education.
We must maintain in good order
the property we are privileged to use,
protecting the environment and natural resources.

Our final responsibility is to our stockholders.
Business must make a sound profit.
We must experiment with new ideas.
Research must be carried on, innovative programs developed
and mistakes paid for.
New equipment must be purchased, new facilities provided
and new products launched.
Reserves must be created to provide for adverse times.
When we operate according to these principles,
the stockholders should realize a fair return.

FIGURE 4-1. Johnson & Johnson credo. Source: The WWW@http://www.jnj.com

how they perform on the job but on their sexual orientation. Often minority group members have problems based on the **biases** (a prejudiced view based on background or experiences) of others. Such biases can cause **stereotyping** (perceptions or images held of people or things that are derived from selective perception). Stereotyping may be positive or negative. Positive stereotyping allows us to group things or individuals. However, negative stereotyping can cause premature closure to communication and prejudicial behavior that leads to acts of rejection. If an individual has a negative experience with an individual from Russia and then groups all Russians in the same negative category in the future, **prejudice** (a system of negative beliefs and feelings) occurs.

Physically challenged individuals (persons with a physical handicap) often face biases based on their physical challenges. They may be treated differently due to their physical disabilities. None of this discussion is to imply that the ethical organization advocates a policy that ignores performance issues due to gender, physical challenge, race, ethnicity, or sexual orientation. All individuals must perform their jobs satisfactorily. What is extremely important is giving all individuals that opportunity regardless of any type of minority status.

How does the ethical organization deal with diversity issues? Here are several possible ways:

- Ensure that initial employment practices support diversity.
- Ensure that promotional opportunities provide for equal treatment of all individuals.
- Hold managers accountable for supporting and implementing nondiscriminatory policies.

The ethical organization treats all individuals equally, regardless of race, ethnicity, age, gender, sexual orientation, or physical challenge. *Courtesy of © Digital Vision.*

- Assist individuals who have English language deficiencies by allowing them to enroll in courses on-site or off-site at a college or university.
- Provide access for the physically challenged to all facilities and proper equipment and workspace.
- Do not evaluate individuals based on their age.
- Raise the diversity awareness of other managers and individuals by providing seminars on diversity.

Committed to the Community

The ethical organization understands that a business has a social responsibility to contribute to the community. That can mean:

- Contributing to charities
- Participating in the local Chamber of Commerce and other service organizations

- Working with youth groups
- Supporting the inner city in its crime reduction programs
- Assisting schools and colleges on internship programs
- Encouraging employees to participate in their local communities through recognizing and rewarding their community endeavors

Committed to Employees

Promoting employee productivity is important to the ethical organization. Although fear about job performance and security exists at some level in most organizations, the ethical organization takes steps to reduce such fear by:

- Establishing realistic job descriptions
- Helping employees set achievable goals
- Administering performance evaluations fairly
- Supporting employees in learning new skills

The ethical organization supports employees in learning new skills.
Courtesy of © PhotoDisc, Inc.

- Encouraging employees to cooperate with each other
- Rewarding employee creativity
- Providing personnel policies in writing to all employees
- Establishing teams who work on significant company issues

An Establisher of Standards

If ethical behavior is to be carried out in the organization, standards should be established that support ethical decision making and quality delivery of products and services. The ethical organization helps establish these standards.

Standards can be established industry-wide. For example, the **FDA** (Food and Drug Administration) establishes standards for food and drug products that are manufactured in the United States. Those companies that do not follow the standards are subject to quick censure and exposure.

It is also important to establish standards within a company for the delivery of a product or service. Such standardization reduces error and increases efficiency, effectiveness, and safety.

Ethical Change

We don't live in a world in which all individuals and organizations are ethical. However, such a statement is not a negative one. It merely suggests the inevitable—we do not live in a perfect world. We do live in a world in which many people and organizations daily strive to make it better. If an organization is to become more ethical, the people within the organization must behave more ethically. Successful individual change within the organization occurs when the organization supports, enhances, and preserves individual change. The best work settings are those that make positive changes possible for individuals. The process for achieving ethical change in individuals and in organizations requires understanding, a systematic approach, commitment, cooperation, and hard work. In the next section, you will examine factors that impede ethical change and consider pragmatic steps for producing ethical change.

Factors Impeding Ethical Change

Our backgrounds and beliefs often stand in the way of ethical change. As you read the following negative beliefs, ask yourself if you hold any of them.

- Values cannot be changed.
- Organizations are amoral.
- Labels accurately describe individuals.
- The leadership of an organization never behaves ethically.

Now examine each of these statements individually.

Values Cannot Be Changed. Clearly, it is difficult to change values since they are generally beliefs that we have held from childhood. However, change is possible A simple example is the receptionist who can learn the names of customers more quickly by practicing word association techniques, or the office professional who can learn to write effective correspondence by attending seminars on effective writing techniques and then implementing them. Organizations, by giving support to small changes a person makes over time, can help the individual change or redefine his or her values. Workgroups within the organization can also support and encourage value changes within their particular group.

Organizations Are Amoral. Amoral is defined as lacking moral judgment or sensibility, neither moral nor immoral. We generally readily accept that individuals should have ethics, but we are not so clear about what that means for individuals within the organizational framework. You may hear such statements as, "The organization has no right telling me how to behave." Yet, if an organization is to be ethical, the employees within it must be ethical. We can each be held to ethical standards in the workplace that are higher than our individual standards. When the individual enters the workplace, she or he makes a commitment to uphold the standards of the workplace. Managers have a right and an obligation to hold employees responsible for upholding the ethics of the organization, in addition to holding them accountable for technical skills required to produce the product or service.

Labels Accurately Describe Individuals. Generally, when we attach a label to someone, we are not describing that individual accurately. For example, to describe a female by her job title is clearly to leave out much of who she is. Or to describe a person as a "team player" or a "bore" is restrictive of the whole person's qualities and traits. The entire labeling process of individuals is a complex one, but the point to keep in mind here is that labeling hinders rather than helps the change process. Labeling individuals colors our view of them. If we are engaged in ethical change, labels should not be used.

The Leadership of an Organization Never Behaves Ethically. Clearly, there are organizations in which leadership does not behave ethically. However, to automatically assume that all management is bad is negatively stereotyping management. As you have learned earlier in this chapter, you should not negatively stereotype individuals or groups. If we do not want to behave ethically ourselves, it is easy to shift the blame for our lack of performance to management. Your first obligation is to uphold the organizational ethics yourself. Then, if you find through repeated incidences that management does not uphold the organizational ethics, you will probably want to leave the company. When organizational ethics are not lived by management, the company is not a good place to work.

Steps Producing Ethical Change

Now that you have looked at factors that hinder ethical change, consider these steps that can help produce it.

- Determine the ethical change required.
- Determine the steps required to achieve the objective.
- Practice the new behaviors.
- Seek feedback.
- Reward the individual or group involved.
- Evaluate the effects of ethical change.

To help you understand how to apply these steps, a situation involving an employee (Michael) is given, with examples of how the situation might be handled following each step.

Determine the Ethical Change Required.   Consider this situation.

You are chairing a task force that is charged with improving the organization's sexual harassment policy. Michael is on the task force. He always attends the meetings but never says anything during the meeting. He sits and listens. However, once outside the meeting, Michael attempts to sabotage the decisions that were made by going to each person individually who was in the meeting and voicing his reservations with the decisions.

In determining the change required, the specific behavior must be considered.

Not: Michael is not professional in his conduct.

Rather: Michael does not openly express his feelings and thoughts in meetings.

Determine the Steps Required to Achieve the Objective.   The objective in this situation is to get Michael to express his thoughts and feelings in the meetings, not outside. The process that you use here is similar to the decision-making process that you learned in Chapter 1. You may want to go back and review the process now. After you define the problem, you establish the criteria and generate possible alternatives. In this case, you decide to do the following:

- Talk with Michael in private before the next meeting and ask him to express his viewpoints in the meeting. You take a positive approach and tell Michael that his viewpoints are important to the group and need to be heard by the group in the meeting.
- At the next meeting, ask Michael for his comments if he is not forthcoming with them; thank him when he does express his viewpoints.

Practice the New Behaviors.   At each meeting that is held with Michael, behave in the same manner as was identified in the previous section.

Seek Feedback.   Ask a trusted employee to evaluate your behaviors with Michael during meetings and Michael's behaviors with the group and with you. You might also seek help from the outside. For example, you might have a consultant observe the group and offer suggestions to you and the group for change.

Reward the Group and Individuals Involved.   In this situation, when Michael's behaviors change, reward your

ETHICAL CHANGE STEPS

- Write standards and procedures that support ethical behavior.
- Appoint senior-level management to monitor standards and procedures.
- Communicate standards to all employees; train employees on how to live the standards within the work environment.
- Develop an internal mechanism for employees to report ethical violations.
- Consistently reinforce ethical standards. Nonaction in enforcing ethical standards dooms an ethical code as meaningless and superficial.

FIGURE 4-2. Ethical change steps.

own efforts. Add this success to your list of strengths. Reward Michael for the changes in his behavior. In addition to a verbal or written thank-you, the reward might be a small celebration for Michael and for the entire group on successful group decision making.

Evaluate the Effects of the Ethical Change. Take some time to determine how the change in Michael's behavior has impacted him, the group, and the organization. Consider what you have learned from the experience. Ask Michael what he has learned from the experience. Use the evaluation to help make change easier in the future.

Additional suggestions for producing ethical change within organizations are given in Figure 4-2.

Discrimination

You learned earlier in this chapter that the ethical organization does not discriminate due to race, ethnicity, gender, age, sexual orientation, or physical challenge. Unfortunately, however, discrimination does occur in our workplace and in our world. Headlines such as the following attest to the fact that discrimination happens and that it can be costly to an organization.

> $176 Million Race Bias Settlement Gets Tentative Okay
>
> Supermarkets Will Pay $81.5 Million to Settle Bias Suit
>
> Business Pays $87.5 Million for Not Promoting More Women

Although discrimination can take many forms, only sexual harassment and racial discrimination are considered here.

Sexual Harassment

Sexual harassment is defined by the EEOC (Equal Employment Opportunity Commission—an office of the federal government) as harassment arising from sexual conduct that is unwelcome by the recipient and that may be either physical or verbal in nature. Three criteria for sexual harassment are set forth:

1. Submission to the sexual conduct is made either implicitly or explicitly as a condition of employment.
2. Employment decisions affecting the recipient are made on the basis of the recipient's acceptance or rejection of the sexual conduct.
3. The conduct has the intent or effect of substantially interfering with an individual's work performance or creates an intimidating, hostile, or offensive work environment.

When sexual harassment is based on the first two criteria, it is referred to as **quid pro quo** sexual harassment. Quid pro quo is Latin for "this for that." It is a trade. When sex is a prerequisite for getting a job, a promotion, or some type of benefit in the workplace, it is illegal. The third criterion is referred to as hostile environment sexual harassment. In this situation, the employer, supervisor, or coworker does or says things that make the victim feel uncomfortable because of his or her gender. Hostile environment sexual harassment does not need to include a demand for an exchange of sex for a job benefit; it is the creation of an uncomfortable working environment.

The courts have found that suggestive comments, jokes, leering, unwanted requests for a date, and touching can be sexual harassment. Sexual harassment can also occur between people of the same sex, or it can be a woman harassing a man in addition to a man harassing a woman. Victims of sexual harassment can sue and recover for their lost wages, future lost wages, emotional distress, punitive damages, and attorney fees. EEOC guidelines state that harassment on the basis of sex is a violation of Title VII of the Civil Rights Act and that the company has a duty to prevent and eliminate sexual harassment. A federal appeals court ruled that a company:

- Is liable for the behavior of its employees even if management is unaware that sexual harassment has taken place
- Is liable for the behavior of nonemployees on the company's premises

SEXUAL HARASSMENT POLICY STATEMENT

It is against the policy of the company to discriminate against and/or exclude an employee from participation in any benefits or activities based on national origin, gender, age, sexual orientation, or handicap. Harassment on the basis of sex is a violation of the law and a violation of company policy.

FIGURE 4-3. Sexual harassment policy statement.

GRIEVANCE PROCEDURE

Any employee who believes that he or she is being sexually harassed on the job shall file a written grievance with the Director of Human Resources within 24 hours after the alleged sexual harassment has taken place. The grievance will be reviewed by the supervisor and appropriate action taken. If the employee believes that the grievance has not been satisfactorily handled, he or she has the right to appeal to the next level supervisor, with appeal going through the line of authority to the president.

FIGURE 4-4. Grievance procedure.

This means that if a visiting representative or salesperson harasses the company receptionist, the company is responsible. As a result of this responsibility, many companies have published policy statements on sexual harassment. A sample policy statement is given in Figure 4-3.

Once the policy statement is established, it must be communicated to all supervisors and employees, along with a grievance procedure should harassment take place. A sample grievance procedure is given in Figure 4-4.

It is the responsibility of business to educate its employees and its management concerning procedures to prevent sexual harassment in the workplace. Figure 4-5 lists some Do's and Don'ts for Supervisors.

If you are faced with sexual harassment, it is important that you seek help or handle the situation yourself if you deem that appropriate. Suggested steps for handling harassment are given in Figure 4-6. When a company employs you, you should be made aware of its policies in regard to sexual harassment as well as other personnel policies that affect your work. If you are not made aware of policies, you

PREVENTING SEXUAL HARASSMENT IN THE WORKPLACE DO'S AND DON'TS FOR SUPERVISORS

DO

- Educate management and employees as to what sexual harassment is; let everyone know that sexual harassment will not be tolerated.

- Designate a person or office where employees can bring concerns and complaints about sexual harassment.

- Publish options available to employees who feel they are victims of sexual harassment.

- Promptly and thoroughly investigate every complaint.

- Provide leadership by example in applying and promoting high standards of integrity, conduct and concern for all employees.

- Be observant of language and behavior of fellow supervisors and managers; "call" them on what may be perceived as sexual harassment.

- Maintain an environment free of retaliation or punitive actions against a complainant.

DON'T

- Permit sexual jokes, teasing or innuendo to become a routine part of the work environment.

- Allow employment decisions to be made on the basis of any reasons other than merit.

- Allow social behavior to become confused with behavior in the workplace.

FIGURE 4-5. Do's and don'ts for supervisors. Source: The WWW@http://www.womenintrades.org/prevsex1.html, material from *Sexual Harassment: An Employer's Guide for Supervisors.*

STEPS FOR HANDLING DISCRIMINATION

- Know your rights. Know your organization's position on racial discrimination and sexual harassment, what is legal under the EEOC guidelines, and what your employer's responsibility is. Know the laws.

- Keep a record of all sexual harassment and racial discrimination infractions, noting the dates, incidents, and witnesses (if any).

- File a formal grievance with your company. Check your company policy and procedure manual or talk with the Director of Human Resources as to the grievance procedure. If no formal grievance procedures exist, file a formal complaint with your employer in the form of a memorandum describing the incidents, identifying the individuals involved in the sexual harassment or racial discrimination, and requesting that disciplinary action be taken.

- If your employer is not responsive to your complaint, file charges of discrimination with the federal and state agencies that enforce civil rights laws, such as the EEOC. Check your local telephone directory for the address and telephone number of the EEOC office in your city. Your state may also have civil rights offices that can assist you. Check your local directory for these offices.

- Talk to friends, coworkers, and relatives. It is important to avoid isolation and self blame. You are not alone; sexual harassment and racial discrimination do occur in the work sector.

- Consult an attorney to investigate legal alternatives to discriminatory or sexual harassment behavior.

FIGURE 4-6. Steps for handling discrimination.

should ask your supervisor to explain them to you.

Racial Discrimination

In addition to sexual harassment in the workplace, racial discrimination also exists. Why? It is mainly based on prejudice, and prejudice is often the result of ignorance, fear, and/or cultural patterns. As groups of people were viewed in the past in certain roles and with certain characteristics, attitudes were learned by one generation and passed on to the next. Changing learned attitudes is a slow process. Strides toward reducing racial prejudice are being made, but it is imperative that even greater strides be made in the future.

What can be done about racial discrimination? There are laws that protect individuals from racial discrimination, the most important being Title VII of the Civil Rights Act of 1964 that makes discrimination illegal if it is based on national origin, ethnic group, sex, creed, age, or race. Title VII has been extended to cover federal, state, and local public employers and educational institutions by the Equal Employment Opportunity Act of 1972. This amendment to Title VII also gave the Equal Employment Opportunity Commission the authority to file suit in

LAWS GOVERNING DISCRIMINATION

These acts, covering discrimination, make it unlawful to discriminate against applicants, employees or students on the basis of race, religion, color, national origin, sex, age, height, weight, marital status, disability or handicap and set out that sexual harassment will not be tolerated.

    Civil Rights Act of 1965, Title VI and VII

    Title IX of the Education Amendments of 1972

    The Age Discrimination Act of 1975

    The Americans with Disabilities Act of 1990

    Civil Rights Act of 1991

The following acts make pay discrimination based on sex and discrimination on the basis of pregnancy, childbirth, or related medical conditions unlawful.

The Equal Pay Act. This act, a 1963 amendment to the Fair Labor Standards Act, prohibits pay discrimination because of sex. Men and women performing work in the same establishment under similar conditions must receive the same pay if their jobs require equal skill, effort, and responsibility.

The Pregnancy Discrimination Act. In 1978, this act amended Title VII to make clear that discrimination on the basis of pregnancy, childbirth, or related medical conditions is unlawful, including refusal to hire or promote pregnant women or to offer them the same fringe benefits or insurance program.

The Family and Medical Leave Act of 1993, effective August 1993, requires private sector businesses of 50 or more employees and public agencies to provide up to 12 weeks of unpaid, job protected leave to eligible employees for certain family and medical reasons. An employer must grant unpaid leave to an eligible employee for one or more of the following reasons:

- Care of the employee's child (birth, adoption, or foster care)

- Care of the employee's spouse, son or daughter, or parent, who has a serious health condition

- Serious health condition that makes the employee unable to perform his or her job

FIGURE 4-7. Laws governing discrimination.

federal district courts against employers in the private sector on behalf of individuals whose charges were not successfully resolved.

Laws governing both racial and sexual discrimination are listed in Figure 4-7, with steps for handling discrimination listed in Figure 4-6.

Characteristics of the Ethical Office Professional

If you are to be an ethical office professional, you not only need to understand the importance of ethics and ethical leadership, the corporate culture, and how ethical change occurs, but you also need to address consistently your own ethical behaviors. The following paragraphs explain certain characteristics of an ethical office professional.

Makes Ethical Decisions

You have learned that your own ethics are influenced by:

- Your religious beliefs
- Your philosophical beliefs
- The culture in which you grew up

The convergence of these factors, plus the culture and expectations of the business organization where you are employed, can make it difficult to determine what truly is right and wrong in a particular situation. Asking these questions can help you decide what is ethical.

- What are the facts in the situation?
- Who are the stakeholders, or who will be affected by my decision?
- What are the ethical issues involved?

- Are there different ways of looking at this problem? If so, what are they?
- What are the practical constraints?
- What actions should I take?
- Are these actions practical?[5]

If you are still unclear about what you should do, ask yourself these questions:

- If my actions appeared in the newspaper, would I feel okay about everyone reading what occurred?
- Is what I anticipate doing legal?
- Could I proudly tell my spouse, my parents, or my children about my actions?
- Will I be proud of my actions one day, one week, one year from the present?
- Do my actions fit with who I think I am?

Supports Ethical Behavior

Whenever you, as an office professional, encounter someone whose words or deeds indicate that the person does not respond to an ethical organization, take a stand. Be sensitive, but be direct. Let people who are cynical about ethical organizations know that you believe strongly in the concept. Let them know that you feel that honesty, concern for society, concern for the future health of the world, and respect for the rights of others are values that belong in the business organization.

Refuses to Engage in Negative Office Politics

What does **office politics** mean? It means that "who you know" within the office is important. It means that some people

---

[5]"How to Teach Ethics," *Keying In*, Vol. 7, No. 3 (January 1997), 4.

within the organization are more powerful than others. It means that networks exist in which favors are done for people based on the networks. Office politics can be good as well as bad. For example, assume that you believe your computer system in your department is inadequate. You begin to talk with your employer and your coworkers about a more effective computer system. You are able to garner support, and your employer goes to bat with upper management for the money to get the system.

Office politics can also be bad. You learned the meaning of quid pro quo in the section on discrimination. Office politics often uses a quid pro quo mentality; that is, you do something for me and I will do something for you. In the most ethical world, negative office politics would not exist. But unfortunately, we do not live in the most ethical world and probably never will. So what do you do about office politics? How do you handle it? First of all, you are aware. When you go into a new job, notice what is happening around you. Be aware of the power bases. Be aware of who knows whom and what the relationships are. Next, hold on to your own value system. Do your job to the best of your ability. Be respectful and polite to everyone. Do not gossip about people within the office. Use your awareness of the office politics to help get your job done. Generally, if you live your values and do your job well, you will be recognized and respected.

Accepts Constructive Criticism

If your supervisor recommends that you do something differently, do not take his or her remarks personally. For example,

assume that you have recently set up a meeting for your employer at a hotel where lunch was served. It was your first time to plan such a meeting, and you thought you did a fair job. After the meeting, your employer calls you in and tells you that the room arrangement was not satisfactory and that the food choice was not good. How do you respond? First of all, you deal with the issues at hand.

You might say, "Can we talk about it more? What type of room arrangement would have been better? What type of meal would you suggest?"

Keep an open mind; realize that you have much to learn and that all of us make mistakes. You might also suggest to your supervisor that you would like to review the arrangements with her before the next meeting takes place to get her input. With any type of criticism, the important thing is to learn from your mistakes and not make the same mistake twice.

Observes Office Hours

In most offices, the working hours are arranged so that they will be fair to both the employer and the employee. The smooth operation of an office depends to a large degree upon strict observance of these hours by all persons concerned. You may be employed in an office where there is a tendency on the part of employees who have completed their work to spend their time taking care of personal affairs. Avoid joining the crowd. It can hardly be considered ethical for an employee to spend time writing personal letters or receiving and making personal telephone calls during working hours.

Get to work in sufficient time in order to begin work on time. An important project for which you are responsible may

The ethical employee observes the company rules concerning lunch hours. *Courtesy of © PhotoDisc, Inc.*

be held up by your tardiness. There is no surer way to call unfavorable attention to you than by getting to work late.

Accepts Responsibilities

The ethical office professional understands and accepts the responsibilities of the job. He or she performs these tasks to the best of his or her ability. There is never an attempt to pass the blame for not doing a task to another individual; the responsibility is always accepted. Also, you may at times be required to assist someone else in doing a task. You may have to work overtime to get the task done. Again, the ethical office professional accepts these responsibilities.

Maintains Honesty and Integrity

The honest office professional avoids hypocrisy at all costs. He or she does not tell "white lies" to the supervisor or coworkers. Even the smallest white lie can cause major damage to your professional reputation. The honest employee does not blame someone else for his or her errors, or break the rules and then claim ignorance of any rules.

The ethical employee understands that supplies and equipment belong to the company. The ethical employee upholds the tenets of ethical behavior listed here.

- Company supplies (such as pens, pencils, paper clips, disks, and paper) are never taken for personal use.
- Company equipment (such as computers) remains on company property unless express permission is granted for business use at home.
- Personal mail remains personal; company stationery and postage are not used.
- Personal telephone calls (local calls) are kept to a minimum; personal long-distance calls are not made on company time and at company expense.
- Software is the property of the company; it is not copied or taken home for personal use.
- Office copiers are used for the business of the company; personal copies are not made.

Figure 4-8 lists additional ethical behaviors concerning computers.

Respects Privacy

The ethical employee respects the privacy of the employer and his or her peers. Confidentiality is crucial in a business, and the ethical employee understands and upholds this concept. The ethical employee does not share confidential or

TEN COMMANDMENTS FOR COMPUTER ETHICS

1. Thou shalt not use a computer to harm other people.

2. Thou shalt not interfere with other people's computer work.

3. Thou shalt not snoop around in other people's files.

4. Thou shalt not use a computer to steal.

5. Thou shalt not use a computer to bear false witness.

6. Thou shalt not use or copy software for which you have not paid.

7. Thou shalt not use other people's computer resources without authorization.

8. Thou shalt not appropriate other people's intellectual output.

9. Thou shalt think about the social consequences of the program you write.

10. Thou shalt use a computer in ways that show consideration and respect.

FIGURE 4-8. Ten Commandments for computer ethics. Source: Arlene H. Rinaldi and Florida Atlantic University, http://rs60000.adm.fau.edu/rinaldi/net/ten.html.

sensitive information obtained from email, incoming or outgoing mail, or conversations overheard on the telephone or in face-to-face meetings.

Is Open to Change

The ethical employee maintains openness to new directions of the company and to new ideas. He or she understands that technology and global competitiveness require constant change. The ethical employee is willing to grow and change as the workplace demands. This openness to change also means that the employee is willing to be a lifelong learner—one who is eager to attend seminars, take short courses, and engage in other forms of professional development.

Is Loyal

The ethical employee is loyal to the company but not in an unquestioning sense. The important issue for the employee and the company is not blind loyalty but the

commitment to company directions that support the values. Employees must be allowed to constructively disagree with directions, to speak out on issues, and to be heard by management in the process. However, once a direction is decided (accepting appropriate input), employees must be loyal and productive members of the team. Ethics demands this type of loyalty.

Keeps the Faith

The ethical employee keeps the faith. The employee understands that changing behaviors is slow but that the commitment to ethics must be upheld even when the organization seems to be mired in behaviors that do not support the stated ethical policies. Certainly, the ethical office professional may become discouraged at times; discouragement is a very natural and expected reaction. Nevertheless, the ethical employee continues to behave ethically, keeping the faith that others in the organization will catch up with him

Key Terms

- Ethical behavior
- Social responsibility
- Transnational ecology
- Pragmatic
- Ethics
- Protestant ethic
- Business ethics

- Morality
- Moral integrity
- Organizational culture
- Biases
- Stereotyping
- Prejudice
- Physically challenged

- FDA
- Amoral
- Sexual harassment
- EEOC
- Quid pro quo
- Office politics

Professional Pointers

Here are some tips for helping you behave ethically in the workplace.

- Critique ideas—not people.
- Do not publicly criticize your supervisor or your coworkers.
- Do not pass on or even listen to gossip about other individuals within the office.
- Check out information you hear from the grapevine. If you know the information is false, say so without becoming emotional about it. Feed accurate information into the grapevine.
- Communicate when appropriate in person. Even though we live in an electronic age where the majority of our communication is through electronic means, face-to-face communication is valuable in being able to see a person's reactions to the message and in clarifying misunderstandings quickly.
- Be a good listener, but do not pass on everything that you hear. Remember that you need to behave professionally, and professionalism carries with it lack of pettiness and rumormongering.
- When you have a problem, go directly to the source of the problem in an attempt to correct the situation.
- Examine your beliefs about people with different backgrounds and experiences than your own. Be aware that your beliefs are powerful and influence the way you act and react to others.
- Appreciate diversity. Understand that people have different values, abilities, and priorities.
- Practice empathy. Putting yourself in the situation of others (figuratively) allows you to more closely relate to the barriers they face or the feelings they have.
- Show concern for others, even if they are unable to return the behavior.

Office Procedures Reinforcement

1. List and explain six characteristics of an ethical organization.
2. Explain three factors that impede ethical change.
3. How can ethical change be encouraged within an organization? Discuss a minimum of five steps that can be taken in encouraging ethical change.
4. List five steps you can take if you are a victim of sexual harassment or racial discrimination.
5. Explain five characteristics of an ethical office professional.

Critical Thinking Activity

Ahmed Miah recently joined Hazelton & Associates in the management trainee program. The program enables recent college graduates to join the business in an entry-level position and work in a variety of jobs for one year. The trainees gain an overall perspective of the business while learning various job skills.

There are eight trainees in the program. At the end of the year, however, only five will be recommended for full employment. The trainees feel a tremendous sense of pressure and competition for those five available management positions.

Ahmed has witnessed certain behaviors that are of great concern, and he is unsure how to respond. The coordinator of the training program tells ethnically biased jokes on a consistent basis. He loves to gather a group of people in the coffee room and tell his "joke of the day." Many of the office employees encourage him as he verbally and physically acts out his off-color stories. The other trainees also laugh and join in the storytelling. Ahmed, however, is offended by the jokes and the behavior of everyone who engages in this practice without regard to the effect it may have on others.

How should Ahmed handle the situation?

- Should Ahmed ignore the behavior of his colleagues or express his concern? If so, to whom?
- Should Ahmed express concern about the behavior of the coordinator? If so, to whom?
- Will Ahmed jeopardize his opportunity in the management trainee program if he complains about the coordinator's behavior?

Office Applications

OA4-1 (Goals 1, 2, and 4)

Select two of your classmates to work with on this activity. Read two recent articles (within the last two years) on the importance of ethical behavior in the workplace and how individuals can be helped to behave ethically. From your research, analyze how the behaviors advocated affect the workplace. Consider, from your readings, how ethical behaviors impact:

- Management
- Employees
- Customers

Also, from your research, make several suggestions for achieving ethical change within an organization.

Write your findings in a report of no more than four pages and submit it to your instructor.

OA4-2 (Goal 2)

Work with two or three of your classmates on this case. Read the case and answer the questions at the end. Present your suggestions in an oral report to the class.

The CEO of a large pharmaceutical company has just been informed that one of their products (a new drug that has been approved by the FDA as a cancer preventative) may have some serious side effects. Six people who have been taking the drug have died; it is not clear whether or not the drug caused the deaths. The drug has been on the market six months, and no other deaths have been reported. Research is being conducted to determine if there is a problem with the drug. Pulling it from the market immediately will cause some serious problems for the company. The negative publicity alone will cause sales to drop several million dollars. Also, if the deaths are caused by the drug, the company may face huge lawsuits. If the drug is not pulled from the market and there are major problems that can result in death, additional deaths may occur and the lawsuit problem is compounded. However, with so little information to go on, it can also be assumed that the drug may indeed be saving lives. And, if it is saving lives, is it wise to pull a drug that helps people? The company is also in the midst of an annual audit. As part of that process, the chief executive officer and the chief financial officer must sign a letter assuring the auditors that circumstances that could cause a negative financial impact have been disclosed.

Discuss the pros and cons of the following possible decisions:

- Pull the drug from the market immediately and notify the press of its possible effects.
- Notify the auditors that you do have some potential problems.
- Wait until additional research is completed; there is not enough information to say that the drug can cause death. The initial testing of the drug showed no problems, and it is been approved by the FDA.
- Say nothing to the auditors; it is not certain whether or not there is a problem.

As a group, determine what decision should be made in this case. Give reasons for making the decision. Is the decision that the group made an ethical one? Justify your response by explaining how it is or is not ethical. Explain how your own ethics impacted your decision.

OA4-3 (Goals 2 and 3)

Select three of your classmates to work with on the four cases presented here. Answer the questions given below the cases. Prepare a short report with your answers and submit it to your instructor.

Case 1

As an office professional, you make hotel reservations for your employer at least three times a month in Atlanta. You always use the same hotel. He enjoys staying there, and it is close to your Atlanta office. You recently received a certificate from the hotel, offering you and your spouse a weekend getaway special, including a suite and breakfast each morning at no cost to you.

Is it ethical to take advantage of this offer? If so, why? If not, why not?

Case 2

Dave Adams began working for a large company right out of college last year. He had had no performance problems on his job. However, he was recently fired because he used a discount coupon that a software vendor (one that the company has never done business with) dropped off at the company. He didn't ask anyone at the company if it was okay; he didn't even think about it. He had never been given a code of conduct the company expected him to uphold. Also, to his knowledge, the company does not publish a values statement.

- Was his behavior ethical or unethical? Justify your answers.
- Was the company justified in firing him? Why or why not?

Case 3

Susan works in the marketing department of a large company. She has been told that the company has a rule that employees cannot accept gifts from suppliers, customers, or anyone—not even little gifts. However, she has noticed that her employer, along with several other company executives, is invited each year to a golf tournament hosted by one of the company vendors. All expenses are paid, including a very nice meal after the tournament and numerous prizes for lowest golf score, longest drive, and straightest drive. Her employer always comes back raving about the event and showing off any prizes he has won. There seems to be a double standard in the company—one for executives and one for the other employees. Susan likes her job. She enjoys her work, and the company is basically a good place to work.

- Should Susan let her boss know that she feels there is a double standard? If so, how should she approach him on the subject?
- Or should she keep quiet? Justify your answer.

Case 4

One of your coworkers came to you with this story recently and asked your advice on what she should do.

Her supervisor asked her to have lunch with him so they might review the details of a workshop she has the responsibility to set up. He suggested that they go to the hotel where the workshop is going to be held so that she might have a chance to look at the meeting setup possibilities. The lunch was all very businesslike until they started to leave. He suggested that it was too early to return to work, so why didn't they take some time to look at one of the hotel rooms. As he said it, he winked at her; she knew exactly what he was suggesting. She told him that she needed to get back to the office. He responded, with a smile, "I'll give you a raincheck."

She has worked for him for two years; this is the first time he has ever made any advances. She doesn't know what to do. What advice would you give her?

Online Research

ORA4-4 (Goal 1)

Search the Web for articles about companies that have lived their values through specific incidences. For example, try to find stories such as the Johnson & Johnson one given on page 89 of your text. Attempt to find three stories of companies. Begin your search on the Web by inserting the words "ethics and business" into your search engine. Then refine your search as appropriate. Make a copy of the stories and submit them to your instructor. Give an oral report of your findings to the class.

ORA4-5 (Goals 2 and 4)

Select three of your classmates to work with on this project. Using the Web, search for vision/values statements for three companies. In finding these statements on the Internet, you may begin your search by putting in the key words "ethics and business." Then, continue to refine your search until you find the vision/value statements. Print out copies of the statements.

As a team, write a short summary (approximately two pages) of the statements, listing the company names and a critique of the statements. Are the statements clear? Do they spell out sufficiently the values by which the company will operate? Will they inspire support from employees? If you were a manager in charge of helping employees who report to you live the values espoused by these statements within the business, how would you go about doing it? Either report orally to the class on your findings or submit your report in writing to your instructor.

Vocabulary Review

On pages 31–32 of your Applications Workbook is a Vocabulary Review, covering selected items from the vocabulary presented in Chapters 1–4. Complete these sentences and submit a copy to your instructor.

Language Skills Practice

On pages 33–34 of your Applications Workbook are sentences that need to be corrected, using the rules presented in the Reference Section of your text. Correct the sentences as needed and submit your work to your instructor.

Office Technology

CHAPTER 5

Information Processing

To say that our world is a computerized one is almost a cliché. We know it, and we live in it daily. Yet as you begin this chapter devoted to computer technology, think for a few minutes about the changes that we demand of our world due to technology. Let's use the **ATM** (automatic teller machine) to illustrate several changes.

The inspiration for the ATM came from a Dallas marketing executive by the name of Don Wetzel who in 1968 had the idea that turned into the ATM. As he was impatiently standing in a bank line, he reasoned there must be a more efficient way.[1] His brainchild, the ATM, epitomizes some of the changes that have occurred in our world due to technology—ones that

YOUR GOALS

1. Identify methods of creating and inputting information.

2. Define and use storage devices.

3. Output information.

4. Identify projected future computer directions.

---

[1]Jerry Adler, "Three Magic Wands," *Newsweek Extra: 2000 A New Millennium* (Winter 1997–98), 10.

we have come to expect and even demand.

- Availability
- Instantaneous service
- Portability
- Flexibility

The ATM is truly the 24-hour banker; it is available at any time we want to use it. If we need cash at midnight, it is there. If you have ever experienced going to an ATM when it was temporarily "out of service" and felt some of the angst that most of us feel, you realize how important that availability has become to you. The ATM provides us with instantaneous service. With the input of our **PIN** (personal identification number) and a few additional keys on the computer pad, we have our cash. The service has been instantaneous; the cash has been received within seconds. If you have ever had to wait in your car for a few minutes as the person in front of you takes more time than you think appropriate, you realize the expectation you have for instantaneous service. You also realize how important it is to have speedy delivery of the product you seek (your cash).

The ATM is *portable* and *flexible*. It is small enough to be set up at almost any location; it does not have to operate at one fixed location. We have ATMs in the parking lots of banks, in grocery stores, in colleges and universities, in shopping malls, at the airport, in other countries— any place where the consumer needs to receive cash. The ATM does not merely dispense cash; it has quite a bit of flexibility. We can check our bank balances, deposit money, transfer money from one account to another, and receive money from either our checking or our savings account.

As this example illustrates, the computer has not only changed the way we work, but the way we live and our expectations of service. The twenty-first century promises to bring additional technological advances that will impact the way we work, learn, play, and interact with each other. As you live and work in this world, you need some basic understanding of computer technology and equipment. This chapter will help you gain that understanding.

Information Creation

Information is created in the office in a variety of ways. For example, your supervisor may create a longhand draft; key a draft on the computer and hand you a disk to work from in completing the final product; or, in a few cases, use a dictation machine. You may create information directly at the computer, use a symbol or alpha system of shorthand in taking notes from your supervisor, or use a dictation/recording machine to record

ATMs provide instant service, available 24 hours a day. *Courtesy of © PhotoDisc, Inc.*

notes. However, the creation of information through taking shorthand notes and/or machine dictation/recording is used less and less by most office professionals. Computer technology makes these methods less efficient for the most part than direct creation at the computer. There are some areas where shorthand systems are still used extensively. For example, in courts of law, court reporters take shorthand notes using a machine. Also, there are times in the office when a computer is not handy, so the office professional takes shorthand notes. You may work for someone who prefers to dictate to you. In addition, dictation/recording machines may be used to take the proceedings of a meeting.

Information Input

Once the information has been created, it is necessary to input it using some type of input device. The basic input device is the computer keyboard. Another input device for data that is used extensively is the scanner. An emerging input device is **voice-recognition technology.** Major technological advances have been made in this area, and it is anticipated that it will become a major source of input in the future. Input devices used to send instructions to your computer or to input specialized types of data include touch screens, mice and trackballs, touch pads, infrared devices, pen tablets, and pucks.

Computer Keyboards

The most frequently used input device is the computer keyboard. The standard keyboard generally comes in one of two layouts. The one used most frequently is the extended 101-key keyboard, with twelve function keys along the top of the board, a numeric/cursor keypad, and an extra cursor keypad devoted solely to moving the cursor and scrolling within the document. There is also an 84-key keyboard with ten function keys arranged along the left-hand side of the keyboard and no extra cursor keyboard. The numeric keypad becomes a cursor keyboard control keyboard when a special key is activated. The part referred to as the **alphanumeric keypad** is almost identical to the standard typewriter keyboard. Portable computer keyboards generally do not replicate that of the desktop computer due to size restrictions. Portables may have smaller-than-usual keys, and the special keys such as Control, Escape, Alternate, Delete, Help, Insert, Caps Lock, and cursor control keys are generally moved or deleted.

In addition to the standard keyboard, there are a number of ergonomically designed keyboards that have evolved beyond the conventional ones into a diverse array of offerings designed to fit special needs. Some of the features on these keyboards include:

- Split-keyboard designs
- Built-in wrist rest
- Detachable wrist rest
- Chair-mounted keyboards
- Foot-switch support
- Mouse functions through keys

Split-keyboard designs vary, with one design being an alphanumeric section that spreads apart in the middle, rises up tent-like, and tilts forward. You can adjust the keyboard to adapt to your individual arm and hand positions. There are wrist-rest supports that help reduce fatigue and strain, as well as injuries caused by performing the same movements over and over again. Chair systems are also available, with the computer attached to the

Ergonomic keyboards may offer the split keyboard design and a built-in wrist rest. *Courtesy of © PhotoDisc, Inc.*

- Adjusting the image size
- Retouching, cropping, and manipulating photos in various ways
- Editing the scanned copy

In addition to these software options, document management software is available that allows you to file the scanned document.

Multifunction scanners allow you to print, copy, fax, and scan. These scanners are designed for small offices and home use. Although they are generally sheetfed, some of the multifunction units have scanners that can be detached and used by hand for scanning bound pages.

The cost of a scanner depends on the features available and the number of pages per minute that can be scanned. Although scanners are available at less

chair. These ergonomic workstations support your arms, wrists, back, and neck. On some keyboards, the numeric keypad can be positioned on the left, yielding greater comfort and accessibility for left-handed individuals. Timing devices are available to remind the user to take periodic rest breaks from the keying operation.

Scanners

Scanners allow information to be input directly into the computer without the traditional keystroking. Scanners can scan text, drawings, graphics, and photos. Scanners come in two basic designs—**flatbed scanners** and **sheetfed scanners.** Flatbed scanners are able to handle bound documents since they operate in a similar fashion to copy machines; that is, you may lift the top and place the document face down for scanning. Sheetfed scanners handle stacks of paper that are loaded automatically. Scanner software is available that allows you to modify the copy by:

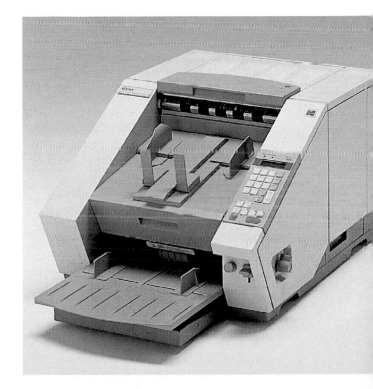

Sheetfed scanners handle stacks of paper that are loaded automatically. *Courtesy of Eastman Kodak.*

than $100, these scanners do not have the features and speed that are needed in middle- to large-size organizations. They may be used in very small businesses or home offices. Scanners used in larger organizations generally run from slightly over a thousand dollars to several thousand dollars. For example, a low volume scanner (from 5–20 pages per minute) costs approximately $1,000, with a medium volume scanner (from 21–50 ppm) costing over $4,000 and a high volume one (over 51 ppm) costing almost $7,000. Prices probably will continue to go down. However, the point you need to understand is that even though scanners can be purchased for under $100 they presently do not have the capacity to serve the needs of most organizations.

A number of specialized scanners, including optical and magnetic ink character readers and barcode scanners are available. These scanners are explained in the next section.

OCR (Optical Character Reader) Scanners.

An OCR can read keyboarded or typewritten information and handwritten documents. This technology is used widely in United States Postal offices to scan mail for quick distribution, rather than having to hand-sort each piece of mail. The OCR reads from the bottom of the address upward, reading the ZIP code, state, and city first, then the street address and company name.

MICR (Magnetic Ink Character Reader).

The MICR is used extensively by banks to read the magnetic ink numbers preprinted on checks and deposit slips. This process provides high-speed reading of financial information and transferring to disks or tapes where the data can be stored and manipulated in further preparing statements and reports.

Barcode Scanners.

Barcode scanners are the most common form of automated data entry. You cannot walk into a retail establishment without encountering the **UPC (Universal Product Code)** that is found on practically every product. Barcodes may be fixed or variable. An example of a **fixed-data barcode** is the barcode found on grocery products. By scanning the barcode, information is fed into the computer, which then computes the customer's grocery bill. The information is also used for inventory purposes in replacing stock.

A lottery ticket is an example of a **variable-data barcode.** The code identifies information unique to one particular ticket. Variable barcodes are used on all kinds of documents and labels. For example, a shipping waybill contains barcodes that allow for the tracking, sorting, and expediting of shipments.

Handheld Scanners.

Handheld scanners are used by a variety of retail

Barcode scanners may be used to record the barcode printed on grocery items. *Courtesy of © PhotoDisc, Inc.*

establishments, such as department stores (reading in prices of items to the computer) and mail delivery businesses (document tracking). Handheld scanners may also be used in the home and in small offices where either scanning is specialized or needs are limited.

Speech/Voice-Recognition Technology

Although voice-recognition technology has been used with mainframes and mini-computers for approximately 20 years, it has not been a real option for the microcomputer (PC) user. Today it is an option due to a breakthrough called **continuous speech recognition,** in which the user can speak normally and the computer decodes the voice. In the past, voice recognition systems used what is referred to as **discrete voice recognition** (the user had to pause between each word spoken). Obviously, this system was cumbersome. The continuous speech recognition technology allows the user to speak at approximately 160 words per minute. As you are aware, good keyboarders can keyboard at approximately 100 to 120 words per minute, with excellent keyboarders at 140 words per minute. In addition to speed, here are some other advantages of voice recognition systems:

- Voice recognition can lessen the problems of carpal tunnel syndrome, even if you don't use it all of the time. By switching between voice-recognition software and keyboarding, the strain to your wrists will be reduced.

- Voice-recognition programs can replace or supplement mouse-clicking duties. Virtually no voice training is needed if you are using the voice-recognition program to supplement the mouse only, since there is a limited vocabulary of commands.

Voice-recognition systems continue to have some disadvantages. The major ones are given here.

- An extended period of training time is necessary for the software being used to adjust to your voice and for you to understand corrections that must be made. Program errors need to be corrected when they are made so that the program can learn the difference between what it did and what you wanted. If errors are not corrected, they are reinforced in the program's mind.

- Considerable computing power is needed for all continuous speech recognition programs—that is, a **CD-ROM** drive with a large amount of **RAM** and hard drive space.

- The system will not work 100 percent of the time; it does not distinguish between such words as *there* and *they're*. In fact, most publishers of these programs claim only 95 percent accuracy, which means that with a 5 percent error rate, 1 in every 20 words will be incorrect. The correction process can be time-consuming and frustrating.

- Outside noise is also a problem for voice-recognition technology, even in a closed-door office. Loud voices in the office can cause errors to occur when attempting to use this technology.

- If you are keyboarding at a rate of 80 to 140 words per minute, voice recognition probably will not speed up your data entry due to the corrections that must be made.

The cost of the hardware for voice-recognition systems will probably decrease in the future, just as all computer technology tends to go down in price. Projections are that the technology will continue to be more

Voice-recognition programs can replace or supplement mouse-clicking duties. *Courtesy of © CORBIS.*

movements. Ergonomically designed mice are available that allow you to use a foot switch or a key that eliminates the "grip-to-click" strain and the unnecessary hand/wrist motion. Cordless mice are also available that work either on infrared or radio frequency technology.

A **trackball** is a stationary ball that you roll with the tips of your fingers to move the pointer on your screen. Trackball rollers are installed on the keyboard or clipped to the side of a laptop or portable.

Both of these devices employ a **graphical user interface (GUI)** rather than being driven by keystrokes. The GUI uses a drop-down menu and various icons for executing commands and choosing program

user-friendly and become the dominant interface with computers in future years.[2]

Mice and Trackballs

A **mouse** is a small hand-controlled device that operates like a remote control box and allows the user to move the cursor and choose menu commands without using the keyboard. When using a mouse, you place the palm of your hand on it and drag it along your tabletop. As you move the mouse, the rubber ball inside the mouse rolls and an arrow or pointer moves about on the screen to match the speed and direction of your tabletop

Touch screens are available in some stores so consumers can learn more about products, pricing, and available services. *Courtesy of International Business Machines Corporation. Unauthorized use not permitted.*

[2]"Voice & Speech Recognition Software: Is It Too Good to Be True?," *PCNovice Guide to Upgrading* (Volume 6, Issue 8), 114–116.

options. The tool bar at the top of your computer is an example of a GUI, with various icons for executing commands.

Touch Screens

With a **touch screen,** the user touches the desired choice on the screen with his or her finger rather than using a mouse or trackball. Touch screens are used in a variety of settings, which include:

- Hospitals, where the M.D. can use it to sign a virtual prescription for a patient
- Fast-food restaurants, where clerks can easily input food items ordered and the amount of the bill
- Gasoline stations, where customers can start the pump by punching in the appropriate type of gasoline
- Office buildings, where the user can find the location of a particular office
- Greeting card stores, where the customer can create his or her own card

Touch Pads

Touch pads are similar to trackballs in operation and look like an Etch-A-Sketch pad. The onscreen cursor follows your movements as you move your finger on the pad. You "click" as you would on a mouse by tapping the pad. Touch pads are comfortable to use since they do not require you to move your entire hand—just your finger.

Infrared Devices

Although **infrared** technology is not new, the use of infrared as an input device is fairly new. An example of infrared that we are familiar with is the remote control that we use to change the channels on the TV. Infrared allows for wireless beaming of data from one device to another. Some companies now make infrared keyboards with built-in trackballs or touch pads. An infrared sensor that comes with the pointing device is attached to the computer and captures infrared signals from the keyboard. For example, if you want to send information from the computer to the printer, rather than clicking a mouse on the printer icon, you send an infrared signal to the computer with the pointing device.

Pen Tablets and Pucks

Pen tablets allow the user to hold the computer with one hand and use a pen with the other to run applications based on a menu. For example, a market research firm that has employees collecting data by doing surveys in malls may use a pen tablet. Also, they may be used to create graphics. If you want more control over the pen, you may use a **puck.** This input device is similar to a mouse, but it has a clear window with built-in openings that provide the user with greater precision. Tablets are hard, plastic devices that look like mouse pads and come in a variety of

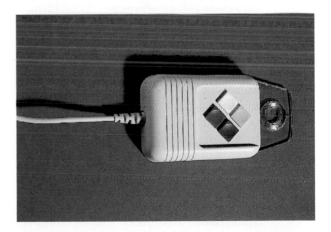

A puck may be used to create drawings. *Courtesy of GTCO Calcomp, Inc.*

sizes. Tablets come with a pen-shaped **stylus** for writing or drawing.

Information Processing

Once information is created and input, the next step is to process that information electronically. Computers are the means for processing.

Computer Classifications

Computers are classified by the amount of storage capacity they contain and the speed with which they operate. There are five main categories of computers:

- Supercomputers
- Mainframe computers
- Minicomputers
- Workstation computers (supermicros)
- Microcomputers

Supercomputers are the largest computers and can operate at the fastest speeds. *Courtesy of © CORBIS.*

Supercomputers. Supercomputers are the Goliaths of the industry. They can operate at 1.06 **teraflops** per second (one teraflop equals one trillion operations). The fastest previous speed on a supercomputer was 368 **gigaflops** per second (one gigaflop equals one billion operations). It is expected that by 2002 supercomputers will be able to operate at a speed of 1 **petaflop** per second (one petaflop equals one quadrillion operations). Although most organizations do not need a computer of this size, very large operations use them. For example, the federal government uses supercomputers for tasks that require mammoth data manipulation, such as worldwide weather forecasting and weapons research.

Mainframe Computers. Mainframes are large computers that accommodate hundreds of users doing different tasks; they

are commonly found in large businesses and government agencies. Main-frames can support a number of auxiliary devices such as terminals, printers, disk drives, and other input and output equipment. They are used in processing company-wide applications such as payroll, accounting, inventory, and purchasing. Mainframes, along with the peripheral equipment such as printers, are usually housed in a separate room with appropriate air-conditioning for heat control and false floors to accommodate the multitude of cables required to connect terminals and peripherals.

Minicomputers. Minicomputers are midrange computers and are generally used in middle-size businesses. They are slower, have less storage capacity, and are less expensive than a mainframe computer. Schools, retail businesses, and state and city agencies are examples of entities that may use a minicomputer. However, a large company may have a centralized mainframe computer and several decentralized minicomputers at various sites such as branch offices. In such a situation, the mainframe and minicomputer are usually **interfaced** (interconnected) so that they can communicate with each other.

Workstation Computers (Supermicros).

Workstation computers (supermicros) are the upper-end machines of the **microcomputer** (discussed in the next section). They have a large amount of process power, approaching the power of a mainframe. They have a high-speed microprocessor, significantly increased memory, and increased hard-disk storage capacity over the microcomputer, and are able to serve several users. Yet they are small enough to sit on a desktop.

Microcomputers (Personal Computers).

Microcomputers are the smallest of the computer systems. The advances in technology in the 1970s, including the manufacture of electronic circuits on small silicon chips, made microcomputers possible. A single miniature chip (called a **microprocessor**) contains the circuitry and components for arithmetic, logic, and control operations. Microcomputers are usually referred to as **PCs (personal computers)** since they are widely used in the home, as well as in business and education. Today, microcomputers are as powerful as many mainframe computers of several years ago; and with the addition of **hard drives** (internal storage capacity) they can store huge amounts of data. Two relatively recent technological inventions, the **Pentium processor chip** manufactured by Intel and Advanced Micro Devices' **AMD microprocessor,** have increased the speed and performance capability of the PC.

In addition to the desktop microcomputer, there are two basic types of portable microcomputers—**notebooks** and **handheld computers.** Notebooks, also referred to as laptops, are capable of performing almost any task that a desktop computer can perform. With the virtual work environment of today, laptops have become indispensable to numerous workers. At the high end of the notebook market is the computer that can deliver as many or more functions than the desktop computer can. Mainly professionals who require heavy-duty computer power as they travel use these notebooks. These machines weigh roughly seven to eight pounds. Smaller notebooks, less expensive and less powerful, are available, weighing from slightly over two pounds to five pounds. Notebooks come equipped with floppy and CD-ROM drives. Since

Handheld computers are the smallest of the portable computers.
Courtesy of © PhotoDisc, Inc.

upgrading them is usually more difficult and costly than upgrading desktop models, it is wise to get as much power and storage as you will need.

Handheld computers are the smallest of the portables. These computers are used for specialized functions such as maintaining calendars and address lists, writing short notes and memos, preparing to-do lists, browsing the Web, and sending or receiving email. They come in various sizes, from large handheld PCs to palm-size PCs to credit-card sized devices. A typical size for a handheld PC is $7'' \times 4''$, with a weight of one pound, and a battery life of from 4 to 8 hours. Data that has been entered on your handheld computer can be transferred to your notebook or desktop PC. For example, calendar information or to-do lists can be transferred from your handheld computer to your desktop computer for further manipulation.

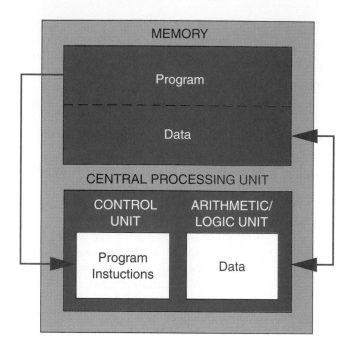

FIGURE 5-1. The CPU manipulates data.

Computer Internal Processing and Storage

Once data has been input into the computer through the various input media mentioned earlier (keyboards, scanners, voice recognition, and so forth), processing takes place in the central processing unit of the computer. The unit has two basic parts—the control unit and the arithmetic/logic unit. The central processing unit interacts closely with primary storage (also called memory), referring to it for both instructions and data. These functions are explained in the next section.

Central Processing Unit.   The **central processing unit (CPU)** is the brain of the computer system. It accepts the data from the input device, processes the data according to the program, and delivers the results through some type of output device. Figure 5-1 depicts this process.

The CPU of a mainframe is housed in a fairly large unit. However, the CPU and memory of a microcomputer are smaller than thumbtacks. The CPU and memory in a microcomputer are on silicon chips, which are referred to as the microprocessor.

Arithmetic/Logic Unit.   The **arithmetic/logic unit** performs all mathematical calculations. It adds, subtracts, multiplies, and divides. It handles logic operations by comparing both alphabetic and numeric data. For example, it makes such comparisons as greater than, less than, and equal to an identified number. The unit can also draw conclusions. Consider this example. You are working with a personnel program that records leave time for employees. You record five days of vacation for an employee, but the employee has only three days of vacation available. The arithmetic/logic unit will let you know that the employee is not eligible for five days and will give you the number of days available.

Control Unit. As its name implies, the **control unit** regulates the different functions of the computer system. All instructions to the computer are interpreted here. For example, the unit directs the input-output devices, giving them instructions as to when to input data and when to output data. It also interprets instructions for all arithmetic-logic operations. It tells the arithmetic/logic unit when to add, subtract, multiply, and divide. The unit tells the arithmetic/logic unit when and how to classify and sort data, and it coordinates the transfer of data to and from the main computer storage.

Memory. Computers use two main types of storage components: primary and secondary storage. Secondary storage consists of floppy diskettes, optical disks, hard disks, and magnetic tapes. Primary memory is contained in the computer itself.

Memory is referred to as **primary storage** since it holds data until it is processed and/or transferred to an output device. Data within computer memory are stored in the form of a code that utilizes a 1 or a 0. These 1s or 0s are called **binary digits** or **bits**. The reason for storing pieces of data in bits is that the computer circuitry is electronic in nature, and electronic devices can be turned either "on" or "off." Combinations of bits are put together to form a **byte**, which represents a character (letter, number, or symbol) in a computer. For example, eight bits are put together to form the letter A; the combined bits are called a byte. A byte is the smallest unit of computer storage.

The memory or storage capacity of different computers is not the same; how-ever, each computer does have a fixed memory capacity. Memory capacities are expressed in thousand-byte units called **kilobytes (KB)**, million-byte units called **megabytes (MB)**, billion-byte units called **gigabytes (GB)**, and trillion-byte units called **terabytes (TB)**. The size of the memory capacity varies by computer. The storage capacity of computers has increased over the years and will likely continue to increase.

The two most common categories of memory are **random access memory (RAM)** and **read-only memory (ROM)**. Both RAM and ROM are present on all computers. RAM memory is necessary for manipulation of data, and ROM is necessary to keep permanently etched in the computer's memory vital information concerning its overall operation. ROM allows you to turn your computer on and off. The contents of ROM cannot be modified; it can only be read—not changed. RAM allows you to change data. When you work with a word processing document, you are using RAM.

Storage Devices

Secondary storage is commonly used since the internal capacity of the computer is always limited. The most popular auxiliary storage devices are:

- Floppy disks
- Zip disks and drives
- Optical or laser disks
- Hard disks
- Magnetic tape

Floppy Disks. Disks (also referred to as **diskettes**) are an indispensable storage medium for the computer. The first size available was a 5.25-inch disk; however, it is rarely used today. The size that is used

or her. A total commitment by all employees to upholding ethical standards makes a company not only a great place to work but also a success with its clients and customers.

SUMMARY

To reinforce what you have learned in this chapter, study this summary.

- Ethics is the systematic study of moral conduct, duty, and judgment—what is right and what is wrong. Ethical business behavior means doing what is right, not merely what is profitable. Business ethics requires that judgment be exercised about a proposed act and its anticipated consequences. It means that individuals within an organization, collectively and singularly, are socially responsible for their conduct and are focused on what is right.

- The ethical organization is:
  a. Environmentally responsible
  b. Internationally aware
  c. Culturally committed to behaving ethically
  d. Honest
  e. Committed to diversity
  f. Committed to the community
  g. Committed to employees
  h. An establisher of standards

- Factors impeding ethical change include the belief that:
  a. Values cannot be changed.
  b. Organizations are amoral.
  c. Labels accurately describe individuals.
  d. The leadership of an organization never behaves ethically.

- Steps that can produce ethical change include:
  a. Determine the ethical change required.
  b. Determine the steps required to achieve the objective.
  c. Practice the new behaviors.
  d. Seek feedback.
  e. Reward the individual or group involved.
  f. Evaluate the effects of ethical change.

- Two forms of discrimination include sexual harassment and racial discrimination. Sexual harassment is defined as harassment arising from sexual conduct that is unwelcome by the recipient and that may be either physical or verbal in nature. Racial discrimination is based on prejudice, which is often the result of ignorance, fear, and/or cultural patterns. There are laws that protect individuals from racial and sexual discrimination, with one of the most important ones being Title VII of the Civil Rights Act of 1964.

- Characteristics of the ethical office professional include the following:
  a. Makes ethical decisions
  b. Supports ethical behavior
  c. Refuses to engage in negative office politics
  d. Accepts constructive criticism
  e. Observes office hours
  f. Accepts responsibilities
  g. Maintains honesty and integrity
  h. Respects privacy
  i. Is open to change
  j. Is loyal
  k. Keeps the faith

almost exclusively is the 3.5-inch disk. Both disks are referred to as **floppy.** The 3.5-inch disk is housed in a nonremovable, rigid plastic case. The amount of data that can be stored on a disk is expressed in terms of **density.** The label on the disk should tell you whether it is a high- or low-density disk. On the 3.5 disk there are two small notches in each corner for the high density and only one notch for the low density. Another helpful hint in determining density on disks is the labeling. A high-density disk is labeled Double Sided High Density. A low-density disk is labeled Double Sided Double Density. The density capacity on a 3.5 disk is as follows:

3.5-inch low density   720K
3.5-inch high density   1.44MB

To help you understand what this means, a typical printed page, using single spacing, contains 2,500 to 3,000 characters. Thus 1MB holds 400 pages of single-spaced text.

When purchasing a disk, you also need to check whether or not it is **formatted.** Formatting is defined as the process of organizing a disk so that it can be recognized by the computer and used to store data. When a disk is formatted, its storage space is organized into a collection of data compartments, each of which can be located by the computer operating system so that data can be sorted and retrieved. Disks may be purchased that are formatted for either IBM (or compatible) or MacIntosh systems. Disks may also be purchased that are not formatted. If you purchase such a disk, you can format it by following the instructions in your computer user's manual.

Additional information, including disk care and the write-protect notch, is provided in Chapter 6.

Zip Disks and Drives.   A **Zip drive** is a small, portable disk drive developed by Iomega Corporation primarily to meet the needs of mobile users. It allows for true portability, enabling users to take files and applications anywhere they carry their notebook computers. Each **Zip** disk (used with a Zip drive) holds 100MB of data (the equivalent of 70 floppy disks). It allows the user to:

- Store unusually large files, with graphic images
- Archive old files that are not used anymore but must be maintained
- Exchange large files with other users

Technological developments continue to provide for increased storage capacity of the portable drives and disks. Two additional drives include the **HiFD drive** (200MB capacity) and the **UHD144 drive** (144MB capacity). These drives combine floppy and high-capacity removable storage into one unit. Owners of older computers can use floppy-replacement upgrade kits to add removable storage systems to their computers.

In addition to the external storage provided by the drives mentioned in the previous paragraphs, increased internal storage is available for personal computers in the form of **Jaz drives and disks.** These drives and disks provide for 1GB of storage.

Compact Disk Storage.   A compact disk is a storage medium for digital data. The disk is read by an optical scanning mechanism that uses a high-intensity light source, such as a laser and mirrors. Compact disks come in several types, including:

- **CD-ROM (compact disk read-only memory)**
- **CD-R (compact disk—recordable)**
- **CD-E (compact disk—erasable)**

- WORM (write once, read many)
- DVD-ROM (digital versatile disk— read-only memory)
- DVD-R (digital versatile disk— recordable)
- DVD-RAM (digital versatile disk— random access memory)

One use of the CD-ROM is to supply software packages such as word processing, spreadsheets, graphics, and databases to the computer; it can be read but not edited. Most computers now have CD-ROM capability that allows the user to access libraries of information, including graphics and video.

The CD-R is a type of CD-ROM that can be written on a CD recorder and read on a CD-ROM drive. The erasable disk (CD-E) can be reused by writing over the data that is there. Thus, it is suitable for applications that call for temporary document storage.

The WORM disk gets its name from the fact that it is written only once and read any number of times. A WORM disk is nonerasable and is used in applications that require the data to be written once as a permanent record. For example, banks and accounting firms use WORM as a means of maintaining a permanent, unalterable audit trail.

The DVD disk is the newest of the ones mentioned previously. A DVD-ROM will hold up to 4.7GB of data, or seven times more than the 650MB capacity of a CD-ROM. It offers faster access and response times, factors especially important in business applications. The first DVD adopters were corporate users who use CD multimedia for training and sales presentations. It allows organizations to make longer and higher-quality, full-screen multimedia presentations.

HiFD and UHD144 drives provide for greater personal computer storage capacity. *Courtesy of © PhotoDisc, Inc.*

Hard Disks.   Hard disks (also called **magnetic disks** or simply hard drive) are secondary storage for mainframes and minicomputers. However, the hard disk that is of more importance to you as an office professional is the one that operates as an internal storage device for the PC. You will often store information on the hard disk drive. Even if you intend to transfer information to a floppy disk at a later point, the usual process is to store it on the hard drive first. In fact, most software programs automatically store the information you are keying to the hard drive and let you determine how often you want it saved. This device allows quicker access to stored information than the floppy disk. Once you have stored information on the hard drive, it is a good idea to also store it on a floppy disk or other devices such as the Zip disk as a backup,

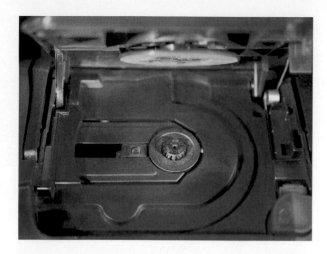

The DVD disk offers fast access and response times and can handle large-scale multimedia presentations. *Courtesy of © PhotoDisc, Inc.*

particularly if the information is extremely important.

Magnetic Tape. **Magnetic tape** has been used as a storage medium for mainframe computers for years, and it is still used today. Tape can also be a storage medium for minicomputers and microcomputers. The basic usage of tape consists of transferring information to tape for archival or replacement purposes. For example, software programs produced **in-house** (within the company) may be transferred to tape to provide a backup if something happens to the program stored on the hard drive. Tape drives for microcomputers may be internal drives that are installed in an empty bay in the front of your computer or external drives that are self-contained units that plug into a connector on the back of your computer.

Information Output

The main two output devices are **monitors** and **printers**. If you want **soft copy** (copy shown on the monitor only—a printed copy is not necessary), the video display monitor is appropriate. If you want hard copy (paper), use the printer.

Monitors

The standard monitor since computers became a fixture in the office has been the **cathode ray tube (CRT),** which is also the technology of the monitor on the standard TV set. CRTs for computers come in a variety of sizes, ranging from 9 to 21 inches, with 14- to 17-inch monitors being the standard size used for desktop PCs. The smaller 9-inch is used on portable computers. The larger 19- to 21-inch monitors are able to display a two-page spread for a desktop publishing program; this size screen is also important if your work requires several open windows at once. The quality of the information portrayed on the screen is referred to as **resolution.** The resolution is measured in **pixels** (short for picture element). One pixel is a spot in a grid of thousands of spots that are individually painted to form an image on the screen. The minimum resolution recommended is 800 x 600 for a 15-inch screen; 1024 x 768 pixels or higher is needed if graphics are going to be displayed. High-performance monitors have a maximum resolution of 1600 x 1200 pixels.

Monitors are available in black-and-white, **monochrome** (one color), or color. The three most popular one-color alternatives are green, blue, or amber. These hues have been found to be the easiest on the eyes over long periods. Color monitors use three primary colors: red, green, and blue. Using these three colors and mixing them in various combinations or proportions, every other color of the spectrum is

Color monitors allow the office professional to determine how the color design will look before printing. *Courtesy of* © *PhotoDisc, Inc.*

possible in tints, tones, and gradations from very dark to very light.

The most recent development in monitors is the **LCD (liquid crystal display).** This monitor has been developed for a few years, but it has been too expensive for most users, often costing several thousand dollars. The LCD can now be purchased for slightly under a thousand dollars, which is still roughly twice the price of the CRT. However, the LCD has some distinct advantages over the CRT. The LCD is also referred to as the flat-panel display since it is very narrow compared to the CRT. A typical 15-inch CRT runs 15 inches in depth, compared to a depth of 7 inches for the LCD. Refer to the photo on page 128, which shows a flat-panel screen; notice how slim it is. This narrow depth allows for the conservation of desk space; in addition, LCDs come with built-in speakers and microphones that allow you to conserve even more desk space. Some of the LCDs also allow you to pivot between **portrait** (document shown across the narrower dimension of a rectangular sheet of paper) and **landscape** (images shown sideways—the width greater than the height) views. The LCD's clarity lets it handle higher resolutions than comparable CRTs can, which allow you to pack more text or spreadsheet cells on your screen. LCDs are also using digital rather than analog technology, which boosts image quality.

Image Quality and Size

Better image quality has been proven to reduce symptoms such as headaches, sore eyes, light sensitivity, and neck strain by up to 66 percent. Research also shows that if the quality of the display on the screen is improved, so will productivity.[3] When purchasing a monitor, you should compare the image quality of several models, using the applications typical of your environment.

In addition to image quality, size is also important. Monitors smaller than 17 inches inhibit the user's ability to see more than a few cells on a spreadsheet and to read from multiple applications at one time. Nineteen- and 21-inch screens provide 50 to 60 percent more workspace than 15-inch monitors.

Printers

The most commonly used output device is the printer, with the two most frequently used types being the laser and the inkjet. Their popularity in companies and in the home office makes it useful to explain these printers in more detail in this section. The dot-matrix printer, an **impact printer** (a device that prints characters on paper by physically impacting or hitting the paper) was one of the first printers to dominate the market years ago. It is still used for some applications, mainly in-

The LCD monitor has a flat-panel screen that allows for the conservation of desk space. *Courtesy of © PhotoDisc, Inc.*

house where continuous-feed paper is used. The laser and inkjet printer are both **nonimpact printers** (make marks on the paper without mechanically striking it).

Inkjets. With the inkjet printer, characters are formed on the page by tiny streams of ink spraying through a nozzle onto the paper. In the past these printers were considered the province of home users due to the lower quality of their print output and relatively slow speed. Today, however, with the text quality approaching the output of laser printers, and

---

[3]Kent A. Blake, "Buying Office Equipment: How the Insiders Do It," *Managing Office Technology* (November 1997), 17.

as **network** (a group of computers and associated devices that are connected by communications facilities) capabilities are added, they are being used more extensively by businesses.

When buying an inkjet printer, check these items:

- Speed—Some inkjets print at a speed of 7.5 **PPM** (pages per minute) for monochrome and 3.5 PPM for color; this speed is equal to the lower-end laser printer.

- Print quality—The quality is measured by print resolution, with inkjets ranging from approximately 720 x 360 **dpi** (dots per inch) to 1440 x 720 dpi. This print resolution is extremely close to the laser printer.

- Ink type—Solid ink is more durable than liquid ink or electrostatic.

- Consumables—Cost of consumables such as color ink cartridges

- Paper costs—Special coated papers designed to bring out the best in inkjet

The inkjet printer is capable of producing text quality that approaches the quality of the laser printer. *Courtesy of © PhotoDisc, Inc.*

print quality are more expensive than the cut-sheet paper used on laser printers and add to the lifetime cost of an inkjet printer.

- Image quality—Quality of photographic images (if needed).

- Cost—Inkjets are available for less than $100 dollars. In fact, multipurpose units which include a printer, color copier, and detachable color scanner are available for less than $500 dollars. However, these printers are suitable for the very small office or the home office—not for the mid- or large-size office. Inkjet printers (when used in larger offices) are several hundred dollars. Laser printers, however, remain the best way to produce professional documents quickly in a demanding business environment.

Lasers. The laser printer uses a beam of light to form images on light-sensitive paper. Laser printers print at extremely fast speeds and produce a high-quality product. They are the printer of choice of most offices due to the speed and quality of the copy produced.

When buying a laser printer, consider these factors:

- Speed—Determine how many pages per minute a laser prints; this can be as many as 24 pages per minute. High speeds are desirable if you are producing multipage documents and share a printer. Color documents print far slower than do black and white ones—approximately one-fourth of the speed.

- Print quality—Print resolution on a laser can be as high as 1200 x 1200 dpi. For standard use, 600 dpi should be enough; however, for camera-ready copy, a printer with 1200 dpi is needed.

- Capabilities—Be certain the printer can handle different paper weights, paper stocks, and typefaces. If printing envelopes and labels is important, buy a machine that handles this function without excessive operator intervention. Find out about the paper tray capacity. Lasers are capable of printing on both sides of the page and holding thousands of sheets of paper, with optional paper bins for unattended operation.
- Consumables—Make certain that changing consumables, such as color cartridges, is easy. Check out the price of the color cartridges and standard toner.
- Cost—Laser printers designed for large offices generally cost a few thousand dollars; models for small office use can be purchased for a few hundred dollars.

In addition to understanding the factors listed here for both inkjets and lasers, it is a good idea to do a needs analysis before purchasing any office equipment. You might want to have an experienced consultant from outside the company come in and do this analysis. Then the next step is to check out various equipment against your needs.

Multifunction Peripherals

Multifunction machines are available that print, scan, copy, and fax. These machines are used more in small businesses and home offices. If you are thinking of purchasing a multifunction peripheral, consider these factors:

- Space available—Multifunction devices take far less space than the several machines they replace and can be installed more easily since one hookup takes care of numerous functions.

- Capacity needed—Multifunctions are available with varying speeds, print resolution, and so forth.
- Cost—The cost can range from a low of several hundred dollars to a high of several thousand dollars, with the capabilities and speed of the machine determining the cost.
- Downtime—When a multifunction device goes down, you lose all functions—the copier, printer, scanner, and fax. This is an important factor to consider, especially in a small business or home office where there are no backup machines.

Networked Printers

Many businesses network (a printer attached to a local area network) or link several computers to one printer. Depending on the needs of the business, networked printers can be a cost savings to the business. For example, if color or specialized functions are required in one department of a company, the department might use a network printer. This printer can provide the capabilities needed—color, stapling, bundling, hole punching, specialized paper size, print speed, and so forth—for a group of people rather than having a printer attached to each computer. To help you understand more about local area networks, read the next section.

Computer Networks

Computers and other peripheral equipment such as printers, as you have just learned, can be linked through networks. These networks may be:

- **Local area networks (LANs)** that link various types of technological equipment within a building or several buildings within the same geographic area such as a business or a college campus with multiple buildings

- **Metropolitan area networks (MANs)** that link technological equipment over a distance equal to the size of a city and its surroundings (approximately 31 miles)
- **Wide area networks (WANs)** that link technological equipment in an area of hundreds of thousands of miles

Almost all desktop computers are networked via LANs, MANs, or WANs. These connections allow computers to talk to each other over distances. For example, a LAN allows for email to be sent between computers within an office. Networking through MANs or WANs allows electronic mail to be sent to computers at distant locations.

The growth of technology and the need for sharing information worldwide have spawned worldwide networks. The **Internet,** a worldwide network, and the **World Wide Web,** one of the features of the Internet, are being used extensively by business and individuals.

Internet

The Internet is the world's largest group of connected computers, allowing people from all over the world to communicate. Solid estimates of the number of computers connected to the Internet are difficult to get; however (as this textbook is printed), there are more than 40 million computers connected to the Internet in the United States alone.

The Internet was created in the 1960s as a project of the U.S. Department of Defense. Since that time, it has grown exponentially, and that growth is expected to continue both in the United States and worldwide. When accessing the Internet, people talk of "going on the Internet." However, no one is ever "on" the Internet as you are "on" an airplane, for example. The Internet is a vehicle for delivering information back and forth between computers around the world. All of the computers speak the same electronic language so they can exchange information; that language is **Transmission Control Protocol/Internet Protocol (TCP/IP).**

In order to access the Internet, there must be some type of line that allows information to go from your computer to other computers. The main access is through a **modem** (short for **mo**dulator/**dem**odulator). The modem sends information from your computer over regular telephone lines to other computers. In addition, office networks and individuals may use **ISDN (Integrated Services Digital Network)** or **DSL (Digital Subscriber Line),** offered by regular telephone companies. ISDN lines achieve greater speed and reliability than modems and regular telephone lines by using digital format. With digital format, the information moves faster and with fewer errors. The single biggest drawback to ISDN is cost. Purchasing an ISDN adapter and paying for service can be expensive compared to the low cost of dialing a local Internet service provider or an online service through regular phone service. Some home users may access the Internet through cable lines. The home user pays a nominal fee (approximately $20 per month) to access the Internet through such services as America Online®, CompuServe®, and Prodigy®.

DSL only became widely available in 1999. Eventually, DSL services are expected to deliver speeds of 1.5**Mbps (megabits per second)** or more routinely;

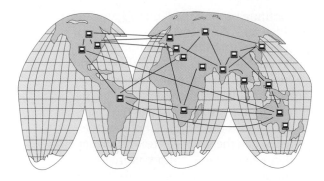

FIGURE 5-2. The Internet is the world's largest group of connected computers, allowing people from all over the world to communicate.

this speed is approximately 30 times faster than the 56**Kbps (kilobits per second)** modems and more than 10 times faster than ISDN.

The phone company is not alone in offering high-speed access. Cable TV is offering it also. Although cable Internet service is available in approximately 10 percent of the U.S. today, that number is expected to steadily increase. Cable services can deliver Web pages at a fast speed (3 to 10Mbps), with a possibility of 40Mbps for a relatively low cost. Cable modems are still being refined.

World Wide Web

The Web is a huge collection of computer files (more than 100 million Web pages and growing daily) scattered across the Internet. The Web is a portion of the information available through the Internet. For example, in addition to the Web, the Internet contains news articles, weather information, entertainment, email messages, travel information, and encyclopedia information, to name a few.

The Web was created by Tim Berners-Lee, a consultant at the Swiss research laboratory CERN, as a tool for physicists to share research data. It was not used by the general public until the creation of Mosaic, **a Web browser.** From this first browser, a number of other browsers have been developed, including Microsoft Internet Explorer and Netscape Navigator. A browser lets users gain access to and navigate the Web. The Web has spawned a new technical vocabulary; some of the Web terms that you need to know are given in Figure 5-3.

In less than five years, the Web has changed the way people all over the world communicate. It is possible to find nearly anything that one can imagine on the Web.

Here is some of the information available.

- Research—Government institutions, universities, and libraries all use the Web as a means of getting information to the public.
- Mail-order catalog (the world's largest)—The Web allows any business to market itself to a global audience.
- Publication—Computer users can create their own Web pages, allowing individuals and businesses to share their opinion and visions with the rest of the online world.
- News—Worldwide news is available almost as it happens.
- Travel services—Reservations may be made at any hour of the day or night.
- Jobs—Worldwide job listings are available.
- Chat rooms—Through chat rooms, individuals may talk with other individuals across the world about particular topics of interest.

Figure 5-4 shows a Web screen with some of this information listed.

When using the Internet and the

WEB TERMS

Hit—Each request made of a World Wide Web server. For example, if you are doing research and ask for "monitors and LCD," the number of responses (articles) that you receive are referred to as hits. You will get a response that states something like, "the first 10 of 178,899." You can continue to pull up as many of the articles as you want to review.

Home page—The startup or introductory page of a Web site.

Hyperlink—A connector between one Web page and another.

Hypertext Markup Language (HTML)—The standard language used for creating and formatting World Wide Web pages.

Search engine—Special Web sites that take words and phrases keyed by users and respond with Web sites and Web pages matching the description. Yahoo® and Excite™, for example, are search engines. Search engines are the best way to find information on the Web.

Uniform resource locator (URL)—The addressing system that helps users locate Web sites on the Internet. It gives the name of the server where the files are stored, the files' directory path, and the file name. An example of a URL is http://www.americawest.com.

Web browser—Software that provides users with a graphical interface for accessing and navigating the Web. Internet Explorer, for example, is a browser.

Chat rooms—Online areas where members may meet to communicate and interact with others.

Server—A host computer that sends Web page information to other computers.

Hypertext Transfer Protocol (HTTP)—The standardized method used to transfer documents from a host computer or server to Web browsers and individual users.

FIGURE 5-3. Web terms.

World Wide Web, here are some things to remember:

- The Internet is public. Even though you may be sitting at a computer in your office or home, other people on the Net can observe you. They can eavesdrop on chat room conversation; they can read information posted on bulletin boards.
- Email is not private. Others can read your email communication unless you use **encryption** software (encoding an email so that others may not gain access).
- Avoid giving out private information such as name, address, phone number, credit card information, and your Social Security number. Someone

could use this information to perpetrate a fraud against you.

- The validity of information posted needs to be checked. For example, if you are doing research, you need to check the validity of the source. As you know, anyone can get on the Internet and publish anything. You do not want to believe or pass on incorrect information. You are responsible for checking the validity of the source.
- Files downloaded from the Internet may contain **viruses,** and you must protect against them. You will learn more about viruses in Chapter 6. You should make sure that your computer has antiviral software.
- Harassment can be common in chat

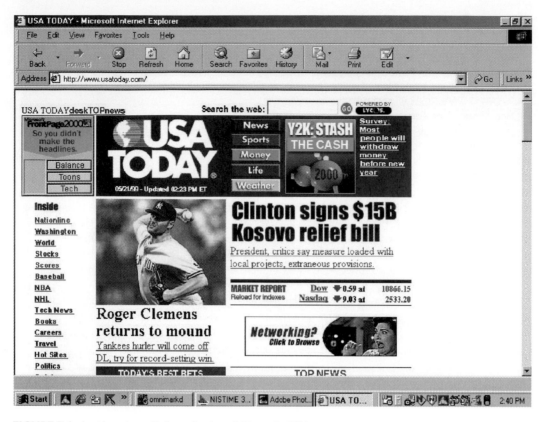

FIGURE 5-4. A wide variety of information is available on the Web.

rooms, particularly for women. The harassment ranges from rudeness and verbal abuse to serious sexual harassment. If you are not comfortable with what is happening in a chat room, use the Escape key to get out.[4]

Intranet

An **intranet** is a network that allows businesses to provide access for their employees to the Internet without allowing outside people to have access to the information within the company. The intranet resides behind a firewall that has been technologically built to keep access limited to the intended members. To help you understand the relationship between an intranet and the Internet, think of the Internet as a worldwide network of computers and an intranet as a business network of computers. People from an intranet can break through the wall to access information from the Internet, but individuals from the Internet cannot break through the wall to access the information on an intranet.

---

[4]Just Like the Real World . . . Use Common Sense to Stay Safe Online, *PCNovice: Guide to Internet Basics* (Volume 6, Issue 10), 96–98.

Extranet

An **extranet** also operates behind a firewall, but the firewall allows the inclusion of selected individuals, companies, and organizations outside the company itself. You can access an extranet if you have a valid username and password. Your identity determines which parts of the extranet you can view. Financial institutions have used an extranet to provide clients with account information and performance reports. The World Bank's massive library, for example, provides fast retrieval of data on every country, along with finance, development, and social policy topics. Health institutions have used an extranet to access medical records. Figure 5-5 illustrates the intranet and extranet concept.

Future Directions of Computer Technology

Trying to make refined predictions of the technology of the future is perhaps an exercise in futility, since the biggest changes will probably come from technological

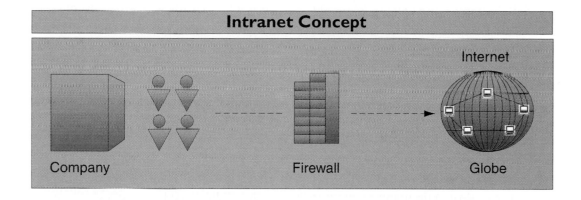

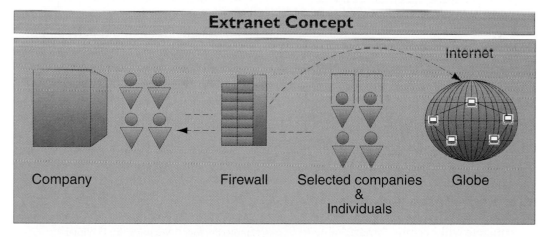

FIGURE 5-5. Intranet and extranet concept.

innovations that we haven't thought about or perhaps have only dreamed about. However, here are several predictions that can be made with some certainty.

- The future will continue to be dominated by technology.
- The growth area jobs of the future (the next ten years) will be in health-related and computer industries.
- The Internet of the future will bring 3-D graphics and full-motion video.
- There will be virtual reality systems that allow you to see, hear, and touch computer-generated 3-D images.
- Due to technological advances, people will live longer and will work into old age, with middle age being approximately 60.
- Technology will require increased levels of education; most jobs will require education beyond high school.
- Household appliances will operate from verbal instructions.
- Car computers will enable people to stay in touch with the outside world; use traffic information to find the fastest route to a destination; monitor the mechanical functions of the car; and, in the case of an accident, transmit the car's exact location and summon emergency workers.
- Digital television will offer pictures of unprecedented clarity and allow a seamless connection to the Internet.
- Nanotechnology (tiny medical robots tinkering with molecules) will patrol the bloodstream, killing cancer and viruses, and scraping out arterial blockages.
- Through **MEMS (micro-electro-mechanical systems)**, materials such as concrete will become "smart," able to adapt to shaking in an earthquake.

- Houses will be programmed to adjust their energy requirements to the needs of their inhabitants.[5]
- **MRIs (magnetic resonance imaging)** will be able to explore any area of our body to find the source of illness and remove it.
- Through the mapping of human genes, researchers will be able to look for ways to treat diseases before they occur.
- Chips may be implanted in our bodies that serve as a combination credit card, passport, driver's license, personal diary, and so forth.

Technology clearly will impact every area of our lives—our work, our home, and our health.

SUMMARY

To reinforce what you have learned in this chapter, study this summary.

- Information is created through longhand drafts, computer drafts, and to a lesser degree, shorthand notes and machine dictation.
- Information is input through computer keyboards, scanners, voice-recognition technology, mice and trackballs, touch screens, touch pads, infrared devices, and pen tablets and pucks.
- Computer classifications include supercomputers, mainframe computers, minicomputers, workstations or super microcomputers, and microcomputers.

---

[5]Adam Rogers and David A. Kaplan, "Get Ready for Nanotechnology," *Newsweek Extra* (Winter 1997–98), 52–53.

- The central processing unit is the brain of the computer system. It accepts the data, processes it, and delivers the results to the output device. The other parts of the computer are the arithmetic/logic unit, the control unit, and memory.
- Computers have two main types of storage—primary and secondary. Primary storage is the main general-purpose storage region to which the microprocessor has direct access. Secondary storage consists of floppy disks, Zip disks, compact disks, hard disks, and magnetic tapes.
- Output devices include monitors, printers, and multifunction peripherals.
- Computers within a company may be linked through networks. These networks may be LANs, MANs, or WANs.
- The Internet is the world's largest group of connected computers.
- The World Wide Web is a huge collection of computer files scattered across the Internet.
- An intranet is a network that lets businesses provide access for their employees to the Internet without allowing persons from the outside to have access to the information within the company.
- An extranet allows the inclusion of selected individuals, companies, and organizations outside the company itself to have access to company information.
- Technology will continue to impact every area of our lives in the future, changing the way we work and live.

Key Terms

- ATM
- PIN
- Voice-recognition technology
- Alphanumeric keypad
- Flatbed scanners
- Sheetfed scanners
- OCR
- MICR
- Barcode scanners
- UPC (Universal Product Code)
- Fixed-data barcode
- Variable-data barcode
- Handheld scanners
- Continuous-speech recognition
- Discrete voice recognition
- CD-ROM
- RAM
- Mouse
- Trackball
- Graphical user interface (GUI)
- Touch screen
- Touch pads
- Infrared
- Pen tablets
- Puck
- Stylus
- Supercomputers
- Teraflops
- Gigaflops
- Petaflops
- Mainframes
- Minicomputers
- Interfaced
- Workstation computers (supermicros)
- Microcomputer
- Microprocessor
- PCs (personal computers)
- Hard drives
- Pentium processor chip
- AMD microprocessor
- Notebooks
- Handheld computers
- Central processing unit (CPU)
- Arithmetic/logic unit
- Control unit
- Memory
- Primary storage
- Binary digits/bits
- Byte
- Kilobytes (KB)
- Megabytes (MB)
- Gigabytes (GB)
- Terabytes (TB)
- Random access memory (RAM)
- Read-only memory (ROM)
- Disks
- Diskettes
- Floppy
- Density
- Formatted
- HiFD drive
- UHD144 drive
- Zip disks and drives
- Jaz disks and drives
- CD-ROM
- CD-R
- CD-E
- WORM
- DVD-ROM
- DVD-R
- DVD-RAM
- Hard disks
- Magnetic disks
- Magnetic tape
- In-house
- Monitors
- Printers
- Soft copy
- Cathode ray tube (CRT)
- Resolution
- Pixels
- Monochrome
- LCD (liquid crystal display)
- Portrait
- Landscape
- Impact printer
- Nonimpact printer
- Network
- PPM
- Dpi
- Local area networks (LANs)
- Metropolitan area networks (MANs)

- Wide area networks (WANs)
- Internet
- World Wide Web
- Transmission Control Protocol/Internet Protocol (TCP/IP)
- Modem
- ISDN (Integrated Services Digital Network)
- DSL (Digital Subscriber Line)
- Mbps (megabits per second)
- Kbps (kilobits per second)
- Web browser
- Encryption
- Viruses
- Intranet
- Extranet
- MEMS
- MRIs

Professional Pointers

Technology, especially in the computer field, is drastically affecting the work of the office professional. Opportunities made available by technology are allowing office professionals to redefine their roles. Keep these tips in mind as you prepare to enter or re-enter the job market in the twenty-first century.

- The competitive pressures of businesses require that new and more efficient methods continually be sought. As an office professional, you may be a part of restructuring and redesigning your organization. Be willing to learn and keep an open mind about how your work may be reorganized and redesigned.
- Office professionals will be critical links in accessing, manipulating, and sending information. You need to keep current on office technology.
- Be knowledgeable about new software packages on the market; be willing to help others learn new software.
- The office professional will be required to possess not only word processing skills, but also a command of graphic arts, interactive video techniques, telecommunications, and computer software installation. Keep current on new developments in these areas through short courses or seminars.

Office Procedures Reinforcement

1. Identify three methods of creating and inputting information.
2. Define and explain the various classifications of computers.
3. Define and explain four storage devices.
4. Explain how you output information.
5. Explain the difference between the Internet and the World Wide Web.

Critical Thinking Activity

Riverfront Properties is a small, locally owned real estate firm. Richard Lapsley, who has his real estate license and handles some sales, also manages the office for the owner and president, Candice VanPelt. There are two additional salespeople and one part-time clerical employee.

Richard realizes that the volume of sales has increased to the point that a computer for the office is a must. Before making the request to the president, however, Richard must do some research.

1. What type of computer would you recommend Richard buy for the business and why?
2. What type of printer would you recommend Richard purchase and why?
3. Should Richard recommend a scanner? If so, why and what type of scanner?
4. Should Richard recommend voice-recognition software?

Office Applications

OA5-1 (Goal 1)

For two or three days, observe from your regular daily routine different methods of how data is created, input, and output. There are examples all around us that we usually don't notice. For example, a cash register tape or receipt is the result (or output) from data that was created by a sale. The sale was input into the cash register, with the tape as the output. Make a list of the methods you observe and the equipment used to record the data. Try to determine how the data is handled or processed by the computer system. In other words, what happens to the data that is input? You may find examples at your local post office, bank, movie theater, and department and grocery stores. If the type of equipment used is not readily apparent to you, ask an employee or manager of the business. Present an oral report of your findings to the class.

OA5-2 (Goals 2 and 3)

Assume that you have a temporary assignment in the Computer Information Systems Department of your company. The CIS staff provides technical support and computer training sessions for all company employees. Among other duties, the office staff assistant is responsible for maintaining scheduling logs. One log is used to schedule employees for training sessions, and another log shows which training rooms are used for each day of the week.

On your student template disk, file OA05-2.doc, is a format for entering all of the scheduled courses for the next training period. Using the information provided in your Applications Workbook on page 35, enter the course information on a database file.

You may need to abbreviate course names based on the spaces available. For the instructor field, enter last names first.

Query the database by instructor and date, and provide a training schedule for each of the four instructors for the month of November. Submit your schedule to your instructor.

OA5-3 (Goals 2 and 3)
Query the database file you created in OA05-2.doc by room number, which will serve as a schedule for the three training rooms for the month of November. Based on requests, additional sessions may need to be scheduled. Develop a chart to show the available rooms for each of the following dates and times:

November 2, 8:30–12:30

November 12, 8:30–10:30

November 12, 1:30–4:30

November 16, 1:30–4:30

November 20, 1:30–4:30

November 21, 8:30–4:30

Make a backup of the chart on a floppy disk. Print one copy and submit it to your instructor.

OA5-4 (Goals 2 and 3)
In your Applications Workbook on pages 36–38 you will find the rough-draft copy of an article for the company's newsletter. Key the copy, making the corrections as indicated, using graphics, and formatting the document in two columns. Make a backup of your data on a floppy disk. Print a final copy and submit it to your instructor.

Online Research Applications

OA5-5 (Goal 4)
Using the Internet, research the advances in voice recognition. Write a short report of your findings, identifying you sources, and submit it to your instructor.

OA5-6 (Goal 4)
Attempt to discover, through Internet research, how computer technology is expected to impact our lives in the next five to ten years. Write a short report of your findings, identifying your sources, and submit it to your instructor.

CHAPTER 6

Computer Software

In Chapter 5, you learned how information is created, input, processed, and output. Although your role as an office professional does not require that you have a detailed knowledge of the inner workings of a computer, it does require that you have an expert knowledge of the particular software packages that you use in the office. Not only will you use software packages daily, but you are also expected to select or help select appropriate ones for the office.

Although the intent of this chapter is not to give you detailed information on any particular software package, it is designed to give you an overview of the various types of software packages that are available. It is expected that you have taken or will be taking a

YOUR GOALS

1. Demonstrate an understanding of operating systems and applications software.

2. Troubleshoot software problems.

3. Describe how to care for hardware and software.

4. Explain how to select software

5. Use applications software in performing tasks.

course that helps you become proficient in one or more sofware packages. Additionally, you will learn how to select and properly care for computers and software in this chapter.

Software Programs

As you work with software, there are two major categories that you need to understand—**operating systems software** and **applications software.** Operating systems software is a set of programs through which the computer manages its own resources such as the central processing unit, memory, secondary storage devices, and input/output devices.

Applications software is the software that you will use daily in producing documents. It allows you to:

- Calendar information
- Produce letters and memorandums
- Create business forms
- Key tables and reports
- Create presentations
- Create a Web page
- Produce graphics
- Query databases

It also allows you to perform numerous other tasks that you do frequently. Both operating systems software and applications software are explained in more detail in the following sections.

Operating Systems Software

Operating systems software controls the systems of your computer, keyboard, printer, mouse, and other peripheral devices. A general knowledge of this software will help you understand how your

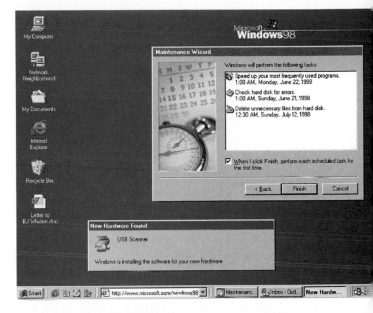

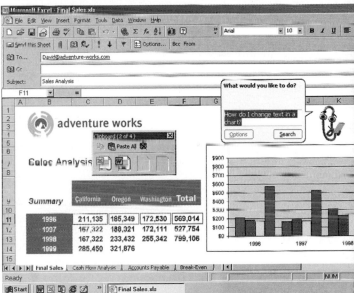

There are two major categories of software—operating systems software and applications software. *Screenshots reprinted by permission from Microsoft Corporation.*

computer functions. An operating system is a program that enables your computer to read and write data to a disk, send pictures to your monitor, and accept keyboard commands. Without an operating system, you cannot perform any of the tasks required, for example, in your word processing program or other applications software programs.

In understanding how an operating system works, consider this analogy. When you turn the key on your car, the motor starts. You merely perform the one function, without being aware of the various electronic parts and the interrelationship between them that it takes for the motor to start. You are then ready to perform a whole series of other steps—putting the car in gear, stepping on the gas so that the car will move, turning on the heating/air conditioning, turning on the

radio or CD player, and so forth. In other words, once the motor starts, you give the car additional instructions as to what you want done. When you turn on your computer, the operating system begins working for you. It gets the computer ready to receive your additional commands. These commands may be to open your word processing or spreadsheet package, to pull up a screen so that you can begin to key a report, or any number of other commands. You have not seen the operating system work, but without it you cannot give the computer any other orders.

There are a number of operating systems, with the major ones being:

- DOS®
- Windows®
- Windows NT®
- OS/390 and OS/400
- UNIX®
- Mac™ OS

DOS. DOS (disk operating system) is an older operating system that was produced by IBM and has been widely used for a number of years. DOS was used for mainframe computers and in microcomputers also. Although Windows has virtually replaced DOS on microcomputers, DOS is still being used on larger computers. In fact, a newer version of DOS called DR DOS is being used by a number of users in **embedded** (software that is built into its carrier) systems. One of the main advantages of its use is that developers worldwide are familiar with DOS.

Windows. Windows is an operating system that was developed by Microsoft. There have been a number of iterations of Windows that are used on microcomputers, including Windows 3.X, Windows 95, and Windows 98. By the time you read this book, there will probably be a new

Windows NT is available for both workstations and servers.
Courtesy of © PhotoDisc, Inc.

iteration of Windows out. Windows also has an operating system that is used with palm-sized computers known as Windows CE.

Windows NT. Microsoft's **Windows NT** is available as NT 5.0 for workstations or NT 4.0 for **servers** (computers that are networked to other computers and peripheral devices). It is a more powerful operating system than Windows 98. The server version is designed specifically for larger network environments, where several computers and peripherals are connected.

OS/390 and OS/400. OS/390 is a disk operating system produced by IBM and used on larger computers such as mainframe computers. OS/390 makes it possible for graphical user interface systems such as Microsoft's Windows to reach the mainframe directly. It uses a graphical user interface that allows it to handle multiple applications at the same time. For midrange computers, IBM has released **OS/400**. Both OS/390 and OS/400 are part of IBM's goal to make a common set of technologies and products available across all of its desktop, workstation, and server systems.

UNIX. UNIX was developed in 1969 at AT&T® for use on Bell's minicomputers. Now it runs on supercomputers and mainframes. It is a very powerful operating system that, because it is written in C **language** (a common computer language), is less machine-specific than other operating systems.

Mac OS. Mac OS was developed by Apple Computer, Inc., for use on the MacIntosh system. This system has been used more in schools and homes than in businesses. However, Apple now makes systems that can run both Mac OS and Windows applications.

Operating System Functions

The operating system for a microcomputer is on a CD-ROM or floppy disk. It must be loaded into the computer before any software programs can be loaded. Once the operating system is loaded, it resides on the hard drive of the computer. When the computer is turned on, the operating system is loaded into the memory. The three main functions of operating systems are to:

- Control computer system resources
- Execute computer programs
- Manage data

Each operating system utilizes memory and storage capacity on the computer. For example, Windows needs at least 16 megabytes (MB) of random access memory (RAM), with 32MB of RAM being more desirable. It also requires anywhere from 120MB to 300MB of hard drive

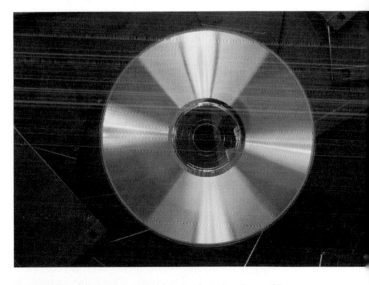

An operating system for a workstation is often placed on a CD-ROM. *Courtesy of © PhotoDisc, Inc.*

space. As other versions of Windows are developed, more memory and hard drive space may be necessary.

As an office professional, you will communicate with your operating system in two main ways. For example, you might need to install a new software program. While this installation in a large office is usually done by a computer technician, you may be responsible for doing so in a small office. Your first step is to locate the installation disk, which is generally on a CD-ROM. You insert the CD-ROM into the CD-ROM drive. From this point, usually the program takes over, asking questions as necessary and prompting you on what you need to do.

Another example of how you might communicate with the operating system is in installing add-ins on your software package. Assume that you have Microsoft Excel® on Windows 98 and you want to sum data from selected lists. To do so, you choose Tools and Add-Ins. The Add-Ins dialog box appears. You then select Sum Wizard, which helps you create formulas to sum selected data in lists. Your operating system, Windows 98, has assisted you in this process.

Applications Software

Through applications software programs, you can tell the computer how to perform a specific task that you need done. For example, you can produce a table through the use of word processing software or a brochure through the use of graphics and word processing software. You can take film from your digital camera and, using photo-editing and image-editing software to modify it if necessary, add a photograph to the brochure. There are numerous applications software packages available; the major categories are given in the following sections, along with several specific software packages in each category. However, software programs are revised frequently and new programs are added constantly; the ones listed are a few that were available at the time this textbook was printed.

Word Processing.　The most commonly used applications software for the office professional is word processing. Word processing allows you to create letters, memorandums, reports, and numerous other documents quickly. You may produce complex documents with tables and graphics, revise the documents extensively, and print a quality product with relative ease. You may insert, delete, and rearrange text without rekeying. Word processing software has greatly improved the productivity of office professionals and has become a standard feature of the computer workstation.

Additional features of word processing programs are add-on features that may be part of the package or added on. Some of these features are:

- Grammar and spelling programs. A grammar and spelling program can help you with your writing. For example, in addition to spelling errors, it can report possible problems such as passive verbs, pronoun errors, punctuation errors, subject/verb agreement errors, and so forth. The program allows you to review the error and makes suggestions for changes; you then decide whether or not to change the text. Grammar and spelling programs can also show overall readability of writing, sentence length, and word complexity. For example, we know that the average reading level used in most publications is tenth grade. If you have written a document that is above this grade level, you may want to use words with fewer syllables and/or reduce the length of your sentences.

- Thesaurus programs. A **thesaurus** is a collection of selected words that mean the same thing (synonyms) and words that have opposite meanings (antonyms). Such a program gives you access to a powerful vocabulary electronically. Figure 6-1 shows a thesaurus screen.

- Language programs. These programs allow you to change the text to another language available on the program. Most programs feature several languages.

Bundles. Programs that are sold with a computer as part of a combined hardware/software package are called **bundled** **software** programs. Computer manufacturers provide these, in part, to attract buyers. A common software bundle includes word processing, spreadsheet, finance, Internet online service, and reference works. If you are purchasing a computer with bundled software, here are some items you should consider in regard to the software:

- What programs do you need? Try to find a bundle that fits your needs.

- What support is offered? Most vendors provide free support during installation. Others support the software that is preinstalled on the computer through subscription service plans and telephone access.

- Do you need Internet access? Some vendors offer up to 50 hours of free

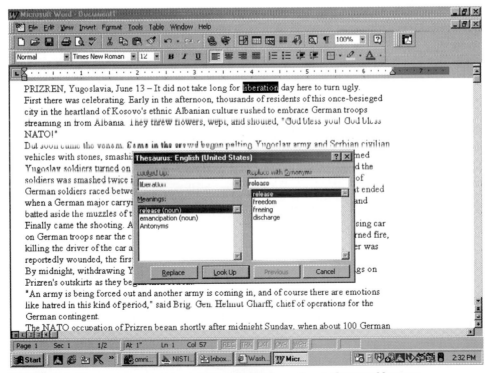

FIGURE 6-1. Thesaurus programs are available on applications software. *Courtesy of Symantec.*

Integrated software includes several applications in one program. *Courtesy of © PhotoDisc, Inc.*

Internet access through AOL (American Online), Prodigy, or other online services.

If you give careful consideration to the programs you need, having bundled software preloaded on the computer can be helpful. Most computer makers do extensive testing to be certain the bundled software will work together. Generally the retail value of bundles and services is several hundred dollars.

Integrated Software or Office Suites. **Integrated Software** is a set of software that typically includes several applications within one program. These integrated packages or suites generally include word processing, spreadsheet, database, presentation, and information management programs. Some suites now include speech-

recognition components. Since the programs are integrated, you can move contextual matter from one program to another quickly and easily. For example, if you are working on a word processing program, you can easily add spreadsheets to your document and then move all the data to a presentation program.

Some of the office suites available are:

- WordPerfect® Office 2000
- Microsoft Office 2000®
- Lotus SmartSuite® (includes speech-recognition component—letters and reports may be dictated into the word processing components and figures may be read from receipts for doing an expense report in the spreadsheet portion)

Graphics. With graphics being used in word processing documents, on spreadsheets, in presentations, and on Web pages, graphics software is one of the major growth areas. Graphics software is available in either image-editing programs or illustration programs. Image-editing programs are designed to work with **bitmapped images;** illustration programs are designed to handle **vector graphics.** A bitmapped image consists of thousands of small squares called **pixels.** Bitmaps are typically used for photographs or painted images. The two major disadvantages of bitmaps are that they require more system resources and when magnified, they appear jagged.

Vector graphics are made up of objects such as shapes, lines, and fronts that are defined mathematically—not by pixels. Vectors are better suited to graphics composed of basic shapes, as in a corporate log. They require less system resources than do bitmaps, and they can be shrunk or magnified without a loss of detail.

Figure 6-2 shows both a bitmap and a vector, with an enlargement. In addition to graphics, photo-editing software is available that enables the user to create professional-looking output with photos by adding color and/or modifying the photo. Here are a few of the graphics and photo-editing software packages available.

- Adobe™ Photoshop (image editing)
- CorelDRAW™ (illustration)
- Microsoft Picture It!™ (photo-editing software)
- Software Publishing ActiveOffice®
- Software Publishing Serif DrawPlus®

Office suite programs and graphics programs provide the capability needed to produce newsletters, brochures, sales documents, booklets, and company periodicals.

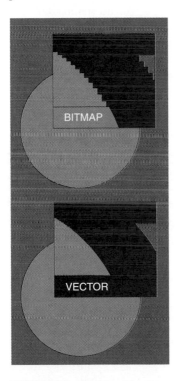

FIGURE 6-2. Graphics software uses both bitmapped and vector images.

Spreadsheets. In its simplest terms, a **spreadsheet** is a grid of rows and columns in which you enter numbers and text. With spreadsheet programs, the computer does mathematical calculations. Basically, a spreadsheet works in this manner. You begin by entering the raw data in the spreadsheet with formulas that indicate the types of calculations you need. For example, assume that your employer asks you to total the amount of office expense in your department for the last six months and project the expense for the next five years using a 3 percent increase in the first year, a 5 percent increase in the second year, and a 7 percent increase in the third through the fifth year. This fairly complex problem can be handled quickly by using a spreadsheet program.

The spreadsheet program you use will most likely be a part of your office suite program. However, if it is not, stand-alone programs are available. Some examples are:

- Microsoft Excel®
- Lotus® 1-2-3
- Quattro Pro®

Personal Information/Contact Managers. You were introduced to PIM software in Chapter 3 because of its time management features. PIM software is also referred to as **contact management software** since it helps you manage your contacts. Additionally, this software allows you to organize your day by:

- Keeping your calendar
- Scheduling appointments
- Managing your to-do lists
- Establishing tickler files
- Finding phone numbers
- Keeping an address list
- Tracking business expenses
- Keeping notes through a notepad that stores text and graphics

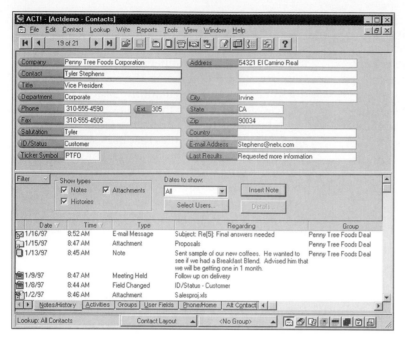

Personal information/contact manager software helps you organize your daily tasks. *Courtesy of Symantec.*

Database Managers. A **database program** helps you store and manipulate data in a manner that allows fast and easy access to it. The program acts as an efficient filing system and an organizer of multiple types of data. The data may be business names, categories of businesses, dates, dollars, or specifications. For example, assume that you want to answer this question: How many applicants are applying for each job posting within the company? The data are the applications that have been received. The information needed to answer this question may be hardcopy applications in file drawers within all the departments of the company. With the assistance of a database program, you can assemble this data so that the question may be answered for the present situation. And once the database program has been set up, the answer to this question may be obtained quickly and easily for future job postings.

A database program allows you to:

- Set up the information needed in a database format called a **table**
- Locate data
- Change or delete data
- Select portions of data for special purposes
- Organize the data into different sequences, such as alphabetic, geographic, or financial order
- Design reports that show the information in the format you need
- Produce reports and other printed output
- Generate statistics

- Accessing email and messaging directories
- Sharing calendars and information with other individuals
- Computing basic mathematical calculations
- Keeping files on customers

One of the latest trends for contact management programs is the addition of Internet-based features. Some programs allow you to connect through the Internet to share calendar information with other businesses or groups, for example. Other programs provide the ability to create address books on the Web.

Software packages include:

- Lotus Organizer® Premium Edition
- Symantec's ACT!™
- WebCal® Personal Interactive Calendar
- GoldMine® Software

Obviously, you can manipulate data manually. For example, in answering the question about the job applicants given previously, an individual in each office could manually count the applicants. However, such a method would be time-consuming and difficult to maintain for ongoing analysis. You can also decide to query the database for specific information at some later point; for example, the breakdown of men and women who applied for the positions. The main advantages of using a database program include the following:

- Speed
- Increased accuracy of data
- Consistency in data recording
- Ability to manipulate and query data

Most office suites contain a database program. For example, Microsoft Office contains Access® a database program. Database programs may also be purchased as a stand-alone. In addition to being part of an office suite, Access may be purchased individually. Here are some other database programs:

- Corel's Paradox®
- Computhink's™ The Paperless Office™

Voice Recognition. In Chapter 5, you were introduced to voice recognition as an input device. As you learned, with the continuous speech recognition process now used, voice-recognition programs are more effective than ever before. Also, these programs are expected to continue to improve in the future, with voice recognition becoming a major input device in the office.

Voice recognition is also infiltrating our lives in other ways. For example, if you call directory assistance, you are likely to get a prerecorded voice that asks: "What city please?" and "Listing, please?" A computer is interpreting your words and finding the number that is then shown on a

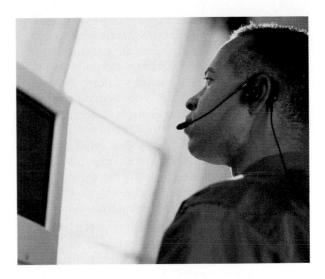

Voice recognition is expected to become a major input device in the office. *Courtesy of © PhotoDisc, Inc.*

computer screen for a human operator to give the number to you.

Three voice recognition programs are:

- Dragon Systems' Dragon Naturally Speaking™
- IBM's ViaVoice
- Lernout & Hauspie's Voice Xpress™

These programs have various capabilities, with some of the major ones being:

- A vocabulary of over 200,000 words
- Accepting continuous dictation at up to 140 words per minute, with 95 per cent accuracy
- Natural language commands—for example, you can ask the computer to "put this sentence in italics," and it will interpret your command
- Editing by voice of previously keyed documents

Remote Access. You learned in Chapter 1 that the virtual office has become a reality for many people today, and it is expected that the number of people working in remote locations will continue to increase. This situation often means that you need access to data at a location other than the one where you are working. How do you get that data? With the right hardware and software, you can exchange information between a remote computer and the host computer (possibly located in an office) and have the information saved on both systems. This ability is known as **remote file exchange and synchronization.** Remote access software allows you to:

- Use the keyboard and screen of a notebook to run programs that are on a computer at another location as if you were seated in front of that computer

- Use a resource such as email that is on the office local area network as if your computer were directly connected to that network

- Communicate by keyboard or by voice with individuals at distant computers

Remote access software includes:

- Netopia's® Timbuktu®
- Symantec's® pcANYWHERE™

Another possibility of remote access is from subscription services that are designed to store and synchronize information through the Internet. These services allow you to store a digital briefcase of information on the Web site for a few dollars a month. When you are working in your virtual location, you may access the information through a Web browser such as Netscape® Navigator® or Internet Explorer®.

Presentation Software.   Presentation software allows you to present your ideas through using drawings, animations with sound, and photographs. Studies have shown that the addition of visuals helps the audience understand what you are saying and increases their retention of the in-

formation. You will learn about presentation techniques in Chapter 11. This section is designed only to make you aware of some of the software available.

Most office suites include presentation software; however, it can also be purchased as a stand-alone product. The software generally contains a wide variety of preexisting **layouts** (arrangements of common slide elements, such as titles and bulleted lists). **Templates** (a predesigned document that contains formatting) provide the design framework for a presentation—the colors, patterns, and pictures for the words that can give your presentation audience appeal.

Here are three presentation software packages available:

- PowerPoint
- Astound®
- Adobe Persuasion®

Privacy Software.   The technology age has brought us numerous advantages as well as some disadvantages, one being our loss of privacy. To give you some idea of the magnitude of this problem, read the information in Figure 6-3. The computers that we use daily and the World Wide Web access that we have allow information on companies and individuals to be available to numerous audiences. The way this information is used by companies and individuals is an ethical question that all of us need to be concerned about. Remember the importance of ethical behavior as presented in Chapter 4. As we, as individuals and as employees and managers of companies, are privy to greater and greater amounts of information, the way in which we use that information must be examined in light of our individual and company ethics.

Large companies that are data aggregators maintain information on millions

PRIVACY ISSUES

- Chance that a U.S. citizen believes his or her privacy has been violated: 1 in 4
- Annual losses from credit-card fraud: $700 million
- Number of state and federal wiretaps issued in 1997: 1,186
- Estimated corporate losses from computer crime in 1997: $136 million
- Number of phone conversations employers eavesdrop on each year: 400 million
- Increase in the number of U.S. workers under electronic surveillance since 1991: 275 percent
- Number of privacy bills introduced in state legislatures in 1997: Over 8,500
- Number of pieces of junk mail delivered each day by the U.S. Postal Service: 600 million
- Number of information executives who think information security is important: 84 percent
- Number of companies who have security policies: 80 percent

FIGURE 6-3. Privacy issues. Sources: Jeffrey Rothfeder, "You Are For Sale," *PC World* (September 1998), 106. Michael J. Major, "Network Security Poses Mind-Boggling Challenges," *Managing Office Technology* (April 1998), 12.

of people. Their databases store information concerning when we were born, what we buy, the drugs we use, who we call, how much money we make, the jobs we hold, our bank accounts, and our medical records. Hackers break into company files, retrieving confidential information. In 1997 there was a 42 percent increase in intrusions by both outsiders and insiders in company files, as opposed to a 16 percent increase in 1996.[1] The greatest threats are perceived to be:

- Computer terrorists (28 percent)
- Authorized users (26 percent)
- Former employees (24 percent)
- Unauthorized users (23 percent)[2]

Although you cannot control the ethics of other individuals, you can be sure that you are behaving ethically with the information that is available to you. You can also protect yourself and your company by using certain security measures that make it more difficult for unethical individuals to obtain the information. Here are some software packages that can help.

- Microsoft's free System Policy Editor®—Prevents unexpected visitors from viewing your files or running applications.
- Computer Sentry Software's™ CyberAngel®—Asks for a password. If the thief does not respond correctly, CyberAngel makes the system seem disabled, and secretly dials Computer Sentry, which traces the call.
- PGP™ for Personal Privacy—A program that secures email from outsiders.
- SecureWin™—An encryption program that scrambles data into a private code.

Numerous other security software packages are available. There are also certain steps you can take in addition to using software packages; some of them are listed in Figure 6-4. Terms that will help you in understanding security issues are given in Figure 6-5.

Internet Software. As you are well aware, both companies and individuals use the Internet frequently. Internet use is expected to continue to increase as more and more businesses market their products on the Internet and go online to seek

[1] "Network Security Poses Mind-Boggling Challenges," *Managing Office Technology* (April 1998), 12.

[2] "Network Security Poses Mind-Boggling Challenges," 12.

SECURITY STEPS

- Don't share personal information—your name, address, phone number, date of birth, social security number, mother's maiden name—until you know who you're dealing with and what they plan to do with the data.
- Don't expect your employer to safeguard your privacy.
- Strengthen your computer's log-in service. Remove or encrypt private files and communications. Learn how to browse the Internet and send email messages without leaving a trail.
- Before you place any sensitive information on your PC, consult your human resources or information systems department for details about your company's privacy policy.
- Don't conduct personal communications on your computer at work.
- Select and guard your passwords well.
- When traveling, place your notebook in a case that doesn't look like it is built for a computer; there are few valuables more attractive to a thief than a computer.
- If you don't want your personal information shared, don't sign guest books or otherwise volunteer information about yourself when using the Internet.

FIGURE 6-4. Security steps. Sources: Carole Lane, "Going Private," *PC World* (September 1998), 115–118.

and provide all types of information and service. Individual use will continue to increase as we keep up with the latest news, check the weather, shop for goods for ourselves and as gifts, research information, use chat rooms to talk with others, and so forth. In order to improve our Internet experience, there are a number of software packages available. These programs can help make you more effective and efficient as you search for information. Two of the software browser programs available are:

- Netscape Navigator
- Microsoft Internet Explorer

Online services such as American Online, CompuServe, and Prodigy use built-in browsers, which are some of the same ones mentioned above.

Although the browser programs listed previously combine browsers, email readers, and newsgroup readers into one package, there are other software packages that separate the functions. Email readers, newsreaders, and Internet **accelerators** (packages that let you download information to your computer at faster speeds) are:

SECURITY TERMS

- Authenticate—To verify that the person attempting to send a message or access data is who he or she claims to be.
- Ciphertext—Scrambled, unreadable contents of an encrypted message or file.
- Cookie—A block of text that is placed in a file on your hard drive by a Web site when you visit it. A cookie is used to identify you the next time you access the site.
- Decrypt—To decode data from its protected, scrambled form so it can be read.
- Digital Signature—Text data, usually added to the main body of an email message, that can be used by the recipient to authenticate the identify of the sender.
- Encrypt—To scramble data into a private code.
- Password—A private and unique series of numbers, letters, or both that enables the person who uses it to gain access to data. A longer password is called a **passphrase.**
- Spam—Unsolicited and unwanted email, usually sent by advertisers.

FIGURE 6-5. Security terms. Source: Carole Lane, "Going Private," *PC World* (September 1998), 142.

- Eudora® Mail
- Pegasus® Mail
- Procomm Plus®
- NetAccelerator™
- PeakJet™

There are also a number of specialized information sites on the Internet in the areas of finance, travel, and business. Here are a few of the sites, with their addresses.

- Fortune Investor: http://www.fortuneinvestor.com
- Money: http://www.money.com
- Morningstar: http://www.morningstar.net
- Internet Travel Network: http://www.itn.net
- Rail Europe: http://www.raileurope.com
- Travelocity: http://www.travelocity.com
- Knowledge Space: http://www.knowledgespace.com
- U.S. Postal Service: http://www.whatis.com
- The World Bank: http://www.worldbank.org

Troubleshooting

As you work with both computer hardware and software, problems are going to occur. One of your tasks as an office professional is to be able to solve as many of your problems as possible. You need to become adept at **troubleshooting**. Here is some general information that you need to know so that you can become an efficient troubleshooter.

- Know how your computer system works.
- Know what operating system your computer uses.
- Know how the software you use should function.
- Learn to recognize text, visual, and audible clues that indicate potential problems.
- Be patient; be willing to learn.
- Know what assistance is available to you within the company. Is there a computer technician who can help you? If not, is there an office professional who is extremely competent on the package you are using?
- Does the software vendor provide assistance? If so, what number do you call?
- Does the computer vendor offer assistance?

When you are working on a particular software program and encounter problems, there are certain troubleshooting steps that you should take. You will need to know your software package, but all packages offer help. As an example, these troubleshooting helps are available on Office 97.

- *Office Assistant* enables you to type in a question and select from several possible types of help. Figure 6-6 shows the *Office Assistant.*
- *Help Contents and Index* is a database of information about topics that you can search by typing in a term or choosing from broader categories of information.
- *What's This?* is a feature that turns your mouse pointer into a help tool. When you've selected it, you can click any one-screen element and a brief description of its function appears.
- *Microsoft on the Web* offers several ways to get online help from Microsoft's Web page.

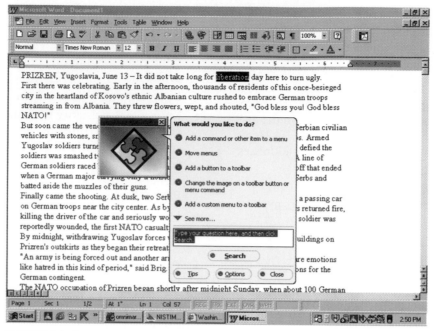

FIGURE 6-6. The *Office Assistant* provides help in troubleshooting problems.

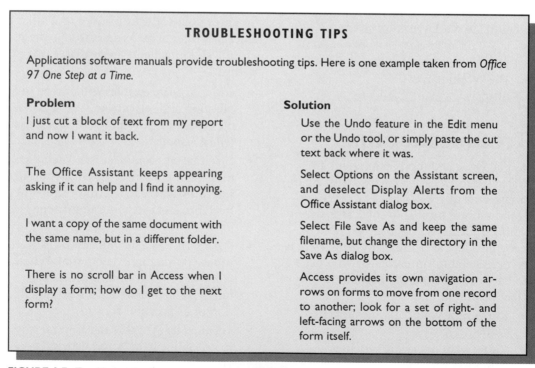

TROUBLESHOOTING TIPS

Applications software manuals provide troubleshooting tips. Here is one example taken from *Office 97 One Step at a Time.*

Problem

I just cut a block of text from my report and now I want it back.

The Office Assistant keeps appearing asking if it can help and I find it annoying.

I want a copy of the same document with the same name, but in a different folder.

There is no scroll bar in Access when I display a form; how do I get to the next form?

Solution

Use the Undo feature in the Edit menu or the Undo tool, or simply paste the cut text back where it was.

Select Options on the Assistant screen, and deselect Display Alerts from the Office Assistant dialog box.

Select File Save As and keep the same filename, but change the directory in the Save As dialog box.

Access provides its own navigation arrows on forms to move from one record to another; look for a set of right- and left-facing arrows on the bottom of the form itself.

FIGURE 6-7. Troubleshooting tips.

- Microsoft provides a telephone number that you may call for assistance from 6 a.m. to 6 p.m. each weekday.
- Manuals are available that provide answers to your questions. For example, Figure 6-7 gives information available on troubleshooting from one section of *Office 97 One Step at a Time*.[3]

Computer Ergonomics and Ethics

You learned in Chapter 3 that ergonomics means the bringing together of the physiological factors that make an effective work environment with those factors that explain how workers react to their environment. Computers have introduced new ergonomic factors into our environment. You learned in Chapters 2 and 5 that ergonomically designed office furniture and equipment are available, including such items as split keyboards, wrist rests, foot rests, adjustable chairs, and mice.

In addition to ergonomic furniture and equipment, there are techniques that you can use to help your productivity and comfort levels as you work on your computer. Several techniques are given in the following section. Also, suggestions are given on how to select and care for software, along with security procedures. Software copying is presented as an ethical consideration, along with the unauthorized use of a disk that may result in a computer virus.

---

[3]Nancy Stevenson, *Office 97 One Step at a Time* (Chicago: IDG Books Worldwide, Inc., 1998), 61.

Productivity and Comfort Suggestions

- Use indirect lighting if possible. Such lighting does not produce a glare on the screen.
- Turn the screen away from windows to reduce glare.
- Keep the top edge of your monitor at eye level or below, so that you are able to look down slightly as you read copy from your monitor. The monitor should be 20 to 30 inches from your eyes.
- Your wrists should never be higher than your elbows and they should be straight—not flexed upward or bent downward. If you cannot achieve this position, your desk may be too high or your chair seat too low. Adjust the height of your chair.
- Do not lean the heel of your hand on the desk. A padded wrist rest may be helpful.
- Angle your keyboard so that the back is slightly higher than the front.
- Your feet should touch the floor. The angle between your thighs and spine should be 90 degrees or more. In fact, human factor engineers have discovered that a sitting angle approaching 128 degrees is more relaxing and less stressful.[4]
- Keep your mouse close to the keyboard so you do not have to reach far to use it. Use a padded wrist rest for the mouse, a foot switch, or a key that eliminates the "grip-to-click" strain.
- Rest your eyes periodically (every 20

---

[4]Jamie L. Nichols, "Hidden Perils in the Computerized Office," *Today's Chiropractic* (May/June 1994), 74.

minutes) by focusing on a distant object and blinking often.

- Be certain your chair provides support for your lower back and is fully adjustable. You should be able to change both the height of the seat and the angle of the seat and back.

- Engage in **isometric exercise** at your desk. Do shoulder and neck exercises by raising and lowering your shoulders and turning your head from side to side. Exercise your fingers by making a fist and then opening and closing it.

Indirect lighting does not produce a glare on the computer screen.
Courtesy of © Digital Vision.

Stretch your legs and move your feet back and forth.

- Take scheduled breaks of approximately ten minutes for every two hours' work at the computer if at all possible.

- If you are using the computer and the telephone at the same time, use a telephone shoulder cradle that is designed to fit around the shoulder. Place the phone within arm's reach in front of you—not behind you.

- Adjust screen contrast and brightness throughout the day as needed.

- Clean the monitor regularly.

- Turn the monitor off when it is not being used for a long period. Most screens now have screen savers that automatically turn monitors off when they are not being used.

- Keep your computer clean. Dust is a problem because it causes heat buildup in the components it covers. Every so often, vacuum every horizontal surface of your computer, giving the vents special consideration.

- Keep the keyboard clean. If you need to clean the surface, put the cleaning solution on a cleaning rag and wipe the surface. Do not spray the keyboard. The best procedure is to purchase a can of compressed air to spray between the keys to remove dust. Tiny computer vacuums that are specially designed for this task can also be purchased.

- Keep the mouse clean. Use alcohol on a cotton swab to wipe the rollers. The ball inside the mouse should be cleaned with lukewarm, soapy water and dried thoroughly.

- Cover the entire computer when it is not being used for a long period. System covers are available from computer stores.

Isometric exercises relieve tension while working at the computer.
Courtesy of © PhotoDisc, Inc.

- Do not have food or drink near the computer. A spill of a soda or crumbs getting inside the keyboard can cause the keyboard to malfunction.
- Turn off the monitor periodically and wipe your screen clean with a static free cleaner.
- Do not smoke near a computer. Smoking adds tar and particle matter to the air. These particles can find their way into the computer.
- Delete files you no longer need from your hard drive from time to time. If you think you might need the files at a later time, put them on a floppy disk or other storage device.
- Defragment your drive with a **disk defragmenter.** The defragmenter is a utility that gathers the fragments of files that the operating system has scattered across the surface of your hard disk and reassembles them, so that each file's data is contiguous (with no empty spaces between files). The defragging improves disk performance.
- Make certain you have a **surge suppressor** or an **uninterruptible power supply (UPS)** so that power fluctuations will not be able to cripple your computer equipment.
- Install antivirus software; you will learn more about viruses in the last part of this chapter.
- Install a utility that prevents crashes. A number of utility software packages are available including Norton's Crashguard® Deluxe and TouchStone's CheckIt®.
- Install backup software that protects your computer if there is an unavoidable shutdown. One such software package is American Power Conversion's® Back-UPS Pro® 280.

Software Selection

As an office professional, you may be asked to select or have input into the selection of software your company plans to use. Figure 6-8 gives some questions you should ask when selecting or upgrading software.

Software Care

When working with floppy disks, you need to store and protect them properly.

SOFTWARE CONSIDERATIONS

- Do you have the hardware, memory, and storage requirements needed for the software? Will the program run on your existing operating system? Do you have the memory capacity to support the software?

- Does the program offer the software features you need?

- What documentation is available? The program should have an instruction manual that is well organized and easy to read. An index, a glossary of terms, a quick reference guide, illustrations, and examples are helpful.

- What software support is available? Support may be in the form of tutorials and/or hotline assistance.

- Is the program **user-friendly** and **ergonomically sound.** User-friendly means that the package should be almost as easy for the beginner to follow as it is for the experienced user. Ergonomically sound means that the software is designed to reduce human fatigue.

- Does the vendor have a reputation for providing good service? Is the vendor reliable? How long has the vendor been in business? Will the vendor assist you during package implementation? Does the vendor have a hotline to answer questions?

- What is the reputation of the software? You can check with individuals who have used the software. You can also read reviews in computer periodicals such as *PC World* and *PC Computing.*

- Will there be conversion costs? When investing in software, there may be much more to consider than the initial purchase. Do you have old files that must be converted to the new software? If so, how long will the conversion take?

- Is the software compatible with other programs you use?

- How much does the software cost? Will there be productivity improvements as a result of using the software?

- Are you going to be working with others in the office? If so, talk with these individuals and agree on a package that will serve all of your needs.

FIGURE 6-8. Software considerations.

Carelessness can destroy untold hours of work on a floppy disk. You should always do the following:

- When labeling a disk, write on the adhesive label before applying it to the disk cover. Remove old labels on a disk before applying a new label.

- Store the 3.5-inch disk in a specially designed container to keep it free of dust and smoke particles.

- Magnets can erase information on floppy disks, so keep them away from disks. Also, keep paper clips away from disks; paper clips have some magnetic characteristics.

- Do not store disks close to a telephone. A ringing telephone can create a magnetic field.

- Keep floppy disks away from water and other liquids. Dry them with a lint-free cloth if they should get wet.

- Keep floppy disks out of direct sunlight and away from radiators and other sources of heat.

- Write-protect a disk if it contains data that you do not want changed. On a 3.5-inch disk, there is a tiny latch in the upper-right corner that is usually closed. To write-protect the disk, turn it over and slide the latch downward so that a small window appears in the corner.

Security Procedures

Several steps can be taken to prevent destruction of computer software. A few steps are listed here.

- Back up data by copying it. Back up material that is on the hard disk with a floppy disk or other storage device.

- Frequently change your password or

PASSWORD DO'S AND DON'TS

- Don't use real words. A combination of eight or more alphanumeric characters is much more difficult to guess or break than a dictionary word or proper name. Use both uppercase and lowercase characters, and avoid simple sequences of letters and numbers such as ABC123. Don't use birth dates, social security numbers, names of pets, or any other bit of data from your real life as a log-in name or password.

- Be original. Don't use the same log-in ID and password on every system or Web site you visit.

- Find a mnemonic that works. It's practically impossible to keep track of dozens of unique alphanumeric passwords that aren't words. Your PC, your Internet, and your LAN server accounts deserve strong passwords. Other sites do not. For those lesser sites, you may want to employ a collection of medium-strength user Ids and passwords that are easy for you to remember but hard for others to guess—foreign-language terms or license-plate-like phrases. Here's a trick: To create a unique password from one you already use, simply move you fingers to the right or left by one key.

- Stay fresh. Change the default password your system gives you right away; then continue to change your password every two or three months.

- Don't be lazy. Windows and many email programs let you store your password, then enter it for you automatically the next time you log in to the server. Unfortunately, that gives anyone with access to your computer the ability to log in to those servers that you use.

- Keep quiet. Remember, your password is supposed to be a secret. Make sure you keep it that way.

- Store a written copy of your password in a safe place, such as in a locked file cabinet. Do not store your password on your computer.

FIGURE 6-9. Password do's and dont's. Source: Carol Lane, "Going Private," *PC World* (September 1998), 123.

access code. Figure 6-9 gives some do's and don'ts for selecting passwords.

- Password-protect your screen saver to keep your computer secure when you are away from your desk. A password prompt comes up when anyone touches your mouse or keyboard.

- Log off email when you leave your desk. If you do not, anyone can read your private mail and send messages to other people in your name.

- Put confidential files in hidden directories.

Software Copying

You learned in Chapter 4 that the ethical office professional supports ethical behavior within the organization and maintains his or her own honesty and integrity. What relationship does ethical behavior have to software copying? The answer is that there is a direct relationship. The honest office professional does not engage in software copying nor sit quietly by and watch others within the company do so.

Software copying is a pervasive problem in our society. According to an article in *Managing Office Technology*, 35 percent of business software in the United States is obtained illegally.[5] Organizations and individuals that illegally copy software can be tried under both civil and criminal law. Title 17 of the United States Code specifies that it is illegal to make or distribute copies of copyrighted material, including software, without authorization. Title 18, passed in 1991, instituted criminal penalties for copyright infringements of software. Penalties include imprisonment for

[5]"The Value of Using 'Real' Software," *Managing Office Technology* (April 1998), 34.

up to five years and fines of up to $250,000 for the unauthorized reproduction or distribution of 10 or more copies of software with a total retail value exceeding $2,500. There is one exception to copying—one backup copy of software may be made.

In addition to the copying of software being unethical and illegal, copying can bring viruses into the system, thereby causing major problems for computer systems. Also, companies and individuals that copy software deprive themselves of the benefits of technical support and training provided by many software companies and the ability to buy upgrades at reduced rates.

Computer Viruses

A **computer virus** is a program with unauthorized instructions that are introduced without permission or knowledge of the computer user. It is called a virus because it is contagious. It can pass itself on to other programs in which it comes in contact. Viruses range from annoying but harmless creatures that pop up stupid messages on the screen to beasts that can trash all the data on your hard disk and crash your computer. Basically, viruses are of two different types.

- Boot sector viruses that reside on the part of your hard disk where the computer stores the files it needs to start up. These viruses become active each time you turn on your computer.
- Program infectors that attach themselves to any file that runs a program. These viruses are activated whenever the file is run. Program viruses can be contracted from floppies, electronic bulletin boards, and networks.

Figure 6-10 illustrates infection from a computer virus.

To protect yourself from viruses, follow these suggestions.

- Educate yourself about computer viruses.
- Make backups of your files immediately—before you have a virus. Backups are the single most important action you can take to protect against viral attack.
- **Download** only from sources you trust. Download, in this context, means to receive a file from another source and transfer the information to your hard drive or receive a file via modem from a bulletin board or online service. Accept programs only from people you know and trust.
- Install an antiviral scanning program on your system, such as Dr. Solomon's Software™ Anti-Virus Deluxe™.
- Ask the computer service professionals in your company to alert you when a new virus occurs.
- Do not allow programs to be loaded on your system without your authorization.
- Purchase all software programs in tamper-proof packaging.
- Always boot from a write-protected disk.
- When you get a new program, write-protect the master disk before inserting it into a drive.
- When using bulletin boards and outside programs, use a stand-alone computer only so that virus checks can be made routinely.
- Do not use unsolicited demo disks.

As you have learned in this chapter, software is a valuable asset for the office professional. It not only increases the productivity of the office employee but also

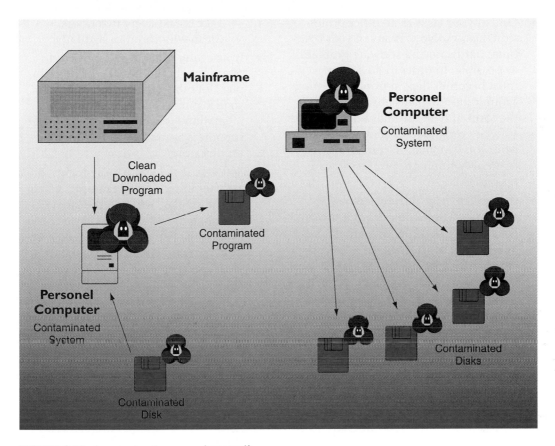

FIGURE 6-10. A computer virus can replicate itself.

improves the quality of the work. With proper care of your computer and your software, you will avoid time-consuming breakdowns, frustrations caused by the inability to get your work done, and loss of productivity.

SUMMARY

To reinforce what you have learned in this chapter, study this summary.

- There are two major categories of software programs—operating systems software and applications software.

- The purpose of operating systems software is to control computer system resources, execute computer programs, and manage data.

- Operating systems include DOS, Windows, Windows NT, OS/390, OS/400, and UNIX.

- Applications software programs tell the computer how to perform a specific task. These programs include word processing, bundles, office suites, graphics, spreadsheets, personal information managers, database, voice recognition, remote access, presentations, privacy software, and Internet software.

- One of your tasks as an office professional is to solve as many of your computer hardware and software problems as possible. In order to do so, you must become adept at troubleshooting. Troubleshooting aids are available in the form of help tutorials built into the software program, telephone assistance from software manufacturers, and manuals written on specific software programs.
- Computers have introduced new ergonomic factors into our environment. For example, in order to be more productive and comfortable as you work at the computer, here are several suggestions:
  - Use indirect lighting if possible.
  - Keep the top edge of the monitor at eye level or slightly below.
  - Keep your wrists straight.
  - Do not lean the heel of your hand on the desk.
  - Keep your feet on the floor.
  - Keep your mouse close to the keyboard so that you do not have to reach far to use it.
  - Engage in isometric exercise at your desk.
  - Take breaks every two hours.
  - Clean your monitor regularly.
- In selecting software, a number of questions should be asked. For example: Does the program offer the software features you need? What documentation is available? What software support is available? Is the program user-friendly?
- Software should be handled appropriately to protect it. For example, when labeling a disk, write on the label before applying it to the disk, store disks in specially designed containers, keep disks away from water and other liquids, and keep them out of direct sunlight.
- Steps should be taken to prevent destruction of software. These steps include backing up data, frequently changing passwords, and placing confidential files in hidden directories.
- Unauthorized copying of software is not only unethical but also illegal.
- Proper procedures should be taken to control computer viruses. For example, an antiviral scanning program can be installed on the system.

Key Terms

- Operating systems software
- Applications software
- DOS (disk operating system)
- Windows
- Windows NT
- Servers
- OS/390
- OS/400
- UNIX
- C language
- Thesaurus

- Bundled software
- Integrated software
- Bitmapped images
- Vector graphics
- Pixels
- Spreadsheet
- Contact management software
- Database program
- Table
- Remote file exchange and synchronization
- Layouts

- Templates
- Accelerators
- Troubleshooting
- Isometric exercise
- Disk defragmenter
- Surge suppressor
- Uninterruptible power supply (UPS)
- User friendly
- Ergonomically sound
- Computer virus
- Download

Professional Pointers

New software programs and upgrades on existing software come on the market frequently. As an office professional, you should be committed to keeping current on software. Here are several ways to do so.

- Ask to be placed on software vendors' mailing lists for updated literature and announcements of new products.
- Read computer journals and magazines.
- Enroll in continuing education courses or workshops on new software.
- Learn from others about the software programs they use.
- Visit computer retail stores and observe demonstrations of available software.

Office Procedures Reinforcement

1. Explain the term "operating system" and name three commonly used operating systems.
2. Name and describe five types of applications software.
3. Explain what troubleshooting means; list three troubleshooting helps that are available on software packages.
4. Explain the relationship between ethics and software copying.
5. What is a computer virus? List six ways that you can protect your software from them.

Critical Thinking Activity

You and a team of office professionals were asked by your supervisor to recommend an updated office suite package for use in the company. The team completed its assignment. Your supervisor was asked to attend the last meeting of the team to hear the recommendation from the group. As chair of the committee, you made the recommendation to your supervisor along with the rationale. She congratulated you on doing a fine job and stated that the package would be purchased. She also asked that as soon as the software was received, the committee act as trainers for other people in the company. She asked that you continue to chair the training group and that you make 20 copies of the software so that everyone in your company could have a copy.

You were extremely surprised when she asked that you copy the software. However, you were so shocked that you did not say anything. The team made no comment. As everyone left the room, you felt "sick." You wonder how you are going to handle the situation.

Discuss this case with three of your classmates; then answer the following questions.

- Is there an ethical problem? If so, what is it?
- Is there a legal problem? If so, what is it?
- How should you handle the situation? Should you keep quiet and make the copies? Should you discuss the issue with your supervisor? Should you discuss the issue with your supervisor's boss? Should you talk with the team about it?

Before answering these questions, you may want to review Chapter 4 on Ethical Behavior.

Office Applications

OA6-1 (Goal 1)

In order to become familiar with the newest applications software packages available, visit a computer store. Pay particular attention to these types of software: office suites, voice-recognition software, graphics, and personal information/contact managers. Select three of your classmates to work with on this project. Be prepared to report your findings to the class.

OA6-2 (Goal 2)

You are having these problems with your software package. Using the troubleshooting helps provided with your software, determine how you would solve the problem. Using the memorandum form on the student template disk in file OA02-1b.doc, write a note to your instructor, giving your solutions and the resources you used to find the answers; for example, a manual, the help icon on your computer, and so forth. Save the memo with a new name and submit the memo to your instructor.

Problems

- I have so many windows open I can't see my desktop; how do I quickly get rid of the clutter?
- I have 355 records in my mailmerge. How can I find the preview of just one of them?
- My monitor does not work.
- I applied a border on my copy, but it just underlined the text.

OA6-3 (Goals 3 and 4)

You work in a small office and your software needs upgrading. Research the types of office suites that are available; determine what you would recommend purchasing and why. Using the memorandum form provided on the student template disk in file OA02-1b.doc, write a note to your instructor, explaining what you would recommend and the rationale for your recommendation. You are also responsible for taking good care of your computer and your software. Explain to your instructor, in the same memorandum, what steps you would take in caring for your computer and your software. Save memo with a new name.

OA6-4 (Goals 3 and 4)

On page 41 of your Applications Workbook is an illustration. Describe what is wrong with the picture, using what you have learned about ergonomics. When you complete your answers, check them by referring to your student template disk in file OA06-4.doc.

OA6-5 (Goal 5)

In your Applications Workbook on page 42 is the draft of an announcement about a physical fitness program your company is beginning. The announcement will be distributed to all employees. Prepare a flyer to be printed on half sheets of paper (8½" x 5½") Make the flyer attractive and professional by using font enhancements, a border, and graphics. Print a copy and submit it to your instructor.

OA6-6 (Goal 5)

In your Applications Workbook on page 43 is a handwritten memo from the director of the Information Systems Department. Key the memorandum, making the necessary corrections. Use the memorandum form provided on the student template disk in file OA02-1b.doc. Save as a new file. Print a copy of it and submit it to your instructor.

Online Research Application

ORA6-7 (Goal 1)

Using the Internet, research the current operating systems, Internet, and privacy software available. Choose two of your classmates to work with on this project. Be prepared to present your findings to the class.

CHAPTER 7

Reprographic Resources

Have you ever thought about the number of copies that are made each day in the office? If you have, you probably realize that the number is staggering. The Information Age, rather than spawning the paperless office as was predicted a number of years ago, has seen a huge increase in the amount of paper that is generated each day in the average office. In addition to hard-copy mail received through the U.S. Postal Service, we receive:

- Faxes from both within and outside our company
- Computer printouts of all types of information
- Email, which we sometimes print out to have a record

YOUR GOALS

1. Identify the types of copiers and fax machines available.

2. Explain the features available on copiers and fax machines.

3. Demonstrate knowledge of copier maintenance and selection.

4. Demonstrate an understanding of ethical and legal considerations when copying materials.

5. Use copiers.

- Copies of information made on the various copy machines that are readily available in the office
- Information from the Internet, which we often print for future reference

All of these copies are made with relative ease and great speed—merely by pushing a button or two. In other words, the Information Age has produced information "junkies." We exist with mountains of paper stacked around us daily, with the size of the mountains growing exponentially.

This chapter, in addition to helping you learn about the various categories of copiers available and their functions, will assist you in understanding copying abuses and ways to control these abuses. You will also learn how to select and maintain copiers. By studying and practicing the insights gained from this chapter, you will become a more knowledgeable and ethical office professional.

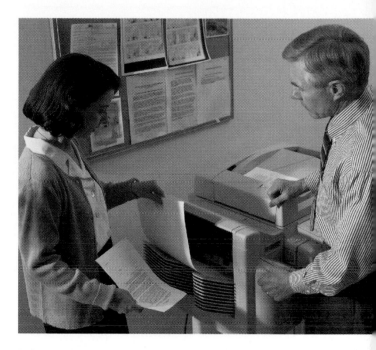

Reprographics is the process of making copies of documents.
Courtesy of © PhotoDisc, Inc.

Reprographics—A Definition

Reprographics is the process of making copies of documents. It refers to any piece of equipment that produces multiple copies of an original document. This process is not confined to one type of copier or even to copiers only. In addition to copiers, copies are made on fax machines, printers, and multifunction units.

Copiers

There are basically four categories of copiers available—low-volume, mid-volume, and high-volume copiers, and copier/duplicators. The category a copier falls within is determined by the monthly copying volume and the speed of the machine. In addition to the basic categories of copiers, technology advances are making possible several additional types of copiers, including digital copiers and multifunction units.

Low-Volume Copiers

Low-volume copiers typically produce from 12 to 30 **cpm (copies per minute)** and run from 500 to 20,000 copies per month. These copiers are one of the fastest-growing segments of the copier market due to their use in small businesses and the growing home market. Some of the features of low-volume copiers include:

- Automatic document feeding
- Duplexing

Low-volume copiers typically produce from 12 to 30 copies per minute. © *EyeWire*.

- Collating
- Stapling
- Flexible paper supply configurations
- Zoom reduction and enlargement

Mid-Volume Copiers

Mid-volume copiers generate between 25 and 56 copies per minute and produce as many as 70,000 copies per month. These machines generally have a few more features than the low-volume copiers; these include:

- Large toner capacity
- Large-capacity paper tray options
- Automatic magnification selection
- Auto tray switching

High-Volume Copiers

High-volume copiers are used in a **centralized copy center** where they can serve

an entire organization. You will learn more about these centers later in this chapter. These copiers are capable of producing over 90 copies per minute, with monthly volumes from 20,000 to 150,000 copies. High-volume copiers are usually equipped with very efficient copy-production capabilities, including:

- Microprocessor-controlled job recovery
- Large paper capacities—4,000 sheets and more
- Sophisticated message displays
- Speed, with first-copy time of 5 seconds or less as compared to low-volume and mid-volume copiers having a first-copy time of 7.5 seconds
- Remote diagnostics

Copier/Duplicators

Copier/duplicators can produce approximately 150 copies per minute, with

Copier/duplicators can produce approximately 150 copies per minute. © EyeWire.

monthly volumes of over 50,000 copies. These copiers possess production-oriented capabilities, with sophisticated user control panels. Some of their features include:

- Ability to run almost 10,000 copies in a single run as opposed to slightly under 1,000 copies in a single run for high-volume copiers

- Five hundred (or more) built-in user access codes

Digital Copiers

Copiers in the past have been analog, and the large majority of copiers today are still analog copiers. However, the copier market, like the TV market, is moving to digital. **Digital** technology allows for data to be transferred as a series of bits rather than as a fluctuating **(analog)** signal. Notice Figure 7-1, which illustrates the differences in the signal appearances of

digital and analog. Digital technology, although it remains more expensive than analog, provides for faster, clearer, and higher-quality output. Digital copiers can create originals from data downloaded from a connected computer or network, with great flexibility in the manipulation of images in terms of editing.

Digital copiers generally appeal to companies that wish to replace old-style copiers with digital systems and add fax, printing, and scanning capabilities, as their older fax, scanners, and printers become obsolete. Through the addition of fax, printing, and scanning modules, the digital copier becomes a multifunction unit. Digital copiers are also appealing to the business that operates a decentralized print shop. Some of the features of a digital copier are:

- Ability to handle difficult originals such as photographs and drawings

- Internal trays that accommodate letterhead, transparencies, envelopes, and labels

- Ability to print and scan the fronts and backs of documents

- Ability to print copies at 120 pages per minute and up

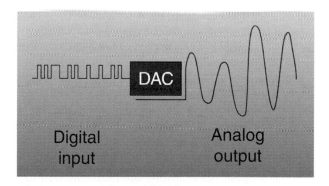

FIGURE 7-1. Digital technology transmits data as a series of bits; analog technology transmits data as a fluctuating signal.

- Configuration for multicolor printing in up to 11 colors

If you are printing copies on a digital copier directly from the computer, you need a computer interface. However, the quality of the copy is from 10 to 15 percent better than if you print directly from hard copy.

The digital copier is not expected to supplant the analog stand-alone copier in the immediate future due to:

- The increased cost of a digital over an analog

- Computer platform compatibility issues

- Reliability concerns when the digital is used as a copier/printer—for example, when the copier breaks, the printer also breaks

It is anticipated that the price of digital copiers will continue to fall and that their use in the office will continue to increase.

Multifunction Units

You learned in Chapter 5 about multifunction machines that print, scan, copy, and fax. Also, you have just been introduced to digital copiers that have the ability to become multifunction units, with the addition of fax, scanning, and printing modules. Multifunction units, by combining capabilities, can save time, steps, and floor or desk space. They can even save user frustration by consolidating time-consuming supply changing and stocking. The multifunction unit's capabilities have basically the same range as the standard copier. For example, the multifunction copier may copy only 10 copies per minute and provide limited features or

copy over 100 copies per minute (as the previously mentioned digital copier is capable of doing), with a wide variety of features. It may be a black-and-white copier only or a color copier. The use of multifunction peripherals is expected to continue to grow, with digital units increasing in use also.

Copier Features

Copier features vary depending on the size and price of the copier. You learned earlier about some of the features on the various categories of copiers. However, the basic features are the same on most copiers. Some of those features are presented in this section, along with some of the special features.

Basic Features

Copiers usually handle the two standard sizes of paper—8½ x 11 inches and 8½ x 14 inches. Most copiers (with the exception of small, low-volume copiers) handle paper sizes of up to a maximum of 11 x 17. The paper tray, which feeds the paper through the machine, may be adjusted for different paper sizes or there may be separate trays. If there are separate trays, one size holds the 8½ x 11-inch paper, one tray holds the 8½ x 14-inch paper, and another tray holds the 11 x 17 paper. The trays snap in and out of the copier for reloading the paper. If there is a single tray, the appropriate paper size for the task being performed must be placed in the tray.

Another basic feature of copiers is the copy counter. Before starting to copy material, the counter is set for the number of copies needed. When the appropriate number has been reached, the copier will automatically stop. Also, copiers are equipped with an exposure control that regulates the lightness or darkness of the copies. For example, if a copy is too light, a button can be pushed instructing the machine to make the copies darker.

Copiers are also equipped with a feature that shows the cause of a machine malfunction, generally with a code number displayed. If the paper path is jammed, the copier will indicate the problem. If the toner in the machine needs to be replaced so that clear, dark copies can be produced, the machine will let the operator know that also.

Special Features

Due to technological advances, many special features are available on copiers. A number of these special features are explained here.

Reduction and Enlargement. This feature allows you to reduce the size of the original document by degrees, usually expressed as percentages. For example, you can reduce an original by as much as 200 to 500 percent. Reduced copies can be made of large documents so that all filed copies are uniform in size. Computer printouts that measure 11 x 17 inches, for example, can be reduced to fit 8½ x 11-inch paper for easier handling and filing.

An enlargement feature allows an original document to be enlarged as much as 500 percent. Reductions and enlargements can be made in 1 percent increments. Fine details on an original can be made more legible by using the enlargement feature. Also, if it is necessary to reduce or enlarge a copy less or greater than the maximum percent allowed by the copies, the copy originally reduced or enlarged (rather than the original) can

then be copied and reduced or enlarged again. Figure 7-2 shows copy that has been enlarged.

Duplexing. Copying on both sides of a sheet of paper is known as **duplexing.** This feature saves paper and reduces the number of sheets of paper to be stored in the files. Copies may be made on both sides of the paper by merely pushing the proper buttons. There is no need for the operator to intervene.

Color Reproduction. Some copiers offer more than one color of ink in the machine at any given time, allowing the operator to change ink colors simply by pressing a button. Several colors are shown in the document depicted in Figure 7-3.

Document or Digital Editing. Copiers that have an editing function scan the image and convert it to digital signals. Then

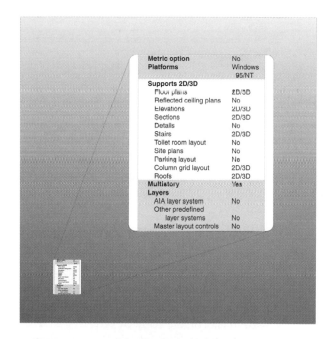

FIGURE 7-2. The enlargement feature of a copier allows for an increase of size up to 500 percent.

Utility
To change layers

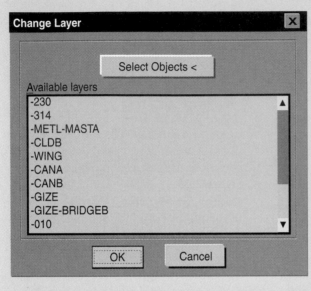

Change Layer ☒

Select Objects <

Available layers

-230
-314
-METL-MASTA
-CLDB
-WING
-CANA
-CANB
-GIZE
-GIZE-BRIDGEB
-010

OK   Cancel

The DDCLA Program :

This utility is used to change the layers dynamically and user friendly. The available list of layers are displayed in the list box. The user can interactively select or remove entities from the selection set by clicking the Select Objects button.

Executing DDCLA :

Load the program and type DDCLA in the prompt. The dialog is displayed after selecting the objects. From the available list, select the destination layer and click OK. The program exits after changing the layer of the selected entities.

Code

```
showlayer : dialog {                      : list_box {
    label = "Change Layer";                   label = "Available layers" ;
    : boxed_column {                          mnemonic = "A";
                                              key = "a_layers";
    : button {                                width =  50;
      label = "Select Objects <";             height = 10;
      mnemonic = "S";                         multiple_select = false;
      key = "sel_obj";                            }
      fixed_width = true;                 }
      alignment = centered;             ok_cancel;
      }                               }
```

FIGURE 7-3. Copies can be produced in numerous colors.

using control keys or a **wand** (similar to a wand used in retail stores to scan letters and numbers on price tags), the operator can mask (delete copy by covering), move, and manipulate the copy to alter the image.

Diagnostics. Some copiers are equipped with microprocessors that monitor and identify copy status and problems and display the findings on a readout panel. These machines can automatically call a remote service center via a **modem**

The remote diagnostic feature allows for problems to be detected and corrected by a technician at a distant location. *Courtesy of © PhotoDisc, Inc.*

(electronic device that converts computer signals into telephone signals) and relay the problem, which can be repaired remotely through the modem. Other problems can be corrected by the service center dispatching a local service person.

This feature eliminates the need for some service calls by recognizing such problems as paper jams and pulled plugs. Also, it helps eliminate more serious problems by recognizing when a machine needs a service check. When a problem in the copier is detected, the system can instantly dispatch a technician to service the copier before a more serious problem occurs. This feature minimizes copier downtime and allows dealers to be proactive instead of reactive to problems.

Collate and Staple. Copiers will collate only or collate and staple sets of materials.

Interrupt Key. This key is a device that permits the operator to stop the copier at any point in the copying process. The key is useful in emergency situations when the operator wishes to discontinue the copy cycle. For example, if the operator is running a long job, the employer may need three copies of another document immediately. The operator can interrupt the long job, make the three copies, and then resume the copy process without starting over.

Help Button. This user-friendly feature allows the inexperienced operator to get help. The help button will flash instructions in step-by-step order so that the operator can produce copies correctly.

Job Recovery. The job recovery mode stops the copier and remembers how many copies have been made. When you are ready to finish the project, the machine automatically picks up where it left off and makes the required number of copies. For example, assume the paper path becomes jammed during a job. Without job recovery, you have to reprogram the machine and start the job over, losing time and effort. With job recovery, once the problem area is cleared, the job can be finished without reprogramming and without wasting a lot of copies.

Automatic Folding. Some copiers will fold 11 x 17-inch copies to an 8½ x 11-inch size. With this feature, drawings and schematics can be kept in a convenient format for handling and distribution. The fold can also be **offset** (not folded to the edge of the paper) so that folded materials can be placed in three-ring binders.

Touch Control Screen. Some copiers have a color CRT that lets you program any job just by touching various icons on the screen. The kinds of jobs you can do are illustrated on the screen.

Programmable Memory. If you perform certain complex copy jobs frequently, you can program them in the copier one time and then call them back when needed. For example, if you copy many long reports in which you begin each section of the report on the right-hand page and insert and copy onto divider sheets, this information can be programmed once and called back with each report you print. Other programmable examples include inserting preprinted tabs or colored paper, copying onto special stocks such as cardstock, and controlling copy quality for a page of graphics. Programmable memory allows you to save time and effort.

Book Copy. With book copy, you can place an opened book on the copier without having to turn the book around to copy facing pages. This feature saves considerable time if you copy from books frequently.

Online Binding. Books can be bound with thermal adhesive tape. The tape is available in various colors to coordinate the binding with cover stocks, tabs, and dividers. With this feature, turnaround time on bound work can be quite fast.

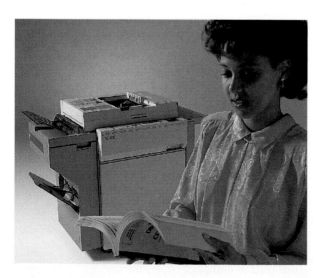

Books can be bound at the copier. *Courtesy of Xerox, Inc.*

Image Shift. When binding books, the image shift allows you to automatically add one-half inch (or whatever is needed) to the left margin for binding. Also, if you are going to place the material in a pre-purchased binder, image shift allows you to make the left margin wider so that the pages may be hole-punched.

Transparency Production. Transparencies may be made on most copiers in much the same way as you make a paper copy. The transparency film is substituted for the paper in the copier's paper feed tray.

Toner and Paper Changes. Some copiers permit toner and paper changes while they are running. These capabilities allow for jobs to be completed without interruption.

Environmentally Friendly Features. Many copiers incorporate organic photoconductors, recyclable materials, toner-save modes, and energy-save modes. Some vendors offer their own brands of recycled paper and other media transparencies, as well as programs that make it easy for customers to recycle their toner cartridges.

Copy Quality

Millions of copies are made each day in offices across our nation at considerable expense to the businesses. These copies certainly should be of high quality. Yet they are not always quality products. You no doubt have received copied documents that have pages missing, are incorrectly collated, or cannot be read, and so on. These errors may be caused by machine malfunctions or inappropriate procedures used by the operator. When you are making copies, check the quality carefully by following these procedures.

- Check the screen of the copying machine to see that it is clean. Be certain there are no spots on the screen that will in turn cause spots on the paper being copied.
- Keep paper clips and staples away from the copier in order to prevent scratching the glass or causing any copier malfunction.
- Run one copy; check it before continuing. Ask these questions about the copy:
    - Is the copy free of spots?
    - Is the copy easy to read? Is the ink dark and clear?
    - Is the copy straight on the page?
    - If the original was in pencil, can the copy be read?
    - If color was used, did the color reproduce well?
- If you are running several pages that must be collated, check to see that:
    - All pages of the document have been copied.
    - The pages have been collated correctly.

When you finish your copying job, leave the room or copy area clean for the next person. Be certain that you have returned all extra paper or supplies that you may have out to the appropriate cabinet. Tear or shred any copies that are inappropriate for use.

Copier Maintenance

Broken office copiers can have a major impact on office productivity. The downtime from nonworking copiers can be extremely costly, along with the cost of service, whether it be in the form of a maintenance contract (that can be purchased from the vendor when the copier is leased or purchased) or direct service

Always leave the copy area clean for the next person's use. *Courtesy of Eastman Kodak.*

charges when a maintenance contract is not used. To keep maintenance to a minimum, there are certain responsibilities for both the office professional and management. Some of these steps are listed in this section.

Responsibilities of the Office Professional

- Store paper properly. Paper should be stored in dry conditions, away from extremes of heat or cold. Keep the paper flat, and if possible, on shelves or pallets above the floor. Since paper is affected by humidity, keep it wrapped and boxed until you need to use it. Rewrap and seal partly used reams.
- Check the paper before you load it into the machine. Some machines will accept different weights of paper; others will not. Damaged, curled, wrinkled, folded, or damp paper can cause paper

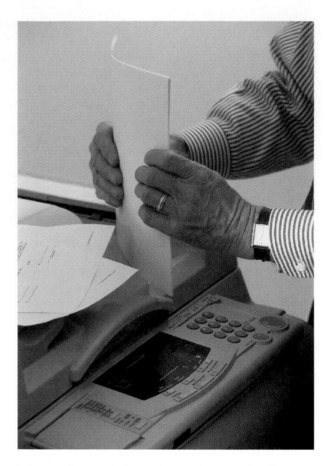

It is wise to fan paper before loading it in the tray so that sheets will feed through singularly. *Courtesy of © PhotoDisc, Inc.*

during use. If you attempt to make a minor repair or retrieve a jammed sheet, you must be very careful. Jewelry can cause your hand to become caught or lodged in the equipment, and touching certain areas inside the machine may result in burns.

- Trust the control panel warning. When the control panel instructs you to add toner, you should do so. Operating a copier with little or no toner is like driving a car with little or no oil. The quality of the copies will surely be affected, as will the internal mechanics of the machine.

- Look for consistency. When a particular problem consistently occurs, the operator can inform the technician of the malfunction. If you have made a list of the types of problems or how the machine reacts in certain situations, you will save repair time and cost.

- Designate a key operator, in conjunction with management if appropriate. One person who is located near the copier should be responsible for simple repairs, such as paper jams, malfunctions, replenishing supplies, and determining when a repair call is justified. Consistent care will add to the operating life of office equipment.

- Determine how the key operator will be trained; management may need to be involved in helping make this decision. The vendor usually has personnel who will provide initial training. Check to see if this training is available. If it is not, check the information provided in the copier manual.

- Establish a schedule for the key operator to train office personnel who will be using the copier.

jams. Paper has an "up" side and a "down" side. Look at the label for the arrow that shows the down side of the paper. The paper should be loaded into the machine with the top side up. Paper that has been packaged has little air. It is wise to fan the stack before loading it in the tray so that sheets will feed through singularly.

- Be cautious. Copiers have moving parts and parts that may become very hot

Responsibilities of Management

Although management will most likely make the decisions about maintenance contracts and where the copier is located, you may be asked for input. This section will help you understand the types of issues you need to consider.

- Choose an appropriate location. A copier needs proper ventilation and adequate temperature control. The user needs sufficient space to place paper and other supplies so that the top of the copier is not abused. Paper clips and staples that fall into the machine can cause major repair bills.

- Determine how often preventive maintenance is needed. Preventive maintenance is to your copier what a tune-up is to your car. It increases the productivity of the copier in the long run by decreasing the number of copier breakdowns. Preventive maintenance should occur approximately every three months.

- Determine whether or not a maintenance contract is cost efficient. What services does it provide? Compare the cost of doing preventive maintenance (hourly rate of technicians) with the cost of a maintenance contract.

- Are remote diagnostic systems available? These systems can detect copier problems before they occur and fix them remotely using an off-site computer. The benefits of copiers with remote diagnostic systems include:
  - Increased equipment uptime
  - Reduced key operator responsibilities
  - Potential for lower service costs
  - More efficient use of the technician's time if a technician must be called

Centralized copy centers serve large-volume copying needs of an organization. *Courtesy of © PhotoDisc, Inc.*

Decentralized copy centers allow for small numbers of copies to be made quickly and conveniently. *Courtesy of © PhotoDisc, Inc.*

COPIER SELECTION

When making a copier selection, ask these questions.

- What materials will be copied? What percentage of copying will be made on letter-size paper? What percentage of copying will be on legal-size paper? What percentage of copying will be made on ledger-size paper? What percentage of copying will be stapled? Will you run card and cover stock, recycled paper, or transparency film? Will forms, directories, reports, and manuals be produced?

- How many copies per month will be run? Do you project an increase or decrease in copy volume over the next five years?

- Will your volume requirements fluctuate during certain times of the year? If so, what are the lowest and highest volumes you can anticipate?

- What space limitations exist for the copier? If there are space limitations, the size of the copier becomes an issue.

- Should you purchase a maintenance contract?

- Ask for a demonstration of the copier. Ask these questions as the machine is being demonstrated.

    —What is the quality of the copy?
    —Are the copies clean and crisp?
    —Is there a clear definition between black and white areas?
    —Are the grays in photos clear?
    —If it is a color copier, are the colors clear?
    —Is the machine easy to operate?
    —Is the interior easily accessible for removing jammed paper and replacing toner?

- What features do you need in a copier? Ask the potential users of the copier what their needs are. A survey is an appropriate vehicle for determining the needs of the employees.

- Is color needed? If so, what will be the cost per copy? What colors are available?

- What is the purchase price of the machine?

- What is the cost of supplies, especially toner?

- Ask the dealer for a loaner (for a trial period) before you buy or lease.

- How reliable is the dealer/vendor?

    —Is the vendor authorized to sell and service the model being considered?
    —How long has the dealer/vendor been in business?
    —Does the vendor carry parts for the brand?
    —Does the vendor provide quick and reliable service?
    —What is the cost of service?
    —Ask the vendor for references and call them to inquire about their experiences with the dealer/vendor.
    —Has your organization done business in the past with the vendor?
    —Is key operator training available?
    —What is the vendor's service response time to your location in hours?
    —What is the vendor's financial stability?
    —Are there any unresolved complaints against the vendor listed with the Better Business Bureau?

FIGURE 7-4. Copier selection.

Copier Selection

Since a copier is used so extensively, it is important that consideration be given to the type of copier that will best serve the needs of the business. Management will have the primary responsibility for making the decision; however, as an office professional, you may be asked for input. You may also be asked to serve on a committee to make a recommendation for copier selection to management. Figure 7-4 on page 180 lists some questions to be asked before selecting a copier.

Centralized and Decentralized Centers

Centralized and decentralized copy centers serve different functions and exist for different reasons. Small organizations may have only decentralized copiers, with large organizations often having both centralized and decentralized centers.

Centralized Copy Centers

Centralized copy centers exist to serve the large-volume copying needs of an organization. For example, if you routinely need 500 copies of reports, with each report ranging from 25 to 50 pages in length, it would not be cost effective or efficient to have the office professional make the copies. Such copying projects would tie up his or her time and reduce the number of other duties that could be handled. If you work in a large organization where there are 200 people each day needing this volume of copy work, you can quickly understand that a centralized center would be the most efficient way to produce the

work. Additional advantages and also several disadvantages of centralized copy centers are given in Figure 7-5.

Although the main job function of employees in a centralized center is producing copies, they do have other responsibilities. For example, some personnel may be graphic artists, preparing graphics and artwork for the documents being produced. Other duties of centralized center personnel include:

- Scheduling projects within the center so that the times established by the individuals needing the work can be met
- Ordering and maintaining supplies
- Supervising the personnel in the center
- Maintaining equipment

Some companies combine the printing function and the mailroom function; thus employees need to have knowledge of mailing equipment and procedures. Employees in a centralized center might prepare mail for distribution internally as well as externally. For example, if you

---

ADVANTAGES AND DISADVANTAGES OF CENTRALIZED COPY CENTERS

Advantages

- Tighter cost controls over equipment and supplies
- Reduction of outside printing costs
- Less unauthorized copying

Disadvantages

- Dependence on one unit; no backups
- Higher personnel costs; dedicated operator; more walking time
- Longer total job turnaround time
- Underutilization of the equipment with some jobs

FIGURE 7-5. Advantages and disadvantages of centralized copy centers. Source: "How to Buy Photocopiers," *Library Technology Reports* (March-April 1998), 58.

want all managers within the company to get a certain report, the center would reproduce the document and send it through interoffice mail to all managers. In addition to these functions, the copy center personnel are also responsible for maintenance of the equipment, assuring that it is in top working condition at all times so that breakdowns are kept to a minimum.

When the office professional takes material to a centralized copy center, complete and accurate information must be given to insure that the job is correctly done. Usually a preprinted form is provided by the center personnel so that the user may check off the type, size, and color of paper needed; the number of copies to be run; any special instructions such as enlargement; and so forth. Completing this form accurately insures the saving of time and money by avoiding redoing a job.

In addition, the office professional is responsible for taking correct copy to the centralized center. If there are errors (factual, typographical, grammatical, and so forth) made in the copy, hundreds of copies may have to be discarded. The cost in time and money to the business can be considerable.

Decentralized Copy Centers

Both large and small companies use **decentralized copy centers,** in which copying machines are located in proximity to the employees. For example, there may be one copying machine located in each department of the company. Employees then have immediate access to a copying machine. Small numbers of copies can be made quickly and easily. Any employee in the area can make a copy; it is not neces-

---

> ### ADVANTAGES AND DISADVANTAGES OF DECENTRALIZED COPY CENTERS
>
> *Advantages*
> - Backup copiers always available
> - Greater user convenience
> - Lower personnel costs; no key operator; less walking time
> - Faster job turnaround
>
> *Disadvantages*
> - Higher total equipment, supplies, service costs
> - More unauthorized copying

FIGURE 7-6. Advantages and disadvantages of decentralized copy centers. Source: "How to Buy Photocopiers," *Library Technology Reports* (March-April 1998), 58.

---

sary to wait for someone else to do it for you. Advantages and disadvantages of decentralized centers are listed in Figure 7-6.

Copying Abuses

As you learned in Chapters 5 and 6, we have had the technology to reduce the amount of copies in the office with the advent of the computer, email, voice mail, scanning technology, the Internet, and so forth. However, the reverse has been true. Businesses produce more copies than ever before. Billions and billions of copies are made each year in businesses, and many of them are unnecessary. For example, an employee may make 20 copies of a document when he or she knows that only 15 are needed. The additional copies are made "just in case" they are needed. Most of the time the employee winds up throwing them away. Additionally, employees sometimes make personal copies on office copiers. Such behavior calls into consideration the personal ethics of the employee.

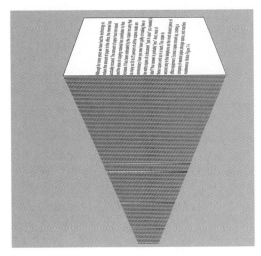

FIGURE 7-7. Excess copies are run frequently in the office.

Think back about what you learned in Chapter 4. The ethical office professional is honest. He or she does not spend company time or resources in copying personal documents. Also, there are ethical and legal considerations inherent in copying due to the Copyright Law. As an office professional, you need to be aware of what you can and cannot copy. The next sections give you an overview of the Copyright Law and legal and ethical elements that should be considered when making copies.

Copyright Law

Since you will be responsible for a great deal of copying, you need to be informed about the law, highlights of which are given in Figure 7-8. Pay particular attention to the fair use clause. This clause means that individuals do have the right to reproduce copyrighted materials without permission under certain fair and reasonable circumstances. Whether the copy-

ing to be done falls within the fair use provision must be decided on an individual basis.

Further technological advances have impacted the copyright process even more. Almost all software is copyrighted. Statements are included on software that spell out the copyright restrictions. For example, under the copyright laws, neither the documentation nor the software may be copied, photocopied, reproduced, translated, or reduced to any electronic medium or machine-readable form without prior written consent from the company. You learned in Chapter 6 that there are abuses in copying software. These abuses are both legally and ethically wrong.

In 1994, the National Information Infrastructure Working Group on Intellectual Property Rights asked the U.S. Patent and Trademark Office to address the shortcomings of the 1976 Copyright Act. The task was to determine if copyright holders and "fair users" of copyright material could agree to a new set of guidelines that address technological trends in education. The result was the establishment of the Conference on Fair Use (CONFU). This group addressed the multimedia, distance learning, visual archives, and digital libraries. The guidelines established by CONFU address the recent technological trends.

Ethical and Legal Considerations

Each employee in a company should be extremely ethical in the use of copying machines. Each employee should also be aware of the legal restrictions on the copy of certain documents. Behaving ethically and legally in copying means:

THE COPYRIGHT LAW

The copyright law is more than 60 pages in length. Here are some of its highlights:

- Money, postage stamps, United States bonds, Federal Reserve notes, or other securities of the United States may not be reproduced.

- Birth certificates, passports, draft cards, naturalization and immigration papers may not be reproduced.

- Driver's licenses, automobile registrations, and certificates of title may not be reproduced.

- Documents that contain the personal information of an individual are protected by the Right of Privacy Act. They may not be reproduced without the individual's permission.

- Material that retains a copyright may not be reproduced without the owner's permission. The fair use provision allows some exceptions to this provision.

Source: House Committee Report, P.L. 94-553.

Fair Use

In order to determine what constitutes a fair use, the factors considered include:

(1) the purpose and character of the use, including whether such use is of a commercial nature or is for nonprofit educational purposes;

(2) the nature of the copyrighted work;

(3) the amount and substantiality of the portion used in relation to the copyrighted work as a whole; and

(4) the effect of the use upon the potential market for or value of the copyrighted work.

Under the doctrine of fair use, it is not an infringement of copyright for a library or archives, or any of its employees acting within the scope of their employment, to reproduce no more than one copy or phonorecord of a work, or to distribute such copy or phonorecord . . . if

(1) the reproduction or distribution is made without any purpose of direct or indirect commercial advantage;

(2) the collections of the library or archives are (a) open to the public, or (b) available not only to researchers affiliated with the library or archives or with the institution of which it is a part, but also to other persons doing research in a specialized field; and

(3) the reproduction or distribution of the work includes a notice of copyright.

FIGURE 7-8. Excerpts from copyright law. (Top, Source: *House Committee Report, P.L. 94-553*. Bottom, Source: *The Guide to American Law* (New York: West Publishing Company, 1984).

- You do not copy documents for your own personal use.

- You do not copy cartoons, jokes, and similar types of information to be distributed to your office colleagues.

- You do not make copies of documents that you need for an outside professional group, such as a service club, unless you have approval from your company to do so.

- You are consistently prudent in making the appropriate number of copies of documents needed within the office.

- You do not copy restricted materials (explained in the copyright section).

Control Systems

To curb copying control abuses, one solution that offices have instituted is the installation of a copy control device. Each system operates somewhat differently but the same basic features exist in all systems. For example, if a keypad system is used, the user enters an account number into a keypad and access is granted to the copier. With a card system, the card is good for a set number of copies. When the card is inserted into the machine, copying costs can be automatically charged back to the appropriate department or division. Each department or division of the company can then check copy costs against a specific account. If abuses are occurring, appropriate action can be taken.

Public entities such as libraries and schools control copying costs by using coin-operated copiers. The user of the copier pays for the copies directly by inserting money into the copier or by purchasing a debit card that has a specific value. As copies are made, the cost is deducted from the card.

Shredders

For those times when a machine malfunctions and copies must be destroyed, businesses often place a shredder in proximity to the copier. A **shredder** is a machine that cuts paper into strips or confetti-like material. Today, shredded paper is recycled by many businesses as packing material. Since mailrooms of businesses process a large amount of paper and often pack materials for shipping, shredders are used in mailrooms also.

The shredder market has increased tremendously over the last few years due primarily to the impact of technology. You have learned that many times addi-

tional copies are made that are not needed. These copies, often with confidential or sensitive information, are tossed into trashcans. People with unethical agendas can use this information to the detriment of the company. Consider these very real possibilities within an office when sensitive data is tossed into trashcans.

- Social Security numbers and birth dates can be (and have been) used to create false identity papers and open fake checking accounts.

- A company competitor may retrieve sensitive documents from the trashcans of the business; this information can then be used to damage the company. For example, a company bid that is placed in the trash may get in the hands of a competitor who then underbids the first company.

- Information about new technology that is being developed by the company may get in the hands of information criminals who use it to the detriment of society.

Your responsibility as an office professional in shredding papers is to.

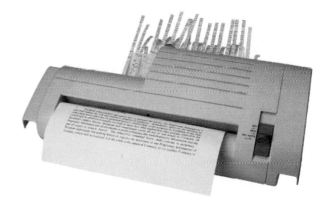

Shredders are used to destroy sensitive or confidential information by cutting paper into strips or confetti-like material. *Courtesy of ©️ PhotoDisc, Inc.*

- Know your company policies on shredding
- Know when a document is confidential or sensitive
- Never toss unneeded copies in the trash without questioning if they are confidential or sensitive
- Shred all appropriate, unneeded copies

Fax Machines

A **fax (facsimile)** machine is a type of copier that electronically sends an original document from one location to another via communication networks. With a fax, you may communicate with other persons within the same building, in the same city, across the nation, or across the world. The first commercial fax machine went into service in 1964. When the prices on the fax machine began to drop below $2,000 in the 1980s, the fax boom began.

A fax machine is a copier that electronically sends an original document from one location to another location via communication networks. *Courtesy of © PhotoDisc, Inc.*

The fax process combines copying technology and telephone or satellite communications. There are two basic steps in the fax transmission.

- The original document is placed on a fax machine. Then the document is converted into electronic signals that are transmitted over communication networks to a receiving fax machine.
- The receiving unit converts the electronic message to its original form and prints a copy of the received document.

The fax has become a standard piece of office equipment, with sales increasing each year and no end in sight. In fact, the fax machine ranks second only to the computer as the most widely used technology in the office. However, some experts predict that email and the Web will make both the fax and photocopier redundant, but not for another two decades.

Fax machines may be purchased as either plain-paper or thermal-paper units. However, the plain paper copier is by far the most used. Thermal paper is slick, curls quickly, and cannot be written on easily. Print speed of a fax is measured in pages per minute (ppm). Mid-range faxes typically print between 4 and 8 ppm. However, some fax machines can print as many as three pages per second. Since most fax machine transmission is through telephone lines, the faster the machine prints, the lower your phone bill is generally. A Gallup/Pitney Bowes poll found that an average of 37 percent of mid- to large-size companies' phone bills is actually fax calls.[1] A faster fax often will pay for itself by reducing long-distance charges. However, if you transmit at a fast speed, yet the receiving unit (over which you have no control) cannot receive at a

---

[1] "Focus on Fax Machines," *Modern Office Technology* (March 1998), 9.

fast speed, you will not be able to reduce your costs proportionately.

Fax Features

Numerous features are available on fax machines; a few of them are given in the following section.

Fax Broadcasting. Fax broadcasting is the ability to personalize and transmit to multiple locations simultaneously. You fax a single document, and then a computer individualizes and faxes it to hundreds or thousands of recipients in minutes. Broadcasting is often accomplished at a fraction of the cost of direct mail or overnight services. Transmissions can be scheduled 24 hours a day. However, most are sent after business hours when telecommunication rates are lower and fax machines are not busy. The message sits in the recipients' machines, ready to be read first thing the next morning.

Dual Access. Dual access means that the fax can perform a number of tasks at one time. For example, the operator can scan a document into memory while transmitting or receiving another document from memory. You cannot, however, receive and send a fax at the same time. If you wish to do that, you have to add a second phone line to your unit.

Fax-on-Demand. Fax-on-demand is the service of storing information for instant retrieval via telephone and fax. It allows you to automate your organization's repetitive actions. For example, customers may call asking for product literature, specification sheets, or price lists. Callers follow a voice-prompted menu to choose documents, and then enter their choices and fax numbers on their telephone keypads. The documents are sent to the designated fax machine.

Color Fax. Color fax makes it possible to scan any high-resolution color image and transmit it anywhere in the world in a few minutes via standard telephone lines. Images can be edited and output to a full-color printer, color display monitor, or other output device.

Autodialers. Autodialers automatically redial a busy number after a minute or two and store from 20 to 200 numbers into memory for one-button code dialing. Some devices can dial numbers when line charges are the lowest so you can transmit information at the cheapest rate. This feature is called **delayed send.**

Portable fax machines are available for use while traveling. *Courtesy of © PhotoDisc, Inc.*

Portable Fax. A **portable fax** (a telephone handset and a small fax machine) will fit in a briefcase. If the executive is traveling and does not have a portable fax machine, machines are available in hotels across the country. Many office supply and copying stores also offer fax machine services.

Elimination of Junk Fax. Businesses have had problems with junk mail clogging up their fax machines. With a special device attached to the fax machine, you can eliminate the receipt of junk faxes. The device requires that the sender know your security code as well as your fax number. If the sender does not know the security code, the machine blocks the message. Another way of controlling junk fax is to purchase a fax machine that allows only communication with user-selected numbers stored in the machine's memory.

Internet Fax

The growth of the Internet has spawned Internet-capable fax, which has the ability to bypass the PSTN (Public Switched Telephone Network) by diverting fax traffic to the Internet and thus reducing fax costs. There are no telephone charges. Fax transmission over the Internet operates like email messaging. The message from the fax is forwarded to an email address, and the user picks up the message as an email message is picked up. The major disadvantage of Internet fax through a service provider, such as America Online, is the immediacy of receipt can be sacrificed. Internet fax may arrive within seconds, minutes, or even hours after the initial transmission. Also, everyone is not connected to the Internet at all times and therefore may not receive messages in a timely fashion.

Multifunction Units

As you have learned earlier, multifunction machines allow the combination of two, three, or four functions. A fax may be a multifunction machine, combining printing, faxing, copying, and scanning or two or three of these functions into one machine, such as faxing and copying. In fact, copying ability is a common feature of most fax machines.

Fax Selection

In selecting a fax, here are some questions you should ask before making the purchase.

- How will I be using the fax? What are my applications? Will I be sending more documents or receiving more documents?

- How much memory will I need? What features do I need?

- What type of image quality is needed? Is faxing photographs or graphics a priority?

- Do I need document security? **Confidential mailboxes** (mailboxes to which no other person has access) are available if document security is an issue. Security devices are also available that enable the user to send **scrambled signals** (signals in code).

- What is the vendor's reputation? How long has the company been in business? Is the service quick and efficient? If the company's home office is not in your city, is there a service center where you are located?

SUMMARY

To reinforce what you have learned in this chapter, study this summary.

- Reprographics is the process of making copies of correspondence, reports, and various other documents. It refers to any piece of mechanical or electronic equipment that produces multiple copies of an original document.

- There are basically four categories of copiers—low-volume, mid-volume, and high-volume copiers; and copier/duplicators.

- The copier market, like the TV market, is moving to digital. Digital technology provides for faster, clearer, and higher quality output.

- Copiers may be multifunction units that fax, scan, and print, in addition to copying.

- Basic features of copy machines include:
  - Handling two to three sizes of paper
  - Automatically counting copies
  - Lightness and darkness controls
  - A feature that shows the cause of a machine malfunction

- Special features on copiers include:
  - Reduction and enlargement of copy
  - Duplexing
  - Color reproduction
  - Document editing
  - Diagnostics
  - Collate and staple
  - Interrupt key
  - Help button
  - Job recovery
  - Automatic folding
  - Touch control screen
  - Programmable memory
  - Book copy
  - Online binding
  - Image shift
  - Transparency production
  - Toner and paper changes
  - Environmentally friendly features such as toner-save modes, energy-save modes, and ability to use recyclable materials

- Copy quality must be maintained. It is important to check the original copy run for quality control.

- Because nonworking office copiers can have a major impact on office productivity, office professionals need to know and use proper maintenance procedures.

- When selecting a copier, a number of questions should be asked. These questions include: What materials will be copied? How many copies per month will be run? What copier features are needed? What is the cost of supplies? How reliable is the dealer/vendor?

- Centralized copy centers serve the large-volume copying needs of an organization.

- Decentralized centers, providing for copiers at various locations throughout the organization, serve low-volume copying needs and ensure quick access by the user.

- Copying abuses are prevalent. Some of these abuses include copying of personal information, making too many copies of documents, and copying material that is protected by copyright laws.

- Behaving ethically and legally when copying documents means that:
  - You do not copy documents for your personal use.

- You do not copy cartoons, jokes, and similar types of information to be distributed to your office colleagues.
- You do not make copies of documents that you need for an outside professional group.
- You are consistently prudent in making the appropriate number of copies of documents needed within the office.
- You do not copy restricted materials.

- Copy control devices are installed on copiers to control copy abuses.

- Unneeded copies of sensitive and confidential information should be shredded.

- A fax machine is a type of copier that electronically sends an original document from one location to another via communication networks.

- Special features available on a fax machine include:
  - Broadcasting
  - Dual access
  - Fax-on-demand
  - Color fax
  - Autodialers
  - Portable fax
  - Elimination of junk fax

- The growth of the Internet has spawned Internet-capable fax, which has the ability to bypass telephone lines by diverting fax traffic to the Internet and thus reducing fax costs.

- Before purchasing a fax machine, ask these questions:
  - How will I be using the fax machine?
  - What features do I need?
  - What is the vendor's reputation?

Key Terms

- Reprographics
- Low-volume copiers
- cpm (copies per minute)
- Mid-volume copiers
- High-volume copiers
- Centralized copy center
- Copier/duplicators
- Digital
- Analog

- Duplexing
- Wand
- Modem
- Offset
- Centralized copy center
- Decentralized copy center
- Shredder
- Fax
- Fax broadcasting

- Dual access
- Fax-on-demand
- Color fax
- Autodialers
- Delayed send
- Portable fax
- Confidential mailboxes
- Scrambled signals
- Plagiarism

Professional Pointers

It is illegal to quote or copy the work of another individual or organization without giving proper credit for the material. Apply the following procedures when you are keying or reproducing copyrighted material.

- A direct quotation of four or more lines should be single-spaced and indented five spaces from the left margin. Quotation marks are not required when using this format.
- A direct quotation of less than four keyed lines should follow the established line length. Quotation marks should be used at the beginning and end of the quoted material and at the conclusion.
- If you must photocopy a published report, table, or other material for distribution to others, be sure to credit the original source of the material. You should review the copyright law so that you will know what constitutes fair use of someone else's work.
- **Plagiarism** is the act of representing another person's work or ideas as your own. Ideas expressed in copyrighted material of another author must be properly credited when used. Quotation marks are not necessary if you paraphrase someone's writing; however, a footnote reference should appear with any expression of ideas not your own.
- Sometimes giving credit for another person's work is not enough. You may need to obtain permission from the individual or organization to use the materials.

Office Procedures Reinforcement

1. Define the term "reprographics," and describe the four categories of copiers.
2. Name and describe four special features available on a copier.
3. Explain how the office professional can help reduce copying abuses.
4. Describe the advantages and disadvantages of a centralized copy center.
5. Explain the importance of a shredder and its relation to office technology.

Critical Thinking Activity

Roberto Rodriquez is an assistant in the sales department of Patal, Incorporated. He is responsible for making all the photocopies for his workgroup. Roberto's supervisor has been asking him to make 20 copies of a monthly newsletter and distribute it to everyone in the department. Roberto has done so, but he does not believe he is behaving ethically. The company orders only one copy from the publisher. The newsletter has a statement that reads: "No part of this publication may be reproduced in any form without the prior written permission of the publisher." Roberto is becoming more and more concerned about his supervisor's request and his own complicity in the process. Is what Roberto is doing illegal? What responsibility does the supervisor have? What should Roberto do? Should he continue to copy the materials or refuse to do so? If he decides to refuse to copy the materials, whom should he talk with about the problem?

Office Applications

OA7-1 (Goals 1 and 2)
As a team of five (four of your classmates and you), visit a technologically up-to-date office to discover the types of copiers and fax machines used in the office.
Ask these questions:

- What type of copiers do you have?
- What are the features of the copiers that you use?
- Do you use digital copiers?
- Do you use multifunction units?
- Do you have both centralized and decentralized copy centers?
- What type of fax machines do you use?
- What are the features on your fax machines?

Prepare a written report of your findings and submit it to your instructor, giving the name of the organization you visited. Use the interoffice memorandum on the student template disk in file OA02-1b.doc in writing the memo to your instructor. Save with a new name. If there is a fax machine available to you, and your instructor has access to a fax machine, fax your memorandum to your instructor. Write a thank-you note to the organization you visited. Be prepared to present your findings to the class as an oral report.

OA7-2 (Goal 3)

You have been asked, along with two of your classmates, to serve on a committee to recommend a copier for your department. There are 30 people in your department, with a number of copying needs; two copiers may be needed to meet these needs. Explain how you would go about making the recommendation. What selection criteria would you use? Your committee is also responsible for making recommendations about maintenance. Include your maintenance recommendations as part of the report. Submit your report to your instructor.

OA7-3 (Goal 4)

You have been with your company for six months; you are an assistant to one of the vice presidents. Before joining this company, you worked as an office professional for a period of five years. You like your supervisor, he has supported you, and he has told you that he thinks you are doing a good job. However, you have growing concerns with what is happening in the company and in your office. In your previous job, you encountered none of these requests; you also did not encounter the management behaviors you have seen. Here are some of your concerns.

- The first month of your tenure at the company you were asked by your employer to make three copies of a new software package for the other office professionals in your area. You made the copies.
- Repeatedly, your supervisor has given you articles from magazines and books to make several copies; he then has told you to send the articles out to his colleagues across the nation. You have done so.
- Today, the president of the company came into your office from a meeting he was in with your supervisor; he handed you a book chapter to copy and asked that you send the 15 copies to a list of administrators. You made the copies and mailed them.

Remembering what you have learned in Chapter 4 and now in this chapter, answer these questions.

- Have you behaved ethically? Why or why not?
- Has your supervisor behaved ethically? Why or why not?
- Has the president of the company behaved ethically? Why or why not?
- What should you do about your growing concerns?

Write a note to your instructor using the interoffice memorandum on the student template disk in file OA7-3, giving your thoughtful answers to these questions and a rationale for your answers.

OA7-4 (Goal 5)

You have been assigned to a project team to develop an office procedures manual. As a member of the team, part of your assignment is to design a cover. The manual will be reproduced on a high-volume copier and will be bound on the left. The cover will be reproduced in blue ink. Include the name of the document (Office Procedures Manual) and the company (People First International). You are to use different type styles and graphics to make the cover attractive. Make copies of your cover for members of your class and submit one to your instructor.

OA7-5 (Goal 5)

A section on printing services for the office procedures manual has been drafted. Part of the text appears on your template disk, file OA07-5.doc. Revisions and additions to the text are provided in your Applications Workbook on pages 45–47. Key the document, making the necessary changes, and print a copy for your instructor.

Online Research Application

ORA7-6 (Goals 1 and 2)

Using the Internet, search for the latest information on copiers and fax machines. Write a report on your findings, giving your sources. Submit your report to your instructor.

CHAPTER 8

The Virtual Office

YOUR GOALS

1. Describe the virtual office.
2. Identify the qualities needed to be successful in a virtual environment.
3. Explain how to establish a virtual office.

You learned in Chapter 1 that technology has spawned the virtual concept, which means that through technology an individual may be physically in one location and virtually present in another. The growth of technology that supports this concept has resulted in our present workforce viewing the nature of work in new and different ways. In other words, the traditional nine-to-five office, although still very present in our work world, has a challenger in the virtual office for millions of people.

The virtual office has a number of variations. For example, it may be one in which an individual is:

- Employed by an organization and works at the organization's office for a portion of a day or a week and at his or her home for the remainder of the time

- Employed by an organization but works full-time from the home
- Self-employed and contracts his or her services to individual organizations
- Self-employed and produces a product or service that is sold to the public

Each of these situations requires that the individual view the job in different ways than in the past. It requires that the individual give careful consideration to goals, personality traits, needs, and home situation. In this chapter you will learn more about the virtual office, some of the characteristics it takes to be successful in the virtual environment, and how you can set up a virtual office.

Virtual Office Growth

The number of people working in virtual office situations has grown tremendously in the last few years, and projections are that the growth will continue and even escalate. Here are a few of the statistics:

- Home-based workers can be found in over 30 million households in the United States.
- The number of U.S. households with a computer is roughly 40 percent.
- Millions of people worldwide use cellular phones.[1]
- According to Pew Research Center, more than 25 percent of Americans use the Internet every day.
- A 1998 study revealed that more than 10 million people had bought something over the Internet in 1997, with the expectation of over 17 million in 1998.[2]
- More than 11 million Americans are telecommuting at least one day a month.
- Government officials have projected that by the year 2002, the federal government will have 15 percent of its workers working from home.[3]

What do all these seemingly diverse statistics have to do with the virtual office growth? Their relevance and relationship are considered in the next sections.

Organizational Interest

Dramatic changes have occurred in the workplace. Organizations, even some of the world's largest ones such as General Motors and Ford, are downsizing, outsourcing and **off-loading.** Off-loading is another name for outsourcing, meaning that part of the work of the organization is done by outside contractors. In today's international economy, organizations must stay as flexible as possible. Businesses must be able to compete internationally. Downsizing and outsourcing or off-loading provide organizations with flexibility; they are not constrained by a large, full-time workforce. A great deal of their work can be done by individual contractors or by people employed part-time by the organization to produce a particular service or product. In either example, the people may work in virtual environments.

---

[1]David H. Bangs, Jr., and Andi Axman, *Launching Your Home-Based Business* (Chicago: Upstart Publishing Company, 1998).

[2]Gary Hamel and Jeff Sampler, "The E-Corporation," *Fortune* (December 7, 1998), 82.

[3]"Telecommuting Grows in Popularity," *Managing Office Technology* (October 1997), 8.

One way in which organizations maintain flexibility is through outsourcing. *Courtesy of © PhotoDisc, Inc.*

Technological Growth

The growth of computers, fax machines, cellular phones, email, and other technological equipment that you learned about in Chapter 5 has given us the possibility of working at almost anyplace and at anytime. The continued decrease in cost of this equipment has made it possible for the average American household to own and use numerous pieces of technological equipment. The 40 percent of American households that own computers underscore the fact that computers are affordable for the average American. The millions of people worldwide who use cellular phones attest to the popularity of such technological equipment. The amazing growth of the Internet, with more than 25 percent of Americans using it daily, is an example of how technologically competent we have become and how willing we are to embrace the use of technology. The 17+ million people who purchased something from the Internet in 1998 as compared to 10 million in 1997 (a 70 percent increase) reinforces the willingness of individuals and organizations to use technological tools.

Worker Interest

There are several factors that contribute to worker interest in a virtual working environment, some of which are:

- The growth of women in the workforce, with presently 46 percent of the labor force being women and the number projected to increase
- The growth in the number of two-career families, with both husband and wife working
- The need for child care for young children
- The increasing longevity of our population that brings with it the care of the elderly, which is often the responsibility of two-career families
- The growth of our cities that often causes transportation problems in getting to and from work
- The relocation of companies to other cities, with the resulting possibility of some workers not relocating but becoming virtual employees of the company

All of these factors make the flexibility of the home-based virtual office attractive to a large number of our workforce. The statistics of more than 30 million households having a home-based worker and 11 million Americans telecommuting are evidence of how popular this trend is. In addition, the government's projection of 15 percent of its workers telecommuting by 2002 indicates that the growth of virtual workers will continue. Also, as more and more organizations continue to downsize and outsource part of their work, many workers have had to rethink their definition of work. No longer is lifetime employment at one company likely. In many cases, workers have had to analyze what situation will ensure financial security for themselves and their families. Sometimes the answer is found in the virtual work environment.

The Future

The future for virtual work is bright. The factors that have been presented in the previous sections are not expected to change. All projections are that the interest in virtual work will continue and the actual numbers of people working in this environment will increase. In fact, some futurists are predicting that in the twenty-first century many jobs will be home based, with meetings taking place via wall screens. In such future scenarios, knowledge robots may handle much of the routine work. For example, the office worker may tell the robot to do a search on international markets and provide a report on one of the screens in the virtual worker's home.[4] The virtual worker then compiles the information into a report for the executive.

Your Goals and Personality Traits

Before you decide to become a virtual employee of an organization or be a self-employed virtual worker, there are a number of questions you need to ask yourself. If you are going to be successful in such an environment, you need to understand what your goals are. You need to spend some time thinking objectively about what you hope to accomplish. You also need to be clear about what traits you have. For example, do you enjoy working alone? Are you a self-starter? This section will help you think about what you want to do and whether or not you have the characteristics to be successful in a virtual environment.

Goal Identification

What are your goals? Do the goals listed below match your own? If so, you may be interested in pursuing the possibility of working in a virtual environment.

- Independence
- Flexibility
- Control
- Ability to set the work schedule
- Family time—time with children, spouse, and parents

If you had trouble answering whether or not these are your goals, perhaps you need to spend some time thinking about what your goals are. Stephen Covey, a well-known authority in the area of establishing goals, suggests asking these questions as you begin to think about what you want to do.

---

[4]Brendan I. Koerner, "Plugging in Einstein," *U.S. News & World Report* (January 4, 1999), 72.

- What do I feel are my greatest strengths?
- What strengths have others who know me well noticed in me?
- What have been my happiest moments in life? Why were they happy?
- When I daydream, what do I see myself doing?
- When I look at my work life, what activities do I consider of greatest worth?
- What quality-of-life results do I desire that are different from what I now have?[5]

Once you ask and answer these questions, Covey suggests that you write a **mission statement** to clarify your goals. A thoughtful mission statement:

- Fulfills your own unique capacity to contribute
- Includes fulfillment in physical, social, mental, and spiritual dimensions
- Is based on quality-of-life results
- Deals with both vision and values
- Deals with all the significant roles in your life—personal, family, work, community
- Inspires you to achieve[6]

To understand more about how a mission statement is written, notice Figure 8-1, which shows one person's mission statement. If you are self-employed and have established a company, it is also a good idea to write a mission statement for the company. Such a statement helps you keep focused on the direction you have determined for the company. Two organizational statements are shown in Figure 8-2—one for a nonprofit organization and one for a for-profit organization.

[5]Stephen R. Covey, Roger Merrill, and Rebecca R. Merrill, *First Things First* (New York: Simon & Schuster, 1994).
[6]Covey, *First Things First*.

PERSONAL MISSION STATEMENT

My mission is to:

Discover and use all of my talents and abilities.

Treasure my family.

Live true to the principles I hold dear (self-sufficiency, honesty, integrity, and giving).

Be an outstanding worker—one who contributes to my employers and clients.

Provide adequate income for my family.

FIGURE 8-1. Personal mission statement.

Personality Traits

In addition to understanding your goals and being clear about them by writing a mission statement that will guide you in the pursuit of those goals, you need to be realistic about who you are. What personality traits do you have? How do you like to work? What traits do you have that contribute to your success?

If you are interested in working in a virtual environment, these traits are important to success.

Disciplined. Do you have **discipline?** Are you able to work when there are many distractions? Working in a virtual home environment means that there are generally a number of distractions. The telephone rings. It may be business, or it may be personal. The doorbell rings. The dog barks. FedEx delivers a package. One of your clients or customers calls. Children come in from school, or the baby cries. Being disciplined means that you know how to work with these distractions because you generally cannot eliminate them.

When working from home, discipline includes these activities:

- Set a routine. Just as you would in a traditional office environment,

FIGURE 8-2. Organizational Mission Statements.

establish a routine. For example, check your to-do list each morning and check your email and voice mail two or three times per day.

- Establish times to communicate with the office if you are telecommuting.

- Create a visual signal for your office door or workstation that lets your family know you are working and cannot be disturbed. A red sign on the door may be appropriate. Also, if you are leaving your home office to go get a soda, you might wear a tag that states: "I'm working." This tag is a symbol for your family not to stop you for home duties at this time.

- Shut your office door at night. The virtual worker can overdo the work hours

Being disciplined means that you know how to get work done, even with multiple distractions. *Courtesy of © PhotoDisc, Inc.*

just as the traditional employee can. Determine the number of hours you will spend working, and then stick to your rules. Remember that the most productive worker is a balanced worker—one who knows how to balance work, family, and play.

Self-Starter. Are you a **self-starter?** A self-starter knows what needs to be done and is anxious to get it done. A self-starter is really the opposite of a procrastinator. The procrastinator always has an excuse why a project cannot be started or cannot be completed. If you have worked at all, you have probably met several procrastinators. They are the people:

- Who always have filing to be done
- Whose desk is always stacked with papers that they can never find
- Who never accomplish what is on their to-do list—in fact, they probably don't even have a to-do list

The procrastinator will not be successful in a virtual environment.

The self-starter generally has numerous items on his or her to-do list and not only gets them accomplished, but feels a real sense of satisfaction as he or she is able to mark the items off the list. The self-starter is also eager to begin the next to-do list, enjoying a sense of pride and accomplishment from being able to do a number of tasks well.

Organized. **Organization** is always important on the job, but particularly so in a virtual situation. An individual must be organized in order to juggle numerous tasks and successfully confront many interruptions. A person working in a virtual environment must be able to plan and organize time well, and to implement the time management techniques described in Chapter 3. These include:

- Setting priorities
- Organizing the workstation
- Simplifying repetitive work
- Handling paperwork as few times as possible
- Using time management systems, such as electronic calendaring and scheduling software

Creative. In the traditional office situation, you generally have someone you can go to for help in solving a particular problem or situation. Not so in a virtual environment. You have to be a **creative**

Adam®   **by Brian Basset**

problem solver. If you are working on a report that has graphics and you can't get the graphics software package to work properly, there is no computer expert in the next office to help. You have to figure it out or find someone who can assist you. If your child develops a fever while you are working under a tight deadline on a project, you have to solve the problem. The old proverb "Necessity is the mother of invention" is particularly true for the virtual worker. Whatever occurs, you must be creative enough to find a solution.

Good Communicator. You have already learned that it is important to be a **good communicator** and to continue to grow in your skills in this area. Such skills are crucial to the virtual worker, who must communicate with a variety of people (executives, coworkers, clients, employees at the local print shop, and so forth). You generally do not have the luxury of communicating with these people often enough to know their communication styles well. Also, many times contacts with these people happen through email, voice mail, the telephone, or fax; you may never see them in person. These situations demand that you not only are a good communicator who constantly strives to improve your skills, but also a person who cares about others. When communications go poorly, you must step back and analyze what happened and why it happened. Realize that you can learn from your mistakes. It is a good idea to remember the Golden Rule—treat others as you would have them treat you.

Energetic. The virtual worker must be **energetic.** There is no one to set the time clock, no one to determine the length of breaks or lunchtime. It is important that you set and maintain a schedule that allows you to get your work done. Also, a

The beauty of the virtual environment is that you can work anyplace and at anytime. *Courtesy of © PhotoDisc, Inc.*

project may take you much longer than you had planned. You have to be willing to work long hours if necessary. However, remember that you have already learned that you need to be a balanced worker. You don't work late because you have been undisciplined or disorganized; you do so only occasionally when a deadline demands it. Sometimes, you might even have to take work with you on vacation. And that is not all bad. We can often be more productive working in a cabin at the top of a mountain or a cottage by the sea. The beauty of the virtual environment is that you can work anyplace and at anytime.

Self-Confident. As a virtual worker, you have to know what you do well. When you do something well, you need to take the time to congratulate yourself on your success. You may even set up your own reward system—however small. Maybe the reward is as simple as a 30-minute break for a walk in the park when you finish a particularly tough project that has been done extremely well. You don't have coworkers or a supervisor to tell you when you have done a good job. You must have the **self-confidence** to be your own support system. Additionally, you must have the self-confidence to admit when you cannot do something well. Then you find someone to help you, you decline the job, or you decide you will develop the needed skills.

Challenges

Just as the virtual worker has advantages, so does the virtual worker have challenges to meet. For example, if you decide that you want to work in a virtual environ-ment either full- or part-time, you will need to adjust to the isolation of the environment. You don't have coworkers constantly around you. In addition, the scope of your responsibility is usually much greater; you have to perform all tasks and balance job demands and family demands. All three challenges are addressed in the next section.

Isolation. The number-one challenge for many people, particularly if they have been working in a busy office with numerous coworkers, is the **isolation** of working alone. You miss the ability to take a break and talk with a coworker or go to lunch with several coworkers. You miss the noise of the office. You miss the routine of commuting to work and observing the

If isolation becomes a factor when working from home, form a support group. Invite other at-home-office types over. *ADAM © Brian Bassett. Reprinted with permission of UNIVERSAL PRESS SYNDICATE. All rights reserved.*

hustle and bustle of the outside world. You miss discussing work problems and how to solve them with your coworkers. You miss the opportunity to talk with a coworker about an exciting new project.

As a virtual worker, you must find ways to lessen your isolation. Here are a few suggestions.

- Join a gym; exercise with people; sign up for an aerobics class.
- Make arrangements to have lunch once every two weeks with someone who is in a similar business.
- If you are a full-time employee of a business, take advantage of company-sponsored professional development activities.
- Go to an occasional movie in the afternoon.
- Turn on the television to a news program during your lunch to get in touch with what is happening in the outside world.

Scope of Responsibility. Another challenge for the virtual worker is the **scope of responsibility.** With all the technological support that you have, you still do not have people support. There is no one to open the mail, answer the phone, fix the fax machine, change the toner in the printer, set up a new computer program, and a myriad of other things that a person working in an office generally has help doing. If you have worked as an office professional full-time in an office and then decide to work at home, you may miss having someone to assist you when you have technical problems with your software or equipment. You may also miss having someone to whom you may transfer your phone when you have to leave the office for a short period of time. Here are some suggestions for dealing with this challenge.

- Learn the software manufacturers that have help lines; keep the phone numbers handy.
- Use Internet sources. For example, you can find out where to get technical help, where to get software and equipment information, and how to download library information through on-line sources such as www.smalloffice.com/expert and www.aboutwork.com/experts. These sources also provide advice from experts and chat rooms for talking with others who have similar interests. (As you read this chapter, you will notice that there are several URL addresses given for online assistance. These resources were current at the time of this book's publication; however, Internet addresses do change. If you do not find these resources on the Internet, there probably will be other similar ones that you may reference.)
- Keep handy the help numbers of the manufacturers of your computer, fax, printer, and so forth.
- Know how to get assistance with Internet problems; for example, if you have AOL or some other online service, know the telephone number to call to get technical help.
- Take a short course from your local college on a new software package that you are going to use.
- Call a temporary agency for part-time support if the job becomes too much for you to handle productively.

Job Demands versus Home Demands. Regardless of where you work, juggling **job demands versus home demands** is never easy. There is always the problem of the sick child, spouse, or parent. There is the school event for one of your children that you need to attend during work hours. However, dealing with such conflicting demands is more difficult for the person working at home. The family often assumes that because you are physically present, you can stop at any point and assist with whatever the issue or problem may be. Obviously, such is not true. Unless you help your family understand what you are doing and limit their unreasonable expectations of you, you cannot be successful as a virtual worker. Here are some suggestions to help you solve the problem.

- Hold a family meeting to explain how you will be working and what your work will be.
- Determine a division of household labor. Establish the household tasks that will be done by each member of the family. What are your spouse's responsibilities? What are the children's responsibilities? If you have parents living with you, what are their responsibilities? Who does the cooking? Who buys the groceries? Who cleans?
- Find a house-cleaning service or an individual who can come in if needed; hire someone full-time if the workload becomes overwhelming.
- Determine if you need someone to help with the children for a period of time after they come in from school. If you do, call a child-care referral service and/or ask friends for recommendations. You need to know that you have a competent, caring individual looking after your children.
- Keep the lines of communication open with your family. When you feel someone is not doing his or her fair share, communicate your feelings. You may want to have a family meeting once each week to discuss how the division of responsibilities is working and to reassign if necessary.

- Do the heavy cleaning chores over the weekend when you are not working.
- Do not expect perfection from your family as they perform tasks. They may not do it as well as you would; don't hold them to such a standard.
- Praise family members for doing tasks well.
- Try to keep your home a low-maintenance one. In other words, do not buy furniture or carpet that requires constant cleaning.

A weekly family meeting can be used to assign household tasks.
Courtesy of International Business Machines Corporation. Unauthorized use not permitted.

Company Expectations

Much of the information presented to this point in the chapter has assumed that you are working in a virtual situation most of the time. However, you may be working at an office for much of the time and at home only a few days out of the week or month. If so, your situation has some different nuances. First, you need to be certain that you know your job very well. If you do not, you will have trouble working at home. Next, you need to be very clear with your supervisor about his or her expectations of you. Here are some items you should discuss with your supervisor if you are a full-time company employee telecommuting a few days each week or each month.

- What are your job responsibilities?
- How will you be evaluated on the accomplishment of your responsibilities?
- What meetings are you expected to attend at the office?
- What assistance can you expect from the company? For example, will they provide you with a computer, fax, telephone (with speakerphone capability), copier, online connection, and so forth?
- If a pager or cell phone is not part of the equipment provided, ask for one. You need some way of knowing that someone is trying to contact you if you are not in your virtual office.
- If you are going to be communicating with other telecommuters or the office staff, request the same computer and software that other office workers have so that messages and files can be sent back and forth with no problems.
- If working at home is not satisfactory for you or for your employer, what happens? Can you go back to the office full-time?

Once you have clarity from your supervisor as to what you are expected to do, your next step is to determine how you will keep in touch with your coworkers. You remain part of an office team even if you are a telecommuter. Think creatively about how you might keep in touch; here are several suggestions.

- Suggest to your supervisor that regular conference calls be scheduled for the two of you to discuss directions, issues, and so forth.
- Ask for a contact name from the technology staff that you can call if you have equipment or software problems.
- Schedule specific times to talk with your coworkers. Some of these talks may be through a teleconference or speakerphone; however, it is also important to schedule some in-person meetings.
- Utilize your software capabilities to let individuals in the office know where you are so that you do not miss important meetings or messages. For example, use the "Out-of-the-Office Attendant" in Microsoft Exchange that tells senders of email messages where you are and whether or not you can check your email.
- Attend some functions at the office; these may be professional development sessions or special celebrations, such as the annual company picnic.
- Invite your coworkers to your virtual office for a meeting; this will help them understand how you function in your virtual workplace. It also helps them understand that even though your office is a virtual one, it is one where legitimate work occurs.

Occasionally, work teams may meet in the home of the virtual employee. © *CORBIS*.

The Virtual Office Setup

There are a number of elements you need to consider when setting up your virtual office. What type of work are you going to be doing? Where should your virtual office be? How much space do you need to accomplish your work? What furnishings will you need? What equipment is needed? What types of services will you need? Through studying this section, you will have a much better understanding of how to set up and maintain a virtual office.

Type of Work

Before you think about the location and size of your office, you need to think through what your needs will be. Ask yourself these questions:

- What will my work be?

- Will I be working on highly technical material that requires a distraction-free environment?
- Will I be meeting with coworkers and customers or clients in my workspace?
- Do I need to have a space that will not be invaded by any member of my family?
- Can I share my space with my spouse? For example, if you have a spouse who also telecommutes or works in a virtual situation, is it possible to have a two-person office?
- What environmental factors are important? For example, are you a person who works more productively when close to a window? Can you work in small spaces? Do you need a relatively open environment?

Once you ask and answer these questions, you are ready to consider location and size.

Location and Size

If you need a distraction-free workplace, you will need to locate your office away from the family area of your home. A spare bedroom, a basement room, or an unused formal dining area may be the answer. If clients, customers, and/or coworkers will be meeting with you in person occasionally, the space needs to be as close to an entrance as possible. You do not want these individuals to have to walk through your entire home before reaching your office. If noise bothers you, you also need to give consideration to the neighbors you have. For example, if you have neighbors on one side of your home who are extremely noisy, with barking dogs and yelling children, you will not want to locate your office on that side of your home.

On the other hand, if you work best where there is considerable noise and movement, you may choose to have your office in an area that is close to the family. Your office does not have to be a separate room; it might be a portion of a room, with dividers and screens to partition it off. You also might have an office that closes up when you are not using it. This type of situation can work effectively if you are using the office on a limited basis; for example, telecommuting only one day a week. Figure 8-3 on page 209 shows a desk that holds a computer, printer, monitor, and other office equipment and then closes to become a coffee table. When in use as a desk, it rises up to a 30-inch height (or lower, depending on your needs). In addition, it includes space for files and supplies.[7]

The location you choose needs to have adequate lighting for your equipment. You will remember in Chapter 2 you learned about the ergonomic factors that affect your work, with lighting being one of them. You do not want to locate your computer so close to a window that the outside light causes a glare on your computer screen. Fluorescent lighting produces a more diffuse light. Halogen lights produce clean, natural light that helps eliminate glare.

Your location also needs to have sufficient electrical outlets and telephone jacks to accommodate your equipment needs. The electrical outlets need to be in proximity to your equipment. Stringing extension cords across a room can be dangerous. Even if you have declared your office space off-limits to your children, there will be occasions when they come into the space. You need to be sure that you do not have loose electrical cords and

When working from home, it is critical to stake out your territory. *ADAM © Brian Bassett. Reprinted with permission of UNIVERSAL PRESS SYNDICATE. All rights reserved.*

---

[7]Catherine Greenman, "3 Smart Setups," *Home Office Computing* (August 1998), 76–77.

FIGURE 8-3. Convertible work center.

seat of your chair should be adjustable. The ergonomic factors that you were introduced to in Chapter 6 apply here. Your desk should be deep enough to place your monitor at a comfortable viewing distance, 16 to 20 inches.

You should have adequate storage for your materials and supplies. You may buy a desk unit that has storage space built in. Figure 8-4 shows a desk configuration with storage space. Additionally, you will probably need at least one file cabinet, a two-drawer or a four-drawer one depending on your space and your needs. However, do not assume that you will need to file all of your papers in hard-copy form. Take advantage of some of the paperless software that is available. For example, through the use of scanners and CD writers, you can quickly reduce the hard copy paper to technological storage. The falling prices of technological equipment now make it affordable for the home office. Scanners, a good tool for reducing the amount of paper, are illustrative of the falling prices. Today, small scanners can be purchased for under $100, whereas in the past they were five or six times that price.

To give you some idea of how this type of storage can reduce your need for space, present technology allows 54,000 pages of double-spaced text to fit on one CD. You can also transfer material that has been stored on removable hard disks such as Jaz or Zip cartridges to CDs and

unprotected electrical outlets, particularly if you have small children. If you have a separate room for your office, it is a good idea to put a security lock on the door when you are not in the room.

Another important consideration for office location is its proximity to a bathroom. You do not want to spend time climbing stairs or going to the opposite end of the house for bathroom facilities. Locate your office as close to a bathroom as possible. You also need to be able to control the heating and cooling in the room. Working in an environment that is too hot or too cold certainly contributes to lessened productivity.

Office Furnishings

Determine the type of chair and desk that will work best for you. Both the back and

FIGURE 8-4. Workstation with storage space.

sponds to callers with the name of your business or the name of the company for whom you work. It also reduces confusion in the household, particularly if you have teenagers who use the telephone frequently. Separate telephone lines for business use can be deducted on your income tax; more detail is provided about home office deductions later in this chapter.

If you have a cell phone and are making only a few long-distance calls, you may want to use cell cards. For example, if you use your cell phone for a half hour one month, then not at all the next month, prepaid cards will save you money. However, if you make numerous long-distance calls, regular service plans are a better bargain. Cell cards are readily available from local establishments. For example, 7-Eleven® stores sell prepaid cell phone cards for such companies as Cellular One,® BellSouth,® and GTE.®

Remember what you learned in Chapter 2 about color. Color influences your productivity as well as the morale of any of your clients or coworkers. Warm colors such as yellow, red, and orange create cheerful surroundings. Cool colors such as green and blue produce a calm and tranquil atmosphere. Depending on your preferences and the space that you have for your office, you may want to paint the space a color that is pleasing to you.

save money. For example, one Jaz hard disk (at a cost of over $100) can be dumped onto two CDs (at a cost of $4). The costs given here are approximate at the time of the publication of this text. As you read this text, the costs may have dropped even more due to continual decreasing costs on technological equipment and supplies.

If you are going to be using the telephone frequently and/or need to have a modem for online communication, you may want to consider a separate phone line into your home. This approach allows you to have a voice-mail system that re-

Just as you personalize your space in a company office, you will probably want to do the same in your home office. Add whatever family pictures or mementos are pleasing to you. If you get a smile on your face by looking at a picture on your desk of your son or daughter, keep it there. However, don't clutter your desk or space with personal items to the point that you do not have enough workspace.

Equipment

How do you determine the equipment that will meet your needs? First, educate yourself about the possibilities. Read computer periodicals such as *Home Office Computing, PC World*, and *PC Computing*. There is a wealth of information there concerning all types of equipment—computers, printers, fax machines, copiers, scanners, and so forth. There is also software information in these and similar publications. Generally, your hardware does not have to be as expensive as what you would buy in an office. For example, your needs are not as great for storage capacity; your copier does not need to perform as many different functions; and your printer will not be in use as much. These differences mean that you can buy hardware at a fraction of the cost of that used in the traditional office.

In addition to reading periodicals, here are some other steps you can take to help you learn more about equipment.

- Conduct online research; many equipment and software manufacturers advertise their products through the Internet.
- Shop your local computer stores.
- Talk with people who use the tech-

nology; for example, discuss the best buys with the computer technicians at the office or friends who are computer literate.

Once you decide what equipment you need, arrange it in an efficient manner. For example, your computer, printer, fax, scanner, and copier need to be in proximity to each other. An L-shaped arrangement, shown in Figure 8-5, can provide immediate access to all of your main equipment.

FIGURE 8-5. L-shaped workstation.

Invest in a **UPS** (uninterruptible power supply). This device connects between your computer, other electronic equipment, and a power source to protect your equipment and software in case of a power outage. It is inexpensive and well worth the investment.

Software

The type of software you will need is dependent upon the tasks that you will be performing. As an office professional, you can assume that you will need an office suite package. You learned in Chapter 6 that these packages include word processing, spreadsheet, database, presentation, and information management programs. Generally, all of these programs will be helpful to you in your virtual office.

If you need a specialized package for a short period of time, you may choose to rent it through the Internet. You can rent enhanced-productivity business tools that were formerly available only to large corporations. For example, if you are involved in a one-time publishing project and do not want to pay several hundred dollars for a software package, you can rent the software for a few dollars a month. Although the rental possibilities through the Internet are limited at the present time, this market is expected to be much larger in the future.

The virtual worker no longer has to be concerned about affixing postage to correspondence. SmartStamp®, a software package from Information Based Indicia (IBI), allows you to download postage from the Internet, output the data to a standard printer, and affix the printout as you would an ordinary stamp. Each SmartStamp has a unique digital signature to prevent tampering or duplication. You

SmartStamp allows you to download postage from the Internet, output to a printer, and affix the printout as you would an ordinary stamp. *Courtesy of Pitney Bowes.*

can print stamps on labels or envelopes. The company is also marketing an optional scale that attaches to your computer and calculates postage automatically. The E-Stamp Internet Postage sells for slightly less than $200 and is available for Windows and NT operating systems.[8]

Certain software can be downloaded from the Internet. Both http://www. smalloffice/com/expert and http://www.aboutwork.com/experts have software that can be downloaded. In the future, it is projected that additional software will be available as a download from the Internet.

Supplies

If you are telecommuting, you will be furnished with supplies from your company, such as letterhead, memorandum forms, envelopes, business cards, and so forth. If you are self-employed, you will probably want to design your own stationery and business cards. One of your local office supply stores or printing businesses can assist in the design and print the items relatively inexpensively and quickly. The growth of such businesses as Kinko's, PakMail, Office Depot, and other similar businesses attests to the number of people who are working in virtual office situations and need assistance quickly and inexpensively.

Other supplies that you will need include toner for your printer and fax, printer paper, filing supplies, mailing labels, filing labels, and disks. As you are setting up your office, find out where you can get these supplies. Keep extras on hand, so that you do not have to chase supplies when you are pressured to get out a project.

Services

What types of services do you need as a virtual worker? Make a list of those services and then find out where you can get them. Hopefully, they can be found close to your home so that you do not have to waste time on the highway. Here are two services that you will likely need.

- Mailing services
- Printing and copying services

For example, if you are engaged in a project in which you will be printing and binding several hundred copies of a document, a printing service can perform this task quickly and fairly inexpensively. You just learned about a software package that is available for calculating postage. However, if you are not sending out large mailings, you may find it to your advantage to use a local mailing service. The service can send items by FedEx or UPS; they can also package your materials.

Tax Benefits

Your virtual office can provide some tax benefits for you. The **IRS** (Internal Revenue Service) rule is that a deduction is allowed for a home office if it is used exclusively on a regular basis as:

- Your principal place of business
- A place of business for meeting or dealing with patients, clients, or customers in the normal course of business

You also may be able to claim an accelerated depreciation deduction and a first-year expensing deduction for your home computer provided you use the computer over

---

[8]"U.S. Postal Service Goes Digital," *Home Office Computing* (August 1998), 17.

SOME DEDUCTIBLE HOME-OFFICE EXPENSES

- Expenses you pay to:
  - —Produce or collect income
  - —Manage, conserve, or maintain property held for producing income
- Legal fees
- Insurance
- Mortgage interest
- Rent
- Utilities and services
- Telephone services
- Repairs
- Security systems
- Depreciation
- Certain travel expenses; i.e., gasoline, airline fares, food, and lodging in relation to travel for your business

Note: This list is a partial one. Check with the IRS or a CPA for a complete and updated list of business expenses.

FIGURE 8-6. Deductible home-office expenses. Source: *IRS Publication 587: Business Use of Your Home.*

50 percent of the time for business. In addition, you may deduct certain other expenses when these are expenses you pay to:

- Produce or collect income
- Manage, conserve, or maintain property held for producing income

Figure 8-6 lists some of the expenses that are deductible.

Additional information on IRS deductions can be obtained from the *IRS Publication 587: Business Use of Your Home.* It is a good idea to check with a CPA as you set up your virtual office, since it is necessary to maintain careful records if you plan to deduct them on your income tax.

Health, Life Insurance, and Retirement Benefits

In the past if you were employed full-time by a company, you were assured of health benefits, with the company paying almost all of these benefits. Today, the situation is very different. Most companies still pay certain benefits; however, the employee is assuming a larger and larger portion of the benefit package. For example, you may pay 50 percent of your health benefits. If you are self-employed in a virtual situation, you will need to pay for your own health insurance. Finding a health benefits package that meets your needs and your family's needs is not an easy task. It must be researched carefully. Figure 8-7 lists several questions that you should ask before deciding on a package.

Life insurance may or may not be offered to you if you are working full-time for an organization. If you are self-employed, it will be your responsibility to determine if you need life insurance; and, if so, what type. It is a complex issue and demands your attention and careful study.

QUESTIONS TO ASK BEFORE PURCHASING HEALTH INSURANCE

- What type of coverage should I get?
- How much will the various types of coverage cost? What will be the yearly and monthly cost?
- Do I need to cover my family or is my family covered by my spouse?
- What is the cost of covering my family?
- Does the chamber of commerce or any professional association offer health insurance plans to members?
- What is the reputation of the insurance carrier?
- How would my health be rated?

FIGURE 8-7. Questions to ask before purchasing health insurance.

Several items that need to be considered before purchasing life insurance are given in Figure 8-8.

In addition, you must be concerned about retirement benefits, since fewer and fewer companies provide retirement packages that will cover your expenses during your retirement years. Also, all projections indicate that there will not be enough money in the not too distant future to provide for the following U.S. government programs unless additional dollars are funneled into the area by our government. How to solve this problem has been an ongoing debate at the federal level for a number of years.

- **Social Security**—A U.S. government program financed by employer and employee payments that provides retirement insurance, disability benefits, and unemployment compensation.
- **Medicaid**— A U.S. health care program reimbursing hospitals and physicians for care of those individuals needing financial assistance.
- **Medicare**—A program under the U.S. Social Security Administration that reimburses hospitals and physicians for medical care provided to qualifying people over 65 years of age.

Although the scope of this chapter does not allow for detailed information about retirement options, you must be concerned about providing adequately for you and your family during the retirement years. Options include **IRAs** (individual retirement accounts) and investments in **mutual funds** (funds that include a combination of stocks and bonds purchased through a mutual fund company) or individual **stocks** (ownership in a company) and **bonds** (a debt owed by an organization), to name a few. You should research carefully the various options available to you and plan accordingly.

> ### QUESTIONS TO ASK BEFORE PURCHASING LIFE INSURANCE
>
> - Do I need life insurance? Life insurance does not directly benefit you; it does benefit those you determine as beneficiaries—your family, organizations, and so forth. Before you decide abou purchasing life insurance, you need to ask yourself if someone depends on you for his or her income. If so, you will probably want to purchase life insurance.
>
> - How much life insurance do I need? Families with one wage-earner and a spouse who stays at home, will need to have higher levels of coverage than those families where both spouses work. Single individuals who support elderly parents or relatives will have different needs.
>
> - What kind of life insurance do I need? Life insurance generally comes in two types—**term life** and **permanent** policies. Term life insurance is insurance protection for a specific period time. It usually has a low payment and no cash value. The death benefit is paid only if the insured dies while the policy is in force. Permanent insurance is basically of two types—whole life or universal life. Permanent life insurance offers lifetime protection, cash or loan values, paid-up insurance options, and possible dividends.

FIGURE 8-8. Questions to ask before purchasing life insurance.

Professional Growth

As a virtual worker, it is doubly important that you continue with your professional growth. The isolation from the busy office and your coworkers can make you feel that you do not know what is happening in the world. In order to keep current, here are several suggestions:

- Network with other virtual workers. Attend seminars in your field; make an effort to meet people at these seminars. Get their business cards; call them for lunch. In other words, keep in touch with your peers. You can also talk with other virtual employees online through http://www/smalloffice.com.

- Join professional organizations. IAAP was suggested in Chapter 1. Seek out other organizations that might be of interest to you such as the Business and Professional Women or a local service club. Stay involved in your community.

- Take classes. With the virtual colleges and universities that have begun as a result of the technological capability to be online, you may prefer to take a virtual course. Although these courses do not satisfy a need to see people face-to-face, many of them have chat room capabilities that allow you to "talk" with other students via the Internet. A number of courses are available from computer classes to liberal arts studies. In addition to colleges and universities, corporations such as Bell South's World Class Campus (http://www.bstwcc.com) offer courses. Topics include computer software, conflict resolution, interviewing techniques, and time management, to name a few.

- Read. Computer periodicals were suggested earlier in this chapter. Also, read in your field. Visit your local bookstore; check out the latest books available.

SUMMARY

To reinforce what you have learned in this chapter, study this summary.

- The number of people working in virtual office situations has grown tremendously in the last few years; projections are that the growth will continue and even escalate.

- The growth of the virtual office is due in part to organizational interest, technological growth, and worker interest.

- Certain characteristics are needed to be successful in a virtual environment; some of these characteristics are:
  - Disciplined
  - Self-starter
  - Organized
  - Creative
  - Good communicator
  - Self-confident

- Challenges that must be overcome when working in a virtual environment include:
  - Isolation
  - Scope of responsibility
  - Job demands versus home demands

- If you are anticipating working virtually, know what your company expects of you and what they will provide you.

- Remain a part of the team as a virtual worker.

- Determine the type of work you will do before setting up your virtual office.

- Give consideration to the following factors when setting up your virtual office.
  - Location and size of the office
  - Office furnishings
  - Equipment and software
  - Supplies
  - Services
  - Tax benefits
  - Health insurance, and retirement benefits

- It is important that you continue with your professional growth when working virtually. Some of the ways you may do this are:
  - Network with other virtual workers.
  - Join professional organizations.
  - Take classes.
  - Read.

Key Terms

- Off-loading
- Mission statement
- Discipline
- Self-starter
- Organization
- Creative problem solver
- Good communicator
- Energetic
- Self-confidence
- Isolation
- Scope of responsibility
- Job demands versus home demands
- UPS
- IRS
- Social Security
- Medicaid
- Medicare
- IRAs
- Mutual funds
- Stocks
- Bonds

Professional Pointers

Here are some questions to ask yourself as a virtual employee.

- Am I a good problem solver?
- Am I independent?
- Do I communicate well?
- Do I set regular break times for myself?
- Am I flexible?
- Do I control my stress?
- Do I exercise frequently?
- Do I set clear limits on my work?
- Does my family understand my job and my expectations of them?
- Do I hold regular meetings with my family to discuss issues?
- Do I allocate appropriate time for both my job and my family?

Office Procedures Reinforcement

1. Describe a virtual office.
2. List the qualities needed in order to be successful as a virtual worker.
3. Explain why understanding goals is important to the virtual worker.
4. List three challenges that the virtual worker faces.
5. Explain how you can continue to grow professionally as a virtual worker.

Critical Thinking Activity

Maria has been working as a telecommuter for her company for one month. She was very pleased when her employer suggested that she could work at home. The only stipulation was that she was to attend one monthly meeting at the company. Maria has two small children—ages 2 and 4. She wanted to spend more time with her children, and she felt being a telecommuter gave her a unique opportunity for more family time. However, after one month Maria is not certain she made the right choice in deciding to work at home. Here are the problems she has faced.

Maria and her husband are splitting the child care. Her husband works from 12 noon to 8 p.m. Maria works in her home office from 7 a.m. until 12 noon and from 9 p.m. until 12 p.m. Her husband is responsible for the children from the time they wake up in the morning (approximately 7:30) until 12 noon. Maria is responsible for them from 12 noon until 8 p.m. However, the past two weeks both children have been ill; both Maria and her husband are very stressed and tired. There never seem to be enough hours in the day to get the job done. Maria missed the monthly meeting at work due to the children's illnesses. Her employer was not happy. Maria and her husband also have no help with the housework. They have not divided the duties, and they seem to scream at each other frequently about who does what. Maria feels that she has been getting her work done in a satisfactory manner; however, she feels very isolated. She has had no contact with her coworkers. Several problems have come up that she has not known how to deal with, but she coped. She feels she needs to sit down and talk with her employer about his expectations of her. Also, her company did not provide her with a fax machine, and she feels that she needs one. She doesn't know whether she should ask for it or buy it herself. Maria chose to establish her office next to the children's room. The noise is distracting for her; she works better in a quiet area.

What suggestions do you have for Maria? Should she ask to go back to the traditional office setting? Should she discuss her concerns with her employer?

Office Applications

OA8-1 (Goals 1, 2, and 3)
Select two of your classmates to work with on this project. Interview two people who are working in virtual environments. You may discover people to interview through Internet resources. Ask them to respond to these items:

- Describe your virtual office situation.
- What personal qualities are necessary in order to be successful?
- If you are a telecommuter, what does your employer provide you?
- Where is your virtual office located? What equipment do you have?
- What software do you use?

- How do you continue to grow professionally?
- What tips would you give a virtual worker?

Write up your findings and present them orally to the class. Submit your written report to your instructor.

OA8-2 (Goal 3)
Using the periodicals mentioned in this chapter or others that you identify, write a short report (two or three pages) on establishing a virtual office—equipment to use, software, furniture, supplies, and so forth. Identify your sources; submit your report to your instructor.

Online Research

ORA8-3 (Goal 3)
Choose two of your classmates to work with on this project. Using the Internet resources given in this chapter or others that you identify, determine the helps that are available to the virtual worker on the Internet. Give an oral report to the class on your findings.

Vocabulary Review

On pages 53–54 of your Applications Workbook is a Vocabulary Review, covering selected items from the vocabulary presented in Chapters 5–8. Complete these sentences and submit a copy to your instructor.

Language Skills Practice

On pages 55–56 of your Applications Workbook are sentences that need to be corrected using the rules presented in the Reference Section of your text. Correct the sentences as needed and submit your work to your instructor.

3 Office Communication

CHAPTER 9

The Communication Process

Communication is vital to the effective office; getting work done depends on it. Communication in the workplace takes several forms:

- Verbal face-to-face communication
- Nonverbal face-to-face communication
- Written communication through email, fax, computers, letters, memorandums, reports, and various other written materials
- Verbal technological communication through telephone, voice mail, and pagers
- Oral presentations

After studying this chapter, you will understand more about the communication process, including both verbal and nonverbal communication. You will also

YOUR GOALS

Your goals as you study this chapter are to:

1. Describe the relationship between communication and self-concept.
2. Explain the communication process.
3. Identify communication barriers and techniques for reducing the barriers.
4. Use effective communication techniques.

learn about communication barriers and how these barriers might be reduced. In Chapters 10 and 11, you will learn how to communicate effectively in writing and through oral presentations. However, it is important that you understand as you begin to study these chapters that developing effective communication is an ongoing process. You cannot study three chapters in this book (or in any book) and assume that you have become an effective communicator. You must continue to pay attention to the process of communication—the people with whom you are communicating, the situations in which you are communicating, the cultural differences that exist, and the most effective techniques to use.

Communication and Self-Concept

Communication is defined in the dictionary as the ability "to make known; to im-part; to transmit information, thought, or feeling so that it is adequately received and understood." **Self-concept** is defined as the way you see yourself—who you believe you are, what your strengths and weaknesses are, and how you believe others see you.

As you begin the study of the communication process, it is important to understand the relationship between communication and self-concept. The two are intrinsically linked, that is, an inevitable part of each other and incapable of being separated. Your self-concept affects the way in which you communicate, and your communication is affected by your self-concept. For example, assume one of your coworkers, Carlos, makes this statement: "I don't have the ability to learn the new software; technology always throws me." A portion of Carlos's self-concept is evident through his communication—he feels inadequate when attempting to deal with technology. Figure 9-1 demonstrates

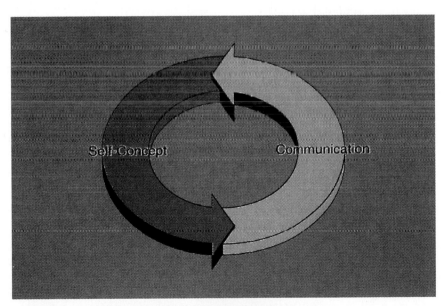

FIGURE 9-1. The intertwined nature of self-concept and communication.

the intertwined nature of self-concept and communication.

As a young child you begin to develop your self-concept. It is formed through your experiences and the feedback you receive from significant others in your life, such as your parents, siblings, close friends, and peer group. Just as communication is a growth process, so is self-concept. If you are open to learning from new experiences and from the feedback that you receive, your perception of who you are grows and changes.

Experience

Through experience you learn what your strong points are and what you like and dislike. Each day you have different experiences that contribute to your self-concept. For example, if you made excellent grades in biology and chemistry in high school, you most likely decided that you were good in the sciences. This knowledge may even have influenced your choice of career; you may have decided that you want to work as an office professional in the health field. On the other hand, if you did not do well in the sciences, you probably decided that you had no ability in the area and that you did not want to build a career that had anything to do with the health professions. In other words, your lack of success in these courses may have made you feel inadequate in this area.

Feedback from Others

Your self-concept is also built on how others see and respond to you. Suppose that you have been constantly told since you were a small child that you have beautiful blue eyes. If so, you probably look at yourself in the mirror each day and feel good about your beautiful eyes. You may even play up this part of your appearance by wearing colors that accentuate your blue eyes. Or suppose that when you took your first speech course, your teacher told you that you were an excellent debater and rewarded you with A's throughout the course. You were reinforced in your skills as you participated on the debate team and won most of the time. Now you probably seek out opportunities to use your debate skills. You may even enjoy a good debate on various issues with your coworkers.

Other people's comments validate, reinforce, or alter our perceptions of who we are and what we can do. The more positive comments you receive as you engage in new experiences, the more positive your self-concept becomes. Conversely, negative comments can hurt your self-esteem and contribute to the development of a negative self-concept. These positive or negative feelings then transfer to our communications with others. We often engage in negative or positive talk about ourselves based on what we have heard or believe others think of us. Consider the following examples of vocabulary and relationships with others for individuals who have positive and negative self-concepts about particular areas of their lives.

Vocabulary.   There is a connection between one's self-image and one's speech habits and voice inflection. Consider the following self-pitying remarks that may reveal a low self-concept.

- "I never could do that."
- "I just can't seem to get anything right."
- "No wonder no one likes me; I do everything wrong."

People with low self-concepts also frequently voice complaints such as these:

- "Mary got the promotion because her uncle is president." (The fact that Mary attended night school for five years to prepare for the job is never mentioned.)
- "Of course Deborah can travel every summer; she makes more money than I do." (The fact that Deborah lives frugally all year in order to afford the trips is overlooked by the complainer.)

In contrast, people with positive self-concepts make statements such as:

- "I can't wait to try that; it's fun to try something new."
- "I know I will be successful."
- "This job is going to be a challenge; I love a challenge."

Not only are the statements of people with good self-concepts positive, but their tone of voice is enthusiastic and their body language projects a self-confident manner. For example, these people stand straight and tall; they walk with an energetic stride.

Relationships.   The person with a positive self-concept develops positive relationships with others. They seek out others and enjoy interpersonal relationships. They believe they will get good feedback from others, and this feedback reinforces their positive self-concept.

Self-Concept Strengtheners

How can you strengthen your self-concept? One way is to be open to new experiences rather than focusing on the past. Consider this example.

Nelda has never seen herself as a creative person. Recently, however, she solved an office problem in a unique way. Her employer complimented her on her creative approach. If Nelda is able to absorb this experience into her consciousness, her self-concept will be strengthened. She will think twice in the future before she belittles herself for her lack of creativity.

Another way that you can strengthen your self-concept is to set your own directions. Recognize that all perceptions that people have of you are not necessarily correct. For example, assume someone makes this

Know your own strengths; do not accept a negative comment as the truth about your abilities when you are merely having a bad day.
Courtesy of © PhotoDisc, Inc.

statement to you after a volleyball game where you played poorly.

"You don't play volleyball very well, do you?"

Rather than accept that person's observation and immediately agree that you do not, ask yourself, "What do my past experiences tell me about how I play volleyball?" If you have been successful at volleyball in the past, you may conclude that you merely had a bad day. All of us do. Do not accept the person's statement. You may respond in this manner:

"I usually play volleyball very well; I just had a bad day as we all do from time to time."

Never accept every statement that others make about you. Evaluate their statements based on what you know about yourself and the experiences that you have had.

Verbal and Nonverbal Communication

Verbal communication is the process of exchanging ideas and feelings through the use of words. **Nonverbal communication** is the process of exchanging ideas and feelings through the use of gestures. Both can be the source of many misunderstandings due to differences in the background and experiences of people who hear the communication. As you learned in Chapter 1, our population is becoming more and more diverse. We have greater diversity in race and ethnicity as well as in age, with people living longer than in the past. This diversity adds to the complexity of our verbal and nonverbal communication. Not only do our native languages differ many times in our diverse popula-

tion, but also the meaning we give to the same words and gestures is often very different from culture to culture. You will learn more about cultural differences in communication, along with nonverbal and verbal communication barriers later in this chapter.

The Communication Process

Communication involves the exchange of ideas and feelings through the use of symbols, such as words or gestures. It contains several elements—the originator, the message, the receiver, and the response. These elements are standard in all forms of communication.

The Originator

The originator is the sender of the original message. The originator transmits information, ideas, and feelings through speaking, writing, or gesturing. Although the originator is often a person, the originator may be a company, a committee, or even a nation. In the ads you see on television about a particular product, the company is the originator of the communication. You get a feel for the company through the message that is conveyed. For example, in our health-conscious world, one might believe that the Quaker® Oats Company cares for our health as it communicates the healthful benefits of oats through its commercials.

The Message

The message is the idea being presented by the originator. The process of turning an idea into symbols that can be communicated is called **encoding**. The symbols used are usually words. However, they may be gestures, such as hand signals, or a combination of words and gestures.

Once the originator mentally encodes the message into symbols, these symbols are transmitted. They may be transmitted through face-to-face exchanges, telephone conversations, written communications (for example, letters and reports), or through electronic transmission such as computers, email, and television.

The Receiver

The person for whom the message is intended is the receiver. The receiver takes the symbols and **decodes** them into meaning. The process of encoding and decoding usually takes place subconsciously. It is not something we give much thought. Because of this tendency, the message that is decoded by the receiver is not always the same message that was encoded by the originator. Since we live in a multicultural world, the differences in language may contribute to this incorrect decoding. However, incorrect decoding can also occur with what we normally consider as very simple concepts. Consider this example of a simple communication.

> John is cold; he asked Bob to turn down the air conditioner. John did not tell Bob that he was cold. The air conditioner temperature is set at 72 degrees. Bob turns the air conditioner to 68 degrees, believing that John wants the temperature turned lower than it is. About 20 minutes later when the room has become even colder, John yells at Bob, "Why didn't you do what I asked you to do?"

Is this an unusual situation? Probably not. Another person often misunderstands what one person considers a simple communication.

The Response

A receiver decodes a message and responds to it. The **response** (feedback) of the receiver lets the originator know whether the communication was understood. The response may be verbal or nonverbal (a nod of the head, a smile, a lifting of the eyebrows). If the response of the receiver indicates to the originator that the communication was misunderstood, then the originator can send the message again, perhaps in a different manner. However, in some instances, it may take some time to determine the response of the receiver. In the previous example, John did not know that Bob had misinterpreted the communication until 20 minutes later. In the television advertisement, Quaker Oats does not know how its message is perceived until sales reports are available or a marketing study is done. Although it is not always possible to get an immediate response, the communication improves markedly as more interaction takes place. The transmitter and receiver are interrelated in the communication process.

Nonverbal Communication

Although what we say and what we write are important parts of communication, another important area is nonverbal communication. We use a variety of nonverbal communication methods to convey meaning. Consider the following.

Body Language

Various body motions or gestures have meaning. Notice the photo below of an individual at a meeting. Would you say that the individual is involved in the meeting? No doubt, your answer is "no." The nonverbal body language of the individual sends a signal that we interpret as lack of involvement in what is going on in the room.

Although body language is extremely important, one gesture by itself does not have significant meaning. All the gestures a person makes must be considered, along with what is being said. Also, in our multicultural society, body language does not have the same meaning in all cultures. For example, eye contact is extremely important for Americans. We tend to believe that people who do not make eye contact with us have low self-esteem, are shy, or uninterested in what we are saying. Conversely, people from Asian, Latin American, and Caribbean cultures feel that it is a sign of respect to avoid eye contact. In our multicultural world, it is important to continue to learn about the body language of people from other cultures rather than to make assumptions based on the American culture.

Nonverbal body language can send a message about people's interest in the subject being discussed. *Courtesy of © PhotoDisc, Inc.*

Voice Quality

A loud tone of voice is usually associated with anger, a soft tone with calmness and poise. If two people are talking softly with each other, it usually indicates that they are at ease. The loudness or softness of the voice and the pitch of the voice are nonverbal behaviors that may reveal something about the individual. For example, a person's voice usually will be pitched higher when he or she is tense, anxious, or nervous. A person usually talks faster when angry or tense. In contrast, a low pitch and a slow pace usually indicate an intimate or relaxed tone. Other forms of nonverbal voice communication include the nervous giggle; a quivering, emotional voice; and a breaking, stressful voice.

Voice quality is so important that individuals whose voices are important to their success or failure on the job, such as TV and radio newscasters, spend time and effort to be certain that their voice

Voice quality is extremely important, particularly when your voice is being broadcast to millions over television. © EyeWire.

important as it is in America. Being 30 minutes late to an appointment is perfectly acceptable. Lingering over a cup of coffee at an outdoor café in Italy is expected any time of day. The wait staff does not pressure you to leave; in fact, they often do not bring you a check until you ask for it. In contrast, in America once our food is served, we eat quickly, expect to have the check by the time we have finished eating, pay for our food, and leave immediately. There is very little lingering over our meals, unless we are taking a leisurely evening out with friends.

Space

Do you have a certain desk in a classroom that you consider yours? Do you feel pushed out of your place if someone else occupies that desk? Do you consider particular areas in your home your territory?

does not cause people to switch to another station. For example, a nasal or very high-pitched voice may be irritating to the listener.

Time

Another important nonverbal communicator is time. Think about the implication time has for the American people. Being punctual for an interview lets the prospective employer know that you care about the position. Being late for an interview sends the reverse message. In a school situation, a late paper or project may result in a penalty for the student.

In other cultures, time may not have the same meaning. For example, in Spain, Greece, Mexico, and Italy, time is not as

In Italy, it is assumed that people will linger over their meals. © EyeWire.

The act of laying claim to and defending a territory is termed **territoriality.** **Proxemics** is the study of the personal and cultural use of space.

Americans use space in particular ways in all areas of their life. For example, the offices of vice presidents of a particular company will all be the same size, with the same size desk and office furnishings. The president's office will generally be larger, with a more expensive desk and furnishings. Office support personnel usually do not have individual offices but workstations with modular walls. In other words, the higher up the organizational ladder one climbs, the more space that is generally provided by the company. With the increased cost of space, some companies today are moving away from this concept to a degree, using modular workstations for people with a wide range of jobs. However, the president and upper-level administrators generally maintain their offices.

Another example of how Americans use space can be seen in our relationship with others. If we do not know someone well or if the relationship is an impersonal one, we tend to stay a foot or two away from the individual while talking. We do not close this spatial gap except in intimate relationships. If we see two people talking at close distances, we assume there is some type of close relationship. In contrast, people from Mexico and South America tend to get very close to someone when they are talking, even if that person is not a longtime friend. With Americans, such closeness is considered an invasion of the person's space and not viewed positively.

Americans assume that when people talk at close distances there is some type of intimate relationship. © *CORBIS.*

Communication Barriers

Barriers often exist that impede communication whether we are communicating with others of the same culture or of different cultures. A few of these barriers are listed in this section.

Language Usage

The language we use often prevents clear communication. Words in isolation have no meaning. They have meaning only because people have agreed upon a particular meaning. You may say, "But what about the dictionary? Doesn't it contain the correct meaning of words?" Yes, it contains the correct meaning as agreed on by **etymologists** (specialists in the study of words). This meaning can be called the objective meaning of a word, and we use the dictionary to determine it. Again, however, cultural differences impact the meaning that certain words have for individuals. In England, even though both Americans and the British speak the same language, words may be used in different ways. For example, when we have to wait in line at a theatre for tickets, we refer to this behavior as "standing in line," while the British refer to it as "queuing up." In Britain, an elevator is called a "lift."

Meanings of words also change with time. New words come into existence, and other words become obsolete because of their lack of usage. The computer era has generated different applications for certain words. Remember when a bulletin board meant only a board that was hung on a wall to which notes were attached? Now a bulletin board can mean a public-access message system through computer linkage. A chat room in computer terminology does not mean a "room" at all in the standard definition of the word, but a location where people all over the world, connected by the World Wide Web, can *talk* with each other via computers.

Consider still another example of how words mean different things to different people. The following example is a conversation between an employer and an employee.

Employer: "I need you to take notes at the staff meeting next week; be certain that all participants get the notes as soon as possible after the meeting."

Employee: "Certainly."

One day after the meeting, one of the staff called the executive to say that he did not have the notes. The employer (apparently upset) asks the employee, "Why don't you have the notes out?" The employee (frustrated) responds, "I'm sorry; I am getting the notes out this afternoon. I assumed that getting them out within two days after the meeting would be okay." Thus, a communication problem has occurred due to the same words ("as soon as possible") having different meanings (different interpretations) for the employer and the employee. Both the employer and the employee are upset. Both intended to be clear with the communication, but neither one was.

It is a good idea to check with the originator of the message if there is any concern that the meaning is not clear. For example, in the situation given above, the employee might have asked, "Will it be okay to have the notes out in two days after the meeting?" If the employer had a problem with that time frame, it could have been resolved immediately.

Evaluation

The tendency to evaluate other people often gets in the way of communication. The following conversation occurred between Su Yang and Elsa Spofford. Elsa took the CPS exam for the first time two years ago. The first year, Elsa passed one part of the exam. The second year, she passed the remaining parts and is now a CPS. Su is taking the examination for the first time next month.

Elsa: "Su, I just heard you are going to take the CPS exam next month. Good luck!"

Su: "Thanks; I feel quite confident. I don't think I will have any trouble. I have taken several review courses and have been studying all year."

Elsa (with a certain amount of disdain in her voice): "If I were you, I wouldn't be so confident. It is a tough exam. I took several review courses too, but I did not pass all parts the first time I took the exam."

Su: "Well, maybe you didn't study hard enough."

In this situation, each individual has passed judgment on the other. Elsa has decided that Su is too confident in feeling that she will pass all parts immediately. Elsa is probably sorry she took the time to wish Su good luck. Su has decided that Elsa did not study hard enough. She also feels that Elsa didn't really want to wish her good luck—probably Elsa only wanted to make her worry by reminding her how hard the exam is.

One of the major barriers to communication is the tendency to judge and to approve or disapprove of the person making the statement. This evaluation is made from the listener's frame of reference and experience. If what is said agrees with the listener's experience, the listener tends to make a positive evaluation. If what is said does not agree with the listener's experience, a negative evaluation may occur.

In order to prevent or reduce the tendency to evaluate other people, you need to listen with understanding. This statement means that you see the ideas from the other person's point of view and try to sense how the other person feels. If you have the courage to listen with understanding, communication will be greatly improved. You may even find that you have learned and grown in the process.

Allness

Communication theorists refer to a communication problem called **allness** that occurs when an individual presumes that what he or she says or knows is complete, absolute, and all-inclusive. To demonstrate this concept, listed below are a few details about one individual. This person is a:

Female
Office Professional
Member of International Association of Administrative Professionals
Tennis player
Mother of two
Pianist

Do these details, even though they seem to be extensive, list all there is to know about the person? No, there is much more to know. The individual may be a single parent, a college graduate, a talented vocalist, and so forth. We cannot know one or even several characteristics, ideas, or details and assume that we know all there is to know or say about a person, subject, or concept. However, that is exactly what we do sometimes in communicating. Two people may take different details from a given situation and assume that they know all there is to know. Then, when they begin to talk about the situation, a tremendous communication problem results.

How can this problem be alleviated? Be aware that you can never say or know everything about anything. Realize that you select and omit details when you communicate. In listening to others, use questioning and restatement techniques to be sure all essential information is

The communication concept referred to as **allness** reminds us that we can never know all there is to know about another person. *Courtesy of © PhotoDisc, Inc.*

obtained. If you are talking or writing, make a habit of adding mental "etceteras" as a reminder that you do not have all the information about the person or subject.

Inference

Inference is defined as the process of deriving logical conclusions from premises known or assumed to be true. The problem that can be caused from making inferences is that individuals may act upon what they believe to be true when it is in fact not true.

Consider this situation. You arrive home from work late one evening and see that all the lights are on in your home. An ambulance is pulling out of your drive. From your observations, determine whether or not the following statement is true

- Someone in your family is very sick and is being taken to the hospital.

Did you answer "yes" to the question? Most of us probably would infer from the situation that the statement is true. However, the statement is not true. A child who lives next door fell on his bicycle and broke his leg. An ambulance was called. Since the neighbor's cars were in their drive, the ambulance driver used your driveway.

People often jump to conclusions or infer things that are not true. Then they may compound the situation by acting on the inference as if it were a certainty. The first step in correcting inference problems is to be aware that you may be making an

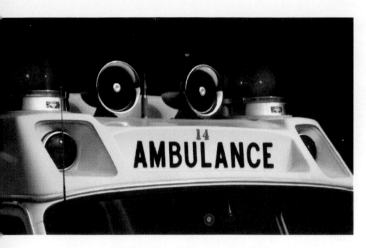

Inference can cause us to act upon assumptions that are not true. *Courtesy of © PhotoDisc, Inc.*

inference. Know the difference between an inference and an observation. Ask the following questions:

- Did I observe the event?
- Or did I infer that it happened?

If you inferred that it happened, what are the probabilities that your inference is correct? Certainly there are times when you cannot observe an event, and it is necessary for you to infer its occurrence. However, it is important to recognize inferences and to realize that they are not always correct.

Categorization

Categorization is the ability to compare, contrast, and classify objects, persons, or ideas. For example, as a small child you learned what a dog looked like and how a dog sounded. As you discovered different breeds of dogs, you were able to see the similarities and the differences in the generic category "dogs." Just as categorization is useful to a child in learning about the world, it is also useful to an adult in

acquiring new information. Categorization provides the means to classify new information with similar facts.

As categorization can assist in the learning process, it also can block the communication process. For example, the tendency to categorize people by their gender can cause blocks. If we are concerned about good communication, we will not assume that because someone is male or female they have certain character traits.

Cultural Differences

You have already learned about several cultural differences in this chapter. Since our population is becoming more diverse and, as a nation, we are becoming more international, we must continue to be alert to the differences among the world's people. Dresser points out numerous differences in various cultures.[1] Some of these differences are given in Figure 9-2.

Reduction of Communication Barriers

If you want to communicate successfully, you must learn to reduce communication barriers. Due to the number of people you encounter each day and the number of different situations you find yourself in, it is impossible to eliminate all barriers. But you can reduce them by using a variety of

[1]Norine Dresser, *Multicultural Manners: New Rules of Etiquette for a Changing Society* (New York: John Wiley & Sons, 1996).

CULTURAL DIFFERENCES

- In Korean culture, smiling can signal shallowness or thoughtfulness.
- In Japan, a smile may be equated with frivolous behavior.
- In Japan, "yes" does not always mean "yes."
- Japanese are taught to withhold their personal opinions. There is an old Japanese proverb that says, "Silence is a virtue."
- Avoidance of eye contact in Japan means that the person is being polite and nonconfrontational. Mothers often scold their children for staring into peoples' eyes when they speak.
- Because Asians regard teachers so highly, they find it difficult to voice their own views in class; it is almost a sign of disrespect to the teacher.
- In Brazil, the gesture of the thumb and forefinger forming a circle (which means "okay" in America) is an obscene one.
- In France and Mexico, being 30 minutes late to an appointment is perfectly acceptable.
- In Iran, giving someone yellow flowers means that you hate them. In Brazil, purple flowers are associated with death; in China, white is the color of mourning.
- In Indian and Indonesian homes, if the host goes shoeless, the guest should do likewise.
- Asians generally do not approve of public displays of affection.

FIGURE 9-2. Cultural differences. Sources: Norine Dresser *Multicultural Manners: New Rules of Etiquette for a Changing Society* (New York: John Wiley & Sons, 1996) and "When the Japanese say 'Yes,' Is This What They Really Mean?", Internet, http://www.t3.rim.orip/%k7Emike3/yes.html.

techniques, some of which are given here. Others are included in Figure 9-3.

Active Listening

Studies show that most people spend 70 percent of their time communicating. Of that 70 percent, 45 percent is spent in listening. However, most authorities agree that listening is the weakest factor in the communication process. Hearing does not constitute listening. A person can hear the words and yet not understand them. **Active listening** requires that you listen for the meaning as well as the words of the speaker. Here are some suggestions for becoming an active listener.

- Prepare to listen. Drive distracting thoughts from your mind and direct your full attention to the speaker.
- Listen for facts. Mentally register the key words that the speaker is using, and repeat key ideas or related points.

COMMUNICATION TECHNIQUES

- Use mnemonic devices to remember key ideas. A mnemonic device is a formula, word association, or rhyme used to assist the memory.
- Minimize your mental blocks and filters. Do not **stereotype** individuals—evaluate a person or group of people based on a perception or image held of the group to which the person belongs; for example, all CPAs are only number crunchers.
- Use direct, simple language.
- Utilize feedback. When communicating with someone, listen totally to what that person is saying, not only to the words. Remember there are many ways to communicate, including words, gestures, facial expressions, tone of voice, time, and space. If you feel that the other person does not understand what you are saying, try to explain your point in a different manner.
- Time messages carefully. Stop, look, and observe what is going on in the world of the receiver before you attempt to communicate.
- Do not expect people from different cultures to behave the same way you do.
- Commit to constantly increasing your communication skills.

FIGURE 9-3. Communication techniques.

Relate what the speaker is saying to your experiences.

- Listen for feelings. Search beneath the surface. Listen to what is and is not being said.
- Minimize mental blocks and filters by being aware of them. Know your biases and prejudices. Do not let them keep you from hearing what the speaker is saying.
- Take notes. When listening to a presentation or lecture, notes can be beneficial in jogging your memory later. Write only the main points of the message; do not attempt to record each word.
- Question and paraphrase. Ask questions when you don't understand what you have heard. Paraphrase by putting the speaker's communication in your own words and asking the speaker if you have understood correctly.

Person Oriented

As you have learned, words do not have meaning by themselves. They have meaning only because word specialists have agreed upon a particular meaning. This meaning may not be the same for all groups of people. Alert communicators ask: "Do you understand what I'm saying?" In other words, they are **person oriented**—sensitive to what the words mean to the receiver of the communication.

Nonjudgmental

Try to understand the message as the speaker intends it. Be **nonjudgmental;** do not attempt to judge the individual's intelligence, appearance, or any other characteristics. Listen to what the speaker is saying; in other words, give the person a chance to get his or her message across

without forming judgments. Avoid arguing with the speaker. If you are opposed to an idea, do not argue or become emotional. Control your reaction at least until you have heard all the speaker has to say. Regardless of your acceptance or rejection of what a speaker says, your knowledge will increase when you listen—even if you only learn another person's view.

Conflict Resolution

When conflicts occur (and they will), seek to resolve them. Use these **conflict resolution** techniques:

- Acknowledge the worth of the other person and the other person's point of view.
- Acknowledge the other person's emotions and feelings.
- Offer an apology if appropriate.
- Agree with the other person's point of view when you can.
- Express your point of view without denigrating the other person. Use "I" statements rather than "you" statements. For example, you might say: "I think it is important to proceed in this way" as opposed to "You are wrong in the direction you are suggesting."
- Acknowledge differences openly.
- Ask for the other person's advice.
- Build bridges between your differences rather than walls that restrict each person to his or her view.

Communication— A Growth Process

As you learned earlier in this chapter, communication is a growth process. In order to be an effective communicator,

Reduce communication conflicts by building bridges. *Courtesy of © PhotoDisc, Inc.*

you must continue to pay attention to effective communication techniques. As new situations confront you, consider them carefully. Pay attention to what is and is not being communicated. Observe nonverbal as well as verbal behaviors. Consider the people with whom you are communicating. Learn as much as you can about their background and experiences. Attempt to view the world from their point of reference. After a particularly difficult communication situation, evaluate what happened. Determine what went right and what went wrong. Consider how you might correct what went wrong for future communication. Although communication is never easy, by using good techniques, we can continue to become better communicators.

SUMMARY

To reinforce what you have learned in this chapter, study this summary.

- Communication is defined as the ability "to make known; to impart; to transmit information, thought, or feeling so that it is adequately received and understood."

- Self-concept is defined as the way you see yourself—who you believe you are, what your strengths and weaknesses are, and how you believe others see you.

- Communication and self-concept are intrinsically linked—an inevitable part of each other and incapable of being separated.

- Self-concept is formed from your experiences and the feedback received from significant others.

- Individuals with a positive self-concept tend to adopt a positive vocabulary and develop good relationships with others.

- Self-concept can be strengthened through being open to new experiences and setting your own directions rather than allowing others to set directions for you.

- Verbal communication is the process of exchanging ideas and feelings through the use of words.

- Nonverbal communication is the process of exchanging ideas and feelings through the use of gestures.

- The originator, the message, the receiver, and the response are the elements of communication.

- Body language, voice quality, time, and space are all elements of nonverbal communication.

- Communication barriers include:
  - Language usage
  - Evaluation
  - Inference
  - Allness
  - Categorization
  - Cultural differences
- Barriers may be reduced by:
  - Active listening
  - People orientation
  - Nonjudgmental behavior
  - Conflict resolution

- Communication is a growth process. In order to continue to grow in the communication process, you should always consider the situation and the people with whom you are communicating. When particularly difficult communication situations arise, evaluate what happened and learn from the process.

Key Terms

- Communication
- Self-concept
- Verbal communication
- Nonverbal communication
- Encoding
- Decodes

- Response
- Territoriality
- Proxemics
- Etymologists
- Allness
- Inference
- Categorization

- Mnemonic device
- Stereotype
- Active listening
- Person oriented
- Nonjudgmental
- Conflict resolution

Professional Pointers

By working in proximity with other people, as is the case in most workplace environments, working relationships develop. Sometimes these relationships can be difficult due to problems that occur as people work closely and for lengthy periods of time together. Follow these suggestions to improve your workplace relationships.

- Respect cultures and traditions that are different than your own.
- Understand the difference in personal relationships and working relationships; be wise enough to know when you are close to crossing the line.
- Avoid stereotyping or generalizing when assessing others' work habits.
- Maintain high ethical standards.
- Be patient with your coworkers.
- Assume that people can always be trusted until proven otherwise.
- Always seek to understand others and their behaviors.
- Admit mistakes when you make them; apologize if appropriate.
- Refrain from making negative comments to another individual, or about individuals to another person in the workplace.

Office Procedures Reinforcement

1. Explain the relationship between self-concept and communication.
2. Identify and explain the elements of the communication process.
3. List and briefly describe three types of nonverbal communication.
4. Identify and explain three communication barriers.
5. Explain what active listening means, and describe three suggestions for becoming an active listener.

Critical Thinking Activity

Kevin Bartholomew is an account analyst in the offices of Port First Securities. He has been with the company for about a year. Kevin interacts infrequently with other employees in the office except when a project requires the establishment of a team. In team projects, he never takes the lead and rarely volunteers for any portion of the work. In group discussions, Kevin is extremely reserved. He mumbles when he does speak, and he seems to lack self-confidence.

Kevin, however, performs whatever task he has to do very well. The director, Claudette Stevens, is very pleased with his performance. He usually completes assignments well in advance of their due date, and other employees like to work with Kevin on projects because he is so reliable and efficient.

Reporting sessions to corporate executives are conducted quarterly. Ms. Stevens would like to have Kevin participate in the quarterly presentations because of his competence.

- How might Ms. Stevens help Kevin understand the image he projects?
- List the points and recommendations that Ms. Stevens should make to assist Kevin in participating in the presentations.

Office Applications

OA9-1 (Goal 1)

Having to verbalize our personal strengths usually creates an uncomfortable feeling. In OA1-4 you completed a self-evaluation chart on your strengths, weaknesses, and interests. Refer to the chart and choose several strengths or characteristics that you like about yourself. Write a one-page assessment entitled "What I Like About Myself." Include positive physical attributes, personality qualities, skills, and talents. No negative statements are allowed in your evaluation. Share your evaluation with a trusted family member or friend.

OA9-2 (Goals 2 and 3)

As you learned in this chapter, individuals do not always perceive people, situations, or ideas in the same way. To demonstrate this concept, participate in this exercise with your classmates.

1. Divide into groups of eight members.
2. Choose three members from each group who will leave the room (Person A, Person B, and Person C).
3. Your instructor will show the rest of the members of the group a picture. Examine the picture, but do not write down what is in it.

4. Call in Person A from each group. Each group describes the picture to Person A. Person A cannot ask questions; he or she merely listens to the descriptions the group gives.

5. Call in Person B from each group. Person A describes the picture to Person B but without the group's help.

6. Then Person C from each group is called in, and Person B describes the picture to Person C. Person C goes to a flip chart and draws the picture from Person B's description. Compare the drawings from each group. Then compare these pictures with the original picture.

Each group should discuss the following questions:

1. How did the differences in the perceptions of various members interfere with the communication process?

2. What contributes to these various perceptions?

OA9-3 (Goals 3 and 4)

In this chapter you learned about nonverbal behavior. Complete the form provided on page 57 of your Applications Workbook. Compare your answers with one of your classmates; discuss the differences and similarities between how you behave nonverbally and how you observed other people behaving.

Online Research Applications

ORA9-4 (Goals 3 and 4)
Work with two of your classmates on this project. Using the Internet, research communication patterns in Japan, Mexico, and Africa. Present your findings orally to the class.

CHAPTER 10

Written Communications

Written communications can spell success or failure. Consider for a moment the letters you have received from businesses. Have any of these letters:

- Made you angry?
- Made you say you would never do business with a company again?
- Been too intrusive?
- Contained incorrect information?

Most of us have received letters from businesses that have been poorly or incorrectly written due to the carelessness or inability of the person writing the letter.

Letters represent a company, and this representation must be positive so that the reader will respond

YOUR GOALS

1. Apply effective writing principles when composing email, memorandums, letters, and reports.

2. Compose business correspondence.

3. Write collaboratively.

positively and the desired action will occur. To be insensitive to the reader is to invite no response or a negative one.

In addition to correspondence that goes outside the business, many email messages, memorandums, and reports are written to individuals within the organization. On occasion, these may be sent externally. It is important that they be written clearly, concisely, and correctly.

As an office professional, your job many times demands that you compose correspondence. When you first begin working for a company, you may be asked to compose draft copies of correspondence. As you learn your position and the needs of the company, you may send out correspondence under your own signature or write final copy for your employer to sign. Being a competent and careful writer is extremely important to your success. This chapter will give you techniques for writing effective correspondence for both your external and internal audiences.

Types of Written Messages

The basic types of written messages that the office professional produces are letters, email, memorandums, and reports. Although the initial correspondence that you prepare as a beginning office professional may be routine, your employer is likely to increase your writing assignments if you demonstrate the skills and abilities to produce effective correspondence.

Letters

It is good practice to acknowledge each letter that requires a reply as quickly as possible. By responding on the same day

that the letter is received, the executive can present a favorable image for the company that may win a friend or produce a customer. If you are beginning to assume writing responsibilities, you may prepare a draft response to the letter for your employer's review. If you and your employer have been working together for a period of time and your writing styles are compatible, you may be able to prepare the final document for his or her signature without doing a draft. Whatever role you play in the composition of correspondence, the principles you will learn in this chapter will help you be an effective letter writer.

Email

Electronic mail is used extensively in the office due to its ease, speed, and relative low cost. Billions of email messages are sent each year in corporations throughout the world. Although it is used mainly for interoffice communication, it is also used to send short messages to external business constituencies. In fact, we often overuse and misuse email. This chapter will help you learn how to effectively use an excellent communication tool without abusing it.

Memorandums

Although email has become the tool of choice for internal correspondence, memorandums continue to have an important place in office correspondence. For example, a memorandum is more appropriate when:

- A hard copy of the correspondence is needed for future reference
- The memo is relatively lengthy
- A signed document is needed

As an office professional, you will write numerous memorandums. Since they are internal documents, they are not as formal as letters. However, careful attention should be paid to writing a clear, effective memorandum—one where the reader is given all the necessary information and not left with numerous unanswered questions. You will be introduced to the elements of an effective memorandum in this chapter.

Reports

In addition to email, memorandums, and letters, numerous reports are prepared in the office. These may be informal reports of two or three pages, or they may be formal reports containing a table of contents, the body of the report (with footnotes or endnotes), appendices, and a bibliography. You will learn more about report writing in a later section of this chapter.

Collaborative Writing

In Chapter 2, you learned about the importance of project teams in the workforce and characteristics of effective teams. In Chapter 9, you learned about communication barriers and techniques for reducing them. You also learned about the importance of understanding cultural differences in our multicultural world. Just as numerous teams work together daily on various projects within the office in solving problems, making recommendations, and numerous other activities, teams are also used in writing correspondence.

To be an effective member of a writing team, you will need to use some of the same skills that were presented in Chapters 2 and 9, such as active listening,

conflict resolution, and understanding and acceptance of cultural differences. If you are engaged in a team writing assignment, these guidelines will help your team produce a better project.

- Determine the purpose of the writing assignment. What are you to produce? What is the deadline? Are there certain stipulations that are to be met?
- Determine who the audience is. Who is to receive the final report? What is their background? How much do they know about the subject matter? In other words, you need to determine what your style of writing should be and how much information you should give the recipient(s).
- Select a team leader. The team leader is responsible for setting the procedures for the team writing meetings, facilitating the meetings, and helping the group meet deadlines, solve problems, and produce the document.
- Set a work schedule. Decide when and where you are going to meet. Set timelines and stick to them.
- Allocate the work. Define the tasks of each team member. Determine each team member's writing strengths and use these strengths when assigning tasks.
- Monitor the progress. The group must stay focused and produce the written product by the deadline established.
- Reduce the chance of conflicts by:
  - Actively listening to each group member
  - Paying attention to cultural differences that may exist
  - Acknowledging the worth of the other group members and their point of view

Collaborative writing involves using active listening skills. *Courtesy of © CORBIS.*

Effective Correspondence

If a written communication is to accomplish its goal, the purpose for writing must be understood, the content organized appropriately, and certain principles maintained. Following the principles presented here will assist you in producing a quality product—a letter, email, memorandum, or report.

Characteristics of Effective Correspondence

How do you know if correspondence is effective? You know if it gets results and serves the purpose the writer intends. For example, an effective letter of application secures the interview; an effective sales letter sells the product; and an effective email provides the necessary information. Effective correspondence has the characteristics listed in the next section.

Complete. Correspondence is complete if it gives the reader all the information needed to accomplish the results the writer intends. To help you achieve completeness, ask the **W questions.**

- WHY is the correspondence being written?
- WHAT is the goal of the correspondence? What do I hope to accomplish?
- WHAT information is needed before writing the correspondence?
- WHO needs to receive the correspondence?
- WHAT information needs to be included in the correspondence?

Refer to Figure 10-1 for examples of ineffective writing when the W questions were not asked and corresponding examples of effective writing when they were asked.

Clear. After reading a message, the reader should be able to determine without a doubt the purpose of the correspondence. Clear messages reflect clear thinking. Writing clearly requires good organization and simple expression. Each sentence should have one thought and each paragraph one purpose. Business correspondence is not the place to impress a person with your vocabulary. Its aim is to get your purpose across in a simple, concise manner. If a short, easily understood word is available, use it. Your words should express rather than impress.

Unclear writing is costly for the business. Think of the times you have received a memorandum or a report that is not clear. What is your recourse? You probably pick up the phone and call the writer, asking questions such as:

- Where will the meeting be held?
- What is the purpose of the meeting?
- Which sales report is Mr. Quin to bring?

ASKING THE "W" QUESTIONS

Consider the following examples of ineffective writing when the W questions were not asked, and the corresponding examples of effective writing when the W questions were asked.

Ineffective:	Your order will be mailed soon. (WHEN?)
Effective:	Your order will be mailed June 12.
Ineffective:	There will be a seminar on June 2. (WHERE and WHAT kind of conference?)
Effective:	A total quality management seminar will be held in the Green Room at 1 p.m. on June 2.
Ineffective:	The planning meeting was canceled. (WHY and WHEN?)
Effective:	The planning meeting scheduled for July 15 at 2 p.m. has been canceled due to a conflict with the communication meeting scheduled at the same time. The planning meeting has been rescheduled for July 30 at 2 p.m. in the Executive Conference room.

FIGURE 10-1. Asking the W questions.

The unclear communication has cost the business two to three times the amount it would have cost if the communication had been clear. Clarity is not only a matter of consideration but also one of cost savings.

Accurate. Inaccurate communication can also be expensive to the organization. Get the facts before you start to write. Check your information carefully. If you are quoting prices, be certain you have the correct price list. If you are presenting dates, confirm them.

When you are writing, keep your biases out of the correspondence as much as possible. Your task is to write objectively. You learned in Chapter 4 that ethical individuals do not allow their own biases to determine how they view a situation or individuals. Just as ethics are important when dealing with individuals face-to-face, so are they important in writing. Do not slant the information or overstate its significance. Deal with the facts—simply and accurately.

Prompt. The conscientious business correspondent is prompt. Prompt answers to messages say to the readers that the writer or company cares about them. Conversely, late messages convey the impression that the writer or company is indifferent to the needs of the reader or is grossly inefficient. In either instance, a negative message is sent. A rule of thumb is that replies to routine correspondence should be sent within three to five days. Urgent messages such as urgent email or faxes usually should be answered within 24 hours.

Concise. Conciseness in writing means expressing the necessary information in as few words as possible. Say what you need to say without cluttering your communication with irrelevant information, needless words, or flowery phrases. Figure 10-2 lists some questions to ask in helping you be concise.

Courteous. Courteousness in correspondence means using good human relations skills as you write. Treat the reader with respect; write as if you care about the person. Keep in mind that writing is not dissimilar to talking in the message that you are conveying. When dealing with people face-to-face, courtesy and consideration are necessary in order to develop

FIGURE 10-2. Checklist for conciseness.

and maintain goodwill. The same or perhaps even greater concern must be evident in written correspondence since only the written word conveys the message—a smile, a nod, or a friendly gesture cannot be seen.

Never show your anger in a communication. You may be extremely unhappy about a situation, but to show your anger merely compounds the problem. Angry words make angry readers. Both parties often end up yelling at one another through the written word, with little being accomplished. Remember, anger and courtesy do not go together.

Courtesy also means being considerate. If a person is asking you something, respond. If you are unable to give a positive response, explain why. Explanations let others know that you are sincere.

Positive. It is much easier to hear the word "yes" than to hear the word "no." It is much easier to accept a concern than it is to accept a complaint. Using a positive tone will give the reader a favorable association with the writer, the company, and/or the product. A positive tone is set by the words chosen and by the way they are used. For example, some words and phrases possess positive qualities while others possess negative ones. Figure 10-3 gives a list of some positive and negative words and phrases.

Never show your anger in a written communication, even if you are extremely unhappy. © EyeWire.

The Planning Steps

Correspondence that is well planned and organized will be effective. Just as a builder needs a blueprint to build a house, you should develop your thoughts before you begin to write. You may find that making notes on a scratch pad or in the margins of correspondence to which you are responding will help you organize your thoughts. If you are an inexperienced writer, you may want to make an outline to assist you in organizing your thoughts and material. As you become more experienced, you may make only a mental outline. In any case, the important point is to plan carefully what you want to say in

POSITIVE AND NEGATIVE WORDS AND PHRASES

Positive Words and Phrases	Negative Words and Phrases
Congratulations	Apologize
Glad	Complaint
Immediately	Difficult
Pleasure	Error
Qualified	Disappointed
Satisfactory	No
Thank you	Inconvenient
I will	I cannot
Honest	Dishonest
Would you please tell us	You failed to tell us about
Please send your check	You neglected to send your
The order will be shipped	I hate to inform you

FIGURE 10-3. Positive and negative words and phrases.

writing. The steps in the planning process are:

- Analyze the readers
- Determine the purpose
- Organize the content

Analyze the Readers.   A critical element in the writing process is considering who the readers will be. By evaluating them correctly, you are able to communicate more effectively and thus the message will be understood better. Here are some basic questions to ask yourself about the readers.

- What are the values and beliefs of the readers?
- How old are the readers?
- What is the level of education?
- What issues might make the readers angry?
- What attitudes do the readers have? Will they be receptive or resistant to your message?
- Do the readers come from a diverse background? If so, what is that background?
- Are they local or international readers?

- What will the readers do with the document? Will they read only a portion of it? Study it carefully? Skim it?

The Professional Audience.   If you are writing to a professional audience (for example, engineers, physicists, lawyers), your writing style may use technical vocabulary, knowing that they understand the terms. Also, you can deal immediately with the subject, without spending time explaining the background of the material.

The General Audience.   If you are writing to a general audience, you need to use a simple vocabulary and explain any concept that may be confusing. It may be important to include examples to explain your concepts. Concentrate on what your communication will mean to the readers and what you expect the readers to do with it.

The International Audience.   When writing for international readers, you need to be extremely cautious of the words you use. You learned in Chapter 9 that words do not have the same meaning for everyone. For international readers, this concept is particularly true. Consider these examples.

FIGURE 10-4. Analyze the reader when writing.

- Nova, the model name of a GM car produced in the late 80s, sounds in Spanish like the phrase "No va," which means "It doesn't go."
- When the American Stores Company changed the name of Sav-On Drugstores to Osco, Spanish-speaking customers were dismayed since "osco" sounds like "asco," which means something disgusting that causes nausea. When the company changed Osco back to Sav-On, business increased.[1]

[1]Dresser, Norine, *Multicultural Manners* (New York: John Wiley & Sons, Inc., 1996), 156–157.

When writing for an international audience, make sure that words do not offend or translate into incorrect meanings to different cultures. It is a good idea to have what you have written edited by a person within the particular international community. Figure 10-5 gives several general principles for writing international correspondence. However, it is important to keep in mind that customs vary from nation to nation.

Determine the Purpose. Once you have determined who the reader will be, you need to determine your purpose.

GENERAL PRINCIPLES FOR INTERNATIONAL CORRESPONDENCE

- Use relatively formal language. Phrases such as "Very Honored Professor Dr. Fruer" and "Your honored servant" are used in some countries.

- Do not use expressions unique to the United States; do not refer to events that are common only to the United States.

- Use the dictionary meaning of a word; do not use slang.

- Always use the title of the individual with whom you are corresponding. First names should not be used.

- Be extremely courteous; use "thank you" and "please" often.

- Be complimentary when appropriate (but always sincere).

- Ask questions tactfully.

- Practice the art of negotiation in writing documents.

- Do not use humor; it may be misunderstood.

- Respect all customs of the country (social, religious, and so forth).

- Learn all you can about the country; read extensively.

- Translate correspondence into the native language of the country.

- Send business cards that are printed in the native language of the country.

FIGURE 10-5. General principles for international correspondence.

Before you begin to write, ask yourself these questions:

- What should this document accomplish? Is your purpose to:
  - Explain
  - Inform
  - Recommend
  - Evaluate
  - Assess
  - Persuade
  - Request

- What should the reader(s) do after reading this document?

- What do I want the reader(s) to know?

Some business messages will have more than one objective. For example, the objectives may be to inform and to persuade. What information will the reader need so that he or she may be informed and willing to say "yes" to your request?

Organize the Content. Have you ever read something and realized that your eyes were following the words, but your mind was somewhere else? You may have begun reading with interest, but you lost that interest soon. The organization of a message affects the reader's interest.

Begin with the Important Information. Don't bury the purpose of the document in the middle of the correspondence. The basic organizational structure uses a three-pronged approach. The first part of the document conveys the purpose of the correspondence. The second supports, informs, and/or convinces the reader. The last indicates the desired results.

Plan the Paragraphs. Effective paragraphs possess unity, coherence, and parallel structure.

- Unity. A paragraph has unity when its sentences clarify or support the main idea. The sentence that contains the main idea of a paragraph is called the **topic sentence.** For example, in this paragraph the topic sentence is at the beginning. However, it may also be at the end of the paragraph. The point to remember is that the topic sentence helps the writer keep focused on the main idea for the paragraph.

- Coherence. A paragraph has coherence when its sentences are related to each other in content, in grammatical construction, and in choice of words. Each sentence should be written so that the paragraph flows from one thought to the next in a coherent fashion. One method of achieving coherence is by repeating key words in a paragraph or using certain words for emphasis. Consider the following use of repetitive words.

> The anthropologist Elena Padilla describes life in a squalid district of New York by telling how much people know about each other—*who* is to be trusted and *who* not, *who* is defiant of the law and *who* upholds it, *who* is competent and well informed and *who* is inept and ignorant.

- Parallel. Parallel structure helps you achieve coherence in a paragraph. **Parallelism** is created when grammatically equivalent forms are used within a sentence. Consider the following illustration of nonparallel and parallel constructions.

> Nonparallel: The position is prestigious, challenging, and *also the money isn't bad.*

> Parallel: The position offers prestige, challenge, and money.

Use Appropriate Sentence Structure.
Sentences should be simple but varied. Use a combination of sentence structures to keep your reader's attention. There is no formula for determining sentence length, but shorter sentences help keep the reader's attention. They are also easier to understand. Consider this sentence.

> January reports indicate that sales in the wholesale market increased by more than 40 percent, which serves to support the proposed plan presented at last week's Board meeting for 20 additional positions.

Did you get lost in its length? The sentence has 32 words. Sentences with more than 20 words tend to lose the average reader's attention. This statement does not imply that you should count the words in each sentence or limit sentences needlessly. However, you should be aware that readability generally is increased when the sentence is shorter.

Eliminate the Passive Voice.
Passive voice is present when the subject of the sentence receives the action or is acted upon. It has three characteristics:

- A form of the verb *to be* (*is, am, are, was, were, be, been, being*)
- A past participle (a verb ending in *ed* or *en*)
- A prepositional phrase beginning with *by*

Notice these examples of passive voice.

- The printer was turned on by Eliza.
- The results of the meeting will be sent to you on Monday.

In contrast, **active voice** is present when the subject performs the action. Now let's take those two sentences and put them in active voice so that you can see the difference.

- Eliza turned on the printer.
- You will receive the results of the meeting on Monday.

Do you see the difference? The active voice is stronger and clearer than the passive voice. Is the use of the passive voice always wrong? No; it does have uses. For example, the person performing the action may not be known. In addition, sometimes the passive voice is used to obscure who was responsible for the action. For example, consider this sentence.

> The decision was made to downsize the company by 15 percent.

The reader does not know who made the decision. The writer may have wanted to be ambiguous about the decision, so the sentence was intentionally phrased in this manner. Although the passive voice has its purposes, it can result in wordy, dull writing. Use the passive voice when you need to, but do not overuse it.

Determine Readability Level.
Readability is the degree of difficulty of the message. These items contribute to a greater reading difficulty:

- Long sentences
- Words with several syllables
- Technical terms

Readability formulas such as the Gunning Fog Index and the Flesch-Kincaid Index provide **readability indices.** The higher the readability index, the less readable the message. As a rule, business messages should be written to achieve a readability index of between the 7th and 11th-grade levels. Certainly, there are exceptions. If you are writing a highly technical report for an expert audience, you may write it with an index of 14 or higher. However, such a report is not written for a general audience but for an audience with the background and educational level to comprehend it.

Utilize Software Writing Aids. Almost all word processing packages now have writing aids to assist you. For example, once you complete a piece of correspondence, you can activate the software writing aid to help you determine:

- Spelling and grammar usage such as
  - verb/subject agreement

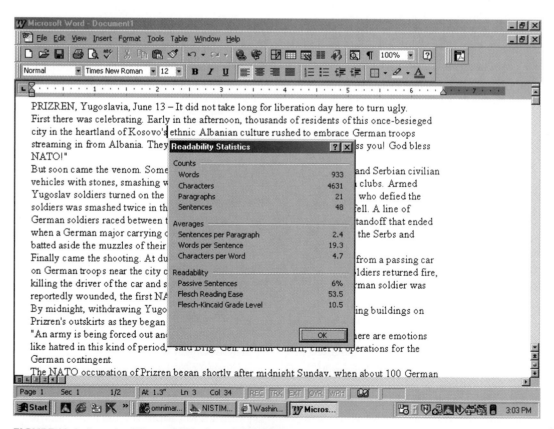

FIGURE 10-6. Example of Microsoft Word's readability scale.

- capitalization
- punctuation
- sentence fragments
- possessives
- Passive sentences
- Readability level

These aids also give you the number of words, paragraphs, and sentences in the document. In addition, you are given averages of the number of sentences per paragraph, the number of words per sentence, and the characters per word. The screen shown in Figure 10-6 shows readability information.

Email, Memorandums, and Letters

The three most frequent types of written correspondence that you as an office professional will write are email, memorandums, and letters. Since there are special considerations when writing each of these types of correspondence, a section is devoted to each one.

Email

As you have already learned, email is used extensively in offices today due to its ease, speed, and cost efficiency. In fact, you probably already use it from your office, if you are presently employed; from your home; and/or from your college or university. However, today, due to the billions of emails that are sent each year (with over 90 percent of major U.S. companies using email), some businesses and individuals are abusing a good communication tool. In addition to overusing it, we often use it incorrectly. Sometimes we do not pay atten-

tion to grammar, proper etiquette, or even good common sense as we send off our email with the click of a key or a mouse.

The characteristics of effective correspondence that you have learned earlier in this chapter apply to email; that is, the email should be:

- Complete
- Clear
- Accurate
- Prompt
- Concise
- Courteous
- Positive

Additionally, there are several general guidelines, as well as guidelines for etiquette and ethics that apply to email specifically. You should pay careful attention to this section so that your email correspondence will be effective and efficient.

Use Proper Guidelines

- Be appropriately formal when writing email. The rule of thumb is to be almost as formal in email as you are in regular memorandums or letters. Most people resent the use of **emoticons,** such as:
    - ⟨G⟩ I'm grinning as I write this sentence.
    - ⟨LOL⟩ I'm laughing out loud.
    - :-) denotes a smile
    - ;-) denotes a wink
    If you must use emoticons, save them for use on your home computer when you are communicating with your best friend or family.
- Use the "subject" line. The subject line should be concise and make sense to both the sender and the recipient. For example, if you are sending an email about a sales meeting at 1:30 on November 15, the subject should read: Sales Meeting, 1:30 p.m., November 15 rather than "Meeting."

- Organize the message and tightly construct it. Email should not be longer than one screen. If you are writing a memo that will take more than one screen, send a hard-copy memorandum. It is much more frustrating to scroll from screen to screen (and often have to scroll back to read something you didn't understand) than it is to read several pages of printed hard copy.

- Edit and proofread carefully. Don't send out an email that contains inaccuracies or incorrect grammar.

- Use complete sentences.

- Capitalize and punctuate properly.

- Do not run sentences together; it is very difficult to read email constructed in this manner.

- Insert a blank line after each paragraph.

- Check your spelling. If your email has a spell-check feature, use it.

- If you have trouble managing your email, you might use tools such as Microsoft Exchange or Eudora to help you. For example, if you get numerous emails from your boss, you can set up a folder called "boss" where these messages will be collected.

Consider Appropriate Etiquette

- Do not use different types of fonts, colors, and clip art and other graphics in email; such an approach merely clutters your message and takes longer to send and receive, particularly if you have included numerous graphics.

- Do not write in all capital letters (known as "shouting" when sending email). Do not write in all lowercase letters.

- Don't respond to a message in anger. In fact, it is a good idea when composing a message to leave the "recipient" field blank until you get ready to send the message. By doing so, you will give

yourself a chance to rethink the situation before keying in the recipient's name and hitting the Send key.

- If you send a message in haste and then immediately realize you should not have done so, use the "unsend" option if it is provided on your email package.

- Answer your email promptly. However, promptly does not generally mean that you should respond within five or ten minutes. Your job will involve much more than answering your email. The general rule is to read and respond to your email once or twice a day (depending on volume). If you receive an email that makes you angry, a response that is too hasty can be dangerous. Use time to think about it.

- Don't send large attached files unless you know the person can receive them; in other words, ask before you send them.

Be Ethical

- Don't send jokes to your family, friends, or coworkers through email; office email is for professional use only.

- When people send you inappropriate email, let them know politely that you cannot receive it. You might say, "I would love to hear from you, but please send any personal email to my home. I cannot receive it at the office."

- Don't use email to berate or reprimand an employee; don't use it to terminate someone.

- Don't use email to send information that might involve any type of legal action.

- Remember that even if you delete email, it may not actually be deleted. Some companies make backup tapes of

TO:

FROM:

DATE:

SUBJECT:

FIGURE 10-7. Memorandum form.

all electronic files. Think carefully before putting something on email.

- Be certain your message is appropriate. Think of email as an electronic postcard. Realize that people other than the recipient may be reading it.

- Don't forward junk mail or chain letters; both are inappropriate in an office.

Memorandums

Although email messages have become the preferred vehicle for communication within the company and short messages outside the company, there are times when a memorandum is more appropriate. For example, when the message is longer than one computer screen or it is important to have a hard copy of it, the memorandum is the better choice.

The characteristics of effective correspondence hold true for memorandums also. They must be complete, clear, accurate, prompt, concise, courteous, and positive. In style, they are slightly more formal than email, but less formal than letters (discussed in the next section). Memorandums are usually written on a preprinted form. This form generally contains the word "memorandum" and the following elements:

- Organizational logo
- *To* line
- *From* line
- *Date* line
- *Subject* line
- **pc** (photocopy) or **cc** (courtesy copy) may be in the heading or listed below the body of the memorandum. Note: Before the computer, *cc* meant carbon copy. After computers, the *cc* became *pc* (photocopy). Today, either *pc* or *cc* may be used on letters, email, and memorandums, with the *cc* meaning *courtesy copy*.

Figure 10-7 illustrates a memorandum form. When filling out the "To" portion of the memo, know what your company preferences are and follow them. For example, here are some general rules:

- Use the first name (or initial) and last name of the individual.

- Use the job title of the individual if it is company policy; many organizations do not use titles in memorandums.

- Do not use *Ms.* or *Mr.*

- List the names in alphabetical order or by hierarchical order within the company (if the company policy dictates).

- List *pc* or *cc* recipients alphabetically or hierarchically, whichever is company policy

If the memorandum is more than one page, the additional pages are keyed on plain paper. The name(s) of the individual(s) receiving the memo, the date, and page number should be keyed at the top of all additional pages.

When writing the memorandum, you need to think through these elements:

- Who is the audience? What does the audience know about the subject?
- What is the purpose of the memorandum?
- How should the content be organized?
- What action is the reader expected to take?

As you write the memorandum, be clear about each of these elements. You may even want to give the sections of the memorandum headings so that the reader can scan the memo quickly and easily. For example, your headings might be:

- Purpose
- Summary
- Action

Figure 10-8 illustrates a memorandum written with headings.

TO: Ernesto Soto

FROM: Juan Menendez

DATE: December 11, 2000

SUBJECT: Paris Operation

Purpose:

I visited our Paris office last week in an attempt to understand why we have experienced such a drastic loss of revenue for the last six months. What I discovered was that we are not working carefully with the companies who are requesting employees. We are not making an attempt to understand their needs. Consequently, we have been sending employees out who have not been trained to do the job.

Recommendations:

I want you to go to Paris next week and spend whatever time it takes to help the office understand how to assess client needs and then train prospective employees to match their needs. I would anticipate that you will need approximately two weeks. Let me hear from you after the first week so that we may discuss progress. When you return, I will expect a full report from you.

FIGURE 10-8. Headings increase readability.

Letters

Letters are much more formal than email or memorandums. A letter represents the company to the outside public—customers, clients, and prospective customers and clients. A well-written letter can win friends and customers; conversely, a poorly written letter can lose customers and make enemies of prospective customers. Regardless of whether the letter is written well or poorly, a letter is a relatively expensive piece of correspondence. The cost of letters continues to escalate each year. According to the Dartnell Report as published in *From Nine to Five*, letter costs have increased $4 per letter since 1990, for a cost in 1998 of $14.56 per letter if by machine or $20.56 per letter if by dictation. A poorly written letter is not only initially costly but can be much more so if it also loses a customer for the company.

Your task as an office professional is to assist your employer with writing effective letters and producing effective drafts or final copy of letters that produce goodwill and positive results for the organization. Before you continue this section on letters, you may want to review the characteristics of effective correspondence and the planning steps that were presented earlier in this chapter. These elements apply to writing letters and are the first steps in the writing process.

Next, you must consider the reader, as of course you do in all correspondence in the planning stages. However, in letters there is an additional step you should take. That step is referred to as the "you approach." Then your next step is to consider the type of letter you will be writing.

Use the You Approach. The **You approach** requires the writer to place the reader at the center of the message. This approach means that the writer must place

herself or himself in the shoes of the reader and attempt to understand the situation from the reader's perspective. It involves using **empathy** in writing. If the writer is trying to sell a product or a service, the writer must look at the benefits it will offer to the reader, not the amount of sales commission the writer will receive. If the message involves something as routine as setting up a meeting, then the writer must stress the benefits of the meeting to the reader. Such writing emphasizes the *you* and *your* and deemphasizes the *I, we, mine,* and *ours*.

To carry out the approach, adhere to two words of caution: *Be sincere.* Do not overuse the you approach to the point of insincerity and even dishonesty. Your goal is not to flatter the reader but to see the situation from the reader's point of view and to respond accordingly. Sincerity dictates that you be honest and empathetic with the reader.

Figure 10-9 gives some examples of how to change the *I-we viewpoint* to the *you viewpoint*. The changes are small, yet the meaning and tone are quite different. The you approach makes the reader's viewpoint important in contrast to the I-we viewpoint, which ignores the reader.

THE YOU APPROACH	
I-We Viewpoint:	We received your order for ten laser printers today.
You Viewpoint:	Your order for ten laser printers arrived July 15.
I-We Viewpoint:	I will be happy to speak at the conference.
You Viewpoint:	Thank you for asking me to speak at the conference. I am delighted to accept.

FIGURE 10-9. The you approach.

Determine the Type of Message.

Generally, letters can be placed into four categories as to the type of message and the anticipated reader response.

Type of Message	Anticipated Reader Response
Favorable	Positive
Routine	Neutral
Unfavorable	Negative
Persuasive	Interested to Indifferent

Favorable messages are those the reader will be pleased to receive. They might include a letter offering a job or a letter of congratulations upon receiving a promotion. **Routine messages** have a neutral effect on the receiver. These messages include requesting information, relaying information, or acknowledging receipt of information. **Unfavorable messages** bring a negative reaction from the reader, such as a letter turning down a job applicant. **Persuasive messages** attempt to get the reader to take some action. For example, a letter trying to convince a busy executive to speak at a local conference is a persuasive letter.

The type of message determines the organization of the letter.

Type of Message	Organization
Favorable	Direct
Routine	Direct
Unfavorable	Indirect
Persuasive	Indirect (persuasive approach)

Direct. If the reader's reaction to your message will be favorable or neutral, you should use the direct approach. Much of the routine correspondence you will write falls into this category. Direct correspondence should:

- Begin with the reason for the correspondence. If you are making a request or inquiry, state it.

"Do you publish an office handbook?"

- Continue with whatever explanation is necessary so that the reader will understand the message.

"If so, I would like to know the title, author, price, and how to place an order."

- Close the letter with a courteous thank-you for action that has been taken or with a request that action be taken by a specific time.

"Please send me the information by November 10."

Figure 10-10 gives a checklist to review when writing favorable and routine messages.

Indirect. When your message to the reader will cause an unfavorable reaction, your best approach is an indirect one. There are times when you have to write correspondence refusing a request or an appointment or in some way saying no to a person. Even so, you want the person to accept the decision and to understand that you are interested and concerned about assisting him or her if at all possible. You want to leave the person with a positive impression. The indirect correspondence should:

- Begin with an opening statement that is pleasant but neutral.

"The appointment you suggested is important to me, and I do want to talk with you about our strategic directions."

- Review the circumstances and give the negative information.

"However, I have an appointment at the time you suggested, and I cannot change it."

- Close the correspondence on a pleasant and positive note.

"Is your calendar free for Tuesday, November 20, at 10 a.m. for a discussion? Let me know as soon as possible

FAVORABLE AND ROUTINE MESSAGE CHECKLIST

- Did you begin the first paragraph with the reason for the correspondence?
- Did you continue with whatever explanation was necessary?
- Did you close with a thank-you for action or with a request that action be taken by a particular date?
- Did you use the "you" approach?
- Is the correspondence clear, concise, and simple?
- Is the correspondence complete? Did you ask the W questions?
- Is the correspondence considerate?
- Is the correspondence timely?
- Is the correspondence positive?
- Do the paragraphs have unity, coherence, and parallel structure?
- Is the readability level appropriate for the intended audience?
- Is the format correct?
- Did you proofread carefully?

FIGURE 10-10. Favorable and routine message checklist.

professional? How to deal with the unhappy customer? How to manage conflict in your office? How to get the multitude of tasks that you face daily handled effectively and efficiently without being stressed out?"

- Continue by creating interest and desire.

"If you answered "yes" to the above questions, our monthly publication, *The Office Professional*, is just what you need. It is packed with effective techniques and suggestions for handling office situations. Each month there is a feature article, with such titles as:

Conflict Can Cause Big Problems

The Office Professional in Touch with the Future

Manage Your Time More Efficiently"

- Close by asking directly for the action desired.

If this date is acceptable for you. I look forward to talking with you concerning our organization's directions."

Figure 10-11 provides a checklist to consider when writing unfavorable messages.

Persuasive. Use the persuasive approach when you want to convince someone to do something (buy a product, give a presentation, and so forth) or change an indifferent or negative reader's reaction. Your goal is to turn a negative or indifferent attitude into a positive position. The persuasive correspondence should:

- Open with the you approach; get the reader's attention.

"Would you like to know all the latest successful techniques for the office

UNFAVORABLE MESSAGE CHECKLIST

- Did you begin with a pleasant but neutral statement?
- Did you review the circumstances and state the negative information as positively as possible?
- Did you close on a pleasant note?
- If you had to say "no" to something, did you offer an alternative if possible?
- Is the correspondence clear, concise, and simple?
- Is the correspondence complete, considerate, and correct?
- Is the correspondence prompt and positive?
- Do the paragraphs have unity, coherence, and parallel structure?
- Is the format correct?
- Did you proofread thoroughly?

FIGURE 10-11. Unfavorable message checklist.

"All this valuable information costs you only $15 per month. What a small amount to pay for information that will help you perform more efficiently on the job! To get *The Office Professional,* merely fill in the information on the enclosed form. We will send you two months free if you purchase an 18-month subscription by December 15."

Reports

The office professional's role in preparing reports will vary. You may have only the responsibility of keying the report, producing the final copies, and distributing the report to the appropriate individuals. Additionally, your role may involve assisting with the creation of visuals for the report (charts, graphs), doing research, and even drafting some or all portions of the report.

The planning steps hold true for reports; that is, the writer should begin by:

- Analyzing the audience who will receive the report
- Determining the purpose of the report

Once these steps have occurred, the writer begins to determine the content of the report by:

- Preparing a summary of what should be included in the report.
- Gathering information for the report. If research is necessary, it is done at this point.
- Preparing an outline of the report. The outline may be a detailed one or merely an informal one the writer prepares to get his or her thoughts organized. Figure 10-12 shows a portion of an outline. Notice that no main head-

PREPARING A BUSINESS REPORT

I. Introduction
   A. Purpose of the Report
   B. Role of the Office Professional
II. Outline
   A. Purpose of the Outline
   B. Organization of Information
      1. Titles
      2. Headings
      3. Subheadings
   C. Report Structure
      1. Definition of Parallel Structure
      2. Example of Parallel Structure

FIGURE 10-12. Preparing a business report.

ing or subheading stands alone. For every *I*, there must be a *II*; for every *A*, there must be a *B*. An outline may be written in topical form (as illustrated) or in complete sentence form. An outline should also be parallel in structure; that is, if roman numeral I begins with a noun, then all roman numerals must begin with a noun.

- Drafting the report. The body of the report should have:
  - An introduction to help the reader understand the purpose of the report
  - A main part that includes all the pertinent information
  - A conclusion or findings and recommendations to help the reader understand what should be done with the report
- Preparing any necessary graphs, charts, and tables.
- Reading and editing the report.

- Making appropriate changes and rereading the report.
- Preparing the executive summary.
- Printing and distributing the report.

Reference Sources

Most reports involve some type of research. This research may be **primary research;** that is, original data collection that is conducted through surveys, observations, or experiments—material that the writer or team creates or discovers. Or the research may be **secondary;** that is, data that is collected through books, periodicals, and various other library materials—material that other people have discovered or created.

Conduct Primary Research.   If you are conducting primary research, you must decide how you are going to gather the information. You may decide to:

- Observe situations and individuals
- Survey or interview groups of individuals
- Perform an experiment

Observational research involves collecting data through observations of an event or of actions. Survey research involves collecting data through some type of survey or interview. An interview may be done face-to-face or by telephone. Sometimes **focus groups** are brought together to talk with an interviewer about their opinions of certain events or issues. A survey is generally done by mail; however, it also may be administered in person. For example, you may decide to assemble several people in your company and pass out a survey to be completed immediately. Generally, there is a much better **response rate** on surveys administered in person than those done by mail.

Focus groups provide primary research data. *Courtesy of © PhotoDisc, Inc.*

Experimental research has generally been used in the sciences; however, it is becoming popular with business. It may involve a researcher selecting two or more sample groups and exposing them to treatments. For example, a business may decide to test a marketing strategy before implementing a marketing campaign. Experimental groups would be selected and the marketing strategy implemented. Based on the outcome of the research, the business would proceed with the marketing strategy, modify it, or select another one.

Conduct Secondary Research.   There are two major sources for conducting secondary research. The traditional one is the library; however, with the amount of information now on the Internet, it is rivaling the library for gathering research. In fact, most libraries today are filled with computers. These computers are connected to the Internet and to various other sources of information. For example, two libraries may be connected to each other through computers, thus eliminating the necessity for having a large number of books physically stored on shelves within the library.

Whether you do traditional library research in the form of reading books, periodicals, and other reference sources, or you use the Internet from your home computer or the library computer, your responsibility as a researcher is to gather credible information and cite your sources. With the traditional library, we have accepted that materials that are published by major publishing companies or major periodicals have credibility. However, we have not had the issue of determining the credibility of our source. We have documented our sources by using the traditional footnote or endnote that is used in this textbook, the **MLA** (author/work) or **APA** (author/year) approach. These different approaches will be explained in more detail in Chapter 11.

With the amount of data now on the Internet, our task becomes a different one. Any person, as you are aware, can get on the Internet and write almost anything he or she chooses. The information may or may not have any validity or reliability. If you are doing research on the Internet, whether it is from sources on the World Wide Web or from local or national sources, it is important that you evaluate the information carefully. For example, here are some questions you can ask.

- Has the person writing contributed to the body of research in the past; that is, has he or she published in the field?
- Does a credible organization or company represent the person?
- Does the person give appropriate support for his or her points?
- Does the person have appropriate educational credentials?

If you accept that the research or data is credible, you must document your source from the Internet. The style of documentation is different; information on this is given in Chapter 11.

Parts of the Report

An informal report might have only one or two parts—the body and an executive summary. Formal reports may contain the following parts:

- Executive summary
- Title page
- Table of contents
- List of tables and illustrations
- Body
- Documentation (Endnotes/footnotes, MLA, or APA)
- Bibliography or reference section
- Appendix

Executive Summary. The **executive summary** is a one- or two-page summary of the document. It is written for the busy executive who:

- wishes to preview the report to determine if there is a portion that he or she wants to read in its entirety, or
- does not need to have a detailed understanding of all aspects of the report, but does need to know the background, major findings, and recommendations.

The executive summary:

- Describes the background—why the report was necessary, what the problem or issue was.
- Gives the major findings—what was discovered as a result of the research.
- Provides the recommendations—as a result of the research, the recommendations that are being made and the actions the organization should take.

Title Page. The title page contains the title of the report; the writer's name, title, and department or division; and the date the report is being submitted.

Table of Contents. The table of contents lists each major section of a report and the page number of the first page of that section. A table of contents is not required; however, when a report is long, it helps the reader find particular parts of the report.

List of Tables and Illustrations. If there are numerous tables and illustrations within a report, it is appropriate to list the title of each one, with the respective page number. This procedure helps the reader quickly locate them and scan the data presented.

Body of the Report. The body is divided into the following major sections.

- Introduction
- Problem statement
- Research methods
- Findings and discussion
- Recommendations
- Conclusion

Footnotes/Endnotes/Internal Citations. Footnotes appear at the bottom of the page where the reference is made. Endnotes are grouped at the end of the document. Internal citations appear within the context of the document.

Bibliography or Reference Section. All references used in a report should be included in a bibliography or reference section. This section includes the complete name of the author(s), the title of the book or periodical, the date of the publication, the publishing company, and page numbers.

Appendix. A formal report may contain an appendix that includes supporting information such as tables, statistics, and other pertinent material. Items in an appendix are lettered *Appendix A, B,* and so forth. The appendix is the last part of the report.

Your communications, whether they are email, memorandums, letters, or reports, can be written well and follow all of the elements of good correspondence. However, if the message is not presented in an appropriate format and free from grammatical or keyboard errors, it will not be well received. In the next chapter you will learn how to effectively present your correspondence.

SUMMARY

To reinforce what you have learned in this chapter, study this summary.

- The basic types of written messages in an office are letters, email, memorandums, and reports.
- Teams are used in writing as they are in various other activities of the office. Collaborative writing demands that team members work together using active listening, conflict resolution, and acceptance of cultural differences.
- Effective correspondence is complete, clear, accurate, prompt, concise, courteous, and positive.
- The planning steps include analyzing the reader, determining the purpose, and organizing the content.
- In organizing the content, the writer should begin with the important information, plan the paragraphs, use appropriate sentence structure when possible, determine the readability level, and utilize software-writing aids.
- When sending email, the writer should use proper guidelines, etiquette, and ethics.

- Memorandums are generally longer than email messages and are useful when a hard copy of the message is needed.
- Letters are more formal than email or memorandums. A letter represents the company to the outside public.
- Messages can be organized into four types—favorable, routine, unfavorable, and persuasive.
- There are two basic approaches when writing letters—the direct and indirect approach.

- In writing an effective report, the writer should:
  - Analyze the audience
  - Determine the purpose of the report
  - Prepare a summary of what should be included in the report
  - Gather information for the report
  - Prepare an outline
  - Draft the report
  - Prepare any necessary graphs, charts, and/or tables
  - Prepare the executive summary
  - Print and distribute the report

Key Terms

- W questions
- Parallelism
- Passive voice
- Active voice
- Readability
- Readability indices
- Emoticons
- pc (photocopy)

- cc (courtesy copy)
- You approach
- Empathy
- Favorable messages
- Routine messages
- Unfavorable messages
- Persuasive messages

- Primary research
- Secondary research
- Focus groups
- Response rate
- MLA
- APA
- Executive summary

Professional Pointers

Here are some pointers to help you write more effective letters and memos. Remember them as the "do's and don'ts" of written correspondence.

- Do not use sexist terminology; it can have a detrimental effect on the development of good business relationships. Terms such as these involve implied or overt stereotyping and should be avoided:

  Chairman (use chairperson)

  Spokesman (use spokesperson)

  Stewardess (use flight attendant)

  Businessman (use businessperson)

  A secretary . . . she (use office professional or secretaries . . . they)

  A nurse . . . she (use nurses . . . they)

- Do use plural pronouns when possible to avoid male/female stereotyping:

  Avoid: Each executive has his assigned space.

  Use: All executives have assigned spaces.

- Do use general job titles rather than specific ones. You may want to refer to the *Dictionary of Occupational Titles* for updated titles.

  Avoid: The mailman does not deliver to this business address.

  Use: The mail carrier does not deliver to this business address.

- Do not use the same word too often in a document. Do use a thesaurus for appropriate synonyms to enhance your writing.

- Do not use redundant expressions (words that have the same meaning), such as *each and every* or *exactly identical*.

Office Procedures Reinforcement

1. Name and explain the common characteristics of effective correspondence.
2. Explain the planning steps of correspondence.
3. What is passive voice? Why should it be used sparingly?
4. Explain the difference between primary and secondary research?
5. What is an executive summary?

Critical Thinking Activity

Darlene Hughes began her career six years ago as a clerical assistant at Lansing Corporation. For the past four years she has been an office services specialist. Darlene has an excellent work record and exceptional composition, keyboarding, and organization skills.

Two months ago several administrative changes occurred in the company. Some managerial positions were eliminated, others were consolidated, and new ones were created. Mark Stevenson was promoted from field engineer to associate director of research and design. Darlene was given the position of administrative assistant to Mr. Stevenson. She was very pleased with the increase in salary and looked forward to the added responsibilities and the challenge of a new job.

Mr. Stevenson's new responsibilities include introducing new product designs, completing routine forms for patents, handling inquiries for research data, and responding to requests for information on new products. In addition to tackling such a demanding job, Mr. Stevenson has also been appointed chairperson of the project team to improve productivity in the manufacturing of new and established products.

Mr. Stevenson has been so busy with his new job duties that he has failed to realize how Darlene can be an efficient assistant and thus lessen his workload. Darlene has done an average amount of document preparation; otherwise, her workload has been relatively light. Mr. Stevenson composes all of his correspondence in handwriting. Many of the letters he writes are replies that could be handled by Darlene.

- Should Darlene admit that she does not keep busy and that her workload is too light?
- How could Darlene approach Mr. Stevenson to discuss a better utilization of her skills?
- What specific responsibilities could Darlene assume for Mr. Stevenson?
- How would you react to a situation such as this one? Would you want to increase your workload?

Office Applications

OA10-1 (Goals 1 and 2)

Load the OA10-1.doc file from your template disk. Analyze the memorandum for words or phrases that you consider inappropriate. Highlight these words or phrases by using a bold format and print a copy. Use the copy to mark the necessary revisions that reflect the principles of effective writing. Revise the memorandum and print a final copy. Submit both the edited draft and final copy to your instructor.

OA10-2 (Goals 1 and 2)

On the student data template disk in file OA10-2 is a simulated email form. Write a memo to Elaine Bordeaux of the Paris, France, office using email. Request a copy of the income and expense statement for the office for the last two years. Elaine Bordeaux's email address is eb@pfi.com. Mr. Menendez needs this information within two weeks.

OA10-3 (Goals 1 and 2)

You have been requested to speak at your local chapter of IAAP on "Effective Written Communication Techniques." The request is for December 15. You will not be able to do so due to your heavy workload at the present time. However, you would like to speak in the future. Write a letter declining the invitation. Use the letterhead provided on the student template disk in file OA10-3.

OA10-4 (Goals 1, 2, and 3)

Choose three of your classmates to work with on this project. Conduct primary research by surveying 15 to 20 students on one of the three issues given below. Write a report of your findings. Use charts and graphs in your report. If you developed a survey to give to the students, provide a copy of it as an appendix to your report. Before you begin your research and writing, review the guidelines for collaborative writing in your text on page 244. After you have finished writing your report, use the evaluation form in your Applications Workbook, p. 61, to determine if your team worked together successfully. Submit your report and your team evaluation to your instructor.

Choose one of the following issues.

- Are ethics a problem in our society? If you believe they are, why do you believe it? If you do not believe ethics are a problem, why not?

- Is it okay to lie under oath? If you believe that it is, is it always acceptable to lie under oath? What issue is it okay to lie about? If you believe that it is not okay to lie under oath, why not?

- Should there be any censure of material on the Internet? If so, what type of materials should be censured and why? If you believe there should be no censure, why not?

Online Research Applications

ORA10-5 (Goals 1 and 2)

Using the Internet, research the characteristics of effective messages. Write a memorandum to your instructor with your findings; use the memorandum form provided on the student template disk in file ORA10-5. List the resources you found, using this format.

Name of author, date of article, title of article, URL

Bowers, K. L. (November 2000). *Effective Letters*, http://www.dev.com.

CHAPTER 11

Presentations

1. Prepare letters and reports using appropriate style and placement.
2. Prepare and deliver oral presentations.

In addition to the writing principles that you learned in Chapter 10, it is important that business documents be presented attractively to the reader. This chapter focuses on presenting letters and reports effectively so that the recipient will want to read the correspondence. Also, as an office professional, occasionally you will have the opportunity to make oral presentations before groups, either as an individual or as part of a team. This chapter will help you develop oral presentation skills.

If you are preparing a letter, you should:

- Format it appropriately
- Be certain that it is free of typographical and grammatical errors

If you are preparing a report, it is important to:

- Present it in an appropriate format
- Integrate tables and graphs to illustrate information and data
- Document primary and secondary research appropriately

If you are making an oral presentation, you should:

- Plan well so that your message is relevant for your audience
- Prepare appropriate visuals
- Deliver the presentation effectively

You probably have been introduced to the formats for letters and reports in keyboarding courses. Thus, this chapter presents a short review of the format, with concentration on using graphics, documenting appropriately, and making oral presentations.

Presenting Letters

We all know that first impressions are important in face-to-face encounters and can be lasting impressions in relationships. Usually, we strive to make a good first impression on people we are meeting for the first time. First impressions can be equally important when receiving a letter. Even if the letter is well written, it will not make a favorable impression if it is presented in an incorrect format or if it contains keyboarding and grammatical errors. One of your goals as an office professional is to present letters attractively and correctly. You should pay careful attention to style, placement, and **mailability** (free of any type of error).

Letter Parts

The basic parts of a letter are:

- Dateline
- Letter address

- Salutation
- Body
- Writer's name and title
- Reference initials

Additional parts of a letter may include:

- Attention line
- Subject line
- Second page heading
- Notations such as enclosure and copy

The correct placement of the parts of a letter is shown in Figures 11-1 and 11-2. In setting margins, the default margins (1.25 for left and right margins) on the software package generally are acceptable. However, if the letter is extremely short, you may need to increase the left and right margins to approximately 2″ by going into the Page Setup dialog box of the word processing software you are using. Another possibility is to leave the default margins alone and use center placement of the letter by activating the center option on the formatting toolbar. Notice that in both Figures 11-1 and 11-2 the letter is framed on the page, with the various parts formatted correctly. This framed look is the one you want to achieve. Additional formatting guidelines are given in Figure 11-3.

Letter Styles and Punctuation.   The two basic letter styles used today are **block** and **modified block**. Figure 11-1 illustrates a block style, and Figure 11-2 shows a modified block style.

Punctuation Styles.   The two punctuation styles used are **mixed** and **open**. In mixed punctuation, a colon is keyed after the salutation and a comma after the complimentary close. When open punctuation is used, there is no punctuation after either of these elements. Open punctuation is shown in Figure 11-1 and mixed punctuation in Figure 11-2.

PEOPLE FIRST INTERNATIONAL
986 Front Street
Detroit, MI 48201-1701
Telephone: 313 555-0199
Fax: 313 555-0178
URL: http://www.pfi.com

October 10, 2000

Mrs. Amelia Santiago
37 Duke Street
Boston, MA 02136-0117

Dear Mrs. Santiago

All lines in the block style letter begin at the left margin. In open
punctuation, as this sample letter shows, there is no punctuation after the
salutation and complimentary close.

The block style letter is efficient, since there is no need to use tabs. You
will find this letter style used quite often in business correspondence

Sincerely

Amanda G. De Vault

Amanda G. DeVault

gt/let/10.10

pc Chi Wang

FIGURE 11-1. Block Letter Style, Open Punctuation.

PEOPLE FIRST INTERNATIONAL
986 Front Street
Detroit, MI 48201-1701
Telephone: 313 555-0199
Fax: 313 555-0178
URL: http://www.pfi.com

October 10, 2000

Rodelski Van Lines
Attention Mr. William Fallen
402 DuBuys Road
Melrose Park, IL 40162-6210

Dear Mr. Fallen:

THE MODIFIED BLOCK STYLE LETTER

The modified block style letter may be written with block or indented paragraphs. The date and closing lines start at the center. An attention line is included in this letter. It is keyed below the company name in the letter address. A subject line is also used in this letter. It is keyed a double space below the salutation.

Notice that mixed punctuation is used in this letter. A colon follows the salutation and a comma follows the complimentary close.

Sincerely,

Jeff C. Fay
Office Manager

Pjw/let/10.15

Bc Roger Zapinski

FIGURE 11-2. Modified Block Letter Style, Mixed Punctuation.

LETTER FORMATTING GUIDELINES

- Use the proper format.
- Use the company's letterhead for letters.
- Place the letter address approximately one-half inch below the date.
- Place the attention line as the second line of the letter address.
- Place the salutation a double space below the letter address.
- Place the subject line a double space below the salutation.
- Place the complimentary close a double space below the body of the letter.
- Place the signature line a quadruple space below the complimentary close.
- Place reference initials a double space below the signature block.
- Place enclosure and attachment notations a double space below the reference initials.
- Place a copy notation a double space below the reference initials or a double space below the enclosure or attachment notation.
- Identify the document with the electronic filename for ease of retrieval.
- Use plain paper for the second page of letters. The second page heading includes the name of the addressee, page number, and date of the letter placed one inch from the top of the page at the left margin.

FIGURE 11-3. Formatting Guidelines

Stationery. Letterhead stationery is used for the first page of letters. The letterhead usually includes the name of the firm, the mailing address, phone number, and fax number printed at the top of the paper. With the number of organizations that now have information on the Internet, URLs (Uniform Resource Locators) sometimes are given in the letterhead. Figures 11-1 and 11-2 show a letterhead on the left side of the page. The letterhead may also be centered or on the right side of the page. Plain bond paper is used for the second page of a letter.

Envelopes. The standard size envelope, which is $9\frac{1}{2}$ x $4\frac{1}{8}$ inches is referred to as a No. 10 envelope. This envelope is the one used with the standard $8\frac{1}{2}$ x 11-inch letterhead stationery. Small envelopes, measuring $6\frac{1}{2}$ x $3\frac{5}{8}$ inches, generally are used for personal letters. However, they may be used for business letters when the stationery is smaller than $8\frac{1}{2}$ x 11 inches.

Since **optical character readers (OCRs)** are used by the U.S. Post Office to scan envelope addresses, the address must be placed appropriately on the envelope. A No. 10 envelope should be formatted in the following manner:

- The address is keyed $2\frac{1}{2}$" from the top of the envelope and 4" from the left edge.
- The address is keyed in all caps with no punctuation.
- Two-letter state abbreviations are used, along with the 9-digit ZIP code.
- Notations to the post office such as REGISTERED are keyed below the stamp at least three lines above the address in all caps.
- Notations such as CONFIDENTIAL and PLEASE FORWARD are keyed a triple space below the return address and three spaces from the left edge of the envelope.

Mailability. Once you have keyed a letter, it is important to proofread it carefully for mailability. Remember, it is most important that there be no keyboarding, grammatical, or formatting errors. When checking your letter for mailability, ask these questions.

- Is the format correct? Do the margins resemble a frame around a picture?

- Have you used an appropriate letter style and punctuation style?
- Is the dateline appropriately placed? Is the date correct?
- Is the letter address correct? Is it appropriately placed?
- Is the salutation correct? Is it appropriately placed?
- Are the complimentary close and signature lines correct and appropriately placed?
- Are the reference initials in the appropriate place?
- If there are enclosures, have they been noted on the letter?
- If there are special letter parts such as an attention line or enclosure notation, are they correct and appropriately placed?
- If a copy is to be sent to another individual, is it noted on the letter in the appropriate place?
- Does the envelope address match the letter address?
- Is the appropriate envelope format used?
- Is the letter free of grammatical and punctuation errors? Is it free of misspelled words? (Have you used your grammar and spell check program?)
- Is the letter folded and inserted in the envelope correctly?

To help you in proofreading your letter carefully, read the "Proofreading Tips" given in Figure 11-4.

PROOFREADING TIPS

- Proofread your document on the screen before you print it. Scroll to the beginning of the document and use the top of the screen as a guide for your eye in reading each line.
- Proofread a document in three steps.

  a. General appearance and format
  b. Spelling and keyboarding errors
  c. Punctuation, word usage, and content

- Read from right to left for spelling and keyboarding errors.
- Use a spell checker.
- If possible, do not proofread a document right after keying it; let it rest while you perform some other task.
- Pay attention to dates. Do not assume that they are correct. Check to determine that Thursday, June 18, is actually a Thursday, for example. Check the spelling of months; check the correctness of the year.
- Do not overlook proofreading the date, subject, enclosure notation, and the names and addresses of the recipients.
- Use the thesaurus if you are not certain a word is appropriate.
- Watch closely for omissions of -ed, -ing, or -s at the end of words.
- If punctuation causes you problems, check a grammatical source after you have completed all other proofreading.
- Be consistent in the use of commas.
- Be consistent in the use of capital letters.
- Check numerals.
- Be consistent in format.
- Keep a good reference manual at your desk to look up any grammar or punctuation rules you question.

FIGURE 11-4. Proofreading Tips

Presenting Reports

A report may be informal containing only a few pages, or it may be formal with numerous parts. You learned about the various parts of a report in Chapter 10. An informal report may be written in a conversational style, using personal pronouns such as "I," "you," "we," and so forth. The formal report generally is written in manuscript format and contains the preliminary and supplementary parts such as:

- Executive summary
- Title page
- Table of contents
- List of tables and illustrations
- Body of the report
- Footnotes/endnotes/internal citations
- Bibliography or reference section
- Appendix

All of these parts were discussed in Chapter 10. Whatever form you choose for a report, you should take care to present it well.

One or more drafts may be necessary before the final version is prepared. Drafts allow the writer to review and edit the report before the final copy is formatted. When preparing a draft, the word "draft" should be placed at the top of each sheet. Also, it is a good idea to date the draft, with the date under the word "draft" at the top of the page. Dating the draft prevents confusion when you are dealing with several versions of a report. You may generate the draft and date notations by using **headers** or **footers** (elements that appear on every page of your document). Word processing packages allow you to add headers and footers easily. They may be added before you begin keying the document or before printing the first draft. Drafts generally are double-spaced so that corrections can be made easily.

Documentation

Documentation is the process of giving credit to the sources used in the report. You learned in Chapter 10 that footnotes, endnotes, or internal citations are all appropriate forms of documentation. This section will show you how to format each type.

Footnotes and Endnotes. Footnotes and endnotes are older forms of documentation than internal citations. Both footnotes and endnotes require superscript numbers within the report. When using footnotes, the documentation for the superscript numbers appears at the bottom of the page on which the superscripts appear. With the endnote format, the documentation for the superscript numbers appears at the end of the document in a section titled "Reference" or "Notes." Figure 11-5 shows both footnote and endnote citations.

Internal Citations. Internal citations or **parenthetical documentation** are documented using either the **MLA style (Modern Language Association)** or **APA style (American Psychological Association)** format. Internal citations are placed in the report itself within parentheses. The details of the source are given in a section usually titled "Works Cited" or "References," which is placed at the end of the document. Figure 11-6 gives examples of both the APA and MLA styles of documenting a source.

Internet Citations. The Internet now provides a tremendous amount of information about a vast number of topics. The sources it offers are used extensively by individuals and businesses as they research a topic. The documentation of those sources differs from documentation methods given previously, as shown in Figure 11-7.

FOOTNOTE AND ENDNOTE CITATIONS

Footnote Citation

At the point where the reference is mentioned, a superscript number is placed in the text, and a footnote is placed on the same page as the superscript number. A sample footnote is shown here.

1. Michael G. Dolence and Donald M. Norris, *Transforming Higher Education: A Vision for Learning in the 21st Century* (Ann Arbor, MI: Society for College and University Planning, 1995), 25.

Endnote Citation

The endnote style requires the same superscript number when the reference is noted in the text. However, no information about the work is given until the end of the paper in a section referred to as "References" or "Notes." The reference notes appear in numerical order according to the superscript and are double-spaced within and between notes.

1. Michael G. Dolence and Donald M. Norris, *Transforming Higher Education: A Vision for Learning in the 21st Century* (Ann Arbor, MI: Society for College and University Planning, 1995), 25.

FIGURE 11-5. Footnote and Endnote Citations

APA AND MLA DOCUMENTATION STYLES

APA Documentation Style

According to Bachner (1998), improper lighting conditions that continue over a period of time can cause low productivity and morale.

MLA Documentation Style

John P. Bachner suggests that improper lighting conditions can cause low productivity and morale (16).

Note: When the authority is first introduced, the first name and the surname are used. In subsequent citations by the same authority, only the surname is used.

FIGURE 11-6. APA and MLA Documentation Styles

INTERNET DOCUMENTATION

With the relative newness of Internet data, the guidelines for references are not as clear. Also, many times the information given for Internet data is not consistent. Although you may not always find all of this information listed on an Internet source, here is a suggested documentation method.

DePaul University Institute for Business and Professional Ethics ((http://condor.depaul.edu/ethics/resource.html)

Note: If the author is given, his or her name should be used also.

FIGURE 11-7. Internet Documentation

Bibliography or Reference Section. This section provides the information the reader needs to find the sources that were used in the report. It includes the complete name of the author(s), the title of the book or periodical, the date of the publication, the publishing company and the city of publication (if the reference is a book), and the page numbers. The state of publication may be included if the city is a less common one. Several different forms may be used in preparing the reference list. Figure 11-8 illustrates reference lists for footnotes and internal citations using the MLA and APA styles.

Graphics

Graphics such as tables, line graphs, bar graphs, and pie charts are frequently used in business reports to illustrate data. Graphics provide "pictures" to help the reader understand and remember the information presented in the report. They also help hold the reader's interest. A report becomes much more appealing to the reader when well-designed graphics are used. When deciding when and where to

FIGURE 11-8. References

place graphics in a report, ask yourself these questions.

• Who is the audience?

• Will graphics assist the audience in understanding the message?

• What purpose will the graphic(s) serve?

• Are you presenting the information in the graphics in a straightforward manner? Too much information in a graphic can cause confusion for the reader.

• Is the graphic placed appropriately? Does it follow the text to which it refers?

• Has the appropriate type of graphic been selected? If you have selected a bar graph, for example, does it illustrate the concept well? Or would a pie chart or a line graph be more appropriate? Figures 11-9 and 11-10 show both bar and line graphs.

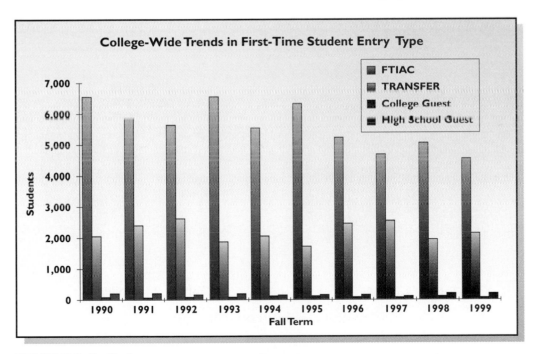

FIGURE 11-9. Bar Graph

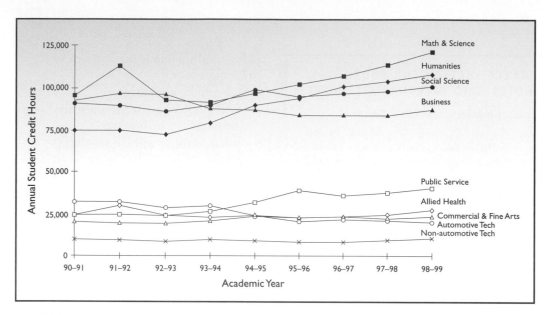

FIGURE 11-10. Line Graph

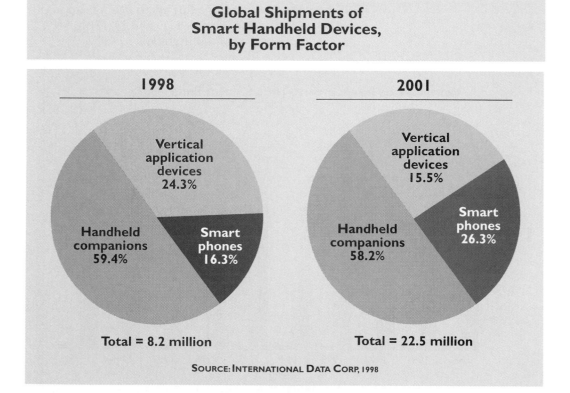

FIGURE 11-11. When using colors in graphs, provide adequate contrasts.

- Will color help get the message of the graphic across to the reader? If so, have you used color? If you have, do not use too many colors. That can cause confusion for the reader. When using color, make certain that the contrasts are great. For example, two shades of one color (with one slightly darker than the other) generally will not provide adequate contrast. When you want to highlight contrasts in data, it is best to use colors of very different hues. Notice the color contrasts in Figure 11-11. Light colors make an object appear larger than do darker colors. In the pie chart in Figure 11-12, the "FICA & Retirement" piece of the pie appears larger to the eye than the "Supplies & Services" piece, although in actuality the "Supplies & Services" is larger.

FIGURE 11-13. Clip art can enhance your document; however, do not overuse it or your document will look cluttered.

Clip Art, Line Drawings, and Borders

Clip art, available on most word processing packages, may also be used effectively in a report. Various illustrations are available and are easily inserted into reports. Figure 11-13 shows several clip art possibilities.

By using the drawing tool bar on your word processing package, you may draw lines and various shapes. The shapes may then be modified (reduced, enlarged, or moved to another part of the page). Figure 11-14 shows several shape and line possibilities.

In addition to the clip art and lines and shapes, borders and columns may also be used effectively in reports. Borders

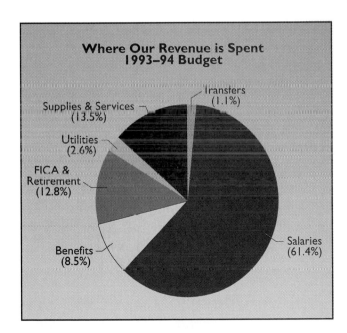

FIGURE 11-12. Light colors make an object appear larger than darker colors.

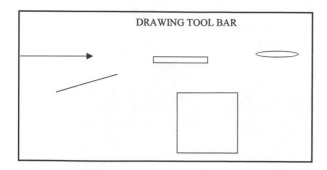

FIGURE 11-14. The drawing tool bars allow you to draw lines and various shapes.

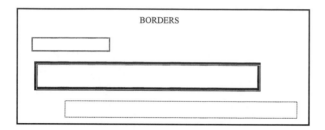

FIGURE 11-15. Borders may be of various widths and designs.

may be of various widths and designs. Figure 11-15 shows several widths.

Margins and Page Numbers

The default margins (1.25″) on your software package are appropriate for reports unless you are binding them. If so, you will need to add .25″ to the left margin to allow for ease of reading. The first page of a report is not numbered. The page number for second and subsequent pages is usually placed at the top right of the page. However, page numbers may be placed at the bottom of the page and centered. If you are **duplexing** (printing on both sides of the paper) and are placing the page numbers on the top right, you will need to alternate the position of the page number for every other page. You may do so

easily by instructing your word processing package to print the page number in alternate positions.

Headings

The title of the report should be in all capital letters and centered on the first page of the report. Side headings are placed at the left margin. The main words begin with a capital letter. A double space precedes a side heading, and a double space follows it. Different sizes of **fonts** (sets of characters in particular sizes, typefaces, weights, and styles) may be used in headings. Figure 11-16 illustrates several sizes of fonts and variations in font appearance.

Paragraph headings may be indented or flush with the left margin. They may be followed by a period and underlined. Paragraph headings are preceded by a double space.

Quotations

Material from other sources may be quoted directly or indirectly in a report. It is necessary to obtain permission to quote copyrighted material when reports are to

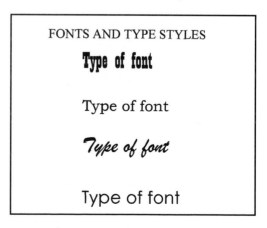

FIGURE 11-16. Various sizes of fonts may be used effectively in reports.

be printed or copied for public circulation. If an indirect quotation is used, a footnote reference is all that is necessary. If the material is a direct quotation, it should be handled in the following manner:

- Quotations of fewer than four lines are included in the body of the report and enclosed in quotation marks.

- Quotations of four or more lines are without quotation marks, single-spaced, and indented one-half inch from the left margin. The right margin of the quotation is the same as that of the document.

- When the quotation consists of several paragraphs, quotation marks precede each new paragraph and follow the final word in the last paragraph only.

- A quotation within a quotation is enclosed in single quotation marks.

- Omissions are shown by **ellipses—** three spaced periods (. . .) within a sentence, four spaced periods at the end of a sentence.

- Italicized words in the quotation may be underlined if an italic font is not available.

Researching and Keying Presentations

When your employer is making a presentation, your role in assisting him or her may be in helping with the research and in keying the presentation. You learned in Chapter 10 that you may conduct primary or secondary research.

If you are conducting secondary research, the Internet can be a source of information. Since the amount of information on the Internet is increasing exponentially, it is a good idea to check what is available on any particular topic. When doing research on the Internet, you need to refine your search as much as possible. State the topic that you are researching in precise rather than general terms. For example, if you are searching for information concerning computer equipment, be specific. Your search words might be "Computer Equipment and Printers." By adding the "and Printers" to your search words, you narrow the search to a specific type of computer equipment. If you are interested in color laser printers, you can be even more precise by adding "and Color Laser Printers." Unless you narrow your search as much as possible, you can receive thousands of **hits (references).** Your search then becomes terribly difficult as you sift through reference after reference that may have little significance to the information that you actually need.

Whether or not you have a role in assisting the executive with research for presentations, you probably will key presentations many times. When keying presentations for the executive or for yourself, you should:

- Key material using a large font size; you may want to check with your employer as to the size font you use.

- Double or quadruple space the presentation.

- Number the pages.

- Place the final copy in a folder. (This folder may be a specially purchased leather one. Such a folder provides a professional and organized method of carrying the presentation when delivering the speech.)

If you or the executive are using visuals in the presentation, number them and refer to each number in the body of the presentation at the point the visual is to be shown. You might want to use a colored felt tip pen to highlight this point.

When preparing visuals, you may want to use a presentation software package to assist you. Presentation software packages allow you to add graphics and other forms of visuals that, if used effectively, can improve the quality of your presentation. Visuals can be created that include these elements:

- Graphics (which you can **import** from spreadsheet software, word processing software, and so forth)
- Clip art
- Resize and move graphics or clip art
- Freehand drawing
- Color
- **Animation** (the copy appears as if being keyed on the screen at the particular point that you are presenting it)
- **Narration** (a sound card and a microphone are needed to add narration)
- Print to paper or transparencies

Preparing and Delivering Oral Presentations

As you have learned earlier in this text, office professionals serve on project teams. These project teams often make presentations of their findings and recommendations, which you, as a part of a team, may have an opportunity to present before a group. You also may have occasion to speak at professional organizations to which you belong. This section deals with preparing and delivering effective presentations.

If your presentation is to be effective, there are several steps that you should follow, as listed in the following sections.

Determine the Purpose

You have probably listened with impatience to speakers who did not make the purpose of their presentation clear. In fact, you may have wondered:

Does the speaker have a point?

If so, when is the speaker going to get to the point?

To keep you from making such an error, ask yourself these questions as you begin to plan your presentation.

- What do I want to accomplish with the presentation?
- What do I want the audience to know as a result of my presentation?
- What, if anything, do I want the audience to do as a result of my presentation?

Determine the Anticipated Audience

Who will be in the audience? For example, if it is a group of office professionals, you know some of their interests. You can use anecdotes or stories that will have meaning for them. If you are speaking to a group of colleagues from your office, again you know some of their interests. You can tailor your message to meet their needs. If you are speaking to a general audience, here are some questions you need to ask and be able to answer as you begin to plan your remarks.

- What will be the ages of the people in the audience?
- Will the audience be **heterogeneous** as to gender? Or will it be **homogenous**— all male or all female?
- What is their education? Are they generally high school graduates or college graduates?
- What knowledge do they have of the subject you will be presenting?
- What will be the size of the audience? Will there be 15 or 50? Numbers do

Determine the anticipated audience. *Courtesy of © PhotoDisc, Inc.*

- When will the presentation be given? In the morning? Right before lunch? Immediately after lunch? In the evening (before or after a meal)?
- Will there be entertainment preceding your presentation or after?
- Will there be other business occurring before or after the presentation?
- Will the presentation be held in an office building, a hotel, a conference center, or a school?
- How will the room be arranged? Will it be a theatre type setting? If the audience will be small, will they be sitting around a table? Will the chairs be set up in a circle?

If you have an opportunity to control the setting, do so. Be certain that the size of the room is appropriate. You do not want to be giving a presentation to 12 people in a room designed for 100 people. It will look as if you gave a party and no one came. Neither do you want to be giving a presentation to 50 people in a room designed for 25. People are not comfortable when too crowded. Be certain that the chairs are comfortable, the temperature is pleasant, the room is clean, the lighting is appropriate, and the acoustics are good.

Gather the Material

Research the topic if necessary. You have already learned about conducting primary research and secondary research. Determine what type of research is appropriate, and gather the material.

Organize the Presentation

An outline is a good way to organize the presentation. The organization should consist of an introduction, body, and

make a difference. A small audience allows greater interaction; questions can be used effectively. With a large audience, there is little chance for interaction other than possibly saving time for a question-and-answer period at the end.

Determine the Setting

The time of your presentation, the location, and any other activities that are occurring around the same time are important to know. Ask these questions in determining the setting.

conclusion. In the introduction, you tell your audience what you are going to say. In the body, you give them the information; and in the closing, you remind them again of what you have said by giving a summary. In other words, you remind the audience three times of the important points of your presentation; such repetition increases the chances that the audience will understand and remember what you have said.

Develop an Opening

The opening should immediately get the audience's attention. For example, you may tell a story, use a quotation, ask a question, or refer to a current event. However, it is important to know what you do best. If you can never remember the punch line of a joke, do not try to tell a joke. Nothing is worse than beginning with an opening that flops. If you do tell jokes well and decide to do so, make sure that the joke is not in poor taste—for example, makes fun of a particular race or ethnicity or is **sexist** (presenting one gender in an inflammatory or derogatory manner).

When you are determining how you will open your presentation, ask yourself these questions.

- Is there a link between the story and the presentation?
- Is it a new story or joke? You do not want to relay one that the audience has heard numerous times.
- Am I telling it as succinctly as possible? You do not want to spend one-third of your time on your opening story.
- If it is a joke, am I timing the punch line well?

Use Powerful Language

- Use language that is comfortable for you and use it in a creative manner. Deliver the message enthusiastically.
- Use direct language. Do not use multisyllable words when a simpler word would be just as powerful.
- Personalize your talk. Address your audience directly; use "you" frequently.
- Talk in a conversational tone. Use the active rather than the passive voice. For example, do not say "It is believed . . ."; say "I believe . . ."
- Use **analogies** (comparing two different things by stressing their similarities) to help explain your ideas. For example, here is an analogy:

Stress is like a rollercoaster ride. © *CORBIS*.

Stress is like a rollercoaster ride; it has numerous highs and lows.

When using an analogy in a presentation, tie it directly to the subject matter of the presentation.

- Speak at an appropriate rate—not too fast and not too slow.
- Speak loud enough so that everyone can hear. Indicate emphasis through variations in tone. Do not speak in a **monotone.**
- Articulate carefully. For example, do not drop the ending of words; say "learning" not "learnin'."
- Use humor. Insert stories throughout your presentation. Too much factual material delivered in a dry manner can put your audience to sleep. Have a good time while you are telling a story; smile and put a bounce in your voice.

Develop a Strong Closing

The closing must tie together the opening with the overall purpose of your presentation. The conclusion is your destination; it is the part of your presentation that should take your audience where you want them to be—to what you want them to learn or what you want them to do. Don't tell your audience you are going to conclude; such an approach is not dynamic. A good conclusion gets the audience's attention. It helps them see the relationship between each part of your presentation—between the opening and the body and the body and the conclusion. It puts the pieces of your presentation together in a creative and interesting way so that the audience leaves feeling that you have helped them learn and/or motivated them. Your conclusions can be a moving statement, a story, a call to action, or even a challenge delivered to the audience. For example, if you are deliver-

ing a presentation on human potential, you might end by saying, "I leave you with three challenges—to be the best person you can be, to constantly grow and learn, to reach the unreachable star."

Pay Attention to Body Language

- When you are being introduced, look at the introducer and then look slowly at the audience.
- As you approach the lectern, walk with confidence. As you reach the lectern, slow down and collect yourself. Place your notes as high as possible on the lectern so that you may refer to them easily. Pause for just a moment before you begin your presentation; let your eyes sweep the room.
- Respond to the introduction, but make your response brief. You may say "thank you very much," exchange a firm handshake with the introducer, and move right into your presentation.
- Maintain eye contact with the audience. As you speak, focus on one side of the room with your message and then (after a period of time) focus on the other side of the room. Maintain eye contact with as many people as you can.
- Watch for nonverbal feedback from the audience. For example, puzzled looks or blank stares are cues that the audience does not understand what you are saying. Modify your presentation as quickly as possible to help your audience understand. Such modification is never easy to do before a large audience, but the accomplished speaker learns to read his or her audience well and make adjustments in the presentation as needed. In addition, focus on the positive body language (smiles, nodding heads, and so forth) coming

When delivering an oral presentation, use natural gestures for emphasis. *Courtesy of © PhotoDisc, Inc.*

from your audience. Let yourself feel good about positive reactions.

- Use natural gestures. You may use your arms and hands to emphasize points. However, it is not a good idea to use constant arm and hand motions. Use these sparingly and for emphasis.

Use Visual Aids

You have already learned that you may use presentation software in presenting visuals. Also, you may use overhead transparencies and handouts. According to research developed by Hermann Ebbinghalls, on average we retain:

- 10 percent of what we READ
- 20 percent of what we HEAR
- 30 percent of what we SEE
- 50 percent of what we SEE and HEAR
- 70 percent of what we SAY
- 90 percent of what we SAY as we DO[1]

---

[1]Bradford Agry, "Self-Managed Teams: Readiness Test," *Dartnell's Teamwork* (September 14, 1998), 2.

When giving a presentation, it is a good idea to include visuals so the audience may both HEAR and SEE what is being presented.

Dress Appropriately

The usual attire for a woman is a suit or a dress. Wear something that you are comfortable in and that looks good on you. Although bright colors for women are acceptable, a darker color such as navy blue or black usually connotes power and conservatism to the audience. The color symbolism chart in Chapter 19 on page 537 can help you in determining the connotations given by various colors. You need to analyze your audience and the image you want to project before deciding what color to wear. To find out more about dressing appropriately, check out the Internet. One site that provides tips on dressing, plus a newsletter entitled *Dressing Well,* is http://www.dressingwell.com. Also, books

When delivering an oral presentation, wear something that looks good on you. *Courtesy of © PhotoDisc, Inc.*

are available from the library and your local bookstores that deal with the topic.

Jewelry should not be too large and overwhelming. Avoid dangling earrings because their constant movement can be distracting. Rings and bracelets are appropriate, but do not wear noisy bracelets that distract from what your are saying.

The usual dress for a man is a suit and tie. It is appropriate for men to wear colored shirts and bright ties. Wear a suit that looks good on you. Do not wear gold bracelets and a number of rings; they can be distracting to the audience. Hair for both men and women should have a well-groomed look and not be in the eyes. Having to throw your head back to get hair out of your eyes in bothersome to the audience.

Rehearse the Presentation

Rehearse the presentation exactly as you plan to give it. If you will be standing at a lectern during the presentation, stand at one during the rehearsal. If you are going to be using a microphone during the presentation, use one during the rehearsal. It is also a good idea to have a trusted colleague hear and critique your presentation as you rehearse. Ask the person to be totally honest with you. It is much better to be able to correct your errors before you present than to be upset about them after the presentation.

Control Nervousness

Realize that nervousness is normal. In fact, surveys have shown that one of the greatest fears that individuals have is the fear of speaking before an audience. Also, realize that a certain amount of nervousness is helpful; it can be a positive source of energy for you. Remind yourself that

you have prepared and rehearsed well, you are knowledgeable about your topic, and you are pleased to be able to present it. A well-prepared and well-rehearsed presentation can eliminate many of your fears. Additional suggestions for controlling nervousness include:

- Arrive early; survey the room; make sure that everything is set up appropriately. Determine where you will place your notes. See that a glass of water is close to the lectern.
- While waiting to present, walk around by yourself. Compose your thoughts. Practice deep breathing. Remind yourself that you are going to enjoy giving the presentation.
- Remember that the audience is your friend. They made an effort to come to hear you present; they want you to do well.

Critique Your Presentation

Within a day after you have given the presentation, critique what happened. Evaluate yourself, using these guidelines:

- Be kind. List the goods and the bads.
- Don't try to solve too many problems at once. Pick one or two things to improve each time.
- Realize evaluation is an ongoing process.
- Build yourself up by thinking of how much you have improved.
- Make notes of your critique to help you the next time you give a presentation.

In addition, get feedback from other people. You may ask a respected colleague to evaluate you. You may also provide evaluation forms for the people in the audience to evaluate you. Do not let yourself

CHECKLIST FOR PREPARING ORAL PRESENTATIONS

- Is the content organized in a logical and persuasive manner?

- Did you include anecdotes or a humorous personal story to support your presentation?

- Did you prepare cue cards to help guide your remarks?

- Have you practiced your presentation so that you won't just read it?

- Did you practice looking at a listener long enough to deliver a complete thought before moving to another individual and repeating the process?

- Did you end your presentation by briefly summarizing key points?

- Did you prepare appropriate visual aids to highlight important points?

- Did you check the visual aids, using the equipment that you will be using on the day of your presentation?

FIGURE 11-17. Checklist for Preparing Oral Presentations.

become upset over a few negative comments. Know that there will always be some negatives. Attempt to learn from them. The checklist in Figure 11-17 will help you review the steps you should take in preparing a presentation.

Presenting as a Team

You have learned in previous chapters that project teams are used extensively in business today; these project teams often present their report as a team. Such presenta-

tions require **collaborative planning.** The techniques presented in the previous section apply to both team and individual presentations. Here are some additional suggestions for team planning.

- **Brainstorm** what the presentation will include and how it will be presented. Brainstorming techniques include:

  Saying each idea aloud as it occurs to you.

  Having a recorder to jot down each idea.

  Listening attentively to others' ideas.

  Piggybacking on the ideas of others.

  Suspending judgment—not critiquing the ideas of others or even your own as they are presented.

- Decide who will present each part of the presentation.

- Determine how you will make the transition from one speaker to another. Usually, it is a good idea for the speaker finishing to mention the next speaker's name.

- Practice your presentation as a group.

- If graphics are going to be used, determine who will prepare them.

- Determine what the dress will be. Each speaker should dress in a similar fashion. For example, all speakers may wear suits.

- Determine how the group will be seated before and after each presentation. Will the speakers be on a stage? In what order will they be seated? It is generally a good idea to have the first speaker the closest to the podium.

To reinforce what you have learned in this chapter, study this summary.

- All office correspondence needs to be presented attractively and correctly to ensure that a favorable impression is made on the reader and that the point of the communication is delivered.

- In presenting letters, consideration needs to be given to correct placement, letter and punctuation styles, mailability, stationery, and envelopes.

- When presenting reports, consideration needs to be given to the necessary parts of the report. With a formal report, the parts may include an executive summary, title page, table of contents, list of tables and illustrations, body of the report, documentation, bibliography, and appendix.

- In order to make the report appealing to the reader, graphics, clip art, drawings, and borders may be used.

- Both primary and secondary research may be used in preparing the report.

Primary research consists of creating or gathering original information. Secondary research consists of gathering information that other sources have prepared.

- When preparing and delivering oral presentations, consideration needs to be given to the following elements:

  Purpose

  Audience

  Setting

  Material to be presented

  Organization

  Opening

  Language (both verbal and body language)

  Closing

  Visual aids

  Dress

  Rehearsal of the presentation

  Control of nervousness

  Critique of the presentation

- Teams are often used in presenting orally. Team presentations require collaborative planning.

Key Terms

- Mailability
- Block style
- Modified block style
- Mixed punctuation
- Open punctuation
- Optical character readers (OCRs)
- Headers
- Footers
- Documentation
- Internal citations
- Parenthetical documentation
- MLA style (Modern Language Association)
- APA style (American Psychological Association)
- Duplexing
- Fonts
- Ellipses
- Hits (references)
- Import
- Animation
- Narration
- Heterogeneous
- Homogenous
- Sexist
- Analogies
- Monotone
- Collaborative planning
- Brainstorm

Professional Pointers

When communicating—whether in writing or orally—the message is affected by the way it is presented. The office professional plays a very important part in this process. As you strive to prepare and assist in the presentation of messages, keep these pointers in mind.

- Be critical of the documents you prepare. Make certain your work is accurate and has a professional appearance.
- Use reference guides for punctuation, grammar, and word usage.
- Continually strive to improve your writing skills. Take writing seminars if possible.
- Develop a manual of preferred document styles and formats for your office if one does not exist.
- Utilize technology to create interesting and professionally prepared documents. Today's readers are accustomed to documents that are enhanced visually by graphics and other formatting capabilities.

Office Procedures Reinforcement

1. Explain two types of letter and punctuation styles.
2. Define mailability and list eight items you should check when proofreading a letter for mailability.
3. Explain the difference between footnotes and internal citations.
4. List five elements that you should consider when planning graphics.
5. List ten steps you should take when planning and giving an oral presentation.

Critical Thinking Activity

The local county government's property assessment office employs a director, two office personnel, and five assessors. Glenna Aiken, one of the office assistants, handles most of the correspondence to county residents concerning their property assessments.

Some of the correspondence can follow a standard format by simply changing names, addresses, parcel numbers, and assessed property values. Most of the letters, however, are written to clarify property transactions and inform residents of increased valuations. Linwood Tyler, the director, has received many complaints from citizens about the letters they have received from the assessment office. Although the initial reaction of people when they receive letters increasing their taxes is negative, the citizens complain that the letters are not well written and contain misinformation, incorrect information, and grammatical errors. Due to the large volume of letters, Mr. Tyler cannot read every word of every letter before he signs them. He has spoken to Glenna about the complaints, but errors continue to be made.

Glenna uses her spelling and grammar tools on her software. She has never tried to check to determine if the increased valuations are correct; she merely keys what Mr. Tyler gives her. A review of her last five letters shows that she has missed errors in word usage, such as *principle* for *principal,* misspelled the taxpayer's name, and incorrectly keyed the increased property valuation.

- What suggestions would you make to Glenna for improvement?
- How might office efficiency and effectiveness be improved?

Office Applications

OA 11-1 (Goal 1)
On page 69 in your Applications Workbook is a handwritten letter that must be prepared for mailing. Check the letter for errors first. Be certain the format is appropriate for a business letter. Key the letter, proofread the document carefully, and print one original on the letterhead provided on the student template disk in file OA11-1. Submit your letter to your instructor.

OA 11-2 (Goal 1)
Select three of your classmates to work with on this office application. Choose one of the following topics to research and prepare a report.

- Student Use of the Internet (Determine how a portion of the students in your school use the Internet.)
- Sexual Harassment in the Workplace
- Communication Patterns of Different Nationalities

You may select a topic other than one on the list if approved by your instructor. Conduct both primary and secondary research on the topic. For example, if you choose the Internet topic, you may conduct primary research through a survey of students. Your report is to have the following parts.

- Title page
- Executive summary
- Body
- Footnotes, endnotes, or internal citations
- Reference section
- Appendices (surveys or documents that were used in collecting primary research)

Prepare a draft of the report for all team members to review and make changes before the final report is keyed. Bind the final report on the left-hand side.

OA 11-3 (Goals 1 and 2)
As a team (with the same classmates you worked with on Office Application 11-2), present the report that was prepared in Office Application 11-2 to the class. Use presentation software (if available) or some type of visuals (transparencies, posters, or graphics) in presenting your report. Use the techniques given in the chapter on presentations to deliver your presentation effectively. Prepare an evaluation sheet for the class to use for your presentation. Submit your written report to your instructor. You do not need to submit the class evaluation to your instructor unless asked to do so; the evaluation is for your own growth.

Online Research Application

ORA 11-4 (Goal 1)

You have been asked to prepare a report on the state of Michigan for 15 employees who will be transferred to People First International, from the Atlanta office. Your report will be included in a packet with information on the company's relocation procedures. The report should include the following topics, along with any others that you consider important.

- Geographic size
- Population
- Climate
- Economic development (major employers of types of business and industry)
- Legislative representatives (U.S. Senate and House of Representatives)
- School system
- Cultural activities

Use the Internet to research this topic. Prepare a report of your findings, using the topics listed as headings. Submit your report to your instructor.

CHAPTER 12

Telecommunication Skills

The term **telecommunications** is used today to describe the electronic transmission of text, data, voice, video, or graphics. Telecommunications is the accurate and quick exchange of information between two or more points. Although the field is rapidly changing, there is one piece of telecommunications equipment that has been with us since the late 1800s: the telephone. Through the years there have been many changes in the appearance and operation of the telephone. Even in our Information Age, we find that direct verbal contact via the telephone both within and outside the company is essential. In fact, verbal contact within the office and with business customers is so important that the executive often has a phone in his or her car and pocket. In our high-technology world, the telephone allows for an added dimension

YOUR GOALS

Your goals as you study this chapter are to:

1. Explain how telecommunications affects the way information is transmitted through networks.

2. Identify telecommunications equipment and services.

3. Develop and use proper telephone techniques.

4. Discuss the impact of telecommunications in the office.

of humanness in our communications. Through hearing the other person's voice, you can detect sincerity, happiness, and even anger. Your effective use of the telephone and other telecommunications equipment is essential to the success of both you and your company.

In this chapter you will learn:

- How information is transmitted electronically
- The nature of telecommunications equipment and services
- The impact of telecommunications on business and society
- Proper telephone techniques

Communications Yesterday and Today

Ways of communicating information have taken many different forms. Think back to the days of the Pony Express where a sure-footed horse and a determined rider were the quickest means of transmitting messages. As our country grew, faster methods of communication were developed.

The first method of transmitting ideas other than by written message was through Morse code. Words were converted to coded dots and dashes and sent as electrical impulses. These signals were transmitted over wire lines that were strung from one location to another. At their destination, messages had to be decoded and put on paper before delivery.

The first telephone conversation, or direct voice communication, was made possible over similar wire lines. On July 1, 1881, Alexander Graham Bell, who was in Boston, had the first telephone conversation with Thomas Watson a few miles away in Cambridge; now you can use the telephone to communicate directly with

Multiple methods of transmitting information are available through telecommunications technology. *Courtesy of © Digital Vision*

another individual almost anywhere in the world.

In a speech presented to the Economic Club of Detroit, AT&T Chairman and CEO C. Michael Armstrong talked about how quickly technology affects our lives today. He discussed the fact that although radio took 30 years to reach 50 million people, television did the same thing in 13 years. In 1998 more than 100 million people used the Internet, and the number of users is expected to reach 250 million by 2003.[1] Developments in

---

[1]C. Michael Armstrong, "Plain Talk: The Future of Telecommunications," *Vital Speeches of the Day* (November 15, 1998), 85.

telecommunications over the past few years have permitted the interconnection of computers, printers, facsimile machines, televisions, and telephone systems. Office personnel are able to make use of all the telecommunications services available to them through the interconnection of office equipment.

Networks

Networks integrate or link systems to expedite the flow of information so that businesspeople can be more responsive to rapidly changing business conditions. In a larger sense, networked systems expand the potential of the workforce by making timely information available in a better organized, more usable form.

How can one mainframe computer link to another mainframe computer? How can one microcomputer link to another microcomputer? How can computers connect to input or output devices such as **OCR (Optical Character Reader)** scanners, laser printers, or facsimile units? How can all types of information systems be linked so that any one can talk to any other?

The answer is through **networks** (the integration or linkage of information systems). The philosophy behind networks is that all types of input/output devices can be connected to one universal system for sharing and exchanging information. These input/output devices may be computer terminals, facsimile machines, printers, copiers, video, or telephones. Networks allow office personnel to send messages electronically and to access common databases (electronic information catalogs). They also allow office personnel to manipulate data and generate reports, share programs, and share expensive storage devices such as large-capacity disk drives and output devices such as laser printers.

Types of Networks

A **local area network (LAN)** links various types of equipment used within a building or several buildings within the same geographic area such as an office park or college campus. **Wide area network (WAN)** connections may be established through the public telephone network. The WAN connections link independent local area networks separated by great distances.

Local Networks (LANS)

The local area network consists of some form of transmission cable (often coaxial cable) to transmit the information, plus interface units to link the various pieces of equipment to the cable. As illustrated in Figure 12-1, **coaxial cable** consists of an insulated wire conductor surrounded by fine copper wire mesh and/or an extruded aluminum sleeve.

There are various configurations and media used in local area networks. A discussion of the different arrangements for organizing a network (also known as configurations) would be quite technical and is beyond the scope of this chapter.

Wide Area Networks (WANS)

Local networks can be expanded into extensive networks that enable companies to send information from city to city, across the nation, and globally. These large telecommunications networks make use of combinations of copper and fiber telephone lines, microwave towers, and satellites to send information.

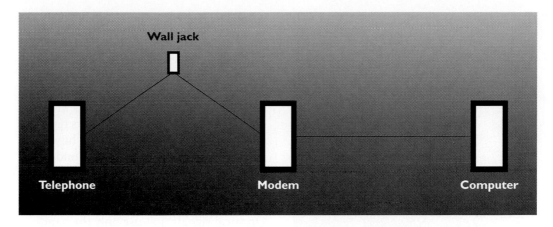

FIGURE 12-1. Modems are used to connect a computer to a remote LAN through a telephone line.

Microwaves are a common medium for long-distance telecommunications. Antennas and "dishes" (similar to those used for television transmission) serve as typical relay stations along the path of transmission. Long-distance telephone companies or "carriers" use a combination of both **terrestrial** (land-based) telephone lines and networks made available through satellites in space. Beaming signals off satellites in space to relay stations all over the world provides instantaneous transmission of information.

Wireless Networks

The wireless network option is rising in popularity in business. Wireless networks work off satellites in space without the necessity of linking to traditional telephone lines. This technology has become more prevalent with the increase in manufacturing of handheld computers and pagers that can receive email messages. Wireless networking enables business communication anywhere in the world without traditional wiring or a phone jack. Though it's not thought of as a computer in the business sense, the **Global Positioning Service (GPS)** is an easy way to grasp this wireless network idea. With a handheld GPS unit, no matter where you are, you can push a button to activate the system. From satellite feeds, your position is documented in longitudes and latitudes.

This same wireless technology coupled with the development of **Internet Protocol (IP)** technology is now being seen in a variety of business applications. IP allows computer systems, operating systems, and software to speak to one another electronically. IP technology allows a television signal, a phone call, and a computer file—because they are all digital—to move across the same lines.

Network Connections

Today, a variety of services exist that will allow users to connect to a network from an off-site location. Driven by remote LAN access, Internet access, and videoconferencing, the demand for high-speed data transmission has never been greater. As

Satellites are used to transmit signals to relay stations all over the world. *Courtesy of © PhotoDisc, Inc.*

Modems

The **modem** has been around for many years. It was one of the first ways individuals could connect to an office computing system from their home computers. Although modem technology has increased in speed, the way it works has not changed. In order to understand how a modem operates, you must first understand how traditional telephone service works. A telephone line providing **Plain Old Telephone Service (POTS)** carries electrical signals that use only the bandwidth below 4000Hz. These frequencies correspond directly to frequencies of sound waves that carry human voices. The telephone converts the air pressure vibrations of the voice into electrical signals that "vibrate" at precisely the same frequency as air. The telephone is connected to a pair of copper wires that lead to a **Local Exchange Carrier's (LEC) Central Office (CO).** Inside the CO, the wires are plugged into a telephone switch, which converts the signal to a digital format. This conversion ignores any frequencies that are out of the voice range.

The development of the modem allowed computers to communicate with each other by converting their digital communications into an analog format to travel through the public phone network. Then the information was changed back to a digital format that the computer could understand. The name *modem* is an acronym that stands for modulate/demodulate. A computer modem "modulates" data so that it can be transmitted on telephone lines in analog form, and it "demodulates" incoming signals so that your computer's digital processor can understand them. Telephone modems are cards inserted into your computer that are connected to a standard telephone line.

more and more individuals choose to work from remote locations or wish to connect to the Internet, the telecommunications challenge will be to provide reliable, high-speed data transmission between a central network location and an end user. This type of technology includes the development and continued advancement of a variety of remote-access equipment and services. Not all of these services are available everywhere in the country. It is important to decide which service will best meet your needs and then determine whether or not it is available in your area.

Integrated Services Digital Network (ISDN)

Today, nearly all voice communication is digital after it leaves your telephone company's central office. The only analog or sound-based service that may exist is the link between the central office and your home or office for your standard telephone service. Converting this line into a format that can transmit digital information is one way of increasing the amount of information that can be sent over POTS. **Integrated Services Digital Network (ISDN)** is a digital connection that allows audio, video, and text data to be transmitted over traditional telephone lines all at the same time.

ISDN service is provided over the same copper wires that are used for your standard telephone service. To access ISDN service, it is necessary for the customer to subscribe with an ISDN service provider. Residential or business customers may also have to purchase a device that will convert the traditional telephone line to an ISDN signal. If the customer already has a digital phone system, the connection may or may not require additional hardware. The greatest advantage of an ISDN line is its ability to allow both voice and data connections over a single line. In other words, you can be talking on your phone while you are connected to the company LAN. In addition, your connection to the organization's network is at a speed far greater than the traditional modem connection.

ISDN service may also provide capabilities not found with standard phone service. For example, it may allow you to assign multiple numbers to one incoming line. Instead of sending a ring voltage signal to ring the bell in your phone, ISDN sends a digital package that tells who is calling (if available), what type of call it is (data/voice), and what number was dialed (if multiple numbers are used for a single line).

A variety of service levels exists for ISDN. This allows the consumer the opportunity to choose the level of service they wish to purchase. Typically, ISDN subscribers are charged a monthly fee and may be billed for access time. Different ISDN services include a variety of access speeds to remote networks. In addition, higher-level ISDN services can support features that you would expect to get on an office PBX line such as multiple lines, conferencing features, voice-mail features, speed call, call pickup, and caller ID. In addition, ISDN is ideal for applications such as Internet access, remote LAN access, WAN connectivity, and videoconferencing.

Digital Subscriber Line (DSL)

The **Digital Subscriber Line (DSL)** is another method of remote access to a network. While interactive video was the initial reason for the development of DSL technologies, interest in high-speed Internet access and telecommuting applications for small office or home office applications has now become the focus. Like ISDN, DSL works through the traditional copper phone wiring. This type of technology does not change the digital information into analog form. Instead, DSL sends digital signals at high frequencies. Because of this, the signals cannot pass through a traditional telephone switch in the CO because the high frequencies will be discarded. Therefore, DSL technology uses special connections at the customer's end to send the digital signals over the traditional copper wiring and special connections at the telephone central office to divert the high-frequency signals through a specially made switch. Often, DSL providers will lease space in the central office and create their own connections to the remainder of the telephone system. Figure 12-2 shows how DSL works.

DSL provides a variety of advantages over traditional modem connection methods. Like an ISDN connection, it provides high-speed, dedicated access to the Internet or remote LANs without interfering with your regular phone services. Because DSL technology uses entirely different frequencies than the POTS line, it is possible to simultaneously carry voice and data over the same single pair of copper wires. Once again, your computer can be connected to your organization's network and you can be using the phone at the same time.

A variety of DSL services exists today, and those choices continue to expand, providing consumers with a variety of options. **Asymmetrical Digital Service Line (ADSL)** is a form of data transmission where most of the data line is devoted to moving information downstream, or retrieving information for the user. Only a small portion of the line is available for upstream transmission. This increased speed allows the telephone line to bring motion video, audio, and 3-D images to your computer.

Because many remote users are just as likely to be sending data as they are to be retrieving it, **Symmetric DSL (SDSL)** services are also available. This type of format is particularly attractive to business customers who need the same transmission rates upstream and downstream. Applications such as Web hosting, LAN interconnect, and file transfers are all common in small to mid-size businesses, and all require symmetrical connections. In addition, multispeed SDSL connections are available that provide a wide range of bandwidths. This allows business customers to start small and upgrade their SDSL bandwidth in increments. Users who outgrow the highest level of SDSL can be migrated to higher-speed **Rate Adaptive DSL (RADSL)** by replacing interface cards.

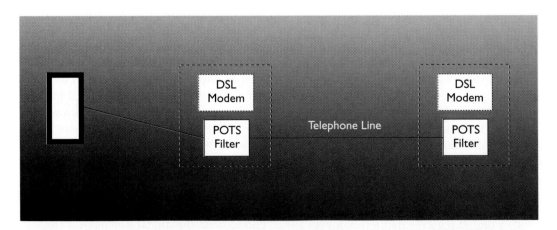

FIGURE 12-2. A digital subscriber line uses special connections to transmit data over traditional telephone lines.

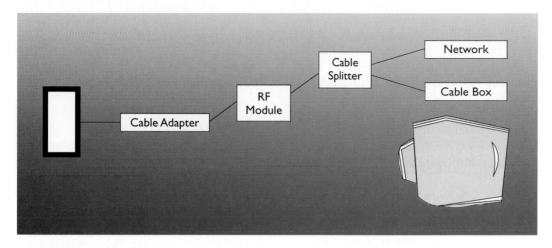

FIGURE 12-3. A cable modem connects the personal computer to a remote LAN through existing cable lines.

Cable Modems

Instead of accessing the Internet through your telephone lines, you may choose to connect through your cable system. A **cable modem** is an external device that connects to your computer. The modems are also attached to a cable TV company coaxial cable line that communicates with a **Cable Modem Termination System (CMTS)** at the local cable TV company office. Cable modems also modulate and demodulate data, converting it from digital to analog and vice versa. They translate your computer's digital information into analog **RF (Radio Frequency)** signals, similar to those used by your television. In addition, cable modems use a **Network Interface Card (NIC),** such as an Ethernet card, which fits into a standard slot in your computer. NIC cards allow for much faster transmission than the standard COM ports used with traditional modems. Figure 12-3 shows how the cable modem works.

A cable modem can also be added to or integrated with a television set box that turns your TV set into an Internet channel. For PC attachment, the cable line must be split so that part of the line goes to the TV set and the other part goes to the cable modem and the PC.

One advantage of cable over telephone Internet access is that it is a continuous connection. Cable modem service is always on. With a cable modem, you will receive a constant stream of information to your computer. You will not experience busy signals or dial up errors, nor will it be disconnected for inactivity. Cable modems also allow multiple users by permitting modem access as well as full cable TV on the same coax connection. Transmission speeds are almost 100 times faster than the traditional modem connection, and it does not tie up your phone line.

The major disadvantage of the cable modem is that the user may share the bandwidth of the cable connection with other users in the area. Since you and your neighbors share the same cable, your information may not travel as fast or you may experience problems with data security. While cable modems may have greater downstream bandwidth than some connection alternatives, that bandwidth is shared among all users on a line and will therefore vary with traffic. Cable modem upstream traffic will in many cases be slower than other connection devices, either because the particular cable modem is slower, or because of rate reductions caused by competition for upstream bandwidth.

A variety of cable modems exist. Some systems include security devices that will encrypt or scramble your information. This makes it difficult for others to acquire your data. Although the majority of cable modems send information upstream faster than downstream, symmetrical cable modems do exist. These modems allow the user to send and receive data at the same speed.

The big difference between digital phone line connections and cable modems, however, is the number of lines available to each. The number of homes equipped to support cable modems is far less than those that have telephone lines. In addition, many businesses are not currently equipped with cable connections. Although the number of cable connections continues to grow, it will not catch up with the telephone lines for many years. For some individuals, digital phone lines that use POTS are more practical.

Telecommunications Equipment and Systems

The most important component of telecommunications in an office is getting the message to the customer in a timely manner. The ability to provide the proper information in time to make appropriate decisions determines the success or failure of a company. The following sections present some commonly used electronic means of distributing information.

The Telephone

Because of rapid changes in electronic technology, telephone equipment has undergone numerous changes in the past several years. In fact, some writers say that the Information Age has now become the Telecommunications Era. Whichever term is used to indicate the office environment of today, automated technology, with the telephone (or voice terminal) being a key piece of equipment, is of prime importance. In 1967 the 100 millionth telephone was installed in the United States.[2] There are more than 190 million telephone units in use today. Globally, about $1 trillion is spent annually on telecommunication products and services, and within the United States the telecommunication industry represents about 17 percent of the economy.[3] With the continued changes in technology in this area, these numbers will continue to increase. In this section you will learn about telephone switching systems, along with the major types of telephones in use today.

Switching Systems

Calls are routed to and from the public lines of the telephone company to the private lines within a company through switching systems. These systems include key systems and **PBX** (private branch

---

[2]Lenore V. Tracey, "30 Years: A Brief History of the Communications Industry." *Telecommunications* (June 1997), 24.
[3]Tracey, 36.

exchange) systems. Due to evolving technology, the life cycle of a switching system is estimated to be from three to five years today. This number is expected to decrease in the future due to increased technological change. There are no longer easily distinguishable dividing lines between key and PBX systems. The highest-end system is the PBX, with the lower-end system being the key one. However, due to computer integration and increases in digital transmissions, some applications that were once available only on higher-end systems are now available on lower-end systems through the use of computer software. Here are some of the differences in the various systems.

Key Systems.   The key system is used primarily by small companies because it offers economy and efficiency. The system can handle up to 80 telephones, with auxiliary units available for additional features. Typically, incoming calls ring at a central location; however, calls can be answered at any telephone. Conference arrangements are available so that a third party can be added to a call. Outside or intercom calls can be announced by a special tone or voice signal. Calls on hold can be connected to background music. A paging system, linked to speakers throughout the business office, can be used to notify employees of calls.

PBX Systems.   The PBX (private branch exchange) is used by large companies. This system can link up to 10,000 telephones (voice terminals). It uses computer software to connect the call with company extensions. Outgoing calls can be made directly by employees dialing a number such as "9" to exit the system and connect to an outside line. Incoming calls are distributed automatically to extensions in the order in which they are received.

The PBX system is a sophisticated computer offering dozens of features such as:

- Handling multiple calls by holding one or more calls while one person is talking to another
- Teleconferencing where several people can hold meetings without leaving their offices
- Redialing busy lines automatically
- Informing an employee that a call is waiting
- Routing calls automatically from one line to another
- Allowing an employee to answer any telephone within a certain work area
- Allowing an employee to send all calls to another answering point

Employees within the business typically call each other by dialing only the last four digits of the telephone number. This number is their PBX extension. If the called party has a display phone, the name and number of the calling party are displayed as the telephone rings so that the call can be answered in a more personal way. In addition, distinguishing rings may indicate whether the call is internal or coming from an outside line.

Centrex.   Centrex (Central exchange) is a service provided by the local phone company that offers PBX-like features to a business without the business purchasing a switching system. This system is ideal for a mid-size business because it eliminates the costly investment of computer software and equipment or the leasing of equipment. Centrex provides **direct inward dialing (DID)** in which all calls go directly to the number dialed. Every telephone extension in the system has its own number devised by modifying the last four digits of the company's main listed

PBX systems often use computer software to link thousands of telephones. *Courtesy of Sprint.*

may be equipped with 10 to 30 buttons. If a call comes in on one line while an individual is talking on another line, the hold button can be utilized to pick up another call. Specialized telephone features and services can also be purchased for a multiline telephone.

Optional Telephone Features. Single and multiline telephone units can also be purchased with additional features. Some of these features include:

- Programmable speed dialing buttons that allow the operator to preprogram frequently dialed numbers.
- A speakerphone with a built-in transmitter and volume control that will permit both sides of a telephone conversation to be amplified. This feature allows more than one person to engage in the conversation. It is also hands-free, allowing the individual or individuals using the phone to move around the room while talking.

directory number. If a caller does not know a particular Centrex extension number, he or she can dial the company's main number and ask the attendant to make the connection.

Telephone Equipment

Single-Line Telephones. Single-line telephones are used in homes and small offices. As the name implies, these telephones have only a single line available. Although many home or small offices have only one incoming line, a variety of special telephone features and services should be considered to increase office efficiency.

Multiline Telephones. Multiline telephones allow one person to handle several telephone lines. These voice terminals

Multiline telephones include 10–30 buttons. *Courtesy of © PhotoDisc, Inc.*

- An answering machine or voice-mail system that allows messages to be recorded when an individual is not able to answer the phone.

Optional Telephone Services. A variety of enhanced services can be purchased for business telephones. This especially assists the office with a single line by helping you juggle calls without purchasing additional lines. These services include the following:

- Call waiting. When you are talking on the phone, you hear a signal that indicates someone else is trying to call you. You can answer the new call and put the original call on hold.

- Caller ID. This feature displays the number (and in some cases the name) of the person trying to call you. To utilize this feature, you must purchase a display or have the capability built into the phone. Caller ID may be used as an answering machine since it will remember numbers of those who have called while you were unavailable.

- Call forwarding. This feature is sometimes called remote call forwarding or call following. By activating this feature, calls to your number can be sent to another phone. If you know you are going to be at another location, you can forward all calls to that number. If you know you will only be available by cell phone, you can forward calls to that number.

- Conference calling. Also called teleconferencing, conference calling allows three or more people to share a conversation.

- Dialing features. Speed-dialing and last-call return are features that can be purchased for additional charges. Sometimes the telephone comes equipped with these features. If not, the feature can be added.

- Voice messaging. This service can be purchased as an optional telephone feature. Although it can function as an answering machine, it also allows the caller to leave a message while you are on the phone, something an answering machine cannot do. Voice mail will be discussed in detail later in this chapter.

A combination of optional features could provide some distinct advantages for the small office. For example, if you are on the phone with your boss and someone is trying to reach you, you will be alerted through call waiting. With caller ID, you can then check to determine if it is a client. If it is a call that can wait, you can let your voice messaging take over. Since these features cost additional money, it is important to determine which ones are necessary for your particular office.

Special Telephone Equipment

There are several types of special telephone equipment available. This equipment can assist office workers in being more productive and in providing for unique needs.

Cellular Telephones. Cellular technology makes it possible to have a fully functional telephone in the car, the briefcase, or even a coat pocket. In a cellular system, there may be 50 or more stations, with each serving one transmitting **cell** (area) from two to ten miles wide. When a customer places a call from a mobile unit, the nearest cell or transmitting station relays it to a central computer that, in turn, directs the call into the local telephone system. When a customer leaves one cell area and enters another, the computer

Cellular technology makes it possible to have a fully functional telephone at all times. *Courtesy of © PhotoDisc, Inc.*

According to a Gallup study, Americans who use cellular telephones believe the communications tool has dramatically enhanced their business success. Where cell phones were once a luxury item, many businesspeople now consider them a necessity. Advantages according to users are increased flexibility, accessibility, and efficiency. Other advantages are increased productivity and the ability to schedule appointments.

New technologies in the cellular communications field include digital cellular service and personal satellite phones. Digital cellular was developed to overcome some of the limitations of the conventional analog cellular equipment. Digital service improves sound quality, makes it harder for your conversations to be intercepted, gives you longer battery life, and enables you to subscribe to optional features. Caller ID, three-way calling, text messaging, and voice mail are available on some digital cell phones. Most digital phones work on both the old analog and new systems; however, the price of the phone itself is more expensive. Personal satellite phones will enable users to speak from anywhere in the world without relying on transmission towers. Reception on this new wireless communications tool, however, is still hampered by bad weather, tunnels, dense buildings, and other obstacles. As new satellite systems are launched, the phones will become more reliable and cost-effective.

Portable Pagers. Pagers are signaling devices that alert the holder to contact a phone number for a message. Pagers are usually clipped to your pocket or belt, and when someone in the office wants to speak to you, the pager sounds. You then call the office from the nearest telephone. The newest generation of pagers has the

automatically switches the transmission to the next nearest cell. This automatic switching is known as **roaming.** Although the quality of the transmission does not lessen with distance, generally the farther you range from home, the more you will pay. There are usually differences in prices according to time of day as well.

Cellular phones can be integrated into the dashboard of a car, contain a speakerphone, be voice-activated, and be totally hands-free. This type of cellular phone provides for greater driver safety since there is no need to dial a number. Cellular fax machines are also available. These can double as copying machines and can be placed on the front seat of a car next to a portable cellular computer and cellular modem.

ability to carry voice messages and email or Web pages.

Cordless Telephones. In the early 1980s the cordless telephone was introduced. These telephones allow a person to communicate over short distances without interconnecting wires. Cordless telephones have a base station and a handset. The base station is a unit with electronic circuits that communicates with the handset. The base station plugs into both the phone jack and an electrical outlet. The handset functions as a portable telephone with a receiver and a transmitter; rechargeable batteries provide power for the handset. The handset may be carried to distances of approximately 900 feet and used as a telephone. Often, cordless phones are used by office professionals so they can move freely around the office while talking.

Just as with the cellular technologies, cordless phones also use two different methods to process the voice signals they transmit. The more expensive digital phones have better sound quality and are much less susceptible to interruptions and eavesdropping from other phones and radios. Prices for cordless phones vary substantially; however, the more expensive models usually have more features that will serve you longer and are easier to use. Manufacturers make cordless units that have the same message answering, caller ID, and memory features available on traditional telephones.

Electronic Messages

An **electronic message** is the noninteractive communication of text, data, images, or voice messages between a sender and a recipient through telecommunication links. Types of electronic messages include email, fax, voice mail, and telegrams. You learned about fax communication in Chapter 7. Email and telegrams will be presented in Chapter 13.

Voice messages are a type of electronically stored message. Since employees are frequently away from their desks or on another call, voice mail has become an efficient way of giving or seeking information with just one call. The first commercial voice messaging system was installed in 1980. Today, it is a growing business, with approximately 85 percent of companies using voice mail. Voice mail automates the delivery of messages in the caller's voice through a telephone network. Voice messaging is used for one-way communicating. Anyone with a telephone on the network can have access to voice mail.

When you reach an unattended phone that is connected to a voice message system, you hear a message. This message may tell you how to reach another extension number or leave a message. If you leave a message, it is stored in the receiver's electronic voice mailbox. By keying an access code, the receiver can pick up his or her messages from the voice mailbox. Messages can be saved, annotated, forwarded, or deleted.

Advantages of voice mail include:

- Speeding communication by getting messages through, even when there are time zone differences. For example, if a user wants to send a message from California to New York at 4 p.m., the New York office will probably be closed since it is 7 p.m. in New York. However, with voice mail, the message can be sent immediately, and the receiver can listen to it when he or she arrives at work the following morning.

- Making office workers more productive by eliminating repeated telephone calls when the individual called is not available.
- Cutting down on extraneous conversation. For example, a normal phone conversation lasts four or five minutes, while a voice message averages 30 seconds to a minute.
- Providing the frequent traveler with the ability to communicate with the office at any time.
- Cutting down on internal memorandums to groups as well as individuals. Most systems will allow you to broadcast messages to multiple recipients.

When creating a message for a voice-mail system, it is important to leave detailed information for incoming callers. The message should include your name and the name of the organization. Although it is important to keep the message short, it should ask callers to leave their name, time, reason for calling, and telephone number. The message may also indicate when you will pick up your messages. This may help eliminate repeated calls from the same individual.

Voice mail should not be confused with voice-recognition systems. Such systems recognize the human voice as input to a computer and thus bypass the need to keyboard information at a terminal for transmission to a computer. You learned about voice recognition systems in Chapter 6.

Unified Messaging

Unified messaging is starting to make an impact in the business market. This type of service integrates voice, email, and fax messaging. For users, this means that one mailbox will include messages in all three formats. The user then has the opportunity to use any format to retrieve and respond to the messages. For example, if the user is traveling, he or she may want to respond to all messages with an email system on a laptop computer. The same user can access messages at home using voice mail. The unified system allows users to respond with the system of their choice, rather than whatever the medium the sender chose to use. At this point, unified message systems are still quite expensive. However, as the price for communications technology decreases, more systems will incorporate more than one message medium. Truly unified messaging will allow Internet access to the message box as well as the traditional land-line access.

Videophones

Although videophones have been available for some time, the latest generation of videophones provides improved video quality (reduction of distortion and improved images) and a new, graphical user interface. Hardware costs are reasonable; and since videophones use standard telephone lines, a video call costs no more than a voice-only phone call. There is also no monthly service or subscription charge. Videophones may be plugged into any standard telephone outlet and connected to a touch-tone telephone or a speakerphone. The hardware includes a digital video camera and a matrix liquid crystal display (LCD). No computer is necessary. Some models use a regular television for display.

Desktop videoconferencing uses a personal computer to communicate with others. © COMSTOCK.

Features of the videophone include:

- Picture-in-picture preview so that you may see yourself in a smaller window within a full-screen display of the image from the other end of the call
- Caller ID display
- Speed dialing
- High-resolution snapshot capability
- Auto answer mode
- Electronic pan, tilt, and zoom

Videophone application in organizations includes:

- Health occupations where health care workers may monitor and interact with patients from their homes
- Schools where nurses may ensure that sick children get medical attention by placing a video call to a pediatrician, who can see the child and prescribe medication, if required
- Convenience stores, gas stations, and fast food restaurants where video-

phones provide an efficient way to monitor operations on a 24-hour basis

- Service organizations that provide information to consumers such as how to perform CPR, save someone from choking, diaper a baby, or prune a rose bush

Selection of a Telephone System

A telephone system will continue to remain very important to a company. And the numbers of options available today are extensive. For these reasons, many companies will employ an experienced telecommunications professional or retain a consultant for advising them on equipment purchases. However, if you are involved in making recommendations about a telephone system, here are some of the items you should consider.

Cost is a primary factor. Although the telecommunication market is very cost-competitive, there are wide fluctuations in cost. It is wise to examine the specifications carefully to determine the cost of the standard and optional features. In addition, the expense of running and maintaining the system should be considered. A reliable system will save maintenance costs. Some suppliers will offer maintenance contracts, which generally charge a flat fee as insurance for multiple service calls. Refurbished equipment is also an option today. It can be purchased at a savings of 30 to 70 percent of the price of new equipment.

Another factor to consider is *system flexibility*. A telephone system should be easy to expand. For example, a software-driven system is more flexible because product enhancements may be implemented more easily and cost-effectively by loading new software than by installing new or additional hardware. The ability to move telephones between systems and facilities is also important. For example, a large company that has locations throughout the nation and frequently adds and moves locations can standardize equipment that can move from one location to another when needed. In addition, if an office needs to expand from a key system to a PBX, the telephones can be retained, thus protecting a capital investment.

Voice and data switching capability is also an important consideration. The company needs to make sure that a telephone system has the capability to meet both existing and future needs. A PBX system equipped with data handling capabilities allows data transmission and reception between users and equipment, such as computers, which are linked to the system.

Another factor to be considered is whether to *purchase or lease the equipment.* Comparisons should be made of the advantages and disadvantages of both purchasing and leasing. There are also a number of long-distance carriers today. Consideration should be given to which carrier will provide the services that are needed at the most reasonable rate. The market changes rapidly, so periodic rate checking should be maintained.

Telephone Responsibilities

The telephone is a very important public relations tool. Although a variety of changes have occurred in the telecommunications field, the phone will continue to be an important tool for the office of the future. Your success in that office will be

determined in part by the phone skills that you develop and use.

Although it is second nature to pick up the phone, using it effectively requires careful consideration. Somehow it is easier to be rude when you cannot see the person to whom you are speaking. How many times have you been angered or hurt by rude treatment on the telephone? How many times has an inconsiderate office employee kept you waiting for an extended period of time? How often have you been told curtly that the person you wanted to talk with was busy? The mistakes made by office professionals over the telephone are numerous and inexcusable, but they can be avoided.

Think for a minute about the attitude you convey on the telephone. How you sound on the phone is five times more influential than what you say.[4] Good telephone techniques will be just as critical in 2010 as they are today.

Telephone Techniques

If you are to be effective on the telephone, there are several techniques that will help you. Study carefully the suggestions given in the following sections.

Develop a Pleasant Voice. Regardless of how busy you are, you should answer the telephone with a smile on your face. If you have a smile on your face, it is reflected in the enthusiasm and tone of your voice. Treat the voice at the other end as you would a person sitting across from your desk. Let the individual know that you are eager to help.

When you are rude and curt in answering the telephone, you set the stage

---

[4]Joseph F. McKenna, "Your Future Is on the Line." *Managing Office Technology* (December 1996), 10.

Answer the telephone with a smile. *Courtesy of © CORBIS.*

for a negative approach to the entire conversation. You may be busy, but that doesn't give you an excuse to be rude. Chances are the person you are talking to is just as busy. Instead, answer the telephone with a smile in your voice that says, "I am happy you called. How may I help you?" so the conversation gets off to a positive start.

Speak Distinctly. Your voice is carried most clearly when you speak directly into the mouthpiece, keeping your lips about an inch away from the transmitter. Be certain that you do not have gum, food, or a pencil in your mouth when you answer the telephone. You cannot speak distinctly with something in your mouth. Speak in a normal tone of voice—do not shout and do not mumble.

Be Helpful and Discreet. When someone calls and your employer is not in the office, tell the caller approximately how long your employer will be gone or ask if someone else can help. Let the person know that you are trying to be of help. Consider this example, Mr. McArthur calls for Ms. Zalapi. Ms. Zalapi is out of the office, and the office professional knows that she will be gone for about two hours. The conversation goes like this:

Mr. McArthur:	This is Ralph McArthur. May I speak with Ms. Zalapi?
Office Professional:	Ms. Zalapi is out of the office.
Mr. McArthur:	When will she be back?
Office Professional:	I expect her back in about two hours.
Mr. McArthur:	Would you ask her to call me then?
Office Professional:	Yes, may I have your number, please?

What is wrong with that conversation? You may be thinking that you do not see any glaring errors. The employee answered Mr. McArthur's questions. But that is exactly the point. Mr. McArthur had to ask all the questions and pull the information from the office professional. Mr. McArthur probably thought the employee was uncooperative. Notice the improvement in this conversation:

Mr. McArthur:	This is Ralph McArthur. May I speak with Ms. Zalapi?
Office Professional:	I am sorry, but Ms. Zalapi is out of the office. I expect her back in about two hours. May I have her call you then?
Mr. McArthur:	Yes, please. My number is 555-3456.
Office Professional:	Thank you; I will give her your message.

How is this an improvement over the previous conversation? The office professional has saved time for both persons involved. This approach would have left a positive impression on Mr. McArthur. He was aware that the employee wanted to help him.

Another important point here is that you should be helpful but also discreet. In other words, do not give unnecessary information to the caller. Consider the same situation.

Mr. McArthur:	This is Ralph McArthur. May I speak with Ms. Zalapi?
Office Professional:	I am sorry, but Ms. Zalapi went over to see Carl Englewood of IPI about an advertising matter. She should be back in about two hours. Can someone else help you or may I have her call you when she returns?
Mr. McArthur:	Yes, please. My number is 555-3456.
Office Professional:	Thank you.

What went wrong? The office professional gave entirely too much information. Was it necessary to tell Mr. McArthur exactly where Ms. Zalapi went and why? Certainly not! The employee may have revealed confidential information. What if Mr. Englewood was Mr. McArthur's competitor? You want to help the caller, but you must also protect your employer.

Ask Questions Tactfully. It is your responsibility to learn the caller's name. Usually the caller will identify himself or herself. But if not, ask the name tactfully. Never say, "Who is this?" Notice the difference between "Who is this?" and "May I tell Mr. Finley who is calling, please?" "May" and "please" completely change the

approach. The caller understands that it is your responsibility to find out who is calling and usually does not resent your asking tactfully. Always try to put yourself in the other person's place, and ask questions the way you would want to be asked.

Take Messages Completely and Accurately. There is nothing more aggravating than getting an incomplete message. It is your job to get all the necessary information from the caller and to get it accurately. You need to get the person's name, company, telephone number (including area code), time of the call, and the message. If you cannot understand the person's name, ask that it be spelled. Repeat the person's name and telephone number so that if you have misunderstood, you can be corrected. It is also important to sign or initial the message so the recipient knows whom to ask if there are any questions. Offices usually supply message pads for recording telephone calls and office visits. If not, these can be purchased for a nominal price at a stationery or office supply store. Figure 12-4 gives one example. You merely fill in the blanks. Some office professionals use email to record and send messages instead of completing message pad forms. This saves time in delivering the message. It also leaves a documentation of the message in case it needs to be accessed later.

Be Attentive. As you are talking with the caller, visualize him or her. Speak "with" the person, not "at" the telephone. Listen politely to what the other person is saying. Don't interrupt or continue to keyboard. If the caller is unhappy about an experience with the company, listen to the story. It is easier to deal with a disgruntled caller after you have heard what he or she has to say. If you are thinking about your

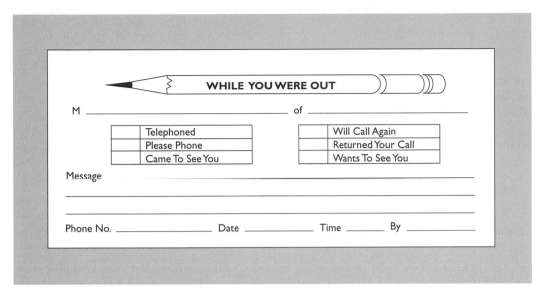

FIGURE 12-4. Telephone message pad.

response while the other person is talking, then you're not hearing everything the other person is saying. Use good listening skills.

- Listen for facts.
- Search for hidden or subtle meanings.
- Be patient.
- Don't evaluate.
- Try to understand the words the caller is using.
- Act on what the caller is saying.

Take notes during a long or involved conversation. This will help you ask appropriate questions and write out the message when you are through.

Remember to say "thank you" and "you're welcome." People always appreciate courtesy, and it is especially important to be courteous over the telephone. Use the words "thank you" and "you're welcome" frequently. They let the caller know that you are grateful and that you care.

Avoid Slang. It is neither businesslike nor in good taste to use slang.

Avoid	Say
OK	Yes
Yeah, yep	Certainly
Uh-huh	Of course
Bye-bye	Goodbye
Huh?	I beg your pardon
	Or
	Excuse me. Could you repeat that?

Use the Caller's Name. It is flattering to the caller to be recognized and called by name. Use the person's name on the telephone. Frequent responses such as "Yes, Mr. Jaksen, I will be happy to get you the information" and "It was nice to talk with you, Mr. Jaksen" indicate to the caller that you are thoughtful and efficient.

Transfer Calls Properly. Frequently it is necessary to transfer a caller to another extension. Before you transfer a call, explain to the person why it is necessary and make sure the caller is willing to be transferred. You may say, "Ms. Dyer is out of the office at the moment, but I believe Mr. Radman can help you. May I transfer you to Mr. Radman?" It is important to give the caller the extension number in case the transfer does not go through. Stay on the line until Mr. Radman picks up and announce the call to him. If Mr. Radman doesn't answer, take a message from the caller. The caller can then call that number without having to call you again.

Terminate Calls Courteously. Use courtesy. Thank the person if a "thank-you" is appropriate. Say "good-bye" pleasantly. Let the person who called hang up first. Treat the handset (receiver) gently; no one likes to have it slammed down in his or her ear.

Keep a List of Frequently Called Numbers. A file of frequently called numbers is an excellent time-saver. These numbers may be kept in a Rolodex file for easy access and quick updating. When changing a number, you merely have to pull the card from the file, complete a new one, and return it to the Rolodex file.

Another method of maintaining frequently called numbers is to list them in a computer database. And if you have PIM software and a modem, you can dial your calls quickly and easily.

Handle Problem Calls. Although most individuals are extremely pleasant over the telephone, sometimes there is a caller who is angry or unhappy. Remember that the individual is not angry with you. She or he is angry at a situation or event. Just as you should be pleasant to the difficult visitor to your office, you should be pleasant to the difficult telephone caller. If the person is angry about something that he or she feels the company has done, it is best for you to listen. An office professional has defused many angry callers by taking the time to let the other person tell his or her story and not becoming emotionally involved in the situation.

Once you have listened to the person, try to assist in getting the problem solved. This approach may mean that you suggest a solution or someone who can solve the problem. It may be necessary to have someone call the person back. It is important not to put the person on hold for a long period of time or to mishandle the call by transferring it to an individual who cannot help. Such approaches merely make the person angry again.

If you have a caller who refuses to give her or his name, it is usually best to put the person on hold while you tell your employer that you are unable to get the person's name. Your employer can then decide whether or not to speak to the individual. Otherwise, you may run the risk of offending someone who is important to your company.

Although you will never be able to solve all difficult situations and make all telephone callers happy, you will be able to handle most people and situations well if you remain courteous and considerate.

Incoming Calls

As an office professional, you will be responsible for handling many incoming calls. Here are some techniques to help you handle these calls efficiently.

Answer Promptly. When your telephone rings, answer promptly—between the first and second ring if possible and certainly before the third ring. You may lose a potential customer if you are slow in answering the telephone.

Identify Yourself and/or the Company.
The company for which you work will usually instruct you as to how to answer the telephone. In large companies the switchboard operator identifies the company and directs incoming calls. When your telephone rings, identify your office and possibly yourself. For example, "Ms. Ogg's office, Carla Geraci speaking" is a typical way to answer the telephone. If you are in an office without a switchboard operator, you will identify the company. "Good morning, Marconi Equipment Company" is an acceptable greeting.

There are times when you may be asked to answer another person's telephone when she or he is not available. In this instance, you need to acknowledge the other person. For instance, "This is Mr. Higgin's desk. This is Carla Geraci. How may I help you?"

Be Prepared. Make sure you have all the necessary equipment within reach before you answer the phone. It is important to have a pen or pencil, writing paper or message pads, and any reference material you may need. Don't make the customer wait while you look for a pen or pencil. You should also have access to a clock, since time is often an important component of a telephone message.

Place Calls on Hold Only After Requesting Permission. A caller may sometimes request information that you do not have at your fingertips; it may be essential for you to check with someone else or go to the file cabinet to get information. When this happens, do not place the caller on hold without his or her permission. You may say, "I need to pull the information from my files. Would you like to hold for a moment while I get it, or shall I call you back?" If the caller agrees to hold, try to get back to the person as soon as possible. Nothing irritates a caller more than to be left on hold. If it is taking longer than you anticipated, check with the caller every minute and ask whether or not he or she would like to continue holding. When you return to the line, let the caller know you are back by saying, "Thank you for waiting." If there has been an unavoidable delay, apologize immediately.

Handle Multiple Calls. You may have more than one telephone line that you must answer. If so, there will be occasions when you will be answering a call on one line and another line will ring. When this happens, you must remember that the caller on the second line does not know you are already on the phone. He or she is expecting to get an answer to the call immediately. Excuse yourself as politely as possible by saying to the first caller, "May I place you on hold for a moment? I must answer another phone; I will be back shortly." Then answer the other phone. If the other call is going to take a while, ask the person if you can have a number so that you may call him or her back as soon as you are off the first call. Then go back to the first caller with, "Thank you for waiting." Your responsibility is to handle all calls as quickly and efficiently as possible.

Screen Calls. Many executives have one telephone number that is published for callers and an inside number that is not published. This inside number is used by the executive to make outgoing calls and may be given out to a few close professional friends. The office professional is usually expected to screen the calls that come from the published number. For example, when the executive receives a call, the office professional is expected to determine who is calling and why. The executive may tell the office professional that there are certain calls that he or she will not take. Rather than taking the initiative to automatically screen calls, the office professional should always ask the executive whose calls are to be screened. Then, if it is your job to screen calls, you should use extreme tact. Even though your employer may not talk to a certain individual, you should never be rude. If there is someone else in your company who can talk with the individual, transfer the call to that person. If there is no one, let the person know courteously that your employer is not interested. Certainly, each situation will vary but one response might be, "I appreciate the information; however, Mr. Whitehall is not interested in pursuing the matter with you at this time."

Leave a Message When You Leave Your Desk. If you have to leave your desk, forward your calls to a coworker or to voice mail. Tell the coworker who will answer your telephone where you can be reached and the time you will be back. If your employer is also gone, tell the coworker in general terms where your employer is and when he or she will return. There is no need to be specific. "Mr. Whitehall is at lunch; he will be back at one." Or "Mr. Whitehall is in a meeting and will be back in the office around three." Both answers are informative yet discreet. You may also wish to leave a note on your desk or door for walk-in customers. This note should indicate when you will return.

Follow Through on Promises. If you make a promise to call back with additional information, do it. A broken promise can cause a canceled order or a lost customer. A kept promise can enhance a reputation for reliability and trustworthiness. Help your employer remember promises that he or she may have made. If you know of information that your employer has promised a customer and there has been no follow up, remind her or him tactfully of the need to follow through. Your employer will appreciate you for the reminder.

Keep a Log of Incoming Calls. Telephone message pads are available with second sheets of **NCR** (no carbon required), which allows you to keep a record of all incoming calls and only write the information one time. If your supervisor loses a number or misplaces some information about a call, you can quickly go

TELEPHONE DIARY OF INCOMING CALLS

Date: _____

Time	Name of Caller	Affiliation/ Company	Message or Purpose	Disposition	
				Spoke With	(Call Back) Telephone #

FIGURE 12-5. Telephone diary.

to your duplicate copy and retrieve the needed information. When the executive is away for several days, you might prefer to keep a telephone diary. Figure 12-5 shows a diary.

Outgoing Calls

As an office professional, you are often responsible for making business calls or placing calls for your employer. Just as incoming calls must be handled effectively, so must outgoing calls. Here are some hints for facilitating outgoing calls.

Plan Your Call. Take a few moments before you make your call to plan it. Know the purpose of your call and what you intend to say. Make notes in advance and follow them during your call. The person you call will appreciate your organization, and you will save yourself and the company time and money. This is also very helpful if you reach the other person's voice mail.

Know the Number. Your file of frequently called numbers should be up-to-date and readily available at all times. If the number you need is not in your file or if you are not sure of the number you have, check the telephone directory. If the number is not in the directory, check with directory assistance for the correct number and record it in your file.

Allow Time to Answer. After you have called a number, give the person you are calling six to eight rings to answer. You may be saved another call if you give the caller time to answer.

Keep a Record of Outgoing Calls. If you are placing numerous outgoing calls, it may be important to keep a record of these calls. You can develop a log for recording the name, date, time, and reason for the call. For example, if your em-

ployer asks you to call ten executives requesting information, a record of the calls will help you know whom you have reached, who needs to call back, and whom you need to call again.

If you make numerous outgoing calls, you might want to take advantage of the efficiencies provided by PIM software. With PIM software, it is possible to type a keyword, and the telephone number of the individual appears on the screen. In addition to the telephone number, you can see the customer's file while talking to him or her on the phone. The process gives you valuable information about the customer and lets you carry on an informed discussion.

Long-Distance Calls

Although most calls will be local, you may also be making long-distance calls. In order to dial long distance correctly, you should be familiar with the different types of long-distance services available.

Direct Dialing. In most areas you can call long distance by **Direct Dialing (DD).** You do not have to go through an operator because you dial the number directly.

Wide Area Telecommunications Service. The company you work for may have a **Wide Area Telecommunications Service (WATS)** for making long-distance calls. With this service, a subscriber pays a fixed charge for long-distance calls to a particular area and may make any number of calls to or from numbers within a WATS area. To control costs, many companies require employees to log the long-distance calls they place, whether they are WATS calls or DD, and the department is charged for the cost of each call. **Inward WATS** allows callers to a particular business to call toll free. For example, some hotel chains have toll-free numbers to use when making reservations. With this service, an 800, 877, or 888 number is used. Employees who encourage friends or relatives to call them on the WATS line not only are abusing company resources, but they are also limiting available lines for potential customers.

Operator-Assisted Calls.   If you are dialing long distance, you may wish to place operated-assisted calls. One example is a person-to-person call, which is used when you must talk to a particular person. Charging begins when the called person answers. In most areas, person-to-person calls are initiated by dialing the prefix 0 plus the area code and the telephone number. When you have completed dialing, the operator will come on the line and ask for calling information. You then give the operator the name of the person you are calling. Keep in mind that whenever you must use an operator, the call will be more expensive. Other examples of operator-assisted calls are collect calls or calling card calls (although both of these systems often use a voice messaging system instead of a traditional operator).

Remember Time Differences.   It is important to remember time zone differences in placing long-distance calls. There are four standard time zones in the United States: Eastern, Central, Mountain, and Pacific. There is a one-hour difference between neighboring zones. For example, if it is 10 a.m. in New York City (Eastern Standard Time), it is 9 a.m. in Dallas (Central Standard Time). If you are calling from New York to California, you would not want to call at 9 a.m. Eastern Standard Time because it would only be 6 a.m. in California (Pacific Standard Time).

Under the Uniform Time Act, which became effective in 1967, all states, the District of Columbia, and U.S. possessions are to observe Daylight Saving Time beginning at 2 a.m. on the first Sunday in April and ending at 2 a.m. on the last Sunday in October. Daylight Saving Time is achieved by advancing the clock one hour in the spring. To return to regular time in the fall, the clock is set back one hour. Any state, by law, can exempt itself. Arizona, Hawaii, Puerto Rico, the Virgin Islands, American Samoa, and part of Indiana are now exempt. As you place calls during Daylight Saving Time, you need to be aware of those areas of the country that are not observing it. Figure 12-6 gives a time zone map of the United States.

There are also international time zones. For example, the person who places a call from New York to London must remember that when it is 11 a.m. in New York, it is 4 p.m. in London. If you are placing many international calls, you need to become familiar with these time zones also.

Choosing Long-Distance Service

Although your local telephone service is capable of providing long-distance service, it is important to check out other options. In a large metropolitan area, you may have a variety of sources to choose from. Cost should be the top priority when choosing a service. Because of increased competition in this market, there are few other differences among competing services.

Costs for long-distance rates usually depend on the volume of calls and the frequency of peak or off-peak usage. Many programs charge more if you don't meet a

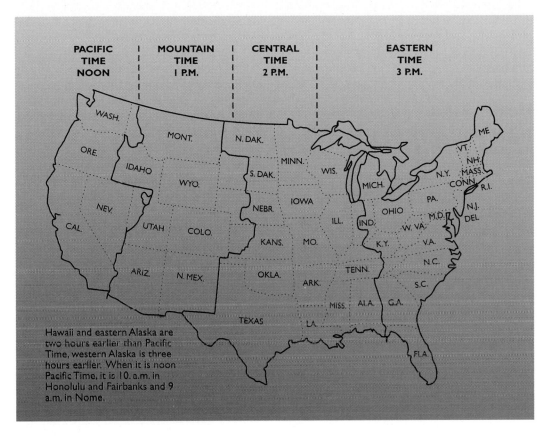

FIGURE 12-6. Map of time zones.

minimum volume. In addition, many carriers offer discounts for frequently called places and for long-term commitments. However, don't commit to a program for more than two years; less expensive options usually become available. In addition, package deals, which provide a variety of services, may include further discounts.

Telecommunications and Society

The structure of our society is heavily influenced by telecommunications. The uses of telecommunications have already influenced work patterns, job opportunities, banking procedures, education, and many other areas. A discussion of a few areas affected by electronic communications follows.

Telecommuting

Working from home on an occasional or full-time basis has become a reality in the business world of today. Advances in telecommunications technology such as ISDN or DSL lines have allowed increased remote access to corporate networks. Today, your office can be wherever you can tie into a network through a telephone line and connection device. This "virtual office" was discussed extensively in Chapter 8.

Health Care

Telecommunications technology is finding many applications in the health care industry. **Telemedicine** is becoming an effective mechanism for delivering quality health care to patients in both remote and urban locations. For example, doctor's notes, patient information, and photographs for a dermatology patient can be transmitted over the Internet from a primary physician to a specialist. Often, a diagnosis can be made without the patient ever seeing the specialist. A physician who has a patient with a heart problem could email notes, transmit a video of the patient's electrocardiogram, and send an audio capture of a stethoscope to a cardiologist. The specialist would have appropriate information to make recommendations without ever meeting with the patient. These types of arrangements are more efficient for the office staff of both the specialist and physician, because there is no need to set up an appointment. In addition, the patient doesn't have to travel or take time off work for a second appointment. Telemedicine gives patients access to the most appropriate provider regardless of their location.

One of the most widely accepted telecommunications applications of telemedicine is **teleradiology,** which is the transmission and reading of X rays, CT scans, and MRI's in digital form. This process involves sending a digital computer file to an organization that then locates the most appropriate specialist to read the image. The process increases the precision

of diagnosis without raising the cost to the patient or insurance provider.

Another practical example of telemedicine has been implemented in the nursing field. Patients who are recovering from surgery or who are chronically ill often require frequent visits from home nurses. In one of the newest uses of this technology, instead of requiring the nurse to make a home visit, the nurse and patient communicate through a videophone connected to a regular telephone line. With the addition of specialized equipment, the nurse is provided with online measures of the patient's heart rate, blood pressure, or even a video examination of a wound. Because the video "visit" can be initiated by either the patient or the nurse, potential complications may be recognized at an earlier stage. This early intervention can often eliminate the need for an additional appointment with a doctor or trip to the emergency room.

Education

Classroom instruction through telecommunications technology for students in a place or a time different from that of the instructor is typically referred to as **distance learning.** Although interactive video has been available to link educational institutions to businesses for a number of years, the availability of distance learning opportunities has significantly increased with recent advances in technology. One category of distance learning includes Internet courses, or Web-based education.

Students enrolled in Web courses may be asked to read material from a textbook, complete writing assignments that appear on the Web, engage in chat room or bulletin board discussion groups, and review video and textual information presented on the Web. Web based or Internet courses are classified as **asynchronous** (telecommunication signals travel at different times). The instructor may post questions or discussion topics at any time, and the students respond at a time and location that is convenient for them.

A second type of distance learning is **synchronous** (telecommunication signals go back and forth simultaneously). Interactive video instruction is synchronous. Although the students are in a distant location from the instructor, they can see and talk in real time. For example, as the instructor explains a concept, a student at another location may raise a question and have that question answered immediately by the instructor. There is no time lag between the interactions of the instructor and the students. Educational entities are now offering both types of distance learning—asynchronous and synchronous; it is anticipated that there will be an increase in distance learning opportunities in the future.

SUMMARY

To reinforce what you have learned in this chapter, study this summary.

- Telecommunication is used to describe the electronic transmission of text, data, voice, video, or graphics.
- Networks integrate or link systems to expedite the flow of information.
- Local area networks link various types of equipment used within a building or several buildings within the same geographic area. Wide area networks link independent local area networks separated by great distances. Wireless networks utilize satellites to transmit information.

- Modems are cards installed in your computer that allow users to transmit digital computer information over ordinary copper telephone wiring.
- Integrated Services Digital Network is a digital connection service that can be purchased from a service provider. This type of connection allows audio, video, and text data to be transmitted over traditional telephone lines at the same time at speeds greater than the traditional modem connection.
- The Digital Subscriber Line allows remote users to access a network. This system sends digital information at high frequencies over traditional copper wiring. There are a variety of types and speeds of DSL service available including asymmetric and symmetric formats.
- Cable modems allow users to connect to the Internet or remote networks through a traditional cable television line. This connection translates the computer's digital information into analog RF signals, similar to those used by your television.
- Long-distance telephone companies use a combination of both terrestrial (land-based) telephone lines and networks made available through satellites to carry information.
- Telephone systems include key systems and PBX systems. Key systems are used primarily by small companies that need 80 stations or less. Large companies use PBX (private branch exchange) systems.
- Centrex is a service provided by the local phone company that offers PBX-like features to a business, without the business purchasing a switching system.

- Single-line telephones have only one line available and are used in homes and small offices. Multiline telephones can be equipped to handle up to 30 lines and are used in medium- to large-size offices.

- Additional features available on telephones include programmable speed dialing, speakerphones, and answering machines.

- Optional telephone services include call waiting, caller ID, call forwarding, conference calling, and voice messaging.

- Cellular technology makes it possible to have fully functional telephones in the car, the briefcase, or even a coat pocket. Cellular technology includes analog, digital, and satellite services. Special features are also available for cellular telephones.

- Pagers are signaling devices that alert the holder to contact a phone number for a message.

- Cordless telephones allow a person more freedom to communicate at short distances from the main telephone equipment.

- An electronic message is the noninteractive communication of text, data, images, or voice messages between a sender and a recipient by utilizing telecommunication links.

- Voice messages are a type of electronic message. Voice mail allows you to reach an unattended phone and hear and leave a message.

- Unified messaging creates one mailbox for voice mail, email, and fax messages. Users can then respond to the messages with the medium of their choice.

- The latest generation of videophones provides improved video quality, with the use of standard telephone lines and a digital video camera or TV. Health occupations, schools, convenience stores, and service industries are a few of the organizations that are now using videophones to improve their service and efficiency.

- In selecting a telephone system, cost, flexibility, and voice and data switching capabilities are important considerations.

- Techniques that will help you be effective when talking over the telephone include developing a pleasant voice, taking messages completely and accurately, transferring calls properly, and terminating calls courteously.

- In answering incoming calls, you should answer promptly, identify yourself and the company, screen calls, and follow through on promises.

- In placing outgoing calls, you should plan your call, allow time to answer, remember time differences, and place long-distance calls correctly.

- When choosing long-distance services, it is important that you do your research. There are many options available for businesses.

- Telecommunications has influenced the way we deliver health care and education. Telecommunication technologies such as telecommuting, telemedicine, and distance learning are changing the way we work, learn, and live our personal lives.

Key Terms

- Telecommunications
- OCR (Optical Character Reader)
- Networks
- Local area network (LAN)
- Wide area network (WAN)
- Coaxial cable
- Terrestrial
- Global Positioning Service (GPS)
- Internet Protocol (IP)
- Modem
- Plain Old Telephone Service (POTS)
- Local Exchange Carrier (LEC)
- Central Office (CO)

- Integrated Services Digital Network (ISDN)
- Digital Subscriber Line (DSL)
- Asymmetrical Digital Service Line (ADSL)
- Symmetric DSL (SDSL)
- Rate Adaptive DSL (RADSL)
- Cable modem
- Cable Modem Termination System (CMTS)
- RF (Radio Frequency)
- Network Interface Card (NIC)
- PBX

- Centrex
- Direct Inward Dialing (DIP)
- Cell
- Roaming
- Electronic message
- Voice messages
- Unified messaging
- NCR
- Direct Dialing (DD)
- Wide Area Telecommunications Service (WATS)
- Inward WATS
- Telemedicine
- Teleradiology
- Distance learning
- Asynchronous
- Synchronous

Professional Pointers

Because businesses must continuously learn new ways to be efficient, message management has become a recent area of study. Until voice-mail systems and electronic mail systems came into wide use, almost 75 percent of all business calls were not completed on the first attempt. There is vast waste in employee productivity when phone calls must be placed and messages taken repeatedly. Keep in mind the following pointers when you use voice or electronic mail systems, so that your efficiency will be at its optimum:

1. Program a phone so that callers can reach a person if they need special attention or choose not to leave a message on the voice-mail system during normal business hours.
2. Learn all of the features of an electronic voice system, and use them effectively.
3. Be certain to include necessary information on fax transmittals. This includes the voice number and fax number of the sender in case there is trouble in transmission.

4. Know the laws that pertain to electronic messaging. For example, voice mail (via telephone systems) is deemed to be private by the U.S. government, but electronic mail (via computer systems) has not yet been included in the Federal Communications Privacy Act.

Office Procedures Reinforcement

1. Describe the differences between the three main types of networks.
2. Name and describe three optional telephone services.
3. Describe the advantages of voice messaging over a standard telephone answering machine.
4. Explain unified messaging and its impact on future electronic communications.
5. Explain how to place outgoing calls efficiently.

Critical Thinking Activity

Thomas, Thomas, Batollini & Hazelwood, a local law firm, employs 15 people. Three individuals provide office support for ten attorneys and two legal assistants.

The firm has handled two notable and well-publicized cases in the past year, and business has been brisk. Due to the tremendous increase in calls, the support staff cannot keep up with their workloads. The attorneys are rarely available to take incoming calls, so a great deal of time is spent in taking duplicate messages.

Latonya Moyers, who generally serves as the lead receptionist and has been with the firm for nine years, has suggested that a voice-mail system be purchased. The senior partners have agreed that Latonya should investigate the capabilities of a voice-mail system. Latonya will make a recommendation at next month's staff meeting about the appropriateness of a voice-mail system for the law firm, its advantages and disadvantages, and approximate cost.

1. What is Latonya's first step in justifying that a voice-mail system is needed?
2. How can Latonya learn what features would best suit the needs of the office?
3. List several features of voice-mail systems that would support Latonya's recommendation at the staff meeting.

Office Applications

OA 12-1 (Goals 1 and 4)
Select one of the following topics to research:
Local Area Networks
Wide Area Networks
Wireless Networks

Using three current periodicals, prepare a summary of the articles; list your references. Present your findings orally to the class. Prepare a cover memorandum for your instructor using the memorandum form on the student template disk in the file OA12-1 Explain in the memorandum why you chose the particular topic that you did and how you might use the information you received in your present job or in a future job. Turn in both the memorandum and the report to your instructor.

OA 12-2 (Goal 2)
Choose two of your classmates to work with on this project. Using the information given in this chapter on cellular telephones, contact two cellular telephone providers in your area. From each provider, find out the following information:

- Is it possible to purchase analog service, digital service, or both?
- What kinds of enhanced features are available with the cellular telephone?
- How far can you travel before you are charged roaming fees?
- What are the rates for peak and off-peak calls?
- Are there any other fees associated with the telephone?
- Are there any "perks" or special deals that come with the telephone?
- What kind of contract must be signed?
- What is the penalty for breaking a contract?

Write up your findings and present them orally to the class. As part of the written report, indicate which cellular service provider you would choose and give supporting information for that decision. Submit your written report to your instructor.

OA 12-3 (Goal 3)
Amanda St. James substituted at the receptionist's desk for the Sales Division yesterday afternoon. All employees with ten or more years with the company were required to attend a health benefits seminar.

Refer to the telephone messages on pages 73–74 of your Applications Workbook. Each of these messages was incomplete or needs additional information. Supply the answers to the questions provided on page 74 of your Applications Workbook.

OA 12-4 (Goal 3)

It has been a busy morning. In fact, the phones have been ringing off the hook. Gloria has just answered one call when the second phone line starts to ring. She asked the first person to hold so she could answer the second call.

Gloria:	XYZ Office Supplies, this is Gloria. You'll have to hold while I get the other line.

It was about 2 minutes before Gloria gets back to the second line. At this point, the individual seems a bit upset.

Gloria:	How can I help you?
Mr. Silva:	This is Hector Silva and you can help me by taking care of my problem.
Gloria:	What kind of problem do you have?
Mr. Silva:	Well, I ordered two dozen printer ribbons three weeks ago and they still aren't here. Better yet, I got the bill for them today and it says that it's already past due.
Gloria:	Well, I'm not in charge of shipping so you'll have to call them to find out when they were supposed to be mailed. As for the bill, you better pay it if you want to avoid a finance charge.
Mr. Silva:	I ordered the parts from your supervisor. Why can't you take care of this for me? Let me talk to your supervisor.
Gloria:	He's not here right now. You'll have to call him sometime tomorrow.
Mr. Silva:	You better believe I will. Good-bye.

1. Was the telephone call effective? Why or why not?

2. What could Gloria have done differently in the beginning of the conversation that would have set a better tone for the conversation?

3. According to information presented in the chapter, list all the mistakes Gloria made in handling this telephone call.

4. Rewrite the conversation in a way that corrects all mistakes you identified in question 3.

OA 12-5 (Goals 3 and 4)

Northwest Savings Bank recently merged with another regional bank. Now there are 28 branch offices throughout the state, and services have been expanded to a great extent. Leon Pavilottus is the newly appointed vice president of customer service.

Mr. Pavilottus will be instituting an evaluation of the bank's services by its customers. He will be seeking several long-term customers to be "shoppers" for various on-site and telephone services provided by the bank. The shoppers conduct normal business transactions and provide an evaluation of the service they received. The customers who serve as shoppers do so anonymously—in other words, the bank's employees do not know which customers are "shoppers." As manager of the division, Mr. Pavilottus will use the surveys as positive feedback and overall improvement of services.

On page 75 of your Applications Workbook is the information that needs to be included on the evaluation. Design a form with the information that the shoppers will find easy to use.

Online Research Applications

ORA 12-6 (Goals 1 and 2)

Search the Internet for information on long-distance telephone services. Choose two companies and compare their business telephone rates and packages and find out what kinds of networking opportunities and equipment they provide. Write a short summary of your findings and submit it to your instructor. Here are three possible Internet addresses for your use:

- www.att.com
- www.mciworld.com
- www.sprint.com

CHAPTER 13

Office Mail

The amount of mail received by companies today through the United States Postal Service (USPS) and private carriers is on the increase rather than the decrease, while at the same time email services are expanding. According to the USPS, it delivers hundreds of millions of messages and billions of dollars in financial transactions each day to eight million businesses and 250 million Americans.[1] Mail volume has increased over 300 percent in the past two decades,[2] and the cost of handling it is a significant expense to

---

[1] "History of the US Postal Service," http://www.usps.gov/history.
[2] Group I Software, "Address Accuracy Delivers Greater Benefits," *Managing Office Technology* (April 1995), 34.

YOUR GOALS

1. Identify mail classifications and mail services.

2. Process outgoing mail.

3. Process incoming mail.

4. Describe projected future mail trends.

The United States Postal Service delivers hundreds of millions of messages and billions of dollars in financial transactions each day to millions of businesses and individuals. *Courtesy of the U.S. Postal Service.*

businesses. In fact, mail expenditures have grown to 9.2 percent of total operating expenses at the average **Fortune 500 companies** (the largest 500 companies in the United States).[3]

The way mail is prepared and processed can have an effect on operating costs. Company profits may suffer if mail operations are inefficient. For example, assume that you allow a letter that contains an important order to remain on your desk unopened for several days. Two possibilities are likely. The customer will not receive the order on time, will become upset, and will never buy from your company again. Or the customer may even cancel the order. In either situation, your company may lose a valuable customer due to the improper handling of mail. Additional improper mail handling procedures that can contribute to increased company costs include failure to

- Address mail properly
- Use the proper postage
- Use the appropriate zip code
- Choose the appropriate mail service

Efficient handling of office mail, both incoming and outgoing, is expected of the office professional. This chapter will help you learn how to process mail efficiently.

U.S. Postal Mail Services

The United States Postal Service, a governmental agency, is the major mail service provider within the United States. The **USPS** began in 1775 when Benjamin Franklin was appointed by the Continental Congress as the first Postmaster General.[4] Today the USPS lists its mission as follows:

The Postal Service shall have as its basic function the obligation to provide

---

[3] Mary S. Malik, "The Hard Facts on Mailroom Software," *Managing Office Technology* (April 1995), 31.

[4] "History of the US Postal Service," http://www.usps.gov/history.

postal services to bind the Nation together through the personal, educational, literary, and business correspondence of the people. It shall provide prompt, reliable, and efficient services to patrons in all areas and shall render services to all communities.[5]

The 1999 goal statements developed by the USPS are

- Improve customer satisfaction by offering superior customer value in each market and customer segment that we target.

- Improve employees' and organizational effectiveness by having the right people in the right place with the right tools at the right time to consistently provide superior customer value and ensure commercial viability in a dynamic market.

- Improve financial performance to assure our commercial viability as a service provider for the worldwide movement of messages, merchandise and money.[6]

Postal classifications, special mail services, and international mail services available from the United States Postal Service are described in this section.

Postal Service Classifications

If you work in a small office, you may be required to know the current postal classifications and rates. You may keep current by obtaining pamphlets from your local post office or visiting the USPS Web site at http://www.usps.gov. The size, weights,

[5] "Looking to the Future, USPS 5-Year Strategic Plan," http://www.usps.gov/history/five-year-plan.
[6] "1999 Annual Performance Plan," http://www.usps.gov/history/app99.

and postal rates given in this text became effective on January 10, 1999. Brochures are available from the United States Postal Offices in your city and from the USPS Web site that give the most recent information as to size, weights, and postal rates.

Express Mail. Express Mail is the fastest service available from the USPS. Express Mail is delivered the next day by 12 noon to most destinations, with delivery 365 days a year. There is no extra charge for Saturday, Sunday, or holiday delivery. All mail sent by Express Mail must bear an Express Mail label. Items must weigh 70 pounds or less and measure 108 inches or less in combined length and girth. Express Mail envelopes, labels, and boxes are available at no additional charge. Features of this service include:

- Tracking and tracing
- Delivery to post office boxes and rural addresses
- COD (collect on delivery)
- Return receipt service
- Waiver of signature
- Insurance at no additional cost up to $500
- Additional merchandise insurance up to $5,000
- Pickup service at an additional charge

Figure 13-1 gives the charge for Express Mail for several different weights.

Priority Mail. Priority Mail offers two-day service to most domestic destinations. Items must weigh 70 pounds or less and measure 108 inches in combined length and girth. Priority Mail envelopes, labels, and boxes are available from USPS at no additional charge. There is an additional charge for pickup service.

First-Class Mail. First-Class Mail includes letters, greeting cards, postcards, bills, and so forth. There is a charge for the first ounce of First-Class Mail and an additional charge for each ounce, plus an additional charge for nonstandard size dimensions (over 11½" long, 6⅛" high, ¼" thick; or the length divided by the height is less than 1.3 or more than 2.5). Postcard dimensions are a minimum of 3½" x 5" x .007" thick and a maximum of 4¼" x 6" x .016" thick. A partial listing of postal charges for First-Class Mail is given in Figure 13-2.

Periodicals.   Publishers and registered news agents are the only people who may mail publications at the **Periodicals** rate. The public may mail publications at the applicable Express Mail, Priority Mail, First-Class Mail, or Standard Mail rate.

Standard Mail (A).   Standard Mail (A) consists of mail weighing less than 16 ounces and is used primarily by retailers, catalogers, and other advertisers to promote products and services.

Standard Mail (B).   Standard Mail (B) is used for mailing items such as books, circulars, catalogs, and other printed matter and parcels that weigh 16 ounces or more. Packages must weigh 70 pounds or less and measure 108 inches or less in combined length and girth.

Parcel Post.   Parcel Post mail consists of pieces exceeding 108 inches but not

FIRST-CLASS MAIL RATE CHART

Weight	Charge
First ounce	$0.33
2 ounces	.55
3 ounces	.77
4 ounces	.99
5 ounces	1.21

FIGURE 13-2. First-Class Mail Rate Chart

more than 130 inches in combined length and girth. Parcel Post is composed of four subclasses:

- Parcel Post
- Bound Printed Matter
- Special Standard Mail
- Library Mail

Special Mail Services

In addition to being familiar with USPS mail classifications, you also need to know what special services are available. By being aware of these services, you will be able to process outgoing mail effectively.

Certificate of Mailing.   A certificate of mailing provides evidence that the item has been mailed. There is a minimal charge for this service, and the certificate may be purchased at the time of mailing.

Registered Mail.   Registering mail provides maximum protection and security for valuable items. **Registered mail** is available only for First-Class or Priority Mail. When you register an item with no declared value, no insurance is necessary. However, if you declare a value on the item, insurance is mandatory. Figure 13-3 gives the fee in addition to postage on

EXPRESS MAIL RATE CHART

Weight	Charge
Up to 8 ounces	$11.75
Over 8 ounces up to 2 pounds	15.75
Up to 3 pounds	18.50
Up to 4 pounds	21.25

FIGURE 13-1. Express Mail Rate Chart

REGISTERED MAIL RATE CHART

Declared Value without Postal Insurance			Fee in Addition to Postage
$ 0.00			$ 6.00

Declared Value with Postal Insurance			Fee in Addition to Postage
$ 0.01	to	$ 100.00	$ 6.20
100.01	to	500.00	6.75
500.01	to	1,000.00	7.30
1,000.01	to	2,000.00	7.85

FIGURE 13-3. Registered Mail Rate Chart

registered mail with no declared value and registered mail with various declared values. Registered mail may be combined with COD, restricted delivery, or return receipt (services mentioned in the next section).

Restricted Delivery. With **registered delivery,** the mailer sends the item by direct delivery only to the addressee or addressee's authorized agent. The addressee must be an individual who is specified by name. This service is available only on certified mail, COD mail, registered mail, or mail insured for more than $50. There is an additional fee for restricted delivery.

Return Receipt. **Return receipt** is a service that provides a mailer with evidence of delivery. It is available only for:

- Express Mail
- Certified mail
- COD
- Registered mail
- Mail insured for more than $50

The return receipt may be requested at the time of the mailing or after the item is mailed. Generally, you would request a return receipt before the item is mailed.

However, if you decided after it was mailed that you do need a return receipt, it may be requested. The cost of requesting a return receipt after the item is mailed is approximately six times as much as requesting it when the item is mailed, with the cost being $1.25 at the time of mailing and $7.00 if requested after the item is mailed. The receipt shows:

- To whom the mail was delivered
- The signature of the person receiving the mail
- The date the mail was received
- The addressee's address

Collect on Delivery (COD). Collect on delivery (COD) allows the mailer to collect the price of goods and/or postage on the items ordered by the addressee when they are delivered. COD service may be used for merchandise sent by the following classes of mail:

- First-Class Mail
- Registered Mail
- Express Mail
- Priority Mail
- Standard Mail (B)

COD service is not available for international mail or for **APO (air postal office)** and **FPO (fleet postal office)** addresses. Both APO and FPO are military postal addressees.

Figure 13-4 shows a listing of charges for COD mail, which includes insurance.

Certified Mail. For materials that have no monetary value but for which you need a record of delivery, use **certified mail.** The mailer is provided with a mailing receipt, and a record is kept at the recipient's post office. Certified mail is available only for First-Class Mail and Priority Mail. An additional fee above postage is charged.

COD MAIL RATES

Amount to be Collected or Insurance Desired			COD Fee
$ 0.01	to	$ 50.00	$ 4.00
50.01	to	100.00	5.00
100.01	to	200.00	6.00
200.01	to	300.00	7.00
300.01	to	400.00	8.00
400.01	to	500.00	9.00
500.01	to	600.00	10.00

FIGURE 13-4. COD Mail Rates

Insured Mail. Insured mail provides for coverage against loss or damage. Coverage may be obtained for up to $5,000 for Standard Mail (B), as well as Standard Mail items mailed at Priority Mail or First-Class Mail rates. Items may not be insured for more than their value. For items insured for more than $50, restricted delivery and return receipt service are available. Figure 13-5 gives the fee in addition to postage for items insured at various amounts.

Money Order. You may obtain money orders from the post office. This service

INSURED MAIL RATES

Insurance Coverage Desired			Fee in Addition to Postage
$ 0.01	to	$ 50.00	$0.85
50.01	to	100.00	1.80
100.01	to	200.00	2.75
200.01	to	300.00	3.70
300.01	to	400.00	4.65

FIGURE 13-5. Insured Mail Rates

provides for safe transmission of money to individuals or institutions; amounts are available up to $700. There is a minimal fee charged for money orders.

Authorization to Hold Mail. The USPS will hold mail at the post office if a mailer requests this service. The mailer must fill out an **Authorization to Hold Mail** form; the service is limited to a 30-day period.

International Mail

International mail is divided into four different classifications:

- **Letters/Letter Packages**
- **Express Mail International Service**
- **Postcards and Stamped Cards**
- **Aerogrammes**

All international letters, letter packages, postcards, and stamped cards receive First-Class Mail service by the most expeditious transportation available in the United States. In the destination country, airmail or priority handling service is used. Mailers should mark international mail as "Air Mail" or "Par Avion." Rates for letters/letter packages (up to six pounds) for both Canada and Mexico and all countries other than Canada and Mexico are shown in Figure 13-6. These rates went into effect May 30, 1999.

Express Mail International Service is a high-priority mail service that is available to nearly 200 countries and territories. This service offers speed, reliability, and convenience to the mailer. Rates vary by weight and destination country, with a starting rate of $15.

Additional information about international rates and services may be obtained at http://www.usps.gov/consumer/int530.htm. and at the Postal Explorer Web site and the Global Delivery Services Web site.

INTERNATIONAL RATES

CANADA AND MEXICO

Weight	Charge—Canada	Charge—Mexico
0.5	$0.48	$0.40
1.0	0.55	0.46
1.5	0.67	0.66
2.0	0.76	0.86
3.0	1.00	1.26
4.0	1.20	1.66
5.0	1.40	2.06
6.0	1.60	2.46

ALL COUNTRIES EXCEPT CANADA AND MEXICO

Weight	Charge
0.5	$0.60
1.0	1.00
1.5	1.40
2.0	1.80
2.5	2.20
3.0	2.60
3.5	3.00
4.0	3.40
4.5	3.80
5.0	4.20
5.5	4.60
6.0	5.00

FIGURE 13-6. International Mail Rates

Private Mail Services

There are several private companies across the United States that offer fast and effective mail services. Four well-known ones are Federal Express® (FedEx), United Parcel Service® (UPS), DHL Worldwide Express®, and Airborne Express®. These companies offer service worldwide, and information about them is available on the Internet. Listed here are a few of the services provided by FedEx (similar services are also provided by the other companies).

Service within the United States

- Priority Overnight—Delivery by 10:30 a.m. the next business day to thousands of U.S. cities, by noon to most other areas, and by 4:30 p.m. to most remote locations
- Standard Overnight—Delivery by 3 p.m. the next business day to thousands of U.S. cities and by 4:30 p.m. to many other areas
- 2Day—Delivery in two business days by 4:30 p.m. and 7:00 p.m. to residences
- Express Saver—Delivery within three business days within the continental U.S. by 4:30 p.m. and by 7 p.m. to residences
- First Overnight—Delivery by 8 a.m.

International Services

- International Priority—Delivery typically in one, two, or three business days to more than 210 countries
- International Economy—Delivery in four to five business days to major world markets

Freight Services

- FedEx Overnight Freight—Delivery by noon the next business day in most U.S. cities; delivery by 4:30 p.m. to most other areas including Alaska
- International Priority Freight—Delivery typically in one, two, or three business days for single pieces, with shipments having at least one piece weighing 151 pounds or more

Additional services are available from FedEx including computer software and bundled hardware and software packages. These packages are designed for medium and large shipping departments or mailrooms and enable businesses to streamline the shipping cycle.

A mailer may also use the FedEx Web site to prepare a document for shipping. For example, through the Web site, you may:

- Prepare your shipping documentation
- Print out the FedEx label to be attached to your package
- Find the nearest drop-off site with the Dropoff Locator
- Get the rate for the shipment
- Check the status of your shipment once it is on its way through the tracking function provided

minder of its importance in the office of today.

Email

A study by the IceGroup of Wakefield, Massachusetts, reported that the average email user spends five to ten hours each week on his or her email, with an inbox of between 250 to 500 items. According to the study, most people are not managing their email well. Here are suggestions for helping you manage your email more effectively.

- Keep messages concise.
- Never send email in the heat of the moment; give yourself time to rethink what you need to say and how you say it.
- Make sure you know to whom you are sending the message; sending a

Electronic Messages

An **electronic message** is the communication of text, data, images, or voice messages between a sender and recipient by utilizing telecommunications links. As you have already learned, many of our communications today are sent through electronic messages. In Chapter 12, you learned about voice mail, which is a type of electronic message. In Chapter 10, you learned about email, another type of electronic mail. Since the coverage of email was relatively extensive in Chapter 10, the information on email given here is intended merely to serve as a re-

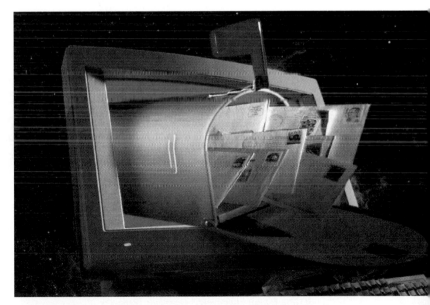

Office professionals receive numerous email messages on a daily basis.
© Comstock, Inc.

message to a wrong person can be devastating.

- Read, act, and then file or delete the email.
- Do not forward junk mail.[7]

Fax Mail

Another type of electronic message is a fax message. The fax process was covered in Chapter 7. You may recall that the fax machine is one of the most widely used technologies in the office today. Even though it has been projected that the growing use of email may lessen the use of fax in the future, fax will remain a prominent means of electronic communication for the foreseeable future.

Fax messages are considered important messages and should be immediately delivered to the addressee, as speed of delivery is one of the reasons for using a fax. You can assume that all fax messages take top priority unless your employer tells you otherwise.

Telegrams

A **telegram** is also an electronic message. Although the telegram is used infrequently today, it still has a place in the office. Telegrams are considered top priority mail and should receive immediate attention by the recipient. According to information provided by Western Union, telegrams have an 89 percent open rate and are opened first more than twice as often as First-Class mail.[8]

Telegrams can be sent any time of the day or night. Western Union guaran-

Western Union® branded mail products can be delivered same day, over night or in several days.

tees delivery of telegrams to major U.S. cities within five hours by messenger (if a delivery service is available in the area) or two hours by telephone. The minimum charge is based on 15 words, excluding the address and signature. An additional charge is made for each additional word.

Additional services provided by Western Union include:

- Broadcast fax—sends a message to thousands of individuals
- Fax-on-Demand—allows access of documents via phone from anywhere at any time
- Web-to-Fax—faxes documents from any Internet browser
- Electronic transfer of funds
- Free software such as DeskMail 2000 that allows the user to transmit to Western Union via modem any time of day
- Mailgrams, priority letters, and custom letters

---

[7] "Using E-Mail Effectively," *Dartnell's Teamwork* (October 12, 1998), 3.
[8] Western Union, "Commercial Services Messaging" (http://www.wucs.com/about.htm).

Outgoing Mail

An office professional's responsibilities for handling outgoing mail will vary. In a large company, he or she is responsible for preparing the mail for processing by mailroom employees, who in turn determine postage requirements, affix postage, seal the correspondence, and sort for the Postal Service. In a small company, the office professional usually has the responsibility for both preparing and processing the mail for the Postal Service. Several steps that will ensure you handle outgoing mail properly are described here.

Check Enclosures

An enclosure or attachment notation at the bottom of a letter serves as a flag to the recipient. Attachment is used when the item is attached to the letter by a staple, paper clip, or in some other form. Enclosure is used when the item is merely placed behind the letter without being attached to it. If there is more than one enclosure or attachment, the number should be placed in parentheses after the word "enclosure" or "attachment" or itemized as shown below.

Enclosures (2)

or

Enclosures

Annual Report

Sales Forecast

When you prepare documents for mailing, be certain to indicate any enclosures or attachments. If the enclosure is the same size as the letter, you can fold it with the letter. If it is smaller than the letter (smaller than 8½ x 11), place it in front of the letter. If it is larger (larger than 8½ x 11), place it behind the letter. Automatic canceling machines are equipped to process only envelopes containing flat contents. If you do enclose bulky items, such as pens, pencils, keys, and so forth, key "Hand Cancel" on the outside of the envelope.

Prepare Envelopes

Your responsibility as an office professional is to choose the correct size envelope for the correspondence that is being mailed. Envelopes that are too large for the items they contain cost the company extra money. Most outgoing correspondence is mailed in No. 10 envelopes. If you need to mail correspondence in a special size envelope, check with the Postal Service as to any restrictions. Be aware that special sizes of envelopes can cost more money to mail.

Address Envelopes. An incorrectly addressed envelope can cause the delay of an important letter or document and a subsequent loss of money to the company. Always compare the letter and envelope address of outgoing correspondence. Check the address against the letterhead of previous correspondence to be sure the address is accurate. If you keep a mailing list of frequently used addresses, be certain it is up-to-date.

Adhere to Automation Requirements. The Postal Service uses automated equipment designed to handle the steadily growing volume of mail. As an office professional, you are responsible for seeing that outgoing mail is properly prepared for this equipment. Two such machines installed in large post offices throughout the country are the **optical character recognition (OCR)** and **barcode sorter (BCS)** machines. Some companies preprint a barcode on their correspondence; you may do so quickly and easily

FIGURE 13-7. Envelope addresses must be keyed to meet OCR requirements.

with a software package. For example, many utility companies print a barcode at the bottom of the return envelope. If you have not noticed this barcode, you might check the return envelope received with your next utility bill.

When addressing envelopes to be read by OCR machines, follow these guidelines:

- Key the address in all caps. Although OCR machines can read a large number of handwritten addresses, a keyed address in all caps is much easier to read. There are also a number of handwritten addresses that cannot be read by machines and must be processed manually. It costs the USPS $5 per thousand to process envelopes that are keyed as opposed to $45 per thousand to manually process envelopes. One of the goals of the USPS is to read more than 70 percent of all handwritten envelopes by the end of this millennium. Annual mail volume processed by the USPS is expected to reach more than

210 billion pieces by 2002, with 17 percent of those pieces still likely to be handwritten.[9]

- Key an attention line as the first line of the address.
- Key any special notations to the USPS such as "registered" and "special delivery" below the stamp, three lines above the address in all caps.
- Key any on-receipt notations such as "confidential" or "hold for arrival" a triple space below the return address, three spaces from the envelope's left edge.
- No punctuation should be used except the hyphen in the ZIP +4 designation.
- For best results, the address should be printed in black, preferably on white paper.

Figure 13-7 shows a correctly addressed envelope.

Seal and Stamp

If you work in a medium to large office, you usually are not responsible for sealing and stamping the mail. The outgoing mail

---

[9] "Clearing Up Public Penmanship," http://www.usps.com/dtf.

is sent to a mailroom where sealing and stamping are done with automated equipment. If you work in a small office, you may seal and stamp envelopes using a postage meter. Envelopes are fed into the meter and are stacked, sealed, weighed, meter-stamped, and counted in one continuous operation. The metered-mail imprint serves as postage payment, postmark, and cancellation mark. A postage meter prints either directly on envelopes or on adhesive strips that can be affixed to packages. Postage is purchased for the postage meter from the USPS. Postage meters can be replenished electronically through telephone line connections to the USPS or by removing the postage meter head and taking it to the USPS for refill.

Another possibility in a small office is to seal and stamp mail manually. To seal a number of envelopes quickly, place them in a row on the desk with the flaps facing up. Run a moist sponge across the flaps and press down the flap for each envelope. You may also save time by purchasing stamps in rolls. Place the envelopes to be stamped face up on the desk. Pull the stamp and place it on the envelope. Self-adhesive stamps may also be purchased in sheets. They are a little more difficult to handle when stamping several envelopes at once than are stamps in rolls.

Establish a Schedule

Determine how often and at what times the local post office dispatches the mail. Outgoing mail can be delivered more quickly if it is deposited before the established collection times. If the company has a central mail department, there are usually periodic pickups of outgoing mail from individual offices. In some offices there are outgoing trays at a central loca-

Learn the schedule for mail pickups and have your outgoing mail ready on time. *Courtesy of the U.S. Postal Service.*

tion from which the pickups are made. Learn the schedule for these pickups and have your outgoing mail ready on time.

Maintain Current Mailing Lists

Most companies have correspondence that they send to a certain group of individuals on a fairly frequent basis. As an office professional, it is your responsibility to see that a current mailing list is maintained. Periodic updating of addresses is essential, as is adding new names to the mailing list occasionally. By maintaining your mailing lists on the computer, you can update them quickly and easily. Address labels and/or envelopes can also be printed from the mailing lists.

Prepare Mail for Automated Processing

Under the 1996 USPS Mail Classification Reform, mailers who prepare mail that meets automated processing requirements can save on postage rates. For example, a

First-Class letter rate can be reduced approximately 6 cents per letter by conforming to the USPS address quality standards. Under the Classification Reform, all automation rate mail requires:

- Properly addressed, 100 percent valid delivery point barcoded mail
- Certified software to develop and maintain all mailing lists
- Barcodes for tray and sack labels[10]

In addition to bar coding, it is also important to meter your mail. Mail that has been both metered and barcoded will reach its destination sooner because it will bypass several steps within the post office.

Reduce Mailing Costs

Preparing mail for automation is one way of reducing costs, as you have just learned. Here are several other suggestions:

- Consolidate materials into one envelope; it is less expensive to pay the increased cost per ounce on a heavier package than to send an additional envelope.
- Design mail to conform to letter size. Some firms send such items as promotional materials, newsletters, and monthly billing statements in larger envelopes. In order to save money, fold the material to fit into letter envelopes that meet USPS automation requirements (minimum 3" x 5"; maximum $6\frac{1}{8}$" x $11\frac{1}{2}$" and a maximum thickness of $\frac{1}{4}$"). Mailings that fit into letter envelopes can be sent at reduced rates over the larger envelopes and may also qualify for automation discounts.
- Use postcards when possible. Postcards offer these related cost benefits in addition to lower mailing costs:

Lower staff expense. There are no envelopes, no enclosures to insert, and less staff time needed to prepare the mailing.

Immediate impact. If the message is well written, with graphics if appropriate, the reader gets the message without having to open an envelope.

- Eliminate return receipts unless these receipts are absolutely necessary. Certified mail may provide all the proof of mailing that you need at a reduced cost.
- If you are mailing a bulky document with copy printed only on one side of each page, reduce the size of the document at the copier and duplex it (copy on both sides of the paper).
- Educate yourself. Know the USPS regulations and private mailer regulations.[11]
- Address mail correctly. According to USPS surveys, more than 30 percent of all mail pieces have misspelled street or city names, improper state abbreviations, missing or incorrect ZIP codes, or other inaccurate or incomplete information that slows delivery.[12] Software is available that can scan addressed labels and check them against USPS addresses to make sure the addresses are accurate.

Use Software Programs

In addition to the software that can scan addresses and check their accuracy, here is a sample of other software that can help make mailing more efficient.

---

[10] "Postal Classification Reform Isn't Going to Go Away . . .," *Managing Office Technology* (July 1997), 7.

[11] David A. Pina, "Sorting Through Mail Costs," *Journal of Accountancy* (November 1996), 77.
[12] "Mailroom Automation Is Today's Necessity," *Managing Office Technology* (August 1996), 30.

- Software packages are available that can presort addresses for special rate discounts.
- Software for coding incoming mail allows an operator to scan the name on any piece of mail, both keyed and handwritten; look up the name in a database of employees; and print out a label with the employee's information. An average piece of mail can be scanned and coded in two seconds or less.
- Software is available that allows organizations tighter control over mailing efficiency. For example, from a networked computer, management can determine which mailing machines and operators are most efficient.
- When handling a large number of records, such as checks and credit card statements, software can identify missing documents for reprint and insertion.
- Pitney Bowes has a number of software and Web-based products; some of the capabilities of these products are:

  Postage may be downloaded from the Internet and printed onto an envelope.

  Mailing lists for more than 95 million consumers and 11 million U.S. businesses may be downloaded.

  Mailings of 200 pieces or more may be automatically sorted by ZIP code.

  Rates for FedEx, UPS, USPS, DHL, and Airborne (private mail and shipping services) are consolidated on one Web site.[13]

Use Internet Services

Internet services are available through the USPS and private mailers. For example, the USPS is testing two new Internet-based services—PostOffice Online and Post E.C.S. (electronic courier service). With PostOffice Online, users electronically transmit documents and business correspondence with their mailing lists to USPS. USPS then electronically sends the documents to commercial printers where the information is downloaded, printed, put into envelopes, and addressed. The mail pieces are then deposited into the mail stream for delivery. Post E.C.S. is a test of a global document delivery service in which Canada and France are cooperating partners. Post E.C.S. will offer security, tracking, delivery confirmation, sender and receiver authentication, mail list management capabilities, and portable document format technology.[14]

Private mail services such as FedEx and UPS also offer mailers Internet services. The FedEx service that allows mailers to address labels, determine rates, and track mailings on the Internet was mentioned earlier. It is anticipated that Internet mailing services will increase for both USPS and private mailing services.

Incoming Mail

Responsibilities for handling incoming office mail will depend largely on the size of the company. As an office professional in a small firm, you personally may be expected to receive and process all the mail. Most large companies, on the other hand,

[13] "Pitney Bowes Demonstrates New Inter-Based Mail Solutions for Small Offices at 1999 International Consumer Electronics Show," http://www.pitneybowes.com.

[14] "Postal Service Merges onto Information Superhighway; Introduces Internet-Based Services," United States Postal Service, http://www.usps.gov/news.

have a central mail department that receives and distributes the mail.

You need to establish a schedule for handling incoming mail. Know when to expect the mail, whether it is delivered directly to you by:

- the mail carrier (USPS or private carrier),
- the company's mailroom attendant, or
- an electronic car, which is a self-powered, unattended, robot-like cart that uses a photoelectric guidance system to follow paths painted on carpeting, tile, or other floor surfaces.

Set aside time each day to promptly handle the incoming mail. Follow the steps described here when you process it.

When incoming mail is received, sort it by the individual addressed. © EyeWire.

Sort

Once you receive the mail in your office or department, you must do a preliminary mail sort. If several individuals are in the department, sort the mail according to the person addressed. An alphabetical sorter is handy if you are sorting for a number of individuals. Once the sorting is done, place the mail for each individual into separate stacks. When this preliminary sort is completed, sort each person's mail in the following order.

- Personal and confidential. The office professional should not open mail that is marked personal or confidential on the outside of the envelope. Place this mail to one side so that you do not inadvertently open it.
- Special delivery, registered, certified, or telegrams. This mail is important and should be placed so that the individual to whom it is addressed will see it first.

- Fax mail. Most fax mail takes top priority. However, your company may receive some "junk fax mail." If so, learn to discard this mail or place it at the bottom of the stack, depending on your supervisor's wishes.
- Regular business mail (First-Class Mail)
- Interoffice communications
- Advertisements and circulars
- Newspapers, magazines, and catalogs

Open

Mail may be opened in the mailroom (the envelope slit by a machine) or in the individual's office. Mail opened in an individual's office is usually opened by hand, using an envelope opener. Even if a machine has opened the envelope, you will need to follow most of the procedures listed here.

- Have the supplies that you need readily available. These supplies include an envelope opener, a date and time stamp, routing and action slips, a stapler, paper clips, and a pen or pencil.
- Before opening an envelope, tap the lower edge of the envelope on the desk so that the contents will fall to the bottom and will not be cut when the envelope is opened.
- Place envelopes face down with all flaps in the same direction.
- Open the correspondence by using a hand envelope opener or running it through a mail-opening machine.
- Empty each envelope. Carefully check to see that everything has been removed.
- Fasten any enclosures to the letter. Attach any small enclosures to the front of the correspondence. Enclosures larger than the correspondence should be attached to the back.
- Mend any torn paper with tape.
- If a personal or confidential letter is opened by mistake, do not remove it from the envelope. Write "opened by mistake" on the front of the envelope, add your initials, and reseal the envelope with tape.
- Stack the envelopes on the desk in the same order as the opened mail in case it is necessary to refer to the envelopes. It is a good practice to save all envelopes for at least one day in case they should be needed for reference; then the envelopes may be thrown away, except as noted in the next section.

Keep Selected Envelopes

Envelopes should be retained in the following situations.

- An envelope with an incorrect address—You or your supervisor may want to call attention to this fact when answering the correspondence.
- A letter with no return address—The envelope usually will have the return address.
- A letter written on letterhead with a different return address than that written on the envelope—For example, a person may write a letter on a hotel's letterhead and write the business address on the envelope.
- A letter without a signature—The envelope may contain the writer's name.
- An envelope that has a postmark that differs significantly from the date on the document—The document date may be compared with the postmark date to determine the delay in receiving the document.
- A letter specifying an enclosure that is not enclosed—Write "no enclosure" on the letter and attach the envelope.
- A letter containing a bid, an offer, or an acceptance of a contract—The postmark date may be needed as legal evidence.

Date and Time Stamp

Date and time stamping allows you to verify when the document was received in your office. If the postmark date on the envelope and the date on the letter are at variance from the time you received the letter, you know that the letter was held up at some location prior to getting to you. When dating and time stamping, stack the opened mail by mail categories; for example, First-Class Mail, interoffice memorandums, and so forth. Then stamp each item in the upper right-hand corner to show the date and time received. You

Date and time stamping allows you to verify when the document was received in your office. © Pitney Bowes.

tations about previous actions taken or facts that will assist the reader. You may annotate by writing notes in the margin of the correspondence or by using post-it notes. The advantage of post-it notes is that they may be peeled off and destroyed when you and the executive are through with them. Here are some examples of annotations that might be made.

- The enclosure is missing from the letter. It is a good idea to call the person who sent the letter, letting the person know that the enclosure is missing and requesting that it be sent. Note on the letter that the call has been made and when the enclosure is expected.

- There is a discrepancy between the amount of a bill and the check received.

- The correspondence refers to a previous piece of correspondence written from your office. Pull the previous correspondence and attach it to the new correspondence, noting that the previous document is attached.

- A meeting is suggested at a time that the executive is already committed.

- Annotate periodicals by:

    Checking the table of contents for items that might be of interest to your employer. Place a check mark by the title of the article in the table of contents.

    Reading the articles of interest and highlighting the key points in the article.

    Figure 13-8 shows an annotated letter that has been dated and time stamped.

may use a machine that automatically dates and time stamps, or you may use a manual stamp that prints the date and time.

Read and Annotate

Busy executives need as much help as they can get with the large amount of mail that crosses their desks each day. As an office professional, you can help by scanning the mail for the executive and noting important parts of the correspondence. For example, you might underline important elements with a colored pen or pencil. Such underlining is referred to as **annotating.** Annotating also involves making no-

Organize and Present

After you have completed the preliminary mail sort and have opened, date and time stamped, read, and annotated, you are

AMERICAN HEALTH COUNCIL
28550 Southfield Road, Suite 110
Lathrup Village, MI 48076-6334
248 555-1880 • Fax 248 555-1887

April 9, 2000

Ms. Patricia J. Bevins
President
Ruther Corporation
2481 Opdyke Road
Bloomfield Hills MI 48304-2355

Dear Ms. Bevins:

There will be a special dinner meeting of the Board of Directors on Monday, April 19, at the Park West Inn, 18000 Merriman Road, Livonia. The dinner meeting will begin at 6:00 p.m. Our guest will be Chief Justice Curtis Houser.

We hope your schedule will permit you to join us. Please RSVP by calling Valeria Bracken, 555-1987, with your reply.

Sincerely,

Haifa Karlis

Haifa Karlis
Executive Director

/vb

you have a previous commitment— Economic Club

FIGURE 13-8. Annotated Letter

ready to do a final sort. Here is one arrangement that may be used.

- Immediate action. This category consists of mail that must be handled on the day of receipt or shortly thereafter.

- Routine correspondence. Such mail includes interoffice memorandums and other correspondence that are not urgent in nature.

- Informational mail. Periodicals, newspapers, and other types of mail that do not require answering but are merely for the executive's reading are included here.

Once you have organized the mail into these categories, it is beneficial to place it in folders. For example, there would be an immediate action folder, a routine correspondence folder, and an informational mail folder. You also might color code the folders—for example, red for immediate action, blue for routine correspondence, and yellow for informational mail. The folders are then placed on the executive's desk or in his or her in-basket. If the executive prefers not to have the correspondence placed in folders, you should turn over the top piece of correspondence when placing it on the desk or in the in-basket so that it may not be read by someone walking into the office. The executive may ask that you present the mail one or two times a day. For example, if outside mail is received in the morning and afternoon, the executive may ask that you organize and present it at 10 a.m. and 2 p.m.

Route

It may be important that more than one person read a piece of correspondence. If so, you may make photocopies of the correspondence and send a copy to each individual on the list; or you may route the correspondence to all individuals by the use of a routing slip. The basic question to ask when determining whether to make photocopies is: Is it urgent that all individuals receive the information immediately? If the answer is "yes," it is best to photocopy. If the answer is "no," it is best to use a routing slip, particularly if the correspondence is lengthy. A routing slip also provides a reference for you to know when and to whom you sent the correspondence in case there is a question about who received the document. When each individual on the routing slip has received and read the copy, he or she should initial by his or her name before sending the copy to the next individual on the list. The last person to receive the correspondence generally returns it to the individual who sent it. You save copying costs by routing. A routing slip is shown in Figure 13-9. Notice how initials are placed by the individuals' names to indicate that they have read the copy, and notice that the sender is requesting that it be returned to him or her.

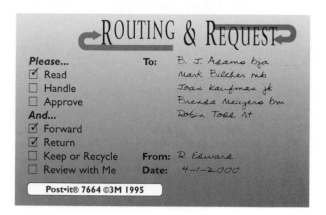

FIGURE 13-9. Routing Slip

Handle Mail When the Executive Is Out

In handling the mail when the executive is away, you need to follow these general guidelines.

- Before the executive leaves, discuss exactly how the mail should be handled; be specific in your questions so that you are clear. Mistakes in handling mail can be costly to the company.

- When urgent mail comes in, be certain that it is handled immediately according to the executive's directions; for example, you may give it immediately to the person who is in charge or you may fax it to the executive.

- Answer mail that falls within your area of responsibility in a timely manner.

- Maintain mail that has been answered (with the answer attached) in a separate folder; the executive may want to review it upon return.

- Maintain mail that can wait for the executive's return in a separate folder. Retrieve any correspondence that has previously been written that will be needed when reviewing the mail; place it in the folder also.

It is the responsibility of the office professional to handle the mail appropriately when the executive is away.

Recyling

You have learned that our Information Age is spawning more paper rather than less. This causes serious problems for our environment, with the loss of our forests and the use of valuable land to establish more landfills. Here are a few of the facts about paper use within offices.

- Typical business offices generate about 1.5 pounds of waste paper per employee per day.
- Financial businesses generate over 2 pounds per employee per day.
- Nearly half of typical office paper waste is comprised of high-grade office

paper, for which there is strong recycling demand.

- Recycling one ton of paper saves about 6.7 cubic yards of landfill space.
- Every recycled ton of paper saves approximately 17 trees.
- Recycling paper reduces the air and water pollution due to paper manufacturing.[15]

Due to the serious environmental issues facing us because of the use of so much paper, recycling programs are becoming common in businesses. Such programs can save millions of tons of paper each year. Organizations often provide recycling bins for paper, and outsource the collection and shredding of paper to a private vendor. The outsource vendor generally does not charge a fee for this service since they are able to collect money for the recycled paper.

In addition to recycling paper, organizations need to use recycled paper products. Recycled paper uses 64 percent less energy and 58 percent less water in the production of the paper than does the production of virgin papers. In addition, manufacturing recycled paper produces 74 percent less air pollution and 35 percent less water pollution than virgin paper production processes.

Organizations also need to take a look at how they can reduce the use of paper in the office. Here are several suggestions.

- Use both sides of the page (duplex documents).
- Convert scratch paper into memo pads, telephone answering slips, and similar items.

---

[15] "Fact Sheet: Reducing Office Paper Waste," http://es.epa.gov/techinfo/facts.

Help save our forests; recycle! © *PhotoDisc, Inc.*

- Print only the amount of copies needed.
- Use electronic mail for sending and receiving messages.
- Review text onscreen to limit mistakes and thus reprinting.
- Put up a central memo board where employees can read interoffice mail.
- Shred used paper and package materials to be mailed with the shredded paper rather than using plastic pellets.

Future Mail Trends

Understanding the projected future mail trends will help you determine what you need to consider as you deal with mail in your own department of an organization. Here are some of those trends.

- Increased use of automation in the processing of mail to generate financial and labor savings
- Increased use of the Internet to deliver mail services and software applications to individuals and businesses
- Outsourcing (contracting with an outside firm) of mail operations for large companies
- Increased technological improvements in mailroom equipment
- Increased use of alternative delivery options in mail such as email and fax-on-demand, with businesses partnering with vendors who understand mail, and alternative delivery options designed to provide the most effective services
- Use of multifunctional equipment to fold, sort, label, and perform other mailroom tasks (This equipment will be modular also so that features can be added as needed.)
- Increased use of software that verifies, cleanses, and maintains mailing lists, combined with hardware that applies the delivery point barcode and addresses envelopes
- Processing of incoming mail via computer imaging and integration of fax and email into an electronic communication system
- Continual changes in the USPS to stay competitive in the delivery of mail
- Increased market share for private mailers and increased technology-based services provided by these mailers
- Increased international partnerships designed to provide more efficient mail services globally

Keeping pace with mail trends is a challenge for the office professional. © Pitney Bowes.

- Continual training of mail personnel so they stay current in the highly technological mail world

  Mail procedures will continue to change as technology becomes more and more advanced and new forms of mail distribution are available. Keeping pace with these changes will be a challenge not only for employees but also for businesses.

SUMMARY

Study this summary to reinforce what you have learned in this chapter.

- Mail is classified by the USPS into Express Mail, Priority Mail, First-Class Mail, Periodicals, Standard Mail (A), Standard Mail (B), and Parcel Post.
- Special mail services include:

  Certificate of mailing

  Registered mail

  Restricted delivery

  Return receipt

  Collect on delivery

  Certified mail

  Insured mail

  Money order

  Authorization to hold mail
- International mail is divided into four classifications—letters/letter packages, express mail international service, postcards and stamped cards, and aerogrammes.
- There are a number of private mail services across the United States that offer fast and effective mail services domestically and internationally.
- Electronic mail includes voice mail, email, fax mail, and telegrams.
- To ensure the proper handling of outgoing mail, these procedures should be followed:

  Check enclosures

  Prepare envelopes

  Seal and stamp

  Establish a schedule

  Maintain current mailing lists

  Prepare mail for automated processing

  Reduce mailing costs

  Use software programs

Use Internet services

- Responsibilities of the office professional in handling incoming mail include:

Sorting

Opening

Keeping selected envelopes

Dating and time stamping

Reading and annotating

Organizing and presenting

Routing

Handling mail when the executive is out

- It is important for our environment that businesses recycle paper.
- Mail trends of the future include greater automation; extensive use of software; outsourcing; increased use of multifunctional, modular equipment; continual changes in USPS services to stay competitive; increased market share for private mailers; increased international partnerships; and continual training of mail personnel to stay current with technological developments.

Key Terms

- Fortune 500 companies
- USPS
- Express Mail
- Priority Mail
- First-Class Mail
- Periodicals
- Standard Mail (A)
- Standard Mail (B)
- Parcel Post
- Certificate of mailing
- Registered mail
- Registered delivery

- Return receipt
- Collect on delivery (COD)
- APO (air postal office)
- FPO (Fleet postal office)
- Certified mail
- Insured mail
- Money orders
- Authorization to hold mail
- International mail

- Letters/letter packages
- Express mail international service
- Postcards and stamped cards
- Aerogrammes
- Electronic message
- Telegram
- Optical character recognition (OCR)
- Barcode sorter (BCS)
- Annotating

Professional Pointers

These pointers will help you deal effectively with the mailing and shipping needs of your office.

- When purchasing mailing equipment, keep in mind that the equipment has a life span of from three to five years; you can extend that life span by investing in upgradeable technology.
- Keep current on USPS and private mailing and shipping services by reviewing the Web sites of the organizations.
- Compare the costs and services provided (time of delivery, convenience of pickup, and so forth) of mailing materials via USPS and private mailing services.
- USPS surveys have shown that more than 30 percent of all mail pieces have misspelled street or city names, improper state abbreviations, missing or incorrect ZIP codes, or other inaccurate or incomplete information. Use mailing list software to check your mailing addresses.
- Western Union® messages may be sent as a Mailgram, Priority Letter, or Custom Letter; keep current on Western Union services by checking their Web site.
- To help maintain our forests and reduce the land needed for landfills, recycle your paper.

- Reduce the amount of paper you use by: printing on both sides of the paper (duplexing), photocopying only the amount of copies you need, single spacing documents, and using email for in-house communication.
- Purchase recycled paper.

Office Procedures Reinforcement

1. Identify and describe the classifications of mail offered by the USPS.
2. Identify and describe six mail services available from the USPS.
3. Describe the responsibilities of an office professional for handling outgoing mail.
4. Describe the responsibilities of an office professional for handling incoming mail.
5. List five projected mail trends.

Critical Thinking Activity

A computer network connects all of the offices of People First International. The computer department staff maintains and services software that resides on the system, troubleshoots for hardware and technical problems, and monitors the agency's communications. Every employee with a computer logs onto the system with a network name, assigned by the computer department, and a secret password, which is chosen by the employee. An employee's electronic mailbox can only be accessed by using both of the assigned code names.

Eva Reid, an administrative assistant who works in the Detroit office, communicates weekly by email with her sister who works in the Atlanta office about personal matters. Two weeks ago Eva sent her sister an email note that she was thinking about resigning; she told her sister that she had received a wonderful job offer with a considerably higher salary. Yesterday at lunch a coworker, from the computer department, approached Eva and asked when she was leaving. Eva was shocked and angry! Eva's sister denied telling anyone about the job offer, and she told Eva that she erased the note as soon as she read it. To Eva's knowledge, no one has access to her electronic mailbox.

1. Are there ethical considerations in this case? If so, what are they?
2. Should Eva tell her supervisor about her job offer before the rumor spreads? Should Eva tell her supervisor that she communicates with her sister via company email?
3. How can Eva learn if someone in the agency has access to her electronic mail? Should she file a complaint if she learns someone has been reading her email?
4. Are there company policies that should be put in place as a result of this situation?

Office Applications

OA13-1 (Goals 1 and 2)

You are given the following items by your supervisor to be sent in the outgoing mail. Explain whether you will use USPS service or private mailing or shipping services. If you are using USPS service, identify the type of service and mail classification of the item. Use the form provided on the student template disk, file OA13-1 to record your answers; submit a completed copy of your form to your instructor.

- A letter to be sent to a client in France for delivery the next day
- A book weighing 18 ounces to be sent to a coworker in Atlanta
- A contract with a new client; proof that the contract is received is necessary
- A check for $250 for your supervisor's AMA dues
- A report (100 pages) that must reach your Paris office by tomorrow
- A contract that must reach your New York office by 10 a.m. tomorrow
- A letter that must reach California within two days
- A congratulatory note to the recently promoted vice president of the Frankfurt, Germany office
- A memo that must reach your Paris office within the next 30 minutes.

OA13-2 (Goal 2)

Prepare a fax to be sent to Avion LeFever (Fax No. 011-33-21-655-2318), your counterpart in the Paris office, stating that your employer, Juan Menendez, will be arriving in Paris on American Airlines, Flight 750, on Tuesday, April 23, at 8:15 a.m. Ask that there be someone to pick him up and take him to the Paris office. Request a reply concerning the arrangements by the afternoon. Use the fax cover sheet on the student template disk, file OA13-2. Submit your fax to your instructor.

OA13-3 (Goal 3)

You received the items listed on the student template disk in file OA13-3 in your morning mail. Sort the mail by filling out the form also given in file OA13-3. On pages 79 and 80 of your Applications Workbook are two letters that were received in the morning mail. Annotate these letters. Submit your sorting plan and the letters to your instructor.

Online Research Applications

ORA 13-4 (Goal 4)
Select three of your classmates to work with on this project. Using the Internet, research the services provided by the following mail and shipping services:

- USPS
- Western Union
- FedEx
- UPS

Prepare a report of your findings; submit your report to your instructor.

Vocabulary Review

On pages 83–84 of your Applications Workbook is a Vocabulary Review, covering selected items from the vocabulary presented in Chapters 9–13. Complete these sentences and submit a copy to your instructor.

Language Skills Practice

On pages 85–87 of your Applications Workbook are sentences that need to be corrected, using the rules presented in the Reference Section of your text. Correct the sentences as needed and submit your work to your instructor.

Records
Management

CHAPTER 14

Rules and Procedures

Your job as an office professional in managing and maintaining records is much more complex today than it was in the past. You learned earlier in this text that offices are generating more paper than ever before—not less as was anticipated when the computer age began. Paper records are maintained in abundance in most offices. In fact, it is projected that in 2000, 60 percent of the records filed still will be in paper form, with the conversion to electronic form proceeding at approximately three percent per year for the next decade.[1] Even though paper or manual

1. Learn and use filing rules.

2. Identify and use the four basic storage methods.

3. Determine the types of paper storage equipment available.

---

[1] "Office Equipment: The 21st Century," *Managing Office Technology* (December 1997), 30.

storage still dominates, there are a number of electronic and microimage storage methods in existence. In addition, with the expectation that electronic files will continue to increase and paper files decrease, you need to be knowledgeable of paper and electronic storage procedures, software, and equipment.

As an office professional, you need to know when records should be maintained in paper format and when they should be maintained in electronic format. You also need to understand the basics of records management—filing rules, storage methods, and basic supplies and equipment. This chapter will help you become familiar with the basics. You will learn filing rules and how to use alphabetic, numeric, subject, and geographic methods of storage. In Chapter 15, you will learn about various electronic and microimage storage systems and software.

The Importance of Records Management

A **record** is any type of recorded information. For example, the information may be:

- Written and recorded on paper
- Written and recorded on some type of electronic form or **microform** (generic term for any medium containing miniaturized or microimages)
- An oral record that captures the human voice and is stored on a CD or a tape
- Email stored in an electronic folder
- Movies stored on videotape
- Digital photographs stored on a disk

Whatever the form, these records contain information about an organization—its functions, policies, procedures, decisions, and operations. **Records man-**

agement is the systematic control of records over the **record life cycle,** which is from the creation of the record to its final disposition. This life cycle has five distinct phases:

- Creation of the record
- Distribution of the record to internal or external users
- Use of the record (information gleaned from the record for making decisions, determining directions, and so forth)
- Maintenance of the record (filing and retrieving)
- Disposition (retain or destroy after a period of time)

Records are an asset to a business just as products, services, management expertise, and a good reputation are assets. Records provide a history for the business. Successful organizations appreciate the need for records. They use the information contained in records to make decisions and plan for the future. Additional values of records to business include:

- Legal value by providing evidence of business transactions such as articles of incorporation, real estate transactions, and contracts
- Financial value through records needed in audits and for tax purposes
- Personnel value through such items as employment applications, date of hire, evaluations of employees, payroll records, and employment termination records
- Day-to-day operational value through such records as policy and procedures manuals, organization charts, minutes of meetings, information sent to clients and customers, and sales reports

Well-managed records are essential for all organizations and offer the following benefits:

Well-managed records are essential for all organizations.
© PhotoDisc, Inc.

- Reduction of staff time spent searching the files for misplaced records
- Quick and easy retrieval of information needed in making management decisions
- Financial savings through systems that provide the most efficient and effective methods of materials storage
- Protection and storage of information needed in perpetuity by the business
- Planned records management systems that allow for growth, evaluation, and updating of methods and equipment
- Trained personnel who understand the importance of records and the need for effective systems and procedures
- Efficient use of space by maintaining records in the most appropriate form and determining the proper equipment for storage

Alphabetic Indexing Rules

The rules for filing may vary slightly from business to business based on specific needs of the organization. Find out what filing rules are used in your organization and use them. The Association of Records Managers and Administrators, Inc. (**ARMA**) has set forth rules that are designed to help the office professional perform his or her job more effectively. The rules in this chapter are compatible with ARMA's Simplified Filing Standard Rules and Specific Filing Guidelines.

Rule 1: Indexing Order of Units

A. Personal Names   A personal name is indexed in this order: (1) surname, (2) first name or initial, (3) middle name or initial. If it is difficult to determine the surname, the name is indexed as written. All punctuation is omitted, and a unit consisting of just an initial precedes a unit that consists of a complete name beginning with the same letter. The general rule to follow in all indexing is: *nothing comes before something.*

Filing Segment	*Index Order of Units*		
Name	*Key Unit*	*Unit 2*	*Unit 3*
George H. Carmack	Carmack	George	H
Herschel E. Carmack	Carmack	Herschel	E
Herschel Elias Carmack	Carmack	Herschel	Elias

B. Business Names   Business names are indexed as written using letterheads or trademarks as guides. Each word in a business name is a separate unit. Business names containing personal names are indexed as written.

Filing Segment	*Index Order of Units*			
Name	*Key Unit*	*Unit 2*	*Unit 3*	*Unit 4*
Ed Monaghan Photography	Ed	Monaghan	Photography	
Monahan McNulty Corporation	Monahan	McNulty	Corporation	
Monarch Electric Service Company	Monarch	Electric	Service	Company

Rule 2: Minor Words and Symbols in Business Names
Articles, prepositions, conjunctions, and symbols are considered separate indexing units. Symbols are spelled in full. When the word "The" appears as the first word of a business name, it is considered the last indexing unit.

Filing Segment	*Index Order of Units*			
Name	*Key Unit*	*Unit 2*	*Unit 3*	*Unit 4*
At the Point Grocery	At	the	Point	Grocery
Cintron and Medina Corporation	Cintron	and	Medina	Corporation
The Miller Corporation	Miller	Corporation	The	

Rule 3: Punctuation and Possessives   Disregard all punctuation when indexing personal and business names.

Filing Segment		*Index Order of Units*		
Name	*Key Unit*	*Unit 2*	*Unit 3*	*Unit 4*
Baba's Foundation	Babas	Foundation		
House-Life	HouseLife			
Hughes' Foundation Correction	Hughes	Foundation	Correction	
North-South Foundation	NorthSouth	Foundation		
Nu-Trend Drive Thru Mini-Mart	NuTrend	Drive	Thru	MiniMart

Rule 4: Single Letters and Abbreviations

A. Personal Names   Initials in personal names are considered separate indexing units. Abbreviations of personal names (Wm., Jas.) and brief personal names or nicknames (Dick, Liz) are indexed as written.

Filing Segment	*Index Order of Units*		
Name	*Key Unit*	*Unit 2*	*Unit 3*
Jas. R. Edwards	Edwards	Jas	R
Dick W. Calkins	Calkins	Dick	W

B. Business Names   Single letters in business names are indexed as written. If single letters are separated by spaces, index each letter as a separate unit. Index **acronyms** (words formed from the first or first few letters of several words such as ARMA) and radio and television station call letters as one word. Abbreviated words (Corp., Co.) and names (AT&T) are indexed as one unit regardless of punctuation or spacing.

Filing Segment		*Index Order of Units*		
Name	*Key Unit*	*Unit 2*	*Unit 3*	*Unit 4*
J. M. Guzman	Guzman	J	M	
Josefina Maria Guzman	Guzman	Josefina	Maria	
L M N Corp.	L	M	N	Corp
LRO Radio Station	LRO	Radio	Station	
PTK	PTK			

Rule 5: Titles and Suffixes

A. Personal Names A title before a personal name (Dr., Mr., Ms.), a **seniority suffix** (II, III, Jr.), or a **professional suffix** (DDS, MD, PhD) after a name is the last indexing unit. **Numeric suffixes** (II, III) are filed before **alphabetic suffixes** (Jr., Sr.). If a name contains both a title and a suffix, the title is the last unit. Royal and religious titles followed by either a given name or a surname only (Sister Mary) are indexed and filed as written. If a person's professional title comes after the name, it is referred to as a suffix; for example, CPA, CPS.

Filing Segment	Index Order of Units			
Name	Key Unit	Unit 2	Unit 3	Unit 4
Bruce R. Packard II	Packard	Bruce	R	I
Bruce R. Packard III	Packard	Bruce	R	III
Bruce R. Packard, Jr.	Packard	Bruce	R	Jr
Bruce R. Packard, Sr.	Packard	Bruce	R	Sr
Olivia M. Packard, M.D.	Packard	Olivia	M	MD
Sister Packard	Sister	Packard		
Ms. Rachael Packard, CPS	Packard	Rachael	CPS	Ms

B. Business Names Titles in business names are indexed as written.

Filing Segment	Index Order of Units		
Name	Key Unit	Unit 2	Unit 3
D. Feng's Cleaners	D	Fengs	Cleaners
Sister Mary's Bookstore	Sister	Marys	Bookstore
Aunt Patsy's Cornmeal	Aunt	Patsys	Cornmeal

Rule 6: Prefixes—Articles and Particles

An article or particle in a personal or business name is combined with the part of the name following it to form a single indexing unit. The indexing order is not affected by a space or punctuation between a prefix and the rest of the name; the space and punctuation are disregarded when indexing. Examples of articles and particles are Da, El, La, San., St., Ste., Van, and Von der.

Filing Segment	Index Order of Units			
Name	Key Unit	Unit 2	Unit 3	Unit 4
Keith M. LeFebvre	LeFebvre	Keith	M	
Agnes Ruth St. George	StGeorge	Agnes	Ruth	
Van Alstine	VanAlstine	Car	Wash	Center
Car Wash Center				
Marcus Von der Veen	VonderVeen	Marcus		

Rule 7: Numbers in Business Names   Numbers spelled out in a business name are considered as written and filed alphabetically. Numbers written in digit form are considered as one unit. Names with numbers as the first unit written in digit form are filed in ascending order before alphabetic names.

Arabic numbers (2, 3) are filed before Roman numerals (II, III). Names with inclusive numbers (33–37) are arranged with the lowest number only (33). Names with numbers appearing in other than the first position (Pier 36 Café) are filed alphabetically within the appropriate section and immediately before a similar name without a number. When indexing numbers written in digit form that contain *nd, rd, st,* and *th,* ignore the letter endings and consider only the digits.

Filing Segment		*Index Order of Units*		
Name	*Key Unit*	*Unit 2*	*Unit 3*	*Unit 4*
12 Step AA Club	12	Step	AA	Club
12th Step Group	12	Step	Group	
1212 Jackson Street Garage	1212	Jackson	Street	Garage
Twelve Hills Apartments	Twelve	Hills	Apartments	
Twilight 21 Club	Twilight	21	Club	
Twilight Skating Rink	Twilight	Skating	Rink	

Rule 8: Organizations and Institutions   Banks and other financial institutions, clubs, colleges, hospitals, hotels, lodges, motels, museums, religious institutions, schools, universities, and other organizations and institutions are indexed and filed according to the names written on their letterheads. *The* used as the first word in these names is considered the last filing unit.

Filing Segment		*Index Order of Units*			
Name	*Key Unit*	*Unit 2*	*Unit 3*	*Unit 4*	*Unit 5*
First Bank of Carrollton	First	Bank	of	Carrollton	
Korean First Presbyterian Church	Korean	First	Presbyterian	Church	
Manning White High School	Manning	White	High	School	
Motel LaFont	Motel	LaFont			
Nevada State Teachers Association	Nevada	State	Teachers	Association	
The Rotary Club of Detroit	Rotary	Club	of	Detroit	The
University of Oklahoma	University	of	Oklahoma		

Rule 9: Identical Names   When personal names and names of businesses, institutions, and organizations are identical, filing order is determined by the addresses. Addresses are considered in the following order.

1. City names
2. State or province names (if city names are identical)
3. Street names; include *Avenue, Boulevard, Drive, Street* (if city and state names are identical)
   a. When the first units of street names are written in figures (18th Street), the names are filed in ascending numeric order (1, 2, 3) and placed together before alphabetic street names (16th Street, 20th Avenue, 25th Drive).
   b. Street names with compass directions (North, South, East, and West) are considered as written (North LaSalle Street). Numbers after compass directions are considered before alphabetic names (North 6th, North Main, SE Main, Southeast Main).
   c. If city, state, and street names are identical, house and building numbers are used. House and building numbers written as figures are filed in ascending numeric order (10 Opdyke Terrace, 2480 Opdyke Terrace) and placed together before alphabetic building names (Opdyke Terrace). If a street address and a building name are included in an address, disregard the building name.
   d. ZIP codes are not considered in determining filing order.

Filing Segment				*Index Order of Units*				
Name	*Key Unit*	*Unit 2*	*Unit 3*	*Unit 4*	*Unit 5*	*Unit 6*	*Unit 7*	*Unit 8*
Adrian B. Campillo Denver CO	Campillo	Adrian	B	Denver	Colorado			
Adrian B. Campillo Phoenix AZ	Campillo	Adrian	B	Phoenix	Arizona			
Retail Design Inc., 512 10th St. Houston TX	Retail	Design	Inc	Houston	Texas	10th	Street	512
Retail Design Inc., One Main Street Houston TX	Retail	Design	Inc.	Houston	Texas	One	Main	Street
Richards Fence Co. 811 Main Building Mission TX	Richards	Fence	Co	Mission	Texas	811	Main	Building
Richards Fence Co. 1012 Main Building Mission TX	Richards	Fence	Co	Mission	Texas	1012	Main	Building

Rule 10: Government Names   Government names are indexed first by the name of the governmental unit—country, state, county, or city. Next, index the distinctive name of the department, bureau, office, or board. The words *Office of, Department of, Bureau of,* and so forth, are separate indexing units when they are part of the official name. If *of* is not a part of the official name as written, it is not added.

A. Federal   The first three indexing units of a United States (federal) government agency name are *United States Government*.

Filing Segment   *Index Order of Units*

Name	Key Unit	Unit 2	Unit 3	Unit 4	Unit 5	Unit 6	Unit 7	Unit 8
Department of Labor Employment Standards	United	States	Government	Labor	Department	of	Employment	Standards

B. State and Local   The first indexing units are the names of the state, province, county, parish, city, town, township, or village. Next, index the most distinctive name of the department, board, bureau, office, or government/political division. The words *State of, County of, City of, Department of,* and so forth, are added only if needed for clarity and if in the office name. Each word is considered a separate indexing unit.

Filing Segment   *Index Order of Units*

Name	Key Unit	Unit 2	Unit 3	Unit 4	Unit 5	Unit 6	Unit 7	Unit 8	Unit 9	Unit 10
Department of High-Ways and Public Transportation, Dist. Const. Office Dallas Texas	Texas	High-ways	and	Public	Transpor-tation	Depart-ment	of	District	Construc-tion	Office

C. Foreign   The distinctive English name is the first indexing unit for foreign government names. Then index the remainder of the formal name of the government, if needed and if it is in the official name (China Republic of). Branches, departments, and divisions follow in order by their distinctive names. States, colonies, provinces, cities, and other divisions of foreign governments are filed by their distinctive or official names as spelled in English.

Filing Segment   *Index Order of Units*

Name	Key Unit	Unit 2	Unit 3
Dominion of Canada	Canada	Dominion	of
French Republic (Republique Francaise)	French	Republic	
Republic of China	China	Republic	of

Indexing Rules for Computer Applications

The alphabetic indexing rules are the same whether you are filing the material manually or on a computer. However, you need to give special consideration to how you sort your data. Here are two important steps that must be followed.

Computer Filing Considerations

- Key each filing unit into a separate field. A common list of field names appears on the computer; however, if the field name you wish to use does not appear, you may add the field name.
- Plan how you want the information sorted. For example, if you wish to sort a list of records by *Sales Region*, your first field would be *Sales Region*, your second field would be *Last Name*, and your third field would be *First Name*.

Computer Sorting

To help you understand how a computer sort looks, refer to Figure. 14-1, which shows an alphabetic name sort from a word processing program, and Figure 14-2, which shows a sort from a spreadsheet program. Here are some of the terms

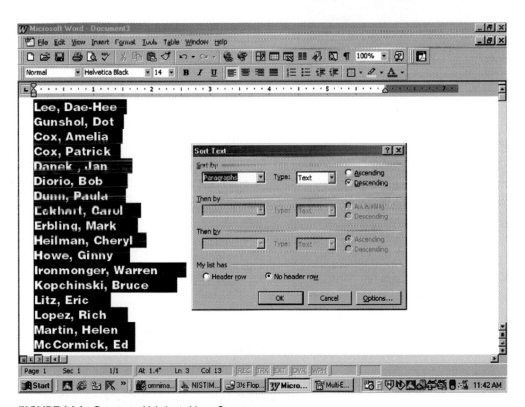

FIGURE 14-1. Computer Alphabetic Name Sort

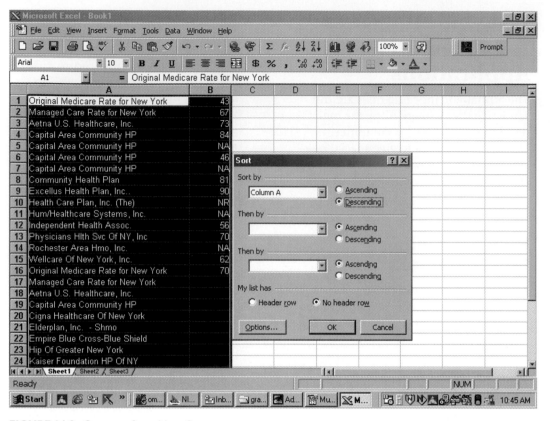

FIGURE 14-2. Computer Spreadsheet Sort

that are important for you to know when filing by computer:

- A **field** is a combination of characters to form words, numbers, or a meaningful code.
- A **computer record** is the total collection of fields or specific pieces of information about one person or one item within a file.

- A **file** is a collection of related records and also may be called a **database.**
- A **filename** is a unique name given to a file stored for computer use.

Storage Methods

As you have already learned, records may be stored in paper, electronic, or image form. The same storage classification system can be used in whatever media the record is stored. In this chapter, the illustrations of records storage will show manual paper systems. As you are learning the classification systems, it will be easier for you to understand by illustrating a manual paper system. Additionally, as you have already learned, paper systems continue to be used extensively. In Chapter 15, you will learn about storing records electronically and in microimage form.

Records storage methods (sometimes called filing methods) are the manner in which records are classified for storage. For example, there are four types of classification systems that are used:

- Alphabetic
- Numeric
- Subject
- Geographic

There are also several variations on the numeric classification method, with four of these methods presented in this chapter. The variations that will be presented in this section are **terminal-digit storage, chronologic storage, block numeric coding,** and **alphanumeric coding.**

Alphabetic Storage Method

The **alphabetic storage method** uses letters of the alphabet to determine the order in which the names of people and companies are filed. This method is one of the most common methods used and is found in one form or another in almost every office. With the alphabetic storage method, the name of the company, the person, or the organization addressed determines the filing order of an outgoing record. The name of the originator (company, individual, or organization) determines the filing order of incoming records. Figure 14-3 shows an alphabetic file. Records are filed according to the basic alphabetic filing rules that were presented earlier in this chapter.

Alphabetic Storage Advantages

- It is a **direct access** system. There is no need to refer to anything except the file to find the name.
- The dictionary arrangement is simple to understand.
- Misfiling is easily checked by alphabetic sequence.
- It may be less costly to operate than other filing methods because of direct access.
- Only one **sorting** (arranging records in a predetermined sequence) is required.
- Papers relating to one originator are filed in the same location.

Alphabetic Storage Disadvantages

- Misfiling may result when rules are not followed.
- Similarly spelled names may cause confusion when filed under the alphabetic method.
- Related records may be filed in more than one place.
- Expansion may create problems. This statement is especially true if the expansion takes place in a section of the file where there is no room remaining for the insertion of more guides and folders.
- Excessive cross-referencing can congest the files.

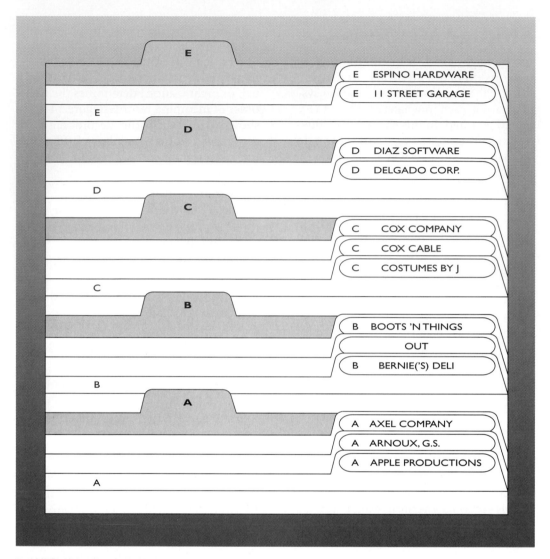

FIGURE 14-3. Alphabetic File

- Confidentiality of the files cannot be maintained since the file folders bearing names are instantly seen by anyone who happens to glance at a folder.

Subject Storage Method

In a **subject storage method,** records are filed according to the subject of the mate-rial. Subject filing is used to some extent in all offices. It is used when the file may be looked for more by a topic than by a name. For example, assume a department is working on cancer research. A file labeled CANCER RESEARCH would place all material on the same subject in one folder. See Figure 14-4.

Although subject filing is useful and

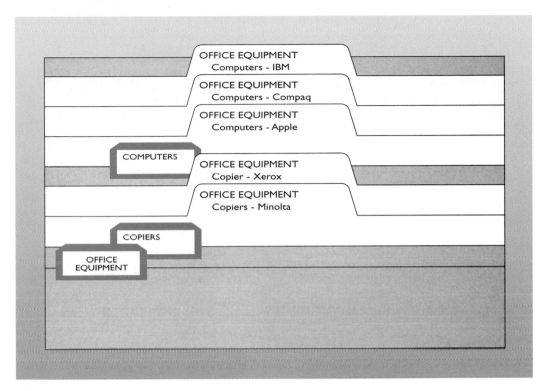

FIGURE 14-4. Subject File

necessary in certain situations, it is the most difficult and costly method of filing. Each paper must be read completely to determine the subject. It is a difficult method to control since two people reading a record may have different views of what the subject is.

A necessary part of a subject file is an index. The index is a list of all subjects under which a record may be filed. Without an index, it is almost impossible for the subject filing method to function satisfactorily. The list should be kept up-to-date as new subjects are added and old ones are eliminated. When new subjects are added, the index provides guidance to avoid the duplication of subjects. The index may be kept on standard sheets of pa-

per and filed in a notebook or on index cards and filed in a card file box.

Subject Storage Advantages

- Records about one subject are grouped together.
- The system can be expanded easily by adding subdivisions.

Subject Storage Disadvantages

- It is difficult to classify records by subject.
- Liberal cross-referencing is necessary since one record may contain several subjects.
- The system does not satisfactorily provide for general records.

- It is necessary to keep an index of subject headings contained in the file.
- It is the most expensive method to maintain since it requires very experienced file clerks.
- Preparation of materials for the subject file takes longer than any other

method since each record must be read carefully.

Numeric Storage Method

Under the **numeric storage method**, file cards and folders are given numbers and

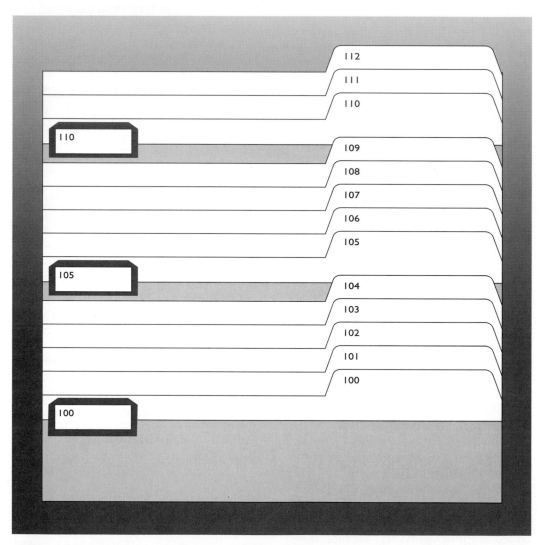

FIGURE 14-5. Numeric File

are arranged in numeric sequence. This method of filing is particularly useful to:

- Insurance companies that keep records according to policy numbers
- Social welfare agencies that maintain records according to case numbers
- Law firms that assign a case number to each client
- Warehouses that stock by part numbers, and real estate agencies that list properties by code numbers

Basic Parts

- Numeric guides and folders
- Alphabetic general file
- Card file
- Accession book

Numeric Guides and Folders. The numeric file houses the records. Behind the primary guide are individual folders with numbered captions. A numeric file is shown in Figure 14-5.

Alphabetic General File. Records are usually arranged alphabetically and filed in the general file. The general file contains a primary guide labeled *General* and individual folders labeled with letters of the alphabet as shown in Figure 14-6.

Card File. After a number is assigned to an item, an index card is prepared, showing the name and the assigned number. This card is placed alphabetically in the card file, shown in Figure 14-7.

Accession Book. The accession book is a record of the numbers that have been assigned. This book shows the next number available for assignment and prevents the assigning of the same number to two different names. An accession book is shown in Figure 14-8.

Storage Procedure. The basic storage procedure in a numeric system is:

- A record is received for storing.
- The card file is consulted to see if the correspondent or subject has been assigned a number.
- No number is assigned when there is only one record for a company or subject. The name or subject is keyed on a card with the letter G (general) keyed in the upper right-hand corner. The card is placed in alphabetic order in the card file. The record is placed in the general file in the appropriate alphabetic folder. When several records from the same source have been accumulated, the records are then assigned a number and placed in the numeric file.

FIGURE 14-6. General File

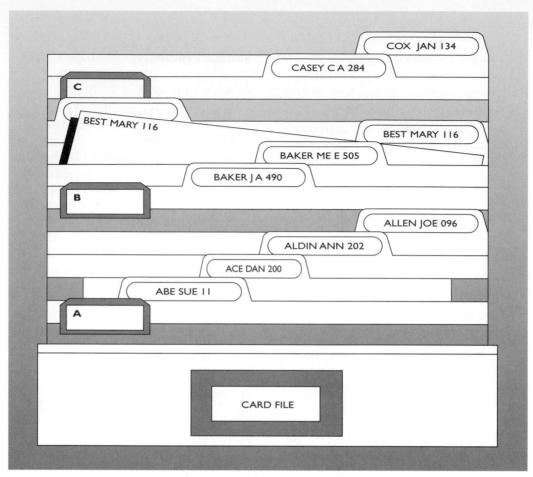

FIGURE 14-7. Card File

Number	Name	Page 105 Date
504	M. E. Baker	3/16/00
505	Browning Supply Co.	3/16/00
506	Jan Chinook	3/17/00
507	Travel World	3/17/00
508		

FIGURE 14-8. Accession Book

Numeric Storage Advantages. Some advantages of the numeric storage method are:

- Expansion is unlimited.
- It is confidential. A card file must be consulted before files on important papers can be located.
- Once an index card is prepared and a number is assigned to a record, filing by number is quicker than filing alphabetically.
- Misfiled folders are easily located because numbers out of place are easier to locate than misfiled alphabetic records.

Numeric Storage Disadvantages. Some of the disadvantages of the numeric storage method are:

- It is an indirect method; the card file must be consulted before a paper can be filed.
- More equipment is necessary, so the cost is higher.

Variations of Numeric Storage. There are several variations of the basic numeric storage method. Four of these variations are described briefly here.

- Terminal-Digit Filing. In the basic numeric method, as the files increase, the numbers assigned become higher. When the numbers become several digits long, it becomes difficult to file items correctly. **Terminal-digit filing,** which is designed to remedy this problem, is organized by the final digits of the number. The digits are usually separated into groups of two or three. For example, assume you have a file with the number 013746. The last, or terminal, digits (46) identify the file drawer number. The second two digits (37) indicate the number of the file guide. The first two digits (01) give the num-

ber of the file folder behind the file guide. Figure 14-9 illustrates terminal digit filing.

- Chronologic Storage. A **chronologic storage system** is an arrangement in which records are stored in date order, with the most recent date first. Chronologic storage may be used for filing such items as freight bills, daily reports, and tickler files. The term **tickler file** comes from the fact that the file is used to tickle your memory and remind you to take certain actions. For example, when something must be taken care of on a certain date, a card is prepared with the necessary information and placed in date or chronologic order. The file is checked each morning

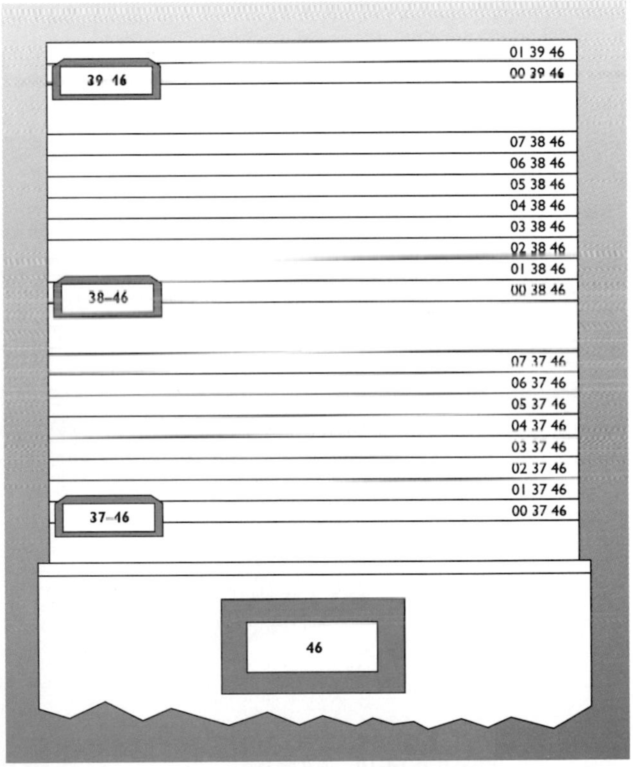

FIGURE 14-9. Terminal Digit File

to see what must be done that day. The basic arrangement of a tickler file consists of a series of 12 guides with the names of the months printed on the tabs and 31 guides with the number 1 through 31 representing each day of the month printed on the tabs. The tickler file is generally kept on the office worker's desk. A tickler file is shown in Figure 14-10.

Chronologic storage may also be used as a supplement to a subject system as a help to finding records filed by subject. You have already learned that a subject system is the most difficult method of filing. You may keep a chronologic index with a subject system. The index would contain the date of the document, the name of the individual or company, and the subject under which the document is filed.

Such a system allows you to find records with limited information. For example, assume your employer says, "I need the letter to Armando Bentances that was written in January." With a

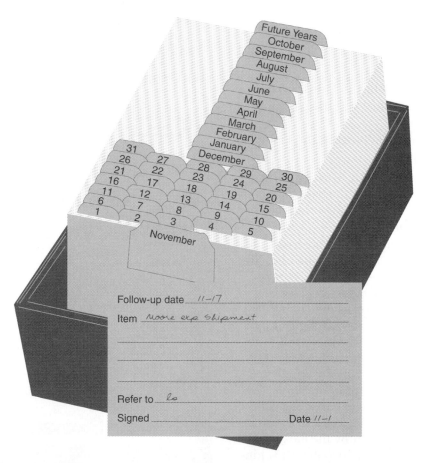

FIGURE 14-10. Tickler File

subject system alone, it would be difficult to locate a record with only the name and date of the letter. A chronologic system allows you to find the letter with the limited information given. A chronologic system also is used within individual folders. For example, the most recent record is always on top so that anyone who opens a folder can immediately see the latest record.

- Block Numeric Coding. **Block numeric coding** is a system based on the assignment of groups of numbers to represent primary and secondary subjects; in other words, it utilizes both numeric and subject filing. Major subject divisions may be assigned a block of numbers such as 100, 200, and 300. Each subdivision is then assigned a block of numbers within the block such as 210, 220, and 230. For example, the guide in the file would have **100 ACCOUNTING,** with the folders having labels such as **110 ACCOUNTS PAYABLE, 120 ACCOUNTS RECEIVABLE,** and so forth.

- Alphanumeric Coding. **Alphanumeric coding** combines alphabetic and numeric characters, with the main subjects arranged alphabetically and their subdivision assigned a number. For example, the file guide may have **RM-01 RECORDS MANAGEMENT,** with the files having **RM-01-01 FILING METHODS, RM-01-02 ELECTRONIC FILING SYSTEMS,** and so on.

Geographic Method

When the files are requested by location rather than by name, geographic filing is advantageous. This method is based first on the location of the originators and second on their names. It is particularly useful for:

- Utility companies where street names and numbers are of primary importance in troubleshooting
- Real estate firms that have listings according to land areas
- Sales organizations that are concerned with the geographic location of their customers
- Government agencies that file records by state, county, or other geographic division

In geographic filing, the main divisions may be states, counties, cities, sales territories, and so forth. The breakdown into geographic divisions and subdivisions must fit the type of business, its organization, and its need for specific kinds of information. In a geographic file by state and city, for example, files guides are used to indicate the state and city. The file folders are arranged alphabetically behind the guides by company or individual. Figure 14-11 shows a geographic filing arrangement.

An alphabetic card file is an essential element of a geographic filing method. Records may be requested by the name of the originator rather than by the address. A file consisting of cards with the names of originators in alphabetic order and their complete addresses gives all the necessary information when the file clerk must locate records without knowing the location. A card from an alphabetic card file is shown in Figure 14-12.

Geographic Storage Advantages

- It provides for grouping of records by location.
- The volume of records within any given geographic area can be seen by glancing at the files.
- It allows for direct filing if the location is known.

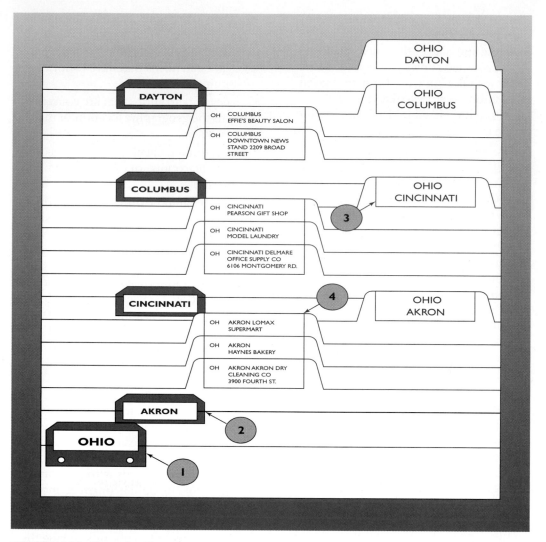

FIGURE 14-11. Geographic File

- All the advantages of alphabetic filing are inherent in this method since it is basically an alphabetic arrangement.

Geographic Storage Disadvantages

- Multiple sorting increases the possibility of error and is time-consuming.

- The arrangement of guides and folders (see Figure 14-11) makes filing more difficult.

- Reference to the card file is necessary if the location is not known.

- It takes longer to set up than does the alphabetic method.

ERICKSON THOMAS B

183 JUNGLE AVENUE
DUNCANVILLE TEXAS 75116-7606

FIGURE 14-12. Alphabetic Card File

Storing Procedures

After you have determined the storage method or combination of storage methods (alphabetic, numeric, subject, or geographic) to be used, the next step is to get the material ready for storage. The steps you should follow in storing records are given in the following sections.

Inspect

Incoming records must not be stored until the record has been reviewed and acted upon (if necessary) by someone in authority, which is usually your employer. Therefore, before storing any incoming record, be sure to **inspect** the record for a release mark. This may be in the form of initials, a stamp, a check mark, the word "file" written on the record, or some other agreed-upon mark. Sometimes records will be placed in the out basket by mistake. If there is no release mark, be sure to check with your supervisor to see if he or she is ready for the record to be stored.

Copies of outgoing records do not need a release mark since the record is usually one that has been generated in your office by you or your employer. For example, assume that your employer gives you a letter that has been keyed on her computer for you to format and edit. Your employer has prepared the letter. Once the original has been signed, the copy can be stored.

Index

Indexing refers to the process of determining the name to be used in storing. For example, consider indexing as applied to an incoming letter. The most likely name to use is in the letterhead. On an outgoing letter, the most likely name to use is in the letter address. Since numerous letters are stored in all offices, here are some suggestions for proper storage.

Incoming Letters

- The letterhead is the most likely name to be used for storage purposes.
- If the letterhead has no relation to the writer (for example, the letter has been written in a hotel on hotel stationery), use the name or company of the writer.
- If the letter is on plain paper, use the name or company in the closing lines.
- The company name is used, except in rare exceptions when the originator is more important than the company and the letter would be searched for first by the name of the originator. When company names are used, you may want to set up folders for individuals after more than seven to nine pieces of information are received for different individuals within the same company. If you do so, the company name is used first in filing, followed by the name of the individuals in alphabetical order.

Outgoing Letters

- The inside address is used when storing outgoing letters, with the name of the company as the indexing unit.
- If correspondence within a company is consistently addressed to one or more individuals, you may want to set up a folder for these individuals. If you do so, the company name is used first in filing, followed by the name of the individual(s) in alphabetical order.

In subject storage, indexing means determining the most important subject discussed in the record. If there are two subjects, the record should be filed under one subject and cross-referenced under the other. In geographic storage, the location to be used must be determined. In numeric storage, the name and number to be used must be determined.

Code

Coding is marking the units of the filing segment (or name) by which the record is to be stored. Coding is important since it saves time in the refiling process. When a paper has been removed from the files and must be refiled, the office professional does not have to reread the document if it has been coded. On outgoing records, coding may be done on the record as it is being prepared. You are already aware that as you input material on a disk you must give the record a filename. The filename is essential in retrieving the record, and it may be printed on the document. On incoming records, coding is done before the document is filed by underlining, circling, or writing on the document the filing segment.

Cross-Reference

When a record is likely to be called for under two or more names, a **cross-reference** is prepared. For example, assume AWB Corporation is owned by Rose Cuffee. Records may be asked for by the name of Rose Cuffee or AWB Corporation. In this case, the main file would be AWB Corporation with the cross-reference under Rose Cuffee. Cross-reference cards or sheets may be purchased from a commercial company, or you may make your own forms. An example of a cross-reference sheet is shown in Figure 14-13. Notice that the notation on the sheet indicates where the original correspondence is filed.

Sort

Sorting is the arrangement of records in the order in which they are to be filed. The records should first be sorted into a few groups, and then into the final arrangement. The first sorting is called **rough sorting.** For example, items may be arranged into groups of A to C, D to H, I to M, N to S, and T to Z. The last sorting, or **fine sorting,** consists of arranging the items in exact alphabetic order. When the fine sorting is completed, the materials are ready to be filed.

To assist you in efficiently sorting materials, a sorter may be used. The guides on each flap of the sorter carry an alphabetic designation. If you do not immediately file materials, it is helpful to have the materials in a sorter at your desk so that they may be located quickly without having to shuffle through a pile of papers.

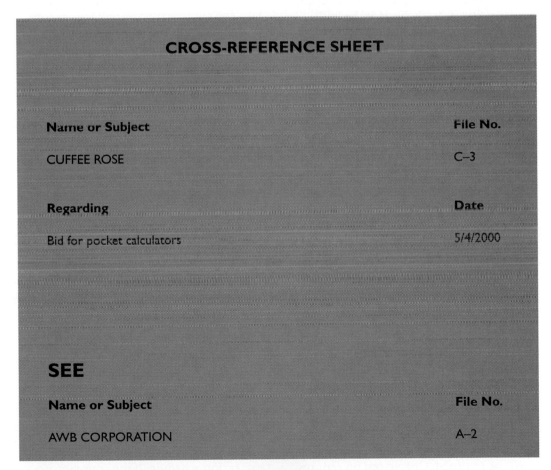

FIGURE 14-13. Cross-Reference Sheet

Store

Storing is the actual process of placing the record in the file folder and the file drawer. Rather than filing one record at a time, which is extremely time-consuming, accumulate several records before going to the file drawer. As you are accumulating enough paper to file, you should keep the papers in order at your desk in case someone needs to refer to a record. When you are ready to file, take the sorter to the file drawer. Each paper goes into the folder with its top to the left. The most recent paper is always placed on top, which means that the oldest piece of correspondence is always at the back of the folder. The final step in this cycle of the life of a record is disposing of the record when it is no longer needed. You will learn more about disposal in the next section.

Manual Records Retrieval, Retention, Transfer, and Disposal

In all filing systems, whether they are manual, electronic, or image, it is important to be able to retrieve records, retain them for the useful life of the record, and transfer them to other locations in order to reduce the size of the active files. Manual system retrieval, retention, and transfer will be explained here. Electronic and image system retrieval, retention, and transfer will be discussed in Chapter 15.

Records Retrieval

If a record is taken from a file, it is necessary to indicate what was taken and when it will be returned. Charge-out procedures using requisition forms and out guides and out folders provide a system for retrieving records taken from the files.

Requisition Form.   A **requisition form** includes a space for identifying the record borrowed, the name and location of the borrower, the date on the borrowed record, and the date the record is to be returned to the files. This form is usually prepared in duplicate, with one copy kept in a tickler file and the other inserted in an out guide or out folder.

Out Guide and Out Folder.   The **out guide** is usually a pressboard or plastic guide with the word OUT printed on the tab. The guide is used to replace a record that has been removed from the files. When an entire folder is taken from the files, papers for a particular originator cannot be filed until the folder has been returned. For continuity in filing, you may choose to use an out folder to take the place of the one borrowed. The out guide or out folder remains in the file until the borrowed record or folder is returned and refiled. Figure 14-14 shows both an out guide and an out folder.

Records Retention

As the cost of office space continues to rise, the need for retention control becomes more and more important. Filling valuable office space with unnecessary documents and file cabinets is not a viable option.

As an office professional, you probably will not make decisions about how long important documents should be kept. The legal counsel for a company is generally consulted here. If the company is large, it may have developed a retention schedule. Figure 14-15 shows a portion of a retention schedule. If the company does

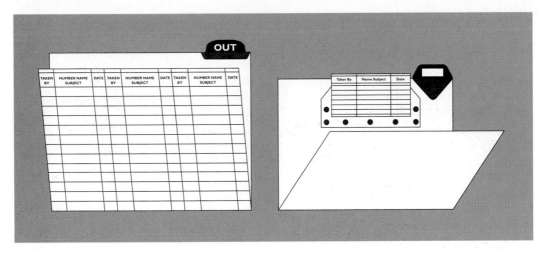

FIGURE 14-14. Out Guide and Out Folder

not have a records retention schedule, the office professional should check with the supervisor before making any decisions about how documents should be transferred or destroyed.

One useful reference on the retention and legality of records is the *Guide to Record Retention Requirements* published by the National Archives and Records Service, available from the Superintendent of Documents, U.S. Government Printing Office, Washington, DC 20402.

Retention and destruction files have taken on additional importance with the approval in December 1993 of the Revised Rule 26 of the Federal Rules of Civil Procedure. Revised Rule 26 requires organizations to make available all relevant records that must be kept in compliance with prevailing statutes and regulations. Delay or failure to find information makes an organization vulnerable to financial loss and adverse legal judgments. Disposal becomes important because records kept past legal retention and disposal periods can be a liability.

To understand more about retention control, consider the following categories of records.

Vital Records. Records that cannot be replaced and should never be destroyed

RETENTION SCHEDULE	
Document	**Retention in Years**
Accounting	
Payroll (time cards)	3
Expense reports	6
Payroll	8
Corporate Records	
Capital stock and bond records	Indefinitely
Contracts and agreements	Indefinitely
Patents	Indefinitely
Personnel	
Disability and sick benefit records	6
Personnel files (terminated)	6
Withholding tax statements	6

FIGURE 14-15. Retention Schedule

are called **vital records.** These records are essential to the effective, continued operation of the organization and should not be transferred from the active section of the storage area. Some examples of vital records are corporate charters, certain contracts, deeds, and tax returns.

Important Records.   Records that are necessary to an orderly continuation of the business and are replaceable only with considerable expenditure of time and money are known as **important records.** Such records may be transferred to inactive storage but not destroyed. Examples of important records are financial statements, operating and statistical records, and board minutes.

Useful Records.   **Useful records** are those that are useful for the smooth, effective operation of the organization. Such records are replaceable, but their loss involves delay or inconvenience to the organization. These records may be transferred to inactive files or destroyed after a certain period of time. Examples include letters, reports, and bank records.

Nonessential Records.   Records that have no future value to the organization are considered **nonessential.** Once the purpose for which they were created has been fulfilled, they may be destroyed.

Records Transfer

At some point in the life of a record you decide either to destroy the record, retain it permanently, or transfer it to inactive storage. Two common methods are **perpetual transfer** and **periodic transfer.**

Perpetual Transfer.   With the perpetual method, materials are continuously transferred from the active to the inactive files. The advantage of this method is that all files are kept current, since any inactive material is immediately transferred to

storage. The perpetual transfer method works well in offices where jobs are completed by units. For example, when a lawyer finishes a case, the file is complete and probably will not need to be referred to often. Therefore, it can be transferred to inactive files.

When distinguishing between active and inactive records, the following categories should be used.

- **Active records** are those records that are used three or more times a month and that should be kept in an accessible area.

- **Inactive records** are those records used less than 15 times a year and that may be stored in less accessible areas than active records.

- **Archive records** are records that have historical value to the organization and are preserved permanently.

Periodic Transfer.   With periodic transfer, active records are transferred to inactive status at the end of a stated period of time. For example, you may transfer records that are over six months old to the inactive file and maintain records that are less than six months old in the active file. Every six months you follow this procedure. This method of transfer works well and is used by most businesses.

Records Disposal

Records that no longer have any use should be destroyed. If the material is not confidential, it may be disposed of by simply dropping it in a basket, with the paper being recycled. However, when the information is confidential, it should be destroyed by shredding. Shredders that cut the paper into confetti-like strips are common in offices. The shredded paper may then be recycled.

Misplaced and Lost Records

Although you may be very careful in your filing, papers do occasionally get misplaced and even lost. When they do, here are some tips to help you find the paper and suggestions about how to handle a lost document.

Misplaced Records

- Look in the folder immediately in front of and immediately behind the correct folder.
- Look between folders.
- Look in the GENERAL folder.
- Check to see if the paper has slipped to the bottom of the file drawer.
- Look completely through the correct folder since a record may be placed out of chronological sequence.
- Look for the second, third, or succeeding units rather than for the key unit.
- Check for misfiling due to misread letters; for example, C for G, K for H, and so forth.
- Check for alternative spellings of words; for example, McDonald or MacDonald.
- Check for the transposition of numbers.
- Look in a related subject file.
- Look in the sorter.
- Look on your desk and your employer's desk.

Lost Records

If you are unable to find the record, try to reconstruct as much of it as you can by asking your employer about the contents and rekeying the information. Key the words "Replacing Lost Record" at the top of the record and store it in its correct place within the file.

Basic Manual Filing Supplies and Equipment

Basic manual filing supplies and equipment include file folders, suspension folders, file guides, labels, tabs, and file cabinets.

File Folders

A file folder is generally a manila one that will hold 8½ x 11" or 8½ x 14" inch paper. Other colors of folders are available including blue, yellow, brown, and so on. The filing designation for the correspondence placed in the folder is keyed on a label that is then affixed to the tab of the folder. Folders are made with tabs of various widths, called **cuts.** The cuts are straight cut, one-half cut, one-third cut, and one-fifth cut.

Suspension Folders

In addition to standard file folders, **suspension folders** are available. These are sometimes called **hanging folders** because small metal rods are attached to the folders, allowing them to hang on the sides of the file drawer. Plastic tabs and insertable labels are used with the folders. These tabs and labels may be placed in any position using the precut on the folder.

File Guides

A file guide is usually made of heavy pressboard and is used to separate the file drawer into various sections. Hollow tabs on the top of the guide provide for a name, number, or letter that represents the section of the file drawer to be inserted. This type of guide is shown in Figure 14-16.

File Folder Labels

File folder labels may be purchased in various configurations including continuous folded strips, separate strips, rolls in boxes, or on pressure-sensitive adhesive labels. Different colored labels can speed up the process of filing and finding records and eliminate much misfiling. It is very easy to spot a colored label that has been misfiled since that color stands out from the other colors that surround it.

Some of the ways that colored labels may be used are to:

- Designate a particular subject (for example, green labels may designate budget items, blue labels personnel items)
- Indicate geographic divisions of the country
- Designate particular sections of the file

When preparing labels for files, consistency should be observed in keying them. Suggestions for preparing labels are:

- Key label captions in all capital letters with no punctuation.
- Begin the caption close to the left edge of the label.
- Always key the name on the label in correct indexing order.
- Use the same style of labels on all fold-

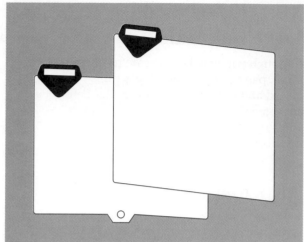

FIGURE 14-16. File Guides

ers. For example, if you decide to use labels with color strips, be consistent; if you decide to use colored labels, be consistent.

- Key wraparound sidetab labels for lateral file cabinets both above and below the color bar separator so that the information is readable from both sides.

Equipment

Vertical files are the conventional storage cabinet. These files are available in one-to-five drawer sizes. They are also available in sizes to accommodate cards and letter-size records.

Lateral files are similar to vertical files except the drawer rolls out sideways, exposing the entire contents of the file drawer at once. Less aisle space is needed for a lateral file than a vertical file. A lateral file is shown on page 387.

Movable-aisle systems consist of modular units of open shelf files mounted on tracks in the floor. Files are placed directly against each other. Wheels or rails permit the individual units to be moved apart for access. Movable systems may be manual, mechanical, or electrical. Manual systems are small, with two to four carriages. They require no power; the user merely pushes the files apart. Mechanical systems operate by turning a crank. Electrical systems move carriages with motors. A movable-aisle system is shown on page 388.

Because movable systems take less space than standard files, they are being used more frequently. Features that provide safety for both file contents and the people who work with them are of top priority for companies using the system.

The most basic protection device is a key-operated carriage lock that prevents the system from rolling on the rails. Another safety device is a strip that runs the length of the file cabinet at floor level. Pressure of more than a few ounces stops cabinet movement. Still another safety device is an infrared photoelectric beam. If a person or object breaks the beam, the system stops movement. When the person or object is no longer breaking the beam, the system resets itself. To ensure safety of materials, users may have a badge that is swiped through a badge reader to allow entrance to the system, or users may enter a password code. Some systems can be fitted with locking doors.

Lateral file drawers roll out sideways.

Movable-aisle systems consist of modular units of open shelf files mounted on tracks in the floor. *Courtesy of Tab Products Company.*

SUMMARY

To reinforce what you have learned in this chapter, study this summary.

- Records management is the systematic control of records from creation to final disposition.

- The Association of Records Managers and Administrators, Inc. (ARMA) has set forth alphabetic indexing rules designed to help the office professional perform his or her job more effectively. Ten rules, compatible with the ARMA rules, are presented in this chapter.

- When indexing for the computer, there are certain special considerations to conform to computer processing standards.

- The types of storage methods are alphabetic, numeric, subject, and geo-

graphic. The alphabetic method is the most commonly used method of storing materials.

- Variations of the numeric storage system include terminal-digit filing, chronologic storage, block numeric coding, and alphanumeric coding.

- Storage procedures include inspecting, indexing, coding, cross-referencing, sorting, and storing.

- Out guides and out folders allow for the retrieval of records taken from the files.

- Records retention involves deciding how long records should be kept. In retaining and storing records, consideration should be given to the classification of records. These classifications are vital records, important records, useful records, and nonessential records.

- Records may be transferred to storage using perpetual or periodic transfer methods.
- Confidential records should be disposed of through shredding.
- When records are lost or misplaced, a consistent process should be undertaken to attempt to locate the paper that includes looking in the folder immediately in front of and immediately behind the correct folder, checking for misfiling due to misread letters, checking for alternative spelling of words, and so forth.
- Basic manual filing supplies and equipment include file folders, suspension folders, file guides, file-folder labels, and file cabinets.

Key Terms

- Record
- Microform
- Records management
- Record life cycle
- ARMA
- Acronyms
- Seniority suffix
- Professional suffix
- Numeric suffix
- Alphabetic suffix
- Field
- Computer record
- File
- Database
- Filename
- Records storage methods
- Terminal-digit storage
- Chronologic storage
- Block numeric coding
- Alphanumeric coding
- Alphabetic storage method
- Direct access
- Sorting
- Subject storage method
- Numeric storage method
- Terminal-digit filing
- Chronologic storage system
- Tickler file
- Block numeric coding
- Alphanumeric coding
- Inspect
- Indexing
- Coding
- Cross-reference
- Sorting
- Rough sorting
- Fine sorting
- Storing
- Requisition form
- Out guide
- Vital records
- Important records
- Useful records
- Nonessential records
- Perpetual transfer
- Periodic transfer
- Active records
- Inactive records
- Archive records
- Cuts
- Suspension folders
- Hanging folders

Professional Pointers

You may have the opportunity to be involved in recommending, implementing, or expanding a records management system. If so, keep these pointers in mind.

- Define the needs of the organization—office, department, division, or entire company. Know the types of records used, how long they are to be retained, who can have access and the capacity needed for storage.
- Conduct research and seek information. Based on your identified needs, collect recommendations from representatives of records supplies and systems firms. Solicit input from other organizations similar to your own as to the system they use.
- Ensure that everyone has adequate training on the system that is chosen.
- Give a list of the filing procedures/rules as a reference source to all individuals who have access to the files.
- Include a method for ongoing evaluation of the records management system. Efficiency and cost effectiveness are vital to the success of the system and the business.

Office Procedures Reinforcement

1. Define records management and describe the value of records to a business.
2. List the advantages and disadvantages of the alphabetic and numeric storage methods.
3. Describe the steps in proper storing procedures.
4. Name and briefly describe the four categories into which records can be classified.
5. List at least six tips to use in locating misplaced or lost files.

Critical Thinking Activity

Franklin Brezenski is employed by HBJ Insurance Corporation; he has worked for the company for four years as a records clerk in the Records Management Department. His supervisor is Janie Townes. Ms. Townes believes that Franklin is an outstanding employee. He is very thorough and accurate; he is dependable. He is always punctual and has only missed two days of work in the four years of his employment. If there is work that must be done outside regular hours, Franklin is always willing to work overtime to get it done. He is well liked by the entire staff; he is seen as a team player by the individuals within the department. He is bright and willing to learn. When new systems or new equipment have been installed, Franklin is the first to learn them. In fact, he is a good teacher—helping others to learn. Ms. Townes has always given Franklin excellent evaluations.

Approximately six months ago, an employee from another department informed Ms. Townes that a piece of paper concerning a confidential matter had been given to one of the insurance salespersons in his department. Furthermore, said he that although he could not prove it, he believed that Franklin had given the paper to the individual. Ms. Townes told him that surely he must be mistaken, but that she would check it out. She checked the out records to see if the piece of paper had ever left the office; there was no record of it having been taken out. Since the paper involved a confidential matter, she also checked to see if the individual who supposedly had the paper was on the list of approved persons. He was not. She waited a few days and then asked Franklin about the situation. She told him what she had heard, although she did not give Franklin the name of the individual who told her. Franklin vehemently denied taking out the record. He reminded Ms. Townes that he knew the system and that he always checked out material. Franklin also stated that he would never give a confidential document to someone if he or she was not approved to receive the document. Ms. Townes believed Franklin and let the matter drop.

In the last month, Ms. Townes has discovered that two complete file folders are missing from the office. There is no record of the files being checked out. Both files contain confidential information. Ms. Townes called all the people together who work in the department and told them the files were missing. No one knew anything about it. Ms. Townes reinforced with everyone that nothing must leave the office unless it has been properly checked out. The files have not shown up. Ms. Townes is puzzled, and she decides that she will be more diligent about checking to see that procedures are followed.

Last evening Ms. Townes asked Franklin to work overtime since the department was behind on paper work. As usual, Franklin was cooperative and agreed to work. Ms. Townes left the office at 5 p.m. but returned at 7 p.m. to work for awhile. Franklin did not know she would be returning. When she came into the department, Franklin was handing several files to a salesperson. The salesperson left immediately after Ms. Townes came in with the files; the salesperson was the same one that Ms. Townes had been told earlier had received confidential files from Franklin. Ms. Townes went to her office and began working; Franklin left at 8 p.m. Ms. Townes checked the out records at 8:30 p.m. to see if any files had been recorded as checked out. Nothing was recorded; Ms. Townes did not know what files were taken.

Ms. Townes was very concerned. She spent a sleepless night thinking about the problem. She decided she would discuss the situation with her supervisor, one of the vice presidents. When she told him the situation, he said that upper management had reason to believe that one of their competitors was getting confidential information concerning HBJ. He further stated that management has no idea how the information is being leaked, but maybe Franklin and the salesperson are the sources. The vice president asked Ms. Townes to suggest a plan of action for addressing the issues and bring her plan to him by tomorrow morning.

- What advice would you give Ms. Townes for handling the situation?
- Prepare a suggested plan of action to give to the vice president.

Discuss your suggestions and plan of action with the class.

Office Applications

OA14-1 (Goals 1 and 2)
On the student template disk in file OA14-1.doc is a list of clients. Print the list to use as a working copy on which to mark the indexing units for a paper storage system. Rearrange the list into proper order by city for a geographic file, and print a final copy for review. Submit your copy to your instructor.

OA14-2 (Goals 1 and 2)
In your Applications Workbook on page 89 is a list of client names. Correspondence from these clients is to be placed in a numeric file. Assign numbers to the clients, beginning with No. 100 for the first name on the list. After the numbers are assigned, prepare 3 x 5 cards for the card file by listing the clients' names in indexing order and placing the appropriate number on the card. Arrange the cards in alphabetical order. Submit your cards to your instructor.

OA14-3 (Goals 1 and 2)

The company for which you work is switching from a manual or paper records storage system to an electronic system. Create a database and enter the records of clients from OA14-1.doc. Change the field for the states to the two-letter state abbreviation. Add a field for the ZIP code. Several records need to be added to the list; refer to page 90 of your Applications Workbook for the additions. Make the necessary revisions. Sort the records by customers' names, and print a copy. Submit your copy to your instructor.

OA14-4 (Goals 1 and 2)

Your student template disk contains several letters and memorandums that are to be placed in a subject file. The files are OA14-4a.doc, OA14-4b.doc, OA14-4c.doc, OA14-4d.doc, OA14-4e.doc, and OA14-4f.doc. Print a copy of each document, index, and code, and sort the correspondence in preparation for filing. Cross-reference the letter to M. Holms; a cross-reference form is provided on page 91 in your Applications Workbook.

OA14-5 (Goals 1 and 2)

On your student template disk in file OA14-5.doc is a list of customers. These names have been properly indexed and listed in alphabetical order. On page 92 of your Applications Workbook is another list of customers. Index this list of names and merge them with the first list for one consolidated list in alphabetical order. Print a copy and submit it to your instructor.

Online Research Application

ORA 14-6 (Goal 3)

Using the Internet, research the following:

- Types of manual storage equipment available
- Types of information available from ARMA

Prepare a short synopsis of your findings, listing the sources used. Submit your synopsis to your instructor.

CHAPTER 15

Records Management Technology

The Information Age has greatly changed the process of storing records. At one time records were stored only in paper form. Today, in addition to paper, records are stored electronically and in microimage form. Although paper storage is still the main storage medium for business records, the number of records being stored electronically or in microimage form continues to grow. In an increasing number of companies, computers serve as electronic file cabinets that store digitized images of documents that can be retrieved and instantly displayed on a screen. Consider the benefits of electronic storage over paper storage in space and equipment needed. A standard

YOUR GOALS

Your goals as you study this chapter are to:

1. Describe and use electronic and microimage systems.
2. Identify examples of the integration of computer and microimage systems.
3. Explain future trends in records management.

four-drawer filing cabinet may hold up to 10,000 pieces of paper. Advanced CD-ROMs are now able to store as much data as a warehouse of file cabinets, or about 300,000 pages of paper copy. Other benefits of using electronic storage are:

- Increased productivity through more efficient workflow
- Better and faster customer service
- Reduced paper and photocopying expenses

Some of the pioneers in implementing electronic storage of records have been the paper-intensive insurance and finance industries. Insurance companies use electronic systems to process claims, answer customer inquiries, or write new policies. Hospitals, law firms, and government agencies are making increasing use of electronic storage systems.

Since you will probably be using electronic or microimage technology in storing records, it is important that you have some knowledge of the technologies available. Electronic systems, microimage systems, and the trends in records management are presented in this chapter.

Information Management Systems

An information management system includes:

- Inputting data
- Processing the data through integration with other data, modifying, editing, deleting, and sorting
- Outputting the data
- Storing and retrieving the data

Information in an automated system is entered into the system, processed, stored, and retrieved in different ways than in a manual system. For example, information in an automated system is entered into the system through a personal computer. This information may be keyed, scanned, or inputted through a voice-recognition system. Once the information is entered, it is available to be processed. This processing may include performing arithmetic computations, sorting numbers, sorting alphabetic lists, and so on. Output may be stored on tapes, hard drives, compact disks, digital versatile disks, or on microimages such as microfilm and microfiche. It can then be retrieved through the personal computer. Figure 15-1 illustrates this concept.

Electronic Database Systems

The records storage methods and the storage procedures that you learned in Chapter 14 are applicable to electronic systems as well. In other words, it is still essential to plan how to file the correspondence and follow the necessary steps of indexing, coding, and storing. Just as in a paper system, if you do not know where an item is filed, you cannot retrieve it. However, by using correct records management procedures, electronic systems allow you to store and retrieve information almost instantly.

Database Software. A **database** is a collection of records organized in related files. A **database management system** (also referred to as a **relational database management system**) is the software that allows the user to perform a variety of records management functions. With a database management system, the user can organize, enter, process, index, sort, select, link related files, store, and retrieve

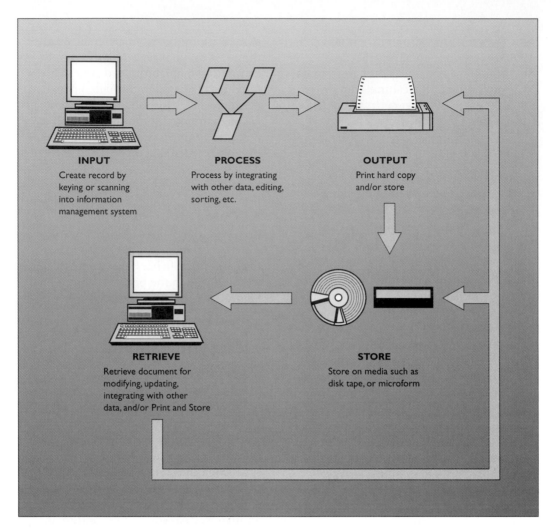

FIGURE 15-1. Information Management Systems

INPUT
Create record by keying or scanning into information management system

PROCESS
Process by integrating with other data, editing, sorting, etc.

OUTPUT
Print hard copy and/or store

RETRIEVE
Retrieve document for modifying, updating, integrating with other data, and/or Print and Store

STORE
Store on media such as disk tape, or microform

information. Figure 15-2 illustrates the process.

When using a database, the information is generally stored in the order in which it is entered. The next record is assigned the next available record number. **Indexing** sorts the records and stores the information based on one or more key fields. The **primary key** or **keyword** is a unique identifier chosen by the user. For example, if you are working in a human resources department and entering employee information, the keyword might be the employee's social security number.

In addition to entering employee names and social security numbers in the database, you will probably enter other information such as date of employment, age, address, salary, and so on. From there, you can **query** (ask) the database to display the information in a variety of ways. For example, you might ask for

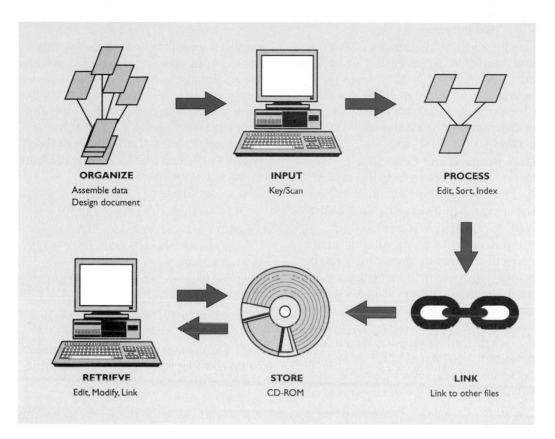

ORGANIZE
Assemble data
Design document

INPUT
Key/Scan

PROCESS
Edit, Sort, Index

RETRIEVE
Edit, Modify, Link

STORE
CD-ROM

LINK
Link to other files

FIGURE 15-2. Database Cycle

employees who are making a certain salary level or employees who have been employed for a specified period of time. The design of the database allows the user to ask for information efficiently and receive it in a useful format. **Integrated packages** combine database software with spreadsheet and word processing software so users can easily move stored information from one application to another.

Database management software can use optical (laser) disks as the storage medium. If you have no need to edit or modify the document in any way, you may store information on a **CD-ROM** (compact disk—read only memory). Hundreds of thousands of pages of data

A CD can be used to store information. © *PhotoDisc, Inc.*

may be stored on these types of disks, and that number keeps increasing. In addition, information stored on this media cannot be erased or manipulated. It is not susceptible to changes in temperature, erasure, or exposure to viruses; and its life expectancy is over 100 years.

Decentralized and Centralized.
Decentralized storage refers to information that is stored by individual office assistants on their disks or tapes. A **centralized storage** system is one in which computers are linked together through a network and files on the network can be accessed by more than one person at a time. The network may be a LAN (local area network) or a WAN (wide area network).

Most businesses use a combination of centralized and decentralized systems. For example, as an office professional, you will generally store the documents you key on a disk. These documents may be reports, spreadsheets, letters, and so forth; other individuals in the office will not usually need to access this information for editing or use in other documents. This storage is an example of a decentralized system. Personnel information is an example of work that may be stored on a centralized system. This information needs to be accessed by a variety of departments—the payroll department in writing checks or the benefits department in determining insurance coverage, vacation leave, and sick leave.

Storage and Retrieval. When setting up your decentralized electronic filing system, you need to make two decisions. You must determine how you will file the disks or tapes, and you must decide on the naming system and the standards you will use to store any documents. You can use the alphabetic, subject, numeric, or geo-

graphic method for both of these items. For example, let's assume you are going to use an alphabetic system. You work for six executives. First, you decide that you will use subdirectories for each executive. You have a letter written to B. J. Valentine on November 5, 2001; Carla Jung is the originator. You index, code, and store the letter in the following manner.

Jung/BJV110501 (Jung—subdirectory, BJV—name of addressee, 110501—date)

Some software systems allow you to key full names. In that case, you could store the letter in the following manner.

Jung/BJValentine110501 (Jung—subdirectory, BJValentine—name of addressee, 110501—date)

There are many other options you could consider when storing information. The most important thing is to be consistent. Make sure you always name your documents using the same procedure. You should also label each disk with a general classification. For example, in the illustration given above, you might label the disk "Letters." Make sure you also include the date of the information saved on the disk label.

If you are using a centralized electronic system, you must follow the standards within the system. A centralized system allows you to store information for your private use only or to make the information available to all people on the network. Within the electronic system, storage can be compared to cabinets, drawers, and folders. A collection of files could be referred to as a cabinet. You may create drawers (folders) within the cabinet and smaller sections (additional folders) within the drawers. Accurate indexing is key to the success of an electronic filing system. And, as electronic filing incorporates computer-generated documents such as email, word processing files, presentation slides, and electronic spreadsheets, everyone in the organization must learn to consistently identify and tag their documents so they can be accurately indexed and retrieved by a variety of users.

Safety and Security.   Records must be protected from physical hazards as well as from unauthorized access. Here are some suggestions for safety and security.

Safety

- Store electronic media at room temperature, out of direct sunlight.
- Copy electronic files as a backup system; store the copies in a fireproof cabinet.
- Store electronic files at an off-site location. When doing so, you may want to

use barcode technology. For example, each magnetic tape may have a barcode label so that it can be quickly identified and retrieved when needed.

- Protect against viruses. Several suggestions for protecting against viruses were given in Chapter 6; you may wish to review those suggestions now.
- Keep tapes stored in their cases when they are not in use. Do not touch the tape with your fingers.
- If you want to ensure that your disk files will not be erased by another office worker, use the write-protect feature on the disk.

Security

- Protect the data stored on the disk or tape from unauthorized use by assigning passwords to employees. Only

Electronic files may be stored at an off-site location. © *CORBIS*.

individuals with the appropriate passwords can retrieve information.

- Develop a security policy that ensures safe and reliable operation of the records system.
- When an employee leaves the company, immediately eliminate his or her password from the system so there is no access to the data.

Document Management Systems

Document management systems essentially act as advanced corporate libraries. They provide employees with easy access to document storage facilities while still maintaining control over individual documents. An electronic document management system typically incorporates one or more key technology components, including document imaging or archiving, workflow software, and computer output to laser disk. Document management is the process that converts paper information to digital data. This digital information can then be indexed and retrieved in a topic-specific fashion.

In the past, the solution for organizing document information was to use a database. Although the database continues to be an essential business tool, companies realized that they needed a system to store computer-generated documents such as memos, faxes, email, bills, and invoices. This type of material is often called "unstructured data" since it can't be reduced to fields and records that are stored in a traditional relational database. The problem of managing unstructured information led to the development of document management software.

Document Management Software.
Software may be purchased that will help you manage electronic, digital, microimage, and paper systems of storage. Some of the features of a document management software system include the ability to:

- Log in documents
- Print file labels
- Track active files, inactive files, vital records, and off-premise storage
- Provide an inventory of all records
- Follow up on overdue files
- Track nonpaper documents such as disks and microforms
- Generate activity reports by department and user
- Generate records retention and disposal guidelines

The escalating cost of maintaining files, mismanaging, and misfiling (with the average cost of retrieving a misfiled document being about $200) has led to increased use of document management software. As these systems become easier to use and the variety of storage media continues to change, it is projected that document management systems will become increasingly important within organizations. Future software systems will allow records that are stored on a variety of media to work together in accessing information.

Digital Archiving. Digital archiving is the practice of converting paper documents to digital format that can be stored on a variety of media and retrieved electronically. This method is also called **document imaging.** Using appropriate equipment, information is transferred to optical media. A LAN-based document system provides all users on the network with instant access to documents through their desktop computers. Instead of looking through paper file folders, employees can access an index on their computer screen.

They no longer have to find a document, copy it, and return it to the filing system. Instead, this type of system saves valuable time since employees can view, print, or fax a document without leaving their desks.

The components of a digital archiving system include a computer, a scanner, a storage medium, a printer, and application software. Optical disks using **WORM technology** (write once, read many) prevent any alteration to the original document once they are converted to an image. Two methods of converting information to digital images exist. The first scans the paper document and replicates the document in digital format. After documents have been scanned, they are annotated with identifying information such as name, date, account numbers, and so on. Documents can then be referenced and re-trieved through the use of computer-based index and search criteria. The images can be viewed using a variety of file-viewing mechanisms.

A second method of converting documents to digital images uses **optical character recognition** (OCR) to capture data from scanned documents. This method scans in documents and converts the contents into computer-readable format (text) using special software. These text files can then be indexed, as the images files are, and located using a contents search. The text approach uses less storage space than imaging filing.

Some organizations use a combination approach: filing some documents as images and others as text documents. Regardless of the approach used, document image processing technology is used for capturing document images and

Digital archiving can be used to change paper documents to digital information. *Courtesy of Hewlett Packard Company.*

storing them away for future retrieval and distribution. Both the image and text-conversion techniques allow you to electronically disseminate documents (such as email), annotate them, and otherwise treat them as computer files.

Storage Methods. At one time, choosing a storage medium was a straightforward task. Users who needed high capacity at the lowest price went with tape. Others who needed an unalterable format or random access chose optical disk, while those who needed speed and price turned to magnetic disk. Now a variety of storage media exist with options that overlap in terms of price, performance, capacity, reliability, and other key requirements. Although magnetic storage using hard drives like those in regular computers is an option, most digital archiving today uses **compact disk (CD)** or **digital versatile disk (DVD)** media. Within each product category there are new varieties of technology, plus a large number of different media formats within each technology. This often leaves users faced with the task of determining which storage mechanism will be most effective in meeting their needs.

Compact Disks (CDs). Because a single CD can hold the same amount of information as an entire filing cabinet (about 15,000 to 25,000 pages), it has been used extensively in document management systems. Specifically, **CD-R (CD-recordable)** technology has become very popular in digital archiving. Because CD-R media is purchased blank and is a WORM medium, the user can store archival data in a method that is fairly secure. Because the CD-R is a write-once medium, information stored this way cannot be modified. In addition, because CD-Rs cannot be erased, archival data will last as long as the disk. Blank CD-R media typically have a 25- to 100-year warranty depending on the brand name and storage technology used. **CD-RWs (CD-rewritables)** are also available. This type of technology is not considered secure for archiving data since it offers up to a thousand rewrites per disk. At this time, CD-RWs are more prone to damage because they are not stored in a cartridge. In addition, they are currently more expensive than a CD-R.

CDs have become a popular storage mechanism for a variety of reasons. First, CD technology represents an established standard so that CD-R media can be read in any CD-ROM drive. Second, CD-R drives and storage media are inexpensive permanent storage devices when

A DVD can store 7–28 times the information stored on a CD.
© *PhotoDisc, Inc.*

compared to DVDs or laser technologies since CD-Rs can't be erased. In addition, CDs offer rapid retrieval since data is written to only one side of the disk.

Digital Versatile Disks (DVDs).

Although a single CD-ROM can store up to 250,000 pages of text, newer optical data storage technologies, such as digital versatile disk (DVD) can store much greater amounts of data and images. Current DVDs can store seven times the information as a conventional CD-ROM, and it is expected that future DVD disks will be double-sided and double-layered, and will be able to store 28 times the current capacity of a CD.

A variety of DVD formats are available to meet the needs of digital archiving. A **DVD-ROM** has been developed as read-only storage intended for use on PCs. There are **DVD-RAM,** a DVD format which supports write-many, ready-many storage; **DVD-RW;** and **DVD+RW** formats, which are also rewritable high-density optical formats. DVD technology also includes the DVD-R (recordable), which is similar to the CD-R. This DVD format supports WORM technology, which prevents any alterations to the original information.

Because DVD is a higher-bandwidth technology, it provides higher-resolution images, better audio quality, and theater-quality video. DVDs have 7–28 times the capacity of current CD technology, and they are entirely backward compatible with today's CDs, which will allow users to access information that has been stored on CD-ROMs, CD-Rs and CD-RWs. At this time, DVD technology is considerably more expensive than CDs.

Advantages of Document Management Systems. Changing from traditional paper filing systems to document management systems provides an organization with many opportunities for cost savings and increased productivity, as follows.

- Electronically filed documents decrease the amount of necessary filing space. With this decrease in used space, the organization can reallocate traditional filing space for other uses.

- Organizations can increase productivity of employees by eliminating or reducing the amount of time employees will spend storing, retrieving, or tracking documents.

- Increased retrieval speed is also a major benefit. In addition to improved customer relations, increased access speed helps cut costs by reducing the need for additional staffing to handle growth or seasonal surges in volume.

- Electronically filed documents do not need to be removed from their filing location, which will decrease or eliminate the possibility of missing documents.

- Using multiple indexes, documents residing anywhere in the system can easily be found by users. In addition, electronically filed documents can be accessed by multiple users concurrently.

Microimage Systems

Electronic records management systems can reduce the amount of space required to keep records and can provide for almost instantaneous retrieval of records. However, in some instances it is more cost-effective to store some records in other ways. For example, banks need to retain copies of canceled checks. Personnel departments need to retain copies of employment information. Schools need to retain copies of grade reports. Government agencies need to retain birth certificates. Although this information could be maintained on document imaging systems, in some instances microimage systems provide a more cost-effective method of storage.

Microforms. There are two main types of microimage forms, microfilm and microfiche.

Microfilm. Microfilm is a roll containing a series of frames or images much like a movie film. Each record is photographed and reduced to fit the frames of the film. It is magnified on a screen when it needs to be viewed by the user.

Microfilm may be stored on reels or in cartridges, cassettes, or jackets. Reels are desirable for storing large volumes of records that do not change. Microfilm that is stored on reels needs to be threaded through a machine when it is being viewed. Microfilm on cartridges and cassettes requires no threading and is thus easier to use. Still another method of storing microfilm is by cutting it into strips and placing the film in a jacket. The jacket storage method allows portions of a file to be updated easily, since a strip of film can be removed and replaced with a new strip.

Microfiche. Microfiche is a sheet of film containing a series of images arranged in a grid pattern. Microfiche is usually shortened to **fiche** (pronounced "feesh"). Fiche permits direct access to any record without having to advance a roll of film to the appropriate location. Ultrafiche is a variation

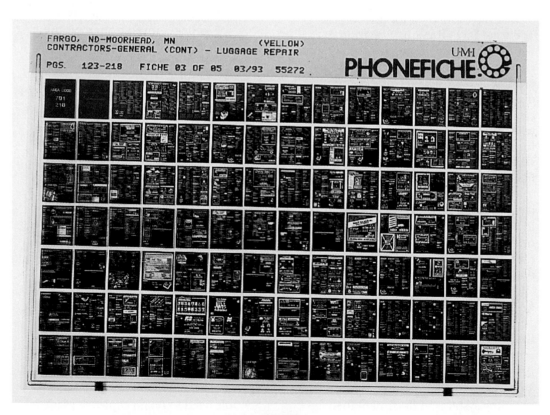

Microforms include microfilm and microfiche. © *Jeff Greenberg/MRp.*

of microfiche. The standard size microfiche contains 98 frames or images. One ultrafiche can store thousands of images.

System Elements.   In order to produce and use microforms, it is necessary to have a microimage system that encompasses the following phases.

- Converting the records to film
- Processing and duplicating the film
- Displaying and reproducing the film

Converting to Film.   Although some companies photograph records in-house, many hire service bureaus to assist in the conversion of documents to microform. Even if your organization outsources this process, you as an office professional may have the responsibility for getting the documents ready for filming. All paper clips and staples must be removed from the records. Attachments to records such as routing slips and envelopes should also be removed. And records should be batched and placed in sequential order. Once this has been done, they are ready to be converted.

Processing.   After the material has been filmed, the film must be processed. Again, many organizations use an outside company for this. However, inexpensive processors do exist if a company decides to process in-house.

Duplicating.   Sometimes more than one copy of the microforms may be required. For example, a company may have several branches and need the same records at each location. Or it may decide to have the records stored in two places for safety and security reasons. Thus, the microforms must be duplicated. Although, as an office professional, you will not be involved in the actual duplication, you may be involved in finding a company that will do it for you.

Displaying and Reproducing.   To read a microform, you must place it in a projector called a reader or viewer. A reader displays the microform in an enlarged form on a screen so that it can be easily read. The typical reader is a desktop unit designed to accept either microfiche or microfilm. There are multimedia readers, however, designed to accept two or more different types of microforms. Readers are also available in a variety of magnifications determined by the reduction ratio of

A reader/printer is used to view and print a microform. *Courtesy of Eastman Kodak.*

the microform and the size of the viewing screen. Many readers have interchanging lenses to satisfy various user requirements.

Portable readers are also available that are lighter in weight and less expensive than desktop readers are. Lap readers can be purchased for use in cars, at outside job locations, or by an executive on the road. Since these readers are so inexpensive (some costing less than $100), they may be used at home as a supplement to existing office equipment.

Often a person viewing a microform needs a paper copy of the record. This copy may be obtained through the use of a readerprinter. The microform is inserted in the readerprinter, and each image is portrayed on the viewing screen. If the viewer desires a hard copy, he or she can push a button on the machine and produce a copy in seconds.

Storing. Various storage containers are available for each type of microform. These storage containers include trays, cabinets, carousel units, and rotating desktop stands.

Legal Aspects.   The Uniform Photographic Copies of Business and Public Records as Evidence Act of 1951 allows microforms of certain business documents to be admitted as evidence in courts of law. Federal and state agencies often have their own regulations concerning the substitution of microforms for hard copies. The Securities and Exchange Commission allows filming if the duplicate of the microform is stored separately from the original. Many states consider microforms inadmissible in court when the record involved is a negotiable instrument such as a stock or bond. If a company plans to microform records, both state and federal laws should be checked to determine the legality of these forms if they are needed in court proceedings.

Evaluation of Micrographic Systems.
When evaluating whether or not to store information on microforms, consider the following points and determine answers to the following questions.

- The cost of the microforms
  - Is the equipment available

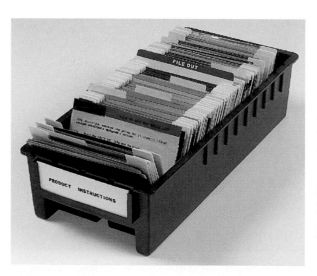 

Microform storage includes trays, carousel units, and cabinets. *Left, Courtesy of Luxor Corporation; right,* © *Fellowes Manufacturing Co.*

in-house? What will be the cost of copying (both machine and personnel costs)?

- What is the cost of having a service bureau film the documents? Is it less than in-house processing? What is the reputation of the service bureau? What is the turn-around time on the document processing?
- If an off-site storage facility is to be used, what is its cost? If an in-house storage facility is to be used, how much space will be needed? What type of storage cabinet is best?
- Are duplicate copies of the microforms needed? If so, what will the cost be?
- The legality of microforms
  - What records can be legally filmed?
  - What records cannot be filmed?

Integration of Electronic and Microimage Systems

Computer and micrographics technologies have come together in the form of computer-output microfilm (COM), computer-input microfilm (CIM), and computer-aided retrieval (CAR). These combinations of micrographics with the computer have made the storage and retrieval of microforms a speedy, inexpensive, and efficient operation.

Computer-Output Microfilm (COM). One of the big problems of processing data by computer is the enormous amount of paper printouts that are created. If such paper is stored, the storage can be expensive. One result of using the computer in conjunction with micrographics is **computer-output microfilm (COM)**. With COM, no paper documents are produced; instead, documents are pro-

duced on microforms, which may be microfiche or microfilm.

Here is how the COM process works. Information from the computer is sent directly to microfilm, never being printed on paper. Images may be created on COM in one of the following ways:

- By displaying the image on a video display screen, which the COM camera photographs.
- With a laser, which writes on the film like a laser copier.
- With an electron beam, which creates dots that make up the image.
- With LEDs (light-emitting diodes) and a fiber optics bundle, which produce the image photographed by the COM camera.

Computer-Input Microfilm (CIM). Computer-input microfilm (CIM) is COM in reverse. Plain language data on microfilm is converted into computer-readable data for use in a computer. A CIM device converts information into a form that the computer can read. Often COM and CIM come together in one system to exchange both input and output between the computer and the microform system.

Computer-Aided Retrieval (CAR). Computer-aided retrieval systems are designed to solve two common problems encountered in records systems—the high expense and the difficulty of finding documents that are filed manually. Drawing on a combination of micrographics and computer technology, CAR can result in more effective and economical approaches to document storage and retrieval. With CAR, accesses to randomly filed documents on microforms are facilitated by the use of the computer.

Here is one example of how CAR works. Documents are indexed by the entry of such data as the date, author, and subject into a computer. As data is transmitted to the computer, software establishes and/or updates a series of indexes maintained online with a disk drive. In retrieving documents, the user may request all documents written on a particular date, by a particular person, and dealing with a particular subject. The user has the option to narrow, broaden, or otherwise change the search. The final outcome is the identification of one or more microfilm addresses containing the desired documents. The user selects the reel (or cartridge or cassette), mounts it on a reader or readerprinter, and advances the film to the indicated frame position. Or the readerprinter may operate online with the computer. In other words, once the appropriate reel, cartridge, or cassette is mounted, the frame selection is automatic.

As an assist in the CAR process, barcoding is now being used. Barcoding consists of placing an identifying unit (such as a name, social security number, or invoice number) on a document in barcode format, which reduces an identifier to a series of bars. Here is an example of how barcoding might work in a micrographic system. A barcode is placed on the computer document. As the document is transferred from the computer to the microform, the barcode also appears on the microform. Then, during the CAR process, the image is retrieved by a CAR cartridge reader or readerprinter that has barcoding scanning and encoding abilities.

Integration of Fax and Micrographics.

Technology now exists that combines the cost savings and convenience of microfilm and the immediacy of electronic delivery. Here is an example of how such technology works. The office assistant keys an image address and then inserts the roll of microfilm. The computer automatically retrieves the image and positions it on a screen. The office assistant verifies the image and faxes the image to the appropriate location. The image may also be printed on a laser printer. Automatic cropping and edge detection make it easy to print only selected information and protect confidential data. Optional annotation capabilities give the office assistant the ability to add important routing information. With this technology, an office assistant can take a micrographic image, manipulate it, and send it via a fax environment anywhere in the world. The document may also be set up to be faxed after business hours, when the rates are cheaper. Figure 15-3 depicts how an image from a workstation can be delivered to a laser printer, a fax unit, and then to optical or digital storage.

Benefits of the Integration of Electronic and Microimage Systems.

The integration of computer and micrographics technology allows records to be stored in an effective and efficient manner. Here are some of the benefits.

- Space savings. By using microforms for document storage, the space required by a paper filing system can be reduced up to 98 percent. This is an important consideration with the continually escalating cost of floor space. Still, another cost savings results from the elimination of file cabinets and filing supplies.

- Cost savings as compared with a manual system. In a paper-based system, it has been estimated that between 125 and 175 documents can be filed manually in an hour. The time typically spent in filing 2,000 documents is more than 11 hours. With integration, up to 2,000 documents can be filmed

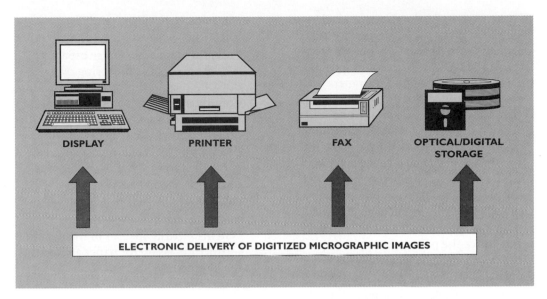

DISPLAY   PRINTER   FAX   OPTICAL/DIGITAL STORAGE

ELECTRONIC DELIVERY OF DIGITIZED MICROGRAPHIC IMAGES

FIGURE 15-3. Electronic delivery of micrographic images

and the appropriate index information input on a computer in about three hours. Retrieval time is also greatly reduced as compared with a manual system.

- Increased productivity. By using an integrated system, the laborious and time-consuming tasks involved in manual sorting, filing, retrieving, refiling, updating, and eliminating outdated records are eliminated. Employees are able to increase their productivity and take on other assignments.

- Elimination of lost or misfiled papers. It is estimated that typically between 4 and 8 percent of all paper documents in a manual system are lost. With electronic filing systems, problems of lost and misfiled documents are virtually eliminated.

- A secure and easily duplicated storage medium. Microforms and electronic media are difficult for an unauthorized person to access. These forms of storage may also be reproduced easily and inexpensively so that copies of important records can be stored off company premises for protection in case of fire or other catastrophe.

Computer Output to Laser Disk (COLD) Systems

Many organizations are moving toward **COLD systems,** which originally stood for Computer Output to Laser Disk, to organize information that was historically stored on microfiche, paper, or on mainframe computers. Today, COLD is defined more by the process it represents than by the storage media that is used.

Storage Process. COLD technology takes report files and rewrites them onto magnetic or optical disks in a special format, which can be redisplayed to a variety of system users. As the data are "read" into the system, the associated software builds an index by extracting information from the reports. With COM technology, information from mainframe computers is systematically copied on microform. The microform is then manually filed and must be retrieved in order to access the information. With COLD technology, the information is still copied to a storage media but remains accessible to authorized users on the system. This gives users instant access to information. COLD technology brings us closer to the "paperless office" since the printing, copying, and filing steps of the COM system are eliminated.

Storage Methods. Although original COLD technology stored information on laser disks, updates to the technology allow the user to store information using a variety of formats including networks, CDs, optical disks, DVDs, or the Internet. The CD or CD-R (CD-recordable) has become a popular storage solution for COLD data. As mentioned before, CD-R media are an established standard, are inexpensive, and offer rapid retrieval.

Advantages of COLD Technology. COLD technology provides users with a variety of advantages over the traditional COM system, as follows.

- Provides instant access to information and eliminates the cumbersome and time-consuming tasks associated with microform retrieval.
- Eliminates all microfilm costs associated with film production, distribution, and retrieval.
- Provides instant access in branch offices or remote sites to current COLD data through network storage instead

of having to duplicate and distribute microfilm reports.

- Provides increased storage capacity. CD-Rs are capable of storing over 800,000 pages of information. In addition, most systems come with compression technology; you can store 50 percent more information on your chosen storage medium. DVDs are capable of storing seven times more information than CD-Rs.
- Confidentiality of information is controlled through normal information systems security instead of the physical security necessary for paper and microform records.

Records Migration

Organizations maintain records for a variety of reasons, as discussed in Chapter 14. Whether for legal reasons, financial reasons, or to provide historical data, it is important that those records can be accessed and used in the future. As technology changes rapidly, many applications and file formats for records that were used just a few years ago now are difficult or impossible to support. As organizations adopt and implement new technology, the challenge of **migrating records** to these new technologies becomes very important. Organizations must make sure that the technology they use today will allow them to access their records ten years from now. Because of this, many organizations that previously disliked microfilm and microfiche now look to it as a medium that will guarantee perpetual access to documents and avoid major migration challenges.

Trends in Records Management

The volume of records will probably continue to rise at a rate faster than the rate of disposal. Because of the increase in the amount of information that needs to be stored, as well as continued changes in technological advances, you can expect some of the following trends in records management for the future.

- The need to quickly retrieve records from an ever-growing amount of records will likely increase. Because increases in technology lead to greater and greater expectations of that technology, pressures for immediate response may lead to errors and access problems with records.
- COLD technology will increase in use. Remember, with COLD technology, the information always remains accessible to authorized users on the system in addition to being stored for future access.
- The increase in the number and variety of computer-based systems available for records storage will continue to grow. This growth will result from the increased availability of computerized records management systems. In addition, an increasing number of companies will offer a wide variety of document and records management systems.
- Increased reliance on computerized systems in organizations will require that records managers become more involved with the technical computer issues and systems. This may require a merger of information systems staff with records management staff. Such a merger will allow businesses to effectively perform the work since both departments will have a better understanding of the entire electronic record process.
- Records management standards will continue to be developed throughout the industry. Such standards will assist companies in managing their records. These standards will continue to include a broader legal definition of the types of storage media acceptable in litigation.
- The use of combination systems, which include a wide variety of electronic technologies, will increase. Systems will continue to be produced that will provide for the merger and combination of various technologies. It will be important for the organization to continue to update their stored records so that they can continue to be used with new innovations.

SUMMARY

To reinforce what you learned in this chapter, study this summary.

- An information management system includes inputting data; processing the data through integration with other data; modifying, editing, deleting, sorting, and so on, outputting the data; and storing and retrieving the data.
- Many offices store records on electronic systems. It is still essential to plan how to file the correspondence and follow the necessary steps of indexing, coding, and storing.

- Database software allows the user to perform the records management functions of organizing, entering, processing, indexing, sorting, selecting, linking, storing, and retrieving within a specific software program.

- Decentralized storage refers to information that is stored by each individual office assistant on his or her disks or tapes. A centralized storage system is one in which computers are linked together through a network, and files on the network can be accessed by more than one person at a time.

- Records must be kept safe and secure by protecting them from physical hazards and unauthorized access.

- Document management is the process that converts paper information to digital data. The digital information can then be indexed and retrieved.

- Digital archiving or document imaging systems include a computer, scanner, storage mechanism, printer, and application software. Two methods of converting information exist. Document imaging stores the actual image, whereas OCR changes the information to text. Some organizations use a combination approach.

- Most digital archiving will use compact disk or digital versatile disks as their storage media. Within the compact disk category, there is a large variety of media formats including CD-ROM, CD-R, and CD-RW. DVD technology includes DVD-ROM, DVD-RAM, DVD-RW, DVD+RW, and DVD-R.

- An organization that changes from traditional paper filing systems to document management systems has many opportunities for cost savings and increased employee productivity.

- Microimage systems provide a suitable storage alternative for many records. These records are placed on microforms—microfilm and microfiche.

- There are laws that determine what types of records may be stored on microforms and still be acceptable in a court of law.

- Computer and micrographics technologies have come together in the form of COM, CIM, and CAR. Numerous benefits have occurred as the result of the integration of micrographics and computers.

- Fax and micrographics have been integrated, combining the cost savings and convenience of microfilm and the immediacy of electronic delivery.

- The expectation for the future is that there will be even greater integration of micrographics with other technologies. Such integration will provide for more effective and efficient storage methods. There will also be widespread use of local area networks and RIM software. More versatile storage equipment will be available. In addition, there will be a merger of computer systems staff with records and information management.

- Computer Output to Laser Disk (COLD) technologies will continue to be an important records management tool. This technology will continue to evolve and impact how records are stored and retrieved.

- Records migration will continue to be an important challenge faced by organizations. Because technology changes rapidly, organizations must make sure the technology they use to store their records will be supported when they need to retrieve those records.

Key Terms

- Information management system
- Database
- Database management system
- Relational database management system
- Indexing
- Primary key
- Keyword
- Query
- Integrated packages
- CD-ROM
- Decentralized storage
- Centralized storage
- Document management systems
- Digital archiving
- Document imaging
- WORM technology
- Optical character recognition
- Compact Disk (CD)
- Digital Versatile Disk (DVD)
- CD-R (CD-recordable)
- CD-RWs (CD-rewritables)
- DVD-ROM
- DVD-RAM
- DVD-RW
- DVD+RW
- Microfilm
- Microfiche
- Fiche
- Computer-output microfilm (COM)
- Computer-input microfilm (CIM)
- Computer-aided retrieval (CAR)
- Computer Output to Laser Disk (COLD) systems
- Migrating records

Professional Pointers

Here are several suggestions to help you manage records more efficiently.

- Determine any problems that your organization has in managing records properly. Seek solutions to problems from employees who work closely with the process.
- Prepare a records management manual. This manual should describe the job responsibilities of records personnel and the equipment and systems used for controlling records. This manual could be stored on a network, allowing all employees access to the most current information.
- Maintain effective operating procedures.
- Measure the efficiency of each process; discard unnecessary procedures and improve necessary ones.
- Develop and adhere to strict records retention policies.
- Seek new technology that will enhance productivity and improve overall efficiency of managing records. Make sure to update stored records to accommodate new systems.

Office Procedures Reinforcement

1. Describe the four parts of an information management system.
2. Describe the differences in a decentralized and a centralized electronic storage system.
3. List the advantages associated with document management software.
4. Describe the computer-micrographics technologies called COM, CIM, and CAR.
5. Explain why COLD technology is important as a storage system.

Critical Thinking Activity

Karla Mikimoto has just been promoted to records manager. She has been reviewing the files during the past week and has discovered numerous problems:

1. Files are misplaced.
2. Labels are not consistently prepared.
3. Color coding is not consistently used.
4. Folders and file cabinets are overcrowded.
5. Material may remain in a file clerk's in-basket for two weeks before being filed.
6. File sorting is not done.
7. There is a tremendous backlog of records to be converted to microfiche.

There are five clerks in the center. Karla called a meeting to talk with them about the problems she noted. She explained the problems as they appeared to her and told the file clerks that she expected their immediate response in cleaning up the situation. Three file clerks immediately became defensive and irate. The other two said nothing. Since it was evident that Karla would have trouble getting the file clerks to cooperate, she lost control and told them that she was the boss and they would do as she said. Since the meeting was held, one of the clerks has turned in a resignation.

1. What should Karla do now?
2. What suggestions can you give Karla to prevent this situation from becoming worse or from happening again?

Office Applications

OA 15-1 (Goal 1)

Karla Mikimoto, records manager, has made revisions to the records retention and disposition schedule to be submitted for review at this week's executive officers' meeting. Using the document on the student template disk, OA15-1.doc, make the revisions indicated on pages 95–97 of your Applications Workbook. Use the strikethrough feature to show material to be deleted, and underline all new wording. This will aid the reviewers in understanding revisions to the document. Identify the document as Draft 2.

OA 15-2 (Goal 1)

Karla Mikimoto has asked you to prepare a database that includes information about all employees in the Records and Information Systems Department. Each employee has completed a form listing a variety of personnel information. The completed forms can be found on pages 98–99 in your Applications Workbook. Create a database that includes the information from the forms. Print a copy of the database for your instructor.

OA 15-3 (Goals 1 and 2)

Select two of your classmates to work with on this project. Visit two companies or organizations in your area, and determine what type of records management systems are used. Include descriptions of the types of records and storage mechanisms. Also briefly describe any safety, security, or retention policies they have in place. Write up your findings, and be prepared to present them orally to the class. Submit your written report to your instructor.

OA 15-4 (Goals 1, 2, and 3)

Choose one of the trends in records management listed at the end of this chapter. Find three current periodical articles and summarize their content using a report format; list your references. Present your findings orally to the class. Prepare a memorandum to your instructor describing how you feel this topic will impact records management policies or procedures within organizations. Use the memorandum form on the student template disk in file 15-4. Turn in both the memorandum and report to your instructor.

Online Research Applications

ORA 15-5 (Goals 1, 2, and 3)

Search the Internet for information on one of the following topics:

- microimage systems
- document imaging
- COLD systems

Choose two vendors with similar technology packages, and compare and contrast their packages. You may want to consider the following questions when making your comparisons.

Are the prices similar or quite different?

What kind of equipment is necessary to implement this system?

What kinds of user support and/or training does this organization provide?

What kinds of advantages does the vendor state will come from the implementation of this technology?

Write up your findings and present them orally to the class. As a part of the written report, indicate the impact this technology will have on records management. Submit your written report to your instructor.

Vocabulary Review

On pages 103–104 of your Applications Workbook is a Vocabulary Review, covering selected items from the vocabulary presented in Chapters 14–15. Complete these sentences, and submit a copy to your instructor.

Language Skills Practice

On pages 105–107 of your Applications Workbook are sentences that need to be corrected using the rules presented in the Reference Section of your text. Correct the sentences as needed, and submit your work to your instructor.

Meetings, Travel, and Financial Documents

CHAPTER 16

Meetings and Conferences

A great deal of organizational time is spent in meetings. Approximately 50 percent of the upper-level executive's time may be spent in meetings. For lower-level managers the figure is 25 to 35 percent. With the team approach that is now being used in many organizations, the office professional also may spend a number of hours each week in meetings. Since all of these hours are costly to the business or organization, it is important that meeting time be spent as productively as possible. Yet a survey of middle managers conducted by Inc. magazine revealed these meeting horror statistics:

YOUR GOALS

1. Explain the elements of an effective meeting and use appropriate techniques in conducting them.

2. Identify and explain electronic meeting alternatives.

3. Define the responsibilities of the office professional for meetings and conferences.

4. Prepare minutes.

- In 34 percent of the meetings, there was no agenda.
- In 38 percent of the meetings, not all of the items were addressed even when there was an agenda.
- In 41 percent of the meetings, no follow-up action was assigned.
- In 54 percent, nonessential personnel were involved.
- In 64 percent, no time frames were set for the meetings.[1]

As an office professional, you will have the responsibility of helping your supervisor plan and schedule all types of meetings and conferences. This chapter will help you develop the knowledge and skills to assist your supervisor in holding meetings that are productive for all members and, thus, an efficient use of organizational time.

Meeting Effectiveness

The effective meeting is one in which:
- There is a definite need for the meeting.
- The purpose is stated and clearly understood by all participants.
- The appropriate people are in attendance at the meeting.
- An agenda is prepared and adhered to.
- All members participate.
- There are outcomes achieved as a result of the meeting.

Although these criteria seem relatively straightforward, few meetings satisfy them. Many people schedule meetings

---

[1] "Why Replace Meetings?" http://www.locustcreek.com.

that are not necessary, with no specific purpose and little thought as to the people who need to be in attendance.

Unnecessary Meetings

Have you ever been engaged in or overheard this type of conversation about a meeting:

"Are you going to the staff meeting on Friday."

"Sure, it's a command performance, isn't it?"

"I guess so, but we never accomplish anything. I don't know why we even have the meetings."

"I guess one of these days the group will figure out what they are trying to accomplish, but don't hold your breath. It may be awhile."

Most of us have been involved in such conversations and have attended numerous meetings that were totally ineffective. Many times, meetings are called that are not appropriate and should never be held. Meetings are not a good idea when:

- There is no clearly defined purpose for the meeting.
- No consideration has been given to the people who need to be in attendance.
- Confidential or sensitive personnel matters must be addressed.
- There is inadequate data for the meeting.
- There is insufficient time to prepare for the meeting.
- The information could be communicated more effectively by memo, fax, email, or telephone.

Many times meetings are called that are not appropriate and should never be held. © *PhotoDisc, Inc.*

- There is a considerable amount of anger and hostility in the group and people need time to calm down before coming together.

Necessary Meetings

Calling a meeting can be appropriate when:

- A group needs to be involved in solving a problem or making a decision.
- An issue arises that needs clarification.
- Information needs to be given to a group.
- Communication needs to occur quickly with a large number of people.

Notice that in each of the situations given above there is an underlying purpose for the meeting. Once a purpose is identified, considerable planning needs to occur before the meeting. The meeting leader has a role to play if the meeting is effective; he or she must understand the role and be well prepared for the meeting. The participants also have a role to play. The participants must understand the need and purpose of the meeting, prepare before the meetings, and be active participants during the meeting.

Role of Meeting Leader

If a meeting is to go well, there must be a leader who is skilled in running a meeting. She or he must understand the need and purpose of the meeting and have the ability to engage people in an effective conversation around the issues. The leader also must be able to bring closure to the agreed-upon objectives.

Make the Purpose and Objectives Clear. As you have already learned, the purpose of the meeting must be clearly established. The leader of the meeting does not necessarily establish the purpose. For example, assume that an executive of the company calls a meeting. He or she determines what the purpose is before the meeting and makes that purpose clear in writing. Although the executive may be the leader of the meeting, he or she may choose to have someone else preside at it. Once the purpose of the meeting is established and sent out in writing to the participants by the executive, it is the leader's responsibility to reiterate the purpose at the beginning of the meeting. The leader should also let the participants know the objectives of the meeting—what must be accomplished at the meeting and what must be done after it.

Adhere to the Agenda. The leader must keep the participants focused on the agenda. If they stray from it, the leader is responsible for sensitively but firmly bringing them back to the agenda. The leader might say, "Thank you for your comments about that issue; we might want to put it on the agenda for a future meeting. Now, let's continue on with the agenda for today."

Manage Time. The leader must begin the meeting on time, even if several people are not present. Waiting for others to arrive is not fair to the individuals who have made an effort to be on time. Just as important as starting on time is ending on time. The leader must be sensitive to other time commitments made by the participants. Time frames, both beginning and ending, should be established when the

If the meeting is to start at 9 a.m., begin promptly at 9. Do not wait for the latecomers. © *PhotoDisc, Inc.*

notice of the meeting is sent out. The leader is responsible for maintaining these time commitments.

Encourage Participation. Before invitations are issued, considerable thought should be given to who should be at the meeting. Determining the participants is the role of the executive; this role will be discussed later in the chapter. Once the meeting begins, the leader is responsible for seeing that all individuals participate. If, as the meeting gets under way, several people have not spoken, the leader might say, "Maria, what direction do you think we should take to satisfy our needs in the twenty-first century?" or "Jack, we haven't heard from you on this issue. What is your opinion?"

Let the participants know that you and the group value their opinions. Help them feel comfortable enough to speak up. Make it easy for everyone to contribute. Respect each comment that is made. Never say such things as "That's a bad idea," or "Why on earth would you make such a comment? It doesn't have any relevance at all to our topic." Do make such statements as, "Thank you for that contribution," "That's an excellent idea," or "Thanks, can you expand on that direction? It sounds as if it has possibilities for us."

Lead a Balanced and Controlled Discussion. In leading a balanced and controlled discussion, the leader should:

- Keep the participants focused on the agenda.
- Encourage participation from everyone, even if the opinions being expressed are about highly volatile issues.
- Limit the domination of any one person in the meeting.
- Positively reinforce all individuals for their contributions.
- Keep the discussion moving toward the objectives and outcomes determined.

Handle Conflict. You learned in Chapter 9 about several ways of handling conflict; you may wish to go back and review those suggestions now. Here are a few additional strategies.

- Make the role of the participants clear at the beginning of a meeting; state that conflict will be addressed using

Clarify communication barriers if a conflict arises. Ask that participants define their terms if they are not clear. © *CORBIS*.

conflict resolution techniques. If it is anticipated that the meeting will be particularly volatile, the leader may want to pass out conflict resolution guidelines.

- Clarify communication barriers if a conflict arises. Ask that participants define their terms if they are not clear to the group.

- Concentrate on building a team with the group; stress collaboration rather than competition.

Bring Closure to the Objectives. Have you ever left a meeting wondering "What is going to be done next? How will the steps that we discussed be implemented?" Most of us have. Remember that every effective meeting has a purpose and objectives, from which outcomes occur. For example, assume that you are setting directions for your department for the next year. One of your directions is to increase the number of customers by 5 percent. How are you going to meet this objective? What steps will you take? Merely saying that a direction is to increase the number of customers does not help the direction get accomplished. Detailed steps as to how, when, and by whom it will be done bring closure to the objective.

Evaluate the Meeting. Generally, with informal meetings within the organization, no formal evaluation is done; however, an informal evaluation by the leader (and possibly the participants) should always be done. Many times the attendees are very forthright. They may even tell the leader that they found the meeting a waste of their time. If any attendees make such a statement or a similar statement, the leader should always seek clarification on exactly what is meant. If no participants say anything to the leader, the leader may want to ask participants individually how

they felt the meeting went. In any case, the leader should ask questions such as the following of himself or herself after the meeting.

- Were the attendees participatory?
- Was the nonverbal behavior positive?
- Were the participants creative problem solvers?
- Did the participants exhibit a high energy level?
- Was the purpose of the meeting satisfied?
- Were appropriate decisions made?
- Can I improve on how I handled the issues, the people, or the meeting in general?

If the meeting is a relatively formal one, the leader may ask participants to fill out an evaluation form, as shown in Figure 16-1.

Role of Meeting Participants

Just as a leader has responsibilities, so do the participants. Their roles are much broader than attending the meeting. Their responsibilities begin before the meeting and continue after it.

Before the Meeting. Participants are responsible for:

- Responding to the meeting notice in a timely manner
- Reading any materials sent out before the meeting
- Evaluating the materials sent out in relation to the purpose of the meeting
- Calling the executive to clarify any questions that they might have before the meeting

During the Meeting. Participants are responsible during the meeting for:

MEETING EVALUATION FORM

Item	Yes	No
1. Were the purpose and objectives of the meeting clear?		
2. Were the purpose and objectives of the meeting accomplished?		
3. Was the agenda received in time to prepare for the meeting?		
4. Did the leader adhere to the agenda?		
5. Did the leader encourage participation of all members?		
6. Did the participants listen to each other?		
7. Were the appropriate people included in the meeting?		
8. Did the meeting start on time?		
9. Did the meeting end on time?		
10. Were decisions made that were consistent with the purpose and objectives of the meetings?		
11. Did the leader help bring closure to the objectives?		
12. Additional comments		

FIGURE 16-1. Meeting Evaluation Form

- Being on time
- Adhering to the agenda
- Making contributions
- Listening to other participants' contributions and responding
- Respecting the leader's role
- Not dominating the discussion
- Being nonjudgmental of others' comments
- Being courteous to each individual in the meeting
- Taking notes, if necessary

After the Meeting. Once the meeting is over, the participant's responsibilities do not necessarily end. The participant may be responsible for some research, study, or action before the next meeting. The participant may also be asked to work with a small group of people in bringing back a recommendation to the next meeting. Whatever follow-up is necessary by the participant, he or she must be committed to carrying out those responsibilities.

Meeting Types

Meetings may be classified into two types—traditional and electronic. Both are discussed in this section.

Traditional Meetings

Meetings that are traditional include staff meetings, committee meetings, project team meetings, customer/client meetings, board of directors meetings, seminars, conferences, and conventions.

Staff Meetings. An extremely common type of meeting is one in which the executive meets with a member of his or her staff. These meetings are usually scheduled on a regular basis. For example, the executive may have six people reporting to him or her and meet with these people as a group every week. The purpose of these meetings is usually to handle the routine problems that occur and to review directions, plans, and assignments.

Committee Meetings. In most businesses, there are committees or task forces operating. A **tast force** is formed to deal with a specific issue or problem. Once the problem is handled, the task force is disbanded. In other words, the task force has a beginning and ending time. It is organized for a purpose; once the purpose is accomplished, it no longer exists. A **committee** may be established for an ongoing purpose. For example, your company may have a Safety Committee that meets regularly (perhaps every month) to identify and address safety concerns. Since safety is an ongoing concern, the committee functions from year to year.

Project Team Meetings. You learned earlier that project teams are used frequently in organizations today. These teams are organized around a specific project to be accomplished. For example,

a project team may be organized to determine the type of automation to be used in the mailroom or to implement quality control within the company. Once the project has been completed, the team may be disbanded or take on another project to be accomplished.

Customer/Client Meetings. Your employer will probably hold meetings with customers or clients. These meetings generally will be with only one or two people. For example, a lawyer may meet with the client to discuss the evidence in a case. An engineer may meet with a customer to discuss the design of a product.

Board of Directors Meetings. Most large corporations and organizations operate with a board of directors. There are usually **bylaws,** written policies and procedures that clearly delineate how board meetings are to be conducted. Boards meet once a month or less. The chairman of the board conducts the meeting, and strict procedures are usually followed. An agenda is sent out before the meeting,

Parliamentary procedures should be followed in a board meeting.
© *PhotoDisc, Inc.*

noting the items to be covered. If the organization is a public entity in which an open meeting rule applies, notice of the meeting is posted according to legal procedures. Parliamentary procedures as set forth in *Robert's Rules of Order Newly Revised* are generally followed closely.

Conventions and Conferences. **Conventions** are usually formal, annual meetings of members of a professional group. A convention can involve hundreds or even thousands of people. Planning and executing a convention is so complicated that meeting consultants are often hired to assist in carrying out the details.

A **conference** is a meeting in which there is a discussion on certain issues or topics. For example, a conference or seminar may be held on topics such as conflict management, written communications, and union negotiations.

Electronic Meetings

The growth of teamwork, national and international organizations, and communications technology has contributed to our need for and ability to communicate with individuals in remote locations. According to a 3M Network survey, 50 percent of work being done today is conducted in teams, up from 20 percent just ten years ago. Of those teams, 25 percent include members who communicate remotely.[2] Telecommunications technology provides alternatives to face-to-face meetings through several electronic options referred to as **teleconferencing.** Teleconferencing is a general term applied to a variety of technology-assisted, two-way (interactive) communications via telephone lines, fiber

optics, or microwaves. The three main types of teleconferencing are audioconferencing, videoconferencing, and data conferencing. Many of the meetings listed in the previous section as traditional meetings may also be conducted in an electronic format.

Audioconferencing. Audioconferencing is a type of conference in which an unlimited number of participants use an audioconferencing unit to participate in a meeting. This unit may be as simple as a telephone with speakerphone capabilities, which provide hands-free communication and the amplifying and projecting of the speakers' voices. These phones today have superior sound quality that allows speakers to participate from almost any part of the room. A conference operator may also assist individuals by setting up a call among a group of individuals. You may set up this call by contacting the conference operator through your local telephone service, giving the individual the date, time, names, and numbers of the people who will be participating in the audioconference. Advantages of the audioconference include the ability to:

- Assemble individuals on short notice, assuming their schedules allow
- Connect individuals at any location, nationally or internationally
- Use telephone technology that is readily available to almost everyone

A primary disadvantage of audioconferencing is the lack of visual input. However, visual input can be achieved through the use of facsimile equipment such as a fax machine. In addition, visual messages can be written on an **electronic blackboard.** This blackboard allows individuals to write on the surface and the information to be transmitted over telephone lines to a distant location.

___

[2] "Getting Together—Anytime, Anyplace," *Meeting & Conventions* (December 1998), 16.

Participants can add or change the visual input through an electronic blackboard that has been set up at their locations. In other words, the blackboards allow for **interactivity** (information transmitted from one location to another and acted upon by participants at any location).

Videoconferencing. Videoconferencing is a system of transmitting audio and video between individuals at distant locations. Videoconferencing may be transmitted from a PC-based application (referred to as **desktop videoconferencing**) or by the use of numerous pieces of equipment that have been set up in a specially equipped room. The equipment includes cameras to transmit pictures of people and graphics, monitors to pick up people and graphic images, microphones and speakers for audio interaction, and facsimile units for hard-copy transmission of documents. Videoconferencing is **interactive** (participants at all locations can see and respond to other participants). Although the specially equipped room is costly, desktop videoconferencing is relatively inexpensive, costing approximately $1,000 per user with the price expected to continue to drop. With desktop videoconferencing, you can hear the voice of the person with whom you are conferencing and see his or her image on the window of your desktop computer. A kit is needed that includes a camera installed on the top

Videoconferencing may be transmitted from a desktop computer or by the use of numerous pieces of equipment that have been set up in a specially equipped room. © *PhotoDisc, Inc.*

of the PC, speakers, a microphone, and software to compress the audio and video files.

Data Conferencing. Data Conferencing enables two or more people to communicate and collaborate as a group in real time using the computer. Software is available to assist you in data conferencing. For example, Microsoft has a program called NetMeeting® that may be downloaded free from the Internet. This software allows participants to:

- Share a program running on one computer with other participants in the conference. Participants can review the same data or information and see the actions as the person sharing the application works on the program.

- Exchange information between shared applications through a shared clipboard, transfer files, and collaborate on a shared whiteboard.

- Send files to conference participants.

- Chat with other conference participants by keying text messages or record meeting notes and action items as part of the collaborative process. One participant may have a private conversation with another person using the "whisper" feature of the software.

NetMeeting also has applications for video and audioconferencing. With NetMeeting, you can send and receive real-time visual images using any video for Windows-compatible equipment. NetMeeting also allows you to engage in audioconferencing by making voice calls to associates and organizations around the world over the Internet or corporate intranet.[3]

---

[3] "NetMeeting Features," http://www.microsoft.com/netmeeting/corp.

Virtual Conferencing. Virtual conferencing links participants through the Internet and chat rooms to transmit information and discuss issues. A chat room is a special area established on the Internet that allows a group of people to converse on issues. The participants may be within the United States or at locations across the world. Virtual conferencing is similar to video conferencing in that it provides for both audio and video delivered over telecommunication networks. However, virtual conferencing as defined here is more comprehensive and more sophisticated in that it allows participants to enter and move around electronically through rooms. Here are examples of types of virtual conferences that have occurred.

A virtual conference that was set up from London, England, allowed participants to observe priceless works of art at unique angles. The participants could "fly" around sites and see, for example, the Sistine Chapel ceiling as Michelangelo saw it, observe it face to face, or levitate above the altar at Stonehenge.

Another virtual conference conducted over a period of two weeks served more than 20,000 delegates from all over the world. The conference also reached a far wider audience than registered delegates, with 100,000 people gaining access to 150 preconference papers, which could be downloaded via the Internet. The conference was set up to resemble a real conference village where delegates could visit a coffee bar to exchange views; in addition, participants were able to post questions for speakers.

Although only two examples are given, our technology today provides the ability to deliver almost anything you can imagine via a virtual environment. However, projections for future technology suggest that the possibilities for virtual conferencing will be even greater than most of us can imagine.

Advantages and Disadvantages of Electronic Meetings. Advantages of electronic meetings include:

- Savings in travel costs, travel time, meals, and hotel rooms
- Presentation of a considerable amount of information concisely through sophisticated audio and video technology
- Bringing together people with expertise in a number of different areas to discuss problems of mutual concern with a minimum of effort
- Providing information from the conference to individuals who are not in attendance at the conference
- Huge environmental savings in less polution of air through cars, planes, and trains

Disadvantages include:

- Less spontaneity between individuals due to a fairly structured environment
- More formal in nature
- Inability to see body language of all participants at any one time; inability to pick up small nuances of body language over the monitor
- Little or no socializing time between participants
- Less chance for effective brainstorming on issues

International Meetings

As you have learned previously, with the multinational corporations that exist today, international meetings are becoming quite common. These meetings may be either face-to-face or electronic. In either situation, you cannot forget that cultural differences do exist. If the meeting is to be successful, such differences must be understood and respected. Otherwise, you might have an international incident rather than the resolution to a problem. International meetings are more formal in nature. Hierarchical considerations must be known and dealt with appropriately.

Being prepared for cultural differences is crucial. For example, language has different meanings in different cultures. Even though the British speak English, they do not speak American and vice versa. For example, in the United States "tabling" means postponing a discussion. In England, to table a subject means to put it on the table for present discussion. In other countries, many values are also different than those values held in the United States. Americans value honesty and directness. However, Asians are more concerned with the quality of an interaction; they do not expect and do not want your complete candor. Silence is also a form of speech in some cultures. For example, the Swedes value silence, whereas Americans are often uncomfortable with silence. When you are assisting with an international meeting, you need to research carefully the culture and speech patterns of participating countries before the meeting. Your local bookstore generally will have books that will assist you. You may also find someone in your company who is from that particular country and can help. Here are a few general suggestions for what to do and what not to do in international meetings.

- Greet each person properly. Do not ignore greetings merely because the meeting is electronic. Greetings become doubly important in such a situation.
- Do not use first names of participants. Even though it is our custom in

Be aware of cultural differences when participating in an international meeting. © PhotoDisc, Inc.

- Do not use slang.
- Avoid gesturing with your hands. Many people take offense at such gestures.
- Watch your body language; remember that this differs from one culture to another. Make certain you do not communicate something you do not mean through your body language.
- Use an interpreter if necessary.
- Do not mistake a courteous answer for the truth—"yes" does not always mean "yes" and "no" may not mean "no."

The Executive's Role in Meetings

The executive has several roles in meetings, which include determining the purpose of the meeting, setting objectives, deciding who should attend, planning the agenda, and setting the time and place.

Determine the Purpose

Every meeting must have a purpose; without it, there is no need for a meeting. It is the executive's role to determine the purpose. When the meeting notices are sent out, the purpose needs to be stated clearly so that all individuals will understand why the meeting is occurring.

Set the Objectives

The executive should have a written set of objectives. Objectives more clearly define the purpose and delineate what is to be accomplished in the meeting. For example, if the general purpose is to determine the training needs of the organization, the objectives might be to:

America, it is rarely appropriate in other countries.

- Recognize the leader of the other groups. For example, if the presidents of companies are involved, they should be recognized first and speak first.
- Take time for the amenities before beginning the meeting. Shake hands with the participants or bow (whatever is appropriate for the culture) if in a face-to-face meeting.
- Dress conservatively.
- Do not ask personal questions; keep the conversation general (even at the more informal times such as over lunch).
- Disagree agreeably; it is generally offensive to flatly contradict people from another country.

- Establish training needs for each department
- Determine whether the training needs are to be done by people within the organization or by an outside consultant
- Determine the amount of time necessary for training
- Determine the budget for training

These objectives should be shared with the attendees before the meeting.

Determine Who Should Attend

The persons who should be invited to the meeting are those who:
- Have knowledge that can contribute to meeting the objectives

A heterogeneous group can bring varying views to the problems discussed in a meeting and encourage creative thinking. © PhotoDisc, Inc.

- Will be responsible for implementing the decisions
- Represent a group that will be affected by the decisions

You also need to consider the backgrounds of the people who are being considered. For example, a **heterogeneous group** (a group having dissimilar backgrounds and experiences) can often solve problems more satisfactorily than a **homogeneous group** (a group with similar backgrounds and experiences). A heterogeneous group can bring varying views to the problem and encourage creative thinking through the diversity that is present. However, an extremely heterogeneous group demands a skilled facilitator to make the meeting productive.

Determine the Number of Attendees

The ideal number of attendees at a meeting is based on the purpose of the meeting and the number of people who can best achieve it. The ideal size for a problem-solving and decision-making group is from seven to ten people. This size group also allows for creative **synergy** (the ideas and products of a group of people developed through interaction with each other). This size group provides enough people to generate divergent points of view and to challenge each other's thinking.

Small groups of five or less people are necessary at times. For example, if the purpose of the meeting is to discuss a faulty product design, the product engineer, the manager of the engineering section, and two or three line technicians may be the only people in attendance.

Plan the Agenda

The executive's role is to plan the agenda. The agenda, which is distributed before the meeting, provides participants with the purpose and objectives of the meeting. It is an outline of what will occur at the meeting. In addition, it provides the:

- Order in which the objectives of the meeting will be presented
- Person responsible for presenting the agenda item
- Action expected on agenda items
- Background materials (if needed)
- Time frames for various agenda items

Establish the Time and Place

The executive is responsible for establishing the approximate time of the meeting and the general place of the meeting. For example, he or she may tell the office professional that the meeting should take place on Tuesday morning. It then becomes the office professional's responsibility to check the calendars, through PIM software, of the people who are to be in attendance to determine the most appropriate time on Tuesday morning. The office professional should also contact the office assistants of the people who will be attending the meeting. Such a practice is a courtesy to the office assistants in keeping them informed of meetings that are occurring; and, in addition, it provides some additional help—the office assistants can remind the people of the meeting. The executive may also inform the office professional that the meeting will be on-site at the company or at an off-site location such as a hotel conference room. The office professional's responsibility is to find an appropriate on-site or off-site room.

The Office Professional's Role in Meetings

As an office professional, you have a number of responsibilities in planning meetings, whether face-to-face or electronic. You must work closely with your supervisor so that you will understand his or her general expectations and the meeting purpose. You can handle the other responsibilities on your own; however, you must understand your supervisor's preferences in these areas.

Before the Meeting

The office professional has a number of responsibilities before the meeting. All of these responsibilities involve careful planning at each step and following up to determine that everything is going as planned. Lack of planning and follow-through can cause both you and your employer aggravation and embarrassment.

Discuss the Purpose, Objectives, and General Expectations with the Executive. When you first join an organization or begin to work with a different supervisor, it is essential for you to spend a significant amount of time with that person before each meeting to understand his or her preferences. Once you begin to understand how your supervisor works, you will have less need to discuss details. However, it is always essential that you discuss the purpose of the meeting, objectives, and the general expectations. Without this overall understanding on your part, you may make some decisions on details that will lessen the effectiveness of the meeting. For example, you may not select the right room or room arrangement.

The office professional must discuss with the executive the purpose of a meeting, the objectives, and the general expectations. © *Digital Vision.*

Gather Information.   As you begin to gather information for the meeting, set up two file folders—one for you and one for the leader of the meeting. Your folder contains all the information about the meeting, including meeting notices, agenda, attendees, room requests, and so forth. The folder for the meeting leader includes the meeting agenda, a list of the people who will be in attendance, handouts (in order of presentation), and any special notes. These folders help you keep organized; without them, you may find yourself with notes on various sheets of paper that are scattered all over your desk and office.

Make Calendar Notations.   You should mark your calendar with any notations that will assist you in planning. For example, if equipment is needed for the meet-

ing, make a note on your calendar concerning when to request the equipment. Also note on your calendar when the meeting notice should be sent. You will want to send out the notice early enough so that participants have time to plan for it. Usually, a week before the meeting is scheduled is adequate time. You will probably want to make your calendar notations on the computer rather than keeping a paper calendar.

Reserve the Meeting Room.   When you have the date and time of the meeting, immediately check to see that a room is available. If the meeting is to be held at the company location, there will usually be several conference rooms of varying sizes. Be certain to reserve a room that is appropriate for the size of the group. If you choose a room that is too large, the participants may feel "lost" in the room. Conversely, if you choose a room too small, the participants will feel crowded. If a meeting is to be held at a location outside the company, arrangements must be made well in advance. In addition to assuring that the size of the room is appropriate for the meeting, make certain that the room has the appropriate facilities, such as:

- Tables
- Comfortable chairs
- Proper lighting and ventilation
- Speaker's table, lectern, or podium (if needed)
- Space and electrical outlets for whatever equipment may be needed

Notify Participants.   If the meeting is an in-house one, you may choose to notify the participants by electronic mail. By using calendaring software, you can check the schedules of the meeting participants to determine if they are free at the designated time. Be certain that the notification gives the participants all the information they need, such as date, time, and place of the meeting. A sample meeting notification memo is shown in Figure 16-2.

Prepare the Agenda. An **agenda** is an outline of procedures or the order of business to be followed during a meeting. Participants should receive a detailed agenda at least a day, and preferably a week, before the meeting. It is good practice to send out the agenda with the meeting notice. The agenda should include the:

- Name of the group
- Date of the meeting
- Starting and ending times
- Location of the meeting
- The agenda items in order of presentation
- Background materials (if appropriate)

For each agenda item, the person responsible for presenting the item should be listed. You might also wish to allocate a particular time period for each item on the agenda. Although this process is not absolutely essential, it usually does remind people of the importance of time and adhering to a schedule. The order of the agenda items can vary. Some people feel that the most difficult items should be presented first; others feel that they should be presented last. You should check with your supervisor to determine the order that he or she prefers.

The action that is expected on the agenda item should be noted. You will notice in Figure 16-3 that the word "action" is listed after specific agenda items. This word denotes that a decision will be made on the item. This approach helps participants know that they should come

---

MEETING NOTIFICATION MEMO

MEMORANDUM

TO: All Managers

FROM: Juan Menendez

DATE: April 5, 2000

SUBJECT: Meeting Notice, April 20

There will be a planning meeting on Thursday, April 20, to review our accomplishments for the last six months, the proposed budget for next year, and the goals for the next six months. The meeting will be held in Conference Room C, beginning at 9:00 a.m. until approximately 11:30 a.m. Please bring copies of your accomplishments to the meeting for distribution to all participants. A meeting agenda is attached.

It is most important that everyone be in attendance. However, if there is an emergency that prevents you from attending, please call Tien Su by April 18.

Attachment

FIGURE 16-2. Meeting Notification Memo

MEETING AGENDA

Planning Meeting

Conference Room C

April 20, 2000

I.	Review of accomplishments on department objectives for last six months (30 minutes)	All Managers
II.	Proposed budget for next year (20 minutes)	Juan Menendez
III.	Goals for next six months (1 hour) ACTION	All Managers
IV.	Objective Planning Timelines (15 minutes) ACTION	Juan Menendez

FIGURE 16-3. Meeting Agenda

to the meeting prepared to make a decision. If an item is for discussion only and a decision will be made at a later point, the word "discussion" may be placed by the item.

As you learned earlier in this chapter, participants have a number of responsibilities during the meeting, including being prepared for the meeting and keeping focused on the agenda. An agenda, properly prepared and distributed along with any necessary backup materials, can help participants fulfill their responsibilities.

Prepare Materials for the Executive. Materials for the executive should include:

- The meeting notice with a list of the people who will be in attendance
- Materials that have been sent out before the meeting
- Notes that are needed at the meeting
- Visuals or handouts

If the executive is a participant of a meeting off-site, you may also need to include directions to the location. Most large cities have detailed maps available of the city. Also, maps for particular locations can now be obtained on the Internet. For example, you put in your address and the address of the meetings; the computer draws a map for you.

Prepare Materials for Attendees. Background materials, as you have just learned, should be sent to attendees with the meeting notice and agenda. However, you may have handouts or other materials that need to be distributed during the meeting. If the handouts have several pages, it is helpful to place them in individual folders. Sometimes attendees are expected to take notes; if so, you might provide a pad of paper in the folder. Extra pencils and pens may be placed on the table or at a convenient location for the attendees in case they are needed.

Order Equipment. Determine what equipment, if any, is needed for the meeting. Follow through to see that it is available. It is a good idea to make a list of the equipment and note on the list what arrangements have been made. List who is responsible for obtaining each item; if it is your responsibility, note that. Before the meeting begins, take your list to the room and check it against the equipment present.

Determine the Seating Arrangement. The seating arrangement of the room depends on the objectives of the meeting. The five basic seating arrangements are:

- Rectangular
- Circular
- Oval
- U-shaped
- Semicircular

These room arrangements are depicted in Figure 16-4.

The **rectangular arrangement** allows the leader to have good control because she or he sits at the head of the table. This arrangement is also good if it is important

to have individuals talk in groups of two or three. Individuals seated next to or opposite each other have a chance to discuss. However, if discussion is important, the table should not be too long. A long table may make communication difficult due to the inability to see the nonverbal behavior of all the participants. The rectangular arrangement is most effective in formal meetings.

The **circular** and **oval arrangements** work best when the purpose of the meeting is to generate ideas and discussion and the meeting is relatively informal. These arrangements encourage togetherness, shared communication, and participation. It is easy to make direct eye contact with everyone in the group. Communication channels are considered fairly equal among all participants since there is no one person who is in a dominant position.

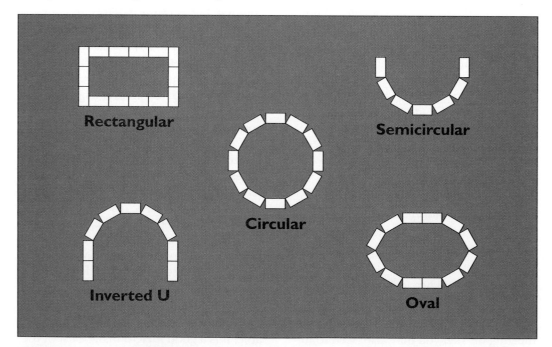

FIGURE 16-4. Room Arrangements

The **U-shaped** and **semicircular arrangements** work well for small groups of six to eight members and when the meeting is a semiformal one. The leader has moderate control since he or she can be positioned in a fairly dominant position. These two arrangements are also good for showing visuals because the visual can be set up at the front of the configuration.

Always make certain that you have the appropriate number of chairs for the participants who will attend. You do not want to have extra chairs; they merely get in the way of the participants, and it appears that some people failed to attend. You also do not want to have too few chairs; it appears you have not planned properly.

Order Food and Beverages. If it is a morning meeting, your employer may request that there be coffee, juice, cold drinks, and/or some appropriate snack. Water should also be available. If it is an afternoon meeting, you may want to provide coffee and soft drinks. However, it is not necessary to provide beverages or snacks; find out your employer's preference.

For a luncheon meeting, you will probably have the responsibility of selecting the menu, calling the caterer, and arranging for the meal to be served. The lunch should be light if you are expecting people to work after lunch; a heavy meal often makes people sleepy.

If it is a dinner meeting, you may have the responsibility of working with an outside caterer or with the hotel staff if the meeting is held in a hotel. If you know the attendees, you should consider their preferences in food. If not, ask the caterer or hotel staff to recommend several menus from which you may select.

Whether you are providing beverages and snacks or a full meal, be certain to check with your supervisor as to budget allocations. You do not want to overspend the budget nor order so sparingly that you appear miserly.

Follow Up on the Meeting Notice. Although you ask people to let you know if they will not be able to attend, you can be certain that not all people will respond. Thus, it is your responsibility to email or telephone the people who have not responded to determine whether or not they will be present. You also need to let your employer know who will be at the meeting and who will not. He or she may want to know the reason the person is not attending. If someone is going to be late for a meeting, that should be noted also.

Check the Room Temperature. Check the temperature controls before the meeting. Remember that bodies give off heat, so the room will be warmer with people in it. A standard rule is to aim for about 68 degrees. Be certain that you know

Check the room temperature before the meeting begins.
© *PhotoDisc, Inc.*

whom to call if the temperature gets too hot or too cold during the meeting. Nothing can be worse than a hot, stuffy room or a room that is icy cold when you are trying to make important decisions.

Consideration should be given to the smoking policy before the meetings. Many organizations now prohibit smoking in the building or restrict it to designated areas. If your company does not have a smoking policy, the executive in charge of the meeting may want to make the smoking rules clear at the beginning of the meeting.

Prepare to Present. Sometimes it is necessary for the office professional to do a short presentation about the logistics of the meeting—coffee break times and so forth. If so, you should plan carefully what you need to say so that you can give the information in a concise, informative manner.

During the Meeting

Usually, your major responsibility during the meeting is to take notes or minutes of the proceedings. Other responsibilities include greeting guests, handling any special problems, and assisting the chairperson in observing parliamentary procedure.

Greet Guests. If you are having guests at the meeting, your employer may expect you to greet them. Your role is to make them feel comfortable and welcome. Keep a smile on your face, and introduce the guests to the appropriate individuals. Make sure that they also know where to hang their coats and the location of the nearest restrooms.

Assist the Leader in Observing Parliamentary Procedure. Parliamentary procedure usually is not observed in informal meetings. However, in formal

meetings (such as board meetings) it becomes important in assuring that the proceedings go smoothly. Knowledge of parliamentary procedure can help you not only in your job but also in your professional activities outside of work, such as IAAP (International Association of Administrative Professionals) meetings.

Parliamentary procedure has been defined as common sense used in a gracious manner. Its purpose is to arrive at a group decision in an efficient and orderly manner. A variety of books is available that will help you understand parliamentary procedure. One good source is *Robert's Rules of Order Newly Revised.*

Take Notes and Minutes. Always take time before the meeting begins to look over the agenda and any handout materials. If you are familiar with what is going to happen, you will be able to take better notes. A laptop computer can be an efficient way for you to record the proceedings of a meeting. By recording on the laptop, you can have the minutes almost ready to print (with minor editing) and distribute once you leave the meeting. Another method of recording minutes is to use a tape recorder and transcribe the minutes after the meeting has adjourned. If you do use a tape recorder, you will want to note the names of individuals who make motions, second motions, and so forth or ask each individual who speaks to identify himself or herself. Without some identification of the individuals, you will not be able to complete the minutes properly.

It is a good idea to sit next to the person who will conduct the meeting so that you can hear what is being said. You will want to note the names of the people in attendance and those who are absent.

If you are taking notes for a meeting that is relatively informal in nature, you will follow a different format than if you are taking minutes for a board meeting, for example. Notes from informal meetings should include the following:

- Date, time, and place of the meeting
- Members present and absent
- Actions that were taken at the meeting
- Follow-up necessary after the meeting and the individuals responsible for doing the follow-up
- Date of the next meeting (if determined)

If you are taking minutes of an organizational meeting such as a board meeting or a professional group (for example, IAAP), the proceedings are recorded in a more formal manner. Minutes should contain a record of important matters that are presented in the meeting. Although you do not need to record the minutes verbatim, you must record motions verbatim and all pertinent information from the meeting. Items that should be included in the minutes are the:

- Date, time, and place of the meeting
- Name of the presiding officer
- Members present and absent
- Approval or correction of the minutes from the previous meeting
- Reports of committees, officers, or individuals
- Motions made, with the name of the person making the motion, the name of the person who seconds it, and an indication of whether it passed or failed
- Items on which action needs to be taken and the person responsible for taking the action
- A succinct summary of the important points of each discussion

- Adjournment of the meeting
- Name and title of the person who will be signing the minutes (the secretary of the organization or board), along with a signature line (if the minutes are to be signed)

See that Food and Beverages Are Served. Be alert to the time that food needs to be served (mid-morning, noon, mid-afternoon, and so on) so that you can check with the caterer immediately if the food does not appear when planned. Also, it is a good idea to call the caterer a few hours before the meeting is scheduled to confirm the date and time of the service.

Handle Special Problems. Special problems sometimes occur during meetings. For example, you may have difficulty hearing or understanding a speaker. If the meeting is large, it is a good idea to prearrange some type of signal with the person presiding in case you need to have something repeated. If the meeting is small, you can inform the speaker that you are unable to hear. If a motion is made and you are unsure who made it, immediately ask for the person's name. It is better to interrupt at this point than to try to find out after the meeting.

There are times when an emergency message must be delivered to someone in the meeting. If it is your responsibility to deliver the message, do so as unobtrusively as possible. Get up quietly, answer the door, and deliver the message to the recipient. If you do not know the recipient, give the message to the person presiding. If you have several responsibilities during the meeting (such as taking notes, delivering messages, and so forth), it may be necessary for you to have an assistant help you.

After the Meeting

Once the meeting is over, your responsibilities do not end. You must see that the minutes are prepared and distributed and that all routine follow-up duties are handled.

Prepare the Notes or Minutes.
Minutes from a board meeting are shown in Figure 16-5. As you have learned previously, notes of a meeting are not as formal as minutes. There is no set form for minutes; however, here are some general guidelines.

- Minutes may be single- or double-spaced. Margins should be at least 1 inch. If the minutes are to be placed in a bound book, the left margin should be 1½ inches.

- Capitalize and center the heading that designates the official title of the group.

- Use subject captions (the agenda's subject captions generally may be used) for ease in locating various sections of the minutes.

- Establish when the meeting was called to order; indicate whether it was a regular or a special meeting.

- Give the name of the presiding officer.

- Capitalize words such as *company, corporation,* and *committee* in the minutes when they refer to the group conducting the meeting.

- Use businesslike language. Do not include personal opinions or comments. If gratitude is expressed for an individual or a group, it should take the form of a resolution.

- Give the name of each speaker and a summary of what the speaker discusses.

- List any motions made verbatim.

- Minutes may or may not be signed. Minutes of board meetings are signed, and generally minutes of professional associations are signed. However, routine minutes of meetings within a business are not signed. If minutes are to be signed, a signature line should be provided.

- Strive to complete the minutes in final form and distribute to the participants within 24 hours of the meeting.

If you are preparing minutes of a corporate meeting, you should follow the rules outlined in the bylaws of the corporation. If the bylaws do not spell out the method to follow, check the minutes of previous board meetings and adhere to the format established.

Perform Routine Follow-Up Duties.
Some of the duties you need to perform after the meeting are:

- Check the meeting room to see that it is left in good order. All equipment should be returned. Tables and chairs should be restored to normal room arrangement. Pick up all papers and materials left in the room. Some of the excess material may be confidential and should be shredded.

- If the room needs to be cleaned, notify the cleaning staff.

- Any individuals who were not present but were given duties or assignments at the meeting must be notified.

- Items that require future attention should be written on your electronic calendar.

- Forms should be processed for those participants who have incurred reimbursable expenses.

- Any items that need to be considered at the next meeting as a result of the proceedings of the current meeting should be noted on the next meeting agenda.

MINUTES

BOARD OF DIRECTORS MEETING
MANAGEMENT SOCIETY

Detroit Chapter

April 25, 2000

TIME AND PLACE OF MEETING

The regular monthly meeting of the Board of Directors Meeting, Management Society, Detroit Chapter, was held on Tuesday, April 25, 2000 in the Tiffany Room of the Wonderlin Hotel at 6 p.m. The meeting was called to order by the president, Ronald Anderson. All twelve members of the board were present.

READING OF THE MINUTES

The minutes of the March meeting were approved without reading since each member had received a copy prior to the meeting.

TREASURER'S REPORT

The treasurer's report (copy attached) showing a balance of $2,895 as of March 31 was read, received, and filed.

UNFINISHED BUSINESS

Ronald Anderson reported receipt of acceptance from H. R. Princeton to speak at the October meeting and that publicity items have been turned over to the Publicity Committee.

NEW BUSINESS

Chapter Merit Award Qualifications. It was suggested that the merit award qualifications be included in the Chapter bulletin for the first week of June.

Speakers Bureau. Silas Stohr, Chairperson of the Speakers Bureau, said that he and the Bureau are planning to increase the number of speakers at the winter seminar so that the programs can be expanded.

Information Service Committee. Mildred Gary, chairperson of the Information Service Committee, said that she has written to the national office about the Chapter's willingness to participate in any survey proposed by the national Office; to date no reply has been received.

Publicity Committee. Percy Atwater reported the approval on the solicitation of ads for the roster and the bulletin was received. He explained that the format of the bulletin will have to be changed to accommodate the inclusion of the ads. The Board of Directors approved this action.

ADJOURNMENT

As there was no further business, the meeting was adjourned.

Arthur M. Grant
Arthur M. Grant, Secretary-Treasurer

FIGURE 16-5. Minutes

Responsibilities of the Office Professional for Conferences and Conventions

A conference or convention is much larger in scope and number of participants than a meeting. For example, a company or companies may hold a national sales conference each year to introduce and market the company's new products. As an office professional, you may be involved in helping to plan a conference or convention. If so, your duties are usually varied and time-consuming. Planning a national convention, for example, takes months of work. You will not have the total responsibility for planning this type of function, but you may be involved in a number of tasks that take numerous hours to complete.

Before the Conference

The planning you do before a conference is extremely important. Good planning will assure a smooth, successful conference; poor planning will result in a disorganized, ineffective conference. You must know your role in conference planning and carefully consider all the details.

Arrange for Meeting Facilities.   In planning the arrangements for the meeting facility, it is important to know how many people are expected for the conference. It is also important to know approximately how many people will be attending each session so that rooms large enough to accommodate the attendees may be reserved.

Another responsibility is determining what equipment is needed for the pre-

sentations. A large room usually requires a microphone. The microphone may be attached to a podium, or a lapel microphone may be needed if the presenter plans to move around the room. If the presentation is a panel discussion, it may be necessary to set up a table at the front of the room with microphones for each panelist. Other equipment needed may include computers, video presentation equipment, flip charts, floor microphones (if the audience is going to be invited to participate), and so forth. The hotel or conference center staff usually sets up the equipment. It is your responsibility to check the room before the meeting begins to see that all equipment is set up and is in working order. If there is non-working equipment (either before the meeting begins or failure occurs during the meeting), audiovisual technicians are usually available to correct the problem. You should get their names and telephone numbers before the meeting begins.

Contact Outside Speakers.   If someone outside the company is to speak at the conference, you will probably be asked to assist in making the arrangements. Since some professionals book their speaking engagements months in advance, you should contact them as early as possible. Before making any final arrangements, determine the speaker's fee. Ask the speaker to provide you with a resume (to be used in introducing the person), a photograph and a biographical sketch (for publicity purposes if needed), and information about any special room arrangements and equipment. Give the speaker the following details:

- Date, time, and location of the conference
- General information about the organization

- Purpose of the conference
- Number of people expected to attend
- Nature of the audience expected (gender, age, interests)
- General guidelines or subject matter for the presentation, if they exist (length, question-and-answer period if needed, suggested subject matter)
- Expenses that will be paid (hotel, meals, and transportation are standard)

Make Hotel and Travel Reservations.

When out-of-town speakers or special guests come to a conference, you may be expected to make their hotel and travel reservations. You should determine the type of accommodations required—price, room arrangements (single, double, queen or king-size bed, smoking or non-smoking); method of travel (air, car, train); class of travel (first class, business, or coach); and arrival and departure times. A confirmation number or a written confirmation should be obtained from the hotel. The receipt of tickets will serve as confirmation of travel arrangements. If an individual is expected to arrive late at a hotel (after 6 p.m.), the hotel should be notified to hold the reservation for late arrival. Determine if someone from the company will pick up the guests when they arrive in town. If so, the designated person should be given the name(s), times of arrival, flight numbers, hotel accommodations, and any other necessary information. The speaker or special guest also should be given the name of the individual who will be meeting him or her. Since the speaker or guest will probably not know the person, the individual may carry a sign with the name of the organization or the conference. Let the speaker or guest know if a sign will be carried and what notation will be on the sign.

Plan and Conduct Registration.

Usually there is a preregistration period during which people can register for the conference (perhaps at a reduced cost). You may be responsible for designing the registration form, mailing it out, and receiving the forms. You should keep a record of all persons who preregister and the money received. You might prepare a database from which name tags can be prepared in advance and folders or envelopes containing program schedules, tickets for special events, and other literature such as information about the city can be assembled.

Registration of participants at the conference requires careful planning several months in advance. Generally, you will not be in charge of the total registration process, but you may be asked to assist. Persons to staff the registration tables should be selected prior to the conference and their duties explained in detail. A list should be made of all supplies needed at the registration table; for example, pens, registration packets, and name tags. Signs

Registration of participants at the conference requires careful planning several months in advance. *Photograph by Alan Brown/Photonics.*

should be made directing the participants to the registration desk; the hotel or conference center will generally handle these signs. If the conference is large, the registration packets should be divided into separate alphabetical sections with each registration assistant responsible for a certain section of the alphabet. Signs should be made to indicate the location of each alphabetical section.

Assist with Planning and Arranging Meals and Receptions.   You may also be asked to help with planning and arranging luncheons, dinners, and receptions. The hotel or conference staff is of great assistance here. If you give them a price range, they will suggest various menus.

Prepare Evaluation Forms.   Many times evaluation forms are provided for participants at conferences and conventions. Evaluations may be done of the en-

tire conference and/or of particular sessions of the conference. You may be responsible for helping to design this form and distributing it at the conference. Evaluations should be short and simple. Figure 16-6 shows an evaluation form for a specific session.

During the Conference

Your responsibilities during the conference may include running errands, assisting in getting messages to participants, and being on hand to help solve any problems that occur. During a presentation, for example, a speaker may have trouble with a computer or a piece of multimedia equipment. Your job may be to get a technician to repair the equipment. You may also be asked to deliver emergency messages to individuals during the conference. Other responsibilities may include:

CONFERENCE SESSION EVALUATION FORM

Please rate the items on a 1 through 5 basis by circling the appropriate number. The highest possible rating is 5, and the lowest possible rating is 1.

1. The topic of the session was appropriate for the conference.   1   2   3   4   5
2. The speaker was well prepared.   1   2   3   4   5
3. The speaker was enthusiastic about the subject matter.   1   2   3   4   5
4. The visuals used were appropriate to the topic.   1   2   3   4   5
5. I learned from the speaker.   1   2   3   4   5
6. I would recommend the speaker to others.   1   2   3   4   5
7. The room was arranged appropriately for the meeting.   1   2   3   4   5
8. Media equipment was in good working order.   1   2   3   4   5

Comments _____

_____

_____

FIGURE 16-6. Conference Session Evaluation Form

PEOPLE FIRST INTERNATIONAL
986 Front Street
Detroit, MI 48201-1701
Telephone: 313 555-0199
Fax: 313 555-0178
URL: www.pfi.com

April 27, 2000

Mr. Eduardo Martinez
Detroit Enterprise
1834 Elm Drive
Detroit, MI 48231-3502

Dear Mr. Martinez:

Thank you for speaking at the Management Conference last Thursday. Your topic, "Management in the 21st Century," was timely and well received by the audience. I heard numerous comments that the suggestions you offered for increasing managerial effectiveness were practical.

The conference was one of the best we have had, and your presentation helped make it successful.

Sincerely,

Eric Johnson

Eric Johnson
Program Chairperson

cd

FIGURE 16-7. Letter of Appreciation to a Presenter

- Escorting speakers to the appropriate room
- Preparing and distributing an attendance list
- Collecting evaluation forms
- Maintaining expense records

At a conference, you are a representative of the company or organization for which you work. You must present an outstanding public relations image at all times. Keep a smile on your face and handle even the most difficult situations with poise and confidence.

After the Conference

After the conference, your basic duties involve responsibility for cleanup and follow-up. You may need to see that:

- Out-of-town guests and speakers are assisted with transportation to the airport.
- Letters of appreciation are sent to presenters.
- Expense reports are processed by conference participants.

Figure 16-7 shows a sample letter of appreciation to a presenter.

You also may be responsible for seeing that the proceedings of the conference are published and mailed to the participants. Generally, you will not be responsible for the actual writing of the conference proceedings, but you may be called upon to work with the conference reporters in producing a comprehensive report based on taped conference sessions. Participants may be charged a fee for a copy of the conference proceedings. If individual sessions are taped, the participants who are interested in receiving a copy of the tape may be charged a fee for it. If papers are read at a conference, each speaker usually is asked to submit the paper prior to the conference. Copies of the paper may then be provided for the participants at the meeting. As a final responsibility, you may be asked to keep a record of problems that occurred and make recommendations for future conferences.

SUMMARY

Study this summary to reinforce what you have learned in this chapter.

- The effective meeting is one in which there is a definite need for the meeting, the purpose is stated and clearly understood by all, the appropriate people are in attendance, an agenda is prepared and adhered to, all members participate, and there are outcomes achieved as a result of the meeting.
- Unnecessary meetings are ones in which:

  There is no clearly defined purpose.

  No consideration has been given to who needs to be in attendance.

  Confidential or sensitive personnel matters must be addressed.

  There is inadequate data for the meeting.

  There is insufficient time to prepare for the meeting.

  Information could be communicated in writing or by telephone.

  There is a considerable amount of anger and hostility in the group.
- The role of the leader in meetings is to make the purpose and objectives clear, adhere to the agenda, manage time, encourage participation, lead a balanced and controlled discussion, handle

conflict, bring closure to the objectives, and evaluate the meeting.

- The role of participants before and during the meeting is to prepare by carefully reading the materials sent out, participate in the meeting, listen to others' points of view, be nonjudgmental, and be courteous to each individual.

- The role of participants after the meeting is to follow up on any responsibilities assigned during the meeting.

- Types of meetings include traditional and electronic. Traditional meetings include staff meetings, committee meetings, project team meetings, customer/client meetings, and board of director meetings. In addition, there may be conventions and conferences.

- Many of the traditional meetings may be conducted in an electronic format. The types of electronic meetings include audioconferencing, videoconferencing, data conferencing, and virtual conferencing.

- Advantages of electronic meetings include savings in travel costs, ability to present a considerable amount of information concisely through audio and video technology, and ability to bring together people with expertise in a number of different areas to discuss problems of mutual concern with a minimum of effort.

- With the multinational corporations that exist today, international meetings are becoming quite common. These meetings may be face-to-face or electronic. In either situation, consideration needs to be given to cultural differences that exist.

- The executive's role in meetings is to:
  Determine the purpose

  Set the objectives
  Decide who should attend
  Determine the number of attendees
  Plan the agenda
  Establish the time and place

- The office professional's role before the meeting occurs is to:
  Discuss the purpose, objectives, and general expectations with the executive
  Gather information
  Make calendar notations
  Reserve the meeting room
  Notify participants
  Prepare the agenda
  Prepare materials for the executive
  Prepare materials for attendees
  Order equipment
  Determine the seating arrangement
  Obtain food and beverages
  Follow up on the meeting notice
  Check the room temperature
  Prepare to present

- The office professional's role during a meeting consists of:
  Greeting guests
  Helping the person conducting the meeting to observe parliamentary procedures
  Taking notes and minutes
  Seeing that food and beverages are served
  Handling special problems

- The office professional's role after the meeting consists of:
  Preparing the notes or minutes
  Performing routine follow-up duties

- The responsibilities of the office professional for conferences and conventions include:

Arranging for meeting facilities

Contacting outside speakers

Making hotel and travel reservations

Planning and conducting registration

Assisting with planning and arranging meals and receptions

Preparing evaluation forms

Cleanup and follow-up duties after the conference, such as assisting out-of-town guests and speakers with transportation to the airport, writing letters of appreciation to the presenters, and processing expense reports

Key Terms

- Task force
- Committee
- Bylaws
- Conventions
- Conference
- Teleconferencing
- Audioconferencing
- Electronic blackboard
- Interactivity
- Videoconferencing
- Desktop videoconferencing
- Data conferencing
- Virtual conferencing
- Heterogeneous group
- Homogeneous group
- Synergy
- Agenda
- Rectangular arrangement
- Circular arrangement
- Oval arrangement
- U-shaped arrangement
- Semicircular arrangement
- Parliamentary procedure

Professional Pointers

As an office professional, you may be presenting at some meetings within the company and in professional meetings outside the company. Here are some pointers to help you present effectively.

- Thoroughly research the topic you are presenting well in advance of the meeting.
- Secure supporting data and documents that may be used to help clarify the information you are presenting.
- Anticipate the kinds of questions that may be asked about the subject. Write the questions down and outline your answers. This approach will help you remember the issues and be better prepared when a question is asked of you.
- Explain your topic in terms that the group will understand.
- Be familiar with parliamentary procedure so that you will not be caught off guard by breaching a parliamentary procedure.
- Be concise; do not ramble.
- Exhibit confidence in yourself and your topic.

Office Procedures Reinforcement

1. Describe the role of participants in a meeting.
2. Describe the types of electronic meetings.
3. What is the executive's role in meetings?
4. List the functions of the office professional in meetings.
5. List the responsibilities of the office professional in conferences and conventions.

Critical Thinking Activity

Bess Franklin has been working for People First International for six months. On several occasions during this time, Bess has been asked to set up meetings. Most of the meetings have been for only three or four people, usually within the company. She merely called the employees and gave them the date, time, and location of the meetings. No one asked her to do anything else.

Last week Bess's employer asked her to set up a meeting with five executives at Hazel Thomas and three executives from People First. Bess has never had the responsibility for planning a meeting. She used her calendaring software to arrange the meeting with the executives in the company, and she called those executives outside the firm. She gave them the date, time, and location of the meeting over the phone. No other arrangements were made.

When it was time for the meeting to begin, the conference room was occupied by another group. Her employer had to find Bess (who was on her morning break) to learn why the conference room was not scheduled. Equipment for the showing of a video entitled "Forecasting for 2010 and Beyond" was not ordered from the media department. Bess quickly found an available conference room on another floor. She called the media department for the equipment, and it was delivered in 20 minutes. Her employer convened the meeting; Bess returned to her desk. There was no one to record the minutes of the meeting. Once again, her employer called Bess and asked her to join the meeting.

At the conclusion of the meeting, Bess transcribed the proceedings and gave them to her employer. When her employer asked Bess if copies had been sent to the other attendees, Bess said that they had not. Her employer "hit the ceiling." She accused Bess of lacking professionalism and not understanding the poor impression made by improperly planned meetings. As she left the office, she turned and told Bess that she had not even had the foresight to order coffee.

- What steps should Bess have taken in planning the meeting?
- How might Bess have helped her employer in making a more professional appearance to the attendees?
- Does Bess's employer have any responsibility for the poor meeting? If so, what are her responsibilities?
- What should Bess's reactions to her employer's comments be?

Office Applications

OA16-1 (Goals 1 and 3)

Choose six to seven of your classmates to work with on this project. Your task is to conduct an effective meeting before your class members. Plan the meeting and determine who will be the leader. The purpose of the meeting is to plan a training session for your department on one of the following topics:

- Effective Written Business Communications
- Effective International Communications
- Effective Conflict Management

The group is to prepare a meeting notice (giving the date, time, place, purpose, and objectives of the meeting), an agenda, written materials (if necessary), and an evaluation form. The meeting notice, agenda, and written materials are to be given to the entire class before the meeting. Once the meeting has been held (before the class), your group and the other class members are to fill out the evaluation form. A copy of the meeting notice, agenda, written materials, and a compilation of the responses to the evaluation are to be submitted to your instructor.

OA16-2 (Goal 4)

Attend a professional meeting (for example, International Association of Administrative Professionals or a meeting of an organization on campus of which you are a member) and take minutes. Key the minutes in an acceptable format and submit a copy to your instructor.

Online Research Application

ORA16-3 (Goal 2)

Using the Internet, search for current software and/or new developments in audio, video, and data conferencing. Prepare a brief report of your findings, including sources, and submit a copy to your instructor.

CHAPTER 17

Travel Arrangements

Travel in today's fast-moving, international business world is an integral part of most executives' work. You have learned about the sophisticated telecommunications systems such as videoconferencing, computer conferencing, audioconferencing, and electronic mail, which make it possible for people around the world to communicate without travel. However, even with these systems, there is still a need for executives to communicate face-to-face with associates in negotiating business deals, exchanging information, and learning new techniques.

The way travel arrangements are handled will vary by company. Many larger organizations will

YOUR GOALS

Your goals as you study this chapter are to:

1. Make travel arrangements.

2. Prepare itineraries.

3. Describe the duties to be performed while the executive is traveling and when he or she returns, prepare an expense report.

contract with travel agencies to handle all the travel for the company. Other organizations have their own in-house travel department. Small companies may expect executives to make their own travel arrangements. Whatever the situation, you, as an office professional, will usually have a major role in assisting the executive. It is imperative that you be aware of company procedures concerning travel and your employer's preferences regarding airlines, hotels, rental cars, and other matters. You also need to keep current on the travel services available.

Methods of Travel

Since time is so important to the busy executive, most business travel over long distances is by air. If your employer plans to travel by train, you may obtain information from the toll-free Amtrak number listed in your local directory or from the *Official Railway Guide*, published by the National Railway Publication Company. Information concerning bus travel may be obtained from your local bus lines. If your employer makes frequent trips by auto, he or she may find it helpful to pay an annual fee to join an automobile club such as the American Automobile Association (AAA). Such clubs can help you plan the automobile trip and provide you with maps marked for the recommended routes.

The basic travel duties, such as making reservations, preparing the itinerary, gathering materials for your employer's trip, and completing an expense report, are the same regardless of the method of travel. Since air travel is the most common means of travel, the concentration in this chapter is on air travel. Some information is provided on car and train travel.

Air travel is the most common means of business travel. © PhotoDisc, Inc.

Domestic Travel

As you have already learned, executives travel most frequently by air. This section will concentrate on the types of flight classifications, reservations, and other information you will need in making air travel arrangements. In addition, there is information on making hotel and car reservations, plus a brief section on car and rail travel.

Air Travel

Today an air traveler can have breakfast in San Francisco and dinner in New York (the flight only takes approximately 5 hours, but time zone differences preclude you from arriving in New York in time for lunch). The air traveler can travel from Chicago to Frankfort, Germany, in approximately 8½ hours and from Portland, Oregon, to Seoul, Korea, in approximately 11 hours. And during this time on the plane, the executive can prepare business briefs and reports on a laptop computer and make calls back to the office from the telephone on the plane. Once the reports have been finished and the executive is on the ground, the completed report can be sent to the office via a modem, a fax, or by mail. If the report was sent on disk, the office professional can edit, print, and distribute the report to the appropriate individuals. Technology allows the busy executive to continue his or her work while traveling across the nation or the world.

Flight Classifications. When you make flight reservations, you need to know your company's policy regarding the classes of air travel. Airlines have two basic classes available—first class and coach. Since first class is more expensive than coach, some organizations have a policy that only chief executives travel first class. This will usually include the chairperson of the board, the president, and sometimes executive vice presidents. First class is located at the front of the plane. Some airlines also provide business class, located directly behind first class or in front of coach class.

Executives can use laptop computers to prepare reports while traveling. © *PhotoDisc, Inc.*

First-class accommodations are more luxurious than coach or business class. The seats are wider, farther apart, and provide more legroom than those in the coach section. Several flight attendants are available to take care of your needs. Elegant meals and generous refreshments, including alcoholic beverages, are served free of charge. Some airlines allow you to eat the meal at anytime you ask. You may even eat the meal that you would have had on the plane in the airport lounge before flight time and then go right to sleep on the recliner seats in the plane. Headsets are often provided to block out engine noise.

Business class is usually available on international flights and on some domestic flights. It is slightly more expensive than coach but less costly than first class. The business-class section on a plane is located in front of the coach class—at the front of the plane if first class is not offered or directly behind first class. Accommodations may include more spacious seating than coach, complimentary alcoholic beverages, headsets for listening to music, video screens that swing out of armrests, recliner seats with extra legroom, amenity kits, and better food than coach class.

Coach accommodations provide snacks, soft drinks, tea or coffee, and meals free of charge. However, seats are closer together, more people use the coach section, and fewer attendants are available. In short, the atmosphere is not as luxurious nor is the service as attentive as that in first class or business class. Such items as alcoholic beverages and headsets are available in coach but there is usually a charge for these services.

Special Services. Several special services are provided by airlines and by airports. For example, an airline may have a shuttle service that runs from a location in the downtown area or from various strategic locations across the city. Tickets can often be purchased at these shuttle locations through self-ticketing machines or through airline employees on duty. The shuttle will take customers to the departure gate, pick them up at the airport, and return them to the shuttle location. Vehicle parking is provided at the shuttle location.

Shuttle service is available from an airport parking location to the airlines. © *PhotoDisc, Inc.*

Airports also offer parking for a fee. Generally, there is some type of covered parking close to the airport that is charged at a daily rate. This is usually the most expensive. Other parking locations are provided at areas some distance from the airport. A shuttle service often is provided to take you to your departure gate and to return you to your car after the trip.

Private parking services are often available in proximity to the airport. The traveler drives to the parking service and parks his or her car; then a shuttle service takes the traveler to the airline terminal. Upon returning to the airport, the traveler is picked up by the parking service shuttle and returned to his or her car. These services are reasonably priced and assist the traveler in getting to the airlines quickly.

Airline Clubs.   For the frequent business traveler, membership in an airline club may be a worthwhile investment. Although membership is usually not free, a variety of travel perks accompany an airline club membership. Members usually have access to special airport lounges that are equipped with a variety of business equipment and facilities, including computers, fax and copy machines, conference rooms, and telephones. Members also have access to current periodicals and newspapers. In addition, clubs may offer complimentary soft drinks, juice, coffee, pastries, and light snacks. Other clubs offer assistance with airline reservations, seat selection, and boarding passes. Airline clubs are available for both the domestic and international business traveler.

Changes or Cancellations.
Occasionally, it may be necessary to cancel or change flight reservations. However, if you have purchased a flight through some type of special fare, you may be charged a penalty for changing the flight. When arranging for a special fare, be certain to ask if the flight may be canceled or changed. Sometimes your money is not returned on a special fare that you cancel. If your employer is prone to make frequent changes, it might be wise to seek fares that do not have a penalty for changes. Even though they may be more expensive initially, you can probably save money in the long run.

Ground Transportation.   Once the executive arrives at his or her destination, some type of ground transportation is generally necessary. That transportation may be as simple as taking a taxi or shuttle service to the hotel. Since taxi service is generally the most expensive method of ground transportation, it is a good idea to check taxi costs and availability of shuttle services when making the travel arrangements. Some hotels provide free shuttle service to and from the airport. Private vendors also offer shuttle services that are generally less expensive than taxi service. Limousine service is available at many airports, at about the same price as taxi service.

If it is necessary for the executive to attend meetings at several locations during his or her stay, a rental car may be the most economical and convenient method of ground transportation. Toll-free numbers for car rental agencies are listed in the telephone directory, or cars may be rented through the airlines or travel agent. When renting a car, specify the make and model preferred and the date and time the car will be picked up and returned.

When arriving at the destination airport, the executive picks up the car from the rental desk (generally located next to the baggage claim area). The cost of a rental car may be based on a daily or weekly rate. Some offers include unlimited mileage, while other packages include an additional charge for mileage. Company policy may dictate that the executive rent a

A car may be rented if the executive needs to travel extensively within the destination city. © 1999 Hertz System, Inc.

car no larger than midsize. Prices from rental agencies are determined by the size of the car, and the classifications include:

- full-size (the most expensive)
- mid-size (middle price range)
- economy (the least expensive)

Car Travel

If an executive is traveling 300 miles or less, she or he may prefer to travel by car. Most top level executives have company-owned or leased cars. Some companies also have a motor pool where cars may be signed out to an individual for the duration of the trip. If the executive does not have a company-owned car or access to one for a trip, he or she may drive a personal car and be reimbursed by the company for mileage, or rent a car from an agency.

Your responsibilities for a car trip may include determining the best route to follow, where to stop for the night, and so forth. Although you could use a road map to chart the most direct route to the loca-

tion, many resources are now available to help you do this. A variety of computer software packages are available to plan your trip, or you may use these same types of resources that are available on the Internet. Software packages generally ask for a starting point and a destination as well as the number of days you will be traveling. The software program then provides you with the most direct route to your destination. It will also give you alternate routes that you could use.

It is also important to get good directions to the hotel or motel sites and the meeting locations. If the hotel or motel has a Web site, you could use the Internet to print a map that provides directions to their site. These may also be obtained by calling the sites and asking for specific directions.

Rail Travel

If the executive is traveling short distances, he or she may find it more convenient to take a train than to go by car or by air.

Train stations are generally centrally located, and their fares are usually less expensive than airfares. First-class and sleeping accommodations are available on trains, along with coach accommodations for more economical travel. Dining cars are also available; meals are delivered in first-class accommodations. To find out about train service in your area, look under "Railroads" in the Yellow Pages or call Amtrak.

Hotel Reservations

The *OAG Business Travel Planner*, North America Edition, published by OAG Guides, provides information about hotel and motel accommodations. The publication includes a variety of details on hotel and motel listings such as ratings; prices; number of rooms; phone numbers; and amenities such as cable TV, health clubs, fax service, photocopy service, and meeting rooms.

When arranging for hotel accommodations, specify the preferred room rate, choice of accommodations (king- or queen-size bed), the number of persons registering, date and approximate time of arrival, length of stay, and how the bill will be paid. Most hotels will ask for a credit card number as confirmation. Many hotels now provide entire "no smoking" floors. Ask the hotel about their policies if your employer is concerned about smoke. If the executive is going to arrive late in the day, you will need to make a guaranteed reservation. With such a reservation, the hotel will hold the room until your employer arrives. Otherwise, it is the policy of many hotels to hold the room only until a designated time—around 6 p.m. If your employer will be arriving late, you should request a confirmation number. If the hotel does not have time to mail you a confirmation, they may fax it to you or give you a confirmation number over the phone. This confirmation number or written confirmation should be included on the executive's itinerary in case there is some problem at check-in.

Many hotels now offer rooms that are equipped for the business traveler. These rooms may include specially designed desks, ergonomically correct chairs, two phone lines, and sometimes even a selection of office supplies. Some hotels offer these rooms at the same rate as other rooms, while other hotel chains charge a small additional price. A continental breakfast is often included in the hotel charge.

In addition to a room, the executive may require a suite or meeting rooms at the hotel in which to conduct business or provide professional entertainment. If so, the office professional must be aware of the size of the room needed and any special arrangements that must be made.

International Travel

Today, with many companies conducting business all around the world, it is not uncommon for executives to make trips abroad. As an office professional, you need to know how to make arrangements for an overseas trip.

Cultural Differences

If the executive is planning a trip to a country for the first time, he or she needs information about the customs and cultures of the people. The phrase "ugly American" has come about in part because we have not been sensitive to the customs and cultures of other people as we have traveled in their countries.

Consider these situations in which Americans have made mistakes merely because they did not understand that differences exist.

Situation 1: A president of an American company meets Lo Win Hao, the president of a Chinese company. The American president extends his hand, with a big smile, and says: "Hello, Mr. Hao." The Chinese president quickly knows that the American does not understand much about his culture. In China, the surname comes first and the given name last. The correct approach would have been a reserved, slight bow, and a greeting such as "It is good to meet you, President Lo."

Situation 2: An American visiting Saudi Arabia gives a gift to the president of the company on first meeting him. It is appropriate to give gifts in Saudi Arabia but never on the first meeting; it may be interpreted as a bribe. Gifts should also never be given to the spouse of a business acquaintance; however, gifts for children are enthusiastically welcomed.

Similar situations can occur frequently if a person has not traveled in a particular country. It is wise to study the culture before traveling abroad. Help is

The executive needs to be sensitive to international customs and cultures. © *PhotoDisc, Inc.*

available through travel agencies and books carried by libraries and bookstores. In large cities, consular offices (offices representing the country abroad in the United States and staffed with personnel from the country) are another source of information about customs and cultures. If the company is establishing a new location abroad, it will sometimes conduct seminars for its people. Short seminars may also be available at community colleges or universities. There are some very practical aspects of other cultures that travelers will want to be aware of before traveling to other countries. They include such considerations as:

- What is an appropriate greeting?
- When leaving, what is an appropriate farewell?
- At local restaurants, hotels, and airports, is tipping expected or acceptable? If so, what is the appropriate amount?
- What is the appropriate dress when attending a business function? A banquet? Sightseeing?
- Are there special considerations for a female executive traveling abroad?

Appointments

If you are involved in assisting the executive in setting up appointments, remember to take into consideration time zone differences. **Jet lag** is a true medical condition that results in prolonged periods of fatigue. It upsets metabolism and medication schedules, in addition to eating and sleeping cycles. Because of this, jet lag can greatly restrict an executive's effectiveness. Since it takes the body about a day for each time zone crossed to adapt to the new environment, it is a good idea to give the executive an extra day before meetings begin to recover from the trip.

If the executive does not have the luxury of a full day before scheduling appointments, there are some techniques that will generally help with jet lag. For example, if the executive is traveling west, for two days before the flight he or she should postpone bedtime by two or three hours. If the executive is traveling east, he or she should retire a couple of hours earlier. At the same time, the executive can also start shifting mealtimes in the direction of those of the destination city. The body clock will not be fully adapted to the new time cycle upon landing, but the executive will have made a start in the right direction.

Business Cards

It is a good idea for the executive to take business cards with his or her name, company affiliation, and address in English on one side of the card and in the language of the country visited on the other. Most executives of businesses in other countries have cards and will expect to exchange them with the executive. In Japan, the exchange of business cards is quite a ceremony. The Japanese executive will take time to carefully read the visiting executive's card and then store it in a special case. It is considered rude to simply take the card and put it in your pocket.

Small gifts are also appropriate for business executives—a nice pen or some similar item is usually appropriate. However, before giving any gift, research customs and taboos of the destination country.

Air Travel

International air travel is basically the same as domestic air travel. Classes of flight are the same—first class, business class, and coach. (Coach is also referred to as tourist or economy class.) Weight and size restrictions for luggage may vary slightly from one airline to another.

Passports

A **passport** is an official government document that certifies the identity and citizenship of an individual and grants the person permission to travel abroad. A passport is required in most countries outside the United States. Check with your local travel agent to determine if the country being visited requires a passport.

Passport application forms can be obtained from a travel agency, a passport office, some federal and state courts, some county/municipal offices, and some post offices. You can find your local passport office telephone number by looking under "United States Government, Passport Information" in the government section of your local telephone directory. In order to obtain a passport for the first time, you must appear in person before an authorized agent and present the following items:

- A completed application
- Proof of United States citizenship through a certified copy of a birth certificate, baptismal certificate, or certificate of naturalization. (If such proof is not available, the applicant must submit a notice that no birth record exists and secondary evidence such as census records, family Bibles, school records, or affidavits of persons with personal knowledge of the applicant's birth.)
- Proof of identification through such documents as a valid driver's license, government or military ID, or a previous U.S. passport

- Two identical black-and-white or color 2" x 2" photographs taken by a photographer within the past six months
- The passport fee

It is suggested that you apply for a passport several months in advance of your departure. It is possible to apply for an emergency passport at least five days before your departure. In addition to the items listed above, you will also need to present your tickets or itinerary from an airline and pay an additional fee.

A passport is valid for ten years from the date of issue. As soon as the passport is received, the information requested on the inside cover should be completed and the passport should be signed. While traveling abroad, the passport should always be carried by the traveler. It should never be left in a hotel room.

Visas

A **visa** is a document granted by a government abroad that permits entry and travel within a particular country. A visa usually appears as a stamped notation on a passport indicating that the bearer may enter the country for a certain purpose and period of time. Most countries require a visa, but if you have any doubt as to whether or not a visa is needed, you should contact your travel agency or the consulate for the particular country.

Currency

Money can be exchanged from certain banks and currency exchange offices for the currency of the country being visited before leaving the United States. The rate of exchange for various countries is published in the newspaper. If the executive prefers, he or she may exchange only a small amount of money in the United

International currency. © *PhotoDisc, Inc.*

States and exchange additional money when arriving at the country of destination. If all of the currency has not been used by the end of the trip, it may be exchanged for U.S. currency. It is always a good idea to be aware of the exchange rates before going to the country and to pay attention to the exchange rates once in the country. For example, the exchange rate at a bank may be more favorable than the exchange rate at the airport.

Euro Dollars

On January 1, 1999, the Euro became the standard currency of Belgium, Germany, Spain, France, Ireland, Italy, Luxemburg, the Netherlands, Austria, Portugal, and Finland. In the beginning of 1999, the new monetary unit could be used by consumers and retailers in the form of checks, traveler's checks, bank transfers, credit cards, and electronic purchases. By July 2002, the Euro will gradually displace national currencies in the form of seven Euro notes and eight Euro coins. A businessperson traveling to any of these countries will no longer have to worry about currency exchange. This means business executives will no longer have to pay exchange commissions or waste time on price comparisons or shopping around for the best exchange rate.

Health Precautions

Before leaving for a country abroad, it is smart to check with a physician concerning any vaccines or medical precautions necessary for the particular destination. Keep in mind that the environmental factors are usually different from the ones experienced in the United States, and it is easy to develop some type of illness as a result of food, water, or even the particular climate of the country. A physician may prescribe medications that can be taken to help you recover from stomach-related illnesses or colds. In some countries, it is important that you not drink the water unless it has been boiled or purified in some manner. In these countries, you should rely on bottled water for all activities, including brushing your teeth. Because raw fruit is usually washed in water, another health consideration is to avoid eating raw fruit or vegetables unless they have been peeled. In addition to your physician, travel agents can make suggestions as to precautions you should take when visiting certain countries.

Hotel Reservations

Hotel reservations can be made either through a travel agent, an airline, or directly with the hotel. If secretarial assistance or a meeting room is needed at a hotel abroad, a travel agent can also arrange for these services.

Local Transportation

Once the executive arrives in the country, he or she may need to travel extensively. If so, it may be necessary to rent a car or take advantage of the rail transportation

Car Rental. Cars are readily available for rent. A travel agency can arrange for the rental, or it may be done once the executive arrives in the country. In most countries, a United States driver's license is sufficient. You may obtain an International Driver's License from AAA (American Automobile Association). The telephone number of AAA can be found in your local directory. It is important that the traveler obtain appropriate insurance and become familiar with the driving regulations of the country. Conditions are often quite different from those in the United States—from the side of the car on which the steering wheel is mounted to the speed limits on the highways.

Rail Transportation. Many countries have excellent rail service (particularly in Europe). Service is frequent and relatively inexpensive. A traveler can get from one city in Europe to another in a relatively short period of time with a limited amount of inconvenience. Underground rail transportation within cities such as

London is quite good and an inexpensive way to travel. In addition, bus transportation within large cities is good and inexpensive. Rail passes and special rates are often available in certain countries. Check with the travel agent prior to leaving about special rates. For example, the Eurorail pass cannot be purchased after you arrive in Europe; it must be bought prior to leaving the United States.

Travel Arrangements

Since company policies on making travel arrangements vary, it is important for you to learn the specific procedures followed by the company. Is an outside travel agency used, or is there an in-house travel department? Is the executive expected to make his or her own arrangements? Does the executive have a company credit card? How is the executive reimbursed for travel expenses? Is there a set **per diem** (per day) amount for travel? Is a travel advance granted the executive? Exactly what are your responsibilities in making travel arrangements?

In making travel arrangements, you should obtain the following information from the executive:

- The dates and times for travel
- Cities to be visited; times and locations for appointments or commitments
- Hotel preferences: single or double room, size of bed (double, queen, or king), number of nights, price range, smoking or nonsmoking room or floor
- Car rental: type of car, size, make, model; number of days of usage; pickup and drop-off locations
- Company account number or the executive's credit card number

- Transportation preferences including to the airport or train station—will the executive drive, take a taxi, or use a shuttle service?

     Other items that need to be determined include:

- Appointments—Are there appointments to be made? With whom? When? Where?
- Funds—Is a travel advance needed? If so, how much?
- Materials—Are materials needed for the trip? If so, what and how many copies?
- Person in charge—Who will be in charge while the executive is away?
- Correspondence—How will it be handled while the executive is away?

     If the executive is traveling by air, you should have the following information in addition to that given above:

- Preferred airlines if he or she has one, along with his or her frequent flyer number. (A frequent flyer program is an incentive program offered by most airlines. It provides an opportunity for a variety of awards, including upgrading from coach to first class and free airline tickets after accumulation of a specified number of mileage points. Because of this, you would want to use the frequent flyer airline whenever possible.)
- Class of flight—first class, business class, or coach
- Preference as to aisle or window seat
- Special food preferences—low-calorie meal, low-cholesterol meal, salt-free meal, and any other special needs
- Ticket delivery—Are tickets to be picked up at the airport? Sent by courier? Mailed? (If a travel agency is used, most deliver the tickets to the business.)

- Timeline for arriving at airport—*at least* one hour before the flight departs is standard arrival time for domestic flights and two hours is standard for international flights
- Corporate policies regarding air travel—For example, some organizations require that top executives take different flights even though their destinations may be the same. The reason for this is the fear that the company would be at a loss if there were an accident and all top executives were on the same flight.

     If the office professional is dealing directly with the airlines rather than a travel agency, there is usually a toll-free number listed in the phone book for the airlines.

Travel Agencies

Travel agencies will make all travel arrangements for the executive. They will schedule the flight, obtain tickets, make hotel reservations, and arrange car rental. The agency will also see that airline tickets are delivered to your business. Part of their service includes providing a complete **itinerary,** which gives flight numbers, arrival and departure times of flights, hotel reservations, car rental, and any other arrangements that were requested Figure 17-1 shows an itinerary prepared by a travel agency. Also, travel agencies (through the use of computer software) can give you a list of all airlines leaving at the approximate time the executive wishes to travel and provide an analysis of the lowest fare. Figure 17-2 illustrates the type of information that can be provided. The company can make arrangements with the travel agency to bill directly to the firm, or the travel agency will accept major credit cards.

Marvin Cook

1. CUSTOMER

```
669401  ITINERARY INVOICE
        PAGE NO.  1
INV. NO.    PNR: 1P-7QU4PS
```

FULLER ELAINE DR
2480 SQUARE LAKE RD
BLOOMFIELD HILLS MI 48304

FULLER ELAINE   DR

AGENT	CONTACT	STATEMENT INFO.	ACCOUNT NO.	DATE
		25121720	01"8105"32	15APR93

DAY	DATE	CITY - AIRPORT	TIME	CARRIER	FLIGHT - CLASS STATUS	SERVICE - AMOUNT
A SA	05JUN	LV DETROIT/METRO	450P	NORTHWEST	48H OK	DINNER
	06JUN	AR LONDON/GATWICK	715A			1STOP D10
			SEAT	23-B **RESERVED**		
				FULLER ELAINE .DR		
			SEAT	36-H **RESERVED**		
				FULLER ELAINE .DR		
A TH	10JUN	LV LONDON/GATWICK	1220P	NORTHWEST	49H OK	DINNER
		AR DETROIT/METRO	546P			1STOP 747
			SEAT	35-H **RESERVED**		
				FULLER ELAINE .DR		
			SEAT	23-H **RESERVED**		
				FULLER ELAINE .DR		

```
              TICKET NUMBER(S):  0121512110632

                               AIR FARE               623.00
                               TAX                      20.45
                               TOTAL AIR FARE          643.45
                               AMOUNT                  643.45

THIS AMOUNT WILL BE CHARGED TO CREDIT CARD. AX

FOR EMERGENCY SERVICE AFTER NORMAL HOURS PLEASE CALL
THOMAS COOK AT 1 800-555-4282
THIS RESERVATION HAS BEEN MADE FOR YOU BY PAMELA ROE
HAVE A NICE TRIP.
YOUR MEMBERSHIP ID CODE IS NW-1QS-OAKL
US CITIZEN/VALID PASSPORT
EMERGENCY SERVICE OUTSIDE THE US CALL COLLECT 708-555-6191
CHANGE TO RETURN RSVN/TKT PERMITTED FOR $ 75.00




P8N 00173 04.151552
```

CODE: A-Air H-Hotel T-Tour C-Car S-Surface V-Other Travel Service	CLASS: F, P-First, C, J-Business Class Y, B, H, M, Q, K, S, V, L-Coach/Economy	STATUS: OK-Confirmed TO-Request WL-Wait List

RECONFIRM RETURNING AND CONTINUING RESERVATIONS 72 HOURS IN ADVANCE FOR INTERNATIONAL FLIGHTS AND SUGGEST 48 HOURS IN ADVANCE FOR DOMESTIC FLIGHTS. CAUTION: TICKETS HAVE VALUE. IF UNUSED PLEASE RETURN FOR CREDIT OR REFUND.

FIGURE 17-1. Travel agencies prepare brief itineraries.

Marvin Cook
EXPRESS PLANNER™

For:
COLLEEN FINLAY
MARVIN COOK TRAVEL

Requested By:
COLLEEN FINLAY
313-555-4314

DEPART: *Detroit (Wayne Co), MI to Atlanta, GA*   *Tue, Apr 6 - 9:00a*

Max Penalty Reqested: 100% _____   CONNECTION _____
Class Requested: Coach

	FLIGHT	EQP	DEPART		ARRIVE/DEPART	FLIGHT	EQP	ARRIVE		MEAL	CLS	ON-TIME	TRAVEL TIME
A	DL 201	M80	128a	DTW	——(non-stop)——>			310p	DTW	L	C	6	1:42
B	NW 798	D9S	200p	DTW	——(non-stop)——>			355p	DTW		C	8	1:55
C	TW 774	72S	324p	DTW	——(non-stop)——>			518p	DTW		C	9	1:54
D	DL 490	D9S	400p	DTW	——(non-stop)——>			548p	DTW		C	9	1:48
E	NW 798	767	501p	DTW	——(non-stop)——>			645p	DTW	D	C	3	1:44
F	TW 498	D9S	540p	DTW	——(non-stop)——>			732p	DTW	S	C	8	1:52
G	US 780	D9S	650p	DTW	——(non-stop)——>			845p	DTW	D	C	7	1:55

RETURN: *Atlanta, GA to Detroit (Wayne Co), MI*   *Sun, Apr 11 - 4:00p*

                                  CONNECTION _____

	FLIGHT	EQP	DEPART		ARRIVE/DEPART	FLIGHT	EQP	ARRIVE		MEAL	CLS	ON-TIME	TRAVEL TIME
1	DL 252	M80	128a	ATL	——(non-stop)——>			310p	DTW	L	C	6	1:42
2	NW 798	D9S	200p	ATL	——(non-stop)——>			355p	DTW		C	8	1:55
3	TW 774	72S	324p	ATL	——(non-stop)——>			518p	DTW		C	9	1:54
4	DL 490	D9S	400p	ATL	——(non-stop)——>			548p	DTW		C	9	1:48
5	NW 798	767	501p	ATL	——(non-stop)——>			645p	DTW	D	C	3	1:44
6	TW 498	D9S	540p	ATL	——(non-stop)——>			732p	DTW	S	C	8	1:52
7	US 780	D9S	650p	ATL	——(non-stop)——>			845p	DTW	D	C	7	1:55

FARES: *As of 2:52p CST, the lowest round-trip fare is $196*

	A	A	A	A	A	A	A	RESTRICTION CODES
1	254 ab	490 ac	490 ac	254 ab	490 ac	490 ac	490 ac	CANCEL PENALTY: a = 100%
2	340 ac	*196* ab	340 ac	340 ac	*196* ab	340 ac	340 ac	PURCHASE BY: b = Mar 10 c = Mar 11
3	390 ac	390 ac	216 ab	390 ac	390 ac	216 ab	390 ac	
4	340 ac	*196* ab	340 ac	340 ac	*196* ab	340 ac	340 ac	
5	*196* ab	340 ac	340 ac	*196* ab	340 ac	340 ac	340 ac	
6	340 ac	*196* ab	340 ac	340 ac	*196* ab	340 ac	340 ac	
7	340 ac	340 ac	*196* ab	340 ac	340 ac	*196* ab	340 ac	

AIRLINE & AIRPORT INFO

AIRLINES
DL   *Delta Air Lines*
NW   *Northwest Airline*
TW   *Trans World Airlines*
US   *USAIR*

AIRPORTS
ATL   *Atlanta, GA*
CLT   *Charlotte, NC*
DTW   *Detroit (Wayne Co), MI*

For reservations or further information, contact your Marvin Cook reservation center.
For assistance with Marvin Cook Express, call our Help Desk at 1-800-555-5556.
Fares are subject to actual seat availability at the time of your booking. Fuel / terminal surcharges may apply.

FIGURE 17-2. Travel agencies have access to flight information through computer software.

Ask the travel agency to check with several airlines to determine the least expensive flight available. Airlines are extremely competitive today, and reduced prices are often available. Regardless of the level of the executive's position, he or she is usually interested in the lowest price available. Also ask the travel agency to get the best flight connections possible. Usually, the executive prefers to travel on a direct flight (nonstop) to save time. However, a direct flight may not always be available or the executive may choose to save money by using connecting flights. Another money-saving feature involves the day of the week of travel. For example, if it is convenient for the executive to travel at night or over a Saturday night, special lower prices usually are available. Planning several weeks in advance can also save money since you may be able to take advantage of special offers.

Travel agencies receive commissions from airlines, hotels, and other service industries when they sell services; therefore, the agency generally does not charge a fee to the business for making the travel arrangements. If you ever have the task of helping to select a travel agency for your company, determine which agencies specialize in business travel and get references from other businesses using travel agencies.

Arrangements by the Office Professional

If the executive is expected to make his or her own arrangements, you have a major responsibility. After getting directions from the executive as to trip dates, times, and so forth, you work directly with a specific travel agency the executive wishes to use; with the in-house travel department; or individually with the airlines, hotels or motels, and car rental agencies.

If you are working with individual airlines, you may wish to subscribe to the *Official Airline Guide* published by Official Airline Guides, Inc. Information on fares, schedules, aircraft, and other services is provided in the guide. The guide is available in hard copy format, or an electronic edition is available for use on your computer. Figure 17-3 hows a screen from the electronic edition of the *Official Airline Guide*. Notice on the screen there is a flight from Los Angeles to Washington leaving at 7:10 a.m. from LAX (Los Angeles International Airport) and arriving at DCA (Washington National Airport) at 4:45 p.m. The flight is NW 330; breakfast is served; there is one stop; and the travel time is 6 hours and 35 minutes. (Keep in mind that flight arrival and departure times are given for the local time, which

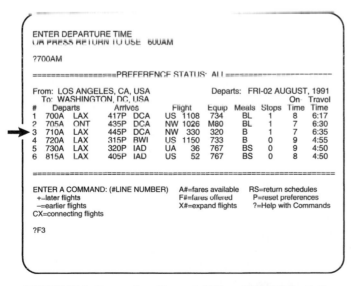

FIGURE 17-3. Screens from Electronic Edition of *Official Airline Guide*

is why this particular flight appears to be 9 hours and 35 minutes.) Airline flights are also available on the Web. You can check the schedules and reserve a flight via the Internet.

You may choose to do much of the travel arranging through the Internet. A variety of sites exist that will allow you to take care of all of your travel needs from one location. These comprehensive sites allow you to make airline reservations, reserve hotel rooms, as well as book rental cars. Some examples of comprehensive sites include:

http://home.netscape.com/travel

http://expedia.com

http://www.lycos.com/shopnet/travel

Specific hotel, car, or airline sites may also be useful to you in making travel arrangements. For example, if your supervisor belongs to a frequent flyer club with a specific airline, you could access that airline's Web site and make reservations. If your supervisor always stays at a Marriott hotel, you can access the site at http://www.marriott.com to make room reservations.

Responsibilities Before the Trip

As you have already learned, you will be involved in helping the executive plan the trip and making the appropriate reservations. Your responsibilities are very important and must be completed carefully. One incorrect flight time or the wrong accommodation at a hotel can cost an executive considerable time and stress.

In addition to the duties already mentioned, there are additional responsibilities you will have. These include:

- Preparing the itinerary
- Obtaining travel funds
- Preparing materials for the trip
- Making calendar notations
- Confirming appointments
- Assembling items for the trip
- Understanding how matters are to be handled while the executive is away

Prepare an Itinerary

The **itinerary** is a must for you and your employer. As you have already learned, the travel agency will prepare a brief itinerary covering items such as flight number and departure and arrival times. This itinerary is helpful, but a comprehensive itinerary that includes appointments, hotel and motel reservations, and helpful reminders, along with the flight information, is invaluable. Figure 17-4 shows a clear, concise itinerary set up in an easy-to-read format. Notice that it includes various time zones since the traveler is going from one time zone to another. If your employer is traveling in only one time zone, you need not include the time zones. Ask your employer if he or she would like additional copies of the itinerary to share with his or her supervisor or family.

As you begin to plan a trip, it is a good idea to set up a travel folder with the location and date of the trip on the label. Place all information that you receive concerning the trip in the folder. When you are ready to prepare the itinerary, you will have all the necessary information in one location. In addition to the itinerary, some executives also want a separate appointment schedule that isolates the appointments on one form. An appointment schedule, as shown in Figure 17-5, provides a quick and easy reference for the executive.

```
                    ITINERARY FOR PAUL FORREST

                        March 5-6, 19--

                      Trip to San Francisco


MONDAY, MARCH 5 (DALLAS TO SAN FRANCISCO)

  9:30 A.M.   CST   Leave Dallas--DFW Regional Airport on American
                    Flight 55 (pick up ticket at airport).

 10:30 a.m.   PST   Arrive San Francisco--San Francisco Interna-
                    tional Airport (pick up rental car at airport;
                    hotel reservations at Hilton, 300 Airport
                    Freeway, telephone: 555-3100).

  2:00 p.m.   PST   Appointment with Peter Nelson of Nelson & Nelson
                    in his office, 1214 Harwood Avenue, telephone:
                    555-5418 (correspondence file in briefcase).


TUESDAY, MARCH 6 (SAN FRANCISCO TO DALLAS)

 10:00 a.m.   PST   Appointment with Roger Hall of San Francisco
                    office (reports in briefcase).

  2:00 p.m.   PST   Appointment with Carla Hampton of San Francisco
                    office (reports in briefcase).

  5:00 p.m.   PST   Leave San Francisco International Airport on
                    American Flight 43.

 10:00 p.m.   CST   Arrive Dallas--DFW Regional Airport.
```

FIGURE 17-4. Itinerary

PAUL FORREST
APPOINTMENT SCHEDULE

City	Date/Time	With	Telephone	Location	Remarks
Chicago	Thursday, April 13, 10:00 a.m.	Max Goldberg	555-5620	Room 212 Oil & Gas Building	Blue folder contains papers for meeting.
Chicago	Friday, April 14, 8:30 a.m.	Betty Martin	555-8900	To be arranged	Call Betty Martin Thursday afternoon to determine meeting locating.

FIGURE 17-5. Appointment Schedule

Obtain Travel Funds

Companies differ as to how the expenses are handled. Some companies give the employees cash advances, along with a company credit card. Other companies expect the employee to pay the bill and submit an expense account for reimbursement. Whatever the company policy, you need to assist the executive in obtaining funds.

Cash Advances. When a cash advance is given, the company will require that some type of request form be submitted to the company business office. There will probably be a limit on how much cash can be obtained. Part of your job is to know company policies—how much cash can be obtained, what procedure is to be followed and what form is to be filled out. You should keep copies of the requests for your records.

Traveler's Checks. Traveler's checks are available from the American Express Company, most banks, and travel agencies. They come in denominations of $10, $20, $50, and $100. Since they must be signed at the time of purchase, the person who will use them must purchase them. Traveler's checks come with two receipts that serve as records of the check's serial numbers. One copy of the receipt should be kept in your files and the other copy should be given to the executive so that if checks are lost, the individual may be reimbursed. The receipts should be kept separately from the checks.

Credit Cards. Some companies issue company credit cards to executives. Other executives use their personal credit cards and are reimbursed by the company. Cards such as VISA, American Express, and MasterCard are accepted by most businesses in the United States and abroad. You may be responsible for requesting new credit cards when old ones expire and keeping a record of the credit card numbers. If a credit card is lost or stolen, it is important that the credit card company be notified immediately. To do so, you need to have the credit card number readily available.

Prepare Materials for the Trip

Your employer may need to take business correspondence on a trip. If so, it is a good idea to supply just the necessary copies rather than the entire file folder. By making copies of the correspondence, you retain the original files in the office in case they are needed in your employer's absence.

The executive may also want to take a laptop computer on the trip. If so, make sure that files and programs needed are loaded on the computer. Although computers may be used on planes, there is a period of time on takeoff and landing that the attendants ask that computers not be used. Most executives carry a phone card with them to save on phone costs; you might check to see that the executive has the card. Make sure to include any necessary office supplies that your employer may need while he or she is away, including folders, paper clips, and extra business cards. You may also provide the executive with a list of telephone numbers of people he or she may need to contact while away.

Check the Calendar

Check your employer's electronic calendar and your desk calendar to see if appointments have been scheduled for the period in which your employer will be gone. If so, find out if they are to be canceled or if someone else in the company will handle them. Then notify the people involved. Also check other files such as tickler files or pending files to see if there are matters that should be handled before the executive leaves.

Confirm Appointments for the Trip

Write or call persons whom your employer plans to see during the trip to confirm the appointments. It is wise to do this before preparing the itinerary. Get correct addresses and directions from the hotel to the location of the meeting; make a note of these addresses and directions on the itinerary.

Assemble Items for the Trip

Various items are needed for a trip. A representative list includes the following:

- Plane tickets
- Copy of itinerary
- Travel money, credit cards, phone cards
- Business cards
- Office supplies
- Hotel confirmations
- Copies of correspondence, speeches, and so forth
- Information on companies to be visited
- Reading materials

Know How Matters Are to Be Handled

Find out who will be in charge during your employer's absence. Check to see if your employer is expecting any important papers that should be forwarded. Be sure you understand how to handle all the incoming mail (both electronic mail and traditional mail) and other daily duties.

Responsibilities While Employer Is Away

You have worked hard and efficiently to facilitate your employer's departure. What happens now? Is it playtime for you? Not quite. Your pace may moderate slightly while your employer is out of the office, or it may accelerate. Your responsibility is to handle the office routine smoothly and efficiently during your employer's absence. Your employer may want to set up a date and/or time when she or he will be checking in with you. In this way, you and your employer can discuss anything that needs to be addressed before the employer returns.

Handle Correspondence

There may be correspondence that you will need to forward to your employer. It is a good idea to send copies of the correspondence rather than the original; keep the original in your files.

Answer any routine mail that you can. If you receive mail that needs immediate attention but that you are unable to handle, you can usually refer it to someone else in the office (after you have made a copy for your files) who has been designated by your employer. This person should furnish you with a file copy of the reply so that your employer will be informed as to how the matter was handled. If you are not sure how to handle something and you know your employer will be checking in with you at a specific time, you may want to ask your employer for specific instructions. In addition, you may be required to check your employer's email while he or she is away and respond when appropriate.

Make Decisions

You have the responsibility of making wise decisions within the scope of your responsibility during your employer's absence. You should know which matters to refer to someone else in the company and which matters to refer directly to your employer through a telephone call or fax. Certainly you do not want to place an excessive number of calls to your employer while she or he is away. But there may be matters that your employer must be informed of immediately. Your responsibility is to make the appropriate decisions.

Keep a Record of Visitors and Telephone Calls

It is important to keep a log of individuals who have visited or telephoned for your employer during his or her absence. When your employer comes back to the office, you do not have to relay all the information verbally—you can merely have the log available for review. An example of such a log is shown in Figure 17-6.

PAUL FORREST
VISITORS AND TELEPHONE CALLS

March 5-6, 19--

Date/Time	Visitor	Telephone	Reason for Call	Action
March 5 8:45 a.m.	Reese Vaughn Maxwell & Co.		Personal	Told him you would be back Wednesday and suggested he call you Friday
March 5 9:00 a.m.		Martin Steel 555-5118	Expansion plans	Will call Friday
March 5 9:30 a.m.	Clara Campbell Allhome Insurance		Insurance policy	Will telephone for appointment on Thursday
March 5 9:42 a.m.		Connie Novak Ext. 345	Marketing report	Referred her to Carl Quinn

FIGURE 17-6. Visitors and Telephone Call Log

Set Up Appointments

While your employer is away, you will probably need to set up appointments for persons who want to see your employer after the trip. Remember, when you are setting up the appointments, your employer will probably already have a full day of work in the office to handle on the first day back. Thus, it is not a good idea to schedule appointments for that day. If you must do so, however, remember to schedule as few appointments as possible and to keep the timing convenient for your employer.

Use Time Wisely

Assume that you have handled all routine correspondence and all special matters. Your workday is from 8 a.m. to 5 p.m., and it is now 2 p.m. What should you do? There are many things that you can catch up on while your employer is away—filing, transferring inactive files, replacing file folders, or a number of other tasks.

What about your employer's desk? Do things need to be straightened? Don't indiscriminately throw things in the trash. The key is to straighten the desk—not to clean out and discard everything in sight.

Do you know what is happening in the company? Now is a good time to read company publications, to acquaint yourself with any new products, any newly acquired subsidiaries, and so on. You can use this time to review general business and economic conditions in magazines like *Forbes*, *Business Week*, or *Fortune*.

An efficient office professional does not waste time. Every minute is utilized. There is always something you can do to

Office professionals use time efficiently and wisely to catch up on paperwork. © PhotoDisc, Inc.

increase your own personal knowledge and efficiency.

Duties When the Executive Returns

Once your employer returns from a trip, there are a number of tasks that must be accomplished. For example, an expense report is filled out and correspondence related to the trip is handled.

Expense Reports

Regardless of whether your employer received funds in advance from the company or used personal funds for which he or she will be reimbursed, careful records must be kept of all expenses. Most companies require receipts for hotels, registration fees, car rental, plane tickets, and other major expenses. The traveler's word is usually taken for meals, taxi fares, and tips under $25. Obviously, you and the executive need to know the company's policy before he or she travels.

Expense forms are provided by the company and should be filled in correctly with the amounts totaled. An example of an expense report is shown in Figure 17-7. You should key the expense report carefully, double-checking all figures and totals. You should also be certain that the necessary receipts are attached and that the figures on the expense report match those on the receipts.

Correspondence

Your employer will probably need to write several thank-you and follow-up letters as a result of contacts made on the trip. These letters may be dictated to you, or you may have the responsibility of composing some of the letters with your employer indicating to you what should be said.

ENTER ONLY ONE AMOUNT PER LINE, PER DAY.

Raython, Incorporated — WEEKLY EXPENSE REPORT

NAME: Paul Forrest
SAVE NO.
ENDING SPEEDOMETER
CHANGED DRIVER'S LICENSE NO.
TR. NO.

WEEK ENDING SATURDAY May 12		SUNDAY	MONDAY	TUESDAY	WEDNESDAY	THURSDAY	FRIDAY	SATURDAY	TOTALS
PERSONAL MOTEL OR HOTEL	Hollaran Inn								
CITY	Chicago								
STATE	Illinois								
ROOM CHARGE (ATTACH RECEIPT)	11		110 00	110 00					220 00
BREAKFAST			7 00	6 00	6 50				
LUNCH			8 00	15 00	11 50				
DINNER			12 00	-15 00	15 00				
TOTAL MEALS	12		27 00	36 00	31 00				94 00
OTHER PERSONAL	13								
COMPANY OWNED AUTOMOBILE GAS-OIL	14								
OTHER OPERATING (INCLUDE PARKING, TOLLS, TAXES, AND FEES)	15		8 00	15 00					23 00
PARTS AND REPAIRS	16								
MISCELLANEOUS ENTERTAINMENT (EXPLAIN-ATTACH RECEIPT IF OVER $25.00)	17								
OTHER TRANSPORTATION (INCLUDE USE OF PERSONAL CAR)	18								
MISC. OTHER (EXPLAIN-ATTACH RECEIPT IF OVER $25.00)	19								
TOTAL FOR DAY			145 00	161 00	31 00				EXPENSES 337 00

EXPLAIN OF ENTERTAINMENT AND MISCELLANEOUS:

INCREASE MY ADVANCE	21	
DECREASE MY ADVANCE	22	
ISSUE CHECK	23	337 00

TRAVELER'S SIGNATURE _Paul Forrest_

FIGURE 17-7. Expense Report

SUMMARY

To reinforce what you have learned in this chapter, study this summary.

- Practically all business travel over long distances is by air. Travel over short distances may be made by car or by train.

- The two basic flight classifications are first class and coach, with a third option—business class—offered on some flights.

- In addition to making flight reservations, the office professional usually is responsible for making hotel and transportation arrangements once the executive has arrived at his or her destination.

- Due to our global economy, executives travel abroad fairly extensively. When making international travel arrangements to a country not previously visited, cultural differences should be researched. Passports are usually needed for travel abroad, and a visa may also be needed. Money may either be exchanged in the United States or at the airport, hotels, or banks when reaching the destination.

- Travel arrangements are usually made through a travel agency or by the office professional.

- The office professional's responsibilities before the trip include:
  - Arranging for all flight, hotel, and car reservations
  - Preparing an itinerary
  - Obtaining travel funds
  - Preparing materials for the trip
  - Checking the calendar and tickler files for matters that need to be handled before the executive leaves or for appointments that must be canceled
  - Confirming appointments for the trip
  - Assembling items for the trip
  - Understanding how to handle matters while the executive is away

- The office professional's responsibilities while the employer is away include:
  - Handling correspondence
  - Making decisions
  - Keeping a record of visitors and telephone calls
  - Setting up appointments
  - Using time wisely

- The office professional's responsibilities when the employer returns include:
  - Preparing expense reports
  - Handling correspondence

Key Terms

- Jet lag
- Passport
- Visa
- Per diem
- Itinerary

Professional Pointers

The world is a global marketplace. International trade and investment among businesses is greater today than ever before. Traveling to other countries for business purposes or hosting foreign business representatives in your own country often requires the presentation of a gift. It is important to understand the cultural or religious customs of a customer or business associate who is a native of a foreign country.

These examples illustrate the necessity of learning about culture and customs of different countries.

- In Japan, gifts of less than 10 items should be presented in odd numbers. The numbers "4" and "9" to many Japanese are synonymous with death and suffering; therefore, avoid gifts or mementos bearing those numbers.
- Giving food items requires special caution. Certain cultures do not eat many of the meats that Americans enjoy. Members of the Hindu religion of India do not consume beef, for example, since cows are considered sacred.
- A gift of chrysanthemums in Italy would symbolize mourning. Likewise, the color purple in Italy signifies death.
- Do not write your gift card to a Chinese person in red ink. Using red ink means that you wish to dissolve a friendship.
- A gift of a family portrait to a Moslem may not be received in the manner in which it was given. In the Arab world, one's family is very private.

Office Procedures Reinforcement

1. Describe the advantages of joining an airline club.
2. Describe the responsibilities of the office professional if the executive is traveling by car.
3. What kinds of information are necessary when making hotel reservations?
4. Name and explain five considerations for international travel.
5. What is an itinerary, and what should it include?

Critical Thinking Activity

Brad Venditti recently accepted his first full-time position as an office support technician; he has been working for two months. Last week Brad's employer, Judith Harris, asked him to make arrangements for her to go to Orlando. Brad received the necessary travel information from Ms. Harris and made the flight reservations. Ms. Harris requested a rental car for three days while in Florida. She indicated that she had three appointments scheduled. She left the names of the people she was seeing and the times of the appointments.

Brad handed Ms. Harris a handwritten list that included flight numbers, times, and dates of the departure and return flights. Ms. Harris took one look at the list and asked why the appointments had not been included. She asked if this was his idea of an itinerary. Brad admitted that he did not realize that Ms. Harris would need anything but the flight information and that he really did not know how to prepare an itinerary.

When Ms. Harris arrived at the airport in Orlando, she called Brad and told him that the rental car agency had no record of the booking. Brad was afraid at that point to tell Ms. Harris that he had forgotten to make the arrangements, so he led her to believe that the car rental agency had made the mistake.

While Ms. Harris was away, Brad thought he didn't have any office work to do, so he read a book most of the time. Several of the employees remarked about "having it made" to Brad, and he felt relieved to have some quiet time without his employer around.

When Ms. Harris returned from Florida, she found that the mail had not been sorted, nor did she have a record of who had called or visited the office. Ms. Harris told Brad that his job was in jeopardy if his work did not improve.

1. How should Brad have prepared for Ms. Harris's trip?
2. What should Brad have done while Ms. Harris was away?
3. What can Brad do to improve the impression his employer has of him and his work?

Office Applications

OA 17-1 (Goal 1)

A group of five executives (three men and two women) from your company will travel to France and Germany to investigate opportunities for expansion of the company's operations. The cities they will visit are Paris and Frankfurt. You will assist one of the travel team members, Juan Menendez, who is responsible for handling the trip's arrangements. In a group of three to five classmates, choose one of the countries planned for the trip, and research its customs and culture. Make a list of the steps you suggest are necessary in preparing for this trip. Prepare one written report for the group (citing all references used). The report should include the current exchange rate, visa/passport requirements, travel restrictions, an appropriate gift to take, time zone differences, airlines from your area that serve the country, recommended ground transportation, and any current events that may be of political or economic interest to the visiting group. The group should make an oral presentation to the class on its report.

OA 17-2 (Goals 1 and 2)

Your supervisor, Juan Menendez, will be traveling to Chicago from a meeting in Richmond, Virginia, January 21–23. Use the following information to prepare an itinerary for his trip.

- Mr. Menendez will leave Richmond Airport on US Air Flight 253 at 7:35 a.m. He will arrive in Pittsburgh at 8:50 a.m. and will board US Air Flight 307 to Chicago at 9:35 a.m. Breakfast will be served on this flight. He will arrive in Chicago at O'Hare Airport at 10:15.

- For his return flight, Mr. Menendez will leave Chicago from O'Hare Airport on US Air Flight 1708 at 12:30 p.m. He will arrive in Detroit at 12:44 p.m.

- Mr. Menendez has rented a car from Budgett Car Rental to be used while in Chicago. His confirmation number is 235292.

- Mr. Menendez has reservations at Downtown's Central Plaza for January 21 and 22. His hotel confirmation number is AR452038.

- Mr. Menendez has a variety of appointments while in Chicago. On January 21 he will have lunch with Kellouy Men Ho of Mendelsohn Machinery and a business meeting with Ho from 3–5 p.m. On January 22, Mr. Menendez has a meeting with Ken Martinez, of Martinez Machinery, at 9 a.m. He will make a presentation to the Board of Directors of Martinez at 2 p.m. That evening (7 p.m.) he will be a guest of Martinez and Fred Yousef for dinner and the opera. On January 23, Mr. Menendez has a breakfast meeting (8 a.m.) in the hotel restaurant with Jeana Boziki of Rivers Corporation.

- Mr. Menendez has an appointment on January 23 when he returns from Chicago. He will meet with Dr. Barnardski at 3:30 p.m. in his office.

OA 17-3 (Goal 3)

In your Applications Workbook, page 111, is the form to be used in recording travel expenses. Using the expenses itemized on pages 112–113 of your Applications Workbook, complete the travel reimbursement form for Mr. Menendez. His airfare was $645, and a travel advance of $500 was received for his trip.

Online Research Applications

ORA 17-4 (Goals 1 and 2)

Choose a city within the United States to visit for one week. You will be driving to this city, and while you are there you will visit some of the local attractions. As a part of this project, you will need to complete the following:

1. Use one of the map services available on the Internet to print driving directions from your home to the destination. A variety of these services are available. You may want to use one of the following:

   http://www.mapquest.com

   http://www.lycos.com/roadmap.html

   http://mapblast.com

2. Find hotel accommodations on the Internet. Determine the location of the hotel and a description of the services they provide.

3. Find one specialty restaurant that you would like to visit while in the city. Include the name of the restaurant, types of meals they offer, and price ranges.

4. Find at least three local attractions to visit. Include the name of the attraction, a description of it, hours of operation, and admission price.

   Prepare a written report for your instructor that includes a printed copy of the driving directions, an itinerary for the trip, and descriptions of the items listed above.

ORA 17-5 (Goal 1)

Using the same destination listed above, search the Internet to find airline flights to the city you chose above. Find at least two flights that will get you from your home city to your destination. Compare the two flights and determine which one you would choose. Prepare a memo to your instructor listing the two options and indicating which flight schedule you would choose and why.

ORA 17-6 (Goal 2)

Using the information obtained in 17-4 and 17-5, prepare an itinerary of the trip that you have planned. Turn a printed copy of this itinerary in to your instructor.

CHAPTER 18

Financial Documents

The office professional's responsibilities in providing financial assistance vary depending on the scope of the job and the size of the company. All companies keep banking, accounting, payroll, investment, and insurance records. If the company is large, there are special units that handle these functions. If the company is small, there may be an accounting or bookkeeping department that handles most of them. However, a general knowledge of financial transactions will be helpful to you in understanding the operations of a company. Such knowledge also will be helpful to you in keeping your own personal records.

In this chapter you will learn:

- How consumers and the banking industry are affected by electronic technology
- The types of banking documents used in business
- The types of financial statements used in business
- How payroll laws and taxes affect accounting documents

YOUR GOALS

Your goals as you study this chapter are to learn to:

1. Describe electronic technology used in the banking industry.

2. Explain the basic financial statements and the various parts of the statements; prepare the following types of banking documents:

   • Checks

   • Deposit slips

   • Bank statement reconciliation

3. Explain payroll and other tax laws

4. Define basic investment instruments and terminology

Electronic Banking

The most important change in the banking industry in the last few years has been in the use of electronic technology. Today, numerous banking transactions can be performed electronically. Customers can obtain money, transfer funds from one account to another, deposit money, and pay bills without the use of checks or the services of bank personnel. These services are performed through **electronic fund transfers (EFTs).** Simply stated, with the use of computers, money can be moved from one account to another electronically—without the need for checks or any other written form of payment. EFT services are available in many forms; some of the main forms are discussed in the following sections.

Automated Teller Machines (ATMs)

Traditional **automated teller machines (ATMs)** allow a customer to obtain cash, make deposits, transfer funds, and pay for purchases without writing a check or going to a bank. Shopping malls and supermarkets are popular locations for ATMs. The ATM market now includes college campuses, hospitals, movie theaters, and cruise ships, to name a few.

To use an ATM, you insert an EFT card (a magnetically encoded plastic card similar to a credit card) into the terminal, enter your secret password or **personal identification number (PIN),** and make the desired transaction. The terminal, which is connected to a computer at another location, may serve a bank that is across the street or miles away.

Multifunction ATMs, sometimes called **new technology ATMs (NT-ATMs),**

Automatic Teller Machine. © *PhotoDisc, Inc.*

are now becoming popular. In addition to performing the traditional functions of an ATM, these new machines can communicate in languages other than English and perform 150 functions. Customers can buy traveler's checks, pay bills, and monitor three months' worth of activity on a variety of accounts. In addition to providing service far faster than the previous technology, some NT-ATMs will sell stamps, cash checks to the penny, give cash back on check deposits, or print and bind checkbooks. Customers with brokerage accounts can use NT-ATMs to make stock trades, look up stock quotes, or invest in mutual funds. The goal of ATM equipment continues to be to allow the customer to conduct as much of his or her banking needs as possible without ever entering the bank branch.

Sophisticated Kiosks

Sophisticated Kiosks are another vehicle being presented by the banking industry to assist consumers in completing their banking transactions without ever having to enter a bank. A sophisticated kiosk may include interactive video, telephone, electronic capture of signatures, and imaging in addition to a "regular" ATM. Sophisticated kiosks offer basic services such as balance inquiries, money transfers, and check clearing statements. In addition, they may assist consumers in completing other transactions such as opening accounts and issuing cashier's checks, money orders, and loans.

Debit Cards (Bank Cards)

Debit cards are a type of automated payment of bills. Debit cards are accepted by most merchants who will accept credit cards. Rather than writing a check for a particular purchase, you merely present your debit card to the merchant. The money is transferred from your bank account to the merchant's account. Debit cards can also be used at ATMs to make deposits, cash withdrawals, and transfer money from one account to another. Debit card transactions appear on your monthly bank statement.

There are two types of debit cards: online and offline. Online debit cards require the use of a PIN to initiate the transaction. With this system, online debit transactions are sent through ATM net-

Debit cards can be used instead of writing a check. © *PhotoDisc, Inc.*

works and subtract funds from accounts immediately. Offline debit cards are very similar to credit cards; in fact, the transactions flow over the credit card network. With offline debit cards, the transactions are not immediate; they usually require a few days to settle or for the payment to transfer.

Debit cards provide advantages for all parties involved. For the consumer, they provide a convenient and safe way to make purchases without having to carry cash or checks. For the merchant, they lower the costs associated with bank deposits and check processing, make the funds available earlier, and decrease the number of bad checks. Banks that use a debit card system see a reduction in checks, lower transaction costs, and the opportunity to provide a wider range of services to their customers.

Smart Cards (Stored Value Cards)

Smart cards, or stored value cards, are an alternative method of paying for business transactions. These types of cards are being used at colleges, at libraries, and in the transportation and hospitality industries. Some of these **stored value cards,** such as prepaid phone cards, are disposable. This means that after the monetary value of the card has been used, they can be thrown away. Other systems use permanent (or reloadable) cards. In this type of system, individuals must access a special machine that will accept cash and convert it to stored value on the smart card. For example, a permanent card allows consumers to add value to the card as often as they wish. This type of system is similar to a debit card and has been used in a variety of college settings. Students or employees can load monetary value on their card and then use it at a variety of locations within the system just as they would cash or checks.

Smart cards may work within an open or closed system. With a closed system, purchases are restricted to a single merchant or a limited number of merchants, and there is limited flexibility. A

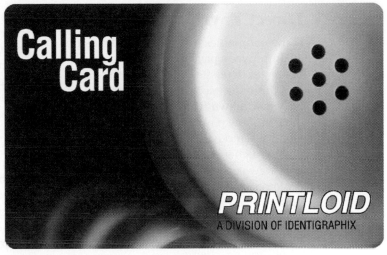

Smart cards can include a computer chip that can store a variety of types of information. *Printloid Division of IdentiGraphix.*

closed system card is often used by the transportation system where the card is used only for a specific type of transportation within a city or area.

With an open system, multiple merchants may participate in the program, providing more flexibility to the consumer. An open system is often used in a college setting. In this setting, students can use a smart card at local retailers instead of carrying cash or checks. The retailer accepts the smart card for payment, and the amount of purchase is automatically deducted from the chip on the card. Retailers are paid through the bank that issues the card.

The use of smart cards, which include a computer chip that can store a variety of types of information including your current bank balance, your medical history, and so forth, is increasing. It is expected that smart cards will be used more extensively in the future.

Direct Payroll Depositing

Many companies provide direct deposit of an employee's paycheck. The employee's net pay is deposited directly into the employee's bank account and is automatically withdrawn from the bank account of the company paying the employee. The employee receives a paper stub or computer voucher showing taxes and other withdrawals as well as the amount deposited to the employee's account. Some of the advantages of direct payroll depositing to the employer are:

- Eliminates the time and expense of writing paychecks
- Lowers security needed in processing and distributing vouchers as opposed to checks
- Reduces postage by not mailing checks
- Decreases the possible loss or theft of paychecks

    Advantages to the employee are:

- Convenience—not necessary to drive to the bank or wait in line to make a deposit.
- Provides for the payroll check to be deposited in the bank even when the employee is on vacation or on a business trip

    In the United States, EFT 99, a provision of the Debt Collect Improvement Act of 1996, required that the majority of federal government payments be made by electronic funds transfer instead of checks. The deadline for the large majority of government programs to convert to electronic systems is 2002. Many instances of electronic payment currently exist. For example, electronic payment is made to companies that provide goods or services to the federal government, and direct deposit of checks has been implemented in a variety of government programs including social security. Under this program, the federal government will deposit social security payments directly to the recipient's bank account rather than preparing and mailing a check.

Direct Withdrawals

Businesses and individuals can also authorize banks or credit unions to withdraw money automatically from their accounts. For example, you can arrange to have house payments, insurance premiums, investments, utilities, and other types of recurring withdrawals made automatically each month by the bank so you do not have to write a check.

Computer Systems and Software Packages

Some banks and other financial institutions also offer computer systems that allow you to handle financial transactions such as:

- Transferring money between accounts
- Checking your checking/savings account balance
- Determining what checks have cleared
- Making a loan payment or other financial transactions

In order to perform these functions, you must have a microcomputer with a modem.

    Software packages are also available that allow you to pay your bills and to balance your checkbook. These packages are available for a nominal amount and can save you considerable time and postage if you have a number of bills to pay each month.

Loss of EFT Card

If your EFT card is lost or stolen, you must immediately report this loss to the financial institution that issued your card. If you report this loss and someone else successfully uses your card, you will not be responsible for more than a small amount of money taken from your account. However, if you fail to notify the bank within two business days, your liability increases tremendously. Thus, it is prudent to notify your bank immediately upon the loss of your card.

The Future of Electronic Banking

Although banking experts agree that the paper check and other forms of paper banking will still be with us in the year 2005, the use of EFTs is expected to increase because of cost savings for the financial institution and increased convenience for the customer. Also, as individuals continue to acquire microcomputers for the home and use the Internet, it is expected that more and more banking transactions and shopping will be done from the convenience of the home. In addition, echecks, the electronic equivalent of a paper check, will become more visible. An echeck contains the same information that is found on a paper check, except it is emailed to the recipient, who in turn electronically endorses the check and deposits it in an account at the bank. At this time there are only a few commercial banks that participate in handling echecks, but that number is expected to continue to increase.

Banking Records and Procedures

Checks

Since checks remain a viable method of transferring funds, you need to understand how to write them properly. Although you may have been writing checks for a number of years, there are consistent procedures that should be followed and are often ignored or not understood. These procedures are presented here.

A check represents an order by the depositor directing the bank to pay money to a designated person or firm. The person or business who orders the bank to pay cash from the account is the **drawer**. The person or business to whom a check is made payable is the **payee**.

In most companies, employees' checks are computer originated. For example, payroll information concerning the number of hours per week an employee has worked, the rate of pay, the deductions to be withheld, and so forth are fed into a computer. The computer then computes the amount to be paid and prints the check or directly deposits the check and sends the employee a voucher. Companies may still prepare some checks manually, however. Also, you will probably write a number of checks personally. When writing checks, these steps should be followed:

1. The check voucher, stub, or register should be filled out first with the date, amount, and purpose of the check. Most companies use a **voucher check**, which has a detachable slip on which the information is recorded (Figure 18-1). A **check carbon** is a carbon

EASTERN PRODUCTS CORPORATION
511 PACIFIC ROAD
DALLAS, TEXAS 75201–7255

NO. 2071

DATE August 7, 20 02

PAY Three hundred forty-seven and 90/100 -- **DOLLARS $** 347.90

TO THE ORDER OF Topcraft Equipment Company
5909 East Colfax Drive
Denver, Colorado 80220–8120

SPECIMEN

EASTERN PRODUCTS CORPORATION

Russel B. Jones

NATIONAL SAVINGS BANK
DALLAS, TEXAS 73211–7201

⑆3 11000 561⑆ 137‴ 10162‴

EASTERN PRODUCTS CORPORATION
511 PACIFIC ROAD
DALLAS, TEXAS 75201–7255

DETACH AND RETAIN THIS STATEMENT
THE ATTACHED CHECK IS IN PAYMENT OF ITEMS DESCRIBED BELOW

	DATE	DESCRIPTION	GROSS AMOUNT	DEDUCTIONS	NET AMOUNT	
	7/3/2002	Invoice #4608	86.97		86.97	
	7/18/2002	Invoice #5087	265.14	4.21	260.93	
					347.90	

FIGURE 18-1. Voucher Check.

copy attached to the original check. The carbon is attached to the spine of the checkbook after the check has been detached (Figure 18-2). A **check register** is a separate form for recording the checks written as well as the deposits made (Figure 18-3). The check carbon and check register are used more frequently for personal transactions, whereas the voucher check is the principal type of check used for business transactions.

2. The date should be entered in the space provided on the check.
3. The name of the payee should be written in full and as far as possible to the left in the space provided. If the name does not fill the entire space, draw a line through the excess space.
4. The amount of the check must be written twice. It is first written in figures after the dollar sign. The figures should be placed as close as possible to the printed dollar sign so that no additional figures can be inserted. The amount of the check is then written on the following line with the words for the dollar amount and figures for the cents. Express cents in fractions of 100. The words should be started as far as possible to the left. If the written amount does not fill the entire space, draw a line through the excess space. If you are writing a check for less than $1, circle the amount written in figures and write "Only" before the spelled out amount.

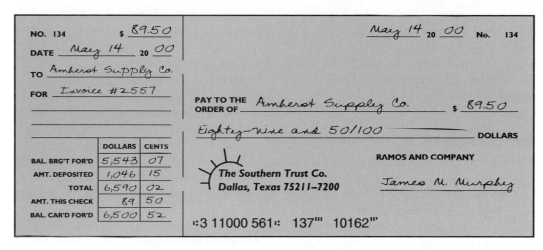

FIGURE 18-2. Check with attached stub.

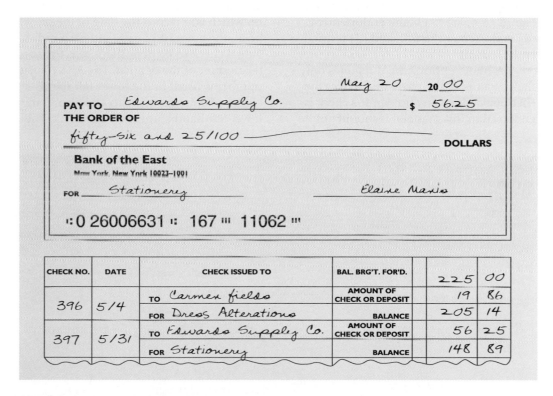

FIGURE 18-3. Check with separate register.

Erasures or changes should be avoided in writing checks. If a mistake is made, write "void" across the face of the check and in the check voucher or register. Do not throw the voided check away; keep it for your records.

Endorsements

An **endorsement** is a written signature by the holder of a check for the purpose of transferring ownership. The endorsement must be written on the back of the check within 1-1/2" from the edge of the check. A rubber stamp endorsement may be used if the check is to be deposited only and not transferred to someone else. The common types of endorsements, as shown in Figure 18-4, are (1) blank endorsement, (2) endorsement in full, and (3) restrictive endorsement.

A **blank endorsement** requires only the signature of the payee and makes the check payable to any holder. If a check is endorsed in this manner, it should not be sent through the mail since anyone can cash it. An **endorsement in full** transfers ownership to another person or business. The name of the person to whom the check is transferred is written before the endorser's signature. When a check is endorsed in this manner, it cannot be cashed without the specified payee's signature. A **restrictive endorsement** transfers ownership for a specific purpose. If you are sending a check through the mail for deposit, a restrictive endorsement should be used.

Deposits

You may make deposits to your company's account or to your own personal account. The bank provides deposit slips on which you record the date of the deposit, the amount of cash and each individual check to be deposited, plus the total amount of the deposit. The ABA transit number is listed in the lower left-hand corner of your deposit slip and also in the lower left-hand corner of your check. The

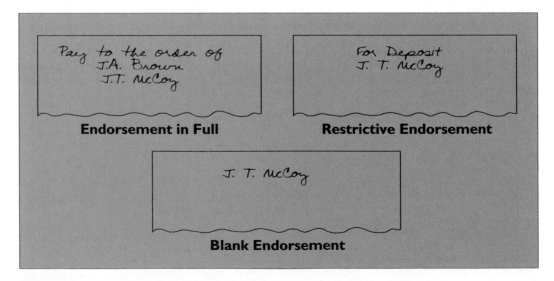

Endorsement in Full

Restrictive Endorsement

Blank Endorsement

FIGURE 18-4. Endorsements.

WITHDRAWAL ⟨⟨========⟩⟩	DEPOSIT				
National Computer Corp. 780 Purant Avenue Grand Rapids MI 49501–2422	CASH	CURRENCY	500	00	74–5/724
		COIN			
	CHECKS LIST SINGLY		2,505	00	
DATE _7-31_ 20 _02_ $ _____ AMOUNT WITHDRAWN			1,682	00	
_____ DOLLARS	TOTAL FROM OTHER SIDE				USE OTHER SIDE FOR ADDITIONAL LISTING
	TOTAL		4,687	00	
SIGN HERE: _____	LESS CASH RECEIVED				BE SURE EACH ITEM IS PROPERLY ENDORSED
	NET DEPOSIT		4,687	00	

OLD TRENT
Old Trent Bank
812 Monroe Street NW.
Grand Rapids, MI 49503–2406

⑆072400052⑆ 6511320111⑈

FIGURE 18-5. Deposit slip.

first set of numbers is the transit number. The next set of numbers is your account number, followed by your check number. If you do not have preprinted deposit slips, you will be asked to record the transit number of your bank on your deposit slip. This number identifies your bank and the Federal Reserve number, which is issued to individual banks by the Federal Reserve. Figure 18-5 shows a properly filled out deposit slip, with the ABA transit number, the customer's account number, and the customer's check number preprinted in the lower left-hand corner.

Make sure that the name of the payee is written on all checks being deposited. If it is not on the check, write it or use a stamp (many businesses have stamps with the company name). Also, make sure that the checks are endorsed properly. A stamped or handwritten endorsement may be made.

Checks and deposit slips are deposited electronically. In order to aid in this electronic processing, the bank's transit number (mentioned earlier), the depositor's account number and the check number are preprinted in magnetic ink characters in a uniform position at the bottom of the checks and deposit slips. Notice the characters on the deposit slip in Figure 18-5. When a check or deposit slip is received at the bank, the amount, the date, and other information are also recorded electronically. Optical character recognition (OCR) equipment sorts the checks and deposit slips and posts the correct amount to the depositor's account.

Bank Reconciliation

Each month banks usually send depositors a statement showing deposits, withdrawals, and changes in connection with their checking and savings accounts. Since the bank statement balance and the checkbook or savings account balance may not be equal, a reconciliation is made to account for the difference and to correct any errors.

Follow these procedures in reconciling the bank statement for the checking account.

1. Look at the check register or stubs to see that all check amounts have been deducted from the preceding balances and that all deposit amounts have been entered and added to the balance.

2. Some banks do not return the checks but use **check truncation** (also referred to as **check retention** or **check safekeeping**). Instead, you get a monthly statement listing the number and amount of each check that has been cashed. You may request a copy of a check you need, or you may use a checkbook in which you automatically make carbon copies of each check.

3. Verify the number of the check on the bank statement with the check register or check stub by placing a check mark on the register.

4. On a separate piece of paper (the bank statement usually provides a form on the back), list the numbers and amounts of the checks that are outstanding. An outstanding check is an issued check that has not yet been cashed by the bank or deducted from the depositor's bank account. Total the outstanding checks.

5. Add the total unlisted deposits to the bank balance.

6. Deduct the total amount of the outstanding checks from the balance shown on the bank statement.

7. Add to the checkbook balance any interest earned in the checking account or any items collected by the bank such as notes receivable. (Banks today offer interest-bearing checking accounts in which interest is paid on the average daily balance of the account.)

8. Deduct from the checkbook balance any service charges or special fees. If there are any charges, they will be shown as separate deductions on the bank statement. The checkbook balance and the balance on the bank statement should now agree.

9. If the reconciliation does not balance after a careful verification, the discrepancy should be brought to the attention of the bank. Errors are seldom traced to faulty bookkeeping by the bank, however. They are usually due to such things as incorrect additions or subtractions in the checkbook, failure to record written checks, failure to add deposits, or transposition errors.

Before notifying the bank of a possible error, take these steps:

- Verify that no deposits or checks were omitted from the checkbook.

- Multiply the difference by two or divide the difference by two and look for an entry in that amount. It could be subtracted when it should have been added or vice versa.

- If the difference is divisible by nine, it might indicate a transposition error. Verify the addition and subtraction in the checkbook register and verify the amounts for each deposit and each check comparing the amount in the register with the amount in the bank statement.

Here is an example that will help you understand how to reconcile the bank balance.

Bank statement balance		$2,002
Add:	unlisted deposits	+500
	Subtotal	$2,502
Subtract:	outstanding checks	−180
Adjusted bank balance		$2,322

Checkbook balance		$1,800
Add:	notes collected by the bank	540
	Accumulated interest	2
	Subtotal	$2,342
Subtract:	service charge	−20
Adjusted checkbook balance		$2,322

Special Bank Services

Banks offer numerous special services that are beneficial. These services include special types of checks and safe-deposit boxes.

Certified Check. A **certified check** is a business or personal check that is guaranteed by the bank on which it is drawn. In order to certify a check, a bank official investigates the drawer's account to see if there are sufficient funds to cover the check. If there are, the word "certified" is stamped on the face of the check and an official signature is added. The drawer's account is immediately charged with the amount of the check. A small fee is usually charged to certify a check.

Cashier's Check. A check issued by a bank and drawn on the bank's own funds is called a **cashier's check.** A cashier's check can be purchased by giving the bank cash or a check for the amount of money desired. A small fee is required by the bank for writing the check. Recommended practice is to have the cashier's check made payable to the purchaser of the check; the purchaser then endorses it to the person to whom payment is to be made. The canceled check becomes proof of payment.

Bank Money Order. A **bank money order** is sold by the bank and states that a certain amount of money is to be paid to the person named on the money order. Normally cashable at any bank in the United States or abroad, the money order is negotiable and can be transferred by endorsement. A bank money order is shown in Figure 18-6.

Traveler's Check. The American Express Company, most banks, and travel agencies issue a special type of check called a **traveler's check,** which facilitates paying for expenses when traveling. Traveler's

FIGURE 18-6. Money Order.

Safety deposit boxes require two keys to open them. © *PhotoDisc, Inc.*

checks are sold in various denominations. A small fee may be charged, depending on the amount purchased. When traveler's checks are purchased, each check must be signed by the purchaser. When cashed, each traveler's check must be countersigned by the purchaser in the presence of the person who cashes the check. When using traveler's checks, individuals should keep a list of the check numbers in a place separate from where the traveler's checks are kept. If the checks are then lost or stolen, the numbers from the checks will be needed to obtain replacement checks.

Safe-Deposit Box. Most banks have large vaults that contain boxes known as **safe-deposit boxes.** These boxes are available for the convenience of individuals and businesses wishing to store articles of value or important papers for safekeeping.

There is a rental charge for the use of these boxes.

The bank has strict rules about access to safe-deposit boxes. At the time a safe-deposit box is rented, the renter must also register her or his signature. The renter is then given a key. Two keys are required to open a safe-deposit box—the renter's and a key kept by the bank. If more than one person has access to the box, each must register his or her signature. Each time the box is used, the person's name must be registered and the time in and out is recorded.

Accounting Records

As an office professional, you will not be expected to have an extensive knowledge of accounting, but you should be familiar with certain accounting statements. The basic financial statements of any business are the income statement and balance sheet. Most publicly held companies issue annual reports, which provide this information for their board of trustees or their stockholders. By reviewing the financial statements of your company, you will learn more about the financial health of the organization.

Balance Sheet

The **balance sheet** shows the financial position of the business on a certain date—how much it owns and how much it owes. The balance sheet is also called a **statement of financial condition.** In order to interpret a balance sheet, you must have an understanding of its major sections. Notice that the balance sheet in Figure 18-7 contains three major sections—assets, liabilities, and stockholders' equity.

BAUGHMAN'S SUPPLY COMPANY

Balance Sheet
December 31, 2001

Assets

Current Assets			
Cash		$ 22,240	
Accounts receivable	$ 41,500		
Less allowance for bad debts	2,500	39,000	
Merchandise inventory		105,725	
Supplies		4,000	
Prepaid insurance		2,900	
Total current assets			173,865
Plant and equipment			
Office equipment	$ 18,000		
Less accumulated depreciation	8,100	$ 9,900	
Factory equipment	$276,000		
Less accumulated depreciation	163,500	112,500	
Buildings	$125,000		
Less accumulated depreciation	20,000	105,000	
Land		35,000	
Total plant and equipment			$262,400
Total assets			$436,265

Liabilities

Current liabilities			
Accounts payable	$ 38,600		
Estimated income tax	15,100		
Salaries and wages payable	1,965		
Interest payable	1,250		
Total current liabilities		$ 56,915	
Long-term liabilities			
Mortgage payable	$ 50,000		
Notes payable, due December 31, 2005	22,500		
Total long-term liabilities		72,500	
Total liabilities			$129,415

Stockholders' Equity

Common stock		$160,000	
Retained earnings		156,850	
Total stockholders' equity			$306,850
Total liabilities and stockholders' equity			$436,265

FIGURE 18-7. Balance Sheet

The **assets** of a company are the properties or economic resources owned by the company. There are two major classifications of assets—current assets and plant and equipment assets. **Current assets** consist of cash and assets that are expected to be turned into cash, sold, or consumed within a short period—usually one year. **Plant and equipment assets** are relatively long-lived assets that are used in the operation of the company.

Another asset category that may be included on the balance sheet is **long-term investments**. Stocks, bonds, and promissory notes that will be held for more than one year are listed under this classification.

Liabilities are the debts of the company. **Current liabilities** are debts that must be paid within one year. **Long-term liabilities** are debts that are not due for a comparatively long period—usually more than one year. Common long-term liability items are mortgages payable, bonds payable, and notes payable.

The **stockholders' equity** section of the balance sheet shows the interest of the stockholders (owners) of a company. The equity of stockholders represents the excess of assets over liabilities.

Income Statement

Another financial statement that reflects the financial health of the company is the **income statement,** also referred to as the **profit and loss statement** or **operating statement.** The income statement covers the results of the operation of a company for a certain period of time. It shows the total amount of money earned and the total amount of expenses involved in earning the money. Figure 18-8 shows an income statement.

The first section of the income statement is the income section. This section shows the total amount of sales the company has made and the cost of the merchandise that was sold. The difference between these two items is the gross profit on sales. If there were no other expenses in connection with the sales, the gross profit would become the net income earned by the business. For example, the employees as well as insurance and utilities must be paid. Notice that these costs are itemized under the operating expenses. The total amount of operating expenses is deducted from the gross profit

on sales to arrive at the net income from operations. All other income and expenses are computed, and the net income is obtained.

Financial Statement Analysis

Before the financial condition of a business truly can be understood, the financial statements must be analyzed. There are many methods of analysis. However, so that you can understand the concept of analysis, two methods are presented here. These methods are called the current ratio and the quick ratio.

Current Ratio.   Bankers and other creditors of a business are mainly interested in the current position of a company. They want to know if the company has enough money to meet its current operating needs and pay its current debts.

One method of determining the current position of a company is to figure the **current ratio.** This figure is obtained by dividing current assets by current liabilities. Refer to the current assets and current liabilities given in Figure 18-7.

$$\text{Current ratio} = \frac{\text{current assets (\$173,865)}}{\text{current liabilities (\$56,915)}} = 3.05{:}1$$

A company's current ratio indicates its debt-paying ability. A current ratio of 3.05 to 1 indicates that \$3.05 in cash is being received for every dollar being paid out within the year. A satisfactory current ratio for a merchandising business is 2 to 1. This ratio should be higher if the company carries merchandise that is subject to abrupt changes in styles. A public utility, which has no inventories other than supplies, is considered solvent even if its current ratio is less than 1 to 1.

Quick Ratio.   The **quick ratio** indicates the extent to which total current liabilities

GOLDSMITH HARDWARE, INC.

Income Statement
For Year Ended December 31, 2001

Sales			$415,100
Cost of goods sold			
Merchandise inventory, January 1		$ 38,500	
Purchases		294,675	
Merchandise available for sale		$333,175	
Less inventory, December 31		51,000	
Cost of goods sold			282,175
Gross profit on sales			$132,925
Operating expenses			
Selling expenses			
Sales salaries and commissions	$28,575		
Advertising expense	19,300		
Miscellaneous selling expense	2,500		
Total selling expense		$ 50,375	
General expenses			
Officers' salaries	$23,000		
Office salaries	8,300		
Depreciation, office equipment	1,800		
Insurance	2,050		
Utilities	2,790		
Total general expenses		38,000	
Total operating expenses			88,375
Net income from operations			$ 44,550
Other expenses			
Interest expense			5,000
Net income before estimated income tax			$ 39,550
Estimated income tax			15,100
Net income after income tax			$ 24,450

FIGURE 18-8. Income Statement

can be liquidated on short notice. It measures the instant debt-paying ability of a company. Cash, notes receivable, accounts receivable, interest receivable, and marketable securities are considered quick assets because they can be turned into cash quickly. Inventories and prepaid expenses are not considered quick assets since they are further removed from conversion into cash than other current assets. The quick ratio is determined by dividing quick assets by current liabilities. The quick assets in Figure 18-7 total $61,240.

$$\text{Quick ratio} = \frac{\text{quick assets } (\$61,240)}{\text{current liabilities } (\$56,915)} = 1.08{:}1$$

The 1.08 to 1 ratio indicates that $1.08 in cash can be quickly received for every dollar to be paid out within the year. This ratio is adequate since a ratio of 1 to 1 is usually considered satisfactory.

Petty Cash Fund

Many times offices will set aside a small amount of money available to office employees for small expenditures and occasional emergencies. This is usually referred to as a petty cash fund. Office employees may use this money to buy stamps, purchase office supplies, or refill coffee supplies. As an office professional, you may be in charge of keeping track of this special fund. In order to make sure that you can account for the money in this fund, consider the following suggestions.

- Start a register (similar to a checkbook register) indicating the initial amount of money allocated to the fund.
- List the date, amount, and description for any expense that is charged to this fund. Update the balance on the register whenever money is removed.
- List the date, amount, and description for any money that is added to this fund. Update the balance on the register whenever money is added.
- Check with your office supervisor to determine whether or not receipts need to be collected when money is disbursed.
- Always store the fund out of sight and preferably in a locked location (office drawer or filing cabinet).

Payroll Laws

It is the primary responsibility of the payroll department to understand the laws and regulations and to compute wages and salaries for each pay period based on these regulations. But even if you never work in a payroll department, you should be familiar with these laws and regulations in order to understand the deductions that are taken from your gross earnings.

Fair Labor Standards Act

The Fair Labor Standards Act of 1938 requires that companies in interstate commerce (engaged in business in other states) keep a record of hours worked and pay a minimum hourly wage. In addition, the law requires that certain employees be paid at a rate at least one and a half times the regular hourly rate for all work in excess of 40 hours during a workweek. Persons in administrative or executive positions are considered exempt employees; they are not governed by the law and do not receive any overtime pay. Although this law does not require that any reports showing hours worked be filed, company records must be kept on file for three years. Government examiners may inspect the records at any time to determine whether the employer is meeting the requirements of the act.

Federal Insurance Contribution Act (Social Security)

Social security provides income upon retirement, disability benefits, and health insurance for retired persons. In order to pay for the benefits that you collect upon retirement, both you and your employer contribute an equal amount of money each pay period to the federal government. The amount of that contribution and the base on which it is paid is revised often by Congress. For example, in 1999, 7.65 percent was levied on a base of $72,600, plus 1.45 percent on salary earned above $72,600. In 1998, 7.65 percent was levied on a base of $68,400, plus 1.45 percent on salary earned above $68,400.

Thus, if you made $40,000 in 1999, you would have paid 7.65 percent of your salary or $3,060 in social security taxes. That same year, if an executive made $120,000, he or she would have paid 7.65 percent of $72,600 or $5,554 and 1.45 percent on the remaining portion of salary.

$72,600 (the base) x 7.65%   = $5,554
   plus
1.45% on 47,400 (total salary
   earned of $120-base of
   72,600 = $47,400)   = $ 687

Total social security   = $6,241

To determine the percentage and the base today, you can check with your local social security office or visit their Web site at www.ssa.gov. The government accumulates the money in an account and pays you benefits when you retire or pays benefits to your survivors and/or dependents in the event of your death.

Under provisions of the Tax Reform Act of 1985, everyone age two or older must have a social security number. To obtain a number, you must file an application with your local social security office or post office. You will then receive a card with your social security number on it. The Social Security Administration recommends that every three years you request a statement of your earnings to make sure that they have been reported properly. In order to get this statement, call your social security office and ask for details.

Federal, State, and Local Income Tax

The amount deducted from your earnings for federal income tax depends on your earnings and the number of dependents you claim. Each employee must fill out a Form W-4 (Employee's Withholding Allowance Certificate), shown in Figure 18-9. The amount of income tax withheld by employers is paid quarterly or monthly to a district office of the Internal Revenue Service. Some states and cities also tax a person's income, while others do not. If there is a state income tax, the deductions are withheld in much the same way as the federal income tax.

Unemployment Compensation Tax

This tax provides some relief to those who become unemployed as a result of economic forces outside their control. To finance the program, all employers covered by the law are subject to a federal and state tax. The state employment rate and the wage base subject to the tax vary from state to state. Provision is made for employers with a favorable record of employment to pay a lower rate than employers with an unfavorable record of employment. For example, all new employers pay the same rate for a period of approximately a year and a half. Then their tax rate is determined by their employment record. If their employee turnover is low, their tax is calculated at a lower rate than if their employee turnover is high. For the exact federal and state tax percentages paid by employers, check with your state employment commission.

Other Deductions

There are several other deductions that may be made from your earnings. Common examples are insurance, hospitalization, union dues, retirement, and employee savings plans. Figure 18-10

Employee's Withholding Allowance Certificate

► **For Privacy Act and Paperwork Reduction Act Notice, see reverse.**

OMB No. 1545-0010
1997

1 Type or print your first name and middle initial	Last name	2 Your social security number

Home address (number and street or rural route)	3 ☐ Single ☐ Married ☐ Married, but withhold at higher Single rate.
	Note: If married, but legally separated, or spouse is a nonresident alien, check the Single box.
City or town, state, and ZIP code	4 If your last name differs from that on your social security card, check here and call 1-800-772-1213 for a new card . . . . . . ► ☐

5 Total number of allowances you are claiming (from line G above or from the worksheets on page 2 if they apply) .	5	
6 Additional amount, if any, you want withheld from each paycheck	6	$

7 I claim exemption from withholding for 1997, and I certify that I meet **BOTH** of the following conditions for exemption:
  • Last year I had a right to a refund of **ALL** Federal income tax withheld because I had **NO** tax liability; **AND**
  • This year I expect a refund of **ALL** Federal income tax withheld because I expect to have **NO** tax liability
  If you meet both conditions, enter "EXEMPT" here . . . . ► | 7 |

Under penalties of perjury, I certify that I am entitled to the number of withholding allowances claimed on this certificate or entitled to claim exempt status.

Employee's signature ►   Date ►   , 19

8 Employer's name and address (Employer: Complete 8 and 10 only if sending to the IRS)	9 Office code (optional)	10 Employer identification number

Cat. No. 10220Q

FIGURE 18-9. Form W-4.

No. 117770	TAZIAM INDUSTRIES	PAY ENDING DATE	CHECK DATE	SOCIAL SECURITY NUMBER
		12 25 --	12 22 --	999-99-9999

HOURS WORKED — **STATEMENT OF CURRENT EARNINGS**

REG. HOURS	OVT. HOURS	REGULAR PAY	OVER LOAD	OVERTIME PAY	MISC. PAY	NEG. ADJ.	GROSS PAY	ANNUITY	ADJ. GROSS PAY	NET PAY
80 00		140673			4620		145293		139711	105015

TAX DEDUCTIONS | **CURRENT DEDUCTIONS** | **SICK TIME** | **VACATION TIME** | **PERSONAL BUSINESS**

	YEAR TO DATE	CURRENT	DEDUCTION	AMOUNT	BANK AS OF JULY 1 DAYS	HOURS	CURRENT BANK DAYS	HOURS	BANK AS OF JULY 1 DAYS	HOURS	CURRENT BANK DAYS	HOURS	BANK AS OF JULY 1 DAYS	HRS	CURRENT BANK DAYS	HRS
FEDERAL TAX	3497 12	132 85	BENEFIT ENHA	96												
STATE TAX	1483 36	56 84	MEMBER INVES	5486	28	5.0	242.0	19	4.0	10	3		1	7.		
FICA	2901 11	111 07	LIFE INS.PRE	4620	LIFE INS.PREMIUMS		46.20									
CITY TAX																

YEAR TO DATE INFORMATION

GROSS PAY	ANNUITY	ADJ. GROSS PAY
37947 50		36447 22

OTHER SCHOOL EARNINGS	COVERED WAGES	M.I.P.
	37923 50	1476.28

No. 117770 COMERICA	**Ti TAZIAM INDUSTRIES**		9-33 720

TAZIAM INDUSTRIES
2400 OPDYKE ROAD
BLOOMFIELD HILLS, MICHIGAN 48304-2266

SOCIAL SECURITY NUMBER	CHECK NO.	00117770
999-99-9999	CHECK DATE	AMOUNT
	12/22/--	PAY $ *1050.15
		VOID AFTER 60 DAYS

TAZIAM INDUSTRIES
PAYROLL ACCOUNT

PAY TO
THE ORDER OF

00117770
DEBRA L. McKENZIE
4841 CALVERT DR
TROY   MI 48098-5009

Bill Larson
AUTHORIZED SIGNATURE

⑈³¹¹⁰⁰⑈ ⑆⁰⁷⁵⁶¹¹³³³⑆ ²⁰⁰⁰⁰¹²²⁷⁰⑈

FIGURE 18-10. Payroll Check.

shows an example of a payroll check with a list of deductions.

Other Taxes

In addition to payroll taxes, there are other taxes that impact a business and an individual. These taxes vary depending on the location and type of business and various other factors. The following are some of the common types of taxes levied on business enterprises and individuals.

Property Tax.   Most property taxes are levied by state and local governments for the purposes of maintaining local governments and schools. A portion is also generally used to pay the expenses of state governments. Two common taxes are real property and personal property tax.

Real property tax is levied on land and buildings. The value of the real estate is determined by periodic appraisal, and the tax is levied on the assessed evaluation. **Personal property tax** is levied on such items as furniture and equipment, automobiles, and machinery.

Sales Tax.   Sales tax is levied on retail sales of most items; however, food and machines are exempt from sales tax. Both the purchaser of the goods and the business pay sales tax. Detailed records must be kept by the business so that amounts may be remitted periodically to the taxing agency.

License Taxes.   Probably the most common **license tax** is the automobile license tax, which is levied by the individual state on all persons obtaining a license. There are, however, many other kinds of federal, state, and local license taxes. Restaurants frequently must purchase several licenses in order to operate. Food stores and nearly all kinds of retail outlets require licenses to operate. Professionals, such as doctors and lawyers, must have a license to practice. A license indicates that permission to operate or conduct a business has been granted by the proper authorities.

Investments

Although you will probably not be involved as an office professional in assisting with any of the company's investments, you do need to have an understanding of investment terminology. Such knowledge can help you in reading and keying reports that contain investment terms and in your personal life as you make investments.

Stocks

Stocks represent shares of ownership in a company. Stockholders invest in a company by buying shares of stock. They are issued stock certificates that show the number of shares owned.

Kinds of Stocks.   Stock in a company can be classified as either **common stock** or **preferred stock**. Common stockholders usually have the right to vote at periodic stockholders' meetings. Common stockholders do not receive a fixed dividend. A **dividend** is a distribution paid to stockholders by the corporation; it is the stockholder's share of the corporation's profits. Dividends may be distributed in cash, other assets, or in the corporation's own stock. If dividends are distributed in cash (the most common method of distribution), the earnings of the corporation determine the dollar amount of dividends paid per share of stock.

Preferred stockholders have preference over common stockholders because dividends are paid on preferred stock before they are paid on common stock.

When dividends are declared, preferred stockholders must be paid in full before common stockholders can be paid any dividends. The preferred stockholders are paid at a set dividend rate. For example, a share of preferred stock with a par value of $200 and a stated 8 percent dividend rate would entitle the owner to $16 yearly. **Par value** is an arbitrary amount assigned to the stock when issued that has no relationship to its actual market value. In rare instances, preferred stock is issued without a stated par value. Such no-par stock has a stated dollar dividend amount instead of a dividend rate.

There are several classes of both common and preferred stocks that give stockholders various rights or privileges. Generally the income on preferred stock is more certain than that on common stock. The market value of common stock may fluctuate more than the market value of preferred stock due to the uncertain amount of dividends on common stock. In periods of high earnings and expansion of a corporation, common stockholders ordinarily receive a much larger share of the increased earnings than preferred stockholders since the income on preferred stock is fixed.

Stock Exchanges. The oldest and largest **stock exchange** is the New York Stock Exchange. Another major stock exchange in the United States is the American Stock Exchange (AMEX). In addition to these stock exchanges, there are various regional exchanges, including Chicago, Boston, and Pacific. In order to transact business on an exchange, an individual broker or brokerage firm must be a member. This membership, called a **seat on the exchange,** allows the person or firm to trade stocks and bonds with others on the exchange. An individual investor does not buy and sell securities on a stock exchange. Instead, the investor deals with a broker who handles the transaction and charges a fee for the service.

The NASD. The NASD (National Association of Securities Dealers) is an **over-the-counter market,** which means that it is not a physical location such as the New York Stock Exchange and the American Stock Exchange but a network of brokers who buy and sell securities. Transactions from the over-the-counter market are listed in the financial section of the newspaper under "NASDQ (National Association of Securities Dealers Automated Quotations) National Market Issues." Also, each day the financial TV channels report market activity of stocks, with the NASDQ and the Dow-Jones averages (performance of 30 U.S. blue-chip stocks) reported.

The Internet. Until recently, the only marketplace for buying stocks was through brokers on the stock exchanges or the over-the-counter market (NASD) and mutual funds companies. Now, however, stocks and mutual funds may be purchased over the Internet. The technology is such that even the beginning investor can buy and sell over the Internet. However, doing so successfully takes time and expertise that most individuals who are employed full-time do not have. Unless you are one of the individuals who understands the stock market very well, you probably will want a broker or a mutual fund company to assist you in your investment strategy.

Stock Quotations. In addition to the Internet, most daily newspapers in large cities and such financial publications as *The Wall Street Journal* carry financial sections that report stock transactions on the major stock exchanges, the NASDQ, and

52 Weeks Hi	Lo	Stock	Sym	Div	Yld %	PE	Vol 100s	Hi	Lo	Close	Net Chg
n 30	$19^3/_8$	FoxEntnGp A	FOX	...	...	...	10812	$28^3/_8$	$26^{13}/_{16}$	$27^3/_{16}$	− $^{11}/_{16}$
$15^7/_8$	$10^3/_4$	FraGrthFd	FRF	2.82e	21.3	...	108	$13^1/_4$	$13^3/_{16}$	$13^1/_4$	+ $^1/_{16}$
$99^1/_8$	$55^1/_4$	FraTelecm	FTE	1.11e	1.4	...	76	$80^1/_2$	80	80	+ $2^1/_4$
28	$20^1/_8$	FrnchsFin	FFA	1.96	8.1	12	1548	$24^3/_{16}$	$23^1/_4$	$24^1/_8$	+ $^1/_8$
$21^1/_8$	$8^7/_8$	FrnklnCovey	FC	...	...	6	674	$9^1/_2$	$9^1/_4$	$9^1/_4$	...
$12^7/_8$	$4^1/_2$	FrnklnElcPub	FEP	...	...	dd	24	$6^1/_4$	$6^3/_{16}$	$6^1/_4$	+ $^1/_{16}$
$10^{13}/_{16}$	$8^7/_8$	FrnklnMulti	FMI	.77a	8.5	...	81	$9^1/_8$	9	$9^1/_{16}$	...
$54^7/_8$	$25^3/_4$	FrnklnRes	BEN	.22	.5	27	6204	45	$43^1/_2$	45	+ $^{15}/_{16}$
$9^{15}/_{16}$	$8^3/_4$	FrnklnUnvlTr	FT	.80a	8.7	...	223	$9^3/_{16}$	$9^1/_{16}$	$9^3/_{16}$	+ $^1/_{16}$
$68^7/_8$	$36^5/_8$	FredMeyer	FMY	...	...	cc	4971	$51^5/_8$	$50^7/_{16}$	$51^5/_{16}$	+ $^{13}/_{16}$
$66^3/_8$	$38^{11}/_{16}$	FredMac	FRE	.60f	1.0	24	15618	$59^{15}/_{16}$	$58^{11}/_{16}$	$59^1/_2$	+ $^3/_8$
$25^3/_4$	$23^7/_8$	FredMacDeb	FWG	.84p	...	...	4	$24^{15}/_{16}$	$24^{11}/_{16}$	$24^{15}/_{16}$	...
$21^1/_2$	$9^3/_8$	FreedomSec	FSI	.20f	1.2	...	151	$16^{15}/_{16}$	$16^5/_8$	$16^3/_4$	− $^1/_{16}$
$16^{13}/_{16}$	9	FrptMcCG A	FCXA	.20j	...	23	614	$14^{11}/_{16}$	$14^1/_4$	$14^{11}/_{16}$	+ $^5/_{16}$
18	$9^1/_8$	FrptMcCG B	FCX	.20j	...	...	6683	$15^3/_8$	$14^{13}/_{16}$	$15^3/_8$	+ $^3/_8$
$22^1/_2$	14	FrptMcCG pfA		1.75	9.5	...	284	$18^3/_8$	$17^7/_8$	$18^3/_8$	+ $^1/_2$
$23^3/_8$	$14^1/_4$	FrptMcCG pfB		1.01e	6.3	...	18	16	$15^7/_8$	$15^{15}/_{16}$	− $^1/_{16}$
$20^3/_4$	12	FrptMcCG pfC		.94E	7.2	...	114	$13^1/_8$	13	13	− $^3/_{16}$
19	$11^3/_8$	FrptMcCG pfD		.84e	6.1	...	3	$13^{13}/_{16}$	$13^{13}/_{16}$	$13^{13}/_{16}$	− $^1/_{16}$
$2^7/_8$	$^9/_{32}$	FrptMcRylty	FMR		...	...	1885	$^5/_{16}$	$^1/_4$	$^5/_{16}$	...

FIGURE 18-11. Stock Quotations.

mutual funds. Figure 18-11 shows a listing of a few stock quotations on the New York Stock Exchange.

Mutual Funds

A **mutual fund** is an investment company that pools individuals' money and invests the money in stocks and bonds (discussed in the next section). Mutual fund companies employ investment advisors, who along with a staff of people, select, buy, and sell investments based on the fund's investment objective. Mutual funds pro-

vide one of the simplest ways for the small investor to buy stocks and bonds, since:

- The investment dollars can be spread over a series of funds.

- A professional management team makes the decisions concerning what stocks and bonds to buy and when they should be bought and sold.

Generally, owning several types of different stocks and/or bonds protects the investor against losses. If one investment in the fund does poorly, there are a number of other investments that can help cushion the loss. Additionally, most individuals do not have the time or expertise to watch the market daily and make the best decisions about what to buy and sell.

Bonds

A **bond** is a certificate that promises to pay a definite sum of money at a specified time with interest payable periodically to the holder of the bond. Thus, bonds do not represent a share of ownership in a company as do stocks but are evidence of a debt owed by the firm. A **bondholder** lends money to an organization and in return receives a bond, which is a preferred lien against the organization. There are several types of bonds that may be purchased—corporate, U.S. treasury, tax-exempt, municipal, and mortgage-backed. Bonds are considered relatively safe investments; however, the market history shows that stocks generally are a better long-term investment than bonds.

Bonds may be purchased from:

- The over-the-counter market
- Mutual funds companies
- Securities dealers
- Fund management companies

In addition, just as stocks may be purchased over the Internet so may bonds.

Bond prices are listed in the newspaper or in such financial publications as *The Wall Street Journal, Investor's Business Daily,* and *Barron's.* Bond information may also be obtained from such sites on the Internet as The Bond Market Association's investor site, www.investing-inbonds.com. General information concerning the price of bonds is given on financial television channels. Figure 18-12 shows a listing of bond price and activity information from *The Wall Street Journal.*

IRAs

An **IRA** (Individual Retirement Arrangement) is a savings plan that permits employees to set aside money for retirement. Although the types of funds that may be purchased through an IRA are restricted by the **IRS** (Internal Revenue Service), generally money may be invested in annuities, money market funds, trusts, and certificates of deposit. Money may not be invested in collectibles such as artwork, antiques, gems, and coins. The amount of money that can be put into an IRA is limited by the Tax Reform Act of 1986. Restrictions depend on whether the employee is covered by an employer-paid retirement plan and on the amount of

CORPORATION BONDS
Volume, $14,471,000

Bonds	Cur Yld.	Vol.	Close	Net Chg
AMR 9s16	7.9	65	$114^5/_8$	$- \quad ^3/_8$
ATT $5^1/_8$01	5.1	30	$99^3/_4$	$+ \quad ^3/_8$
ATT $7^1/_8$02	6.9	61	$103^1/_4$	$+ \quad ^1/_4$
ATT $6^3/_4$04	6.6	112	$102^7/_8$	...
ATT $5^5/_8$04	5.8	120	$97^7/_8$	$+ \quad ^3/_8$
ATT 7s05	6.8	28	$103^5/_8$	$+ \quad ^1/_4$
ATT 8.2s05	7.9	138	$103^3/_8$	...
ATT $7^1/_2$06	7.1	65	106	...
ATT $7^3/_4$07	7.2	78	108	...
ATT 6s09	6.3	27	$95^7/_8$	$- \quad ^1/_4$
ATT $8^1/_8$22	7.7	94	106	$+ \quad ^5/_8$
ATT $6^1/_2$29	6.9	142	$93^3/_4$	$+ \quad ^1/_2$
AlldC zr05	...	20	$66^1/_4$	$- \quad 1$
AlldC zr07	...	30	$57^3/_4$	$- \quad ^3/_4$
AlldC zr09	...	20	49	$- \quad ^1/_4$
Alza 5s06	cv	22	113	$+ \quad ^1/_2$
Amresco 10s03	12.4	65	$80^3/_4$	$+ \quad ^3/_4$
Amresco 10s04	12.1	73	$82^1/_2$	$+ \quad ^1/_2$

FIGURE 18-12.

earned income. IRAs may be deductible from the individual's income tax. This deduction depends on how much the employee makes. Nondeductible contributions may also be made to IRAs.

An additional type of IRA, the **Roth IRA,** was developed to provide some flexibility for investors. With a Roth IRA, individuals of any age with earned income can contribute, but there is a limit of $2000 after-tax dollars for annual contributions. In addition, the Roth IRA provides individuals with the opportunity to withdraw from the account during certain time periods without incurring a penalty. These instances include withdrawals for the first time purchase of a home or for educational expenses. However, the biggest incentive of the Roth IRA for consumers is that the interest gained on the yearly contributions is not taxed. The traditional IRA on the other hand lets you invest money prior to taxes, but all earnings are taxed upon withdrawal from the account.

SUMMARY

To reinforce what you have learned in this chapter, study this summary.

- The most important change in the banking industry in the last few years has been in the use of electronic technology. Examples of this include automated teller machines, sophisticated kiosks, debit cards, smart cards, direct payroll depositing, direct withdrawals, computer systems, and software packages.

- Although technology has made it possible to transfer funds electronically, paper banking in the form of checks and deposit slips is still being used to-

day, and it is projected that they will be used for a number of years.

- When writing checks, certain procedures should be followed, such as: figures should be written as close as possible to the printed dollar sign; the amount in words should be started as far as possible to the left, with a line drawn through any excess space remaining on the line; a check should never be erased or changed—void it and the stub; and the check register or stub is filled out before writing the check.

- There are three types of endorsements—blank endorsement, full endorsement, and restrictive endorsement.

- A bank reconciliation is completed to account for the difference between the bank statement balance and the checkbook balance and to correct any errors that may have been made.

- Special bank services include issuing certified checks, cashier's checks, bank money orders, and traveler's checks.

- The basic financial statements of a business are the balance sheet and the income statement. The balance sheet shows the financial condition of the business on a certain date; the income statement shows the amount of money earned and the total amount of the expenses involved in earning the money for a certain period of time.

- The current ratio and the quick ratio are two ratios that may be used in analyzing financial statements. The current ratio indicates a business's ability to pay debts. A quick ratio indicates how quickly current liabilities can be liquidated.

- Being familiar with payroll laws and regulations will help you understand not only the day-to-day operations of a business, but also the deductions that are taken from your gross earnings. You should be familiar with these laws and regulations: Fair Labor Standards Act, Federal Insurance Contribution Act, Federal and state income tax, and unemployment compensation tax.

- Some additional taxes, in addition to payroll taxes, that impact a business and an individual include real property tax, sales tax, and license tax.
- Your company, your employer, or you may make certain investments. These investments can include stocks, bonds, mutual funds, and IRAs.

Key Terms

- Electronic fund transfers (EFTs)
- Automated teller machines (ATMs)
- Personal identification number (PIN)
- New technology ATMs (NT-ATMs)
- Sophisticated kiosks
- Debit cards
- Smart cards
- Stored value cards
- Echecks
- Drawer
- Payee
- Voucher check
- Check carbon
- Check register
- Endorsement
- Blank endorsement
- Endorsement in full
- Restrictive endorsement
- Check truncation
- Check retention
- Check safekeeping
- Certified check
- Cashier's check
- Bank money order
- Traveler's check
- Safe-deposit boxes
- Balance sheet
- Statement of financial position
- Statement of financial condition
- Assets
- Current assets
- Plant and equipment assets
- Long-term investments
- Liabilities
- Current liabilities
- Long-term liabilities
- Stockholders' equity
- Income statement
- Profit and loss statement
- Operating statement
- Current ratio
- Quick ratio
- Real property tax
- Personal property tax
- Sales tax
- License tax
- Stocks
- Common stock
- Preferred stock
- Dividend
- Par value
- Stock exchange
- Seat on the exchange
- Over-the-counter
- Mutual fund
- Bond
- Bondholder
- IRA
- IRS
- Roth IRA

Professional Pointers

Here are some tips to help you as you work with financial records.
- Double-check figures on all forms that you handle.
- When you key figures, proofread by doing the following:
    - Have someone else read the figures to you.
    - Add all columns of figures that have a total. Even if a column of figures does not have a total, you can add them on the original copy to create a total; then add them on the copy you have prepared to match the two amounts. If they do not match, you have made an error.

- When you are handwriting figures, be certain that you take the time to make the figures legible.
- Keep current on all laws that affect any financial records you might be handling.
- Be knowledgeable of the terminology used in your company. Many financial terms are technical in nature. If you do not understand the meaning of a term, ask someone in the company to explain it to you.
- Utilize available technology in the preparation and maintenance of financial records. Using spreadsheet software, for example, makes calculating and reporting financial documents much more accurate and efficient.

Office Procedures Reinforcement

1. Name and describe the two types of debit cards.
2. List the advantages to employee and employer of direct payroll deposit.
3. Name and explain the difference in the three types of check endorsements.
4. List and describe the types of special checks that are offered by banks.
5. Explain what a current ratio of 2.5 to 1 would indicate about the financial position of a company.

Critical Thinking Activity

Sandi Goldfisher is the office manager for a small insurance company that underwrites a variety of insurance coverage. There are 12 other employees in addition to Sandi.

All of the payroll records are kept by Sandi, and she handles most of the banking transactions. Sandi keeps a petty cash box in her office for small expenditures and occasional emergencies. The petty cash fund is charged out at $250. In the last several months, the office has been extremely busy. For some reason, it seems that many insurance policies cycle around for renewal in January, a lot of new cars are purchased after the first of the year that need new policies, and tax records must be finalized so that W2 forms can be mailed.

Sandi needed to get a certified letter in the mail before 5 p.m., so she went to get $5 from the petty cash box before heading out to the post office. It had been a while since Sandi had used any cash from the fund. Sandi counted the money and found only $63.25. She couldn't believe the fund was so low—and she is responsible for it! She did remember buying a hammer for the office at the local hardware store, and she borrowed maybe $10 for lunch one day. LaMar bought a new coffeepot, and Sandi reimbursed him from petty cash (but she can't remember how much it was). Nedra needed change for a $50 bill one day; and Hazel had asked for a small salary advance—but no, that wasn't from petty cash. The box was in a different location in her office one morning, and she had left it unlocked by mistake. Sandi panicked!

1. What mistakes has Sandi made in keeping the petty cash fund?
2. What steps would you suggest that Sandi implement so that a more accurate accounting of the fund be maintained?
3. How should Sandi handle telling the president that the fund does not balance?

Office Applications

OA 18-1 (Goal 1)
Choose two of your classmates to work with on this project. Select one of the topics discussed in the chapter regarding electronic banking (ATMs, sophisticated kiosks, debit cards, smart cards, stored value cards, and so on). Using three current periodicals, prepare a summary of the articles; list your references. Be prepared to present your findings orally to the class. Turn in your report to your instructor.

OA18-2 (Goal 2)
Your supervisor, Juan Menendez was recently installed as treasurer of the Atlee Rotary Club. The club was chartered one year ago and has a membership of 36 business men and women. The club's fiscal year is July 1 to June 30. You are the administrative assistant for Mr. Menendez, and he has asked that you assist him with his duties as the Rotary Club's treasurer.

   The club's checking account is with Essex Bank. Assist Mr. Menendez by writing checks and making deposits for the club. The forms that you will need for this job are in your Applications Workbook on pages 117–119.

1. The carryover balance from last year, which is stipulated in the bylaws, is $500. Also, 18 members prepaid their annual dues of $100 in June for the coming year. Begin the checkbook register with this total.
2. Complete a deposit slip on July 7 for the following four membership dues received.

Currency	$100
#521	$100
#103	$100
#466	$100

3. Write checks for the transactions submitted by the club chairpersons. Transactions are listed on page 000 of the Applications Workbook. The first four checks should be dated July 10 and should be written to Times Square Florist, FastPrint, Atlee Hardware, and Lipscomb Appliance.

4. On July 31, two members dropped by the office and left checks #301 and #202 for $100 each for their membership dues. Make the necessary deposit. Becky Coviello came in and requested reimbursement for the recycling bins and supplies that she purchased for the Environment Committee. Issue Check #1005 to Becky Coviello for the amount due her.

OA 18-3 (Goal 2)

The July bank statement for the Rotary Club on page 121 in your Applications Workbook just arrived. After verifying the canceled checks with your check stubs, you find that check #1003 for $167 and check #1005 for $414 are outstanding. The July 1 deposit was made after 4 p.m.; therefore, it was not received in time to be recorded on the July statement. Reconcile the account using the form provided in your Applications Workbook on page 122.

The statement does not reconcile with the checkbook balance. You realize the bank's beginning balance for the club's account does not match the beginning balance. A call to Julian Rifige, the club president, revealed that the club's books were audited on June 30 before they were handed over to Mr. Menendez. The audit showed a $25 discrepancy, which was posted on the bank statement in June. Apparently the bank charged the club's checking account a $25 service fee because the balance fell below the $1,000 minimum. Essex Bank was chosen for the club's account because they offer service-free accounts to nonprofit organizations in the community.

Write a letter for Mr. Menendez to Essex Bank to notify them of the error. Follow the instructions listed on the Checking Account Reconcilement form on page 122 of your Applications Workbook. Ask to have the $25 error credited back to the account.

OA 18-4 (Goal 3)

The weekly payroll for People First International's hourly employees has been prepared manually. Mr. Menendez would like you to create a spreadsheet for calculating this weekly payroll. Use the information listed on page 123 of your Applications Workbook to determine each employee's rate of pay, withholding tax rate, and hospitalization deductions. Enter the hours worked by each employee (provided below); determine overtime pay at the rate of time and a half (the hourly rate plus another half); calculate the FICA tax at the rate of 7.65 percent to arrive at net earnings total for the ten employees. Print a copy of the payroll for Mr. Menendez.

Employee	Hours	Employee	Hours
Boone	40	Keith	40
Kay	48	Lane	42
Lin	45	Mark	40
North	44	Park	40
Ramos	40	Stein	40

Online Research Applications

ORA 18-5 (Goal 3)

Contact your local social security office or locate the social security Web site on the Internet to determine the social security percentage and amount of base salary in order to calculate the amount of annual social security tax for the following employee salaries.

Employee Number	Yearly Salary	Amount of Social Security Tax
15-250	$37,550	
12-302	$49,300	
13-269	$57,400	
14-785	$68,204	
13-953	$82,500	
18-734	$102,000	
16-438	$132,000	

ORA 18-6 (Goal 4)

Choose two classmates to work with on this project. Search the Internet for information on traditional IRA accounts and Roth IRAs. Compare and contrast the two types of accounts and summarize them for your instructor. Write a short paper that discusses similarities and differences in the types of IRA accounts available and the restrictions for each of the accounts.

Vocabulary Review

On pages 127–128 of your Applications Workbook is a Vocabulary Review, covering selected items from the vocabulary presented in Chapters 16–18. Complete these sentences and submit a copy to your instructor.

Language Skills Practice

On pages 129–130 of your Applications Workbook are sentences that need to be corrected using the rules presented in the Reference Section of your text. Correct the sentences as needed and submit your work to your instructor.

6

The Office Professional's Career

CHAPTER 19

Employment and Advancement

Finding a good job, one that meets our needs and aspirations, and advancing in our careers are important goals for most of us. It is all part of the American dream.

- We want to achieve a high level of personal and professional satisfaction in whatever career we have chosen.
- We want to make enough money to satisfy our needs and the needs of our families.
- We want to be a contributing member of society—contributing on the job and in our professional lives outside of work.

YOUR GOALS

1. Write a letter of application.
2. Prepare a resume.
3. Complete an employment application.
4. Develop and use interview skills.
5. Review and revise your career plan.

Throughout this course, you have been focusing on developing the knowledge and skills that will help you be successful as an office professional. Before you can put those skills to good use on a job, you must be successful in getting a job. You must know how to write a letter of application and prepare a resume that will call attention to your abilities. You must be able to sell yourself in an interview situation. This chapter will help you develop those skills. Once you land that all-important job, you will want to continue to advance your career. By studying this chapter and using the skills you have developed throughout this course on the job, you will be able to achieve the long-range career goals that you set for yourself.

Sources of Job Information

Now that you are ready to begin looking for a job that will meet your goals and expectations, where do you begin? First of all, you need to be clear about several major issues.

- Within the office professional area, is there a specialty field in which you want to work? For example, do you want to work in the legal field? medical field? computer field?
- Do you want to work for a large or a small organization?
- Where do you want to work? A big city? A small city? An international location? In your hometown?
- What are your long-range career goals? For example, do you want to be an office manager?
- What are your long-range personal goals?

In Chapter 1 you were asked to develop a career plan and to make updates to it as you progressed through the course. Pull that career plan now and review it. Do you need to make changes? The clearer you are about your career path, the more able you will be to make good decisions about where you seek a job.

Once you are clear about your directions, the next step is to find job openings in the area in which you want to work. Sources of information for specific jobs include:

- Newspapers
- The Internet
- Employment agencies
- Professional organizations
- Placement offices
- Personal networks
- Walk-ins
- Temporary agencies

Newspapers

The classified section of newspapers is a major source of job openings. Two kinds of classified advertisements are listed in newspapers—signed and blind. A **signed advertisement** gives the name of the firm placing the advertisement; a **blind advertisement** does not show the firm's name. A post office box number or a telephone number may be the only information given. Figure 19-1 gives examples of signed and blind advertisements.

The Internet

The Internet has become a major source of job information. Several Internet addresses that you might try are:

- http://www.nbew.com
- http://www.ajb.dni.us

SECRETARY

Universal Forest Products, Inc., a nationwide lumber products manufacturer, is seeking a Secretary with at least 2 years experience. Applicant must possess excellent typing, grammar, spelling, interpersonal, organizational and communication skills. A working knowledge of Excel and Word and/or WordPerfect is required. We are an EOE offering a drug free work environment, competitive wages and benefits. Qualified applicants send resume to:

Universal Forest Products, Inc.
2801 E. Beltline, NE
Grand Rapids, MI 49525
Attn: C. Hansen

SECRETARY/RECEPTIONIST—local commercial property management company seeks individual with 3 yrs. secretarial experience. This position requires a gracious and professional approach with tenants, good written and oral communication skills and Microsoft Office computer experience. Previous real estate experience a plus. If you seek challenging work with a progressive company, submit a confidential resume to Box M4383, Care of Press, 155 Michigan N.W., Grand Rapids, MI 49503.

FIGURE 19-1. Signed and Blind Advertisements

- http://www.careermosaic.com

    These sources allow you to seek job sources by company name, job title, job description, and location. International jobs are listed in addition to positions within the United States. Some of these sources provide information on the total job search process, such as:

- The right job for you
- Preparing a resume
- Researching the company and industry
- Preparing for the interview

- Determining what salary is appropriate. Some sites allow you to search by job category and then by state for average salaries—for example, secretaries, except legal and medical, for California. The median salary for the United States is given, along with the median salary for California, using statistics from the Bureau of Labor. Average annual job openings also are listed on some sites, for the United States and the particular state being researched.

    Some local newspapers offer an online version of the newspaper's help-wanted ads—for example, the *Boston Herald's* site at http://www.jobfind.com.

Employment Agencies

There are two types of employment agencies—private and state operated. **State-operated employment agencies** are supported by tax dollars. As a taxpaying citizen, you can take advantage of the services provided by your state-operated agency free of charge. **Private employment agencies** charge a fee for their services. Either you or the employing firm must pay for these services. If you pay the fee, it is usually stated as a percentage of your beginning salary. When the employing firm pays the fee, the agency may advertise the position as **fee paid.** Figure 19-2 shows an employment agency ad in which no fee is charged.

    Generally, you must sign a contract with private employment agencies. Information regarding how the fee is determined should be included in the contract. As with any contract, you should read it carefully before signing.

    Employment agencies screen applicants for the employer. When you go to

FIGURE 19-2. Employment Agency Ad

Professional Organizations

If you are a member of a professional organization, check to see if they maintain a listing of jobs in the area. For example, your local chapter of IAAP may be able to assist you in your job search. Also, you should ask individual members of the organization if they are aware of any openings.

an agency, you should be prepared to complete an application and take several tests. These tests may measure the following:

- Keyboarding speed and accuracy
- Notetaking speed and transcription skills
- Grammar, punctuation, spelling, and proofreading skills
- Mathematical aptitude
- Computer skill
- Specific skills in an area of specialization, such as the legal or medical field

When you go to an employment agency, be prepared to complete several tests.

Placement Offices

Many schools and colleges have placement counselors who aid students in career planning. College placement offices offer a variety of products and services, including:

- Materials about specific careers
- Directories of private industries and governmental agencies
- General occupational information
- Assistance with writing letters of application and resumes
- Assistance with interviewing
- Announcements about available positions

In larger colleges and universities, employers may visit the school to recruit and interview students. You should check with your school to determine if there is job assistance provided, and if so, what is available.

Personal Networks

Networking is defined in this context as the process of identifying and establishing a group of acquaintances, friends, and even relatives who can assist you in the job search process. Most employees are aware of job openings within their company. A number of companies list positions on email, job hotlines, and bulletin boards.

Walk-ins

Although walking into an organization without any knowledge of the job openings that might be available is the least effective method, it can yield results. The

Networking with friends, relatives, and acquaintances can assist you in the job search process. © *PhotoDisc, Inc.*

best approach is to develop a list of large businesses in your area that might employ a number of office professionals and then visit their human resources departments.

If they do not have an opening at that particular point, most companies will allow you to fill out an application. Generally, it will be kept on file for future possibilities. As you talk with members of the human resources department, be extremely clear about what type of position you want and the skills you have. Be concise and pleasant as you state your interests. If there are openings, call back within a week to let them know you are still interested. If there are no openings but they accept your application, you may call back within three to six months to determine if positions have become available.

Temporary Agencies

A **temporary agency** (one that offers temporary work) is not a source of job information in the usual sense. However, if you are not clear about where you want to work, a temporary agency can help you know more about various types of organizations. The agency can place you in a number of different organizations over a short period of time. Without any long-term commitment, you can gain a wealth of information that can help you decide where you want to work full-time.

Temporary agencies also provide an alternative to a full-time job. For example, individuals with young children may decide to work for a temporary agency. As a "temp," you can accept jobs on a part-time basis, allowing for more time with your children.

You have also learned that many companies are downsizing today. With downsizing, they often hire temporary workers. It can be a cost-saving measure for the company since they have fewer dollars tied up in personnel costs. Some organizations may also use temporary agencies as a way to get firsthand knowledge of employees. For example, the organization may hire a temp whose work is so good the company offers the employee a full-time job.

Job Application Process

You may have excellent performance skills but little knowledge and skill in how to apply for a job. Unless you develop these skills, you may become very frustrated during the application process. It is extremely important that you study this section carefully and apply the knowledge you develop as you search for a job.

Company Information

Before you apply for a job with a particular company, find out all you can about the company. This information is needed for two major reasons. First, you need to know if you can meet your goals by working for this company.

- Will the job be challenging?
- Will it provide opportunities for advancement?
- Will the company values and your values be compatible?

Second, you need to know as much about the company as possible in order to be prepared for the interview. One question often asked in the interview is, "Why do you want to work for this company?" Unless you know something about the company, you will not be able to answer this question.

What types of information should you be looking for about the company? Here are some good questions for you to research.

- How long has the company been in business?
- What is the financial health of the company?
- What is the corporate culture?

Before you apply for a job with a particular company, find out all you can about the company. © *PhotoDisc, Inc.*

- How does the company compare to its competitors? Is it an industry leader?
- What is the company's mission?
- What are the company's goals?
- What are the projected areas of growth for the company?
- What characteristics does the company value in its employees?

You can find the answers to these questions through the following sources:

- The Internet-many companies have home pages on the Internet; these pages generally have a wealth of information about various aspects of the organization.
- Industry trade publications and listings of corporations in such publications as *Standard & Poor's, Moody's,* and *Dunn & Bradstreet.*

- Business newspapers and periodicals such as *The Wall Street Journal, Fortune,* and *Forbes*
- Professional associations
- Personal networks

In addition to finding out information about the company, it is a good idea to find out as much as you can about the department of the company where you would be working. This information is more difficult to obtain, and you may not be able to get it unless you or a friend knows someone who works for the company. If so, these are some of the questions you should ask.

- Who will be making the hiring decision? What are the key things this person looks for in a successful candidate?
- What are the department's goals?

- Is the department considered a good place to work?
- What are the issues of the department at the present time?
- What are the responsibilities of the job?
- To whom will I report? What type of person is he or she?
- What are the biggest challenges of the job?

Letter of Application

The letter of application generally is the first contact you will have with a potential employer. The letter of application has several purposes, including:

- Introducing you to the organization
- Providing general information about your skills
- Selling your skills—letting the reader know that you have something to offer the organization
- Transmitting your resume

It makes either a favorable or an unfavorable impression on the person or persons reading it. If the impression is unfavorable, you have little chance of getting an interview. In other words, a poorly written letter of application can prevent you from even getting a chance at the job. The letter makes a statement about you. A poorly written letter can suggest that you are disorganized, sloppy, unfocused, verbose, and ill suited for employment. Conversely, a well-written letter can suggest that you are thorough, conscientious, well organized, focused, results oriented, and take considerable pride in your work.

The letter of application should be concise, consisting of one page containing three or four paragraphs. The elements of the letter are:

- An introductory paragraph that generates interest in you and your purpose for writing the letter
- A second paragraph that highlights your key strengths and abilities
- A summary statement that briefly gives your education and experience
- A statement that compels action on the part of the company
- A statement of appreciation

A good letter of application is shown in Figure 19-3, and a poor one in Figure 19-4. Notice that the poor letter is self-focused; "I" is overused. The writer is pushy and boastful also—none of the characteristics that you want to portray in the letter.

In preparing the letter, follow these tips.

- Key the letter in proper form using an acceptable letter style—either block or modified block. Block is the most commonly used format.
- Be clear and concise.
- Proofread carefully to make absolutely certain there are no spelling, punctuation, capitalization, or grammatical errors.
- Use a good grade of 8½" x 11" white or off-white bond paper. Personal or fancy stationery should not be used.
- Send an original letter (printed on a quality printer such as a laser printer or a letter-quality inkjet) for each application. Never send photocopies of your letter of application.
- Do not copy a letter of application from a book. Make your letter representative of your personality.
- Use your home address for the return address.
- Use an appropriate title for the addressee—for example, *Mr., Ms.,* or *Dr.*

2356 Shady Bend Drive
Detroit, MI 48231
May 5, 2000

Personnel Department
Saud and Wright, Inc.
478 Bellmont Drive
Detroit, MI 48231-1876

Ladies and Gentlemen

Please consider me an applicant for the position of administrative assistant that you advertised in the Sunday *Times Chronicle*. I feel I have the qualifications that match your needs, and I am most eager to work for Saud and Wright.

Your advertisement specifies an individual with excellent grammar, spelling, interpersonal, communication, and computer skills. I can keyboard at 80 wpm and have developed excellent grammar, spelling, and written communication skills through my two-year associate degree program, plus extensive letter and report writing experience on my previous job. My interpersonal skills have been developed through my leadership roles that have included President of the Marketing Club and Vice President of the Student Union Organization.

The middle of this month I will graduate from Michigan Central College with an AAS degree in Office Systems. Courses in business communications, speech, information processing, and office procedures have provided me with knowledge and skills to perform well as an administrative assistant. In addition, I have two years of office experience as a receptionist and secretary, which has helped me understand the importance of teamwork within the work environment. My resume, detailing my school and work experience, is enclosed.

I would like to discuss my qualifications and my desire to work for Saud and Wright, Inc. I will call your office within the next couple of days to arrange for a meeting at your convenience. Thank you for your consideration. I look forward to talking with you.

Sincerely

Edith Medina

Edith Medina

Enclosure

FIGURE 19-3. Good Application Letter

```
2356 Shady Bend Drive
Detroit, MI 48231-1656
May 5, 2000

Personnel Department
Saud and Wright, Inc.
478 Bellmont Drive
Detroit, MI 48201-1876

Ladies and Gentlemen:

I am writing to ask for a job. There are many reasons that I will make an excellent administrative
assistant, and I think it will be well worth your time to meet with me.

I attend Michigan Central College where I will earn an AAS degree in Office Systems this month.
Courses in business communications, speech, information processing, and office procedures have
provided me with knowledge and skills to perform well as an administrative assistant. I also have
two years of office experience as a receptionist and secretary.

I hope that I will hear from you soon and that we can meet personally to discuss how I can be-
come an administrative assistant in your company. I believe such a meeting would be very benefi-
cial for both of us.


Sincerely,

Edith Medina
Edith Medina


Enclosure
```

FIGURE 19-1. Poor Application Letter

Ms. has come to be the acceptable title for either a married or unmarried woman. Do not use *Miss* or *Mrs.* unless you know the individual and know that she prefers one of these titles. If you are sending the letter to the Human Resources Department of an organization but do not have the name of an individual, address the letter to the Personnel Director. If you are addressing your letter to an entire organization, use *Ladies and Gentlemen*.

- Use *Sincerely* or *Sincerely yours* for the complimentary close, since they are considered formal and are the most frequently used forms.
- Sign your letter with a black or blue pen.

Resume

The **resume** is a concise statement of your background, education, skills, and experience. Its purpose is to communicate clearly to prospective employers your job skills. It is your personal marketing document. A well-prepared resume markets your education, skills, and experience so effectively that it sets you apart from the other candidates for the job. Both the format and the content of the resume are critical in its effectiveness.

There are three general types of resumes—**chronological, functional,** and **targeted.** In determining the type of resume you prepare, you must consider your purpose and your background.

The chronological resume is the most popular style; it is illustrated in Figure 19-5. In this type of resume, your work experience and education are listed in reverse chronological format, starting with the most recent experience and education and working backward in time. This style works well for showing progress and growth—for example, if the jobs listed reflect increasing responsibility over time.

The functional resume organizes work experience into categories. It includes the same information as in a chronological resume but organized differently. It allows you to highlight your skills, with employment dates and previous employers of less importance. This format works well for individuals who have recently graduated and people who have a good educational background and good skills, but very little or no work experience. A functional resume is shown in Figure 19-6.

The targeted resume allows the writer to focus on a specific job and let the organization know why he or she is perfect for the job. It combines elements from both the chronological and functional resume. The major problem with this format is that if the prospective employer does not feel you are the right person for the job that you have targeted, you may not be considered for other positions within the company for which you may be qualified. Figure 19-7 illustrates a targeted resume.

Resume Parts. The resume should include six parts, with the possibility of a seventh one—references:

- Heading
- Objective
- Relevant skills
- Work experience
- Education
- Professional accomplishments

Another section that may be added to a resume is references. However, it is not essential on the resume itself. More detail is given about this topic under the "References" section later in this chapter.

Heading. The heading should include your name on the first line, followed by your home address and home telephone number. If you have an email address and/or a fax number at home, you may include this information also. Do not use a work number; it is not ethical to spend time on your present job looking for another job. Notice Figure 19-5, which depicts a well-written resume. The name, address, telephone, and email address are keyed in bold, with the name in all caps. By using all caps, the eye of the reader is quickly drawn to who you are.

Objective. The objective should define clearly the position that you desire. You may also state the department where you want to work. For example, if you are applying for an executive assistant position in the Legal Department, you may state that in your objective. However, you do not want to define your objective too narrowly. Be certain that you only want to

EDITH E. MEDINA
2356 Shady Bend Drive
Detroit, MI 48231-1876
(313) 555-0156
Fax (313) 555-0157
email eem@aol.com

OBJECTIVE: A position as an administrative assistant with the opportunity to use technological skills and communication skills.

RELEVANT SKILLS: Keyboarding at 80 wpm; proficiency in word processing, spreadsheet, graphics, calendaring, and presentation software.

Excellent written and oral communication skills; good team player.

EDUCATION: AAS, Office Systems

Michigan Central College, May 2000

Cum Laude

EMPLOYMENT HISTORY:

June 1996 to July 1998   *WAHRING CORPORATION*   *Detroit, MI*
A large commercial paper products company

Secretary (October 1996 to July 1998)
Reported to the Human Resources Director
- Wrote letters and drafted reports
- Served on the Quality Improvement Team
- Developed a new records management system

Receptionist (June 1996 to October 1996)
Reported to the Office Manager
- Greeted customers
- Answered the telephone
- Keyed correspondence for the Office Manager

LEADERSHIP   President of the Marketing Club

ACCOMPLISHMENTS   Vice President of the Student Union Organization

REFERENCES   Provided upon request

FIGURE 19-5. Chronological Resume

ROGER GALAPOLOS
1800 West Orange Blvd.
Southfield, MI 48034
(248) 555-0102
Fax (248) 555-0103
email rag@aol.com

OBJECTIVE

◆ A position as a computer technician with an opportunity to advance to a supervisory position

COMPUTER PROJECTS

◆ Set up a records management system for a small company.

◆ Trained two coworkers on the system.

TECHNICAL SKILLS

Software:

◆ Microsoft Word, Excel, Microsoft Access, Microsoft PowerPoint

Keyboarding:

◆ 90 wpm

Human Relations:

◆ Team builder

◆ Critical thinker

◆ Problem solver

◆ Self-starter

EDUCATION

◆ AAS, Computer Information Systems

North Central College, May 2001

Summa Cum Laude

◆ Business courses applicable to position include word processing, accounting, computer information systems, Visual Basic language, microcomputer applications, business communications, and management.

EMPLOYMENT HISTORY

◆ ISA Company

3400 Main Street

Southfield, MI 48034

REFERENCES

◆ Provided upon request

FIGURE 19-6. Functional Resume

MERIDITH A. VALDEZ
3095 Cascade Avenue
Grand Rapids, MI 49502
(616) 555-0148
Fax (616) 555-0149
email mav@aol.com

OBJECTIVE

◆ A position as a legal assistant with an opportunity to use research skills

EMPLOYMENT

Legal Secretary, 1999–2000

Kieba, Kieba, and Martin, Grand Rapids, Michigan

◆ Secretary to two attorneys—researched legal questions in law library within the company, prepared legal documents, maintained the filing system, used WordPerfect and Excel

Receptionist, 1998–1999

Howard & Krebs Law Firm, Kalamazoo, Michigan

◆ Keyed legal documents, greeted callers, maintained calendar for attorneys

SKILLS

◆ Legal research skills

◆ Legal terminology

◆ Keyboarding at 96 wpm

◆ Notetaking

◆ Composition

◆ Critical thinking and teambuilding

ACCOMPLISHMENTS

◆ President of Phi Theta Kappa

◆ Who's Who in Communications, Humber College

EDUCATION

Breckenridge College, Kalamazoo, Michigan, 1996–97

30 hours in Legal Assistant Program

Humber College, Clare, Michigan, 1994–1996

AAS, Communications

REFERENCES

◆ Furnished upon request

FIGURE 19-7. Targeted Resume

work in the Legal Department if you say so in your objective. By limiting your objective in this manner, you probably will not be considered for other executive assistant positions that may be available in the company.

Relevant Skills. This section may also be called "Key Qualifications" or "Qualifications Summary." The purpose of this section is to provide a brief (three- or four-line) summary of your job skills. As a person who is interested in the office professional field, you may list the following types of skills in this section.

- Software proficiency
- Hardware proficiency
- Personal strengths, such as team player, critical thinker, self-motivated

Work Experience. This section gives the reader a quick overview of where you have worked and when, along with your key accomplishments in the position. If you have worked in more than one position for the company, you can place the dates of employment with the company (beginning with the most recent employment) on the extreme left side. The dates of various positions held within the company may be placed in parentheses to the right of the department name. Figure 19-5 uses this approach. If you have limited work experience, you can build up the education section by adding business courses you have taken.

Education. Education is generally listed after work experience for someone who has held several jobs. For a recent graduate, education may be listed after the relevant skills. Since the recent graduate probably has very little work experience, the reader's attention is called quickly to what may be the person's most important qualification—education. Education is listed

in reverse chronological order, with the most recent experience listed first.

Professional Accomplishments. This section may also be titled "Scholastic Honors," "Leadership Accomplishments," or even "Professional Interests" for the recent graduate. If you are a recent graduate, you may have few, if any, professional accomplishments. However, you can list outstanding accomplishments during your college days or interests you have. For example, you may have been president of the marketing club, a leader in your dorm, or chairperson of the homecoming committee. All of these activities demonstrate leadership ability. Do not, however, overdo this section; include only those items that have some significance for the position for which you are applying.

References. It is not necessary to include references on the resume. Generally, you should prepare a reference list (being certain that you have received permission from the individuals listed) and take it with you if you obtain an interview. However, you may include a section on the resume for references and merely say that they will be furnished upon request. When you furnish references, follow these guidelines.

- Always ask permission to use a person's name before doing so.
- Be certain that you have the correct address, telephone number, and email or fax number for the reference.
- List people who are employed; they usually are more familiar with what is expected of employees.
- Include people who know you well and, if possible, who are in supervisory or managerial positions.
- Do not list relatives.
- Teachers may be listed if you performed well in the class.

Resume Guidelines. When preparing a resume, follow these guidelines.

- If you are a recent graduate and have held only part-time jobs, list them. Or, if you have not had any paid work experience, list volunteer jobs or leadership positions that you have held. It is never wise to list "none" under the work experience category. If you absolutely have nothing that can be listed under work experience, omit this category from your resume.

- Keep the resume concise—one or two pages at a maximum.

- Tailor your resume for the specific job opening, highlighting those areas of your background or work experience that fit the position for which you are applying.

- Do not use personal pronouns (I, me, you, and so on). They are unnecessary and detract from the impact of the resume.

- Describe your qualifications and skills in specific terms—avoid vague language.

- Use standard 8½" x 11" white or off-white paper.

- Use common typefaces such as Times New Roman, Courier, or Arial. If you are applying for a job in a creative field such as television, you may want to choose a less traditional typeface. However, you should avoid being too creative; some typefaces are difficult to read. Do not use multiple typefaces on the same resume.

- Margins should be from a minimum of 0.6" to a maximum of 1" for the left, right, top, and bottom.

- Print your resume on a high-quality printer such as a laser printer or letter-quality inkjet printer. Never photocopy your resume.

- Use 12-point type for the body of the resume; you may use 14-point type for your name.

- Check your spelling and grammar usage. Many employers will discard a resume if just one spelling, typographical, or grammatical error is found. Do not rely on the spell-check feature of your computer to find every error. Remember that there are a number of errors that spell check will not find. Read and reread the resume several times; then ask someone else who is a good proofreader to read it for you.

- Take advantage of professional help in writing your resume—check the Internet for sources, talk with your placement office at school, or visit a bookstore or the library for materials on how to prepare a resume.

Electronic Resumes. A number of organizations today are using computer tracking systems to search through resumes and narrow the search to a few individuals. If your resume is not easy for the computer to scan, errors can be made. Therefore, if there is a possibility that your resume will be electronically scanned, do not use the format given in Figure 19-5, with bold type and underscoring. Do follow these guidelines.

- Do not use bold, italics, or underlining.

- Use a basic font such as Times New Roman or Courier.

- Use a standard typesize (12 point).

- Use a standard resume format.

- Do not use any abbreviations.

The computer is often programmed to pick up certain key words. Many times these words are listed in the advertisement; you should use them in your resume. For example, an administrative assistant should list specific software programs that he or she can operate—Microsoft Office, WordPerfect, Excel, Lotus, and so forth. If the ad requests a keyboarding skill of 80 wpm, state your keyboarding rate clearly in your resume.

In addition to an organization doing a computer scan on your resume, there are some advantages to having a resume that may be easily scanned electronically:

- You can send your resume by email to a prospective employer.
- You can add your resume to online databases—a free service offered by career-related sites.
- You prove to the prospective employer that you are computer literate.

Employment Application

Either before or after an interview, you may be asked to fill out an **employment application.** If you complete the application in the office, use a black or blue tip pen. Never use a color such as red or green. If an employer mails you an application, you may key it or neatly print it. If you are keying or printing the application, you may want to make a copy of it and fill out the copy before filling in the form you are going to mail back to the company. Using this approach allows you to correct any errors that you make due to misreading the question, spacing problems, and so forth.

A portion of a completed application is shown in Figure 19-8. Here are additional suggestions that will help you in completing an application.

- Read the entire application before completing it.
- When filling in the form by hand, use your best penmanship. Print unless your handwriting is extremely neat.

- Answer every question. If there is a question that does not apply to you (such as military experience), put NA, meaning "not applicable," in the space provided. Leaving a space completely blank may give the impression that you missed the question.
- Be certain to check your spelling. If you are filling out the application at the company, carry a pocket dictionary to ensure that you will not make a mistake or have to ask the receptionist how to spell a word.
- Be prepared to fill out an application at the company. Have all information with you that you will need—dates you attended school, dates of employment, and complete addresses of previous employers and references. Also, you will need your social security number.
- Be honest. Do not falsify any information on the application; to do so is grounds for firing. State accurately the experience and skills that you have. To try to "look good" by adding skills or experiences that you do not have will not serve you well in the long run. If you get the job, you will be expected to perform at the level that you indicated. If you are unable to do so, you will not be able to keep the job. It is important to be honest even if the information that you have to give is negative. For example, a common question is: "Why did you leave your last job?" If you were fired from your job, you must indicate that you were. However, you can say it in a positive manner; your statement might be, "Skills did not match what was needed by the organization." Never be critical of a former employer.
- Some applications provide space for additional comments. This section

EMPLOYMENT APPLICATION

Date of Application _May 22, 2002_

People First International

AN EQUAL OPPORTUNITY EMPLOYER

PERSONAL INFORMATION

Name of
Applicant _Oliver_ _Wendell_ _Carver_
          First   Middle   Last

Social Security No. _012-34-5678_

Present Address _84 West Maple Avenue_

Phone _(413) 623-8749_

City _Danbury, Massachusetts_

Zip Code _21865_

Kind of _Office Manager_

☒ Full Time   ☒ 1st Shift

Work _____

☐ Part Time   ☐ 2nd Shift

Desired _____

☐ Summer   ☐ 3rd Shift

MILITARY INFORMATION

Type of Work	_none_	Entered Mo. Yr.	Discharged Mo. Yr.
Special Training			
Branch	☐ Air Force ☐ Army ☐ Coast Guard ☐ Navy ☐ Marines		

EMPLOYMENT HISTORY

(Please Complete Even If Supplemented by a Résumé)

List Most Recent Position First	MONTHLY SALARY	EMPLOYED		TOTAL MONTHS
		FROM	TO	
1. Employer _Spencer Construction Company_ Address _16 Sudbury Drive_ Name & Title of Supervisor _Madeline Wright/VP_ Your Position and Duties _Secretary to the Vice President_	$ _2,000_	8 98	9 99	13
	REASON FOR LEAVING _career advancement_			
2. Employer _Alpha Sign Inc._ Address _6845 Landview Parkway_ Name & Title of Supervisor _Antonio Anoro_ Your Position and Duties _Office Assistant_	$ _1,400_	6 95	8 98	38
	REASON FOR LEAVING _relocation_			

FIGURE 19-8. A Portion of an Employment Application

gives you a chance to point out your abilities, your desire to work for the company, or your outstanding achievements.

Interview

Assume that you have done well thus far in the application process. Now you will get the chance you have been wanting—a chance to interview. The interview gives you another opportunity to market yourself. It is important that you prepare yourself extremely well for this process.

Portfolio Information.   You may wish to prepare a **portfolio** of your work to take with you to the interview. A portfolio is merely a compilation of samples of your work. The work should be arranged attractively in a binder. Here are some items that you might wish to include:

- Letters that you have written to demonstrate your writing style
- Spreadsheets and graphics that you have prepared to demonstrate your knowledge of software
- Research reports that you have written to demonstrate your ability to conduct research

Location of the Interview.   Be certain you know the exact time and location of the interview. Do not rely on your memory. Write down the time, address, and person's name you are to see and take it with you. When traveling to the interview location, allow time for unexpected delays. It is a good idea to take a practice drive to the location the day before the interview (at the same time the interview is scheduled) so that you can allow the appropriate time for traveling and parking. It is imperative that you not be late for the interview. Excuses made for being late will

not erase the poor impression you have already made. When you arrive at the interview location on the day of the interview, be pleasant with everyone you see— receptionists, administrative assistants, and so forth. Keep a smile on your face and say "thank you" often. You never know who will be asked about you or who will make comments about you.

Number of Interviews.   It is possible that you will have more than one interview. For example, you may be interviewed initially by a human resources professional. Next, you may see the person to whom you will report. Be prepared for this prospect.

Team Interviews.   You have already learned that organizations today are using teams in a number of situations. This team approach often carries over to interviews. For example, the group of people who will work with you may interview you as a group. Usually, the teams consist of no more than four or five people. Although this type of interview sounds intimidating, it need not be so. Follow these guidelines when being interviewed by a team.

- Pay careful attention to each individual's name as he or she is introduced.
- As each person asks a question, focus on that person. Listen carefully and answer the question succinctly.
- When you ask a question, ask it of the group unless one person has said something that you wish to follow up.
- Make eye contact with all individuals if the question or statement is meant for the entire group.
- If you find yourself getting nervous, glance occasionally at the person or persons who have given you positive feedback—the ones who have a

In addition to being interviewed by one person, you may also be interviewed by a team. © *Digital Vision*.

friendly face, open body language, and positive reactions to your responses. Say to yourself, "This person likes me; I am doing well."

- Thank the group after the interview is over.

Virtual Interviews. You have learned throughout this text about the virtual office—one where work may be performed from any place at any time using technology. Some organizations are now using the **virtual interview,** where a prospective employee can be interviewed at any place at any time using technology.

Assume that you are applying for a job in New York. You live in Texas. The company makes arrangements for you to go to a facility in Texas that has teleconferencing capabilities for the interview. The interviewer or interviewers from New York can see you and talk with you, and you can see and talk with them. You are being interviewed virtually in an interactive environment.

Since most of us get a little nervous when we know that a camera is present, it is important that you be extremely well prepared for a virtual interview. Here are some tips in this area:

- Greet the interviewer warmly and with a smile just as you would in person. Repeat the interviewer's name. For example, say, "I'm happy to meet you, Ms. VanAndel."

- Sit back in the chair provided; do not sit on the edge of your chair. Sitting on the edge of the chair may connote nervousness to the interviewer.

- Concentrate on the interviewer, not on the camera. Try to forget the camera is there.
- Dress in colors that look good on you. Remember that black or gray does not generally come across well on camera. Be certain that you are not wearing jewelry that jingles or clangs. This noise is even more noticeable on camera than in person.
- Pay attention to the body language and small nuances of the interviewer. Do not spend an inordinate amount of time answering any one question. Be warm and informative, but also concise.
- Enunciate carefully. Poor enunciation is more pronounced on camera than in person.
- Once the interview is over, thank the person and leave the teleconferencing room.
- Read carefully the hints given later in this chapter for the traditional interview. Many of these hints also apply in a virtual interview.

Pre-Interview Nervousness.   It is both natural and normal to feel nervous before an interview. Most people have such feelings. In fact, nervousness can cause productive behavior—you probably will prepare for the interview better when you are concerned that you will not do well. However, you do want to control your nervousness. Here are some suggestions for doing so.

- Spend your time and energy before the interview in researching the company, reassessing your skills and abilities, and practicing the interview with a friend. Get someone to ask you questions that may be asked during an interview. Frequently asked interview

questions for all job applicants are given in Figure 19-9 and frequently asked questions of the recent graduate are given in Figure 19-10. Review these questions carefully, and think through how you would respond to each one. Frequent mistakes made by interviewees are given in Figure 19-11.

- Do not place all your hopes on one interview. Know that if you do not get this job there are other jobs. As you are conducting your job search, select several companies in which you are interested. If you have had little or no work experience and have not been on many interviews, you may want to go on as many interviews as possible (even if you are not certain you are interested in the job). Such an approach provides a number of learning opportunities for you. However, if you have had several jobs and have been on several interviews, you should apply only for jobs in which you are interested. You do not want to waste your time or the employer's interviewing for a position that you are certain is of no interest to you.
- Plan something to do the night before the interview so that you will not spend the time going over and over the interview. Go to a movie; go out to dinner with a friend.
- Use stress reduction techniques that you learned in Chapters 3 and 11 such as visualization and deep breathing.

Helpful Hints.   These hints will help you make a good impression during the interview.

- Dress appropriately. The safest look is a conservative one, even if you are applying for a creative position. Wear a color that looks good on you. Some industries are typically more conservative

FREQUENTLY ASKED INTERVIEW QUESTIONS

- Tell me about yourself. (Although this is not a question, it is used many times as a conversation starter. It is difficult to respond to this item since it is open-ended.)

- What are your goals?

- What are your strengths?

- What are your weaknesses?

- How would you describe yourself?

- What are your plans for the future?

- What kind of supervisor do you want?

- What do you know about our company?

- How do you define success?

- Why should we hire you?

- Tell me about an ethical dilemma you have faced. (Another request rather than a question; with this request, the interviewer is attempting to assess your integrity and work ethic.)

- What were your responsibilities on your last Job?

- What qualifies you to do this job?

- Are you presently employed? If so, is your present employer aware of your interest in changing jobs?

- If you could have any position, what would it be? Why?

- Which duties performed in the past have you liked the best? the least? Why?

- When working on a team, which role do you usually take?

- In which kind of atmosphere do you work best?

Note on salary: You should have an idea of an appropriate salary before going to the interview. Although salaries are not always listed in job advertisements, your local paper is one source for checking area salaries. Your placement office is another good source for local information.

Also, you can ask the interviewer the starting rate for the company. If you are willing to take that rate, you merely respond that the rate is appropriate. If you feel that the starting salary is below the average rate for that particular type of work, you may reply that you had hoped to start at a slightly higher salary. However, you are primarily interested in an opportunity to show what you can do and take advantage of the chances for promotion (if this is true). If not, you can say you are not interested in the salary offered. However, be certain that you are not interested before you respond in this manner.

FIGURE 19-9. Frequently Asked Interview Questions

FREQUENTLY ASKED INTERVIEW QUESTIONS OF THE RECENT GRADUATE

- How did you choose your college?
- Why did you choose to major in . . .?
- Tell me about your senior project/thesis/other major project.
- How has your college experience prepared you for a career?
- Describe your most rewarding extracurricular experience in college.
- If you had to do it over again, how would you plan your education differently?
- Are your grades representative of your abilities?
- What was your worst grade, and how did it happen?
- Who was your favorite professor, and why?
- Which teaching styles do you learn from best?
- Why didn't you hold any leadership roles in college?
- How did you pay for school?
- How would your classmates describe you?

FIGURE 19-10. Frequently Asked Interview Questions of the Recent Graduate. Source: Michelle Tullier, *The Unofficial Guide to Acing the Interview* (New York: Simon & Schuster-Macmillan, 1999), 255.

not want to wear any perfume or cologne; some people are allergic to it.

- Good grooming is critical; you might want to have your hair styled and a manicure the day before the interview.
- Get a good night's rest before the interview so that you will be alert.
- Carry a briefcase. Females should try to do without a handbag; there is one less item to juggle. Have an extra copy of your resume in your briefcase, along with your references. Have a pad and pen in your briefcase for note taking.
- Stand and walk with your head erect and your shoulders back.
- Greet the receptionist with a friendly smile, stating your name and the purpose of your visit.
- Say "thank you" often—to the receptionist if you are offered a magazine while you are waiting and to the interviewer if you are offered coffee or water.

than others—for example, the banking industry. If you are applying for a job in an area that is considered conservative, you may want to wear a dark blue suit or dress. However, generally such conservatism is not necessary today. Bright colors are acceptable; however, colors do have meanings that may need to be considered. Figure 19-12 gives the symbolism of various colors.

- Keep the amount of jewelry you wear to a minimum. Too much jewelry can cause noise that is distracting to the interviewer. Avoid excessive makeup, perfume, and cologne. In fact, you may

FREQUENT INTERVIEWING MISTAKES

- Lacking interest or enthusiasm
- Emphasizing pay
- Sloppy application
- Criticizing past employers
- Being late
- Not making eye contact
- Failing to express appreciation for the interview
- Having no questions about the position
- A know-it-all attitude
- Vague responses

FIGURE 19-11. Frequent Interviewing Mistakes. Source: Interview Guide, published by Acquinas College. The Grand Rapids Press, Sunday, May 17, 1998, B2.

COLOR SYMBOLISM

Yellow (when bold)	Positive: Power, joy, wisdom, intuitional insight, youth, merriment
	Negative: Cowardice
Green	Positive: Nature, healing, peace, regeneration, fortune
	Negative: Selfishness, jealousy, laziness
Red	Positive: Power, energy, vitality, strength, excitement for life, passion
	Negative: Anger, danger, uncontrolled passion, suffering
Blue	Positive: Truth, harmony, calmness, soothing
	Negative: Depressing
White	Positive: Innocence, purity, perfection, trust
	Negative: Intolerable to people who are deceitful, malicious, jealous, violent
Black	Positive: Absence of light, strength, power
	Negative: Emotional drain, loss, death

FIGURE 19-12. Color Symbolism. Source: Michelle Tullier, *The Unofficial Guide to Acing the Interview* (New York: Simon & Schuster-Macmillan, 1999) 130.

- Give a firm handshake to the interviewer.
- When entering the room for the interview, wait to sit until you are invited to do so.
- Keep your hand gestures to a minimum. Some movement of your hands while speaking is natural, but do not flail your hands and arms around excessively.
- Do not play with your hair or jewelry.
- Don't invade the personal space of others. Maintain a space of three to five feet from the person with whom you are talking.
- Don't furrow your brow or tense your jaw. Keep a pleasant look on your face.

- Don't nod your head excessively, such movement can indicate nervousness.
- Maintain appropriate eye contact. Look at the person talking most of the time; however, do break eye contact occasionally so that you do not appear to be staring at the person.
- Display good humor and a ready smile.
- Be discreet; do not reveal personal confidential information about your former coworkers or employer.
- Show genuine interest in what the interviewer says and be alert to all questions.
- Don't talk too much. When you do talk, take your time. Answer the

questions carefully. When the interviewer asks if you have questions, state them clearly and concisely. Listen to the answers you are given. Some appropriate questions that you might ask are:

Would you please describe the specific duties of the job?

What characteristics are you seeking in the person to fill this position?

What do you consider to be ideal experience for the job?

Can you tell me something about the people I will be working with if I am accepted for this position?

When will you make a decision about hiring for this position?

- Try to understand your prospective employer's needs and show how you can fill them.

- Do not smoke or chew gum.

- Answer questions completely and succinctly. Do not give your life history. Also, do not answer the questions with only one word. Your task is to answer completely without being verbose.

- At the close of the interview, attempt to determine what the next step will be. Will there be another interview? When can you expect to hear the results of the interview?

Interview Follow-Up. Promptly after the interview, write a **follow-up letter** that includes:

- A thank-you for the opportunity to interview

- A recap of your skills and abilities

- A statement of your continued interest in the job

- A reminder of the next steps you agreed on in the interview, such as when the decision is going to be made.

A sample of a letter you might write is given in Figure 19-13.

If no action is taken in regard to your application within a reasonable time (one to two weeks), a second follow-up letter or a call may be advisable. The second letter should merely remind the employer of your having been interviewed and express your continued interest in the job. Depending on the situation, it may be appropriate to make a third contact with the organization. Being persistent can be seen as a plus by the organization since it shows your clear interest in the job. However, you do not want to annoy the employer unnecessarily. Use your good judgment in determining how many follow-ups are appropriate in each job situation.

Of course, it is possible that after the interview you will decide that you are not interested in the position. In such a case, you should promptly send a courteous letter in which you express your appreciation for having been considered and explain why you do not wish the position. Although you are not interested in the present position, you may at a later point be interested in a position with the company. If so, the courteous way in which you decline the first position will help you in being considered a second time. If you are turned down for a job, write a thank-you note to the employer expressing appreciation for the chance to interview and asking that your resume be kept on file for future jobs. Even though you were not selected for the current job, you want to keep the doors open for future possibilities.

Interview Evaluation. If you are interested in the job and do not get it, you will probably be given a standard reason. To avoid potential legal problems, most companies will not give you an exact

2356 Shady Bend Drive
Detroit, MI 48231-1656
May 25, 2000

Ms. Andrea Zipinski
Human Resources Manager
Saud and Wright, Inc.
Detroit, MI 48201-1876

Dear Ms. Zipinski:

Thank you for the opportunity to interview with you this morning. It was a pleasure to meet you and to learn more about Saud and Wright.

Your company is a place that I would enjoy working, and I feel that my skills and experience would be beneficial for your team. My written and oral communication skills are strong, and my technical skills are current. Please give me the opportunity to prove that I can be a valuable employee.

You may reach me at home by calling 555-0156. I look forward to hearing from you soon.

Sincerely,

Edith Medina

Edith Medina

FIGURE 19-13. Follow-up Letter

reason. Also, you will probably not be told of anything you did wrong in the interview. In fact, you may have done very well and still not get the job. It is a good idea to go over the experience in your mind. Play back what happened. Jot down your thoughts on how you did. Note the questions that you had trouble answering. Note any questionable reactions from the interviewer(s). Think about how you might correct any possible errors before the next interview. Review your thoughts and notes with a trusted advisor. Ask him or her how you might improve. Being rejected for a job is no reason to become depressed. Do not lose confidence in your skills and abilities. Learn from each interview situation. Keep trying and maintain a positive attitude.

Even if you are offered the job and do accept it, it is a good idea to evaluate the interview situation. You may not have handled some of the questions as well as you believe you should have. Review how you may do it better the next time. Each interview situation provides a chance for you to learn and grow. If you accept the job, let your network of people who have been helping you in the job process know that you have accepted a position. Thank each individual for his or her help; such thoughtfulness lets your network know that you are sincerely appreciative of their help.

Job Performance

The reward for completing the job search process successfully is getting the position you want. Once you have the position, maintain the same enthusiasm you had when you applied for the position. You were selected because you were considered the right person for the job. Now is the time to prove you can do what you said in the application letter, the resume, and the interview.

Listen, Observe, and Learn

As you begin your new job, listen to what coworkers and your supervisor tell you. Observe what is expected and what is accepted in the office. Observe your coworkers who have the respect of their colleagues. Discuss with these people how they perform various jobs. Ask questions when you do not understand something you have been instructed to do by your supervisor. It is much better to ask than to do it wrong.

Ask about the directions of your department. If a strategic plan has been developed by your organization, ask to read it. Find out if there is a written job description for your position. Study it; if you have questions about the job description, ask your supervisor. Talk with your supervisor about what he or she expects of you. Establish a plan of action for what you intend to accomplish for the next three to six months. Review your plan with your supervisor to see if you both agree with the goals you have established.

Grow from the Performance Appraisal

Good supervisors not only provide you with ongoing feedback about the work you are doing, but they also do formal evaluations of your job performance after you have been on the job for three to six months. Thereafter the evaluation usually is done once each year. These evaluations are called **performance appraisals.** Figure 19-14 shows a sample performance appraisal form. The appraisal may be based on short-range goals that you have established with your supervisor, on items that appear on your job description, or on a standard evaluation form that is used for all office professionals. When you are first employed, find out how you are going to be evaluated. If a form is going to be used, get a copy of it. If you are not receiving any feedback on your job, you may request a discussion with your supervisor about your job performance.

Rather than being afraid to be evaluated, accept the evaluation as a chance for you to learn and grow. Listen openly to

Accept the performance appraisal as a way for you to learn and grow on the job. © *CORBIS.*

SAUD and WRIGHT, INC.
Professional Support Staff Performance Evaluation

Employee Name _____

Job Title _____

Supervisor _____

Assessment

4   Performance demonstrates consistent and important contributions which surpass defined expectations of the position.
3   Performance demonstrates attainment of the defined expectations of the position.
2   Performance has not reached a satisfactory level. Improved performance on this factor is needed to achieve defined expectations of this position.
1   Performance demonstrates deficiencies which seriously interfere with the attainment of the defined expectations of the position.

Organization Skills

Assessment

	4	3	2	1
Prioritizes tasks.	☐	☐	☐	☐
Plans steps to accomplish tasks.	☐	☐	☐	☐
Meets deadlines.	☐	☐	☐	☐
Attends to detail.	☐	☐	☐	☐

Attendance

Assessment

	4	3	2	1
Adheres to scheduled work hours.	☐	☐	☐	☐
Uses leave appropriately.	☐	☐	☐	☐
Uses break period appropriately.	☐	☐	☐	☐
Adjusts work schedule at supervisor's request.	☐	☐	☐	☐

Quality

Assessment

	4	3	2	1
Performs work accurately.	☐	☐	☐	☐
Demonstrates neatness.	☐	☐	☐	☐
Demonstrates thoroughness and attention to detail.	☐	☐	☐	☐

Job Knowledge

Assessment

	4	3	2	1
Uses required job skills.	☐	☐	☐	☐
Demonstrates knowledge of organizational functions needed to perform the job.	☐	☐	☐	☐
Demonstrates knowledge of procedures needed to perform the job.	☐	☐	☐	☐

Cooperation

Assessment

	4	3	2	1
Appreciates and respects responsibilities of others.				
Provides assistance and guidance to others.	☐	☐	☐	☐
Accepts guidance from supervisor.	☐	☐	☐	☐
Works toward workgroup and company goals.	☐	☐	☐	☐
	☐	☐	☐	☐

FIGURE 19-14. Performance Appraisal

SAUD and WRIGHT, INC.
Professional Support Staff Performance Evaluation

Communication

Assessment

	4	3	2	1
Conveys ideas effectively.	☐	☐	☐	☐
Responds to ideas conveyed by others.	☐	☐	☐	☐
Demonstrates appropriate professional courtesy.	☐	☐	☐	☐
Demonstrates sensitivity to a diverse staff.	☐	☐	☐	☐

Problem-Solving Skills

Assessment

	4	3	2	1
Demonstrates the ability to identify the problem.	☐	☐	☐	☐
Demonstrates the ability to select the best solution.	☐	☐	☐	☐
Follows through on chosen solution.	☐	☐	☐	☐
Takes action to prevent future problems.	☐	☐	☐	☐

Supervision Requires

Assessment

	4	3	2	1
Supervision Required.	☐	☐	☐	☐
Does not require supervision to accomplish routine jobs.	☐	☐	☐	☐
Gives constructive feedback to supervisor.	☐	☐	☐	☐
Responds to supervision in a positive manner.	☐	☐	☐	☐

Initiative

Assessment

	4	3	2	1
Seeks additional job knowledge.	☐	☐	☐	☐
Seeks new ideas and methods to improve results.	☐	☐	☐	☐
Develops new ideas and methods to improve results.	☐	☐	☐	☐
Exhibits self-motivation to achieve work group goals.	☐	☐	☐	☐

Supervisor's Comments

_____

_____

_____

_____

Employee's Comments

_____

_____

_____

Employee's Signature _____ Date _____

Supervisor's Signature _____ Date _____

FIGURE 19-14. *(Continued)*

what the evaluator is saying. Here are some other suggestions to help you learn from a performance appraisal and avoid becoming defensive.

- Offer any significant information relating to your performance that the evaluator may not know. Let the evaluator know what you believe you have done well and areas where you want to improve your performance. Before you go into your evaluation session, think through a growth plan that you intend to carry out. Let the evaluator know what you intend to do.

- Maintain eye contact with the evaluator.

- Discuss any issues honestly. Maintain a calm and professional demeanor.

- Ask the evaluator to provide specific examples of general statements such as "Your performance exceeds expectations" or "You have a poor attitude."

- Accept an adverse evaluation as a criticism of your performance, not of you as an individual.

- Resolve to correct your mistakes, and learn from them.

- Accept the evaluation as the organization's way of emphasizing your performance strengths, pointing out any performance weaknesses, and helping you to improve your performance.

If you are certain that your employer is unfairly evaluating your performance, there is usually a grievance policy provided within the organization. You will want to check with the Human Resources Department as to such a policy. However, it is not a good idea to complain after an initial evaluation. You need to realize that you are learning. If after two or more evaluations you are certain that your job performance is good yet you are receiving poor evaluations, then you may want to follow the grievance procedure. Be cautious, however. You do not want the reputation of someone who constantly complains. A better alternative may be to seek a transfer within the company or begin looking for other job opportunities.

Job Advancement

If this is your first job, do not be too eager to move up quickly. Take time to learn your job well and to work well with others. Do not let ambitious thoughts for advancement interfere with the performance of your current duties.

If you have several years of experience, you may begin thinking of advancement opportunities slightly quicker than if you are a beginning employee. Be ready for a promotion should the opportunity occur. Find out if there are established career paths in the company. Be aware of the various positions in the company for which you have the skill and ability.

Advancement Strategies

Whether you are a beginning employee who will not be ready for advancement for a period of time or an experienced employee who might take advantage of advancement opportunities quickly, you will constantly need to develop skills, traits, and knowledge that will prepare you for moving up the employment ladder. These include:

- Commitment
- Communication skills
- Positive attitudinal traits
- Networking

Commitment. Commitment is defined as the state of being bound emotionally or intellectually to some course of action. Commitment in the workplace implies that you understand the directions of the company, and you are committed to working hard to produce both short- and long-term success for your company. You have decided that your goals and the company goals are compatible, and you are willing to use your talents and energy to help achieve those goals.

Communication Skills. You have learned in this course that oral, written, and nonverbal communication skills are important. You have worked on improving your ability in this area. As you continue to learn on the job, remember that the development of communication skills is an ongoing process. You must continue to:

• Accept and respect people of different cultures, races, ethnicities, and backgrounds

• Listen carefully to what people say and what they do not say

• Observe nonverbal behaviors such as gestures, facial expressions, and voice

• Question and paraphrase

• Reserve judgment

Positive Attitudinal Traits. Continue to develop a positive attitude. Be energetic and enthusiastic. Employers, as well as coworkers, are attracted to positive people. No one likes to work with a person who is negative and constantly finds fault with everyone and everything. Be positive about your own abilities. Believe in yourself; believe that you can learn to do almost anything you want to do. Have the courage to continue to learn even if it seems difficult at times.

Networking Skills. Networking is defined in a work context as the process of identifying and establishing a group of ac-

quaintances and friends who reach out and help each other. As you work within a company, you can use your communication skills to successfully network with others. You can offer others encouragement, share information with them, and help them succeed. In turn, others will generally reciprocate with that same help for you.

In addition, it is important to network with people outside your company. It is good to talk with people in your same position with other companies to gain a broader frame of reference for your career area. Also, it is good to network with people who have greater power and influence. By doing so, you will not only learn from them but gain valuable contacts.

Job Change

As you continue in your career, it is important that you review your own personal mission statement and your long-term goals and objectives periodically. You will recall that in addition to learning how to establish goals and objectives in Chapter 1, you learned how to write a mission statement in Chapter 8. After reviewing both your mission statement and your long-term goals, you may decide that they do not match those of the organization where you are presently employed.

Leaving an Organization. If you do contemplate leaving an organization, analyze your reasons carefully. Remember that you have probably put much time and energy into finding the job you have, and you have invested months and maybe years in the company. In analyzing your reasons for wanting to make a change, ask yourself these questions:

• Have I reviewed my mission statement and goals objectively?

- Have I reviewed the goals and directions of the company where I work objectively?
- Are my mission statement and goals realistic?
- Can I find a job that matches my needs?
- Are there problems on my present job that are caused by my own lack of skills or abilities?

A quiz entitled "How Well Does Your Job Match Up with Your Life?" is given in Figure 19-15. If you are presently employed, take the quiz and see how you score.

If, after carefully analyzing all of your reasons for wanting to make a change, you are convinced that it is right for you, leave the organization in a professional manner. Give significant notice to your employer—at least two weeks and more if possible. Make a list of the positive learning experiences you have had in the company. Reflect on the people who have helped you. Take the time to say thank you to these people before you leave. Thank not only the executives with

---

HOW WELL DOES YOUR JOB MATCH UP WITH YOUR LIFE?

Rate yourself by assigning points from one to five for each item. One means that the statement does not describe your situation. Two means that the statement is not very much like your feelings. Three means sometimes "yes" and sometimes "no." Four indicates the statement is a little like your feelings. Five means it sounds a lot like the way you feel.

1. I feel my career expresses the most important aspects of who I am.
2. I feel my decisions are the main things that determine the course of my career.
3. I feel in control of my career.
4. I feel creative at work.
5. I feel the work I do makes a positive difference.
6. I feel I have a good balance between work and family.
7. When I look to the future, I see new and interesting challenges.
8. I am genuinely interested in what I do.
9. I feel that my input and contribution at work are valued.
10. I always feel that I have positive options for myself at work.

Add up your score.

- A score of 45–50: You have a great deal of satisfaction with your career and how it is going.
- A score of 35–44: You are somewhat optimistic about your career.
- A score of 25–34: One or more significant aspects of your life are out of balance with your career.
- A score of 10–24: You seem to have a great deal of dissatisfaction with your career.

FIGURE 19-15. How Well Does Your Job Match Up with Your Life? Source: Jeffrey Spar and Steven M. Warner, *Detroit Free Press*, June 30, 1998, 3E.

whom you have worked, but also your coworkers and people in other departments of the company who have helped you.

Handling the Exit Interview. Many companies ask that employees who are leaving do an **exit interview.** A completed exit interview form is shown in Figure 19-16. An impartial person—often a staff member in the personnel office—usually does the exit interview, not your immediate supervisor. It is not appropriate to make derogatory remarks about your supervisor or to unduly criticize the company in an exit interview. If you have had problems with your supervisor, those problems should have been addressed during the course of your employment. However, this is not to suggest that you should not be honest in the exit interview. State your reasons for leaving clearly and concisely. For example, if you are leaving for a position that is at a higher level than you have now, you might say, "I have decided to accept a position with greater responsibility." As you leave the job, keep in mind the old adage about not burning your bridges. Remember that you will probably need a reference from the company at some point.

EXIT INTERVIEW/TERMINATION FORM

TO BE COMPLETED BY SUPERVISOR:

NAME: Wang   Eileen   S.   297-37-6218.
      Last   First   M.

JOB TITLE *Administrative Assistant*

FULL TIME
HIRE DATE 4/7/19--   TERMINATION DATE
(LAST DAY WORKED) 1/30/19--

ELIGIBLE FOR REHIRE _____ Yes _____ No

COMMENTS *Eileen is a hard working and conscientious employee.*

REASON FOR TERMINATION *Leaving for job with greater responsibilities.*

IF INVOLUNTARY, CHECK BELOW

_____ PERFORMANCE _____ MISCONDUCT

PROPERTY CLEARANCE FORM INITIATED _____
                     Supv. Initials/Date

    Immediate Supervisor

TO BE COMPLETED BY INTERVIEWER

Area of concern discussed during the exit interview should be determined below by interviewer.

SUBJECT AREA	Satis-factory	Unsatis-factory	No Opinion	Comments
1. Work load/ Responsibilities				
2. Working Conditions				
3. Satisfaction Received from Work				
4. Attention to Employee Ideas				
5. Supervision				
6. Employee Benefits				
7. Advancement Opportunities				
8. Other				

INTERVIEWER'S CHECKLIST

_____ Property Clearance Form Completed
_____ Termination Notification Form Completed
_____ Benefits Discussed
_____ Retirement Funds Discussed
_____ Leave Balance   Day(s) Discussed

Paul C. Meeden   1/30/19--
Interviewer   Date
Eileen Wang   1/30/19--
Employee   Date

Post Employment Plans *Position with another company* Not Interviewed _____ Explained _____

Additional Comments *Eileen has been satisfied with position except for advancement opportunities.*

FIGURE 19-16. Sample Exit Interview

Involuntary Removal

You may have to face the situation of not choosing to leave a job but having to leave because you have been laid off or fired. Both situations are presented here.

Dealing with a Layoff

The layoff may have nothing to do with your job performance or your abilities but may be due to a financial situation or change of direction within the company. For example, the company may be downsizing. Whatever the reason for the layoff, it will take a period of time for you to feel okay about the situation. When you have been laid off, it is time to take a hard look at what you want to do in the future and where the job growth is. Here are some questions you can ask yourself.

- What are the growth occupations?
- What companies are hiring?
- Am I willing to relocate? If so, to what part of the country?
- Are there skills that I need to acquire for future employment?
- Do I need more formal education?

Talk with friends and advisers about job opportunities. Consult a career counselor at your local community college or university. Check job opportunities on the Internet and in the newspapers. Check with employment agencies on what jobs are available.

Surviving Being Fired

Sometimes individuals are fired from a job. The firing can occur for a variety of reasons, including:

- Lack of skills or knowledge needed to perform the job
- Ineffective human relation skills such as inability to deal effectively with clients or customers
- Poor attendance and lack of punctuality
- Conflict with the supervisor

Being fired is difficult for anyone to handle. It is normal to feel anger. You may be able to talk through your anger with your family or friends. It certainly is not a good idea to become angry at work and lash out at your employer. Instead, try to express that anger outside of work. Keep in mind that your feelings of rejection and insecurity are normal. However, it is not a time to consider yourself a total failure. It is time to carefully analyze why you were fired.

Listen to what your employer tells you about your performance. What can you learn for the future?

- If the firing is due to your lack of skills or knowledge, what skills and knowledge do you need to develop for the future?
- If it is due to your inability to deal effectively with people, what traits do you need to work on?
- If it is because of poor attendance or lack of punctuality, why were you consistently late or why did you miss numerous days of work?

Strive to get the answers to these questions. You may want to review your situation with a trusted friend or adviser who can help you look as objectively as possible at yourself. Your goal is to analyze your weaknesses and then concentrate on what you may do to improve for the future.

Beginning the Recareering Process

Before you begin looking for another job, spend time analyzing your mission statement, goals, and objectives. Evaluate your strengths and your weaknesses. You may decide that it is time for you not only to change jobs but also to **recareer** (change careers). If you are considering such a move, take the time to determine growth employment areas and career paths within the various fields.

Growth Employment Areas. You might define one, two, or three areas that you are interested in pursuing. Once you have identified these areas, find out what the growth possibilities in each area are. You may do this by:

- Talking with individuals who are in your areas of interest and asking them about the growth potential of the areas
- Reviewing periodicals such as *U.S. News & World Report* and *Fortune* that often carry articles on growth industries
- Checking with the career counseling department of a local college or university
- Checking the Internet

Career Audit. Once you determine a field you are interested in pursuing, conduct a career audit by asking yourself these questions:

- What experiences and skills can I apply to this new career that I already possess? What experiences and skills do I need to develop?

Before you decide it is time for you to change jobs, spend time analyzing your goals. © *PhotoDisc, Inc.*

- Will the career change require additional education? If so, how much? How long will it take me to get the education? How much will it cost? Do I need financial help with going back to school?
- Does the new career fit with my personal goals? Will my family be supportive of my career change?

Whether your final decision is to change careers or to stay in your present one, commit yourself to continual growth throughout your career. Review your career goals often; be certain they are compatible with your personal goals.

SUMMARY

To reinforce what you have learned in this chapter, study this summary.

- Sources of job information include:
  Newspapers
  The Internet
  Employment agencies
  Professional organizations
  Placement offices
  Personal networks
  Walk-ins
  Temporary Agencies
- Before you apply for a job with a particular company, find out all you can about the company.
- The letter of application generally is the first contact that you will have with a potential employer. It has several purposes, including:
  Introducing you to the organization
  Providing general information about your skills
  Selling your skills
  Transmitting your resume
- Resume types include chronological, functional, and targeted.
- Resume parts include the:
  Heading
  Objective
  Relevant skills
  Employment history
  Education
  Professional accomplishments
  Possibly references, with a statement that they will be furnished on request. (It is not absolutely necessary to include references on the resume.)
- Part of the job search includes filling out an employment application. The application should be completed carefully, completely, and accurately.
- Interviews may be done by an individual, a team, or in a virtual setting where one or more people interview the candidate. The interview is extremely important. Review the Helpful Hints and Commonly Asked Questions sections to help you remember how to present yourself well.
- Once the interview is over, it should be followed by a letter that:
  Thanks the interviewer for the opportunity to interview
  Recaps the skills and abilities of the interviewee
  States the interviewee's continued interest in the job
  Reminds the interviewer of the next steps that were agreed on during the interview
- Once you have completed the interview, you should evaluate what occurred by yourself and with a trusted adviser.

- After you obtain a job, it is important to succeed in it. You must listen to what coworkers and supervisors tell you. You must observe and learn what is expected of you and what your job duties are.

- Formal performance appraisals usually are done within three to six months after you begin work. Accept the evaluation as the organization's way of emphasizing your performance strengths, pointing out any performance weaknesses, and helping you improve your performance.

- As you attempt to advance to higher positions in your organization, it is important that you:

  Commit to working hard to produce both short- and long-term success for your company

  Continue to develop your communication skills

  Maintain a positive attitude

  Network with people in your organization

- If it is necessary to leave a job (because it is not meeting your career goals, or you have been laid off or fired), do so in a positive manner. Do not make derogatory remarks in the exit interview. Be factual and brief. Remember that you may need a reference from the company.

- If you have been fired from a job, be kind to yourself. Realize that even though you may have failed at this job, you have not failed at all jobs. It is okay and normal to be angry, but talk out your anger with your family and close friends—not with your employer.

- If you decide to recareer, spend time analyzing your mission statement, goals, and objectives. Take the time to consider growth employment areas and career paths within various fields of interest to you. Make certain there is a fit between your career goals and your lifestyle goals. Determine what types of financial help you might need in recareering.

Key Terms

- Signed advertisement
- Blind advertisement
- State-operated employment agencies
- Private employment agencies
- Fee paid
- Networking
- Temporary agency
- Resume
- Chronological resume
- Functional resume
- Targeted resume
- Employment application
- Portfolio
- Virtual interview
- Follow-up letter
- Performance appraisals
- Commitment
- Exit interview
- Recareer

Professional Pointers

If your job skills are to be marketable in a highly competitive, global world, you must continually sharpen your knowledge and broaden your abilities. Consider these tips:

- Be an educated risk taker; be certain that your risks are based on sound judgment.
- Develop leadership and management skills.
- Learn to work with people from vastly different cultures.
- Never engage in unethical behavior or practices. Live by a set of values.
- Be a good role model. Look and act like someone who can handle a position of significant responsibility. Your likelihood of being promoted rests on the opinion of how others see you and your ability.
- Always be flexible.
- Do not expect everyone to like you.
- Develop your creativity.
- Have a positive attitude.
- Be a team player.
- Maintain confidentiality.

Office Procedures Reinforcement

1. List the elements of an effective letter of application.
2. List and explain the standard parts of a resume.
3. List ten helpful hints for making a good impression during an interview.
4. How should you conduct yourself during a performance appraisal?
5. Explain how you should handle an exit interview.

Critical Thinking Activity

Emily Richards graduated with an AAS degree in Office Systems from a community college a year ago. Emily was an A student; however, she did not take part in any outside activities in school. She is basically a shy, introverted individual. Since Emily graduated, she has been working for a temporary agency. She was not certain what type of firm she wanted to work in full-time, so she used the experiences with the temporary agency to get a feel for what she wants to do. During the year, she has worked for seven different companies. Each one of her supervisors praised the quality of her work. Two of them offered her full-time employment, but she declined because she didn't feel either company fit her long-term goals. She has now decided that she wants to work in the technical field—a computer manufacturing or software company, or some similar type of firm. She has applied for three jobs within the technical field in the last two months. She did receive an interview for all three jobs but has not been offered a full-time position. Here are some of the experiences Emily had during the three interviews.

- When she was asked about her present job, Emily said she didn't have a full-time job. She did say that she had worked for a temporary agency for the last year, but she did not explain why.

- When asked about her college experience, Emily said that she made good grades but didn't do anything outside of her school work.

- When asked what her strengths were, Emily responded that she thought she was a capable employee and that her skills were good. She also said that she knew she had much to learn.

- When Emily was asked by one interviewer if she had any questions, she responded that she had none.

- Emily tried to maintain eye contact, but she did find herself looking at the floor many times.

Emily is discouraged; she wonders if she will ever find a full-time job. She hasn't discussed her situation with anyone. She is afraid to admit that she went on three interviews and was not offered a job.

What advice do you have for Emily? What did she do wrong in the interviews?

Office Applications

OA19-1 (Goals 1, 2, and 3)

Using the newspaper or Internet as sources, find a position in which you are interested in applying. Prepare a letter of application and a resume. Complete the employment application form given on pages 131–132 of your Applications Workbook. Submit copies of your letter of application, resume, and application form to your instructor. Also submit a copy of the job notice that you found, giving the source of the notice. If you are ready to begin your job search, you may want to mail your letter of application and resume to the company once your instructor has evaluated it and you have made the appropriate corrections.

OA19-2 (Goal 4)

Select three of your classmates to work with on this project. Alternate with your classmates in being the interviewer, the interviewee, and the evaluator. Each of you is to answer each question given below as the interviewee. The two evaluators are to evaluate how the interviewee answers the questions by using the evaluation form given on page 133 of the Applications Workbook. The interviewee is to do a self-evaluation using the form provided on page 134 of the Applications Workbook. Once the evaluation has been completed for each interviewee, the group should discuss how improvement can be achieved in each case. In order to answer the question, "What do you know about the company?", the interviewee must do research. Assume the company is Microsoft. Using the Internet, review Microsoft's home page.

- What are your goals?
- What are your strengths?
- What are your weaknesses?
- What do you know about the company?
- Why do you think you are qualified for this position?
- Why did you leave your previous job?
- Do you have any questions?

To help you in answering these questions, review the suggestions given on pages 135–136 of your Applications Workbook.

OA19-3 (Goal 5)

Using the self-evaluation chart that you completed in Chapter 1 and the stress audit that you completed in Chapter 3:

- Do another self-evaluation. Have you increased your strengths and reduced your weaknesses?
- Retake the stress audit. Have you reduced your stress?

Do not turn in either of these evaluations to your instructor; the reevaluation is to help you discover areas where you still need to improve.

Using the career plan that you prepared in Chapter 1, review, analyze, and revise the plan, reflecting your current career goals. Also, write a mission statement. Review the elements of a mission statement on page 199 of Chapter 8. Submit your revised career plan and your mission statement to your instructor.

Online Research Application

ORA19-4 (Goal 4)

Using the Internet, check out one of the job source Internet addresses given on pages 515–516 of your text or other addresses that you find on your own as you search the Web. Research a company that has job openings in your area of interest. Find out all you can about the company. Report your findings orally to the class.

CHAPTER 20

Leadership and Management

YOUR GOALS

1. Define leadership.
2. Identify the major tasks of leadership.
3. Identify and improve your leadership skills.

As you are promoted to higher-level office positions, you may have the responsibility of supervising one or more employees. Being an effective supervisor, one who is able to inspire people to produce at their maximum, demands that you understand and apply effective leadership and management principles. In this chapter, you will be introduced to these principles. Even if you never have the opportunity to supervise personnel, you will find the information presented here helpful. It will give you an understanding of the importance of leadership in our global society. It will help you identify traits that are important for all of us to learn and use regardless of where we might adopt a leadership role—at work, in professional organizations to which we belong, or at home with our family and friends.

Importance of Leadership

You have learned throughout this book that we are living in a time where the issues are both more complex and more divergent than in the past due to a number of factors, with some of the major ones being:

- A global and interdependent economy, with multinational corporations

- Technological innovations that are occurring constantly and reshaping the way we think about health care, education, business, and society in general

- A more diverse workforce than we have ever had—diverse in age, race, ethnicity, and gender

- Value shifts that are impacting both our professional and personal lives

If we are to address these complex issues in ways that will benefit the way we work and live, our society must be capable of producing leaders of vision and courage. Not only is effective leadership essential for the leaders of our world, the **CEOs** (chief executive officers) of our corporations, and our spiritual leaders, but also many of the traits of effective leadership are essential for each of us if we are

to become individuals who live to our maximum potential. Now let's take a look at how leadership is defined and how leadership relates to management.

Leadership vs. Management

Think of leadership and management as part of the same continuum, with leadership encompassing all aspects of management and management being an integral part of effective leadership. Figure 20-1 illustrates this concept, showing leadership as the whole and management as one of the numerous tasks of leadership. The additional leadership tasks will be presented later in this chapter.

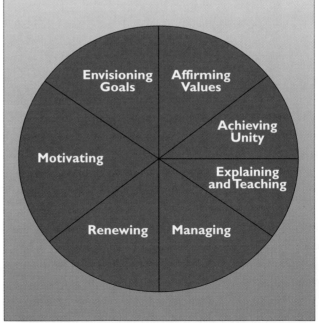

FIGURE 20-1. Leadership encompasses all aspects of management, and management is an integral part of effective leadership.

Leadership Defined

The definition and philosophy of leadership used in this chapter have been impacted by the work of several prominent individuals who have contributed significantly to the field of leadership: John W. Gardner, Peter Drucker, Warren Bennis, Burt Nanus, Peter Senge, and Stephen Covey. Some of their works, which have been recognized and used for a number of years by business, include:

- John W. Gardner, *Leadership Papers*
- Peter Drucker, *The Practice of Management*
- Warren Bennis and Burt Nanus, *Leaders: The Strategies for Taking Charge*
- Peter Senge, *The Fifth Discipline*
- Stephen Covey, *The 7 Habits of Highly Effective People*

Leadership is the process of persuading others to take action that is consistent with the purpose of the leader or the group's shared purpose. When leading, an individual must use the power that he or she has been entrusted with wisely in translating the intentions of individuals or groups into action. **Power** is the ability to act, the strength to accomplish something. Power may be based on:

- The leader's position within an organization
- The leader's knowledge
- The follower's identification with the leader
- The ability of the leader to satisfy the follower's needs
- The ability of the leader to obtain compliance through fear or punishment

Whatever the source of the power, the effective leader uses power well. For example, he or she does not rely on fear or punishment in order to get something accomplished. Rather, the effective leader is true to the vision and directions of the company, leading from a principle-centered approach. Employees can then respond to the leader because they believe in the "right" of what is being done. There is no blind faith or servitude on the part of the employee but thoughtful acceptance or open disagreement (with open discussion) concerning the goals of the organization and the individual. The leader and the employees move forward because of their faith, respect, and trust in each other.

Management Defined

Management in its traditional sense has been defined as the performance of the tasks or activities that are necessary in managing an organization—planning, organizing, leading, and controlling. However, in this text, managing (with its resultant tasks) is defined as one of the activities that leaders perform. Management deals with a bottom-line focus—how can certain tasks be performed efficiently? Leadership deals with the overall picture—what should be accomplished in the organization? According to Bennis and Nanus, "Managers are people who do things right and leaders are people who do the right thing."[1]

To help you understand the difference, consider this situation. A family spends a hot summer afternoon preparing the soil and planting beautiful azaleas around the entire perimeter of the backyard. Within two weeks, the azaleas wither and die because the climate where the

---

[1] Warren Bennis and Burt Nanus, *Leaders: The Strategies for Taking Charge* (New York: Harper & Row, 1985), 21.

family lives is not conducive to growing them. The "managers" prepared the soil well and planted the azaleas properly; they did things right. However, no "leader" emerged to ask the right question—what plants will grow effectively in our climate?

Effective Leadership Characteristics

What are the characteristics of an effective leader? Here are a few important ones. The effective leader:

- Builds a shared vision
- Lives by a set of values
- Uses power appropriately
- Engenders trust
- Rewards risk taking

Builds a Shared Vision

The leader of a department or organization can be a visionary; but unless he or she is able to help others within the organization to see and share that same vision, the vision has little chance of becoming reality. For example, Bill Gates and his friend Paul Allen, as they stood in Harvard Square as college sophomores and pored over the description of a kit computer, had a vision. They were sure that the first truly personal computer would change them as well as the world of computing.[2] They were right. They were able to build an organization (Microsoft) composed of people who shared the same vision, and the world has been changed.

---

[2] William H. Gates, III, *The Road Ahead* (New York: Viking Penguin, 1995), xi.

A vision is shared when individuals have a similar picture in their minds and hearts. When people are united around a vision, they are bound together by a common goal. They understand where they are headed. They may not always know how to get there, but they have the courage to continue to work toward their goal. When individuals have a shared vision, work becomes part of a larger purpose that affects the climate and spirit of an organization. Risk taking and experimentation are common when individuals share a vision. The true leader is able to articulate the vision (the picture in his or her head) and get others within the organization not only to buy into the vision but to feel passionate about it.

Lives by a Set of Values

If we look back over history, we discover that values have been important and a point of discussion among leaders and philosophers. For example, Socrates (469–399 B.C.) asserted that virtue and ethical behavior were associated with wisdom, and he taught that insight into life would naturally lead to right conduct. Plato (428–348 B.C.) carried Socrates' doctrine of virtue as knowledge further by positing the theory of absolute justice. According to Plato, absolute justice exists independently of individuals and its nature can be discovered by intellectual effort. After the rise of Christianity, Catholic theologians—for example, St. Augustine and St. Thomas Aquinas—dominated ethical thinking. Correct behavior in business dealings and all activities was necessary to achieve salvation and life after death.

Today, ethical behavior in business remains the accepted practice. You will recall that in Chapter 4, ethics was defined

A vision is shared when individuals have a similar picture in their minds and hearts. © *PhotoDisc, Inc.*

as the systematic study of moral conduct, duty, and judgment. The tough part becomes how that ethical behavior is lived in the business organization. What practices are ethical? What practices are not ethical? Ethical issues form the basis of many debates—not only in business but also in our world today. On the one hand, we expect ethical behavior from all of our leaders. Yet we are not clear what this means. Each of us has our own definition of what is ethical and what is not. Thus, the debate as to what is right and what is wrong continues. However, few of us would disagree that ethics are important, that our leaders must live by a sound set of **values** (a principle or standard considered worthwhile or desirable).

The contention is made here that our leaders must stand firmly on moral principles. However, leaders must work within the organization to define what those principles are and then to be clear that the principles are being carried out in the daily life of the organization. When the tough decisions must be made, we want leaders who will stand on their espoused values—who in other words will "walk the talk." Although establishing and living a set of values must begin with the top leadership of an organization, it must permeate every level. We want to be a part of an organization that insists that employees also uphold the values established. One of the leadership tasks is to embrace and support an ethical organization.

Uses Power Appropriately

You have learned that power can be achieved through a number of different means. However, power is never limited—in other words, it need not be held in the hands of merely a few people within the organization. Power needs to be distributed throughout the organization. It can be divided without being diminished. The effective leader recognizes that power must be distributed to people throughout the organization. According to Lipman-Blumen, effective leaders

> ". . . see power in strange places: in sharing, in compromising and negotiating, in helping and seeking help, in working together, in entrusting others, in altruism and self-sacrifice—and far less often in authoritarian, individualistic behavior"[3]

The effective leader **empowers** others. Leaders empower people when they

- Provide the employees access to information that will help them do their job better
- Allow employees to take on more responsibility
- Allow employees a voice in decision making

Empowered employees feel a sense of ownership and control over their jobs, responsibility for their work, and ability to get their jobs done. Empowered employees usually are happier individuals—they trust the organization, feel part of it, and enjoy the rewards that the job provides.

The leader who empowers people has a core belief that people are basically good, honest, and well intentioned. This type of leader understands that leadership is doing the right thing, operating from a

The effective leader empowers others. © *PhotoDisc, Inc.*

central core of values even in the most difficult situations.

Engenders Trust

Effective leaders forge bonds of trust between themselves and the people with whom they work. They create a climate of trust throughout the organization. How do they do this? Here are some of the ways in which trust can be engendered.

- Consistently living by a stated set of values
- Being reliable and predictable—doing what you say you will do
- Being unshakably fair in public and in private

---

[3] Jean Lipman-Blumen, *The Connective Edge* (San Francisco: Jossey-Bass, 1996), 241.

FIGURE 20-2. Keys to Successful Risk-Taking

Rewards Risk-Taking

The organization of the twenty-first century, with change as a constant, will face risks daily. The organization cannot take refuge in status quo, conformity to the norm, or security in the past. None of these stances makes sense if the organization is to be successful. The organization must constantly be willing to seek new answers to problems, try new approaches, and be flexible. The organization must have leaders who not only take risks themselves but also encourage others to take risks. Some of the keys to successful risk-taking are given in Figure 20-2.

Leadership Tasks

In order to fulfill your role as a leader, you need to have a thorough understanding of the tasks of leadership. These tasks are:

- Envisioning goals
- Affirming values

- Managing
- Motivating
- Achieving unity
- Explaining and teaching
- Renewing[4]

Envisioning Goals and Affirming Values

Envisioning goals and helping others envision them is at the heart of leadership. A process that is used to help individuals envision goals is called **strategic thinking**. Organizational strategic thinking is the coordination of creative minds into a common perspective (common goals) that enables the organization to proceed into the future through thoughtful analysis of where it should be in three to five years. Strategic thinking allows leaders and individuals within the organization to dream about what the future should be. The strategic thinking process involves analyzing and addressing these organizational elements:

- Values—the values that guide or should guide the organization

- Mission—the nature of the organization, who it serves, why it exists, its aspirations and purpose

- Strategy—the direction the organization should be headed, factors that determine the future products, services, and markets of the organization[5]

The strategic thinking process allows the organization to analyze its values or to develop stated values if none exist.

---

[4] John W. Gardner, *The Tasks of Leadership* (Washington, D.C.: Leadership Studies Program, Independent Sector, 1986), 5–26.

[5] George L. Morrisey, *A Guide to Strategic Thinking* (San Francisco: Jossey-Bass, 1996), 6–7.

Strategic thinking allows leaders and individuals within the organization to plan for the future. © *PhotoDisc, Inc.*

Through the process, leaders have an opportunity to ask the organization to commit to a stated set of values. Value statements are often written down, along with the mission statement of the organization, and posted throughout the organization for people within and outside it to read. In Chapter 8, you were given two examples of mission statements. Figure 20-3 illustrates a mission and a value statement. Through such statements, the organization boldly proclaims that they will live by a set of values. Then the values are reflected in all decisions that are made. Such statements provide a compass for the organization to follow; they point the com-

pany in the right direction when tough times occur.

Long-range and tactical planning follow the strategic thinking process. You will learn more about both of these approaches in a later section of this chapter.

Managing

Leadership includes the ability to manage. In other words, the effective leader not only does the right thing but is also capable of doing things right. Management involves a number of skills such as planning, organizing, recruiting, and training.

MISSION AND VALUE STATEMENT

Merck & Co., Inc. is a pharmaceutical products and services company. In 1999, *Fortune* chose Merck as one of the 10 Best Companies to Work for in America. Here is their mission and value statement.

OUR MISSION

The mission of **Merck** is to provide society with superior products and services—innovations and solutions that improve the quality of life and satisfy customer needs—to provide *employees* with meaningful work and advancement opportunities and investors with a superior rate of return.

OUR VALUES

1. **Our business is preserving and improving human life.** All of our actions must be measured by our success in achieving this goal. We value above all our ability to serve everyone who can benefit from the appropriate use of our products and services, thereby providing lasting consumer satisfaction.

2. **We are committed to the highest standards of ethics and integrity.** We are responsible to our customers, to Merck employees and their families, to the environments we inhabit, and to the societies we serve worldwide. In discharging our responsibilities, we do not take professional or ethical shortcuts. Our interactions with all segments of society must reflect the high standards we profess.

3. **We are dedicated to the highest level of *scientific excellence and commit our* research to improving *human and animal health and the quality of life.*** We strive to identify the most critical needs of consumers and customers, we devote our resources to meeting those needs.

4. **We expect *profits, but only from work that satisfies customer needs and* benefits humanity.** Our ability to meet our responsibilities depends on maintaining a financial position that invites investment in leading-edge research and that makes possible effective delivery of research results.

5. **We recognize that the ability to excel—to most competitively meet society's and customers' needs—depends on the integrity, knowledge, imagination, skill, diversity and teamwork of employees, and we value these qualities most highly.** To this end, we strive to create an environment of mutual respect, encouragement, and teamwork—a working environment that rewards commitment and performance and is responsive to the needs of employees and their families.

FIGURE 20-3. Vision and Value Statement. Source: http://www.merck.com.

Planning.   **Planning** involves setting goals and objectives for the organization and developing plans for accomplishing them. You have already learned that in the strategic thinking process a mission, values, and broad directions for the organization are established. In order to ensure that these broad directions are accomplished, the next step is a planning process that includes both long-range planning and short-range or tactical planning.

Long-range planning is the process by which the ideas from strategic thinking are translated into an action format. It helps turn the ideas into reality. Generally, long-range planning identifies directions that must be carried out within three to five years. In the strategic planning process, the **long-term goals** (what an organization is committed to achieving), primary accountability for the goals, and the resources to carry out the goals are identified.

Tactical planning is the process of making detailed decisions about:

- What the organization or unit intends to accomplish
- How and when it will be accomplished
- Who will be accountable for accomplishing the objectives
- The resources required to accomplish the objectives
- How the accomplishment of the objectives will be evaluated

Tactical planning is generally done for a period of one year.

Now that you have looked at the overall-planning picture—why goals are set and the various components of long-range and tactical planning—let's examine what your role as an office professional supervising support staff might be in planning. You may be asked to help set the objectives of the department where you work. The responsibility for setting departmental objectives rests with the managers of the department, but some organizations include their employees in the planning process. If you have some management responsibilities, the possibility of your being included is greater.

Once you have participated in the setting of objectives for your department, you will have a greater understanding of the objectives and goals of the company. However, even if you do not help in this process, you will engage in planning the activities of your unit. Such planning includes setting objectives. Each person in the unit needs to understand what he or she is expected to produce.

Your role, then, as a supervisor of office support staff is to help your group plan their objectives for the next year. How do you go about this planning process? First of all, you involve the personnel who report to you. You should have a planning session at least once a year to look at what your unit should be accomplishing for the year. Some supervisors choose to have planning sessions more often—for example, every six months. During this planning session, you and the employees you supervise discuss what the unit should be accomplishing and how it should be accomplished. Figure 20-4 illustrates a portion of a tactical plan, giving:

- One objective to be accomplished
- Who is responsible for accomplishing the objective
- When the objective will be accomplished
- The project cost
- How the accomplishment will be evaluated

Organizing. Once the planning has been done, the work must be organized. Organization involves bringing together all resources—people, time, money, and equipment—in the most effective way to accomplish the goals. It involves dividing the work into manageable jobs that can be performed by specific employees. As a supervisor, you will be responsible for dividing the workload. In order to do so, you need to be familiar with some of the concepts of organization.

Span of Control. First, it is important to know how many people you can effectively supervise. **Span of control** refers to the number of employees who are directly

PORTION OF A TACTICAL PLAN FOR HUMAN RESOURCES

Objective: Train employees on the use of OCHRS software.

Actions	Accountability	Completion	Resources	Evaluation
Provide four training sessions of 2 hours each on OCHRS for all employees in the workgroup	Office Manager	March 15, 2001	No additional dollars; training done by representative from OCHRS	Employees' ability to use OCHRS

FIGURE 20-4. Tactical Plan for Human Resources

supervised by one person. There is no formula that rigidly defines the span of control. However, there was in the past. The traditional viewpoint of management held that the ideal number of individuals reporting to one supervisor should be from 4 to 12. The number today is determined more by the philosophy of management and the number of employees that the leader can supervise effectively. You learned in Chapter 1 about a flattened organization structure—one in which there are fewer levels of management. This approach is consistent with other relatively new philosophies of management that include teamwork and quality improvement. With a flattened organization structure, the span of control is broader. There is no "correct" number. However, in determining span of control, these factors need to be considered:

- Leadership philosophy of the organization (Is the organization committed to a flat organization? Or is it hierarchical?)
- Capabilities of the supervisor (Is the supervisor highly skilled and experienced?)
- Capabilities of the workgroup (Are the workgroup members highly skilled and knowledgeable?)
- Similarity of work (Are the jobs that the group is performing similar in nature?)

There is no formula that rigidly defines the span of control.
© PhotoDisc, Inc.

- Extent of clear operating standards and rules (Are there clear standards and rules that govern the tasks to be accomplished?)
- Decision-making ability of the workgroup (Is the workgroup capable of making decisions? Is it allowed to make decisions without checking with the supervisor?)

Job Analysis. A job analysis is a list of the tasks for a specific job and the personal characteristics necessary in order to perform the tasks successfully. Once the information is determined, it is usually compiled into a job description. The **job description** includes skills, training, education necessary for the job, and a list of the job duties. Figure 20-5 shows a job description. Most companies have job descriptions for all employees. Such an approach is helpful not only in the hiring process, but also in letting employees know what they are expected to do.

Work Periods. A third factor to consider in organizing work is the time in which the work is to be performed. In the past, the workweek has been traditionally 8 a.m. to 5 p.m. Monday through Friday.

JOB DESCRIPTION

Job Title: Administrative Assistant

Company: Nowasynski Electronics

Department: Personnel

Reports to: Patricia LaFave

Director of Human Resources

Skills and Training

The position of Administrative Assistant requires excellent organizational and human relations skills. The position requires the ability to screen and establish priorities on projects and to supervise two office support staff. Excellent oral and written communication skills are necessary.

Basic skills include computer (word processing, spreadsheet, presentation, graphics, and calendaring software), records management, grammar and composition, and accurate keyboarding at 70 wpm.

Education and Experience

Two years of office experience; associate degree or equivalent course work.

Duties

1. Inputting personnel records
2. Keying correspondence and reports
3. Composing correspondence
4. Maintaining a records management system
5. Planning meetings and conferences
6. Supervising two office support staffs

FIGURE 20-5. Job Description

However, there are numerous changes today. You learned in Chapter 1 about the flexible workweek (both the compressed workweek and flextime), job sharing, and virtual employment. All of these changes impact the way the supervisor organizes the work for his or her workgroup.

Recruiting and Training.   As a supervisor, you may have the responsibility of recruiting and training new employees. If you are to do so effectively, you must be cognizant of recruitment sources, laws that impact recruitment and interviewing, and effective training techniques. Before you begin the recruitment process, you should pay careful attention to what type of person your organization needs. What skills are needed? What personality traits are needed? For example, if you as a supervisor lack organizational skills, you may need to recruit an administrative assistant who excels in this area. An effective supervisor is able to build a good team of people—a team in which all the skills and traits needed to get the work of the organization done are present.

Recruit and Employ.   Recruitment is the process of searching, both inside and outside the organization, for people to fill positions. In recruiting office workers, a company may use several sources, including:

- Newspaper advertisements
- Employment agencies
- College and university placement offices
- Job openings posted on the Internet
- Employee referrals

Organizations usually establish procedures through their Human Resources departments, which determine how a company will recruit employees. There are certain legal considerations. For example, when placing advertisements, care should be taken that the wording does not conflict with fair labor practice laws. Discrimination statutes prohibit advertisements that show preferences in terms of race, religion, gender, age, or physical disabilities. For example, an employer cannot advertise for a particular age group. Expressions such as *young person* or *retired person* cannot be used in ads. The **EEOC** (Equal Employment Opportunity Commission) requires certain employers

Discrimination statutes prohibit advertisements that show preferences in terms of race, religion, gender, age, or physical disabilities. © *CORBIS.*

(very small organizations are generally not required to meet EEOC regulations) to maintain records on the number of openings in various job groups and the number of applicants, with the applicants listed by race, ethnicity, and gender. As a supervisor, it is your responsibility to find out what EEOC regulations apply to your organization.

Once applicants are recruited, there are three major tools for screening and selection:

- Written application
- Personal interview
- Testing procedures

The cover letter and the resume are written materials that generally are submitted by an applicant. As a supervisor, you should review and screen the written materials carefully to determine which individuals will be interviewed for the job. Before you begin reviewing the applications, make a list of the questions you should ask yourself as you read them. For example, you might ask yourself: What skills does the person need? What level of education is essential? How much experience is essential? With your criteria in mind, screen the applications and select the most qualified individuals to interview.

It is imperative that the second screening method, the interview, be done thoughtfully and with full awareness of all laws that apply to interviewing. For example, laws that prohibit discrimination based on age, race, religion, gender, or physical disability make it unlawful for you to ask questions such as:

- What nationality are your parents?
- Are you married? single? divorced? separated?
- What is the date of your birth?
- Where were you born?

- Is your spouse a United States citizen?
- What does your spouse do?
- To what clubs do you belong?
- What are the ages of your children?
- What church do you attend?
- Have you ever had any health problems?
- Have you ever belonged to a union?
- How did your disability occur?

Keep current on all laws that affect interviewing. Without the latest information, you may place your organization in jeopardy of a discrimination suit. Before you begin interviewing, make a list of questions that you will ask the candidate. Then ask each individual you interview the same questions. Take notes as you interview so you will not forget the answers that were given by each person. By asking the same questions of each interviewee and taking notes so that you do not forget how each person responded to the questions, you are able to be more objective in your analysis. Allocate enough time for a thorough interview; you may need to spend an hour or more with each applicant. Conduct the interview in a place where you will not be interrupted and the noise level is low.

The third screening tool that is used frequently is a test or tests. A common type of written test is the **cognitive ability test,** which measures such items as verbal, numerical, and reasoning ability. Office professionals may also be given a spelling test. Another type of test that is given is a **performance test.** For office professionals, this is usually a test of computer and software abilities, plus keyboarding and accuracy skills. Knowledge of word processing, spreadsheet, calendaring, graphics, and presentation software may be tested. However, legal considerations dictate that

Legal considerations dictate that any test used must measure the person's qualifications for the job for which he or she is applying.

any test used must measure the person's qualifications for the job for which he or she is applying. For example, you cannot ask an office professional to take a math proficiency test unless the use of math is necessary in performing the job.

Train. Once the person has been employed, a training period is necessary. No matter how qualified a person is for the job (what skills and knowledge he or she may possess), procedures and policies of the company must be learned. As a supervisor, you must assist the employee in this job training. For example, an office professional who is a new employee may receive training in how to:

- Handle incoming and outgoing mail
- Set up records management systems
- Handle meetings
- Answer telephones
- Write letters and reports

Additionally, the new employee should receive training on organizational policies and procedures. The employee should be given the company policy and procedures manual, with an explanation of the major policies and procedures within the manual. The new employee should be advised of evaluation procedures—when evaluation occurs, what criteria will be used, and so forth. Evaluation forms that will be used should be reviewed with the employee. Some organizations assign new employees **mentors** (a counselor or teacher). The mentor meets with the new employee regularly, answers questions, introduces the new employee, takes him or her to lunch, and engages in other training activities that will expedite the process of learning the job and the company procedures.

With rapid changes in technology, it also is necessary to provide upgrade training. For example, when the company purchases new software packages, office professionals throughout the company may be given several hours or days of training so that they may utilize its features effectively.

Office professionals may also receive developmental training such as:

- Improving verbal communication skills
- Improving written communication skills
- Addressing conflict
- Becoming an effective team member

As a supervisor, you may also receive developmental training on such supervisory responsibilities as:

- Strategic planning
- Interviewing techniques
- Team building—developing effective project teams
- Motivational techniques
- Stress reduction techniques

Controlling and Evaluating. Controlling and evaluating are two important tasks of leadership. Once directions for the organization have been set, controls must be established to ensure that behaviors and performance meet the standards of the company. Evaluation of products, services, and people must occur to assure that the organization is achieving its goals.

Controlling. Organizations exercise a variety of **control measures**—using procedures, budgets, data, and so forth to measure performance of the organization and individuals within the organization. For example, you learned earlier about planning. Assume that an organization has as one of its goals in the planning process to increase sales by 10 percent for the next year. The organization then builds in measures for evaluating whether or not the 10 percent increase is occurring and if not, it modifies and intensifies its efforts. Assume that when data is collected on sales for the last six months that sales in all but one area have met or exceeded the 10 percent goal. Then the organization must ask why the sales in the one area did not reach 10 percent. What can be done to increase these sales? Is the advertising appropriate for this area? Are the salespersons effective? Organizations such as airlines, insurance companies, telemarketing firms, and telephone companies also may monitor their employees' effectiveness by computer on such measures as number of customers served, length of time required to serve each customer, number of keystrokes per minute, and so forth. If the statistics are not satisfactory, improvement measures are put in place.

Now let's take another control measure—the budget. Assume you are an office manager, supervising three individuals. You need new software to assist in the records management function. When the budget is built, you present your needs to your supervisor. He or she approves your software request, but within certain financial constraints. You cannot spend more than the budget controls allow.

The examples of control given above are of **organizational control**. Three other types of control that exist within organizations are **group control, stakeholder control,** and **individual self-control.** Group control involves the norms and values that groups impose on each other through such measures as group acceptance or rejection. One example of stakeholder control is evident through boards of directors. Boards, along with the CEO, generally look at the "big picture"—issues that are impacting the organization from the outside such as environmental issues, global issues, and ethical issues. Individual self-control is evident through the professionalism of employees. For example, as an office professional you have been acquiring knowledge and skills, along with an understanding of ethics and what is and is not ethical behavior in the workplace. You use your knowledge, skill, and ethical commitment to exercise self-control. You do not use email for personal purposes; you do not falsify your expense account; you do not copy software packages for your home use.

Evaluating. In addition to control measures that are put in place, organizations evaluate the performance of the organization and the people within it. Consider the example given in the previous section of sales quotas not being met in a certain area. Evaluation takes place once the control mechanism alerts the organization to the fact that there is a problem. Are the marketing techniques effective in that area? If not, how can they be made effective?

If you supervise office support personnel, one of your tasks is to evaluate them. As you have learned earlier, the evaluation system should be explained carefully to all new employees soon after they are employed. Evaluation criteria and forms should be reviewed with the new

Some companies monitor the effectiveness of their employees by computer determination of how many customers are served in a certain length of time. © PhotoDisc, Inc.

employee. In other words, evaluation methods should never be a surprise to an employee. Additionally, all evaluation is not formal. Evaluation should occur daily on an informal basis as you observe and talk with the people who report to you. You will engage in formal evaluation of employees every six months or every year. For example, employees may be evaluated every six months for the first year and then once a year thereafter. Whatever the time period for evaluation, it is a crucial management function and must be done well in order to achieve employee growth as well as increased productivity for the company. Figure 20-6 shows a portion of a completed evaluation form.

The following evaluation guidelines will assist you in helping employees learn and grow during the evaluation process.

- Evaluate performance on a day-to-day basis. Employees should always know how they are doing. If there are grammatical errors in a report, let the person who keyed it know immediately. Also, praise an individual for an outstanding job. Evaluation has two prongs—praise and criticism. Do not save the praise or the criticism for a six-month or yearly evaluation session.

- Know yourself. Know who you are, what your needs are, and what your values are. If you come to the office tired or upset, don't vent your irritability on others by criticizing the people or the work when your emotions are the problem. Realize that you are having a bad day. Psychologists call this phenomenon of transferring our problems to others **projection.**

- Allow adequate time for evaluation. The six-month or yearly performance evaluation is important for both the supervisor and the employee. Set aside

enough time on your calendar to do it well. You will probably need to spend an hour or two with each employee. Also, be sure that the place is appropriate. If you are using your office, it is best to have your telephone calls transferred to someone else so that you will not be interrupted as you talk with the employee. Usually, it is best to close the door to ensure confidentiality and keep visitors from dropping in and interrupting you.

- Give credit where credit is due. Be certain that you praise the employee for work well done. Too many managers consider an evaluation period a time for criticism only. It is not. It is a time to look at the total work of the employee. In what areas is he or she performing in an exemplary manner? an average manner? below expectations? Praise the employee for work well done as well as offer constructive criticism for work needing improvement.

- Be fair. Analyze the employee's work based on established criteria of performance, not on how well you like or dislike the employee. Stay away from personality traits. Stress job performance. In discussing errors, suggest ways that the work could have been performed satisfactorily. Give the employee an opportunity to suggest possible alternatives. Let the session be a growth experience for the employee. Give praise before criticism. For example, you might say, "You are doing well in these areas" (then identify the areas), and "you need to work on these areas" (identify the areas).

- Listen to what the person is saying. Too often we listen to others with only half an ear. The employee often comes to an evaluation session with a certain

PEOPLE FIRST INTERNATIONAL

Professional Support Staff Performance Evaluation

Employee Name *Margarate Evans*

Job Title *Administrative Assistant*

Supervisor *R. Martin*

Assessment

4 Performance demonstrates consistent and important contributions that surpass defined expectations of the position

3 Performance demonstrates attainment of the defined expectations of the position

2 Performance has not reached a satisfactory level. Improved performance on this factor is needed to achieve defined expectations of the position.

1 Performance demonstrates deficiencies that seriously interfere with the attainment of the defined expectations of the position

Organization Skills	Assessment			
	4	3	2	1
Prioritizes tasks	☐	☒	☐	☐
Plans steps to accomplish tasks	☐	☐	☒	☐
Meets deadlines	☐	☒	☐	☐
Attends to detail	☐	☐	☒	☐

Quality	Assessment			
	4	3	2	1
Performs work accurately	☐	☐	☒	☐
Demonstrates neatness	☐	☒	☐	☐
Demonstrates thoroughness and attention to detail	☐	☐	☒	☐

Job Knowledge	Assessment			
	4	3	2	1
Uses required job skills	☐	☒	☐	☐
Demonstrates knowledge of organizational functions needed to perform the job	☐	☒	☐	☐
Demonstrates knowledge of procedures needed to perform the job	☐	☒	☐	☐

Cooperation	Assessment			
	4	3	2	1
Provides assistance and guidance to others	☐	☐	☒	☐
Accepts guidance from supervisor	☐	☒	☐	☐
Works toward workgroup and company goals	☐	☒	☐	☐

FIGURE 20-6. Evaluation Form

amount of anxiety and perhaps even hostility. Let the person talk. By talking, the person will usually release much of the anxiety and thus be more receptive to constructive criticism.

- Avoid personal areas. Sometimes a supervisor, even with the best intentions, will become too deeply involved in the employee's personal life. Don't try to counsel an employee about problems that should be handled only by a qualified professional.

- Establish attainable objectives. Help the employee set realistic objectives for improvement. It is a good idea to ask the employee to put these objectives in writing as you discuss them. In fact, if there are several areas that need improvement, a plan of action may be developed, with dates set for the accomplishment of each objective. Then, as the employee works on the plan, your role as supervisor is to check the accomplishment of each objective and make suggestions or let the employee know his or her improvement is satisfactory.

Motivating. Effective leaders understand the hopes and fears of the people within their unit of the organization—what motivates them. **Motivation** is defined as the internal process that moves or energizes individuals to seek various goals. Use sound motivational techniques to achieve an alignment between the individuals' needs and the needs of the organization. Some of these techniques are:

- Set objectives. You have already learned about the importance of setting goals and objectives in the strategic planning process. The effective leader helps employees establish challenging, measurable objectives. Once this is done, the effective leader helps

the employees achieve their objectives. Doing so requires follow-through and planning on the part of the leader/supervisor, who must not only know what the objectives are but also follow up to see that the employees have achieved the objectives.

- Give recognition. As a supervisor, you need to train yourself to become sensitive to the accomplishments of others. There are a number of ways in which you can give recognition—verbal praise for a job well done, a thank-you letter written to the employee, recognition in the company newsletter or at a company dinner, and so forth. The effective supervisor seeks creative ways to give recognition.

- Enrich the job. **Job enrichment** is accomplished by giving employees a greater variety of duties to perform. Enrichment can help make the job more challenging and prepare the employee for advancement. For example, you might give an office professional who has never developed his or her writing skills a chance to do so by assigning routine letters to draft. Once a level of skill is developed, you can assign the individual more complex writing assignments.

- Develop a team. As a supervisor, you can capitalize on the need of individuals to be accepted as part of a team by having them work together on projects. For example, you might ask a team to develop an office procedures manual for the department.

- Pay for the job. Give pay raises to individuals whose performance evaluations are good (assuming the economics allow you to do so). Another method of assuring that you are paying appropriately for the job is to have the job description of employees analyzed

cathy®

by Cathy Guisewite

The effective supervisor seeks creative ways to give recognition. CATHY © Cathy Guisewite. Reprinted with permission of UNIVERSAL PRESS SYNDICATE. All rights reserved.

by an outside consultant every few years Many times jobs change dramatically, with increased responsibilities. Often an expanded job description means that the individual is not being adequately compensated for his or her efforts. An analysis of the job description can point this out, and then the problem can be alleviated. As a supervisor, it is your responsibility to know what your employees do.

- Delegate work. **Delegation** is the process of entrusting the performance of some specific work to another person. Prudent delegation is one of the keys to effective supervision. Most supervisors know this, but they also realize that delegation is not always easy. The reasons for not delegating are many and varied. Some supervisors may not understand their role well and thus cannot delegate what they do not understand. Other supervisors do not trust the people who work for them. They believe that the work will not be done properly unless they do it. Still other supervisors do not have the confidence they need to delegate. They fear competition or loss of recognition if

they delegate work to their subordinates. Clearly, these fears are not the characteristics of an effective leader. Yet we know that not all supervisors are effective leaders. However, supervisors who care are striving constantly to become effective leaders. Delegating work and helping the people who report to them succeed is part of the growth process.

Achieving Unity

In any organization and with any group of people, conflict can and does occur on occasion. Leaders are concerned with resolving the conflict. They must learn and use appropriate conflict resolution skills. Leaders who are skilled in resolving conflict can get to the root of the problem, whatever it might be. They can help the individuals or groups look at what the problem is and possible solutions. In Chapter 9, you learned some conflict resolution techniques. Here are some additional suggestions.

- Initiate a process that examines the conflict from all perspectives.

- Identify points of agreement and work from these points. Then identify points of disagreement.
- Create a safe atmosphere. Provide an environment where everyone is secure.
- Be hard on the facts and soft on the people. Take an extended amount of time to get every detail. Separate fact from opinion. Opinion many times reflects perception rather than reality. Challenge categorical statements by focusing on the facts.
- Involve all team members in finding a solution that will resolve the conflict.
- Identify what is right for the good of the organization.
- If the conflict is an entrenched one, declare a moratorium. Use time as a resource to understand the intentions of the individuals involved and work behind the scenes to ensure the greatest possible resolution to the conflict.
- Separate the people from the problem. When the two are tangled, the problem becomes unmanageable. Concentrate on the problem.

Explaining and Teaching

Part of a leader's job is explaining why something is occurring—why the organization is taking the directions it is, why a certain procedure has been established, why a particular task needs to be done. In explaining, the leader must use good communication skills. You learned several techniques for reducing communication barriers in Chapter 9. A leader is a good communicator; a leader also knows the importance of continuing to refine and improve his or her communication skills.

Good leaders are also good teachers. They understand that each day as they use good communication skills and conflict resolution skills in working with individuals and groups, people are watching and learning from them.

Renewing

In our fast-paced, technological world, we have no option regarding change. Our world does and will continue to change. The way we perform work will change. The problems that we face will change. The good leader recognizes that change is inevitable and helps the people within the organization grow with change rather than become "stuck in the past." Good leaders become "shapers of what can be" rather than holding on to "what is." However, they never support change for the sake of change. Good leaders are capable of analyzing the directions of the external environment and what those directions mean for the organization. They are capable of determining when something within the organization must change.

In order to help employees deal with change, good leaders provide help not only in understanding the directions of the future but also in developing skills for the future. The good leader understands that putting dollars into professional development is a worthwhile use of funds. Good leaders are champions of positive change for the organization and for developing individuals who embrace important new directions.

Leadership—A Growth Process. Just as leaders help others learn and grow, they also realize that it is crucial for them to continue to develop their leadership skills. Effective leaders for the twenty-first century understand that they must develop the ability to:

- Be a visionary, with the realization that their vision is not the only one and that they must be willing to amend their vision based on the thoughtful insights of others

- Handle ambiguity by helping the organization continually seek and interpret information from a variety of sources
- Assemble diverse groups (race, ethnicity, gender, age) to solve organizational problems
- Create alliances even with former antagonists to address organizational issues
- See connections between and among various groups in a diverse and complex world—connections both internationally and with stakeholders outside the business (government, education, environmental groups, and so forth)

These abilities, along with numerous others that will be required to meet the demands of a changing world, point to the challenges that will face leaders and the ever-present need for continual growth and renewal. Whatever position of leadership you find yourself in, whether it is in your work world or in professional organizations outside of your work, the excitement of being able to lead out in thoughtful ways and the challenges of doing so will demand the very best from you.

SUMMARY

Study this summary to reinforce what you have learned in this chapter.

- Leadership is the process of persuading others to take action that is consistent with the purpose of the leader or the group's shared purpose.
- Management is one of the activities that leaders perform. Managers are

people who do things right; leaders are people who do the right thing.

- Effective leadership characteristics include:
  Building a shared vision
  Living by a set of values
  Using power appropriately
  Engendering trust
  Rewarding risk taking
- Leadership tasks include:
  Envisioning goals
  Affirming values
  Managing
  Motivating
  Achieving unity
  Explaining and teaching
  Renewing
- A process that is used to help individuals envision goals is called strategic thinking. Organizational strategic thinking is the coordination of creative minds into a common perspective (common goals) that enables the organization to proceed into the future through thoughtful analysis of where it should be.
- Planning involves setting goals and objectives for the organization and developing plans for accomplishing them.
- Long-range planning is the process by which the ideas from strategic thinking are translated into an action format. It helps turn the ideas into reality.
- Tactical planning is the process of making detailed decisions about how the organization will accomplish the goals established.
- Span of control refers to the number of employees who are directly supervised by one person. It varies based on the philosophy of the organization.

- Job analysis is a list of the tasks for a specific job and the personal characteristics necessary in order to perform the tasks successfully.

- A job description includes the skills, training, and education necessary for the job, along with a list of the duties of the job.

- Recruitment is the process of searching, both inside and outside the organization, for people to fill positions.

- Interviewing must be done as objectively as possible and consistent with the laws that affect interviewing.

- The three major tools used to screen applicants are the written application, the personal interview, and testing procedures.

- One of the supervisor's responsibilities may be to train new employees.

- Organizations exercise control measures (such as procedures, budgets, and data) to measure the performance of the organization toward the accomplishment of its goals.

- One of the tasks of a supervisor is to conduct ongoing and periodic evaluations of employees. Evaluation guidelines include:
  Allowing adequate time for evaluation
  Praising the employee, along with pointing out areas of weakness
  Being fair
  Being a good listener
  Avoiding comments on personal areas
  Helping the employee establish attainable objectives

- Motivation is defined as the internal process that moves or energizes individuals to seek various goals. The effective supervisor understands and uses motivational techniques with employees.

- The leader achieves unity through helping individuals deal with conflict.

- The role of leaders includes explaining organizational directions, teaching individuals through their own action, and helping the organization cope with change through renewal.

Key Terms

- CEO
- Leadership
- Power
- Management
- Values
- Empowers
- Envisioning goals
- Strategic thinking
- Planning
- Long-range planning
- Long-term goals
- Tactical planning
- Span of control
- Job analysis
- Job description
- Recruitment
- EEOC
- Cognitive ability test
- Performance test
- Mentors
- Control measures
- Organizational control
- Group control
- Stakeholder control
- Individual self-control
- Projection
- Motivation
- Job enrichment
- Delegation

Professional Pointers

Effective leaders energize people. Here are some of the ways they do this.

- Effective leaders believe that the opinions, experience, and knowledge of employees are beneficial to accomplishing the organization's goals. They listen to employees.
- Effective leaders promote a spirit of cooperation; they are not controlling or domineering.
- Effective leaders praise employees and workgroups for their contributions and accomplishments.
- Effective leaders function on the premise that the basic human needs of employees are paramount. Employees must feel that an organization cares about them; they, in turn, will care about the organization.
- Effective leaders celebrate the success of individuals and the success of the team.
- Effective leaders initiate unity.

Office Procedures Reinforcement

1. Explain the difference between leadership and management.
2. List and explain five characteristics of the effective leader.
3. Identify seven leadership tasks.
4. Explain the difference between long-range planning and tactical planning.
5. List and explain five effective evaluation guidelines.

Critical Thinking Activity

Jun Saga was promoted to department manager six months ago. Mr. Saga had been assistant department manager for five years. He always worked well with his colleagues, and he was a master at detail. He never had errors in his work. The department manager was very complimentary of his work. In fact, the department manager was not a detail person, and he always turned to Jun to manage the details. The two men were a very good team. When the department manager left, he highly recommended Jun for his job. He was offered the job and eagerly accepted it. He felt he knew the job well from his work with the previous department manager, and he knew everyone in the department.

Now, six months later, morale in the department is at an all-time low. The employees grumble that Mr. Saga does not involve them in any decisions. They have no input into the goals of the department. Mr. Saga never asks for their opinions or suggestions for improvements. If new policies or procedures are put in place, they discover it from people in other departments and have to ask Mr. Saga to update them. Mr. Saga rarely talks with them; he stays "locked" in his office, working on reports. He meets all deadlines of upper management and always gives them quality work. The employees have not complained to upper management; they really do want Mr. Saga to succeed. However, they are beginning to doubt that he has the necessary leadership skills to handle the department.

1. Did upper management make a mistake in promoting Mr. Saga? If so, what should they have considered before promoting Mr. Saga?

2. Should the employees tell Mr. Saga how they are feeling? If so, what should they say?

3. What suggestions would you make to Mr. Saga so that he might become a more effective manager?

Office Applications

OA20-1 (Goals 1 and 2)

Select three of your classmates to work with on this project. Interview two supervisors; ask them the questions given below. Record your findings in a short report, giving the names and organizations of the people you interviewed. Report your findings to the class; submit your written report to your instructor.

- How would you define leadership?
- How did you develop your leadership skills?
- What characteristics does a leader possess?

- Does your organization have a published mission and value statement? If so, how was it developed? (Ask for a copy of the statement.)
- How is the planning process conducted in your organization?
- What process do you use to evaluate employees?
- How do you motivate employees?
- Do you provide training opportunities for employees? If so, what are they?

OA20-2 (Goals 1 and 3)

Using the rating scale on page 137 of your Applications Workbook, rate yourself on your leadership potential. Ask one of your classmates to rate you also. Talk with the classmate about how he or she feels you might improve. Write a short report on ways that you think you can improve your leadership skills.

OA20-3 (Goal 2)

An employee has filed a complaint with the Human Resources director about his supervisor's evaluation of his job performance. Alleged statements made by the supervisor to the employee are as follows:

- "Your performance evaluation is 'below expectations' because you have done a poor job." When the employee asked for reasons, the supervisor responded: "Your work is unsatisfactory; you should already know that. Try to do better next year."
- "Dawson said that you have been complaining about the way vacation requests are approved." When the employee responded that he had not complained, the supervisor said: "I am not going to argue with you; I have reported to you what I heard."
- "When we developed the budget six months ago, I found several errors in the budget that you made as you were keying it." When the employee asked what the errors were, the supervisor responded that he didn't remember.
- "Only two people in the department are receiving excellent evaluations; they obviously work harder than most employees."

The employee also stated in his letter of complaint that the supervisor conducted his appraisal in the office where five other employees work. There are no walls or even partitions to separate the employees' work areas. The appraisal was conducted at 4:45 p.m. (15 minutes before the employee was to get off work).

Write an evaluation of the job performance appraisal based on the information provided here. Include what should or should not have been said or done by the supervisor, and make suggestions for improving the appraisal. Key your evaluation and print a copy for your instructor.

Online Research Application

ORA 20-4 (Goal 2)

Using the Internet, search the home pages of four corporations. Look for their mission and value statements or company background information that gives you some information about the corporation's directions and values. Write a short report of your findings, identifying your sources, and submit the report to your instructor.

Vocabulary Review

On page 140 of your Applications Workbook is a Vocabulary Review, covering selected items from the vocabulary presented in Chapters 19–20. Complete these sentences and submit a copy to your instructor.

Language Skills Practice

On pages 141–143 of your Applications Workbook are sentences that need to be corrected, using the rules presented in the Reference Section of your text. Correct the sentences as needed and submit your work to your instructor.

Reference Section

This section is designed to help you review English fundamentals. It provides a handy and easy-to-use reference to a variety of rules. In addition, there is a section on how to make proper business introductions. The parts of the Reference Section are as follows:

Abbreviations

1. Academic degrees are generally abbreviated; periods are generally not used with an abbreviation.

   PhD   Doctor of Philosophy
   BS   Bachelor of Science

2. Many companies and professional organizations are known by abbreviated names. These abbreviated names are keyed in capital letters with no periods and no spaces between the letters.

   AT&T   American Telephone and Telegraph
   IBM   International Business Machines
   YMCA   Young Men's Christian Association

3. Certain expressions are abbreviated.

   e.g.   *exempl gratia* (for example)
   etc.   *et cetera* (and so forth)
   i.e.   *id est* (that is)

4. Names of countries should be abbreviated only in tabulations or enumerations and should be written in capital letters; periods may or may not be used in these abbreviations.

   U.S.A.   or   USA

5. Abbreviations for government agencies are usually written in capital letters with no periods and no space between the letters.

   FTC   Federal Trade Commission
   CIA   Central Intelligence Agency

6. The personal titles *Mr., Mrs., Ms., Messrs.,* and *Dr.* are abbreviated when written before a name.

   Mrs. Ellen Herrera
   Messrs. Fleming and Brown
   Dr. Joseph Andrano
   Ms. Johnson

7. Other personal titles such as *Rev., Hon., Prof., Gen., Col., Capt.,* and

Lieut. are abbreviated when they precede a surname and a given name. When only the surname is used, these titles should be spelled out.

Prof. Mark Huddleston
Professor Huddleston

8. The titles *Reverend* and *Honorable* are spelled out if preceded by *the*.

the Honorable Marjorie Popham

9. The abbreviations *B.C.*, *A.D.*, *a.m.*, *p.m.*, *No.*, and *$* may be used with numerals.

8:15 a.m. 2000 A.D.
No. 51256 $510

10. The abbreviations *Bro.*, *Bros.*, *Co.*, *Corp.*, *Inc.*, *Ltd.*, and *&* may be used as part of a company name. The official spelling of the company name should be followed.

11. Use only one period if an abbreviation containing a period falls at the end of a sentence. In sentences ending with a question mark or an exclamation mark, place the punctuation mark directly after the period.

The play began at 8:15 p.m.
Does the class start at 9:30 a.m.?

12. Avoid abbreviating the following categories of words unless these words appear in tabulations or enumerations:
    a. Names of territories and possessions of the United States, countries, states, and cities
    b. Names of months
    c. Days of the week
    d. Given names, such as *Wm.* for *William*
    e. Words such as *avenue, boulevard, court, street, drive, road, building*
    f. Parts of geographic names such as *Mt.* (Mountain) and *Ft.* (Fort)

g. Parts of company names, such as *Bros.*, *Co.*, and *Corp.*, unless they are abbreviated in the official company name
h. Compass directions when they are part of an address. (However, abbreviations such as *No.*, *So.*, *E.*, *W.*, *NW*, *NE*, *SE*, and *SW* may be used after street names; before street names, the abbreviations should be spelled out—*East Orchard Lane*.)
i. The word *number* unless it is followed by a numeral.

Capitalization

1. Capitalize the titles of specific courses.

   He took Psychology 131 last semester.

   Do not capitalize general references to academic subject areas.

   She wants to take a course in government.

2. Capitalize titles that precede a person's name and abbreviations after a name.

   General Rodgers
   Mark Jones, Jr.

   Do not capitalize titles when they follow a personal name or are used in place of a personal name. Exceptions are made when high government titles such as *President, Attorney General, Chief Justice*, and so forth are used in formal acknowledgments and lists.

   Robert A. Fidler, president of Dillon Industries, will speak tonight.
   The President of the United States was in Mexico in February.

3. Specific trade names of products should be capitalized.

   He bought a Gateway computer.

4. Capitalize the first word in each line of a poem.

   The doors of the morning must open.
   The keys of the night are not thrown away.
   I who have loved morning know its doors.
   I who have loved night know its keys.

   Carl Sandburg

5. Capitalize the first word of a direct quotation.

   Michael replied, "The sky is the limit."

6. Compass directions are capitalized when they refer to specific regions or when the direction is part of a specific name. Directions are not capitalized when they indicate a general location or direction.

   Northwest Airlines
   I grew up in the East.
   He lives on the east side of town.

7. The first word and all words except articles, prepositions, and conjunctions in the titles of books, articles, poems, and plays are capitalized.

   Les Miserables
   Effective Communication in Business

8. All words referring to the deity, the Bible, the books of the Bible, and other sacred books should be capitalized.

   the Koran
   our Lord and Savior

9. Capitalize names of organizations, political parties, and religious bodies.

   Girl Scouts
   the Presbyterian Church

10. Capitalize names of months, days of the week, holidays, holy days, and periods of history.

    Monday   January
    Christmas   the Middle Ages

11. Capitalize names of geographic sections and places: continents, countries, states, cities, rivers, mountains, lakes, and islands.

    Lake Michigan   Rocky Mountains
    New York   Africa

12. Capitalize names of divisions of a college or university.

    Business Division
    School of Medicine

13. Names of specific historical events, specific laws, treaties, and departments of government are capitalized.

    Vietnam War
    Department of Defense

14. Capitalize names of streets, avenues, buildings, churches, hotels, parks, and theaters

    One Main Place
    The Seasons Hotel

15. Capitalize only the parts of a hyphenated word that you would capitalize if the word were not hyphenated.

    mid-July
    President-elect Blackshear

16. Nouns followed by numbers or letters, with the exception of line, note, page, paragraph, size, and verse, are capitalized.

    Chapter 12
    page 2

17. Names of constellations, planets, and stars should be capitalized.

    Venus
    the North Star

18. Titles of relatives are capitalized when they precede a name or when the title is used as a name. Family titles are not capitalized when they are preceded by possessive pronouns and when they describe a family relationship.

    I telephoned Uncle Ed and Aunt Betty last night.
    Yesterday Mom called me about the tickets.
    My cousin is in town.

19. Every word in the salutation of a letter is capitalized except when dear is not the first word. Only the first word in the complimentary close of a letter is capitalized.

    Dear Miss Edwards   Sincerely yours
    My dear Mr. Smith

20. Avoid capitalizing the following:
    a. Names of the seasons of the year unless the season is personified

        My favorite season is spring because Spring comes in all her glory

    b. Prefixes to proper names

        non-European country

    c. Words that were once proper nouns but which through common usage have become common nouns

        turkish towels
        venetian blinds
        french fries

Numbers

1. The general rule is to spell out numbers one through nine and use figures for numbers ten and over. If a sentence contains a series of numbers any of which is over ten, use all figures.

2. Round numbers are spelled out when they can be expressed in one or two words. If the numbers contained in a sentence or paragraph are in different categories, use consistency in treating them in context.

    Approximately thirty people attended the meeting on Monday, and five people attended the meeting on Tuesday.

3. Always spell out a number that begins a sentence. If the number is large, rearrange the sentence so that the number is not the first word of the sentence.

    Five hundred books were ordered.
    We had a good year in 1981. *Not:* Nineteen hundred and eighty-one was a good year.

4. Form the plural of figures by adding *s.*
    The 2000s will be challenging.

5. Hyphenate spelled out numbers from 21 to 99 and any number that is part of a compound adjective.

    thirty-four hundred
    a two-hundred mile trip

6. Ages of people and things are usually expressed in figures.

    She is almost 18.
    He is 21 today.

7. Use cardinal numbers (1, 2, 3, 4, and so on) to express dates appearing in normal month-day-year order.

    June 12, 2002

    If the month follows the day or is not stated, use ordinal numbers (1st, 2d, 3d, 4th, and so on)

    It happened on the 15th of April.

8. Military dates are stated in day-month-year sequence. In this format, the day is written in cardinal numbers.
   28 October 1994

9. In formal documents, dates should be spelled out.
   May tenth
   Nineteen hundred and eighty-two

10. Decades and centuries should be spelled out in lowercase letters.
    the twenty-first century

11. House or building numbers are usually written in figures. However, when *one* is used alone, it is spelled out.
    One Patricia Avenue
    116 Huntington Avenue

12. Spell out numbered street names from one to ten. Otherwise, use figures. To avoid confusion, use a hyphen preceded and followed by a space when figures are used for both the house number and the street name. When using ordinals in street names, 2d and 3d are preferred to 2nd and 3rd.
    122 Sixth Avenue
    3456-22d Street

13. In legal documents (wills, agreements, and so on) and negotiable instruments (checks, notes, bonds, and so on), numbers are stated in words and figures for clarity and certainty. Legal documents use capitalized words to express sums of money.
    sixteen (16) weeks
    I agree to pay the sum of One Hundred Twenty Eight Dollars ($128)

14. Specific amounts of money are generally expressed in figures.
    $10 $5.25

15. Indefinite amounts of money should be written in words.
    several hundred dollars

16. Round number amounts of $1 million and more may be written as:
    $5 million $10 million

17. When writing money amounts in figures, do not use a decimal point and zeros after even amounts.
    $10 $200
    Exception: Whole dollar amounts take zeros after the decimal point when they appear in the same context with fractional amounts.
    The book was $15.50, but the store offered a discount of $1.00.

18. Amounts of money less than a dollar are keyed in figures with the word *cents* spelled out.
    The small bottle of lotion cost 99 cents.
    a. In formal writing or in stating an isolated amount in cents, spell out the amount and the word *cents*.
       twenty-five cents
    b. In an amount that is less than a dollar but is part of a series in which some amounts are a dollar or more, use $.00 as the form.
       The prices of the items you want are $1.25, $.85, and $3.50 respectively.

19. In general usage, times of day are written in figures with a.m. or p.m.
    12:10 a.m.   3:30 p.m.   8 p.m.
    Note: The abbreviations *a.m.* and *p.m.* are keyed in small letters without spaces.

20. In formal usage, approximate and on-the-half-hour times are spelled out.
    half past three o'clock   eight o'clock
    half after three o'clock

21. Use *o'clock* with spelled-out numbers and *a.m.* or *p.m.* with figures.

eight o'clock in the morning

8:10 p.m.

22. The times *noon* and *midnight* may be expressed in words alone except when these times are given with other items expressed in figures.

Buses run on this route from 5 a.m. to 12 midnight.

23. In general usage, express percentages in figures; spell out percent.

10 percent

In formal writing, spell out the amount and percent.

ninety-eight percent

24. Ratios and proportions are written in figures.

3 to 1   4:1

25. An isolated simple fraction should be spelled out unless it is part of a mixed number.

one-half

$3\frac{1}{3}$

26. Use figures with symbols and abbreviations.

#14   10% $35   18 in.

Often Misused Words and Phrases

1. *A* or *an* before the letter *h*

A is used before all consonant sounds, including *h* when sounded. *An* is used before all vowel sounds, except long *u*.

2. A while, awhile

   a. A while is a noun meaning a short time.

      We plan to go home in a while.

   b. Awhile is an adverb meaning a short time.

      She wrote the poem awhile ago.

3. About, at

   Use either about or at—not both.

   He will leave about noon.

   He will leave at noon.

4. Accept, except

   a. Accept means to receive; it is always a verb.

      I accept the gift.

   b. Except as a preposition means *with the exception of.*

      Everyone left except him.

   c. Except as a verb means to exclude.

      When the sentence was excepted, the committee approved the report.

5. Addition, edition

   a. Addition is the process of adding.

      They plan to add an addition to the building.

   b. Edition is a particular version of printed material.

      This is the fourth edition of the book.

6. Advice, advise

   a. Advice is a noun meaning a recommendation.

      She did not follow my advice.

   b. Advise is a verb meaning to counsel.

      The counselor will advise you.

7. All, all of

   Use all; of is redundant. If a pronoun follows all, reword the sentence.

   Check all the items. They are all going.

8. All right

   All right is the only correct usage. Alright is incorrect.

9. Among, between
   a. Among is used when referring to three or more persons or things.
      The inheritance was divided among the four relatives.
   b. Between is used when referring to two persons or things.
      The choice is between you and me.
10. Bad, badly
    Bad is an adjective and should be used after verbs of sense; badly is an adverb.
    He feels bad about losing. She looks bad.
    The football team played badly tonight.
11. Biannual, biennial
    a. Biannual means occurring twice a year.
       The biannual evaluation will be done next month.
    b. Biennial means occurring once every two years.
       The biennial celebration will occur in May.
12. Capital, capitol
    Capital is used unless you are referring to the building that houses a government.
    Austin is the capital of Texas.
    We toured the United States Capitol in Washington.
    That is a capital idea!
13. Cite, sight, site
    Cite means to quote; sight means vision, site means location.
    She cited the correct reference.
    That is a pleasant sight.
    They sighted a whale.
    The site for the new building will be determined soon.

14. Complement, compliment
    Complement means to complete, fill, or make perfect; compliment means to praise.
    His thorough report complemented the presentation.
    I complimented Jane on her new dress.
15. Council, counsel
    a. Council is a noun meaning a governing body.
       The council meets today.
    b. Counsel as a noun means advice; it also means a lawyer. Counsel as a verb means to advise.
       Dr. Baker's counsel helped Chris overcome her fears.
       Counsel was consulted on the case.
       He is there to counsel you.
16. Farther, further
    Farther refers to distance; further refers to a greater degree or extent.
    The store is a mile farther down the road.
    We will discuss the matter further tomorrow.
17. Good, well
    Both good and well are adjectives. Well is used to mean in fine health; good is used to mean pleasant or attractive.
    I feel well.
    She feels good about her job.
18. Its, it's
    a. Its is the possessive form of it.
       The family had its reunion yesterday.
    b. It's is the contraction of it is.
       It's probably going to rain.
19. Percent, per cent, percentage
    Percent is the correct usage; not per cent. Percentage is also one word.

20. Principal, principle
    a. Principal as an adjective means main; as a noun, it means the main person or a capital sum.
        The principal actor was outstanding.
        The principals in the case are present for their testimony.
    b. Principle is a noun meaning a rule, guide, truth; it never refers directly to a person.
        She held steadfast to her principles.

21. Stationary, stationery
    a. Stationary means stable or fixed.
        The ladder seems stationary.
    b. Stationery is writing paper.
        Order three boxes of stationery.

22. That, which, who
    a. Who is used to refer to an individual person or individual group.
        Mr. King is a man who has a thorough understanding of the situation.
        The administrative assistants constitute the group who will be going.
    b. Which refers to animals and places, and objects.
        Which animals do you mean?
    c. That is used to refer to a class, species, or kind of person or group.
        The book that I read yesterday was good.
        That is the kind of person I like.
        This school is the one that I attended as a child.

23. Who, whom
    a. Who is used as the subject of a verb.

Send it to the people who asked for it.
    b. Whom is used as an object of a verb or preposition.
        Whom shall I ask first?
        Whom did they ask to represent the president?
        The person to whom I gave the information used it improperly.

Plurals and Possessives

1. When a compound word contains a noun and is hyphenated or made up of two or more words, the principal word takes an *s* to form the plural. If there is no principal word, add an s to the end of the compound word.
    commanders in chief   runners-up
    mothers-in-law   forget-me-nots
    passersby

2. The plural of letters is formed by adding *s* or *'s*. The apostrophe is unnecessary except where confusion might result.
    CPAs
    dotting the i's and crossing the t's

3. Singular nouns form the possessive by adding *'s*. If a singular noun has two or more syllables and if the last syllable is not accented and is preceded by a sibilant sound (*s, x, z*), add only the apostrophe for ease of pronunciation.
    the person's   Mrs. Jones's office
    computer
    the department's   Ulysses' voyage
    rules

4. Plural nouns form the possessive by adding an apostrophe if the plural ends in *s* or by adding *'s* when the plural does not end in *s*.

5. When a verb form ending in *ing* is used as a noun (gerund), a noun or pronoun before it takes the possessive form.

Mr. Ware's talking was not anticipated.
Their shouting disturbed me.
I appreciate your being here today.
We were surprised at Helen's leaving.

6. To form the possessive of a compound word, add the possessive ending to the last syllable.

A passerby's scarf blew off.
Her mother-in-law's gift arrived.

7. Joint possession is indicated by adding the possessive ending to the last noun.

We are near Jan and Mike's store.
Drs. Edison and Martin's article was published this week.

8. In idiomatic construction, the possessive form is often used.

a day's work   two weeks' vacation
two dollar's worth   this month's pay

9. The possessive form is used in cases where the noun modified is not expressed.

Take it to the plumber's. (shop)
Stop at the Taylors'. (home)

10. The possessive form of personal pronouns is written without an apostrophe.

This book is hers.
She will deliver yours tomorrow.
The packages are theirs.

Punctuation
The Period

The period indicates a full stop and is used in the following instances.

1. At the end of a complete and declarative or imperative sentence

2. After abbreviations and after a single or double initial that represents a word

acct.   etc.
U.S.   pp.

Some abbreviations that are made up of several capital letters do not require periods.

AAA (American Automobile Association)
YMCA (Young Women's Christian Association)

3. Between dollars and cents
$42.65 $1.45

4. To indicate a decimal figure
3.5 bushels   12.65 bushels   6.25 feet

The Comma

The comma indicates a partial stop and is used in the following instances:

1. To separate independent clauses that are connected by coordinating conjunctions, such as *and, but, or, for,* and *nor,* unless the clauses are short and closely connected

We have a supply on hand, but I think we should order an additional quantity.
She had to work late, for the auditors were examining the books.

2. To set off a subordinate clauses that precedes the main clause

Assuming that there will be no changes, I suggest that you proceed with your instructions.

3. After an introductory phrase containing a verb form or an

introductory adverbial phrase or clause

To finish his work, he remained at the office after hours.

After planning the program, she proceeded to put it into effect.

Although he would have preferred to stay, Peter had to leave the party long before it ended.

4. To set off a nonrestrictive adjective phrase or clause that follows the noun

The beacon, rising proudly toward the sky, guided the pilots safely home.

Our group, which had never lost a debate, won the grand prize.

5. To separate from the rest of the sentence a word or a group of words that breaks the continuity of the sentence

John, even though his work was completed, was always willing to help others.

6. To separate parenthetical expressions from the rest of the sentence

We have, as you know, two persons who can handle the reorganization.

7. To set off names used in direct address or to set off appositives

I think, Mr. Bennett, you will agree with the statement.

Ms. Linda Ming, our vice president, will be in your city soon.

8. To separate from the rest of the sentence expressions that, without punctuation, may be interpreted incorrectly

Misleading: Ever since we have filed our reports monthly.

Better: Ever since, we have filed our reports monthly.

9. To separate words or groups of words when they are used in a series of three or more

Most executives agree that dependability, trustworthiness, ambition, and judgment are required of their office workers.

10. To set off short direct quotations from the rest of the sentence

Mary said, "The play is excellent," and the group agreed.

11. To separate geographical names and dates

Our southern branch is located in Atlanta, Georgia.
The department was divided on February 15,2001, into three sections.

12. To separate abbreviations of titles from the name

William R. Warner, Jr.
Ramona Sandhez, PhD

The Semicolon

The semicolon should be used in the following instances:

1. Between independent clauses joined by a coordinating conjunction when either or both contain internal punctuation

He was outstanding in his knowledge of statistics, computing, and languages; but he was lacking in many desirable personal qualities

2. Between two independent, closely related clauses when the coordinating conjunction is omitted

Many executives now make their own telephone calls; it is faster.

3. To precede expressions such as namely, for example (e.g.,), that is (i.e.), when used to introduce a clause

We selected the computer for two

reasons; namely, because it is a reasonable price and because it has more memory.

There are several reasons for changing the routine of handling mail; i.e., to reduce postage, to conserve time, and to place responsibility.

4. To separate items in a series that are long or complex or that have internal punctuation

When the vote was tabulated, Alvarez won first place; O'Connor, second place; and Schmidt, third place.

The Colon

The colon is recommended in the following instances:

1. After the salutation in a business letter except when open punctuation is used

Ladies and Gentlemen:
Dear Ms. Carroll:

2. Following introductory expressions, such as *the following, as follows,* and other expressions that precede enumerations

The following office equipment is vital for the administrative assistant:

- Computer
- Fax
- Telephone
- Copier

The officers elected were as follows: president, Carol Scott; vice president, Jim Kinney; and treasurer, Jill Goodman.

3. To separate hours and minutes in indicating time

2:10 p.m.   4:45 p.m.   10:15 a.m.

4. To introduce a long quotation

The agreement read: "We the undersigned hereby agree . . ."

5. To separate two independent clauses or independent sentences when the second explains or expands the statement in the first

We selected the machine for one reason: in competitive tests it surpassed all other machines.

The Question Mark

The question mark should be used in the following instances:

1. After a direct question

When do you expect to arrive in Philadelphia?

An exception to the foregoing is a request, suggestion, or command phrased as a question out of courtesy. Use a period at the end of this kind of sentence since the reader is expected to respond by taking action rather than giving a yes or no answer.

Will you please send us an up-to-date statement of our account.

2. After each question in a series of questions within one sentence

What is your opinion of the IBM computer? the Dell? the Hewlett Packard?

Our questions are: When will you arrive? Where will you stay? Will you have transportation?

The Exclamation Point

The exclamation point is ordinarily used after words or groups of words that express command, strong feeling, emotion, or an exclamation.

Don't waste office supplies!
It can be done!
Stop!

The Dash

The dash is used in the following instances:

1. To indicate an omission of letters or figures

    Dear Mr.—

    Date the letter July 16, 2—

2. When strong emphasis is desired

    This book is not a revision of an old book—it is a completely new book. He had spent several hours explaining the operation—an operation that would, he hoped, put an end to the problem.

3. To separate parenthetical expressions that have internal punctuation or when unusual emphasis on the parenthetical expression is desired

    These sales arguments—and every one of them is important—should result in getting the order.

Quotation Marks

Certain basic rules should be followed in using quotation marks. These rules are as follows:

1. When quotation marks are used with a comma or a period, the comma or period should be placed inside the closing quotation mark.

    She said, "I plan to complete my program in college before seeking a position."

2. When quotation marks are used with a semicolon or a colon, the semicolon or colon should be placed outside the closing quotation mark.

    The treasurer said, "I plan to go by train"; others in the group stated that they would go by plane.

3. With more than one paragraph of quoted material, quotation marks should appear at the beginning of each paragraph and at the end of the last paragraph.

    "
    ———————————————.
    "
    ———————————————."

4. To indicate a quotation within a quotation, use single quotation marks.

    The author states, "Too frequent use of 'very' and 'most' weakens the appeal."

5. Quotation marks are used in the following instances:

    a. Before and after direct quotations

        The author states, "Too frequent use of certain words weakens the appeal."

    b. To indicate the title of a published article, a chapter in a book, and an individual poem, essay, or story in a volume

        Have you read the article "Ethics in the Workplace"?

Omission Marks or Ellipsis

Ellipsis marks (. . .) are frequently used to denote the omission of letters or words in quoted material. If the material omitted comes at the end of a sentence, a period is used along with the ellipsis marks (. . . .).

Parentheses

Parentheses should be used in the following instances:

1. When amounts expressed in words are followed by figures

    You must pay twenty-five dollars ($25) as stated in the contract.

2. Around words that are used in parenthetical expressions

    Our letter costs (excluding paper and postage) are much too high for this type of business.

3. To indicate technical references

    Sodium chloride (NaCl) is the chemical name for common table salt.

4. When enumerations are included in narrative form

    Here are the reasons for my resignation: (1) to assume more responsibility, (2) to have a greater chance for advancement, and (3) to move closer to my children.

Proofreader's Marks

Mark	Explanation	Example
⁋	Paragraph	⁋ Start a new paragraph here.
∧	Insert	Insert a letter hᵉre.
ℰ	Delete	Take out this extra word.
stet or	Let it stand	Do not delete these words.
tr or ∼	Transpose	Turn this around sentence.
⌐	Move to the left	⌐ Move this copy to the left.
⌐	Move to the right	Move this copy to the right.
⌒	Close up	Close up the extra spa ce.
Cap or ≡	Set in capitals	Her name is Barbara walters.
lc or /	Set in lowercase	These letters should not be Capitalized.
⊙	Insert a period	Insert a period at this point .
⩔ ⩔	Quotation marks	Bob said, I think she is sick.
⌄,	Comma	Yes place a comma here.
#	Insert space	Space between these words.
=/	Hyphen	They will take a two week trip.
⟨3/	Use superior figure	Place a footnote at the end of this sentence.
[/]	Brackets	[/] John the author wrote the students a letter.
𝓈𝓅	Spell out	Spell out #.
Center or][	Center	CHINN-HART COMPANY

Spelling

1. Put *i* before *e* except after *c* or when sounded like *a* as in neighbor or weigh.
   Exceptions: either, neither, seize, weird, leisure, financier, conscience

2. When a one-syllable word ends in a single consonant and when that final consonant is preceded by a single vowel, double the final consonant before a suffix that begins with a vowel or the suffix *y*.

   run   running
   drop   dropped
   bag   baggage
   skin   skinny

3. When a word of more than one syllable ends in a single consonant, when that final consonant is preceded by a single vowel, and when the word is accented on the last syllable, double the final consonant before a suffix that begins with a vowel.

   begin   beginning
   concur   concurrent

   When the accent does not fall on the last syllable, do not double the final consonant before a suffix that begins with a vowel.

   travel   traveler
   differ   differing

4. When the final consonant in a word of one or more syllables is preceded by another consonant or by two vowels, do not double the final consonant before any suffix.

   look   looked
   deceit   deceitful
   act   acting
   warm   warmly

5. Words ending in a silent *e* generally drop the *e* before a suffix that begins with a vowel.

   guide   guidance
   use   usable

6. Words ending in silent *e* generally retain the *e* before a suffix that begins with a consonant unless another vowel precedes the final *e*.

   hate   hateful
   due   duly
   excite excitement
   argue   argument

7. Words ending in *ie* drop the *e* and change the *i* to *y* before adding *ing*.

   lie   lying
   die   dying

8. Words ending in *ce* or *ge* generally retain the final *e* before the suffixes *-able* and *-ous* but drop the final *e* before the suffixes *ible* and *ing*.

   manage manageable
   force   forcible

9. When a word ends in *c*, insert a *k* before adding a suffix beginning with *e, i,* or *y*.

   picnic   picnicking

10. Words ending in *y* preceded by a consonant generally change the *y* to *i* before any suffix except one beginning with *i*.

    modify   modifying   modifier
    lonely   lonelier

11. Words ending in *o* preceded by a vowel form the plural by adding *s*. Words ending in *o* preceded by a consonant generally form the plural by adding *es*.

    folio   folios
    potato potatoes

12. Words ending in *y* preceded by a vowel form the plural by adding *s;* words ending in *y* preceded by a consonant change the *y* to *i* and add *es* to form the plural.

attorney	attorneys
lady	ladies

Word Division

1. Divide words between syllables.

    moun-tain

2. Do not divide words of five or fewer letters (preferably six or fewer)

    apple   among   finger

3. Do not divide one-syllable words.

    helped   eight

4. If a one-letter syllable falls within a word, divide the word after the one-letter syllable.

    regu-late   sepa-rate

5. If two syllables of one letter occur together within a word, divide between the one-letter syllables.

    continu-ation   radi-ator

6. Divide between double consonants that appear within a word. Also, when the final consonant of a base word is doubled to add a suffix, divide between the double consonants.

    neces-sary   omit-ted

7. When a base word ends in a double consonant, divide between the base word and the suffix

    tell-ing   careless-ness

8. Divide hyphenated compound words at existing hyphens only.

    two-thirds   self-control

9. Avoid dividing a date, personal name, or address. If it is absolutely necessary, maximize readability by doing the following.

    a. Divide a date between the day and the year

    b. Divide a personal name between the first name and surname.

    c. Divide an address between the city and state.

10. Avoid dividing figures, abbreviations, and symbols.

    $20,000   YMCA   #109

11. Do not divide contractions.

    he'll   wouldn't

12. Divide no more than three or four words on a typewritten page.

13. Avoid dividing words at the end of the first and last lines of a paragraph.

14. Do not divide the last word on a keyed page.

15. The first part of a divided word must contain at least two letters; the latter part must contain at least three.

    around (not a-round)

    lately (not late-ly)

Proper Business Introductions

The basic rule to follow in making business introductions is: the most important person is named first, regardless of gender. For example, a customer or client is more important than your supervisor, a government official is more important than your supervisor, and your supervisor is more important than a new employee who is at a lower level on the organization chart than your supervisor. Each person is always introduced to the other. You can achieve this in two ways. By actual use of the word "to."

Mrs. Sinclair, I'd like to introduce you to Mr. Arnold.

Or, by saying the name of the person to whom the other is being introduced first, without the use of "to."

Mr. Santiago, may I introduce Mrs. Komuro.

When introducing people of equal rank in business situations, the social rules for introductions apply, which are a man is introduced to a woman and a younger person is introduced to an older person.

Do not use first names in business introductions unless it is the office custom or if requested to do so by business clients or customers.

When you are introduced to someone, either one of you may extend your hand first. Your handshake should be relaxed but firm. You should look the other person in the eye and say, "I am happy to meet you" or some other cordial greeting. If someone you are meeting backs off as you extend your hand, do not force the issue. Simply drop your hand back to your side, smile, and say "Hello" or some other cordial greeting.

Index

Bylaws, 427
Bytes, 123

C

Cable modems, 301*f*, 301–302
Cable modem termination system
    (CMTS), 301
Calendar, 73–74, 74, 75*f*, 76*f*
    for travel, 472–473
Calendar notations, for meetings, 435
Caller ID, 305
Call following, 305
Call forwarding, 305
Call waiting, 305
Cancellations, with air travel, 458
Capitalization, 584–586
CAR. *See* Computer-aided retrieval
Card file, 373, 374*f*, 377, 379*f*
Career advancement, virtual offices and,
    215–216
Career audit, 548–549
Career decisions, 21–23
Career goals, 20–21
Career, office opportunities, 13–19
Career path, 19–23
Carpal tunnel syndrome, 46–47
Car rental, during international travel,
    465
Car travel, 459
Cash advances, for travel, 472
Cashier's check, 493
Categorization, 234
Cathode ray tube (CRT), 126
cc. *See* Courtesy copy
CD. *See* Compact disk
CD-E, 124
CD-recordable (CD-R), 124, 402
CD-rewritables (CD-RW), 402
CD-ROM, 117, 124, 146
    for records storage, 397–398
Cell, 305
Cellular telephones, 305–306
Centralized copy center, 170, 181–182
Centralized storage system, 398
Central office (CO), 298
Central processing unit (CPU), 122, 122*f*
Centrex, 303–304
Certificate of mailing, 331
Certified checks, 493
Certified mail, 332
Certified Medical Assistant (CMA), 14
Certified Medical Transcriptionist (CMT),
    14
Certified Professional Secretary (CPS),
    19, 20*f*
Change
    leadership and, 576–577
    openness to, 102
Chat rooms, 5, 133*f*
Check carbon, 487

Check register, 488, 489*f*
Check retention, 492
Checks, 487–490, 489*f*
    cashier's, 493
    certified, 493
    payroll, 500*f*
    traveler's, 472, 493–494
Check safekeeping, 492
Check truncation, 492
Chronic stress, 58
Chronological resume, 524, 525*f*
Chronologic storage system, 375–377,
    376*f*
Cigarette smoking, 48
CIM. *See* Computer-input microfilm
Ciphertext, 154*f*
Circular arrangement, 438, 438*f*
Citations
    internal, 263, 275
    Internet, 275, 276*f*
Civil Rights Act, 98
C language, 145
Clarity, of written communication,
    245–246
Clip art, 279*f*, 279–280
Closure, of meetings, 425
CMA. *See* Certified Medical Assistant
CMT. *See* Certified Medical
    Transcriptionist
CMTS. *See* Cable modem termination
    system
CO. *See* Central office
Coach air travel, 456–457
COD. *See* Collect on delivery
Coding, 380
Cognitive ability test, 568
COLD systems. *See* Computer output to
    laser disk systems
Collaborative planning, 288
Collaborative writing, 244
Collation, 175
Collect on delivery (COD), 332
    rate chart for, 333*f*
Colon, 593
Color fax, 187
Color, of office, 43
Color reproduction, 173, 174*f*
Color symbolism, 536, 537*f*
COM. *See* Computer-output microfilm
Comma, 591–592
Commitment, 543–544
    to community, 91–92
    to employees, 92
    of project teams, 35
Committee meetings, 427
Common stock, 501–502
Communication, 222–241
    asynchronous, 11
    barriers to, 230–234
        reduction of, 234–236
    and cultural diversity, 41–42

    cultural diversity and, 234
    effective, 73
    evaluation of, 231–232
    formal, 39
    as growth process, 236–237
    history of, 295–296
    ineffective, 66
    informal, 39–40
    modes of, 66
    nonverbal, 226, 227–230
    organizational, 39–42
    process of, 226–227
    and self-concept, 223*f*, 223–226
    skills needed for, 17
    synchronous, 12
    techniques for, 40–42, 235*f*
    and technology, 4–5
    verbal, 226
    and virtual office, 202
    written, 242–268
Communication skills, and job advance-
    ment, 544
Community, commitment to, 91–92
Compact disk (CD), for records storage,
    402–403
Compact disk (CD) storage, 124–125
Company information, when applying
    for job, 519–521
Compressed workweek, 10
Computer(s)
    classification of, 120–122
    and ergonomics, 157–159
    future of, 135–136
    internal processing, 122–123
    mainframe, 120
    notebook, 121–122
    personal, 121–122
    storage in, 122–123
    troubleshooting, 155–157, 156*f*
    workstation, 121
Computer-aided retrieval (CAR),
    407–408
Computer conferencing, 5
Computer ethics, 102*f*, 152–153
Computer-input microfilm (CIM), 407
Computer keyboards, 114–115
Computer-output microfilm (COM),
    407
Computer output to laser disk (COLD)
    systems, 409–410
Computer record, 368
Computer screen, glare from, 44
Computer services, 7
Computer sorting, 367–368, 368*f*
Computer systems, for electronic bank-
    ing, 486
Computer viruses, 162–163, 163*f*
Conference(s), 428, 444–448
    evaluation forms for, 446, 446*f*
    food and beverages for, 446
    hotel reservations for, 445

Dress
        for interviews, 534–536, 537f
        for oral presentations, 286–287
Drug-Free Workplace Act of 1988, 48
DSL. *See* Digital Subscriber Line; Digital
        subscriber line
Dual access, 187
Duplexing, 173
DVD. *See* Digital versatile disk
DVD-R, 125
DVD-RAM, 125, 403
DVD-ROM, 125, 403
DVD+RW, 403
DVD-RW, 403

E

Echecks, 487
Ecology, transnational, 85
Economic pressures, stress and, 61
Education
        increase in, 6–7
        and telecommunications,
        320–321
Educational services, 7
Education careers, 16
EEOC. *See* Equal Employment
        Opportunity Commission
EFT 99, 486
Electronic banking, 483–487
        automated teller machines and,
        483–484
        computer systems for, 486
        debit cards and, 484–485
        direct payroll deposit and, 486
        direct withdrawals and, 486
        future of, 487
        loss of card for, 487
        smart cards and, 485
        software packages for, 486
        sophisticated kiosks and, 484
Electronic blackboard, 428
Electronic database systems, 395–400
        centralized, 398
        decentralized, 398
        integration with microimage sys-
        tems, 407–409
                benefits of, 408–409
        records retrieval in, 398–399
        records storage in, 398–399
        safety with, 399
        security with, 399–400
Electronic funds transfer (EFT), 483, 486,
        487
Electronic meetings, 428–431
        audioconferencing, 428–429
        data conferencing, 430
        pros and cons of, 431
        videoconferencing, 429–430
        virtual conferencing, 430–431
Electronic messages, 307–308, 335

Electronic resumes, 529–530
Electronic time management systems,
        74–78
Ellipsis, 281, 594
Email, 4, 243, 253–255, 335–336
        ethics and, 254–255
        etiquette for, 254
        organization of, 73f
        with PIM software, 74–77
Embedded systems, 144
Emergency procedures, 49
Emoticons, 253
Empathy, 257
Employees, commitment to, 92
Employee's Withholding Allowance
        Certificate (W-4), 499, 500f
Employer
        obligations to, 35
        obligations to employees, 36
Employment agencies, 516–517, 517f
Employment application, 530–532, 531f
Employment information, sources of,
        515–519
Employment, looking for, 515–539,
        548–549
Empowerment, 32–33, 560
Enclosures, in mailings, 337
Encrypt, 154f
Endnotes, 263, 275, 276f
Endorsement, 490, 490f
Endorsement in full, 490
Energy, 202
Enlargement, by copiers, 173, 173f
Envelopes, 273
        address of, 337, 338f
        keeping, 343
        preparation of, 337–338
Environmentally friendly copiers, 176
Environmental responsibility, 87–88
Equal Employment Opportunity Act,
        98–99
Equal Employment Opportunity
        Commission (EEOC), 95,
        567–568
Equal Pay Act, 98f
Equipment, for meetings, 437–438
Ergonomically sound software, 160f
Ergonomics, 43–46, 46f, 157–159
Ergos, 43
Ethical behavior
        definition of, 84
        support for, 99
Ethical organization, characteristics of,
        87–92
Ethics, 84–109, 558–559
        and change, 92–95
                effects of, 95
                factors impeding, 93–94
                steps producing, 94–95, 95f
        characteristics of, in office profes-
        sional, 99

and commitment, 91–92
and computers, 102f, 152–153
and copier abuse, 182–185
and cultural diversity, 89–91
and decision-making, 99
definition of, 85
and email, 254–255
how of, 87
and organizational culture, 88–89
and software copying, 161–162
why of, 86–87
Etymologists, 231
Euro dollars, 464
Evaluation
        of conferences, 446, 446f
        by management, 571–574, 573f
Exclamation point, 593–594
Executives, role in meetings, 432–434
Executive summary, 262
Exercise, and stress reduction, 62
Exit interview, 546, 546f
Expense reports, 475f, 475–476
Experience, and communication, 224
Express mail, 330
        rate chart for, 331f
Express Mail International Service, 333
Express Saver, 334
External team, 37–38
Extranet, 135, 135f
Eyestrain, 47

F

Fair Labor Standards Act of 1938, 498
Fairness, 37
Family
        and stress, 61
        and working from home,
        204–205
Family and Medical Leave Act, 98f
Fatigue, 47–48
Favorable messages, 258, 259f
Fax broadcasting, 187
Fax (facsimile) machines, 4, 186–188
        features of, 187
        and micrographics, 408
        multifunction units, 188
        and PIM software, 74–77
        selection of, 188
Fax mail, 336
Fax-on-demand, 187
FDA. *See* Food and Drug Administration
Federal Express (FedEx), 334–335
Federal Insurance Contribution Act,
        498–499
Federal taxes, 499
FedEx Overnight Freight, 334
Feedback, 36, 94, 227
        and communication, 224–225
Fee paid, 516
Fiche, 404–405

Information processing, 120–126
Information storage, devices for, 123–126
Infrared devices, 119
In-house, 126
Inkjet printer, 128–129
Inspection, of records, 379
Institutions, indexing of, 365
Insured mail, 333
    rate chart for, 333f
Integrated packages, 397
Integrated services digital network (ISDN), 131, 299
Integrated software, 148
Integrity, 101
Interactive videoconferencing, 429
Interactivity, 429
Interface, 121
Internal citations, 263, 275
Internal Revenue Service (IRS), 213, 504
Internal team, 30–32
    cooperation in, 31
    goals of, 31–32
International Association of Administrative Professionals (IAAP), 19
International audience, for written communication, 248–249, 250f
International awareness, 88
International Driver's License, 465
International Economy, 334
International mail, 333
International meetings, 431–432
International Priority, 334
International Priority Freight, 334
International telecommunities, 7
International travel, 460–465
    by air, 462–463
    appointment setting and, 462
    business cards and, 462
    currency and, 463–464
    health precautions during, 464–465
    hotel reservations and, 465
    local transportation and, 465
    passports for, 463
    visas for, 463
Internet, 5, 131–132
    for job information, 515–516
    and mail, 341
    and PIM software, 77–78
    for research, 281
    stocks and, 502
    and travel information, 470
Internet citations, 275, 276f
Internet fax, 188
Internet Protocol (IP), 297
Internet software, 153–155
Interpersonal skills, of project team, 33–35
Interrupt key, on copiers, 175

Interviews, 532–539, 568
    common mistakes during, 536f
    dress for, 534–536, 537f
    evaluation of, 538–539
    follow-up to, 538, 539f
    frequently asked questions, 535f, 536f
    guidelines for, 534–538
    location of, 532
    nervousness and, 534
    number of, 532
    team, 532
    virtual, 533–534
Intranet, 134, 135f
Introductions, 598–599
Investments, 501–505
    bonds, 504
    individual retirement arrangements, 504–505
    mutual funds, 503–504
    stocks, 501–503
Inward WATS, 317–318
IP. *See* Internet Protocol
IRA. *See* Individual retirement accounts; Individual retirement arrangement
IRS. *See* Internal Revenue Service
ISDN. *See* Integrated Services Digital Network; Integrated services digital network
Isolation, and virtual offices, 203–204
Isometric exercises, 158
Itinerary, 466–469, 467f
    preparation of, 470, 471f

J

Jaz disks, 124
Jaz drives, 124
Jet lag, 462
Job advancement, 543–546
    strategies for, 543–544
Job analysis, 566
Job application, 568
Job application process, 519–539, 548–549
    company knowledge in, 519–521
    from employer standpoint, 567–570
    resumes in, 523–530
Job change, 544–546
Job demands versus home demands, 204–205
Job description, 60, 566, 566f
Job enrichment, 574
Job information, sources of, 515–519
Job insecurity, 60
Job interviews. *See* Interviews
Job performance, 540–543
Job recovery, on copiers, 175
Job sharing, 11

Johnson & Johnson, credo of, 88–89, 90f
Junk fax, 188

K

KB. *See* Kilobytes
Kbps. *See* Kilobits per second
Keeping the faith, 102–103
Keyboards, 114–115
Key systems, 303
Keyword, 396
Kilobits per second (Kbps), 132
Kilobytes (KB), 123
Krinein, 18

L

Labeling, 93
Labor force, diversity in, 5–6, 6f
LAN. *See* Local area networks
Landscape, 127
Language
    clarity of, 41
    and communication barriers, 230–231
    of oral presentations, 284–285
    positive and negative, 248f
Language programs, 147
Laser printers, 129–130
Last-call return, 305
Lateral files, 386, 387f
Layoffs, 547
Layouts, 152
LCD. *See* Liquid crystal display
Leadership, 555–582
    and change, 576–577
    comparison with management, 556f, 556–558
    definition of, 557
    effective, 558–561
    and ethics, 93–94
    and goal-setting, 561–562, 563f
    importance of, 556
    and management, 562–575
    and power, 560
    and risk-taking, 561, 561f
    styles of, 41
    tasks of, 561–577
    and teaching, 576
    and trust, 560
    and unity, 575–576
    and values, 561–562, 563f
    values and, 558–559
    vision and, 558
Leaving employment, 544–549
LEC. *See* Local exchange carrier
Legal careers, 14–16
Letter(s), 243, 257–260
    of application, 521–523, 522f, 523f

Minutes, from meetings, 440–441, 443*f*
    preparation of, 442
Misplaced records, 385
Mission statement, 199, 200*f*
Misused words/phrases, 588–590
Mixed punctuation style, 270, 272*f*
MLA. *See* Modern Language Association style
Mnemonic devices, 235*f*
Modem, 131
    and copiers, 174–175
Modems, 297*f*, 298
    cable, 301*f*, 301–302
Modern Language Association (MLA) style, 262, 275, 276*f*
Modified block letter style, 270, 272*f*
Money orders, 333, 493, 493*f*
Monitors, 126–128
Monochrome, 126
Monotone, 285
Moral integrity, 87
Morality, 87
Morse code, 295
Motivation, management and, 574–575
Mouse, 118–119
Movable-aisle files, 386–387, 388*f*
MRI. *See* Magnetic resonance imaging
Multifunction peripherals, 130
Multifunction units
    copiers, 172
    fax machines, 188
Multiline telephones, 304
Multinational corporations, 7
Mutual funds, 215, 503–504

N

NAEOP. *See* National Association of Educational Office Personnel
Narration, 282
NASD. *See* National Association of Securities Dealers
NASDQ, 502
National Association of Educational Office Personnel (NAEOP), 16
National Association of Securities Dealers (NASD), 502
NCR. *See* No carbon required
Necessary meetings, 422
Nervousness
    during interviews, 534
    during oral presentations, 287
NetMeeting, 430
Networked printers, 129, 130
Networking
    and job advancement, 544
    for job information, 518
Network interface card (NIC), 301
Networks, 130–135
    connections with, 297–302
    types of, 296–297

Newspapers, for job information, 515
New technology ATMs (NT-ATM), 483
New York Stock Exchange, 502
NIC. *See* Network interface card
No carbon required (NCR), 316
Nomos, 43
Nonessential records, 384
Nonimpact printer, 128
Nonjudgment, 236
Nonverbal communication, 226, 227–230
Notebook computers, 121–122
Notes, and PIM software, 77
NT-ATM. *See* New technology ATMs
Numbers
    in digital era, 4
    grammar rules concerning, 586–588
    indexing of, 364
Numeric guides and folders, 373
Numeric storage method, 372*f*, 372–377
    parts of, 373, 373*f*, 374*f*
    procedure for, 373
    variations of, 375–377
Numeric suffix, 363
Nutrition, and stress reduction, 61–62, 62*f*

O

OAG Business Travel Planner, 460
Occupational Health and Safety Administration (OSHA), 46, 87
Occupational Outlook Handbook, 5–6, 14
OCR. *See* Optical character reader; Optical character recognition
Office(s)
    career opportunities in, 13–19
    in Information Age, 3–5
Office environment
    acoustics and, 44–45
    color and, 43
    floor plans for, 45
    furniture and, 45–46
    lighting of, 43–44
    safety and health in, 46–48
    security of, 49
Office hours, observance of, 100–101
Office mail, 328–354
Office politics, 99–100
Office professional
    and copier maintenance, 177–178
    ethical, characteristics of, 99–103
    obligations of employer to, 36
    obligations to employer, 35–36
    role in conferences/conventions, 444–448
        during conference, 446–448
        post-conference, 446–448

        pre-conference, 444–446
    role in meetings, 434–442
        during meeting, 440–441
        post-meeting, 442
        pre-meeting, 434–440
    team with coworkers, 36–37
    team with supervisor, 35–36
    in virtual office, 198–205
Office skills, 17–19
Office suites, 148
Office team
    composition of, 32–37
    coworkers, 36–37
    external, 37–38
    internal, 30–32
    of office professional and supervisor, 35–36
    presentations by, 288
    project team, 32–35
Office visitors, 38–39
Official Airline Guide, 469, 469*f*
Off-loading, 196
Omission marks, 594
Online binding, 176
Open punctuation style, 270, 271*f*
Operating statement, 496
Operating systems software, 143–145
    functions of, 145–146
Operator-assisted calls, 318
Optical character reader (OCR), 273, 296, 337–338
Optical character reader (OCR) scanners, 116
Optical character recognition (OCR), 401
Oral presentations, 282–288
    audience for, 282–283
    and body language, 285–286
    checklist for, 288*f*
    closing of, 285
    critique of, 287–288
    dress for, 286–287
    language of, 284–285
    material for, 283
    and nervousness, 287
    opening of, 284
    organization of, 283–284
    purpose of, 282
    rehearsal of, 287
    setting of, 283
    visual aids in, 286
Organization
    and management, 564–567
    of virtual office, 201
    of work periods, 566–567
Organizational climate, 41
Organizational communication, 39–42
Organizational control, 570
Organizational culture, 88–89
    ethics and, 88–89
Organizational dependency, reduction of, 64
Organizational management, 17–18

R

Race, of labor force, 6, 6f
Racial discrimination, 98–99
Racism, 89–91
Radio frequency (RF), 301
RADSL. *See* Rate adaptive digital subscriber line
Rail travel, 459–460
    international, 465
Random access memory (RAM), 117, 123, 145
Rate adaptive digital subscriber line (RADSL), 300
Readability, 252
Readability index, 252
Reader, for microimage systems, 405–406
Reading, organization of, 72–73
Read-only memory (ROM), 123
Real property tax, 501
Recareering process, 548–549
Receiver, 227
Receptionist, greeting of visitors, 38–39
Recognition, 574
Record life cycle, 359
Records
    coding of, 380
    cross-referencing of, 380–381, 381f
    indexing of, 380
    inspection of, 379
    misplaced/lost, 385
    sorting of, 381
    types of, 383–384
    values of, 359
Records disposal, 384
Records management. *See also*
    Information management systems
    with computer applications, 367–368
    definition of, 359
    importance of, 359–360
    storage methods for, 369–378
    supplies/equipment for, 385–387
    trends in, 411
Records management technology, 394–416
Records migration, 410
Records retention, 382–384, 383f
Records retrieval, 382
    in electronic database systems, 398–399
Records storage methods, 369–378
Records transfer, 384
Recruiting, 567–570
Rectangular arrangement, 438, 438f
Recycling, of mail, 347–348
Reduction, by copiers, 173
References, 281
    for reports, 261–262

on resumes, 528
Reference section
    of business report, 263
    of reports, 276, 277f
Registered mail, 331–332
    rate chart for, 332f
Registration, for conferences, 445–446
Relational database management system, 395–398
Relationships, communication in, 225
Relaxation techniques, 63, 63f
Religion, and ethics, 86
Remote access, 151–152
Remote call forwarding, 305
Remote file exchange and synchronization, 152
Repetitive strain injuries, 42, 46–47
Repetitive work, 71
Reports, 244, 260–263
    body of, 263
    clip art, line drawings, and borders for, 279–280
    documentation of, 275–276
    graphics in, 276–279
    headings of, 280
    margins of, 280
    page numbers of, 280
    parts of, 262–263
    preparation of, 260, 260f
    presentation of, 275–281
    quotations in, 280–281
    references for, 261–262
Reprographics. *See also* Copiers
    definition of, 169
Requisition form, 382
Research
    for presentations, 281–282
    primary, 261
    secondary, 261–262
Resignation, 544–546
Resolution, 126
Respect
    for employee, 36
    for employer, 35
Response rates, 261
Response, to communication, 227
Responsibility
    acceptance of, 101
    and virtual offices, 204
Restricted delivery, 332
Restrictive endorsement, 490
Resumes, 523–530
    chronological, 524, 525f
    education section, 528
    electronic, 529–530
    functional, 524, 526f
    guidelines for, 529
    heading of, 524
    objective of, 524–528
    parts of, 524–528
    professional accomplishments

section, 528
    references on, 528
    relevant skills section, 528
    targeted, 524, 527f
    work experience section, 528
Retirement age, 6
Retirement benefits, with virtual office, 215
Return receipt, 332
Rewards, 94–95
RF. *See* Radio frequency
Risk-taking, leadership and, 561, 561f
Roaming, 306
Role ambiguity, 60
Role relationships, 64
ROM. *See* Read-only memory
Roth IRA, 505
Rough sorting, 381
Routine messages, 258, 259f

S

Safe-deposit boxes, 494
Safety
    with electronic database systems, 399
    in office, 46–48
Salaries, 16–17
Sales tax, 501
Scanners, 115–117
Scanning, 401
Scrambled signals, 188
Screening tools, 568
SDSL. *See* Symmetric digital subscriber line
Search engine, 133f
Seating arrangements, for meetings, 438f, 438–439
Seat on the exchange, 502
Secondary research, 261–262
Securities and Exchange Commission, 406
Security
    with electronic database systems, 399–400
    equipment for, 49
    of office, 49
    personnel for, 49
    of software, 160–161
Self-concept
    communication and, 223f, 223–226
    strengtheners of, 225–226
Self-confidence, 202–203
Self-control, 570, 571
Self-starters, 201
Semicircular arrangement, 438f, 439
Semicolon, 592–593
Seniority suffix, 363
Sentence structure, 251